THE ECONOMIC APPROACH TO POLITICS

HarperCollins Series in Comparative Politics

Series Editors:

Gabriel A. Almond
Lucian W. Pye

THE ECONOMIC APPROACH TO POLITICS

A Critical Reassessment of the Theory of Rational Action

Edited by

Kristen Renwick Monroe

University of California at Irvine

HarperCollins*Publishers*

Sponsoring Editor: Catherine Woods
Project Editor: Diane Rowell
Design Supervisor: Pete Noa
Cover Design: Edward Smith Design, Inc.
Cover Photo: The Bettman Archive
Production: Willie Lane/Sunaina Sehwani
Compositor: House of Equations, Inc.
Text and Cover Printer/Binder: Malloy Lithographing, Inc.

The Economic Approach to Politics: A Critical Reassessment of the Theory of
    Rational Action

Library of Congress Cataloging-in-Publication Data

Monroe, Kristen R., 1946–
    The economic approach to politics: a critical reassessment of the
theory of rational action / Kristen Renwick Monroe.
        p.   cm.
    Includes index.
    ISBN 0–673–46426–1
    1. Political science—Economic aspects. 2. Rational expectations
(Economic theory)   I. Title.
JA77.M66   1991   90–26648
306.2—dc20   CIP

91 92 93 94   9 8 7 6 5 4 3 2 1

In honor of
the contribution of
Anthony Downs

Contents

Preface

This volume offers a careful examination of the economic approach to politics known as the theory of rational action. The volume itself is presented in honor of the contribution to political science made by Anthony Downs. Many of the chapters were delivered originally at a conference marking the 30th anniversary of the publication of *An Economic Theory of Democracy*, Downs's brilliant doctoral thesis that formed one of the cornerstones for contemporary rational actor theory. This book, the first of Downs's prolific writings (over 300 coauthored articles and 15 books), did much to stimulate empirical research applying the economic approach to politics. The goal of the conference was to step back from the particular approach encouraged by Downs's work and to assess the usefulness of the economic orientation when applied to political phenomena. Our assessments are meant to be constructive. We hope to encourage dialogue among those who utilize this approach in their empirical and theoretical discussions of political phenomena and those who find the theory lacking in critical areas. Such dialogue may reveal how best to modify the theory of rational action so it can better explain political behavior; it may also increase our knowledge of those areas in which the theory's application should be curtailed.

In selecting the chapters for this volume, I have tried to be guided by the spirit of Downs's original work, work that is wide-ranging, interdisciplinary, analytically rigorous, fresh in its insights, and motivated by a keen desire to understand and explicate political phenomena lucidly and truthfully, with no commitment to preconceived ideas or traditional wisdom. As is evident by Downs's contribution to this volume, Downs himself has continued to reassess his thinking. His early concern with democracy as a political system that enriches and ennobles its citizens, combined with his scholarly commitment to the examination of significant social problems, animates Downs's current discussion of social values and democracy, a discussion that should further open the way for the introduction of normative concerns into rational models, not the least because such an advocacy emanates from Downs himself.

The timing could not be better for a volume that honors Downs by a careful examination of the theory of rational action. From several directions, social scientists are concerned about the appropriateness of rational models applied outside the conventional province of economics. Much debate, often heated, over the value of this economic approach to politics and social science currently enlivens the discipline. In this preface, I would like to orient the reader to the central themes implicit in this general debate, a debate reflected in microcosm in the selections in this volume. In an editor's foreword, I then summarize each chapter and provide the intellectual background and context for the ideas and controversies that animate the authors in their contributions to the volume.

There are several ways to read the chapters in this volume. One method, of course, is to read each essay as written in critique of or support for the rational model. Read thusly, there are chapters by several well-known critics, such as Gabriel Almond, Michel Crozier, and Harry Eckstein, and chapters by some of the foremost rational actor theorists, such as John Ferejohn, Roger Noll, and Downs himself. My intention in compiling this volume, however, was to move beyond confrontation and toward dialogue and integration. In particular, I sought (1) to provide an accurate overview of the debate over rationality, a debate that touches on some of the most fundamental and exciting issues within contemporary social science, and (2) to stimulate research and focus discussion on critical questions that future scholarship should address.

To best do this, the volume begins with an editor's foreword designed to serve as an annotated reader's guide. The abstract for each chapter is presented and the linkages between the chapters are discussed. I also suggest several ways in which the material in each chapter relates to critical debates within political and social science.

The editor's introduction next presents my own ideas about the exact nature of the theory of rational action. In essence and in its purest form, the theory originates in the classical economics of Adam Smith, and claims that human behavior can best be understood by assuming individuals pursue their self-interest, subject to information and opportunity costs. This assumption carries certain powerful statements about human social behavior, some of which are discussed in detail in both the introduction and the first three chapters of this volume. The introduction also discusses the most frequently used variations on this common definition of rational action. The introduction concludes by summarizing the major criticisms of the theory, criticisms that emanate from a wide range of disciplines but that cluster in four areas: (1) strong disagreements with cultural theory, (2) technical modifications or corrections within economics and cognitive psychology, (3) empirical challenges from experimental psychology, and (4) failures to explain collective political behavior and altruism within political science. Each piece in this volume touches on at least one of these critiques.

The chapters were also selected because each provides insight into one or more of the critical questions currently facing rational actor theorists. Although these questions are discussed more fully in my introductory chapter, let me mention them briefly here, since they form the organizing framework for the volume. (My suggestions on which chapters pertain most directly to each question are noted in parentheses.)

1. How appropriate is the market metaphor for politics? (Almond, Chapter 1; Monroe, Barton, and Klingemann, Chapter 13; Margolis, Chapter 14)

2. Do people actually pursue goals? (Eckstein, Chapter 3; Johnston, Chapter 4)

3. Does collective political welfare emerge from the individual pursuit of self-interest? (Whitehead, Chapter 2; Scalia, Chapter 8; Noll and Weingast, Chapter 9)

4. Is political behavior best understood by assuming political agents act primarily in the pursuit of individual self-interest? (Downs, Chapter 6; Petracca, Chapter 7; Margolis, Chapter 14)

5. Is self-interest the same as utility maximization? (Whitehead, Chapter 2; Noll and Weingast, Chapter 9; Kavka, Chapter 15)

6. Do real people make decisions the way the theory postulates? (Kavka, Chapter 15; Rosenberg, Chapter 16; Wittman, Chapter 17)

7. Do political acts and decisions emanate from a conscious calculus? (Johnston, Chapter 4; Monroe, Barton, and Klingemann, Chapter 13)

8. What is the importance of choice and identity for political behavior? (Johnston, Chapter 4; Crozier, Chapter 12; Monroe, Barton, and Klingemann, Chapter 13)

9. Can political calculus be put into cost/benefit terms? (Petracca, Chapter 7; Scalia, Chapter 8)

10. Does use of the rational actor theory limit our understanding of political action by ignoring the political role of values and institutions? (Johnson, Chapter 5; Downs, Chapter 6; Noll and Weingast, Chapter 9; Grafstein, Chapter 10; Ferejohn, Chapter 11; Margolis, Chapter 14)

Taken as a whole, this volume should provide both a critical reexamination of the theory of rational action and a sense of the dialogue among important critics and practitioners of the theory. The introduction should provide a general outline of the theory itself. The chapters by Almond and Whitehead offer a broad historical perspective. The chapters by Eckstein, Johnston, and Johnson focus on specific and critical theoretical concerns. The central role of self-interest is addressed by Downs, Petracca; Scalia; Noll and Weingast; Monroe, Barton, and Klingemann; and Margolis. The role of institutions is discussed by Grafstein, Ferejohn, and Crozier. Finally, the volume concludes with a comparison by Kavka, Rosenberg, and Wittman of the economic and psychological approach to politics.

ACKNOWLEDGMENTS

In my role as editor, I would like to take this opportunity to thank publicly each of the authors for the extreme care with which they crafted their essays. Edited volumes are not famous for their integration; for that reason, the extra time so generously given to rewrite essays in order to respond to themes presented by other contributors is all the more appreciated. I would also like to express my gratitude to Bernard Grofman, the co-organizer of the original conference honoring Downs's work, and to Dean William Schonfeld for his generous financial assistance for the conference. Additional support came from the University of California Inter-Campus Activities Fund. James Alt, Jonathan Pool, and Stephen Weatherford provided generous and extensive comments on the final manuscript. Conversations with Nancy Bermeo, David Easton, Julius Margolis, and Wil Lampros contributed general intellectual support and direction. Ziggy Bates, Cheryl Larsson, and Jeannie Hawthorne typed the manuscript and Gertrude Monroe read proof. Finally, my thanks to Diane Rowell and Catherine Woods at HarperCollins for providing extraordinarily helpful editorial assistance.

Kristen Renwick Monroe

Editor's Foreword

The chapters in this volume undertake a critical reassessment of the theory of rational action. In this foreword, let me summarize each chapter, explain the intellectual linkages among the chapters and suggest several ways in which the material relates to critical debates within political and social science.

An editor's introduction discusses the concept of rational action and provides the organizing framework for the book. This is followed by two chapters designed to provide a broad overview of the economic approach to politics. The first chapter contains Gabriel Almond's historical perspective on the introduction of economic models into political science. Almond's chapter provides the intellectual context in which rational actor theory first appeared in contemporary political science and examines the ways in which the rational self-interest assumption is presented in some of the exemplars of rational actor theory. Almond divides these rational actor analyses into two categories. The first attributes some degree of realism to the assumption of self-interest; the second replaces the material self-interest assumption with the simpler assumption of goal-directed behavior. Almond asserts that the self-interest assumption has limited value in explicating political action. In particular, while this assumption has substantial heuristic value, and has illuminated constitutional, political party, interest group, and voting phenomena in important ways, Almond argues that it is only when rational actor theory is used in conjunction with concepts and theories drawn from other parts of political and social science that it acquires genuine explanatory power. Furthermore, Almond concludes, the policy-oriented work of some of the writers in this field who opt for the second version of rationality as goal-directed behavior (e.g., James Buchanan, Gordon Tullock, and William Riker) is in fact based on the assumption of short-term material self-interest.

Jaan Whitehead next directs attention to a central fact that is too often overlooked: Rational choice theory grew out of the classical economic thought of Adam Smith, but was modified in critical ways by the marginalist revolution in economics. Whitehead's chapter extends

Almond's historical perspective to address the widespread claim that economic assumptions and models can appropriately be extended to political analysis. Whitehead demonstrates that classical economic theory, as founded by Adam Smith, clearly rejected such a claim. In particular, Whitehead identifies two characteristics of economic activity that Smith believed made it appropriate for the economy to be defined by private interests: (1) stable behavioral patterns based on self-interested emotions, and (2) a competitive market system which regulated that behavior to achieve a public interest. But Smith found neither characteristic present in other realms of life, including the political realm. It was the marginalists who converted classical economic theory to a static theory of rational choice. In doing so, Whitehead argues, they obscured both the emotional basis for behavior and the regulatory role of the market that Smith had emphasized. And it is this theory of private rational choice that has been extracted from its economic context and applied to political behavior.

In doing so, the rational choice model does not produce the same harmonious results it does in economic analysis. There is no "invisible hand" in the political world that regulates self-interested individual behavior to achieve public goals. While the economic approach identifies many of the political problems that result from unconstrained self-interested behavior in the absence of a perfectly competitive market, the assumptions and norms of the economic model preclude many ways of identifying solutions to these problems. By studying how economic approaches to politics developed out of the history of economic thought, Whitehead identifies clear limitations in the usefulness of this approach as a tool for explicating political behavior. Whitehead's chapter illuminates by the depth of its perspective and shows how the classical tradition in economics contains many of the elements most damagingly omitted from contemporary political economic theorizing.

The next three chapters view rational models from a slightly narrower but still essentially theoretical perspective. Harry Eckstein highlights the potentially important category of frustrated, as opposed to motivated, behavior. Essentially, Eckstein addresses the critical assumption on which rational choice theory rests: the assumption that people do pursue goals. Eckstein argues that this assumption may be valid in segments of advanced societies; but because he finds it dubious for most people, in most places, at most times, Eckstein rejects it as a solid foundation for general theory. Instead, Eckstein presents extensive psychological and sociological evidence to demonstrate that human behavior is instigated by frustration, defined as behavior without a goal, or what Eckstein calls analgesic behavior. Eckstein argues that such behavior, while considered sensible from an adaptive, or functional, perspective, cannot be classified as rational. He presents a carefully defined alternative to the rational model and develops it thoroughly so the reader can clearly see what the alternative model produces and why rational choice would not be an accurate characterization for such behavior. In style and spirit Eckstein's essay returns to classical, late nineteenth-century economic theory's concern with poverty and distribution. This chapter thus links to Whitehead's and provides an opportunity for comment on the relation between theoretical presuppostions about human behavior and ideological concerns with social melioration, a concern voiced later in the volume by Petracca.

David Johnston's chapter also takes up the question of how consistently and deliberately people act purposively in everyday life. Johnston argues that there are at least two classes of actions that cannot be accommodated by this orthodox model without straining credibility. The first of these classes consists of role behavior, actions that do not result from choices at all, or that do not result from choices to take the specific actions in question. The second consists of ambivalent actions that are initiated by an agent and whose ends or goals relevant to the action are beset by unreconciled conflicts. Johnston proposes two informal models, based on the ideas of skilled performance and of deliberative choice, to accommodate actions of these contrasting kinds. Johnston contends that these alternatives are of superior value to the orthodox rational model of a human agent, both for the purpose of explaining political behavior in a credible way and for that of evaluating human action from a normative point of view. His notion of counterposing choice to both ambivalence and performance echoes Eckstein's theme in a broader perspective and sets the stage for Crozier's later discussion of trust as a relational boundary of rationality. It also reflects current discussions, by scholars such as Martha Nussbaum and Hayward Alker, that seek to broaden our concept of rationality to include discussions of what it means to be a rational human being, not just a utility-maximizer.

The broader cultural context of meaning into which actions are embedded is also reflected in the chapter by James Johnson. Like Eckstein, Johnson poses a clear alternative to rational choice theory. But unlike Eckstein, Johnson compares interpretive theory with rational choice theory, concluding that the two theories are complementary rather than antagonistic or fundamentally incompatible. In his comparison, Johnson focuses on theoretic representations of the spatial theory of electoral competition as a narrow and highly technical, though central, topic in the rational choice research tradition.

Johnson begins by challenging the orthodox view of rational choice as a positive science. In contrast, he proposes a nonpositivist rendering of rational choice theory, using Jurgen Habermas's concept of reconstructive social theory to argue that interpretative and rational choice theory occupy different but integral positions within a reconstructive enterprise. Johnson then identifies the constraints that interpretation imposes on reconstructive social theory, trying to dispel general qualms about proceeding from the "thick description" of interpretive inquiry to the kind of formal analysis characteristic of rational choice theory. His demonstration of the reconstructive character of rational choice theory explores three common reconstructive techniques employed by rational choice theorists in designing their models. Johnson concludes by indicating the limits that reconstructive considerations impose on the scope of rational choice models.

The chapters by Downs, Petracca, Noll and Weingast, Scalia, Margolis, and Monroe, Barton, and Klingemann all concern the critical role of self-interest in rational actor theory. The chapter by Anthony Downs poses an important reconstruction of his own early economic theory of democracy. In particular, Downs now moves beyond self-interested rationality to call for the inclusion of social values in our models of democracy. His chapter, however, is neither a simple response to critics nor a restatement of the importance of values; rather, it marks an attempt to reformulate election-based models of democratic politics, and it reaffirms Downs's reputation for clear, innovative theorizing. In this chapter, which presages arguments made later in the volume by Scalia and by Ferejohn, Downs considers the critical role of social values in the classic economic approach to democracy pioneered by his own early work. Downs now concludes that certain problems of democracy are insoluble by the economist's reference to preference intensities; a full understanding of democracy can emerge only when we also consider the social values that underline democracy. The significance of such an argument is increased by the fact that it comes from one of the founders of contemporary rational actor theory.

Mark Petracca's chapter is one that readers will praise or denounce, but not ignore. It is included not just for the centrality of its topic but also because, as the most impassioned in the book, it reflects some of the emotional response to rational actor theory that exists in the discipline. This impassioned response was engendered by certain of the more extreme works in rational choice theory, works that—accurately or not—were perceived as expressing an arrogant disdain for scholarship that did not possess their technical rigor.

Petracca examines two of the claims made by these rational choice theorists by asking: (1) Can political behavior best be explained through static models that posit man as a self-interested or profit-seeking being? (2) Can rational actor theory be both celebrated and defended on the grounds that it approaches social, economic, and political phenomena in a scientific and objective fashion? In assessing these claims, Petracca raises uncomfortable and controversial questions for rational actor theorists. He calls into question not only the possible motivation for the current popularity of the rational actor approach to politics, but also the unintended (yet nonetheless significant) consequences of this perspective for the development of democratic politics. In particular, Petracca argues that by assuming that self-interest is an empirically established component of a static human nature, rational actor theory is antithetical to normative democratic theory. Political action that is predicated on such empirical assumptions about human nature, Petracca argues, justifies the prevailing system of political power and privilege under the illusory guise of democratic governance. His chapter identifies the important elements of normative democratic theory that are omitted from political explanation by rational choice theory and discusses the analytical and political consequences of such sins of omission.

In a more historical empirical analysis, Laura Scalia echoes Petracca's concern for the paradigm of democracy that rests on the assumption of self-interest. While critical of Downs's early work, Scalia offers historical validation for Downs's more recent thoughts on democracy through her careful review of the literature assessing republican virtue and self-interest as foundations of democracy and the relation between private interest and public duties. Scalia argues, in effect, that rational choice theorists make democracy a procedure to harness the individual self-interests of both leaders and citizens so that the common good can emerge without anyone expressly pursuing it. Scalia examines the normative consequences of this economic model of democracy and argues that the uncritical acceptance of uncurbed self-interest politics actually destroys the desirability of democracy. She contrasts the contemporary economic model of democracy with early nineteenth-century American perceptions of the consequences of self-interest for republican government. This earlier view accepted self-interest as the norm of political behavior but argued that, if left undirected, self-interested individuals would form factions and administer poor government.

For Scalia, this view suggests that the prevalence of self-interest means effective government can never be wholly democratic. As she demonstrates here, the nineteenth-century debate on self-interest and democracy suggests the contemporary economic model actually developed from an antidemocratic tradition that stressed efficiency. The implications of her analysis suggest we cannot have democratic government that promotes the general welfare if we base that government only on self-interest. We must also introduce a consideration of the common good.

Roger Noll and Barry Weingast disagree. Noll and Weingast first consider the critics who argue that rational choice political economy is necessarily restricted to behavior motivated solely by self-interest. They then address critics who argue that social norms cannot be successfully incorporated into the theory. Noll and Weingast defend rational choice theory by means of an analysis of administrative procedures and bureaucratic cultures. In doing so, their chapter taps centrally into the important debate on methodological individualism and also assesses the role of culture in rational choice theory.

Essentially, Noll and Weingast argue that values do not need to be introduced directly into rational actor models; we need posit only that rational individuals pursue goals that are consistent and stable. (In this, while they disagree with Eckstein, they also underline the potential importance of Eckstein's argument.) Noll and Weingast demonstrate their point by exploring the implications of semi-interdependent preferences as the basis for rational actor theory. They next consider the importance of an individual's normative values in setting the individual's choice of actions. They conclude that a rational actor can rely on—and make use of—this phenomenon in selecting another rational actor to whom will be delegated decisional authority. At the governmental level, they argue that political actors will design administrative procedures and select the problems of administrative agencies; in doing so, rational actors create the set of normative values that the agency will serve. Administrative values thus reflect the policy purposes of the coalition that gave rise to a policy at the time of its creation. And the character of the norms will depend on the political circumstances that originally gave rise to the policy.

Consideration of the relational boundaries of rationality, especially the role of institutions in rational choice theory, discussed by Noll and Weingast, touches on one of the most exciting new areas pursued by contemporary rational choice theory, an area often referred to as the new institutionalism. The chapters by Grafstein, Ferejohn, and Crozier focus directly on rationality and the role of institutions.

Robert Grafstein provides the general intellectual context for this debate. He demonstrates how rational choice theorists, taking their cue from economists, were not initially inclined to build much institutional detail into their study of politics; political outcomes were simply treated as the direct result of aggregating individual preferences in nonmarket situations. In time, rational choice theorists recognized that these political outcomes could not be explained without incorporating institutional variables into the analysis. In correcting this earlier omission, contemporary rational choice theory now looks increasingly neo-institutional.

For Grafstein, the incorporation of institutions, however, raises as many questions as it answers. Though institutions may help explain political outcomes, what explains the existence and efficacy of the institutions? And if institutions are explained as the instrumental choices of rational agents desiring certain stable outcomes, how can the institutions they select have any power over their creators?

One standard answer is that institutions, once in place, create incentives for actors to behave in ways that conform to the rules of the institution. Deviation from institutional rules entails either the risk of punishment or the risk of institutional change, uncertainty, and chaos. Grafstein finds this implied image of rational agents highly implausible. In making their daily decisions, such a scenario requires agents to compare the projected consequences of acts within the existing institution to their imagined consequences within alternative social arrangements. Grafstein's careful and subtle analysis shows that neo-institutionalism typically defines institutions in terms of these internalized models. The net effect is that institutional constraints are explained away be turning them into the intended expression of agents occupying some hypothetically exogenous position. Agents, rather than institutions, wind up doing all the work.

According to Grafstein, this image of rational agents is belied by the very social interdependence the institutionalization of behavior requires. In his chapter, Grafstein demonstrates a way to view the institution not as an object of decision but as one of the constraints, as unavoidable as the decision maker's physical constraints of time, energy, and resources. To recommend this view of rational choice theory, Grafstein argues that this conception passes three crucial tests. First, it solves genuine problems that haunt the standard view, in particular the traditional failure to make satisfactory sense of institutional constraints or (what amounts to the same thing) the excessive demands on the rational agent. Second, Grafstein's conception does not turn the institution into a supernatural *deus ex machina*. Third, while his conception is consistent with fully rational behavior on the part of the participants, full rationality is not demanded by the very definition of institutions. This allows rational agents to have incomplete or even incorrect models of the institutions in which they operate, for under this conception, an institution, like the proverbial tree in the forest, does not require human recognition to rise or fall.

John Ferejohn also considers the usefulness of rational choice theory in examining institutional change. In contrast to Grafstein, however, Ferejohn sets his assessment in the historic context of early Stuart England. As does Johnson, the intellectual explanation Ferejohn chooses to contrast with rational choice theory is interpretive theory. His chapter begins with a valuable contrast of the two theories. Ferejohn's synthetic analysis then takes the given beliefs discussed by Downs as a central part of rationality and shows, with a carefully pursued historical example, how culture fills holes in an otherwise then rational account. In particular, Ferejohn argues that the institutional changes that occurred during the evolution of Parliamentary representation in seventeenth-century England cannot be fully explained by either rational choice theory or interpretive analysis. At best, Ferejohn argues, either type of explanation can eliminate certain patterns of action as inconsistent; but neither theory can fully account for social action. In this, Ferejohn's chapter joins Johnson's in exploring the compatibility of rational choice and interpretive theories of culture. Their work may not satisfy Almond and Eckstein, who pioneered quite different views of culture among political scientists. But it clearly demonstrates the resilience of certain basic concepts and the intellectual vitality of rational actor theory.

At the other end of the debate on institutions and culture stands the work of Michel Crozier. Crozier argues that neither market nor neo-institutional theories can provide satisfactory answers to how individuals resolve choices to further individual versus collective welfare, or even how they resolve choices between their short-term and their long-term individual self-interest. Crozier's chapter addresses the important topic of the role played by social relations between actors and the trust generated by such relations. He turns to the prisoner's dilemma for his example. For Crozier, trust appears to be the key variable that makes it possible to bridge the gap between the self-defeating pursuit of individual self-interest and the common good. In addition to its moral component, Crozier argues that trust has to be understood as a solution to monitoring problems where transactions are costly and actions unobservable.

Crozier argues that people do not maximize their interest in the abstract. Instead, they act as Simon's satisficing model suggests and choose the first solution that makes it possible for them to win or to maintain themselves in the relational game. In this respect, perfect markets must be understood as special cases of rational games in which concrete human relations almost disappear.

Crozier's analysis of game theory emphasizes the extent to which politics deals not with aggregating individual interests, but rather with maintaining and rearranging human games that will have an impact on individual interests. Finally, Crozier argues that the processes by which individuals learn about their self-interests are contextual and deal with their relations with other actors. He argues further that our choices for committing ourselves to specific games and our methods of playing in them make up part of our identity. Our particular identities may carry liabilities; they prevent us from being purely rational and efficient. But they constitute such an integral part of our being that we can neither abandon nor compromise our identities without great cost. Maintaining a posture corresponding to our identity may lead to self-sacrifice; but such sacrifice is not irrational from a particular relational point of view within a specific contextual setting.

The chapter on altruism by Kristen Monroe, Michael Barton, and Ute Klingemann echoes several themes developed earlier in the volume: Crozier's interest in the moral and cultural dimensions of individual choice, and his discussion of the role of identity in delineating human choice; Johnston's discussion of deliberative choice and normative concepts of identity; and the general theme of self-interest that concerns Almond, Downs, Margolis, Petracca, and Scalia. Like the chapters by Crozier, Ferejohn, and Scalia, this chapter offers an empirical assessment of the rational actor explanations of a specific phenomenon. Here the focus is on altruism, long a puzzle for rational actor theorists. The assessment of rational actor explanations of altruism is constructed through interviews with rescuers of Jews in Nazi Europe. The findings challenge the idea that self-interest is the exclusive norm of human behavior. The authors also question the extent to which behavior results from conscious choice and suggest that one's perception of self in relation to others may constitute a critical determinant of political behavior.

While following a quite different tack, Howard Margolis also assesses the importance of self-interest within rational actor theory. Margolis begins with the assumption that in all societies, compliance with laws and social norms is enforced by coercion in one form or another. But this coercion is always incomplete. Compliance characteristically exceeds what could plausibly be accounted for in terms of rational deterrence. Margolis reviews the dual-utilities extension of rational choice developed in his earlier book, and compares the implications of that model in the context of incomplete coercion with those of strictly self-interested rational choice, extended to allow for social motivation though not for dual-utilities. Not surprisingly, it turns out that in general an increase in coercion (stricter enforcement) implies an increase in compliance. But the dual-utilities model, in contrast to either version of the standard model, predicts a response to an increase in coercion even when the change could affect only behavior that is already in compliance. This suggests a set of contexts in which we might devise a particularly sharp empirical test between the dual-utility model and the standard model.

The last three chapters in the volume touch on one of the liveliest debates in political science: the value of the economic versus the psychological approach to politics. The central idea of the economic approach to politics is that we can best describe, understand, and explain the behavior of political actors (e.g., voters, countries, office-seekers, or government bureaucrats) by assuming that they are rational utility-maximizers. Greg Kavka addresses this central assumption and effectively rejects it. For Kavka, however, utility maximization plays a valuable idea-generating role in economic theories of politics, as it does in straight economic theory. In this, Kavka echoes Almond's claim, albeit on a less critical note, that much of the real work in economic theory is done by substantive auxiliary assumptions about human motivation.

The chapters by Rosenberg and by Wittman form a pair of counterposed arguments about social and cognitive psychology and political choice. Shawn Rosenberg provides a theoretical discussion of the potential relevance of the psychological research on cognition for economic studies of politics. Rosenberg's aim is not to deny the value of the neoclassical approach adopted by economists, but rather to delineate when that approach will prove more or less informative and when it will be more or less dependent on the theoretical insights and research of political psychologists. The Rosenberg argument begins with a discussion of the notion of narrow rationality and its dependence on the discipline of the market mechanism. The claim is then made that the political marketplace lacks the particular characteristics needed to ensure discipline among narrowly rational buyers and sellers. The goods are complex and ill-defined. The consequences of choice are remote and unclear. The buyers have infrequent opportunity to make choices. Therefore, economic analyses of politics must necessarily rely on a broader concept of rationality.

With this last point, the cognitive psychological research is introduced as relevant. Rosenberg's review of that research indicates that individuals lack the capacity to reason in a broadly rational manner. They are unable to adequately perceive and understand the objective conditions of their actions, and therefore the political market is unable to discipline them effectively. This result suggests that politics is an arena where objective conditions are importantly mediated and, in the end, powerfully determined by the ways in which individuals understand the world around them. This leads Rosenberg to reaffirm the conclusion reached by others in this volume, that when applied to markets like that of politics, economic analysis must be conducted with reference to theory and research on subjectivity and culture.

In sharp contrast, Donald Wittman challenges the claim of cognitive psychologists (such as Kahneman, Tversky, and Slovic) and critiques the literature in this area, literature often referred to as prospect theory. In essence, Wittman's chapter constitutes a closely specified investigation of the experimental results of cognitive psychology that pertain to political choice and decision making. Wittman begins by suggesting that the experiments in cognitive psychology fail to account for factors such as political institutions and comparative advantage. He argues further that some of these experimental findings, although claiming to reveal faulty human judgment, actually demonstrate optimal decision making within the context of the experiment. Wittman concludes that cognitive psychology fails to encompass a unified body of research and consists of little more than a collection of often internally inconsistent hypotheses and results. His argument is a striking condemnation of the cognitive psychologists' attempts to offer an alternative to economic man, and a plea that political scientists should study political institutions if they wish to understand the biases inherent in individual decision making. Wittman's chapter moves beyond just an argument against prospect theory, however, to address some of the underlying methodological conflicts between economics and cognitive psychology and their relative capacities for explaining political behavior.

These are the topics addressed in this volume. It is hoped that the existing discussion, offered in the spirit of friendly but critical and dispassionate reassessment, will advance our understanding of the usefulness of the economic approach to politics.

K. R. M.

THE ECONOMIC
APPROACH
TO POLITICS

The Theory of Rational Action: Its Origins and Usefulness for Political Science

What exactly is the economic approach to politics known as the theory of rational action?[1] What are the main criticisms of this theory? How useful is the theory for political science? And what should be the focus of research for analysts using this economic approach to explain political phenomena? The chapters in this volume are designed to provide insight on these critical questions.

The first step in our discussion, of course, must be a consideration and a statement of exactly what is meant by rational actor theory. Rational actor theory originated in the classical microeconomics of Adam Smith. In its purest form, it refers to behavior by an individual, be it a person, a firm, or a political entity, designed to further the actor's perceived self-interest, subject to information and opportunity costs. As originally conceived by Smith, the theory provided a powerful and creative mechanism whereby the pursuit of individual self-interest would lead to collective welfare. The genius of Smith's invention—the market mechanism, regulated by an invisible hand—solved a problem which had troubled philosophers since Hobbes made his famous argument that there was one basic human nature and that this nature was self-centered: How can a society of selfish citizens produce collective welfare without authoritarian government? (See Mansbridge, 1990 or Myers, 1983 on the role of self-interest in social theory.)

Smith's work was not originally intended to describe political behavior. Indeed, as is demonstrated later in this volume, Smith found clear and important reasons why his economic approach would not explain political action. As Smith's work was revised, however, especially during the marginalist revolution in economics at the end of the nineteenth century, the broader philosophical context of Smith's political economic thought became less salient and economists introduced other, often more technical, meanings into their basic conceptualizations of rational action.

During the middle part of the twentieth century, rational actor theory blossomed into the subdisciplines of rational choice, public choice, and social choice theory.[2] Distinctions between these specialties are not always clearly defined, and scholars working among the various subfields share key concepts, concerns, and methods of analysis. In general, however, public choice theory emphasizes the way in which decisions are made through nonmarket mechanisms. In economics, it is associated most closely with the work of James Buchanan and the so-called Virginia School and in political science with the work of William Riker and the Rochester School of public choice.

Social choice theory originated in the attempts by welfare economists and mathematicians to develop a formal, axiomatic, and deductive method for analyzing the problems of social decision-making. It focuses on the rules by which individual preferences are aggregated. Typical problems concern the intransitivity of preferences and the construction of formal models of political phenomena, such as voting systems and justice. Its concern with social welfare gives it a strong normative content. Within economics, it is associated most closely with the work of Kenneth Arrow (1951, 1984) and Amartya Sen (1984). Its highly technical place within political science has been ensured by analysts such as Gerald Kramer, Peter McKelvey, and Norman Schofield (1985).

Distinguishing a separate specialty of rational choice within the general field of rational actor theory is even more difficult, in part because the term "rational choice theory" is so frequently used interchangeably with "rational actor theory." I will suggest later that rational choice theory should more aptly be applied to Simon's reformulation of rational actor theory and refers more properly to a decision-making process rather than to actions themselves. But many analysts working in the field do not make this distinction and use the two terms simply as verbal alternatives.

As rational actor theory gave birth to the above-mentioned subspecialties, it also expanded its range of topical purview. By the 1970s, it had developed into one of the dominant paradigms of political and social science, offering insightful, rigorous and parsimonious explanations of phenomena as diverse as voting (Downs, 1957), coalition formation (Riker, 1973), and peasant revolts (Popkin, 1979) to discrimination and marriage (Becker, 1976) and group formation and interactions (Olson, 1965, 1982). During the late 1970s and 1980s, rational actor theorists expanded their original political concerns from arenas such as voting, where it could easily be argued that individual preferences could be aggregated to express the common good, and turned to political puzzles where the economic approach might not appear so immediately relevant. The role of institutions (Fiorina, 1989; Shepsle, 1979; and Weingast, 1979), norms, and culture (Axelrod, 1986) are currently being introduced into rational models and analysts have moved from applications within post-industrial democracies to broader forms of comparative analysis. Throughout this process, distinctions over the definition of the basic concept blurred. In addition to its original meaning, rational action came to refer to the crude pursuit of material self-interest (Buchanan, 1984b:13; Downs, 1957:28), to utility maximization (Buchanan and Tullock, 1962:25–30; Buchanan, 1984b:13; Arrow, 1963:3), to purposive behavior (Riker, 1973:10), and to goal-directed behavior (Riker, 1973).

Given its widespread usage, it was perhaps inevitable that criticisms and qualifications to the theory would emerge. And so they did, emanating from a wide variety of disciplines but clustering around four general areas: (1) strong disagreements with cultural theory, (2) technical modifications or corrections within economics and cognitive psychology, (3) empirical challenges from experimental psychology, and (4) failures to explain collective political behavior and altruism within political science. As will be demonstrated later in the volume, some of these criticisms were quite technical, focusing on explicitly stated postulates about human decision-making; an example of this is Herbert Simon's early work on bounded rationality and satisficing. (See Simon, 1982 for a summary.) Other criticisms were more general, attacking what were seen as implied and erroneous claims about a static human nature, particularly one so exclusively self-interested and bound to the individual as its basic explanatory tool; examples here are the democratic theorists who stress the polity's ability to transform the self through communal deliberation (Barber, 1985; Taylor, 1987; and Sandel, 1984).

As the current decade opened, rational actor theorists who were themselves increasingly critical of specifics within the approach but who sought revision within the general paradigm found themselves with the dual challenge of defending their general approach while seeking to modify its specifics. Notable examples here are economists such as Amartya Sen (1973) and Thomas Schelling (1984) and political scientists such as Jon Elster (1984, 1986a, 1986b, 1989b), Russell Hardin (1982), and Robert Bates (1988). The excitement of all this intellectual ferment carries the richness of conceptual variety; it also entails some conceptual confusion, as rational actor theory now ranges from highly technical axiomatic formalizations to attempts to integrate Marxist and interpretivist theories of culture into the basic rational model.

The current volume includes works which expand upon the above sketch of the origins and basic assumptions underlying rational actor theory. It contains essays which criticize the theory and those which demonstrate the theory's vitality in responding to its critics. In the rest of my introduction, let me fulfill my role as editor by providing an overview of the critical assumptions on which rational actor theory is based. I will then summarize the major critiques and suggest the specific areas I believe future scholars should address in order to modify the theory of rational action so it can be applied more successfully to political phenomena.

KEY ASSUMPTIONS OF RATIONAL ACTOR THEORY

There are seven assumptions of the economic theory of rational action as it developed in classical economics. The first four are foundation assumptions, so widely held in our post-Enlightenment world that they are seldom discussed explicitly. The last three are less basic and are often stated explicitly. These assumptions are as follows:

1. Actors pursue goals.[3]
2. These goals reflect the actors' perceived self-interest.[4]
3. Behavior results from a process that actually involves (or functions as if it entails) conscious choice.[5]
4. The individual is the basic actor in society.[6]
5. Actors have preference orderings that are consistent and stable.[7]
6. If given options, actors choose the alternative with the highest expected utility.
7. Actors possess extensive information on both the available alternatives and the likely consequences of their choices.[8]

The traditional rational actor is thus an individual whose behavior springs from individual self-interest and conscious choice. He or she is credited with extensive and clear knowledge of the environment, a well-organized and stable system of preferences, and computational skills that allow the actor to calculate the best choice (given individual preferences) of the alternatives available. The importance of this model is demonstrated by the fact that "[p]ractically the whole of classical economic theory is constructed within the framework of this [rational] model" (Simon, 1982(1):213).

Rational actor theory contains no discussion about the nature of actors' particular preferences. It assumes little about the way in which actors make probability estimates of uncertain events. It assumes that actors choose the alternative with the highest expected utility, defined as the average of the utilities of all alternatives, each weighted by the probability that the outcome will ensue if the alternative in question is chosen (Simon, 1984:296). The traditional economic theory of rational action ignores the limitations inherent within the actor. It considers only those constraints that arise from the external situation. Once we know an actor's preferences, we can make objective judgments about the extent to which the actor optimally adapts to the situation.

Bounded or Procedural Rationality: Rational Choice Theory as a Modification of Assumptions 5–7.

Bounded rationality shares the same initial intellectual heritage of traditional economic rationality. Perhaps because of this, it also accepts the first four critical foundation assumptions—i.e., that behavior results from individual actors consciously choosing to pursue their perceived self-interest. Its actual birth, however, occurred in cognitive psychologists' reaction to the behavioral movement in psychology. The cognitivists' deemphasis on culture, history, and context meant that their conceptualization of rational action minimized the external situation surrounding an actor (Gardner, 1985). Its emphasis on mental representations or schemata makes rational choice as a method only as effective as the actors' decision-making and problem-solving means permit. To judge whether an act is rational according to bounded rationality, we need to know the chooser's goals, conceptualization of the situation, and abilities to draw inferences from the available information. Because of its origin in cognitive psychology, bounded rationality is thus more concerned with the mental process of decision making itself than with behavior. This contrast with the traditional economic theory of rational action probably accounts for some of the current confusion over whether rational action refers to behavior or to a decision-making process within the actor. Bounded rationality's emphasis on process—not outcome—makes it analogous to the legal concept of procedural due process, which asks whether the procedure that led to the result was fair, rather than whether the outcome itself is fair. This stands in contrast to the traditional economic concept of rationality, which stresses rational outcomes—i.e., outcomes occurring not necessarily from a rational process but *as if* they had resulted from that process. (See Friedman, 1953.) In practice, the terms *rational actor theory* and *rational choice theory* are frequently used interchangeably. Unfortunately, this confusion blurs the important distinction discussed above between rational action and rational choice.

Bounded Rationality Assumptions: Key Points of Difference from Traditional Economic Concept

While it retained the four foundation assumptions (individual action, pursuit of goals, conscious choice, and self-interest), bounded rationality differs from the traditional economic concept of rationality at several critical junctures. They can be noted briefly by stating the assumptions of bounded rationality. (When necessary, I also draw attention to the subtle way in which these assumptions differ from the analogous assumptions of traditional economic rationality.)

1. *Computational limitations.* Actors possess limited computational abilities. For bounded rationality theorists, rational behavior is adaptive within the constraints imposed both by the external situation and by the capacities of the decision maker.

2. *Uncertain and limited information.* Actors search for alternatives, consequences, and information selectively and incompletely. This search is based on limited and uncertain information.

3. *Satisficing.* Decisions are reached once a satisfactory alternative is found; this alternative need not be the optimal one, merely one that satisfies some minimum.

4. *Relevance of cognitive maps.* Predicting behavior requires extensive supplemental knowledge of the actor, particularly the actor's goals and conceptual orientation to the world.

5. *Stress on process, not outcome.* Emphasis on the decision-making process of the unit analyzed (e.g., person, firm, government) means that the process of decision making itself, rather than the outcome of that process, is the hallmark of bounded rationality.

GENERAL CRITIQUES

Despite its widespread use, the theory of rational action has nonetheless received severe criticism, primarily from four different sources.[9] (1) Cultural theorists attack its limited nature.[10] They argue that the theory ignores the limitations on free choice imposed by culture, such as habit, tradition, and societally imposed norms. Furthermore, because values are always exogenous to the model, revealed only through behavior, the theory produces tautological explanations in which any behavior can be deemed "rational" in pursuit of exogenous goals simply unknown to or misunderstood by the outside observer. (In this volume, the chapters by Almond and Eckstein articulate these concerns most directly.) Cultural critics are particularly concerned with the difficulties involved in cross-cultural analysis and fear that the theory's claim to scientific objectivity masks a Western, individualistic bias. (The chapter by Petracca discusses this at length. See also Mansbridge, 1980; Barber, 1984.) (2) The second stream of criticism comes from work at the intersection of economics and cognitive psychology. This critique is best represented by Simon's previously described work on bounded rationality, which argues that the human decision-making process is not one that maximizes utility but rather one that satisfices—that is, actors seek a certain minimum level of satisfaction and thereafter are indifferent among choices.[11] This tradition is represented in this volume by Kavka, who argues that utility maximization serves better as a heuristic than as a true representation of the human decision-making process. (3) More recent critiques emanate from experimental work in cognitive psychology, best articulated by Kahneman, Tversky, and Slovic (1982). This careful empirical work presents striking evidence that neither the existence of preferences, the process by which preferences are pursued, nor the evaluation of information in the basic decision-making process is as consistent or efficient as the rational actor theory posits.[12] This literature is evaluated favorably in Rosenberg's chapter and negatively in Wittman's contribution to this volume. (4) Finally, and of great importance for political science, even scholars working within the rational actor framework admit that the theory has difficulties explaining altruism and collective behavior, both significant deviations from the key assumption of the rational actor theory: the belief that individuals pursue their self-interest. (See Olson, 1965; Margolis, 1982; and the chapters by Margolis, by Crozier, and by Monroe et al. in this volume.) Let me discuss the more important questions raised by these critiques in greater detail, focusing discussion on the theory's viability for political science.

Questions for Future Research

1. How appropriate is the market metaphor for political action? The rational actor theory adopts the rational maximizing actors from economics and transforms them into utility-maximizing voters and politicians who trade in votes and policies just as economic man or woman trades in apples or shoes.[13] Within this volume, this market metaphor is discussed in detail by Almond, who notes its long and legitimate tradition in politics, with scholars from Key (1942) and Schattschneider (1975) to Riker (1962) and Fiorina (1974, 1977) utilizing it to explain American politics. Despite its widespread use, it can be argued (as Margolis does in this volume) that the technical foundation for the market metaphor does not exist in politics, since political goods are analogous to public goods and all the conventional economic theories break down in the presence of public goods. Both Margolis and

Almond remind us that the market is only one metaphor that we should use. Politics as religion, stressing "conversion, prayer, and worship rather than buying and selling as the defining activity," has been employed widely in comparative politics (Almond, page 36 of this volume). Politics as warfare has been frequently used to explain authoritarian movements, such as Fascism and Nazism. Politics as symbolic affirmation of the actors' position, power, or the roles played in society (Geertz, 1953) and politics as a game played for the fun rather than the winning of a particular goal are two other commonly used metaphors. By their insistence that rational models are the only truly scientific models of politics, both Almond and Petracca argue that hard-core rational actor theorists have seriously limited and isolated themselves.[14] On this point, it is interesting that both the severest critics (such as Almond) and the strongest proponents (such as Simon) agree that much of the explanatory power of rational models actually comes from the auxiliary assumptions, assumptions about specific motivations, preferences, and aims of agents within specific contexts:

> . . . actors in the political drama do appear to behave in a rational manner—they have reasons for what they do, and a clever researcher can usually obtain data that give good clues as to what those reasons are. But this is very different from claiming that we can predict the behavior of these rational actors by application of the objective rationality principle to the situations in which they find themselves. Such prediction is impossible . . . because it depends on their representation of the world in which they live, what they attend to in that world, and what beliefs they have about its nature (Simon, 1985:300; also cited in Almond, page 47 of this volume).

All of this suggests that rational models have great heuristic value but may best be used in conjunction with other approaches and certainly with more humility than is too often the case. (The heuristic value of rational models is discussed by Kavka in his chapter).

2. *Do people pursue goals?* Rational actor theory assumes that people pursue goals. Indeed, Downs defines rational action as behavior "reasonably directed toward the attainment of conscious goals" (1957:4). When confronted with convincing empirical evidence of self-sacrificial altruism, some rational actor theorists have recently abandoned self-interest as the heart of their theory, offering up instead consistent goal-directed behavior as the critical component (see also Riker, 1962). Even Simon's bounded rationality, which substitutes satisficing for maximizing and thereby substitutes any good outcome for the best outcome, still assumes that "almost all human behavior consists of sequences of goal-oriented actions" (1984:297). In his wide-ranging examination of this, Eckstein, in this volume, disagrees. He cites exten-

sive evidence, ranging from experimental work with rats (Maier, 1961) to work on Appalachian mountaineers (Gaventa, 1980; Toynbee, 1946; Caudill, 1962; Weller, 1965; Ball, 1968), inner-city blacks (Frazier, 1939/1966) and Puerto Ricans (Moynihan and Glazer, 1966), poverty in Trinidad (Rodman, 1971), and lower-class schools in Britain and the United States (Eckstein, 1984). According to Eckstein, the idea of goal-directed behavior is too limited to work well outside the confines of upper-middle class post-Enlightenment Western societies. The rest of the world, Eckstein argues, exists not in a goal-directed culture but in an analgesic culture. In analgesic cultures actors wish only to avoid pain, decrease precariousness, limit the emotional stress of surviving in a hostile world, and establish some stability in an environment in which it is better to have the predictability of frustration than the bitter disappointment of failing to achieve goals. Such goals result in the frustrated behavior we find in cultures of poverty or aggression. Eckstein asserts that this behavior is not mere risk aversion, although it is certainly that. Rather, action that is known from its inception to be bound to fail "involves acting beyond all consideration of risk. It is not really possible to divorce risks from goals. . . . [But in analgesic cultures, behavior evidences] so high a degree of risk aversion that the difference in degree becomes a difference in kind, at least for theory" (page 84 of this volume).

3. *Does the individual pursuit of self-interest result in collective political welfare?* As formulated originally by Adam Smith, human action emanates in the emotions, not reason, and the driving passion is self-interest (Myers, 1983; Hirschman, 1977). For Smith, some regulation was required in order for the pursuit of individual self-interest to result in the common good. This could come through self-regulation, governmental regulation, or some natural force, such as the market. In the economic realm, Smith located the critical emotion as self-interest and the market as the natural regulatory force. But Smith "did not find either a dependable set of emotions or a reliable natural regulatory" mechanism in the political sphere (Whitehead, page 54 of this volume).

In her contribution, Whitehead demonstrates that it was the marginalists who argued the feasibility, indeed the desirability, of extending the economic metaphor to the political arena. She believes that the marginalists treated individual preferences as assumptions of the model. The marginalists did not try—as did Smith—to explain the preferences themselves. The origin and nature of these preferences became exogenous to the model. Individuals became autonomous actors whose

> diverse emotional motivations for behavior and their need for regulation became masked behind the new static theory of rational choice. . . . The problem is that [if there are no clearly defined collective goals in the political world or if there is no regulatory

mechanism to harmonize self-interested maximizing behavior with such goals], it is no longer clear that self-interested maximizing behavior should be considered rational or that unconstrained individual preferences should be granted sovereignty, as they are in the rational actor model. (Whitehead, page 55 of this volume.)

Thus rational actor theorists assume that individual desires will result in (or at least be compatible with) collective political goals and welfare. Such a relationship is central to the theory. And yet we do not know that individual preferences will result in the collective good or the collective goals of a society or group. Nor do we know *how* these individual drives to pursue self-interest should be regulated if and when they are not compatible with the collective good. It is ironic that the question which compelled Smith to found economics was the very question on which the political theory of rational action may now founder: If it is a scientific given that people are self-interested, how do we achieve the common good without resorting to unacceptable levels of governmental regulation?

A concern with the relation between individual self-interest and collective welfare is of utmost importance to political science and is reflected in several chapters in this volume. Scalia turns to nineteenth-century American debates on self-interest and democracy to suggest that the contemporary economic model actually developed from an antidemocratic tradition that stresses efficiency, not collective well-being. The implication of her analysis suggests that a reliance on self-interest will not produce a democratic government that promotes the general welfare. Noll and Weingast disagree. In their chapter, they argue that government, particularly governmental agencies, develop bureaucratic cultures that reflect societal norms. If the norms are other-directed, that will be reflected in bureaucratic and governmental behavior. Grafstein and Ferejohn also address the role of institutions in rational choice theory, with Grafstein differing with the new institutionalism at several critical junctures and Ferejohn finding this approach more useful than cultural, liberal, or Marxist explanations of political phenomena.

4. *Do political actors actually behave in the self-interested way described by the rational actor theory?* There is a long history in political and social theory that argues that self-interest is a fundamental part of human nature, one that social and political institutions ignore at their peril. Myers (1983) argues that the assumption of self-interest constitutes the heart of economic theory, and Mansbridge (1990) has amply documented the growth within political science of the view that human affairs are shaped almost exclusively by self-interest. The continued existence of altruism, however, has long perplexed theorists—such as rational actor theorists—working within a framework based on the

assumption of self-interest. In recent years, rational actor theorists have responded to this challenge by incorporating altruistic and other-directed behavior into their paradigm. Sen (1977) introduced the concept of metaranking of preferences, whereby actors' sympathy for others and commitment to certain principles might be placed above their more subjective preferences. Others (see Schelling, 1978a, 1978b; Elster, 1979, 1986, 1989a, 1989b; Margolis, 1982) responded by positing the individual as a divided self with the self-oriented part holding a dialogue with the other-oriented part.

Several authors in this volume address this issue directly, and arrive at different assessments concerning self-interest, both as a normative and as a positive tool for political analysis. In my chapter with Barton and Klingemann, I found that even when confronted with the systematic state torture carried out by the Nazi regime, the rescuers of Jews risked their lives and those of their families to save strangers. Clearly, they did not pursue their own self-interest. Nor did psychic gratification serve to disguise a thinly veiled self-interest. Neither honor nor praise was sought, and despite the fact that their actions were well documented by others, all of the rescuers minimized their actions, even as they told us of being arrested many times or of being persecuted for their activities. The existence of such altruistic behavior, no matter how rare empirically, poses a significant theoretical challenge to any theory founded on self-interest. For me, the awareness of altruism suggests limiting the application of the theory of rational action. For others, such evidence indicates the value of incorporating altruism into rational models, an approach advocated by other rational actor theorists and one pursued by Margolis in this volume. Within the volume, both the Margolis chapter and the one by Downs exemplify and discuss the extent to which rational actor theorists are moving away from such exclusive reliance on the concept of self-interest to allow for the inclusion of other social norms.

5. *Is self-interest the same as utility maximization? Does the use of utility maximization locate the theory's drive in the intellect rather than the emotions and thus rob the theory of its vitality?* If utility maximization is not self-interest, which drives the theory? Economists and rational choice theorists like to explain behavior that violates the self-interest assumption by arguing that the theory is based on utility maximization, not self-interest. The few eccentrics like Mother Theresa are then explained as simply having strange utility functions or a preference for altruism. I believe this sleight of hand masks an important intellectual break and renders the theory vacuous. If self-interest is *not* the heart of the model, if rational action is merely consistent goal maximization—and outside observers can know the goals only through an actor's revealed preference—then the model becomes tautological.

Anything and everything can be explained by it; but nothing can be definitively tested and disproved.

The extent to which the rational actor model assumes only goal-directed behavior, or whether it depends upon auxiliary assumptions such as self-interest for its explanatory power raises another issue of current concern: Can you make fewer and fewer assumptions and still retain the theory's predictive power? Proponents answer yes; you can still say things which are important, and which may be even more important because they are universalizeable. Critics argue (1) that we need a more substantive theory of rationality instead of the merely syntactic formal one which economics has stressed, and (2) that the validity of these assumptions is key; if the assumptions are wrong, the economic model itself does not bear the seeds for its own correction.

This critique reflects my own view. Others in this volume disagree, most notably Noll and Weingast, who argue that self-interest is not essential to rational choice political economy. For Noll and Weingast, consistent goal maximization provides a viable model, one that can incorporate norms and one in which the normative values of one person (let us call him Alex) can help other rational actors (such as Will and Nick) choose Alex as someone to whom Will and Nick wish to delegate authority. The Noll-Weingast discussion differs significantly from my own view that sometimes self-interest works and sometimes it won't and that a clever analyst must determine when and how to build it into a model. The issue is of critical importance for political science, however, since it strikes at the heart of the debate on the usefulness of applying the economic approach to politics.

For all of these reasons, I would argue that the debate over self-interest versus utility maximization remains critical. Whitehead's chapter provides an important link in this debate because it documents exactly how the marginalist revolution shifted the theoretical emphasis from Smith's self-interest to contemporary utility maximization, a process that also accompanied the deemphasis I noted above on the emotions as motivating action and focused instead on the action itself. Both Whitehead and Myers identify Smith's genius and the power of his theory in the fact that Smith rooted behavior in the emotions rather than in a conscious calculus. In contrast, the marginalists reduced rationality to a mental process. In attempting to develop a mathematical science, Whitehead argues, the marginalist revolution thus robbed economic theory of its emotional vitality. This process was completed by Simon's work, which further located rational action in a mental process. Instead of Smith's *desires*, we now have *preferences*. The *value* of a good is now *utility*. And the way we transform preferences (Smith's desires) into utility (Smith's values) is no longer through the pursuit of self-interested desires but rather through formulated choices among alternate (usually transitively ordered) goods. Self-interest thus becomes separated from any emotional impetus and becomes instead a rational product of choice. While this contemporary version of the rational actor model has heuristic value, it also carries clear limitations for the model as applied to political contexts:[15]

> The rational actor model can be extracted from the economic context and applied in other contexts as an empirical device to explore if individuals do act in a self-interested and maximizing way in these other contexts. And, the collective consequences of such behavior can be analyzed. But, unless it is assumed that individuals should be able to follow their self-interested desires regardless of the social consequences, then the basic question of how the individual should relate to society again becomes the framework for analysis. This was Smith's basic question and it is not surprising that it is the question underlying many current critical analyses of economic theories of politics. . . . [E]conomic analysis became isolated from the historical and political context in which it previously had been considered. Since government was not an integral part of the market process, it was omitted from the model and was no longer considered explicitly except as part of public finance. Questions of power and coercion within the private economy, which were of concern to classical economists as they looked at the changing distribution of income, were also no longer considered. Nor were societal questions of morality and justice issues of concern. And, perhaps most important, the emphasis shifted to the individual and away from either analytical or normative concern with collective needs and outcomes. But, in political analysis, it is just such a concern with collective needs and outcomes that is required. (Whitehead, page 67 of this volume.)

6. *Do real people make decisions the way the theory postulates?* I have already mentioned the difficulties in translating the market metaphor to political situations. This leaves open a broader critique: Do real people make decisions as the theory specifies? Experimental psychologists from Bartlett (1932) to Kahneman, Tversky, and Slovic (1974, 1982), inter alia, have offered convincing evidence on the individual's limited or bounded capacity to perceive, recall, interpret, and calculate. Happily, this criticism is now being incorporated into economic theory. The chapter by Rosenberg offers a thorough review and a positive assessment of this literature, while the chapter by Wittman dismisses the importance of this literature.

Let me mention just a few of these criticisms briefly, paying close attention to the political arena. (See Nisbett and Ross, 1980, for a more thorough review.) (1) Feedback is not as direct in politics as it is in the marketplace. If I buy a pair of shoes, I soon know if they fit properly. If I vote for a senator because I want someone who is tough on crime, it is more difficult to ascertain whether I have made the right choice. (2) An actor's search for information is incomplete. We know this; Simon addressed it early in his career. But the search for information is also biased by an actor's preconceptions. (3) Actors weigh particular kinds of information (e.g., vivid, personally relevant information) more heavily than others (e.g., pallid statistical data). (4) Actors' abilities to recognize correlational relationships and make causal attributions are severely limited (see Rosenberg, 1988, or Nisbett and Borgida, 1975). This can result from human desires to be consistent (see Heider, 1958; Galambos et al., 1986). (5) Actors use shortcuts or heuristics in making mental calculations (Tversky and Kahneman, 1974). (6) Actors also are extremely sensitive to the way in which choices are framed (Quattrone and Tversky, 1988).

What does all of this mean for political analysis?[16] I believe it suggests the need to determine the actors' views of the world, and in particular actors' views of themselves in relation to others. One promising area currently under exploration entails script or schema theory. Some analysts are exploring script or schema theory that focuses on the definitional computational qualities of the mind itself, apart from any influence of social environments (Heider, 1958; Festinger, 1957; Koffka, 1935; Kahneman and Tversky, 1972). Others explore script or schema theory that emphasizes how the mind's organization of incoming data reflects cultural and historical influences (see Fiske and Taylor, 1984). Finally, the cognitive developmentalists (cf. Kohlberg; Vygotsky; Rosenberg) and the symbolic interactionists (dating from G. H. Mead) find the structure of cognition to be constrained by qualities both of mind and of cultural environments. All of this work should provide links to key psychological theories of human development and to cultural theory.[17]

7. *Do political actions and decisions emanate from a conscious calculus?* The original theory of rational action propounded by Adam Smith required only that decisions proceed *as if* they had originated in a rational calculus. While most contemporary theories of rational *choice*—as opposed to rational *action*—require a conscious calculus, one recent response to criticism on this point has been a movement to deemphasize the commitment to any particular kind of mental process. This seems appropriate, particularly in the political context, where we must ask how much of political action, even political choice, is driven by a conscious process. Consider the process of voting. The original Downsian formulation of voting stresses a conscious calculation of costs and benefits weighted by the voter's belief that his or her vote will actually affect the outcome. One problem for analysts was that fewer people vote in local than in national elections, even though it is in local contests that their votes are more likely to affect the outcome. Faced with this empirical reality, analysts have introduced auxiliary assumptions, such

as civic duty, to explain this phenomenon. Let me suggest an alternative explanation, based on years of close observations of one voter (my mother), an anecdote by Austin Ranney, and my empirical analysis of rescuers of Jews in Nazi Europe.

My mother always votes. But seldom is her party or her candidate elected. Still, she continues to vote. Why? "Well, it's important to vote. What kind of a person would I be if I didn't vote?" This is Mother's standard explanation. Perhaps this is civic duty; but I'd characterize it more as basic identity, a perception of self that defines and limits the options seen as available to the actor.

Anecdote # 2. Long a Democrat, Ranney tells of becoming disgruntled with the Democrats and going into the voting booth determined to send them a clear and direct message by voting Republican. Once in the booth, however, Ranney found his hand would begin to shake as it approached the Republican lever and it would move slowly—as if compelled by a force of its own—back to the Democratic lever. Civic duty? No. Basic identity or self-perception? More likely. Now I have no doubt that Ranney eventually was able to vote Republican. And I imagine there has been—or will be—an occasional election in which my mother fails to vote. I offer these anecdotes only as thought-provoking, not definitive, evidence on the nonconscious extent to which people "decide" to actually vote and on how they reach their particular vote choice.

8. *How much political behavior results from decisions and how much results from an actor's identity perception?* More systematic evidence from in-depth interviews with rescuers of Jews in Nazi Europe suggested to me that certain political acts may be less the result of conscious choice and that our identity constructs effectively limit the perceived options available to actors. For the rescuers, identity was so strong that there was no conscious choice for them to make in the traditional sense of assessing options and choosing the best one for them. Instead, their perception of themselves in relation to others limited the options available *to them*. Certainly they knew that most people did not risk their lives to save Jews and so they knew that theoretically this choice was available. But they did not see this choice as an option existing for them. We asked rescuers how they began their activities, how they made their decision to risk their lives for strangers:

Interviewer You started out . . . talking about making conscious choices. And you said you didn't think you operate that way. Was there really a conscious choice that you made?

Margot I don't make a choice. It comes, and it's there.

Interviewer It just comes. Where does it come from?

Margot I don't know. I don't think so much because I don't have that much to think with. . . .

Interviewer It was just totally nonconscious?

Margot Yes. You don't think about these things. You can't think about these things. It happened so quickly.

Interviewer But it isn't really totally quickly, is it? There's a tremendous amount of strategic planning that has to be done [to do what you did].

Margot Well, I was young. I could do it. Today I don't know. I'd have to try it. But I was 32 years old. That was pretty young.

Interviewer You didn't sit down and weigh the alternatives?

Margot God, no. There was not time for these things. It's impossible.

Interviewer So it's totally spontaneous? It comes from your emotions?

Margot Yes, it's pretty near impossible not to help. You couldn't do that. You wouldn't understand what it means. Suppose somebody falls in the water, as I said before. You want to think, "Should I help or should I not?" The guy would drown! You know, that's no way.

Interviewer How about the repercussions of your actions? Did you think about what might happen because you were doing this?

Margot You don't think about it. No way.

Interviewer You didn't worry about possible consequences for you? For your family?

Margot No. No way. (Monroe, 1991 in press.)

For me, rescue behavior suggests that certain political behaviors—and these may well entail our most significant personal and political acts—are not the result of choice at all. An implication is that work which increases our understanding of how we view ourselves in relation to others should be extremely useful in understanding political behavior, behavior that by its very nature involves others. Since cognitive frameworks may be the link between the theory of rational action and cultural theory, this area should be a major focus for scholars interested in constructing future empirical political theory. Such work may also help us understand which metaphor is most useful in explaining particular political actions and in determining to what extent political conflict results from mixed metaphors and when there are true conflicts of interest. Crozier's chapter in this volume makes a major advance in this direction by offering a theory of rationality that focuses on the relational boundaries of individual choices. In particular, his theory emphasizes the learning processes by which individuals develop impressions of and trust in others. Such processes make our choices contextual, dependent on our own identities and on our perceptions of others. Crozier's analysis, which provides an interesting parallel to Noll and Weingast's discussion of trust, treats rational calculus as the cultural or relational boundary of choice. It provides a creative integration of sociological and moral considerations into rational choice theory.

9. *Can political calculus be put into cost/benefit terms?* Rational choice theory assumes that political behavior results from an economic

cost-benefit calculus. But is this so? To what extent do other, less tangible, more symbolic factors drive political actions, even those that do
result from choice? Again, a consideration of the rescuers of Nazi victims is instructive. For the rescuers, saving someone's life was not something to be subjected to a calculation of cost or benefit. Since these were
significant political acts, we need to know whether other, similar political acts exist. And we need to determine more carefully which political
acts can be explained by an economic cost/benefit calculus and which
political acts cannot. Even political acts that are the product of conscious decision making (e.g., sending troops into the Bay of Pigs or drop-
ping the atomic bomb on Hiroshima) may be better explained by
another model—such as the deliberation model, proposed in the chapter
by Johnston, which expressly allows for ambiguity and the conflicts arising from an individual actor's multiple roles and the values they impose
on human beings (see also Elster, 1986, on the problem of multiple
identities). In this regard, it is of particular note that the chapter by
Downs argues that certain problems of democracy are insoluble without
a full understanding of the social values that underlie democracy. While
others have made similar arguments in critiques of Downs's earlier
work, the mere fact that it is Downs himself who now makes this
argument gives a certain significance and legitimacy to this view.

   10. *Is the theory value-free? Or does its methodological individualism mask a preservation of the status quo?* Rational actor theory
explains political behavior through reference to individual action. This
method of analysis, often referred to as methodological individualism,
stands in contrast to other approaches to politics, such as Marxism's
stress on class structures and class membership or to sociobiology's
emphasis on inherited nature as members of a species. Critics of methodological individualism argue that such emphasis on the individual
causes analysts to neglect deeper sources of political change in favor of
superficial ones. Normative theorists have argued further that this
emphasis on the individual, and on a particular concept of the individual as a competitive, self-interested optimizer, actually preserves and
protects a liberal, self-interested status quo. They argue that in so far as
rational actor theorists assume self-interest as a scientifically established
part of human nature, rational actor theory has perpetuated normative
and empirical consequences which support the prevailing system of political power and privilege.

   This argument is clearly evidenced in discussions of American
democracy. Scholars as different as Pateman (1970) and Wattenberg
(1988) have noted that the rational actor approach to American politics
gained strength just as democratic theorists were disconcerted by
increasing empirical evidence of voting which suggested that the United
States was not a sound democracy in the eighteenth- and nineteenth-
century sense. Pateman suggests this led to revisionist theories of demo-

cracy (i.e., those by Dahl, Downs, or Sartori), designed to bring normative theory more into line with empirical reality. As described by Barber (1984) and Mansbridge (1980), democratic theory as explicated by rational choice theorists shifted its emphasis from explaining political change to justifying political stability. As Petracca suggests later in the volume, the empirical effect of this shift is that we focus too much on voters and pay too little attention to what a vote means. We ask how elections are won but not what elections mean in terms of empowerment. We view citizens primarily as vote-traders and ignore what it means to be a citizen, what citizen obligations entail, and what citizens can expect to achieve in a political system that makes individual self-interest the norm.

So far, there has been too little dialogue between rational actor theorists and normative political theorists over methodological individualism, liberalism and the ideological/scientific nature of rational actor theory. Many critical questions remain unanswered. Within this volume, some of the background on these issues is provided in the chapters by Whitehead and by Scalia. The intensity of the debate is captured in Petracca's chapter. And the chapter by Johnson offers a valuable first step toward the integration of these positive and normative concerns by using Jürgen Habermas's concept of reconstructive social theory to propose a nonpositivist rendering of rational choice theory.

11. *Which is more important for political action—economics or politics? Does the rational actor theory necessitate the primacy of the economic?* As contemporary rational choice theory becomes increasingly classified as a normative rather than a positive formal theory, we return to the debate between scholars who study normative and ancient political theory and those who do contemporary political science: What is human nature and what is its relation to the political? How do our assumptions on human nature affect our empirical findings and the political institutions we construct? On this point, we might recall early work by Cropsey (1977), an economist turned political philosopher, who argues that only modern political theorists (i.e., those after Hobbes and Locke) believed civil law—and social science—should reflect a law of nature. The ancients held no such view, demonstrating a quite different idea of the proper realm of the political as they argued that the polity must shape human nature:

> In confining itself to making explicit what is implicit in man's primitive state, political philosophy caused itself to be supplanted primarily by economics, the discipline that systematically enlarges upon the self-preserving motives of pre-civil man. Political science inherited as its content the ministerial questions pertaining to the support of the essentially economic order of society. In this way, and in the indicated order of rank, economics and political science

arose out of the self-limitation of political philosophy (Cropsey, 1977:43).

Current attempts to introduce the political into rational models—through civic duty or other-directed behavior—represent one attempt to correct this. Both the chapter by Ferejohn and the chapter by Grafstein discuss how political institutions set the context for rational action and assess how rational actor theorists fare in introducing these political institutions into their analyses. Grafstein asks directly how "good" institutions can curb self-interest and argues that the "new institutionalism" still ignores the origin of "good" and "bad" institutions. Margolis's chapter further addresses the concern for others by proposing a model to explain how social preferences mix with private preferences. Finally, the chapter by Downs argues that democracy cannot be adequately explained without reference to social values. This last piece should be particularly significant in legitimizing a paradigm shift that encourages rational actor theorists to introduce values directly into their rational models. Augmenting the models to account for the origin and nature of preferences will be a major challenge for rational actor theorists, one that necessitates closer dialogue between normative and cultural theorists.

CONCLUSION

I have sketched the origins and outlined the essentials of the theory of rational action. I then summarized the wide-ranging critiques of the theory and suggested questions on which future research in this area might profitably focus. Finally, I noted how the chapters in this volume contribute to the general debate in this area. In my conclusion, let me note the three central areas which I believe will be most critical to address in modifying the economic theory of rational action so it can be applied successfully to political phenomena. These center on self-interest, conscious choice, and identity perception.

Self-Interest. It seems clear that self-interest explains much of human behavior. I would not argue that we should discard this construct as part of our theory of rational political behavior. I would, however, claim that the theory's limits are exceeded when it is applied to situations in which individual self-interest is not the dominant force behind behavior and that many significant political acts fall into this domain. While self-interest can remain a basic part of our political theories, it should be balanced by human needs for sociability, defined as a feeling of belonging to a group or collectivity.[18]

To understand when and why we pursue self-interested behavior and when we exhibit more public-spirited behavior—surely a question of some concern to political scientists—we must understand the complex linkages between optimization of an actor's self-interest and an actor's perception of himself or herself in relation to others. Why is individual self-interest sometimes pursued and group interest pursued at other times? The answer may depend on which of the actor's identities is made most salient by external conditions. This is where we could introduce the importance of framing, of social contexts, and the role of culture, thereby responding positively to both the cultural critiques and the cognitive critiques of the rational actor theory.

Conscious Choice. Another limitation in the theory results from its overemphasis on conscious choice; one solution here is to focus more on learned strategies that result in optimal outcomes. Choices may well be less important than strategies that lead to successful outcomes. Furthermore, choices need not be conscious. A successful strategy can originate in unconscious choices, emotions, or chance. The conscious element may enter when the success of a strategy is recognized or learned. Even learning does not require consciousness, however, although in many cases (perhaps even most), consciousness will exist ex poste in recognition of the strategy's successful outcome. While this recognition may be conscious, it need not be; it must be conscious only insofar as it is reproducible in the future, either by the same actor or by another. This posits a close relationship between outcomes and strategies and emphasizes both of these instead of individual choice. Such a treatment would allow for nonconscious forces in behavior (such as emotions and intuition), factors that now have to be introduced exogenously in both traditional and bounded rational models. And it would also revitalize the theory by reinstating the theoretical impetus for political behavior in the emotions.

If we design a theory of political rationality in which the concern is with learned strategies that further particular *outcomes* rather than with the *process* of choice, we allow a role for culture in replicating the strategy that led to optimization. The critical variables would then not be the actual decisions and choices taken by an actor but would instead be the outcomes, intended or fortuitous. The critical component of rational behavior would then be the *process* of evolving toward some stationary optimal point, not an actual decision itself. In this process, critical distinctions should be made between the long term and the short term. Strategies need not be the best (optimal) at any one particular moment, but they must be good enough to allow the individuals following them to survive. Behavior thus need not maximize in the short term, although over the long term it must optimize and do better than all other existing possibilities in order to survive. Optimal strategies, not individual choices, would thus be key. If the emphasis could just as well be on strategies instead of choices, then rationality can be defined (in part) as a strategy that leads through adaptation to survival. Such an approach would incorporate the "muddling through" we all know so well. In the short term, all of this would suggest satisficing rather than maximizing behavior. An emphasis on constant movement and local adaptation, however, would set a theory of political rationality apart from bounded rationality's emphasis on the internal process of choice instead of the outcome of a process and the forces that induce action.

Identities: Individuals and Groups. Finally, we should assume that actors have multiple identities, whose importance varies in response to cultural and situational contexts. (See Elster, 1986.) The key to understanding political behavior would then lie in delineating the actor's constant shift between these identities and the manner in which the actor's perception of his or her identity in relation to others defines the domain of relevant options.[19] To determine when an actor pursues strategies to further individual self-interest and when an agent will act to further interests as a member of a group, we must understand how the perception of a critical identity will affect action. Traditional political economists concerned with collective action have argued that individuals join groups because the group mediates resources for that individual or provides side benefits (Olson, 1965). But other forces also determine group memberships (e.g., parental-offspring bonds or socialization). The logic of social and political (as well as economic) competition is often mediated by a group; and the group to which you give allegiance at a particular moment may be determined by the problems you confront at the time and the way you view yourself in relation to others in the group. The marital relationship offers an instructive example. Husband and wife are a couple, a single unit to deal with mutual problems. But during a fight, each conceives of himself or herself as an individual with conflicting interests. Political negotiation may resolve many marital arguments, but just as many may be resolved by each actor simply deciding whether to remain a part of the marital group. While an economic calculus may explain part of this group behavior, understanding why the group forms and exists is certainly more complex. To understand group formation, we must focus on how groups mediate interests and act to replicate successful strategies.[20] In this process, the perception of one's central identity, and the way actors shift between their individual and their group identities, are crucial.

Parsing out the relevant part of the process by which actors shift from individual to group identity necessarily involves our understanding the cognitive frameworks of different actors. This allows for both internal stability and for changing conditions. It again allows for cultural variations, especially in that most critical variable: the actor's view of the relationship between the individual and society. Both traditional and bounded concepts of rationality reflect a post-Enlightenment framework that separates the individual from the collectivity.[21] Interests are not identified this way in many non-Western societies, however; and even in Western society, individuals have conceptualized their relationships with society quite differently in other historical eras.[22] (This strict differentiation of the individual from society or critical groups may explain why so many Western decision models, based on individualistic assumptions, often fail to predict behavior outside the Western market system.) A successful theory of political rationality should allow for the complex ties among individuals, groups, and society in general. How this can be done is unclear, but the focus on identity perception seems the right route to pursue, not the least because it will reduce the existing theory's individualistic bias and will allow us to focus on the polity's role in shaping both public and private identities.

While much of this introduction necessarily reflects my own ideas about what is needed to make rational actor theory into a more useful tool for political analysis, the reader will find in this volume many views that differ—sometimes quite significantly—from my own. In drawing together such diverse opinions on rational actor theory, written by both some of the major critics and some of the strongest proponents of the theory, it is my intention to stimulate constructive and collegial discussion. It is in this spirit that this volume is offered as a critical reexamination of the theory of rational action by practitioners and friendly skeptics.

NOTES

Acknowledgments: I would like to thank the Earhart Foundation and the University of California, Irvine, Senate Faculty Research Program for their generous support. Many of the chapters in this volume were originally presented at a conference honoring the contribution of Anthony Downs and sponsored by the University of California Inter-Campus Activity Fund. My thanks to the participants of the Downs conference, especially to Bernard Grofman as the co-organizer of the conference. David Easton, Gertrude Monroe, and Wil Lampros provided their usual generous encouragement and support. Jim Johnson, Howard Margolis, Jane Mansbridge, Walter Mebane, Norman Schofield, Eric Uslaner, and Donald Wittman provided particularly thoughtful comments on a draft of this chapter, which was presented at the 1989 Midwest meetings and which also appears in abbreviated form in *Political Science: An Assessment*, edited by William Crotty. Austin Ranney kindly agreed to let me quote from his dinner table repartee. Finally, my thanks to Ziggy Bates, Wilma Laws, Cheryl Larsson, and Susan Pursche for so cheerfully typing the many drafts of the manuscript.

1. Although this volume is entitled *The Economic Approach to Politics*, discussion is limited to one particular approach, that referred to as *rational actor theory*. While this is probably the dominant economic approach within contemporary political science, and is certainly one that has produced both much controversy and much rich analysis, it is not the only economic approach. A discussion of other economic approaches, particularly Marxism, is beyond the scope of this volume, except insofar as some of the Marxist critiques of neoclassical economics are reflected in particular chapters.

2. The major works on which twentieth-century rational choice theory was formulated are usually considered to be Kenneth Arrow, *Social Choice and Individual Values* (1951); James M. Buchanan and Gordon Tullock, *The Calculus of Consent: Logical Foundations of Constitutional Democracy (1952)*; Anthony Downs, *An Economic Theory of Democracy (1957)*; Duncan Black, *The Theory of Committees and Elections* (1958); William Riker, *The Theory of Political Coalitions* (1962); and Mancur Olson, *The Logic of Collective Action (1965)*. See Mitchell, 1988 or Mueller, 1984 for a discussion of the different schools of public choice. See Buchanan, 1984a, 1984b; Buchanan and Tullock, 1962; Buchanan and Wagner, 1977; Riker, 1962; Riker and Ordeshook, 1973; and Riker, 1982 on public choice theory's definitions. See Barry and Hardin, 1982 on the origin of social choice theory in welfare economics and Hardin, 1987 on the theoretical distinctions between social choice theory and game theory, which is utilized by analysts following all of these approaches.

3. Within this volume, see the chapters by Eckstein, Kavka, and Noll and Weingast for a discussion of this assumption.

4. See Smith (1937:14), Mansbridge (1990), and Myers (1983) on the extent to which "the first principle of economics is that every agent is actuated only by self interest" (Edgeworth, quoted in Sen, 1977:317). The twentieth-century specialization of rational choice theory also assumes self-interest as the norm (Harsanyi, 1969; Buchanan and Tullock, 1962; Downs, 1957; Olson, 1965). Within this volume, the chapters by Crozier, Downs, Petracca, Margolis, Noll and Weingast, Scalia, Whitehead, and Monroe et al. address this issue.

5. Traditional economic rationality actually adopts an outcome rather than a process view by use of the "as if" assumption (Friedman, 1953). Within this volume, see the chapters by Crozier, by Johnson, and by Monroe et al.

6. See Mansbridge (1990), Myers (1983), and the chapters by Petracca and by Crozier for discussion of this.

7. Within this volume, Noll and Weingast address this, as do Crozier, Rosenberg, and Wittman.
8. See the chapters by Ferejohn, Grafstein, Johnston, Rosenberg, and Wittman.
9. Even the briefest list of some of the main books in rational choice attests to the theory's importance in applied political science. See, inter alia, Fiorina (1974, 1977, 1981); Popkin (1979); Page (1978); Bates (1983); Calabresi (1981); Bobbitt (1978); Axelrod (1984); Ferejohn (1974); Posner (1977); Hardin (1982); Noll and Owen (1983); Schelling (1978b); or Hechter (1987).
10. See Barry (1970) and Harsanyi (1969) on the distinction between cultural theory and rational actor theory.
11. See Simon (1983, 1985), inter alia.
12. See Kahneman and Tversky (1972); Kahneman, Slovic, and Tversky (1982).
13. Riker's politician as fiduciary agent exemplifies this. Votes are traded for policies. Politicians act as entrepreneurs trying to increase their share of the political market by trading issue positions to put together winning coalitions.
14. "Since politics can take on aspects of a market, a game, a war, a church, a dramatic performance—and the history of the politics of individual societies shows how the explanation of politics over time may require some or all of them—opting for one of them as the realistic or the most realistic model is bound to have costs, [and will] exaggerate some of the potentialities of politics at the expense of others, and at the expense of the dynamic developmental perspective. [Thus] . . . rational choice analysis may lead to empirical and normative distortions, unless it is used in combination with the historical, sociological, anthropological, and psychological sciences which deal with the values and utilities of people, cross-culturally, cross-nationally, across the social strata, and over time" (Almond, page 36 of this volume). See also Turner (1987) on group formation.
15. Part of the Whitehead quotation comes from an earlier version of her chapter in this book.

In a closely related though less critical assessment, Kavka, in this volume, agrees that the central idea of the economic theory of politics is that we can best understand and explain the behavior of political actors (e.g., voters, bureaucrats) by assuming that they are rational utility maximizers. Kavka also agrees with Simon (1984) and with Almond, in this volume, that much of the real explanation in such theories comes from the auxiliary assumptions about human motivation. But Kavka argues that utility maximization acts as the "idea generator" to produce (without logically implying) these assumptions.

16. Rosenberg (1988) concludes that taken as a whole, the research in cognitive, social, and experimental psychology suggests "people do not have the information-gathering, interpretive or computational skills required to properly recognize, comprehend and evaluate the circumstances and consequences of choices made under conditions typical of political life" (Rosenberg, 1988:14).

17. Traditional schema theory may be less useful when we speak of political actors that are not individuals (e.g., parties or nations). Presumably, cultural theories can be useful here in helping us resolve some of the questions (such as whether groups can be said to have goals) that social choice theorists are currently debating.

18. While these two needs vary innately among individuals, both an individual's average position over time and the particular fluctuations along his or her individual continuum are determined by cultural conditions. Specifying how culture (in a general way) and context (in a more immediate way) affect identity will be difficult; but it will do much to specify how an actor's need to advance individual self-interest is balanced by the need to identify with a group or a collectivity.

19. The importance of multiple roles and identities has long been recognized in social science; cf. Rossiter's (1956) analysis of the presidency. How these roles are a function of societal conditions, or aspects of the problem confronted, has been a concern of anthropologists. See, for example, Evans-Pritchard's work on the Nuer (1962).

20. For biologists, traits enabling survival are transmitted genetically. In social science the transmission mechanism is not so clearly identified. Replication of strategies is an evolutionary process, with evolution traditionally said to occur in one of three ways. (1) The more effective individuals survive and reproduce. (2) Trial and error learning occurs, by actors either pursuing their more effective strategies or altering the strategies that were less effective in the past. (3) Actors observe and imitate strategies of more successful actors. In this process, it is the particular strategy followed that is the key to understanding behavior, not the action of any one individual. An understanding of how these strategies are replicated would emphasize both the role of evolutionary change and the way cultural constraints directly affect rational behavior.

21. Ironically, the Enlightenment's passion for individualism has made it difficult for traditional economic concepts of rationality to explain collective and group behavior (Arnhart, 1987). Kolm (1983:62) also notes the extent to which the individualization of society is a legacy of the eighteenth century, one from which contemporary social theory must free itself.

22. A less individualistic, more organic view argues that individual self-fulfillment results from taking part in the life of the polis, or society. (As the child grows into the woman or man, so the individual grows into the citizen.) Individual and group happiness cannot be separated. The good life is the life spent fulfilling civic duties. This organic view corresponds to ideas expressed by Plato and other classical Greek and Roman theorists.

An organismic view of the relationship between the individual's relation to a collectivity is exemplified by medieval theorists such as Aquinas. (As the heart is an organ independent within, but meaningless without, the entire body, so the individual is a separate yet integral part of society.) Each individual has his or her function to play within society; at the same time, each maintains an identity distinct within (but not separate from) society.

REFERENCES

Arnhart, L. (1987). *Political Questions*. New York: Macmillan.

Arrow, K. J. (1951). *Social Choice and Individual Values*. New Haven: Yale University Press.

―――. (1984). *Social Choice and Justice*. Oxford: Basil Blackwell.

Axelrod, R. (1984). *The Evolution of Cooperation*. New York: Basic Books.

―――. (1986). "An Evolutionary Approach to Norms." *American Political Science Review*, 80:1095–1111.

Ball, R. A. (1968). "A Poverty Case: The Analgesic Subculture of the Southern Appalachians." *American Sociological Review*, 33:885–895.

Barber, B. (1984). *Strong Democracy*. Berkeley: University of California Press.

Barry, B. (1970). *Economists, Sociologists and Democracy*. Chicago: University of Chicago Press.

Barry, B., and Hardin, R. (1982). *Rational Man and Irrational Society? An Introduction and Sourcebook*. Beverly Hills: Sage Publications.

Bartlett, F. A. (1932). *Remembering*. Cambridge: Cambridge University Press.

Bates, R. (1983). *Essays in the Political Economy of Rural Africa*. New York: Cambridge University Press.

―――. (1988). *Toward a Political Economy of Development: A Rational Choice Perspective*. (Ed.) Berkeley: University of California Press.

Becker, G. S. (1976). *The Economic Approach to Human Behavior*. Chicago: University of Chicago Press.

Black, D. (1958). *The Theory of Committees and Elections*. New York: Cambridge University Press.

Buchanan, J. (1984a). "Constitutional Restrictions on the Power of Government." In J. M. Buchanan and R. D. Tollison (Eds.). *The Theory of Public Choice—II*. Ann Arbor: University of Michigan Press, pp. 439–452.

———. (1984b). "Politics Without Romance: A Study of Positive Public Choice Theory and Its Normative Implications." J. M. Buchanan and R. D. Tollison (Eds.). *The Theory of Public Choice—II*. Ann Arbor: University of Michigan Press.

Buchanan, J. M., and Wagner, R. E. (1977). *Democracy in Deficit*. New York: Academic Press.

Buchanan, J. M., and Tullock, G. (1962). *The Calculus of Consent: Logical Foundations of Constitutional Democracy*. Ann Arbor: University of Michigan Press.

Calabresi, G., and Bobbitt, P. (1978). *Tragic Choices*. New York: Norton.

Caudill, H. M. (1962). *Night Comes to the Cumberlands*. Boston: Little, Brown.

Cropsey, J. (1977). *Political Philosophy and the Issues of Politics*. Chicago: University of Chicago Press.

Crotty, W. (Ed.). (1991). *Political Science: An Assessment*. Evanston, IL: Northwestern University Press.

Downs, A. (1957). *An Economic Theory of Democracy*. New York: Harper & Row.

Eckstein, H. (1984). "Civic Inclusion and Its Discontents." *Daedalus*, *113*:107–146.

Elster, J. (1979). *Ulysses and the Sirens: Studies in Rationality and Irrationality*. Cambridge: Cambridge University Press.

———. (1982a). *Rational Choice*. (Ed.). Oxford: Basil Blackwell.

———. (1986). *The Multiple Self*. (Ed.). Cambridge: Cambridge University Press.

———. (1989a). *The Cement of Society*. Cambridge: Cambridge University Press.

———. (1989c). *Solomonic Judgements: Studies in the Limits of Rationality*. Cambridge: Cambridge University Press.

Evans-Pritchard, E. E. (1962). *Nuer Religion*. Oxford: Clarendon Press.

Ferejohn, J. (1974). *Pork Barrel Politics: Rivers and Harbors Legislation, 1947–1968*. Stanford: Stanford University Press.

Festinger, L. (1957). *A Theory of Cognitive Dissonance*. Stanford: Stanford University Press.

Fiorina, M. (1974). *Representatives, Roll Calls, and Constituencies*. Lexington, MA: Lexington Books/D. C. Heath.

———. (1977, 1989). *Congress: Keystone of the Washington Establishment*. New Haven: Yale University Press.

———. (1981). *Retrospective Voting in American National Elections*. New Haven: Yale University Press.

Fishburn, P. C. (1973). *The Theory of Social Choice*. Princeton: Princeton University Press.

Fiske, S. T., and Taylor, S. E. (1984). *Social Cognition*. Reading, MA: Addison-Wesley.

Frazier, E. F. (1966). *The Negro Family in the United States*. (Rev. and abridged ed.). Chicago: University of Chicago Press. (Original work published 1939)

Friedman, M. (1953). *Essays in Positive Economics*. Chicago: University of Chicago Press.

Galambos, J., Abelson, R. P., Black, J. B. (1986). *Knowledge Structures*. Hillsdale, N. J.: Lawrence Erlbaum Associates.

Gardner, H. (1985). *The Mind's New Science*. New York: Basic Books.

Gaventa, J. (1980). *Power and Powerlessness: Quiescence and Rebellion in an Appalachian Valley*. Urbana: University of Illinois Press.

Geertz, C. (1953). *The Interpretation of Cultures*. New York: Basic Books.

Hardin, R. (1982). *Collective Action*. Baltimore: Johns Hopkins University Press.

———. (1987). "Rational Choice Theories." In *Idioms of Inquiry: Critique and Renewal in Political Science*. T. Ball (Ed.). Albany, N.Y.: State University of New York Press.

Harsanyi, J. (1969) "Rational Choice Models of Political Behavior vs. Functional and Conformist Theories." *World Politics*, *21*(4):513–548.

Hechter, M. (1987). *Principles of Group Solidarity*. Berkeley: University of California Press.

Heider, F. (1958). *The Psychology of Interpersonal Relations*. New York: Wiley.

Hirschman, A. O. (1977). *The Passions and the Interests*. Princeton: Princeton University Press.

Kahneman, D.; Slovic, P.; and Tversky, A. (Eds.). (1982). *Judgment Under Uncertainty: Heuristics and Biases*. New York: Cambridge University Press.

Kahneman, D., and Tversky, A. (1972). "A Subjective Probability: A Judgment of Representativeness." *Cognitive Psychology*, 3:430–454.

Key, V. O. (1942). *Southern Politics in State and Nation*. New York: Knopf.

Koffka, K. (1935). *Principles of Gestalt Psychology*. New York: Harcourt Brace and World.

Kolm, S. C. (1983). "Altruism and Efficiency." *Ethics, 94*, 1:18–65.

Maier, N. (1961). *Frustration: The Study of Behavior Without a Goal*. Ann Arbor: University of Michigan Press. (Original work published 1949.)

Mansbridge, J. (1980). *Beyond Adversarial Democracy*. New York: Basic Books.

———. (Ed.). (1990). *Beyond Self-Interest*. Chicago: University of Chicago Press.

Margolis, H. (1982). *Selfishness, Altruism and Rationality*. Cambridge: Cambridge University Press.

Mitchell, W. C. (1988). "Virginia, Rochester, and Bloomington: Twenty-Five Years of Public Choice and Political Science." *Public Choice, 56*:101–119.

Monroe, Kristen R. (in press 1991). "John Donne's People." *Journal of Politics*, 53(2) May 1991

Moynihan, D. P., and Glazer, N. (1966). *Beyond the Melting Pot*. Cambridge: MIT Press and Harvard University Press.

Mueller, D. C. (1984). "Public Choice: A Survey." In J. M. Buchanan and R. D. Tollison (Eds.). *The Theory of Public Choice-II*. Ann Arbor: University of Michigan Press.

Myers, M. (1983). *The Soul of Economic Man*. Chicago: University of Chicago Press.

Nisbett, R. E., and Borgida, E. (1975). "Attribution and the Psychology of Prediction." *Journal of Personality and Social Psychology*, 32:932–943.

Nisbett, R. E., and Ross, L. (1980). *Human Inference: Strategies and*

Shortcomings of Social Judgment. Englewood Cliffs, NJ: Prentice-Hall.

Noll, R., and Owen, B. M. (1983). *The Political Economy of Deregulation: Interest Groups in the Regulatory Process*. Washington, DC: American Enterprise Institute.

Olson, M., Jr. (1965). *The Logic of Collective Action*. Cambridge, MA: Harvard University Press.

_____. (1982). *The Rise and Decline of Nations*. New Haven: Yale University Press.

Page, B. (1978). *Choices and Echoes in Presidential Elections*. Chicago: University of Chicago Press.

Pateman, C. (1970). *Participation and Democratic Theory*. Cambridge: Cambridge University Press.

Popkin, S. (1979). *The Rational Peasant*. Berkeley: University of California Press.

Posner, R. A. (1977). *Economic Analysis of Law*. Boston: Little, Brown.

Quattrone, G. A., and Tversky, A. (1988). "Contrasting Rational and Psychological Analyses of Political Choice." *American Political Science Review*, 82:719–737.

Riker, W. H. (1962). *The Theory of Political Coalitions*. New Haven: Yale University Press.

_____. (1986). *The Art of Political Manipulation*. New Haven: Yale University Press.

Riker, W. H., and Ordeshook, P. C. (1973). *An Introduction to Positive Political Theory*. Englewood Cliffs, NJ: Prentice-Hall.

Rodman, H. (1971). *Lower Class Families: The Culture of Poverty in Negro Trinidad*. London: Oxford University Press.

Rosenberg, S. (1988). *Reason, Ideology and Politics*. Princeton: Princeton University Press.

Rossiter, C. (1956). *The American Presidency*. New York: Harcourt Brace and World.

Sandel, M. (1984). *Liberalism and Its Critics*. New York: New York University Press.

Schattschneider, E. E. (1975). *The Semi-Sovereign People: A Realist's View of Democracy in America*. Hinsdale, IL: Dryden Press.

Schelling, T. C. (1978a). "Altruism, Meanness, and Other Potentially Strategic Behaviors." *American Economic Review*, 68:229–230.

_____. (1978b). *Micromotives and Macrobehavior*. New York: Norton.

_____. (1984). *Choice and Consequence*. Cambridge, MA: Harvard University Press.

Schofield, N. (1985). *Social Choice and Democracy*. Berlin: Springer-Verlag.

Sen, A. S. (1977). "Rational Fools: A Critique of the Behavioral Foundations of Economic Theory." *Philosophy and Public Affairs*, *6*(4):317–344.

Sen, A. (1984). *Collective Choice and Social Welfare*. (2nd ed.) New York: North-Holland, Elsevier Science Publications.

Shepsle, K. A. (1979). "Institutional Arrangements and Equilibrium in Multidimensional Voting Models." *American Journal of Political Science* 23:27–59. Fall.

Simon, H. A. (1982). *Models of Bounded Rationality*, vols. 1–2. Cambridge, MA: MIT Press.

———. (1983). *Reason in Human Affairs*. Stanford: Stanford University Press.

———. (1985). "Human Nature in Politics: The Dialogue of Psychology with Political Science." *American Political Science Review*, 79:293–304.

Smith, A. (1937). *The Wealth of Nations*. New York: Modern Library.

Taylor, M. (1982). *Community, Anarchy and Liberty*. Cambridge: Cambridge University Press.

———. (1987). *The Possibility of Cooperation*. Cambridge: Cambridge University Press.

Taylor, S. E., and Fiske, S. T. (1975). "Point-of-View and Perceptions of Causality." *Journal of Personality and Social Psychology*, 32:439–445.

Toynbee, A. (1946). *A Study of History*. New York: Oxford University Press.

Turner, J. (1987). *The Reemergence of the Social Group: A Self-Categorization Theory*. New York: Basil Blackwell.

Tversky, A., and Kahneman, D. (1974). "Judgment Under Uncertainty: Heuristics and Biases." *Science, 185*:1124–1131.

Wattenberg, M. (1988, October 28–29). "Economic, Psychological, and Sociological Theories of Voting." Paper presented at the University of California Conference in Honor of Anthony Downs, Irvine.

Weingast, B. (1979). "Rational Choice Perspective on Congressional Norms." *American Journal of Political Science*. 23:245–262.

Weller, J. E. (1965). *Yesterday's People: Life in Contemporary Appalachia*. Lexington: University of Kentucky Press.

Chapter

1

Rational Choice Theory and the Social Sciences

Gabriel A. Almond

THE PREHISTORY OF RATIONAL CHOICE THEORY

Since this volume, honoring the thirtieth anniversary of the publication of Anthony Downs's *Economic Theory of Democracy*, has sentimental as well as substantive aspects, I ask your indulgence if I reach back for a few appropriate memories. In 1956–1957 I occupied study 14 at The Center for Advanced Study in the Behavioral Sciences. Robert Dahl had occupied that study the previous year, and either he had left me his copy of the dissertation of Anthony Downs, or Kenneth Arrow, who was a fellow that same year, gave me a copy. It was in the form of a report to the Office of Naval Research, which had funded the study. Indeed, it was presented as a dissertation in the form of a Report to the ONR. There was no other version. No changes were made in the manuscript from dissertation to report to published book. Kenneth Arrow chaired Downs's committee, and Robert Dahl and Charles Lindblom were instrumental in getting the dissertation published. I still own that cardboard-bound, mimeographed version of *An Economic Theory of Democracy*, which must now be a collector's item.

Downs's book was the first thing I read at the center in California in 1956. I was then deep in political sociology and psychology, and reading Downs's spare formulations and claims of explanatory power was an astringent experience. But there were aspects of the work which were continuous with a literature with which I was quite familiar. Market-like metaphors were in general use in the analysis of democratic and American politics. The 1950s were the era of the "decline of ideology." Political pragmatism was in the air. T. V. Smith, the homespun philosopher from the University of Chicago, a colleague of the Chicago philosophical pragmatists, and an Illinois state senator, had presented a picture of the successful democratic politician as a somewhat cynical, corruptible, but peaceful resolver of conflicts, as early as the mid-1930s. Pendleton Herring quotes Smith's comparison of the politicians of dictatorship with those of democracy. Smith had written:

> It is precisely that outcome [violence] of intergroup conflicts which the democratic politicians shield us from. If they sometimes lie in the strenuous task, it is regrettable but understandable. If they sometimes truckle, that is despicable but tolerable. If they are sometimes bribed, that is more execrable but still not fatal. The vices of our politicians we must compare not with the virtues of the secluded individual but with the vices of dictators. In this context, almost beautiful things may be said of our politicians—by way of compensation, if not by way of extenuation, of whatever vices attend upon the arduous process of saving us from violence and murder. People elsewhere get killed in the conflicts of interest over which our politicians preside with vices short of crimes and with virtues not wholly unakin to magnanimity (cited in Herring, 1940:135).

On the eve of our involvement in World War II, Pendleton Herring employed market metaphors in describing party politics in the United States:

> Much of our present expectation of governmental aid and relief is only traditionalism expressed in novel terms. There is no great alteration in fundamental attitudes. We had a politics of the handout—free land, mining concessions, shipping subsidies, tariff, and so on. A survey of the nineteenth century reveals continual demands for grants and subsidies. The demands of the little fellows can no longer be met by homesteads and similar concessions. A broader distribution is now demanded. The process, however, involves few niceties of theory or philosophy; it appears as opportunism faintly flavored with humanitarianism. We do not find the ideological conflict which aroused passions so hotly in European countries. In the United States social problems have seldom been related to systematic philosophies, nor has public policy been guided by an abstract formulation of values. Leaders of discontent talk in terms of concrete needs (1940:175).

And again he argues:

> Since major party politicians are not bound by party discipline to follow a definite program, they have much freedom to bargain with interest groups. In this sense the fact that our major parties stand

for so little makes minor parties all the more unnecessary. Through the formation of blocs in Congress sections and states win concessions from party leaders. Special interest organizations control votes that may affect the political life of Democrats or Republicans (1940:187).

In addition Herring anticipated the Downs forecast that, given a normal distribution of voters' ideological predispositions,

> there is a strong tendency for both parties to take the same stand. Once a winning program is discovered, it is equally attractive to both parties. This is well illustrated by the appeal of Senator Arthur Vandenburg during the high tide of Democratic party success. He urged a liberalization of Republican party policy through support of unemployment insurance, retirement pensions, and minimum wage laws.... Republicans will not let Democrats have a monopoly of farmers, workers, and the middle class. Democrats are divided about the wisdom of alienating business. What is good for one party is also good for the other, the differences lying chiefly in matters of personnel, emphasis, and tempo rather than substance. The rivalry really comes down to who is going to manage the rearrangement and fix the terms (1940:193).

Two years later the economist Joseph Schumpeter employed the market metaphor more directly in his analysis of the realistic workings of democracies. Speaking of political leadership, he said:

> This concept presents similar difficulties as the concept of competition in the economic sphere, with which it may be usefully compared. In economic life competition is never completely lacking, but hardly ever is it perfect. Similarly in political life there is always some competition, though perhaps only a potential one, for the allegiance of the people. The justification for this is that democracy seems to imply a recognized method by which to conduct the competitive struggle, and that the electoral method is practically the only method available for communities of any size. But though this excludes many ways of securing leadership which should be excluded, such as competition by military insurrection, it does not exclude the cases that are strikingly analogous to the economic phenomena we label "unfair" or "fraudulent" competition or restraint of competition. And we cannot exclude them because if we did we should be left with a completely unrealistic ideal. Between this ideal case which does not exist and the cases in which all competition with the established leader is prevented by force, there is a continuous range of variation within which the democratic method of government shades off into the autocratic one by imperceptible steps (1942:271).

Downs drew directly on Schumpeter for Adam Smith's "invisible hand" metaphor as well. He quotes this passage from the Harvard economist:

Similarly, the social meaning or function of parliamentary activity is no doubt to turn out legislation and, in part, administrative measures. But in order to understand how democratic politics serve this social end, we must start from the competitive struggle for power and office and realize that the social function is fulfilled, as it were, incidentally—in the same sense as production is incidental to the making of profits (1957:29).

The continuity of Downs's theory with the conventional wisdom of the 1950s is reflected in his acknowledgment of his debt to Schumpeter. "Schumpeter's profound analysis of democracy forms the inspiration and foundation for our whole thesis, and our debt and gratitude to him are great indeed" (1956:29). Other predecessors and contemporaries of Downs in employing these market-like metaphors included V. O. Key (whose leading text on political parties, from its first edition in 1942, stressed the notion of political leadership as involving bargaining and exchanges). Elmer Schattschneider, also a leading interpreter of American parties and elections, repeats the Schumpeter metaphor of the politician as entrepreneur. The task of the citizen is "to learn how to compel his agents to define his options," and the problem for the political system as a whole is

> how to organize [the electoral process] so as to make the best possible use of the power of the public in view of its limitations. A popular decision bringing into focus the force of public support requires a tremendous effort to define the alternatives, to organize the discussion and mobilize opinion. The government and the political organizations are in the business of manufacturing . . . alternatives (1960:139).

The market metaphor, thus, was one of the "literary" metaphors common among students of American politics. Voting was viewed as "like" exchanging votes for policies. And the activities of politicians were viewed as "like" that of entrepreneurs engaged in efforts to increase market share, by trading issue positions and combining resources in search of winning coalitions.

The Downs revolution consisted in converting this literary metaphor into an explicit formal model with all the advantages that such explication conferred. It generated specific hypotheses about party systems which could be tested empirically, and it opened up the possibilities of rigorous scientific work involving mathematization and the use of sophisticated statistics. Since this "will to deductive and inductive rigor" dominated the social sciences of the 1950s and 1960s, it is not surprising that the rational choice and public choice literature flowered in the next decades and into the present, and became the cutting edge of "scientific" political science.

But Downs remembered, just as many of the scholars joining this school tended to forget, that there were costs attendant upon adopting the rational market model. In the pre-Downsian era of literary metaphor, the market metaphor was only one of four or five metaphors found to be useful in the study of politics.

There was politics as religion, with conversion, prayer, and worship rather than buying and selling as the defining activity. Some aspects of French, Italian, Spanish, Latin American, German, and Middle Eastern politics can be captured by this metaphor. Or there was politics as warfare, with paramilitary formations, arms, and fighting for control of the streets. Lenin referred to the leading organs of the Communist Party as the general staff of the revolution. The operating patterns of Nazism, Fascism, Falangism, and other authoritarian movements can also be partly captured by this military metaphor.

We are all familiar with the metaphor of "the game of politics," in which participants become involved because of the fun and excitement, rather than because of the power and policy aspects of political activity. Or, as suggested recently by Clifford Geertz (1980), politics may take the form of play acting, in which the principal goal is edification deriving from the actors' symbolic affirmation of their powers and roles.

Since politics can take on aspects of a market, a game, a war, a church, a dramatic performance—and the history of the politics of individual societies shows how the explanation of politics over time may require some or all of them—opting for one of them as the realistic or the most realistic model is bound to have costs, to exaggerate some of the potentialities of politics at the expense of others, and at the expense of the dynamic developmental perspective. This is the main argument in my essay, that rational choice analysis may lead to empirical and normative distortions, unless it is used in combination with the historical, sociological, anthropological, and psychological sciences which deal with the values and utilities of people, cross-culturally, cross-nationally, across the social strata, and over time.

RATIONAL CHOICE THEORY AS A SCIENTIFIC REVOLUTION

At the time that rational choice theory began to spread out of its native habitat in economics in the late 1950s and early 1960s, the dominant approaches to explanation in the social sciences were sociological theory, culture and personality theory, and social psychological theory. The first, sociological theory, drew on the European tradition of Max Weber, Emile Durkheim, Vilfredo Pareto, and others. The second, culture and personality theory, drew on psychoanalytic and anthropological theory, as in the work of Margaret Mead, Ruth Benedict, Ralph Linton, Harold Lasswell, Abram Kardiner, the Kluckhohns, et al., or on that of the "authoritarian personality" version. Social psychological theory, associated with survey research and small-group experimental methodologies, was advanced by the work of Samuel Stouffer, Paul Lazarsfeld, Rensis Likert, Angus Campbell, Carl Hovland, Kurt Lewin, Dorwin Cartwright, and others.

Nineteenth- and early twentieth-century sociological theory, contra Marx, treated ideas, preferences, and values as of importance in the formation, maintenance, and breakdown of institutions. Norms and values were central to Durkheim's (1973) theories of social integration. Human beings were joined together in societies on the basis of a *conscience collective*, a set of common values and beliefs; suicide was a symptom of normlessness, of *anomie*. Weber (1930) traced the origins of capitalism to the worldly asceticism of the Protestant sects. The will to order one's life, save and accumulate capital, and invest, was based upon the religious view that salvation was somehow associated with success in one's worldly endeavors. For Talcott Parsons (Parsons and Shils, 1951) social action was explained by feelings, beliefs, and values; and social institutions were maintained by socialization processes inculcating these orientations. Culture and personality theory, as in Ruth Benedict (1934), explained the social structure, the politics, and the public policy of different societies in terms of "national character," cultural themes, modal personality, and the like—mixes of beliefs about authority and human relations—which result in part from the ways in which members of these societies were inducted into their adult roles. And social psychological theory treated attitudes and beliefs as important explanatory variables in electoral behavior, as in Lazarsfeld and Berelson (1955); in the morale of the military, as in Shils and Janowitz (1948); in responses to propaganda, as in Hovland (1953); in prejudiced attitudes, as in Adorno et al. (1950); and the like.

The mental, the moral, the attitudinal dimensions were very much in the center of social science discourse in the 1950s and 1960s. This mental and moral world was assumed to be quite complex, dynamic, and generative and not simply reflective. It was a central argument of these literatures that attitudes and values varied substantially, cross-nationally and historically, and that they had substantial explanatory power.

The rational choice literature avoided this complexity. For economists, their intellectual tradition assumed a homogeneous, material-interest, "utility" function. For the generation of political scientists who adopted the rational choice approach in the 1960s and 1970s, there was a deliberate turning toward economics, and a turning away from the other social sciences. While one encounters occasional citations of social science literature in such early works as Anthony Downs's study (1957) celebrated in this volume, Riker's study of coalitions (1962), and the early book of Buchanan and Tullock (1962)—with occasional references to Parsons, Durkheim, Lazarsfeld, Campbell, Horney, Dahl, Easton, and the like—there is a clear break with the intellectual tradition of the social sciences of the 1950s and 1960s.

There is also a self-conscious adoption of the deductive strategy of economics in the analysis of political phenomena. Government and politics are assumed to be similar to markets. Officials, politicians, and voters are short-term, material, self-interest maximizers, seeking benefits in the form of power, legislative and administrative decisions, votes, and the like. Starting with these assumptions, the pioneers in this approach quickly established its power and parsimony in explaining aspects of party systems, constitutional arrangements, and political coalitions. The movement looks so much like the scientific revolution described by Thomas Kuhn (1962), with its abrupt adoption of a new paradigm, not cumulative with previous scientific work, and with its prompt shift to the puzzle-solving of a new "normal public choice science," that one is tempted to conclude that they had deliberately adopted a Kuhnian strategy. The dates of publication, however, rule out such a possibility.

CORE RATIONAL CHOICE THEORY

Rational choice theory is a deductive strategy—purely such, for example, in the work of Downs, Riker, Buchanan and Tullock, and others, or deductive in combination with empirical testing of logically derived hypotheses, as in the work of Fiorina (1981), Ferejohn et al. (1987), Shepsle and Fiorina (1988), and others. It proceeds from assumptions or axioms about human motives and behavior, and draws the logical institutional and policy implications from those axioms. One aspect of this meta-methodological approach is "methodological individualism," which argues that all social phenomena are derivable from, or can be factored into, the properties and behaviors of individuals. A second aspect is that political actors—voters, politicians, bureaucrats—are assumed to be material-interest maximizers, seeking benefits in the form of votes, offices, power, at least cost.

There are a variety of positions taken in the rational choice literature on the nature of these assumptions. Some scholars attribute substantial or "sufficient" realism to the material self-interest assumption. Others argue that the question of realism is secondary, as long as the predictions generated from these assumptions are substantiated. Still others treat the method in purely heuristic terms, as an efficient way of generating hypotheses, starting with simple assumptions, and then complicating them in a controlled effort to increase explanatory power. Some of these scholars have argued more than one position over time.

Milton Friedman, in his early work *Positive Economics* tells us that

> the relevant question to ask about the "assumptions" of a theory is not whether they are descriptively "realistic," for they never are, but whether they are sufficiently good approximations for the purpose in hand. And this question can be answered only by seeing whether the theory works, which means whether it yields sufficiently accurate predictions (1953:40).

And again, he argues that it is not necessary to establish the complete realism of

> any assumption of such theories. . . . A meaningful scientific hypothesis or theory typically asserts that certain forces are, and other forces are not, important in understanding a particular class of phenomena. It is frequently convenient to present such a hypothesis by stating that the phenomena it is desired to predict behave in the world of observation as if they occurred in a hypothetical and highly simplified world containing only the forces that the hypothesis asserts to be important. . . . Complete "realism" is clearly unattainable, and the question whether it is realistic "enough" can be settled only by seeing whether it yields predictions that are good enough for the purpose at hand or that are better than predictions from alternative theories (1953:42).

He attributes a limited realism to the economic-market model, and draws policy implications from it. Friedman also recognizes cultural differences in a limited way. Thus he qualifies his view that price theory was the most robust theory of modern economics, stating that it deserved "much confidence *for the kind of economic system that characterizes Western nations*" (1953:42; emphasis mine).

Buchanan and Tullock, in *The Calculus of Consent*, take a position similar to that of Friedman:

> The ultimate defense of the economic-individualist behavioral assumption must be empirical. . . . Fundamentally, the only test for "realism" of the assumption lies in the applicability of the conclusions (1962:28–29).

But while Buchanan and Tullock stop short of adopting the "individual self-interest norm" as the only "realistic" one, they make a strong argument for its appropriateness in the analysis of politics:

> We know that one interpretation of human activity suggests that men do, in fact, seek to maximize individual utilities when they participate in political decisions and that individual utility functions differ. . . . [S]o long as some part of all individual behavior in

collective choice-making is, in fact, motivated by utility maximization, and so long as the identification of the individual with the group does not extend to the point of making all individual utility functions identical, an economic-individualism model of political activity should be of some positive worth (1962:30).

In his *Theory of Political Coalitions* (1962) Riker defended the realism of the rational self-interest assumption. He argued that while individual behavior may deviate from the self-interest assumption, fiduciary behavior is client-centered. The trustee is obligated to act in the material interest of the client. And since much of politics (e.g., the politician–voter-citizen relation) is based on a fiduciary relationship, the self-interest assumption is applicable to a large part of political action.

In later work Riker (with Ordeshook) defended the assumption on simple meta-methodological grounds:

> the rationality assumption asserts that there is something about people that makes them behave (usually) in a regular way, just as in physical science the mechanical assumption is made that there is something about things that assures us they will (usually) move regularly. In both cases there is an assumption that things behave in regular ways (1973:11).

Riker and Ordeshook go on to argue

> that the notion of rationality plays a fundamental role in social science. It is one of the ways by which we arrive at the regularity necessary for generalization. Whether or not it is better than simple observation is currently the subject of some discussion in political science, being a particular form of the old debate between inductive and deductive methods or between radical empiricism and theoretical science. As is apparent, we side with deductive methods and postulated regularity, largely because we believe them more efficient than their alternative.... [T]he method of postulated regularity is positively more efficient because it permits the easy generation of hypotheses and offers a single parsimonious explanation of behavior. As against this efficiency, the method of observed regularity is ad hoc.... Even if catalogued into hypotheses, behavior appears extraordinarily complex, while with a simplifying and coordinating theory, much of the complexity disappears. On the practical grounds of efficiency, therefore, we prefer postulated regularity (1973:12).

Riker appears to have dropped the issue of realism. The self-interest assumption has become an assumption of goal-oriented regularity.

Downs, in *An Economic Theory of Democracy*, qualifies the rational self-interest assumption. He writes:

> In reality, men are not always selfish, even in politics. They frequently do what appears to be individually irrational because they

believe it is socially rational.... In every field, no account of human behavior is complete without mention of such altruism; its possessors are among the heroes men rightly admire. Nevertheless, general theories of social action always rely heavily on the self-interest maxim [because it tends to be realistic] (1957:9).

In later work Downs adopts a more sociological-historical-philosophical approach to the individual utility problem and assimilates his economic model of democracy into it. He describes his early trailblazing work as involving

a relatively abstract theoretical model of voter and party behavior... gradually introducing certain realistic elements into it, such as the cost of information.... It assumed that all individual preferences were given at the outset. I believe that approach provided an interesting and fruitful way to look at democratic politics. But it was not meant to be either comprehensive or fully realistic (1988:32).

Morris Fiorina quotes from the early Downs approvingly, but adopts the contemporary version of rational choice in economic theory, in which he states that

the assumption of "rational" behavior means no more than the notion that individuals engage in "maximizing" behavior. In any situation the alternatives open to an individual lead to various benefits (typically in some probabilistic fashion). These alternatives entail various costs. The individual chooses so as to maximize the difference between expected benefits and costs, where there are wide varieties of theories about how to calculate those expectations. This is the contemporary generalization of Downs's argument, and, I hope, the perspective of election studies of the future (1981:198).

There is, thus, some ambiguity as to the claims being made for the realism of the rational self-interest assumption. There seem to be at least two different versions. The first is that it is "partly" realistic, or "sufficiently realistic," or that its "realism doesn't make all that much difference" as long as it generates useful or valid predictions. The second version sets aside the material self-interest assumption and replaces it with a rational maximizing assumption in relation to any kinds of goals. But this later version of the assumption is not always adhered to. If we look at the policy-oriented work of Buchanan and Tullock, and Riker, for example, it is clear that policy recommendations tend to get made on the basis of the first version, the one which imputes some degree of realism to the rational self-interest assumption. It also may involve the introduction of other supporting assumptions, the realism of which is affirmed without being demonstrated, as we suggest below.

PERIPHERAL RATIONAL CHOICE THEORISTS

The theorists whose views on the realism of the rational self-interest assumption we have described might be described as core rational choice theorists. They include the founders and leaders of the Rochester and Virginia schools of public choice theory (see below). Others of these schools are not on record as to their views on these methodological questions. There are a number of scholars, such as Terry Moe, Douglass North, Samuel Popkin, Robert Bates, and others, who might be described as peripheral members of the rational choice school, who use the economic model heuristically, employing it in combination with other models.

Thus Terry Moe argues that rational models may be taken as "pretheories, which provide a systematic basis for progress toward the goal of explaining certain social behaviors. In this capacity, they operate as intermediate mechanisms that aid in conceptualization, facilitate analysis through their simplicity and deductive power, point to relevant relationships, and thereby contribute to the development of empirical laws (1979:237). Douglass North, in his interpretation of the economic history of Western civilization, systematically applies the models of neoclassical economic theory to such political questions as the emergence of the state and its role in enhancing and inhibiting economic growth. He describes this as a heuristic undertaking, stating: "We must, of course, be cautious about the limits of neoclassical theory. Public choice theory—economics applied to politics—has at best had only a modest success in explaining political decision making" (1981:21).

Third world development theorists such as Popkin and Bates apply rational choice economic models again quite self-consciously as models. Thus Popkin weighs the alternative rational choice and moral economy models in his study of the Vietnamese peasantry:

> I have modified the two views of peasant society. A free-market economics approach, even when amended to take account of peasant aversion to risk, cannot explain the patterns of stratification and production in the precolonial, colonial, and revolutionary eras in Vietnam without considering collective goods and leadership, political coalitions that shape markets, and the infrastructure of the economic system, including taxes, courts, land titles, law and order, and insurance. The moral economy approach, while fully cognizant of the risks and dangers of markets and the importance of villages and patron-client relations for peasant survival, requires modification as well to take account of the ways in which aversion to risk, conflicts between public and private forms of investment, and conflicts among the peasantry limit the quality and extent of insurance and welfare embedded in peasant institutions (1979:267).

Robert Bates, who has done exemplary work on African and third world political economy, rejects the two major forms of political economy, conventional microeconomics and the "standard" radical or Marxist approaches. He points out:

> The study of agrarian politics reveals the limited relevance of voluntary exchange; economic coercion is a fact of everyday life. The study of rural communities reveals as well the significance of institutions other than markets. And the study of agricultural policy making demonstrates that consideration of objectives other than economic efficiency drives the selection of policies and forms of policy intervention. Clearly, then, conventional economics provides a weak foundation for the study of agrarian political economy. Radical political economy does little better. Consideration of the fate of the peasantry demonstrates that effective class action is problematic. And the analysis of public policy reveals that a theory of politics cannot rest on the presumption of historical materialism; political intervention as frequently retards the growth of productive forces as it promotes it (1987a:185).

Bates recommends a collective choice approach reconciled with culture theory in his most recent work. He recounts his intellectual history, saying that he began his work on the peasantry of the third world

> by shouldering aside, as it were, the contribution of cultural studies. But now at the end, I want to return to this scholarly tradition. For having ventured into the field of political economy, scholars have acquired new tools; and it may now be time for them to return with these tools in hand to analyze the significance of distinctive values and institutions. Who can fail to appreciate the opportunity offered by contemporary game theory to provide a formal structure for kinds of symbolic displays analyzed by Goffman or Geertz, for example? Work on games of imperfect information offers grounds for analyzing their powerful insights into the subjective side of influence and power. And who can fail to appreciate the significance of models of collective choice for the analysis of such institutions as lineage systems, village councils, or systems of traditional authority? Already some scholars have recognized the value of applying these tools. One can hope that the contributions represent but a beginning of a new tradition of research into the properties of significant institutions. . . .
>
> In the early years of political economy, "rational choicers" posed as revolutionaries, attacking their sociologically minded brethren. Now it may be time to promote the synthesis and reintegration of these traditions. Because they work in cultures possessing distinctive beliefs, values, and institutions, those studying the developing areas may be best placed to take this important step (1987b:55–56).

THE CASE OF RIKER'S THEORY OF COALITIONS

It may be instructive to examine coalition theory, exemplified in the work of Wiliam Riker, as an example both of the productivity of the rational choice approach and of its limitations in a general strategy of social explanation. Riker, in reviewing the empirical fate of the size, or minimum winning coalition, principle, concluded that while the theory is deductively sound, "its empirical validity is somewhat less certain" (1983:47–69). He acknowledged that empirical studies of European cabinet formation showed that many coalitions have been larger (or smaller) than minimal. Abram de Swaan (1973) and Lawrence Dodd (1976) demonstrated that ideological similarity was important in European coalition formation, and that this resulted in many deviations from the "minimal winning" expectation. But Riker then goes on to say that when cabinets are examined according to their duration, it has been found that the oversized and undersized coalitions have not lasted as long on the average as the minimal ones, so that the size principle has indeed been supported empirically.

In fact, Dodd found that of all the cabinets formed in Western Europe during the period 1918–1974, 31 percent were minimal winning coalitions and 69 percent were either over- or undersized. Thus the size principle failed on the percentage of tosses of the coin, so to speak, but it predicted better on the question of the duration of cabinets. Dodd found that, on the average, minimal winning coalitions lasted 58 months, while undersized cabinets lasted on the average of 9 to 20 months, depending on how far they fell short of a majority; and oversized ones lasted 13 to 29 months, again depending on the extent to which they exceeded a majority.

There is thus something to the size principle. There is an underlying propensity for coalitions to oscillate around minimal winning size. But this theory misses a lot of what is going on in the world of cabinet coalitions. To understand cabinet formation, we need more theoretical tools than Riker provides for us. Let me review two recent studies which began with Riker's size principle, introduced additional assumptions, and ended up with validated theories of different aspects of European government and cabinet formation.

Gregory Luebbert (1986), in his study of government formation in Europe and Israel, demonstrates a relationship between the structure and culture of political systems, and the kinds of coalitions typically formed in them. Luebbert divides contemporary democracies into four types based upon their degree of legitimacy and consensuality—consensual, competitive, unconsolidated, and conflictual. Consensual democracies are those in which the regime enjoys high legitimacy and the opposition is supportive and cooperative; competitive democracies are characterized by high legitimacy, but the opposition parties are consistently competitive; conflictual democracies are lacking in widespread legitimacy and the opposition is uncooperative, while unconsolidated democracies are those in which there is low legitimacy but in which the parties tend to consensual practices. Luebbert finds that the size principle is sustained only in undominated competitive democracies—that is to say, among those democracies in which there is high legitimacy, in which no party is consistently in the majority, and in which the opposition is consistently competitive. In competitive democracies in which there is one dominant majority party—e.g., Israel (1950–1974), Belgium (1973–1980), the Netherlands (1945–1966)—there is a strong tendency for oversized coalitions to form. Consensual and legitimate democracies, such as Norway, Sweden, and Denmark, have been frequently governed by undersized or minority coalitions, while in conflictual democracies, such as the Fourth French Republic, the Weimar Republic, and Italy, there has been an equal probability of minority and majority government. Thus Luebbert has established that rational self-interest might lead to consistently oversized and undersized coalitions under differing conditions of partisanship and legitimacy. Luebbert concludes:

> The limited relevance of this assumption should now be apparent; it is only in undominated-competitive systems that one finds the need for majorities that is absent in consensual systems; the ability to create them that is absent in conflictual systems; and the urgency that is missing in dominated-competitive systems, where dominance makes creation of majority governments virtually assured (1986:84).

Kaare Strom, in a study of minority governments in post-World War II Europe, shows that minority coalitions may form "... as the result of rational choices made by party leaders under certain structural constraints" (1990:237). Strom isolates two major species of minority governments—those which arise in consensual political systems in which the cost-benefit ratio of remaining outside the government is more favorable for a possible, majority-making coalition partner or partners than the cost-benefit ratio of membership in the governing coalition; and those in which the costs of tolerating a minority government are lower than the systemic costs of opposing it. Strom analyzes coalition formation in Norway and Italy as exemplars of the two types. Both can be explained in terms of rational self-interest, varying according to different structural-cultural constraints.

The implication of the work of Luebbert and Strom is that coalition theory in its pure game-theoretical, size-principle form has to be supplemented by comparative political party theory, if it is to explain coalition behavior in the real world. Thus, as far as cabinet formation theory is concerned, Riker's size principle turns out to have valuable payoffs. It set in motion a productive research program which led to a more rigorous theory of government formation in parliamentary democracies. The intellectual history of coalition theory with special reference to European cabinet formation is reviewed systematically and comprehensively in the recent work of Michael Laver and Norman Schofield (1989).

In an effort to adapt coalition theory to the analysis of political crises and change, Almond, Flanagan, and Mundt (1973) made a number of historical case studies, using a common framework of analysis. The historical studies included the British Reform Act of 1832, the formation of the French Third Republic, in the 1870s; the formation of the Weimar Republic, after the First World War; the Meiji Restoration in Japan, in the mid-1860s; and the Cardenas phase in the Mexican Revolution, in the 1930s. What is relevant to our discussion is that in order to use coalition theory in these historical studies, we had to trace the transformation of political actors, their utilities, and resources as they were affected by changes in the international context and the domestic social structure and culture. From our estimates of these changes we could generate the logically possible coalitions, their policy and resource properties, and the probability of their occurrence at different stages in the development of these crises. The successful coalitions in these historical episodes were not necessarily the most probable ones by strict coalition-theoretic measures. Leadership—as measured by skill in resource mobilization, and/or facility in manipulating, combining, or compromising on issues—had to be factored in, in order to explain the Cardenas victory in Mexico, the Meiji Restoration in Japan, or the collapse of leadership (i.e., missed coalition opportunities) in the Ramsay MacDonald failure in the British crisis of 1931 and the Social Democratic failure in the formation of the Weimar Republic. Thus on the historical problems of the rise and fall of kings and republics, coalition theory has a role, but a relatively modest one. It must be viewed in relation to the often dramatic macro-changes in international and domestic strategic, political, economic, and social structure, which alter the rules and issues of the political game, the identity of the players, and the value of their resources. Even at the micro-level, coalition theory will not take us all the way by any means. It is a useful device enabling us to spell out coalition options under different assumptions and their resource and utility properties. But the properties of utilities and resources cannot be fully captured in hard numbers. They have plastic possibilities which a strong will, insight, and imagination, and a good sense of timing, can enhance, reduce, or otherwise transform.

It is not only the case that rational choice scholars may fudge a bit on the question of the content and realism of their assumptions; in much of their work their inferences turn out to be based more on unacknowledged side assumptions. Thus Herbert Simon, in his comparison of rational choice theory with cognitive "bounded rational choice" theory, comes to the conclusion that

> actors in the political drama do appear to behave in a rational manner—they have reasons for what they do, and a clever researcher can usually obtain data that give good clues as to what those reasons are. But this is very different from claiming that we can predict the behavior of these rational actors by application of the objective rationality principle to the situations in which they find themselves. Such prediction is impossible . . . because it depends on their representation of the world in which they live, what they attend to in that world, and what beliefs they have about its nature (1985:300).

Simon makes the point that rational choice and game-theoretical studies of political phenomena typically rely on assumptions "not derivable from the principle of objective rationality" (1985:298ff.) These assumptions usually have to do with the utility functions of the voters or political actors, their political beliefs, expectations, and calculations, which have to be ascertained empirically.

In a paper entitled "Three Fallacies Concerning Majorities, Minorities, and Democratic Politics" (1989), Ian Shapiro makes an argument similar to that made by Herbert Simon. He criticizes that part of the public choice literature which proposes changes in the American Constitution, restricting the scope of governmental power, or requiring extraordinary majorities before government is able to act. Much of the public choice literature, and particularly that part of it associated with the work of James Buchanan and William Riker, makes additional assumptions regarding the distribution of political resources, as well as transaction costs, that are not factored into their policy conclusions (e.g., James Buchanan and Richard Wagner, 1977, 1978; William Riker and Barry Weingast, 1986). Thus the argument advanced by Tullock and others that justifies the requirement of extraordinary majorities in order to limit encroachments on private economic concentration is based on erroneous or complacent assumptions as to the distribution of political resources and as to the transaction costs of mobilizing extraordinary majorities. Shapiro attributes a central weakness to the failure of this literature

> to deal with the problem of resources, and we can now see that in so doing it ignores most of what politics is really about. For the sense of powerlessness that sometimes motivates political action, and at other times motivates our intuition that political action is warranted, is exactly the lack of resources of individuals and groups to achieve goods and limit harms on their own. . . . While the pub-

lic choice theorists are persuasive that there is no reason to expect majority rule to produce fair or just outcomes, this does not supply a rationale for what is often a utilitarian jurisprudence geared toward wealth maximization (1989:39).

Thus the public choice or rational choice literature may be faulted on the grounds that it often introduces supporting assumptions that are outside the logic of objective rationality, and that it often fails to acknowledge assumptions that are important for their policy conclusions which may be of doubtful validity. These, of course, are serious criticisms if the rational choice assumption serves as a basis for policy conclusions. Where such an assumption is used heuristically and where policy implications are related to empirical tests of actual human values and behavior, the rational choice model may play an important constructive role.

CONCLUDING REFLECTIONS

There are many examples of the productivity of the rational choice approach. Scholars employing its insights and methods have illuminated aspects of democratic party and electoral systems, legislative organization and process, and peasant politics in the third world, and problems of state building and revolution and of international security and diplomacy. But though rational self-interest is a kind of culture, a kind of approach to valuation, rational choice theory has tended to resist drawing on the knowledge and insights of the social sciences that deal in detail with values and culture. I am not the first to make this point. In recent years Aaron Wildavsky (1987), Lucian Pye (1988), Ronald Inglehart (1989) and others have argued the same point. One does encounter anthropological, sociological, and psychological propositions and insights among the peripheral rational choice theorists such as Douglass North, Robert Bates, Samuel Popkin, and others. Along with this goes a more complex explanatory structure, including cultural and institutional differences.

The failure to relate this economic model of rationality in any way to the sociological, psychological, anthropological literatures and particularly to the work of Max Weber, whose great theoretical accomplishment was an analysis of modern civilization and culture in terms of rationality and rationalization, is the most striking consequence of the almost complete "economism" of the rational choice literature. One of the major parts of Weber's sociology dealt with the economic ethics of the world religions. In this careful, systematic comparison of the economic ethics of Buddhism, Confucianism, Hinduism, Islam, Judaism, and Christianity, he explained the origins of modern capitalism by the particular way the Protestant sects associated divine grace and salvation with material success. This theory of the cultural religious origins of "rational self-interest" is alive and kicking today in efforts to explain in part the rapid economic growth of the East Asian NICs (newly industrializing countries) in terms of their Confucian culture.

It was in this connection that Max Weber provided us with a typology of goal-oriented behavior which included, along with the rational self-interest variety, which he called *Zweckrationalität*, or instrumental behavior, *Wertrationalität*, or absolute value-oriented behavior, traditional or habitual behavior, and impulsive behavior. From this perspective we can see what a small part of the reality we, as social scientists, want to explain is captured by the rational choice model. In situations where absolute values come into play, where habit and tradition are important, or where affect and emotion are controlling, hardly rare occurrences, a simple rational choice forecast is going to mislead us.

The rational choice school offers us the alternative view of the self-interest assumption that it is simply a rational maximizing assumption and that it does not have a particular substantive content. As the blank tile in Scrabble can take on the value of any letter, so the rational choice assumption, they seem to be assuring us, can take on the value of any utility imputed to it. Given this viewpoint, it is difficult to defend their neglect of the social science literatures which display the variety of values, preferences, and goals in time and space—in different historical periods, in different cultures and societies, and among different social groupings. Though they make out a most convincing case for including the "micro-level" in the analysis of social and political institutions and processes, and the value of the deductive approach in generating hypotheses explicitly and efficiently, they leave out the disciplines that could specify the content of the utilities that operate at the micro-level in different times and places.

This failure of rational choice theorists to confront these literatures directly, except in a few recent cases, leaves them with theories that cannot travel very far in space and time, and cannot deal effectively with political change.

REFERENCES

Adorno, T.; Frenkel-Brunswik, E.; Levinson, D. H.; and Sanford, N. (1950). *The Authoritarian Personality*. New York: Harper & Row.

Almond, G. A.; Flanagan, S. C.; and Mundt, R. (Eds.). (1973). *Crisis, Choice, and Change*. Boston: Little, Brown.

Bates, R. (1987a). "Agrarian Politics." In M. Weiner and S. Huntington (Eds.), *Understanding Political Development*. Boston: Little, Brown.

_____. (1987b). *Macro Political Economy in the Field of Development*. Duke University Program in International Political Economy. (Working Paper No. 40)

Benedict, R. (1934). *Patterns of Culture*. Boston: Houghton Mifflin

Buchanan, J. (1978). *The Economics of Politics*. West Sussex: Institute of Economic Affairs.

Buchanan, J., and Tullock, G. (1962). *The Calculus of Consent: Logical Foundations of Constitutional Democracy*. Ann Arbor: University of Michigan Press.

Buchanan, J. M., and Wagner, R. E. (1977). *Democracy in Deficit*. New York: Academic Press.

de Swaan, A. (1973). *Coalition Theories and Cabinet Formation*. San Francisco: Jossey Bass.

Dodd, L. (1976). *Coalitions in Parliamentary Government*. Princeton: Princeton University Press.

Downs, A. (1957). *An Economic Theory of Democracy*. New York: Harper & Row.

_____. (1988). *The Evolution of Modern Democracy*. Washington, DC: Brookings Institution. Unpublished manuscript.

Durkheim, E. (1973). *On Morality and Society*. Chicago: University of Chicago Press.

Ferejohn, J.; Cain, B.; and Fiorina, M. (1987). *The Personal Vote*. Cambridge, MA: Harvard University Press.

Fiorina M. (1981). *Retrospective Voting in American National Elections*. New Haven: Yale University Press.

Friedman, M. (1953). *Essays in Positive Economics*. Chicago: University of Chicago Press.

Geertz, C. (1980). *Megara*. Princeton: Princeton University Press.

Herring, E. P. (1940). *The Politics of Democracy*. New York: Norton.

Hovland, C. (1953). *Communication and Persuasion*. New Haven: Yale University Press.

Inglehart, R. (1989). "The Renaissance of Political Culture." *American Political Science Review*, 82:1203–1230.

Key, V. O., Jr. (1942). *Politics, Parties and Pressure Groups*. New York: Crowell.

Kuhn, T. (1962). *The Structure of Scientific Revolutions*. Chicago: University of Chicago Press.

Lazarsfeld, P., and Berelson, B. (1955). *Voting*. Chicago: University of Chicago Press.

Laver, M., and Schofield, N. (1989). *The Politics of Coalitions in Europe*. New York: Oxford University Press.

Luebbert, G. (1986). *Comparative Democracy*. New York: Columbia University Press.

Moe, T. (1979). "On the Scientific Status of Rational Choice Theory." *American Journal of Political Science*, 23(1):237.

North, D. (1981). *Structure and Change in Economic History*. New York: W. W. Norton.

Parsons, T., and Shils, E. (1951). *Toward a General Theory of Action*. Cambridge, MA: Harvard University Press.

Popkin, S. (1979). *The Rational Peasant*. Berkeley: University of California Press.

Pye, L. (1988). *The Mandarin and the Cadre*. Ann Arbor: University of Michigan Press.

Riker, W. H. (1962). *The Theory of Political Coalitions*. New Haven: Yale University Press.

———. (1983). "Political Theory and the Art of Herasthetics." In A. Finifter (Ed.), *Political Science: The State of the Discipline*. Washington, DC: American Political Science Association.

Riker, W. H., and Ordeshook, P. C. (1973). *An Introduction to Positive Political Theory*. Englewood Cliffs, NJ: Prentice-Hall.

Riker, W., and Weingast, B. (1986). *Constitutional Regulation of Legislative Choice: The Political Consequences of Judicial Deference to Legislatures*. Stanford, CA: Stanford University, Hoover Institution (Working Paper Series)

Schattschneider, E. E. (1960). *The Semisovereign People*. New York: Holt, Rinehart and Winston.

Schumpeter, J. (1942). *Capitalism, Socialism, and Democracy*. New York: Harper and Brothers.

Shapiro, I. (1989). "Three Fallacies Concerning Majorities, Minorities, and Democratic Politics." In J. Chapman and A. Wertheimer (Eds.), *Majorities and Minorities: Political and Philosophical Perspectives*. Nomos 32. New York: New York University Press.

Shepsle, K. and Fiorina, M. (1988). "Is Negative Voting an Artifact?" Stanford, CA: Stanford University, Graduate School of Business, unpublished manuscript.

Shils, E., and Janowitz, M. (1948). "Cohesion and Disintegration in the Wehrmacht in World War II." *Public Opinion Quarterly, 12*:280–315.

Simon, H. (1985). "Human Nature in Politics: The Dialogue of Psychology with Political Science." *American Political Science Review*, 79:293–304.

Strom, K. (1990). *Minority Government and Majority Rule*. Cambridge: Cambridge University Press.

Weber, M. (1930). *The Protestant Ethic and the Spirit of Modern Capitalism*. London: Allen and Unwin.

_____. (1978). *Economy and Society* (G. Roth and C. Wittich, Eds.). (Vol. 1). Berkeley: University of California Press.

Wildavsky, A. (1987). "Choosing Preferences by Constructing Institutions. *American Political Science Review*, 81(1):3–23.

Chapter
2

The Forgotten Limits: Reason and Regulation in Economic Theory

Jaan W. Whitehead

Most critical evaluations of the extension of rational actor models from economic to political analysis focus on two questions: (1) do individual political actors behave in the maximizing self-interested way described by rational actor models and (2) if they do, does this lead to desirable collective political outcomes? The first question is an empirical one which asks whether political behavior can be explained by the economic model of individual behavior. The second question is a normative one which asks whether the consequences of such behavior are desirable. In each case, as many of the chapters in this book suggest, serious questions have been raised about the adequacy of the economic model for political analysis. Empirically, other factors appear to determine political behavior besides those contained in the rational actor model. Normatively, self-interested rational behavior often leads to collective political outcomes which offend either democratic norms or ideas of the public good. As a consequence, rational choice theorists now are attempting to expand both their model of individual behavior and their analyses of how individual rational choice can lead to more harmonious collective outcomes.

In this chapter, I will argue that some of the challenges facing rational actor theorists today are the result of constraints imposed on them by the marginalist, or neoclassical, theory on which the rational actor approach is based.[1] I will argue further that the nature of these constraints can be seen by comparing the marginalist model with the classical economic theory which preceded it. When one looks back at the classical formulation of economic behavior, particularly the founding work of Adam Smith, one finds a rich set of questions and analyses about the nature of human behavior and the relation of the individual to society. With the transformation of economic theory to the marginalist model, a number of important changes took place which restricted both the view of human behavior included in the model and the kinds of options that might be considered in relating individual behavior to collective outcomes. The result was a truncated view of both the individual and the individual's relation to society, which, whether appropriate for economic analysis or not, is problematical for political analysis. It is, in part, this truncated view which constrains rational actor theorists in their efforts to understand and meet the challenges of their critics. The classical economists did not have answers to the kinds of political questions facing contemporary rational actor theorists, but they did frame questions in a way which shows the limitations of the later marginalist model for analyzing these questions. By gaining a deeper understanding of the history of economic thought, we can put the current debate in a clearer perspective.

To document this argument, I will look first at Adam Smith's original formulation of modern economic theory. In all of his work, Smith's concern was to identify how people behave and then to analyze how that behavior could be harmonized to produce desirable collective outcomes. The two most important elements of his analysis for current rational actor theory were that he believed that people were motivated by emotions rather than reason in their behavior and that some regulation was needed to produce harmony between individual behavior and desirable collective outcomes. For Smith, this was true in the moral and political realms of life as well as in the economic realm. But it was only in his economic analysis that he was able to identify a set of dependable emotions which produced regularities in individual behavior and a natural and reliable regulatory force which harmonized this behavior with the already defined collective goal of maximizing output. The emotions were those of self-interest, and the natural regulatory force was the competitive market. In the other realms of life, Smith did not find either a dependable set of emotions or a reliable natural regulatory force. Therefore, he would not be surprised to find that political behavior does not necessarily conform to the contemporary notion of individual rationality or that self-interested behavior does not necessarily lead to collective political harmony. Smith would not have expected the special nature of economic activity to be reproducible in political analysis.

The second part of my argument shows that it was the marginalist transformation of economic theory which made it appear feasible to extend rational actor models to political behavior. The key to this transformation was that the dynamic analysis of economic growth of the classical economists was narrowed to an idealized model of static equilibrium. In this idealized model, individual preferences became assumptions of the model rather than variables to be explained, individual behavior based on self-interested emotions was converted to a theory of rational choice, and consumers were elevated to a position of sovereignty in the economic system. In the marginalist revision, individuals came to be seen as autonomous actors and both their diverse emotional motivations for behavior and their need for regulation became masked behind the new static theory of rational choice. It is this theory of rational choice that has been extended to political analysis.

The problem is that, by extracting the rational actor model from its economic context, the factors in the marginalist model which appeared to support the changes in how individual behavior was viewed—namely the presence of the competitive market system as a harmonizing force and the clear definition of the desirable collective goal of maximizing output—were no longer present. Political life does not have such a clearly defined collective goal or a dependable natural regulatory force. Therefore, it is no longer clear that self-interested maximizing behavior should be considered rational or that unconstrained individual preferences should be granted sovereignty, as they are in the rational actor model. The context which appeared to validate these descriptions of individual behavior is no longer present. As we apply the model to political analysis, the questions have to be asked whether individual desires are compatible with collective political goals and, if not, whether they can be regulated to be compatible. These questions, in turn, reopen the questions of how individuals form their preferences, what rationality means in terms of the individual's relation to society, and what the collective goals of society should be.

These, of course, are the questions which originally structured Adam Smith's inquiries but which became lost in the marginalist reformulation of economic theory. The fact that they are also the questions being posed by critics of rational actor theory today reflects, I believe, the inadequacies of the marginalist formulation for political analysis. It is how these inadequacies developed that I want to explore, since I believe that they provide a context for understanding some of the challenges currently being raised to rational actor models of politics.

THE CLASSICAL FORMULATION

Although economic theories have existed throughout the history of recorded thought, the origins of the most important characteristics of modern economic theory are to be found in the work of Adam Smith. It was Smith who identified self-interest as an appropriate motivation for economic activity and maximizing output as the appropriate collective economic goal. And it was Smith who identified the competitive market system as the regulatory force which could harmonize self-interested behavior with this desired collective goal. These parts of his economic analysis laid the groundwork for the development of modern economic theory. However, in that development, Smith's economic views became stereotyped and were taken out of the context of the intellectual framework in which he developed them. Smith's own economic analysis was part of a wider analysis of society which included moral and political studies, and it is only in the context of his wider intellectual approach that the later changes in economic theory can be appreciated.

Smith's concern in all of his work was to examine the relationship between the individual and society. He saw humankind as an emotional being, and he tried to analyze the types and intensities of the various emotions that motivated human behavior. As a result of his analysis, he determined that, left on its own, emotionally driven behavior would result in conflict. From this he concluded that, in order for people to live together in society, their behavior needed to be constrained or regulated.[2] Such constraint could take place through self-regulation, but his study of human beings deemed this an unrealistic basis on which to establish social interaction. Selfish and destructive emotions were too powerful to be reliably tamed by voluntary self-regulation. A second alternative was coercive regulation by government, but, since human beings also make up government and are prone to both mistaken judgment and infringements of personal freedom, this became, for Smith, a last resort if other types of regulation failed.[3]

A third alternative, and the one that Smith favored, was regulation though natural forces that were impersonal but could be relied upon. One of the more interesting aspects of Smith's work is that, although he was a modern thinker in many ways, he also retained elements of older modes of thought. He believed that there was a natural harmony in the world and that it was humanity's job to discover this harmony and, if possible, to conform to it. For Smith, such natural harmony was providential, or God-ordained. However, because he was a Deist and never used direct references to God, he substituted such phrases as the "Great Judge," the "Author," "Nature," and the famous "Invisible Hand" to refer to these providential harmonizing forces. Since self-regulation was undependable and government regulation uncertain and potentially coercive, his analysis of moral, political, and economic behavior became a search for such natural regulatory forces which could produce harmony between the individual and society.

Structuring this search was his analysis of humankind's emotional nature, which was most fully developed in Smith's study of moral life. In *The Theory of Moral Sentiments*, Smith identified three categories of emotions, which he called the social passions, the unsocial passions, and the selfish passions.[4] Both the social passions and the unsocial passions involved relationships between an individual and other people. The social passions were emotions, such as generosity, sympathy, and kindness, which draw people together. The unsocial passions were emotions, such as hatred, envy, and resentment, which drive people apart. The selfish passions, on the other hand, were self-regarding emotions which related to the individual and could be either positive or negative. When emotions were self-regulated and became appropriate to their objects, Smith believed that they could acquire the quality of virtue. From the social passions could emerge the virtue of benevolence, which was the positive quality of helping others, and the virtue of justice, which was the neutral quality of refraining from hurting others. From the selfish passions could emerge the virtue of prudence, or proper concern for one's well-being. And from the unsocial passions could emerge the virtues of forbearance and stoic acceptance.[5] In the development of his work, Smith identified benevolence as the proper virtue of moral life, justice as the proper virtue of political life, and prudence as the proper virtue of economic life.

However, since relying on virtuous behavior was undependable in most cases, the problem, as Smith saw it, was to determine if there were natural forces which could regulate and thus encourage individual behavior toward social harmony. His approach was empirical in the sense that he tried to look at how people behaved and to see whether there were patterns of behavior that revealed such natural regulatory forces. In the moral sphere, he attempted to identify such a natural force, which he called the "Impartial Spectator." The "Impartial Spectator" was a person's projected imagination of how other, less involved, people viewed that individual. Since other people would not sympathize with the individual's emotions to the same extent that they sympathized with their own, the individual would tend to dampen the expression of his or her emotions in order to maintain sympathy from others. Smith believed that this was a natural phenomenon which helped to temper individual behavior and increase social harmony.[6]

The problem was that Smith believed that this particular natural regulative force was not very powerful. In the moral sphere, people's emotions ranged in many directions and the negative emotions often were stronger than the positive desire for sympathy upon which the "Impartial Spectator" relied. Therefore, social harmony was left indeterminate in Smith's analysis.[7] Benevolence was the appropriate virtue in this realm of life, but it was not based on a stable set of emotions and was not supported by a powerful enough regulatory force for it to be dependable.

Therefore, when Smith turned to his analysis of political life, he looked for a stronger mechanism to regulate conflict, since he believed that protection of people and of property were essential to the stability of society. Although we have only student notes on his lectures in this area, since he did not live to complete a full work on the subject, in the work we have he did not find a natural regulatory force to fill this role.[8] He identified justice as the proper virtue associated with political life, justice being the weaker virtue of the social passions, which meant refraining from hurting others. But, since the virtue of justice, like the virtue of benevolence, depended on sympathy, it also could not be relied on. In the absence of a natural regulatory force, Smith turned to government regulation as the only dependable form of constraint in the political world and defined law as the regulator that would curtail behavior which infringed on people's rights. Law backed by coercion was needed to establish the basic security of society so that people could pursue their lives. Smith said that the rules of justice, or laws, were like the rules of grammar, necessary for basic composition and essentially teachable and enforceable. In contrast, the rules of benevolence were like the rules "which the critics lay down for the attainment of what is sublime and elegant in composition."[9] These rules cannot be taught or enforced but can be inspirational guides to help the writer produce more elegant prose. The laws enforcing justice are essential to a stable society, whereas the richer virtues, although not enforceable, are what enhance a society and make it admirable. We cannot know what further analysis Smith might have made of political life if he had lived or if we had a fuller record of his thought, but it is clear that he believed that a strong regulatory force was necessary in political life. Since he did not identify such a natural regulatory force, he recognized law or government coercion as taking its place.

However, when Smith turned his attention to economic behavior in *The Wealth of Nations*,[10] he found a different situation than he had found for either moral or political behavior. In analyzing economic behavior, he identified both a strong set of emotions which motivated this behavior and a powerful natural mechanism which organized this behavior into what he considered to be a desirable societal outcome. The emotions were the self-regarding or self-interested emotions he had identified in *The Theory of Moral Sentiments*. Concern for self-preservation and the maintenance of one's livelihood are, at the most basic level, what produces economic activity in the first place. And appropriate concern for these needs produces the virtue of prudence. In this sense, Smith believed self-interest to be both an appropriate and a realistic foundation for economic activity.[11]

However, more than this was needed to establish a dependable pattern of behavior. One of the key characteristics of self-interested emotions was that, because they were closest to the individual, they were best defined and understood by the individual. If self-interested emotions did come into conflict with opposing emotions, they were more dependable than emotions based on sympathy. And Smith believed that, when given free rein, economic self-interest produced more powerful emotions than just prudent concern for self-preservation. His central proposition was that people basically want to better their economic condition. In part, this comes from the need to sustain themselves and their dependents. But in larger part it comes from the desire to achieve status and the approval of other people.[12] Although Smith did not necessarily approve of economic achievement as the basis for status, he found it to be an extensive and commanding factor of the society he was investigating.[13] This desire to achieve status produced a vigor in economic activity that prudence alone would not produce.

In addition, Smith believed there was a natural propensity in human nature to "truck, barter, and exchange one thing for another."[14] This propensity led to a division of labor which significantly increased productivity and led, in turn, to the development of markets, both for labor and for goods. As markets became more complex, a common currency emerged and price systems developed. Entrepreneurs entered these markets trying to sell at the highest prices and buy at the lowest prices they could attain. The tension between these two objectives led to competition developing among buyers and among sellers, with supply and demand finally setting the market price. As long as everyone continued to act in a self-interested way and as long as the mobility of labor and goods was not restricted, the markets would organize economic activity, encouraging the division of labor and yielding increased output. By observing how people acted if left free to follow the strong emotions of self-interest, Smith discovered that there was, indeed, a natural mechanism that regulated behavior which was the mechanism of the competitive market. In the market process, although people tried to buy at the lowest price and sell at the highest price in order to maximize their goods and income, the market process, in fact, forced the curtailment of these objectives for each individual through the competition of all individuals. This competition led to the most efficient utilization of resources which maximized total output. Although each individual acted in only a self-interested way, the competitive regulation of self-interested behavior led to public benefit in the form of increased total output.

This market transformation of private interest to public benefit was exactly the kind of natural regulatory force that Smith had been looking for. In keeping with his Deist beliefs, in one place he referred to this market mechanism as the "Invisible Hand" by which man is led to "promote an end which was not part of his intention,"[15] the end being an increase in aggregate output and the intention being personal advantage. Smith himself did not fully understand why the competitive market led to the most efficient utilization of resources and the maximization of output. It was not until the development of marginal analysis that the process was fully understood. However, Smith captured the essence of the process and, even after it was more fully explained, his characterization of it not only as a natural process which transforms private interest to public benefit but as a mystical "Invisible Hand" phenomenon remained.

The problem for Smith was that, under the prevailing mercantalist economic doctrines of the 1700s, economic production and trade were heavily regulated by the government so that the benefits of the freely competitive market could not be achieved. The central tenet of mercantilism was that the political power of a state could be enhanced by accumulating specie or precious metals such as gold and silver. In that era of emerging nation states, political power was, to a large extent, conceived in terms of the ability to wage war. The wealth of a country, in turn, was defined as the stock of specie which could be used to pay for such wars. Holding a large stock of specie gave prestige and power to a nation because it defined its military potential. Leaders in that era believed that the way to achieve this goal was to run a positive balance of trade so that there would be a net gain in specie paid into a country. This was accomplished through detailed government regulation of the economy aimed at promoting cheap raw material imports, promoting exports of the resulting manufactured goods, and providing protective duties on imported manufactured goods. The Navigation Acts, which so affected the trade and politics of the American colonies, were part of this general effort to use the economy to attain political goals.[16]

One of the central purposes of Smith's book, the full title of which is *An Inquiry into the Nature and Causes of the Wealth of Nations*, was to challenge this definition of wealth and, therefore, the goal of economic policy.[17] He argued that specie is only a small part of a country's wealth. The true wealth of a country is the output of goods and services available to the people. It is this output that should be maximized, not specie. And for output to be maximized, the natural forces of the market must be allowed to operate freely. Government regulation of production and trade stifled these forces and reduced the growth of output. Although it was some time before his arguments were accepted politically, they eventually became the centerpiece of economic thought, establishing the economic goal of maximizing output rather than the political goal of maximizing specie as the accepted goal for economic activity.

Smith's argument in favor of free economic activity also had an additional attractive aspect for him. Although he believed in a providential natural harmony in the world, he also believed in the modern value of individual freedom. Freedom, for Smith, meant the classical liberal definition of absence from outside interference. His preference was that, as long as people did not interfere with other people's freedom, they should have the liberty to pursue their own lives. This, of course, is the positive statement of his definition of justice, or the refraining from hurting others. The advantage of the market system was that it left people free to pursue their own interests and what regulation did take place was due to the impersonal market rather than the government. As a transitional thinker, Smith adhered to the idea of a social structure of natural harmony, but he peopled that social structure with modern free and autonomous individuals.[18] Where he failed to find strong natural regulative forces to achieve harmony among such individuals in the moral and political spheres of life, he not only described such a regulatory force in the economic sphere but identified it in relation to the self-interested emotions of human beings. It is, of course, because his analysis fit so well the transformation to be caused by the industrial revolution that this part of his thought became so important to later thinkers while his other analyses tended to fall into disuse. But within the context of his whole work, it is clear that economic activity is a special case. It is because there is a natural regulator of behavior that leads to a public benefit that individuals are to be left free to follow their private interests. Such behavior would be inappropriate in either the political or moral spheres of life.

However, even in the economic sphere of life, Smith was never sanguine about people's behavior. As he had said, self-interest involves vanity as well as prudence. And when vanity, or the lust for power and wealth, was carried too far, it would disrupt the economic system. In Smith's era in England, it was business leaders who were most likely to have the power to circumvent the system to their own advantage, since labor, at that time, was unorganized and comparatively weak. Scattered throughout Smith's writings were admonitions to beware of industrialists attempting to distort the market for their own ends. Although Smith wanted government to stop interfering in the internal workings of the market, he recognized the need for government to protect the market from the excesses of its own participants. In addition, Smith believed that government had a direct role in the economy in the provision of public goods, such as roads and educational institutions, that it would not be in the interests of private individuals to supply. Because of the technical nature of these goods, government would be needed to supplement the market.

Of course, Smith also recognized the need for government to be the caretaker of justice through the use of law. Personal liberty was the desired condition but, within a society, it needed to be limited by protection against encroachment on the liberty of others. Behind the free market system must stand a law-abiding society in which individuals' persons and property are protected. The market is like a game in which all can freely participate, but government is needed to set up and enforce fair rules of play.[19]

In setting out his arguments against mercantilism, Smith provided the basis for a new approach to economic theory.[20] Rather than the government organizing economic activity toward the political goal of maximizing specie, economic activity should be left free to organize itself toward the economic goal of maximizing output. Government's role was to set the general framework of external and internal peace for the country, to police abuses of the economic system, and to produce some goods which the market could not provide. If left on their own, people would follow their own economic self-interest in an enterprising way. The market would harness this self-interest and transform it into the goal of maximizing output. Within this market process, people would have the natural liberty to direct their own activities as long as they did not interfere with the liberties of others. What adjustments had to take place in these activities came from the impersonal forces of the market, not government coercion.

However, the approbation that Smith gave to this system depended on the special characteristics of economic activity which he had identified, both the existence of a dependable set of emotions and a natural regulatory mechanism to harness these emotions to attain the collective economic goal. For Smith, there was a special balance between the economy and the rest of society. It would not be appropriate to apply the same analysis to the political or moral spheres of life. Not only were a different range of emotions associated with these other areas of life, but the virtues Smith thought appropriate to these other areas were different. And the other areas did not have strong natural regulatory forces similar to the competitive market which harmonized individual behavior with societal needs. The economy could be dominated by private self-interested modes of behavior because Smith felt they worked well there as long as they were contained within the overall political and moral system. But this economic analysis was empirically and normatively appropriate only to economic activity, not to political or other activity.

What made it possible for contemporary economic theorists to feel justified in extending economic theory to political analysis is that the nature of economic theory changed significantly under the influence of the marginalist, or neoclassical, economists. Smith's analysis had been accepted and expanded by other classical economists such as David Ricardo and John Stuart Mill, who followed him in the early and middle 1800s. The theory which the classical economists built under Smith's influence had a number of defining characteristics. One of these was that the central concern of the classical economists was growth theory, or how economic output increased over time. Their particular interest was in explaining how the factors of production, such as land, labor, and capital, contributed to economic growth. Since the prices received by these factors—namely rent, wages, and profits—affected their costs and availability, how income was distributed among the factors was an essential element in that analysis. Therefore, much of the classical work was aimed at developing theories of income distribution, the emphasis being on the supply side of the market within the dynamic context of economic growth.

Under the influence of the marginalists, the dynamic analysis of economic growth and income distribution which characterized classical thought was transformed into a deductive model of static equilibrium which emphasized the demand side of the economic process rather than the supply side. Consumers became elevated to a position of sovereignty in the model, and their behavior was reformulated into a process of rational choice. This changed the nature of economic analysis so that not only did Smith's concern with the emotional bases of behavior and the need to regulate that behavior become obscured but many of the wider political and social concerns of the classical economists became excluded from consideration. Although the marginalist analysis led to greater precision and contributed significantly to the understanding of the market process, it also resulted in a truncated model of human behavior which had neither the complexity nor the social and political relevance of the classical model.

THE NEOCLASSICAL REVISION

The neoclassical revision of economic thought was based on the marginalist revolution which occurred in the 1870s, with the simultaneous discovery by Jevons, Menger, and Walras of the principle of marginal utility.[21] In contrast to the classical thinkers, the concern of these writers was to explain the behavior of individual consumers in a single time period rather than to explain the factors affecting aggregate growth over successive time periods. Their emphasis, therefore, was on the demand side of economic activity, particularly the role of the consumer. They postulated that consumers would allocate their income among commodities in a way which would maximize the satisfaction, or utility, from them. Their discovery was that it was the last amounts purchased of the goods which were the critical factor in whether utility or satisfaction was maximized. This was called the *marginal amount*, hence the terms *marginal utility* and *marginalism*.

The significance of these discoveries was much greater than would immediately seem apparent. Put in the framework of marginal utility, the problem of maximizing an individual's satisfaction could be reformulated as the basic calculus problem of maximization subject to constraints. The problem, then, became one of maximizing consumer utility subject to the constraints of the individual's available income and the prices of the goods desired. Solving the problem yielded the result that, when a stable maximum was reached, the marginal utility of each good divided by its price must be the same for all goods. This meant that the additional satisfaction derived from a dollar spent on one good was the same for all goods. If this were not so, total satisfaction could be increased by further shifts among goods.

As the use of this mathematical model became accepted, it was applied to the other sectors of the market where the maximization principle was seen to hold. A profit-maximizing model of the firm evolved which was the counterpart of consumer theory. In this model, profits were maximized subject to the constraint of factor prices and availability and the constraint of technology. When this problem was solved, marginal conditions for maximization were obtained analogous to those in the consumer model. From the two models, aggregate demand and supply curves were derived and, eventually, a complete model of market equilibrium.

For this model of market equilibrium to work properly, however, two critical assumptions had to be made. The first was that markets were perfectly competitive. This meant that there were many buyers and sellers so that no one participant could unduly influence the market, that resources and participants had free mobility to enter and leave markets, and that participants had good information about what was taking place in the markets. It was only under the conditions of perfect competition that the market was efficient, allocating the given resources in a way which maximized output and consumer satisfaction.

The second critical assumption was that consumers and entrepreneurs acted rationally. In marginalist theory, this came to mean that individuals, whether consumers or entrepreneurs, could order their desires or preferences in a coherent way and that they could search out and follow the best means to fulfill these desires. In other words, consumers and entrepreneurs could identify and prioritize their goals and act efficiently to maximize them. The goal for consumers, of course, was the self-interested maximization of utility, while the goal for entrepreneurs was the self-interested maximization of profits. If economic actors did not choose these goals or did not choose the best means to achieve them, then the system as a whole would not maximize total output. In effect, the mathematical requirements of the marginalist model defined rationality once the definition of self-interest was established. In order for output to be maximized, preferences had to be well-ordered and individuals had to act in a maximizing way. It was only under these conditions, along with the requirements of perfect competition, that the model worked properly.

An additional characteristic of the marginalist model was that, since the market process was occurring only in one time period, consumer tastes and incomes, technology, and the availability of resources were considered to be fixed. This was significantly different from the classical model, in which the goal was to see how changes in these components affected the growth of output. In the marginalist model, there was no dynamic theory of income distribution. Rather, income distribution was determined in each time period by the market process—that is, wages, profits, interest, and rent were the outcomes of the supply and demand existing in that time period.

This change to a static model with fixed inputs had a number of consequences. One of the most important was that, since consumer preferences were considered a given in any time period, it was no longer relevant to ask how such preferences were formed. Adam Smith had distinguished between the self-interested emotions which fueled economic activity and the behavior which resulted from these emotions. The emotions, themselves, for Smith, were composed of both prudence and vanity and, thus, were neither of a homogeneous nature nor benign. However, they did lead to a regular set of desires—namely, the desire for as many goods as possible. And the behavior resulting from these desires was efficient in the sense that people tried to find the best means to fulfill them. It was the fact that the best means was to buy as much as possible at the lowest price and sell as much as possible at the highest price that set the market process in motion. However, for Smith, the desires themselves had an emotional base which was open to analysis.

Under the marginalists, the emphasis shifted from the emotions motivating economic action to the action itself. Desires were now called *preferences*, a more neutral term. The value to people of the goods they acquired was now called *utility*, also a more neutral term. And an individual's transformation of preferences into utility was recast from one of pursuing self-interested desires to one of formulated choices among alternative goods. Choice, of course, has the connotation of freedom and of rational thought. Thus, in the marginalist formulation, self-interest became disassociated from its emotional base and was transformed into a rational process of choice. In some respects, Smith's prudential aspect of self-interest was expanded to be the dominant quality. As a result, rationality was not only a description of individual behavior but became elevated to be a norm of such behavior, while self-interest became a homogeneous, benign concept, devoid of the potential for abuse that had so concerned Adam Smith. Smith's view of humans as emotional beings in need of regulation was replaced with a view of them as self-contained and rational actors.

This view of the individual as an autonomous and rational actor was further fortified by the way the static equilibrium model elevated the role of the consumer in the economic system. Since the collective economic goal of maximizing output was already defined and since the perfectly competitive market would achieve this goal if it were not interfered with and if individuals behaved rationally, consumers appeared to be the prime motivator of the economic system. Resources and technology were fixed in any given time period, so it was the content of consumer preferences which appeared to drive the system. This, of course, again was a result of how the marginalists organized their model with the emphasis on consumer demand.

However, this view of the consumer was also compatible with the belief in individual freedom which had become an implicit part of economic thought. Not only did the static nature of the model make it appear that consumer preferences determined the composition of final output but it became believed that consumers should determine that composition. The two ideas became combined in the concept of *consumer sovereignty*. Consumers were to be free to determine their own preferences, and these preferences would, in turn, determine the composition of output. Methodologically, it was no longer relevant to ask how consumer preferences were formed, since they were a given for each analytical time period. And, normatively, it was no longer appropriate to ask how they were formed because it became part of individual freedom for each person to determine his or her own preferences. Therefore, the questions of how preferences were formed and whether one set of preferences was preferable to another became excluded from the analysis and consumer sovereignty also became a norm of how the economic system should work. This view of the consumer was, of course, compatible with the approach of methodological individualism which eventually became associated with neoclassical theory.

With this increased emphasis on the consumer as a free and rational actor in the marginalist model, the regulatory role that the market played in the economic system, which had been so central to Smith's analysis, became muted. Although the market was still regulating individual behavior and although that behavior was still based on emotions, both of these factors became masked by the way the model was formulated and by the elevation of rationality and consumer sovereignty to norms of the economic system. The view of people as rational actors appeared to be one that could stand on its own and, therefore, be transferred to other areas of behavior.

However, it is only within the context of an already defined collective goal, the presence of a regulatory mechanism, and the existence of a reliable set of motivating emotions that the deductive and normative qualities of this rational actor model have validity. If these special characteristics are not present in other contexts, then many of Smith's original questions again become relevant. If people have other motivations for behavior than well-defined self-interest or if self-interested maximizing behavior does not lead to desirable social outcomes, then the economic definition of individual rationality has little meaning except in a technical sense and the value of individual autonomy or sovereignty has to be established on other grounds. How preferences are formed and what they are become important both methodologically and normatively. And the question of what kinds of regulatory mechanisms are available to harmonize individual behavior with desirable social outcomes comes back to the forefront of the analysis, as does the question of how to define desirable collective outcomes in the first place.

Under the impact of marginalist reasoning, economic theory took on a new character. The inductive, empirical approach of the classical writers was replaced with a deductive, idealized mathematical model. The classical thinkers had identified many aspects of economic activity which appeared to have analyzable regularities. This made them suitable for scientific analysis as that analysis was being developed in the physical sciences—that is, the explanation of natural phenomena using mathematics and deductive logic. The achievement of the marginalist was to fit such a model to economic activity. However, the gains made in being able to explain economic activity also had their costs. The model became an idealized model of individual behavior and of the market process which not only ignored many aspects of both but distorted how they were interpreted. And normative qualities were assigned to individual behavior which were more dependent on the structure of the model than was recognized.

In addition, economic analysis became isolated from the historical and political context in which it previously had been considered. Since government was not an integral part of the market process, it was omitted from the model and was no longer considered explicitly except as part of public finance. Questions of power and coercion within the private economy, which were of concern to classical economists as they looked at the changing distribution of income, were also no longer considered. Nor were societal questions of morality and justice issues of concern. And, perhaps most important, the emphasis shifted to the individual and away from either analytical or normative concern with collective needs and outcomes. But, in political analysis, it is just such a concern with collective needs and outcomes that is required.

CONCLUSION

The marginalist revolution was not the only factor in the history of economic thought which influenced how economic models became applied to political analysis. The reformulation of welfare economics on

Paretian grounds in order to replace cardinal utility with ordinal utility was another important development which influenced how contemporary theorists formulate political questions in economic terms.[22] However, I believe that it was the marginalist revolution which was responsible for two of the most problematical aspects of the rational actor model, the definition of rationality and the view of the individual as autonomous. The compelling attribute of the full market model has always been that individuals, maximizing their own self-interest, also maximize collective output.[23] It is the dependency among the parts of the model organized by the regulatory role of the market that achieves this result. Individual behavior is only rational because it has collectively rational results. If there is meaning to the idea of reason in economic theory, it is this meaning. But the symmetry between individual behavior and collective outcomes is dependent on the regulatory role of the market. The individual cannot stand alone. It was the marginalist formulation that separated the individual from this interrelated system and attributed to the individual both sovereignty and rationality. The marginalists lost sight of both the wider meaning of reason and the role that regulation plays in it. Economic theory has the analytic potential to contribute a great deal to our understanding of the consequences of self-interested behavior in the political world. But the fruitfulness of that analysis depends, in part, on recognizing the methodological and ideological limitations imposed on the rational actor model by its historical roots.

NOTES

1. The origins of the current extension of economic theory to political analysis are found in problems that were encountered in neoclassical welfare economics in the 1950s. It was the need to reintroduce government in the welfare economics model in cases of market failure which led to William Baumol's *Welfare Economics and the Theory of the State* (Cambridge, MA: Harvard University Press, 1965), which used the rational actor model and the Paretian welfare criterion to establish the legitimacy of government coercion as part of an economic theory of the state. It was the need to choose a societal income distribution in order to complete the welfare economics model which led to Kenneth Arrow's classic work, *Social Choice and Individual Values* (New Haven: Yale University Press, 1963), in which the rational actor model was extended to analyze voting as a method of societal choice. And it was Arrow's work which, in part, inspired Anthony Downs to utilize the neoclassical economic model to analyze actual political activity in *An Economic*

Theory of Democracy (New York: Harper & Row, 1957). Although these works founded different lines of political analysis, they are unified by their common use of economic assumptions and models which acquired their particular formulations in marginalist economic thought.

2. It should be noted that Smith's questions were, of course, similar to those posed by the classical liberal political theorists such as Thomas Hobbes and John Locke, although Smith rejected social contract theory as a way of addressing these questions.

3. For one particularly revealing discussion of Smith's view of the negative aspects of government, see Adam Smith, *The Theory of Moral Sentiments*, ed. D. D. Raphael and A. L. Macfie, Vol. I of *The Glasgow Edition of the Works and Correspondence of Adam Smith* (Oxford: Clarendon Press, 1960), Part IV, Ch. 2, p. 187.

4. Adam Smith, *The Theory of Moral Sentiments*, ed. D. D. Raphael and A. L. Macfie, Vol. I of *The Glasgow Edition of the Works and Correspondence of Adam Smith* (Oxford: Clarendon Press, 1960).

5. For Smith's description of the different types of emotions and their propriety see *The Theory of Moral Sentiments*, Part I, Sec. II, pp. 27–43. For his discussion of virtue see Part VI, pp. 212–266.

6. For an interesting discussion of the "Impartial Spectator," see A. L. Macfie, *The Individual in Society: Papers on Adam Smith*, (London: Allen & Unwin, 1967), pp. 82–100.

7. Religion is, of course, one obvious choice for a regulator in the moral sphere. Smith does not systematically deal with this in his published works or in the notes recovered from his lectures. His missing work on natural theology would probably be instructive here.

8. Two sets of student notes from Smith's lectures at Glasgow University, one from 1762–1763 and one from 1766, are compiled in Adam Smith, *Lectures on Jurisprudence*, ed. R. I. Meek, D. D. Raphael, and P. G. Stein, Vol. V of *The Glasgow Edition of the Works and Correspondence of Adam Smith* (Oxford: Clarendon Press, 1978).

9. Smith, *The Theory of Moral Sentiments*, Part II, Ch. 6, p. 175.

10. Adam Smith, *An Inquiry into the Nature and Causes of the Wealth of Nations*, 2 vols., R. H. Campbell and A. S. Skinner, general ed., W. B. Todd, textual ed., Vol. II of *The Glasgow Edition of the Works and Correspondence of Adam Smith*, (Oxford: Clarendon Press, 1976).

11. A long history of commentary on Smith was started by German writers in the nineteenth century to the effect that there is a conflict in Smith's work between the ethic of benevolence put forth in *The Theory of Moral Sentiments* and the ethic of self-interest put forth in *The Wealth of Nations*. I think that some of this so-called "Adam

Smith Problem" is resolved when his work is analyzed, as it is here, with the emphasis placed on the empirical nature of his study of the relative strengths of these different emotions in their respective spheres and their relation to the virtues appropriate for each sphere.

12. For Smith's discussion of this ambition see *The Theory of Moral Sentiments*, Part I. Sec. III, Ch. 2, pp. 50–61, and *The Wealth of Nations*, Book II., Ch. 3, pp. 341–342.

13. Smith tends to give conflicting signals on this point. He does not approve of vanity in and of itself but he does approve of the enterprise and self-command that is necessary to achieve the goals of vanity and the resulting increase in economic output.

14. *The Wealth of Nations*, Book I, Ch. 2, p. 25.

15. *The Wealth of Nations*, Book IV, Ch. 2, p. 456.

16. For the classic historical study of mercantilism see Eli F. Hecksher, *Mercantilism*, 2nd ed., authorized trans. by Mendel Shapiro (London: Allen & Unwin, 1955). For a more current commentary on Smith and mercantilism see A. W. Coats, "Adam Smith and the Mercantilist System," in Andrew Skinner and Thomas Wilson, eds., *Essays on Adam Smith* (Oxford: Clarendon Press, 1975), pp. 218–236.

17. Smith's arguments concerning mercantilism are scattered throughout *The Wealth of Nations*, but many of his specific arguments can be found in Book IV, Chs. 1–8.

18. Henry J. Bitterman has argued that the natural law or natural harmony aspects of Smith's work are not important and that Smith should be viewed primarily as an empiricist. Although many of Bitterman's points are well taken, I believe he underestimates the continuing influence of natural law on Smith's work. It seems more realistic to view Smith as a transitional figure whose work shows the tensions between the two ways of thinking. See Henry J. Bitterman, "Adam Smith's Empiricism and the Law of Nature," *The Journal of Political Economy*, 48, no. 4 (August 1940), pp. 487–520.

19. Many writers on Smith have tended to underestimate the substantial role that government plays in his work in supporting the economic system. They have, instead, attributed to Smith the extreme laissez-faire doctrine better associated with the physiocrats. For a good discussion of this see Lord Robbins, *The Theory of Economic Policy in English Political Economy*, 2nd ed. (London: Macmillan, 1978), Lecture II, pp. 34–67.

20. Additional useful secondary sources on the aspects of Smith's work discussed here are Joseph Cropsey, "Adam Smith and Political Philosophy," in Andrew Skinner and Thomas Wilson, eds., *Essays on Adam Smith* (Oxford: Clarendon Press, 1975); George J. Stigler, "Smith's Travels on the Ship of State," in M. Skinner and T. Wilson; A. L. Macfie, "The Scottish Tradition in Economic Thought,"

in A. L. Macfie, *The Individual in Society: Papers on Adam Smith* (London: Allen & Unwin, 1967); Joseph Cropsey, "Polity and Economy: An Interpretation of the Principles of Adam Smith," in Macfie, *The Individual in Society*. Additional books of collective readings which are useful are Fred R. Glake, ed., *Adam Smith and the Wealth of Nations: 1776–1976 Bicentennial Essays* (Boulder: Colorado Associated University Press, 1978); Andrew S. Skinner, ed., *A System of Social Science: Papers Relating to Adam Smith* (Oxford: Clarendon Press, 1979); and Gerald P. O'Driscall, Jr., *Adam Smith and Modern Political Economy* (Ames: Iowa State University Press, 1979). Also, Richard R. Teichgraeber's book *"Free Trade" and Moral Philosophy* (Durham: Duke University Press, 1986) includes an interesting discussion of the influences on Smith's thinking, while a thoughtful analysis of the evolution in intellectual thought of the relationship between self-interest and the public interest can be found in Albert O. Hirschman, *The Passions and the Interests* (Princeton: Princeton University Press, 1977).

21. A thoughtful discussion of the marginalist revolution, including an extensive bibliography, can be found in Mark Blaug, *Economic Theory in Retrospect*, 3rd ed. (Cambridge: Cambridge University Press, 1978), pp. 309–342. The presentation of the marginalist economic model can be found in any standard micro-economics textbook.

22. There are numerous texts available on the modern welfare economics that evolved from Pareto's work. However, for critical commentary on this theory, some references are I. M. D. Little, *A Critique of Welfare Economics*, 2nd ed. (London: Oxford University Press, 1957); Maurice Dobbs, *Welfare Economics and the Economics of Socialism* (London: Cambridge University Press, 1969); and Charles K. Rowley and Alan T. Peacock, *Welfare Economics: A Liberal Restatement* (London: Martin Robinson, 1975). Some of the more interesting recent work on Paretian welfare economics can be found in the writings of Amartya Sen.

23. I am referring here only to the theoretical model, not to how an actual market system operates, which can be quite different from the idealized model. In addition, it should be noted that there are other possible collective goals for the economic system besides maximizing output that would change the entire formulation of the model.

REFERENCES

Arrow, K. (1963). *Social Choice and Individual Values*. New Haven: Yale University Press.

Baumol, W. (1965). *Welfare Economics and the Theory of the State.* Cambridge, MA: Harvard University Press.

Bitterman, H. J. (1940). "Adam Smith's Empiricism and the Law of Nature," *The Journal of Political Economy,* 48(4):487–520.

Blaug, M. (1978). *Economic Theory in Retrospect* (3rd ed.). Cambridge: Cambridge University Press, pp. 309–342.

Coats, A. W. (1975). "Adam Smith and the Mercantilist System." In A. Skinner and T. Wilson (Eds.), *Essays on Adam Smith.* Oxford: Clarendon Press, pp. 218–236.

Cropsey, J. (1967). "Polity and Economy: An Interpretation of the Principles of Adam Smith." In A. L. Macfie (Ed.), *The Individual in Society: Papers on Adam Smith.* London: Allen & Unwin, pp. 126–129.

_____. (1975). "Adam Smith and Political Philosophy," In A. Skinner and T. Wilson (Eds.), *Essays on Adam Smith.* Oxford: Clarendon Press, pp. 132–153.

Dobbs, M. (1969). *Welfare Economics and the Economics of Socialism.* London: Cambridge University Press.

Downs, A. (1957). *An Economic Theory of Democracy.* New York: Harper & Row.

Glake, F. R. (Ed.) (1978). *Adam Smith and the Wealth of Nations: 1776–1976 Bicentennial Essays.* Boulder: Colorado Associated University Press.

Hecksher, E. F. (1955). *Mercantilism* (2nd ed.), translated by M. Shapiro. London: Allen & Unwin.

Hirschman, A. O. (1977) *The Passions and the Interests.* Princeton: Princeton University Press.

Little, I. M. D. (1957). *A Critique of Welfare Economics* (2nd ed.). London: Oxford University Press.

Macfie, A. L. (1967). "The Scottish Tradition in Economic Thought" and "Impartial Spectator." In A. L. Macfie (Ed.), *The Individual in Society: Papers on Adam Smith.* London: Allen & Unwin, pp. 19–41, 82–100.

O'Driscall, G. P., Jr. (1979). *Adam Smith and Modern Political Economy.* Ames: Iowa State University.

Robbins, L. (1978). *The Theory of Economic Policy in English Political Economy* (2nd ed.). London: Macmillan, pp. 34–67.

Rowley, C. K., and Peacock, A. T. (1975). *Welfare Economics: A Liberal Restatement.* London: Martin Robinson.

Skinner, A. S. (Ed.) (1979). *A System of Social Science: Papers Relating to Adam Smith*. Oxford: Clarendon Press.

Smith, A. (1960). *The Theory of Moral Sentiments*. In D. D. Rapheal and A. L. Macfie (Eds.), Vol. I of *The Glasgow Edition of the Works and Correspondence of Adam Smith*. Oxford: Clarendon Press.

_____. (1976). *An Inquiry into the Nature and Causes of the Wealth of Nations*. In R. H. Campbell and A. S. Skinner (general eds.), and W. B. Todd (text ed.), Vol. II of *The Glasgow Edition of the Works and Correspondence of Adam Smith*. Oxford: Clarendon Press.

_____. (1978). *Lectures on Jurisprudence*. In R. I. Meek, D. D. Raphael, and P. G. Stein (Eds.), Vol. V of *The Glasgow Edition of the Works and Correspondence of Adam Smith*. Oxford: Clarendon Press.

Stigler, G. J. (1975). "Smith's Travels on the Ship of State." In M. Skinner and T. Wilson (Eds.), *Essays on Adam Smith*. Oxford: Clarendon Press, pp. 237–246.

Teichgraeber, R. R. (1986). *"Free Trade" and Moral Philosophy*. Durham: Duke University Press.

Chapter

3

Rationality and Frustration in Political Behavior

Harry Eckstein

I tried in 1908 to make two points clear. My first point was the danger... especially for the working of democracy... of the "intellectualist" assumption, that every human action is the result of an intellectual process, by which a man first thinks of some end he desires, and then calculates the means by which that end can be attained.
There is no longer [after World War I and subsequent political events] much danger that we shall assume that man always and automatically thinks of ends and calculates means.
.... The vast majority of mankind have had enough to do to keep themselves alive.... An effective choice has only been given to a tiny class of hereditary property owners or a few organizers of other men's labors.

Graham Wallas (1908/1921:192)

ARGUMENT OF THE PAPER: AN OVERVIEW

Rational choice theories in political science have been criticized and modified entirely for the way they specify the process of attaining goals. A more fundamental criticism of the rational choice approach to theory and explanation is to question whether political, and other social, behavior is oriented to achieving goals in the first place. That is what I want to do here.

My argument is that the applicability of the rational choice framework, although intended as a basis of highly general theory, is in fact exceedingly limited by time and culture; it is even substantially subculture-bound in societies where it might serve relatively well. This applies both to its pristine (Simon calls it "Olympian") version and modified versions intended to achieve decent fit with observations. The reason for these damaging limitations is that behavior comes in two fundamentally distinct varieties: Norman Maier (1961) calls them "motivated" and "frustrated" behavior and considers the latter, persuasively, to be "behavior without goals." I suspect that much, perhaps even most, behavior, broadly considered in time, societies, and subsocieties, is of the frustrated kind.

I will argue here that action that is instigated by frustration may be regarded as "sensible," although it takes certain forms we usually consider the height of irrationality. It is sensible because it is well adapted to exigent circumstances that press upon many people, at most times and in most places. By "well adapted" I mean that the behavior performs well certain ineluctable functional imperatives of existence in societies, without the occurrence of destructive personal stress. These imperatives, in fact, explain how frustration instigates distinctive modes of behavior.

Because frustration-instigated behavior can be considered functionally "sensible," rational choice theories might be tempted to annex it to their framework by applying the term "rational" to it. After all, it makes "sense"; one's goal in behavior might sometimes be not to pursue goals at all. Such stretching of the framework is inadmissible: it would involve verbal legerdemain that maintains the framework while draining it of its most important postulate: that behavior is in some way calculated to achieve goals efficiently.

RATIONAL CHOICE AND GOALS

It is hardly possible to imagine rational choices (perhaps "choices" of any kind) that are not intended to achieve goals, or indeed ordered sets of goals. I want to document this point from the political literature about rational choice before discussing the alternate (to us, probably, *prima facie*) implausible view.

In Downs's seminal work applying economic modes of analysis to democratic theory, rational action is generically defined as action "reasonably directed toward the attainment of conscious *goals*" (1957:4; my emphasis). Reasonable is equated with "efficient," which in turn refers to using the least possible input of scarce resources to obtain valued outputs. Downs's summary of his whole perspective of inquiry states:

By *rational* action, we mean action which is efficiently designed to achieve the consciously selected political or economic ends of the actor (1957:20; emphasis in original).

Note the use in both sentences of the word *conscious*. Presumably it is used (in my view, rightly) to avoid equating rationality with *any* effective actions, like actions that satisfy impulsive or reflexive urges, or otherwise adjust unthinkingly to situations that press upon people.

Economics, of course, deals exclusively with highly goal-oriented behavior: its political personas thus are utility-maximizing voters and politicians. The economic view of politicians was anticipated by Schumpeter, in his major work about politics. However, Schumpeter confines the economic analogy to leaders (political entrepreneurs) who, to paraphrase him, deal in votes exactly as business executives deal in oil (1943:285); the mass of voters he treats as hyperirrational, in the manner of the crowd psychologists (1943:262, 263).

A second source of political rational choice theory is the theory of games. Unlike mere play, games are probably the most unambiguously goal-oriented of all activities. Games theory has had a particularly strong influence on another strand of political rational choice theory: the theory of political coalitions first devised by Riker. That theory is solely concerned with winning and payoffs and equated with such analogues as "parlor games, markets, elections, and warfare" (1962:23), all matters in which action is directed at highly specific goals. Riker tries to disarm doubts about working with assumptions drawn from such seemingly far-fetched analogues mainly by equating the position of politicians with that of fiduciary agents, who are morally obligated to act in the maximum interests of their principals (1962: 24–28).

Michael Laver's excellent work on political rational actor theories brings out the same view, a generation's work after Downs (1981:21–38). Rational actor models, he points out, must assume (1) that actors pursue goals weighted in cardinal-utility order and (2) that, in choosing among alternative courses of action, actors also calculate the risks and probable costs of attaining them. The cardinally ordered goals are the first, most fundamental desideratum; consideration of risks or benefits are senseless without them.

In a long series of works that become increasingly focused between 1947 and 1985, Herbert Simon has developed a powerful critique and revision of the postulates of economic theories, especially as applied to administration and politics. Simon moves far along the right track, but still falls short of the most crucial revision needed.

Simon's critique is inductivist: that is, he wants to develop a theoretical model more likely to fit observations than does a "pure" economic model (which proceeds from the postulate of "objective rationality") by being empirically grounded from the outset, chiefly in cognitive psychology. Some theorists probably will disagree with this view for epistemological reasons, concerning the nature and uses of theory. But it will be hard for anyone to disagree with Simon's point (1985:296–302) that if successful predictions derived from a model depend chiefly on the "auxiliary assumption" introduced into it, often ad hoc and dealing with specific observations, then the model is ripe for basic revision. Simon gives a rather crushing recital of such auxiliary assumptions used in economics itself, and, even more, in politics. To cite only one passage:

> [These] examples teach us the same lesson: the actors in the political drama do appear to behave in a rational manner—they have reasons for what they do, and a clever researcher can usually obtain data that give good clues as to what their reasons are. But this is very different from claiming that we can predict the behavior . . . by application of the objective rationality principle. Such prediction is impossible because . . . behavior depends . . . on [actors'] representation of the world in which they live, what they attend to in that world, and what beliefs they have about its nature. The obvious corollary is that rationalism can carry us only a little way in political analysis (1985:300).

Simon's modification of the pure, rational choice model is the notion of "bounded rationality." Such rationality takes into account subjective factors, especially varying levels of knowledge, differences in abilities to compute, completeness or degrees of lack of it in defining out alternatives for action, the extent to which the attention is focused on political issues (a function of the emotions, because they assign degrees of urgency), variable spans of attention, and "education" (following Riker, the artistic, or creative, element in politics that generates alternatives for action in the first place).

Throughout the corpus of Simon's work, what results is the notion of satisficing in place of maximizing or optimizing. Satisficing is pursuing some satisfactory outcome of action—not necessarily the most satisfactory, but one that lies within a range of acceptable attainments. Clearly this is still well within the world of goal-oriented actions. In fact, Simon explicitly writes that, aside from madness, "almost all human behavior consists of sequences of goal-oriented actions" (1985:297). True, goals à la Simon are more broadly defined and good outcomes have taken the place of best or best possible outcomes. Nevertheless, satisficing remains goal-oriented; however much the idea of "efficient" outcomes is loosened and enlarged. Simon's boundedly rational actor still inhabits a world of costs and benefits, punishments and rewards.

In his Madison address of 1985, however, Simon opens the door to something I wish to explore, because it can transcend his revision and lead us to a more fundamental level. The "subjectively rational" actor, Simon argues, not only has internal limitations but adapts behavior to "external situations." Under specifiable conditions, such adaptive behavior has traits that seem to me to preclude considering it rational in any terminology, bounded or unbounded—the reason being simply that the most fundamental, indeed logically indispensable, criterion of rational action, goal-seeking per se, is absent, or present only in a tortured, metaphorical way. This point applies with special force to groups that no doubt are less numerous in the modern West than in earlier Western or other societies. But I suspect that it applies, in varying degrees, to most people, period.

FRUSTRATION-INSTIGATED BEHAVIOR

To a greater or lesser extent, there exists in all modern societies a subculture that cuts across other social divisions: the subculture of the poor. One can dispute about who the "poor" are and how large a proportion of any society they include. Here I do not mean to refer only to the miserable. Degrees of material scarcity lie along curves, though it is undeniably difficult to specify a threshold at which "affluence" ends and "poverty" begins (even if the Department of Labor tells us that about a quarter of Americans live below the "poverty line"). But it is not difficult to identify groups "who have enough to do to keep themselves alive" without going to the Bowery.

The point I want to make is this: the behavior of the poor, even in highly developed, "achieving" societies, conforms more to the generalization that actions are taken to avoid pain, not to attain pleasure: to cope with pain, or minimize it, or to minimize its very perception. There is another way to put this which guards at the start against the argument that avoiding pain is simply the reverse of attaining pleasure—part of the rational calculus—rather than being qualitatively different. Behavior by the poorer segments of societies is more like what Maier (1961) called frustration-instigated behavior than what he called motivation-instigated behavior. In his study of southern Appalachians, Richard Ball (1968) evocatively called such behavior "analgesic"; the word is apt, since *analgesia* literally is a condition of insensibility to pain.

Such behavior should be regarded as not being oriented toward attaining goals at all: what better way to be insensible to failures and resultant frustrations? It is comparable to what Merton (1949) and other writers on social adaptation call "retreatist" behavior: withdrawing into apathy or into small, sheltered worlds of self-limited activity. It appears to have other traits hardly consistent with being motivated to attain goals efficiently, which I will discuss presently.

FRUSTRATED BEHAVIOR IN EXPERIMENTAL SETTINGS

Maier's work on frustrated behavior is part of psychological learning research and theory. The orthodoxy of that field was, and remains, the reward-punishment perspective, a kind of benefit-cost perspective, even though conditioning is emphasized over calculation. Maier's theoretical aim was to show that behavior, and thus its causes, is two-factored (motivated or frustrated) rather than all of one piece—an apparent loss of parsimony, unless one introduces explanatory power into the equation by which parsimony is measured. Maier's point was precisely that the reward-punishment perspective oversimplified and thus actually ended in avoidable, unparsimonious complications, as well as in notions dubious for therapy.

Yates (1962) points out that Maier's work on frustration was unusual in its persistence over a long time span (over 20 years), the sheer quantity of experimental work done, and in Maier's attempt to work out fully the implications of his findings and theory. Yates also emphasizes its importance as an alternative to the somewhat frayed orthodoxy in learning theory—its almost Copernican nature—and, predictably, his profession's extraordinary imperviousness to the work, on the ground of "prejudice and *a priori* convictions" (1962:2), resulting in little follow-up: not exactly unusual in the human sciences.

In the preface to his book's paperback edition (1961), Maier himself remarks rather gently on this "initial opposition." He attributes it to a simple misunderstanding: namely, that people took him to say that frustrated *people* have no goals in the first place—which, of course, would make it difficult to explain why they are frustrated. Instead, Maier tells us that he refers to *behavior* that is not influenced or controlled by goals or that may in fact lead away from initial goals (like stilling hunger). In his theory, such behavior, to be sure, results from prolonged and systematic frustration, in goal-oriented action. However, frustrated people are not a personality type (although susceptibility to the general condition of frustration seems to vary) and it seems possible to go from the frustrated state back to an the earlier motivated state, even if not quickly or without appropriate guidance and exertion. Frustrated behavior has "situational" roots, but, once it is established, it is unusually hard to undo. Under specified conditions, it involves a passage from a general type of behavior to quite another.

Maier came to his distinction between motivated and frustrated behavior through a long series of experiments with rats. His experimental observations, and their interpretations, can only be selectively summarized here. Maier used the Lashley jumping apparatus in his experiments: a platform facing two apertures (cards), marked with different, easily distinguishable symbols: a white circle on a black background and a black circle on a white background. The animal is placed on the platform and induced to jump at one of the symbols. If it chooses the correct symbol, it lands on a feeding platform; if not, it bumps its nose and falls into a net. If food is consistently placed behind a symbol, a consistent preference for the symbol is rather quickly developed, regardless of its position (though rats, for some reason, tend to be position-oriented). If, after symbol learning, the food is always placed to the left or right and the symbol shifted about, the rats readily develop a preference for the correct position. This is typically "goal-motivated" behavior. We are in a world familiar to us, where correct choices lead to benefits and where wrong choices are costly.

What happens if now the location of the food is made random, by symbol and position—that is, unpredictable? What happens is exactly what "rationalists" would expect: after some trial and error, the animals sensibly refuse to jump at all; one might say that rewards being random, they reduce costs to zero.

But what if the rats are forced to jump—for instance, by electric shocks or blasts of noxious air? (Real life, after all, may force human beings to act when doing nothing may be their preference.) The animals now confront an "insoluble problem." Creating such problems for his subjects, in contrast to soluble situations, is the crux of Maier's experiment: one is bound to be frustrated when faced by insoluble problems regarding an inherent need (food). What happens, essentially, is that behavior becomes stereotyped: some animals invariably jump at a symbol, others at a position. Moreover, once stereotypical behavior sets in, it persists regardless of whether all jumps are punished or rewards and punishment are equally divided. Most striking is the fact that the stereotyped behavior persists even when food is placed behind an open aperture. The animals are aware of the location of the food and sniff it, but they then jump in the stereotyped manner anyway. Further, once the subject's behavior has become stereotyped, it seems difficult, and in most cases impossible, to return to the initial world of patterned rewards and punishment. A small proportion of rats did in fact manage the return (viz., to variable behavior), but only after a number of trial jumps vastly larger than before and most readily if they were "guided." (Devices like metrazol injections to induce convulsions were considered to be "guidance"!)

Frustrated behavior, then, is *fixated* behavior. It is invariably repeated action, and highly resistant to change even if the fixated response is directly shown to be ineffective. Punishment, Maier found (1961:78), in fact generally strengthened fixation. And punishment here refers to rather extreme things, like induced convulsions or being subjected to strong blasts of stinking air. It should be evident that the frustrated subject no longer inhabits a world of choice at all. Fixated behavior is an end in itself, insensible to punishment (costs) and rewards (benefits). Maier found, moreover, that such behavior is highly specific, even more so than "habits." Thus it also lies outside any world of limited choice—outside any analogue of satisficing.

Nevertheless, in an odd, hard-to-grasp way, fixation seemed functional to the subject. The fixated rats seemed to be less tense, to respond more readily, to be less susceptible to convulsive seizures than the small minority that did not become fixated through prolonged frustration, or were able to reenter the world of choice. I surmise that the rats preferred a *patterned* world, regardless of what it is, punishing or otherwise, once they come to perceive that rewards and punishments are arbitrary. They avoid the ideal-typical situation of the slave, and they find more peace in invariable pattern than in choice, to the extent that the outcomes of choice are unpredictable.

Maier is quite aware of the links long found between frustration and responses other than fixation, especially *aggression*; he treats that relation at length, with reference particularly to the magisterial work of Dollard et al. (1939).

Aggression as a response to frustration had generally been regarded as goal-oriented. That may, of course, be so, in certain cases. But aggressive behavior also often has characteristics that suggest that it might be behavior without a goal—part of a syndrome, or family, of such actions, of which fixated action also is a part. For instance, Maier (1961:103ff.) notes the following: (1) Aggression seems often to follow frustration even if it is known to be futile. (2) Often it is not directed at the source of frustration but at innocent bystanders (the "bystander" effect is as well documented as "scapegoating"). To quote Maier (drawing on Dollard et al.):

> ...economic frustration leads to violence in the home, strained relationships among friends, crimes against society, lynching, and rioting. As a result problems are not solved and goals are not achieved. But always the innocent bystander is a convenient object.... After the response occurs it is rationalized and justified, but such reasons or justifications are not to be confused with causes or goals. Brutal parents justify abuse of their children by contending that the children are being trained, but the cause of the abusive behavior is their own frustration.

What is attained, no doubt, is some emotional relief (Maier himself makes that point, 1961:105–107; see also Baruch, 1940). One could say that this is a goal, but only by stretching the idea of goals so that they cannot fail to encompass any and all consequences of action; in other words, by being truistic. (3) Finally, and perhaps most telling, even when aggression itself is frustrated, it tends to continue; yet in the reward-punishment perspective, it should decline or be avoided altogether.

Thus aggression, unless directly aimed at the source of frustration, may be considered of a piece with fixation, an alternative goal-less response to frustration. If this is so, one would like to know when one or another option is chosen to cope with frustration, but that is not an important issue here. (Maier does speculate that actors in "free" situations tend to use aggression but become fixated if circumstances are constricted.) Maier also points out that different goal-less responses to frustration often are combined.

The syndrome of such responses includes two other modes of behavior. It includes *regression*: returning to childhood patterns of behavior, like dependency, bed-wetting, tattletale behavior, whining, excessive crying, and nonconstructive play. Such behavior also had generally been treated as "motivated": it was assumed to be a resort to an earlier "rewarding" response when adult behavior was unsatisfactory. However, Maier points out that regression often is merely childish; there frequently is no evidence whatever of a return to anything learned at an earlier stage. He also points out that regressive behavior often ceases abruptly when it relieves frustration—for instance, by "having a good cry." The final set of responses, and the responses that most clearly have no goals, involve *resignation*: undiluted apathy toward one's condition. Resigned behavior has been particularly well described in Allport, Bruner, and Jandorf's study of refugees persecuted by the Nazis (1941) and in Eisenberg and Lazarsfeld's study of the effects of unemployment (1938). These effects included "extreme limitation of all needs; *no plans*; no definite relation to the future; either *no hopes at all or hopes which are not taken seriously*" (quoted in Maier: III; my emphasis). Resignation, which occurred also in some of the experimental rats, clearly is end-of-the-line behavior, the result of especially severe or prolonged frustration on some personalities.

Although Maier might not agree, none of these patterns of behavior seem to me "senseless" in the situations in which they occur: in organisms generally frustrated by having to cope with "insoluble problems," especially over prolonged periods of time. As stated earlier, fixated behavior at least is patterned; it is not anomic. Regressive dependency (the main regressive response) seems to me almost "smart": "If I don't have a decent chance of making a correct choice, you make it for me."

Aggression, even if it achieves no goal, lets off steam; also, aggressive actors at least may enjoy the momentary and dubious pleasures of vengefulness. And resignation surely is not nonsensical when anything done is likely to be wrongly done.

Frustrated behavior is not likely to be *immediately* recognizable as "sensible" action. It has no analogue in human behavior likely to be intuitively meaningful to successful achievers (not excluding successful academic achievers) nor to people blessed by rewards that come even if choices are wrong or no choices are made. If a pattern has not been directly experienced, then, Max Weber has told us, we can only construct a conceptually pure type of it as a crutch to our own understanding: a "concept" to expand limits of empathy and, through empathy, understanding, in the positivist sense.

I want to add three points, very briefly.

First, I part company from Maier on one major point. I consider frustrated behavior to be adaptive; he considered it maladaptive. The difference is only semantic. Maier, like all others in his field, regards only behavior that is successful in its outcomes as adaptive, and links success to goal attainment. I follow Merton's use of the concept, which has had much influence in sociology (1949: Ch. 4). Merton defines adaptation functionally, as coping with situations one cannot alter without suffering avoidable pain or other damage. For that reason, resorting to criminal behavior, retreating from society, acting submissively, and, explicitly, "curbing motivation for sustained endeavor" (1949:139) are, or may be, highly adaptive: functional or situationally logical. Upon that view, frustrated behavior certainly is adaptive, in exigent situations. That may explain why, in most cases, it is hard, or even impossible, to change.

Second, I should, doubtless, address the familiar argument that animals are not people. Experiments like Maier's are heuristic for understanding human behavior. Rats have always served the heuristic purpose well. So has another population, college students. Studies of such students show sufficiently that Maier's theories readily translate to human subjects. For example, Watson (1934) studied 230 college students, one group of whom came from highly strict, "regimented" homes, while the other group had been given "leeway and respect" at home. Of the first group, 81 percent displayed aggression (e.g., rude answers), regression (like weeping spells), fixation (e.g., cherishing past hurts), or resignation (suicidal tendencies). About half of the frustrated students came from "economically deprived" homes, as against very few in the other group—this at a time when poor students were rather rare in colleges. Frustrated parents seem to produce frustrated children. Maier's large bibliography reports numerous such corroborative experimental studies with human subjects.

Finally, frustrated behavior is not mere risk aversion, a phenomenon familiar to economic theory. True, frustrated behavior *is* averse to risks. Yet one aspect of it, aggression that is bound to fail, involves acting beyond all consideration of risk. It is not really possible to divorce risks from goals. Recall that Laver makes the calculation of risks an inherent part of "rational," goal-seeking choice. One could also regard it as so high a degree of risk aversion that the difference in degree becomes a difference in kind, at least for theory.

Frustrated Behavior in a Social Setting

Since we are *social* scientists, we should go on now to analogues of the frustrated condition, and responses to it, in social settings.

One such analogue resembles the experimental situation engineered by Maier in an almost uncanny way. Like experiments, which accentuate conditions, it is an extreme case of persistent frustration in American society: southern Appalachians. Arnold Toynbee traces their experience of failure and frustration back even beyond their migration to America, to Ulster and Scotland:

> The Scottish pioneers who migrated to Ulster begat Scotch-Irish descendants who reimmigrated in the eighteenth century from Ulster to North America, and these survive today in the fastnesses of the Appalachian mountains. Obviously, this American challenge has been more formidable than the Irish challenge. Has the increased challenge evoked an increased response? If we compare the Ulstermen and the Appalachian of today, two centuries after they parted company, we shall find that the answer is in the negative. The modern Appalachian has not only not improved on the Ulstermen; he has failed to hold his ground and has gone downhill in the most disconcerting fashion. In fact, the Appalachian "mountain people" today are no better than barbarians. They have relapsed into illiteracy and witchcraft. They suffer from poverty, squalor, and ill health. They are the American counterparts of the latter-day white barbarians of the Old World Rifis, Albanians, Kurds, Pathans, and Hairy Ainus; but, whereas these latter are belated survivals of an ancient barbarism, the Appalachians present the melancholy spectacle of a people who have acquired civilization and then lost it (1946).

Strong stuff, and no doubt too strong. But the southern Appalachians *have* experienced a history of relentless failure and defeat, by physical and social conditions, and Toynbee captures the consequences for them. Harry Caudill, in *Night Comes to the Cumberlands*, writes:

> Coal has always cursed the land in which it lies. When men begin to wrest it from the earth it leaves a legacy of foul streams, hideous

slag and polluted air. It peoples this transformed land with blind and crippled men and with widows and orphans. . . .

But the tragedy of the Kentucky mountains transcends the tragedy of coal. It is compounded of Indian wars, civil war, and internecine feuds, of layered hatreds and of violent death. To its sad blend, history has added the curse of coal as a crown of sorrow (1962).

Caudill adds that a million Appalachians now (1962) live in squalor, ignorance, and ill health worse than in much of mainland Asia. Other books on the region tell much the same tale of ill fortune and failure, as does Jack Weller's powerful *Yesterday's People* (1965). They all add up to a picture of people who must regard much of life as "insoluble problems."

Richard Ball (1968) has argued that a general analgesic pattern of behavior has been the result. His notion of analgesic behavior is a useful ideal-typical construct for behavior which, in its most fundamental sense, is not motivated toward attaining goals at all—yet, functionally, sensible. He finds "sense" in responses to situations, not just in procedures to attain goals, ruefully pointing out that only ritualistic lip service is paid to Thomas's early emphasis on "the definition of the situation" (1951:572). The developmental condition that produces an analgesic culture, Ball writes, is "the daily experience of inexorable pressure, insoluble problems [sic], and overwhelming frustrations." This, he continues, is "the life situation of the poor generally," but it is encountered in particularly intense, almost "pure," form among Appalachian mountaineers.

Just as the life situation of the mountaineers resembles the laboratory situation of Maier's rats, so do their responses resemble those of the rats. Fixated behavior occurs in the extent to which the Appalachians cling stubbornly to old social ways, to a degree that seems perverse to outside observers, and often clearly against their own "rational self-interest" (as an outside observer might see it). Regression (in a social sense) also is a common pattern, in a considerable variety of ways: intellectually, through hard biblical fundamentalism and pervasive superstition; psychologically, through "chronic dependency," especially on kin structures as ultimate guarantors of minimal needs; economically, by a preference for low, but reliable, welfare payments over less reliable opportunities for getting on, even when the opportunities are available and promising; also, by an impulsive squandering of welfare checks and other quick and short-lived gratifications—a general trait of childishness. Regression occurs, in most blatant form, when those who somehow manage to become migrants to cities, and may in fact have gotten on quite decently, return home "at the slightest misfortune," to a worse, but familiar, life. Aggression takes, among other forms, that of mutually destructive feuding. And there exists pervasive fatalistic resignation, rationalized by fundamentalist religion.

The standard "political" study of the Appalachians (in this case, coal miners and their occupational authority structures) is Gaventa's *Power and Powerlessness* (1980). Gaventa's description of Appalachian political behavior fits nicely with Ball's analysis of the case and the ethnographies of Weller and Caudill. Its themes are apathy and resignation; less and less resistance to abominable work conditions, even when these are perceived as abhorrent; submissiveness; and, sometimes, outbreaks of aggression against domination.

Ball points out that the Appalachians proved strangely recalcitrant and exasperating subjects for "social planners" who came to them, well intentioned, from quite different situations, to improve their lives. To the outside planners, he found, the mountaineers seemed plainly irrational, as well as deviant. In another situation that might have been so. In the past and present situation of the mountaineers, however, one can certainly argue the opposite. At a minimum, their ways have avoided tension and breakdown in a world quite correctly perceived to be hostile and unpredictable. Their nonrational belief systems "explain" that world. Their behavior avoids taking chances on the experience of painful outcomes that are, as they see it, likely to occur. They are, in that way, "realistic." There is, surely, something worse than particular failure: general breakdown.

FRUSTRATED BEHAVIOR AND THE POOR

In discussing the experiences of "social planners," Ball points out that the Appalachians are not at all an isolated case. Similar, apparently irrational resistance to well-meant outside intervention seems to have occurred in a quite heterogeneous set of groups: blacks, the elderly, and a variety of other poor people. The recurrent thread that runs through this apparent variety is continuous failure and frustration and adjustment to their perceived apparent ineluctability.

Here I should refer to the familiar, now wide-ranging, literature on the so-called culture of poverty, a notion which was originated in the 1950s, by Oscar Lewis, in work on Mexican families and American slums (1951, 1959, 1966) and elaborated by other scholars, such as E. Franklin Frazier, who anticipated Lewis in work on black families in the 1930s (1939/1966); Daniel Moynihan and Nathan Glazer's work on blacks, Puerto Ricans, Jews, Italians, and Irish in New York City (1966); and David Matza (1966).

These studies suggest that much that characterizes Appalachia seems to have wide application. Among poor people, sociologists have perceived, above all, negation of the view of action as a subjectively anticipated sequence of behaviors towards a goal altruistic or directed to self-gain. Action seems "impulsive," driven by blind psychological forces rather than by deliberate calculation. The culture of poverty, as well, involves apathy, self-imposed social isolation, tendencies to immediate gratification, unpredictability (of gentle or aggressive behavior), high conformity, suspicion, and fatalism. This is elaborated in a comprehensive way in Charles A. Valentine's *Culture and Poverty* (1968).

Valentine's work criticizes the literature about the culture, or subculture, of poverty, and his criticisms seem to me sound. What is criticized, however, is not the patterns of behavior described in the literature. It is, first, its pejorative nature: in the case of Frazier, for instance, his "direct logical leap from social statistics" (about such things as family desertion, illegitimacy, immoral sex "deviant in terms of middle-class norms") to a "model of disorder and instability" (1968:20–24). What is criticized, second, is the view that the culture of poverty is perpetuated by socialization—which no doubt is so, but is taken to imply that it is nothing but a sort of self-imposed misery which would be quite unnecessary if the poor simply followed the sound American middle-class values of energy, ambition, doing what is required to get on. Former radicals turned neoconservatives have been especially likely to take that line; and small wonder, since the poor seem in fact not to want to help themselves when they can, seem to be recalcitrant and plain deviant, to the exasperation of social meliorists trying to improve their lot.

Valentine criticizes Frazier particularly for ignoring the possibility that the apparently "disordered" life of the poor, in this case blacks, might have its own order and *functions*. Later, he develops theoretical alternatives to explanations of behavior of the poor by "primitive" cognitive structure, lack of ambition, ingrained laziness, and the like; and almost all of the alternatives he argues describe life situations and are functional, in making the case that the described behavior patterns are adaptive to the situations. For instance:

> Low-income urban districts have describable social structures that include . . . some elements that are *specialized adaptations to conditions of socioeconomic disadvantage or marginality* (1968:131).
>
> The domestic group may frequently be unconventional in form and process, but both households and kinship are organized in ways that are *adaptive to externally imposed conditions* (1968:132).
>
> The general contours of individual cognitive and affective orientations to the world are predominantly *realistic and adaptive* (1968:134; my emphases throughout).

Here Valentine lists, as realistic and adaptive, such patterns as dependency, infrequent orientation to the future, resignation and fatalism, and tolerance for behavior others regard as pathological.

FRUSTRATION IN OTHER GROUPS

By now, the beginning of a "literature" about the adaptations of the disadvantaged in a variety of contexts exists. These writings show that the concept of frustrated behavior has wide applicability, and they support the view that its source is adaptation to ineluctable situations. Two examples should suffice.

(1) Hyman Rodman published (in 1971) a splendid account of family life in the lower class of Trinidad. (His account, incidentally, was not originally guided by works on the culture of poverty but became the innocent focus of a severe attack on that literature by others.) Rodman argued that lower-class Trinidadians share the common cultural ideals of marriage and the nuclear family, but that these ideals lack, for them, strong normative control over behavior. The ideals are "stretched" to include alternative marital and familial forms, and some of the stretching is considerable. It includes "promiscuous" sexual relationships, "illegal" marital unions, "illegitimate" children, "deserting" by husbands and fathers, and "abandoned" children—exactly the patterns that led Frazier to conclude that life among many American blacks was plain disordered. Rodman puts quotation marks around the pejorative terms because he does not regard the behavior described by them as *problems* of the lower class but the opposite: "*solutions* [my emphasis] of the lower class to problems that they face in the social, economic, and perhaps legal and political spheres of life" (1971:passim). The "solutions" go so far that words like *promiscuity*, *illegitimacy*, or *desertion* are not even part of the lower-class vocabulary in Trinidad, while less negatively loaded words like "friending" or "outside children" do play a role in it.

Rodman was not aware of Maier's work, so that he does not discuss frustration-instigated behavior directly. He does show that deviant behavior (deviant even from the norms of the actor) and, in that sense, fixated, may be "situationally logical"; and some of the specific behavior patterns he describes (e.g., desertion of wives and children, or promiscuity as a way of life) are not hard to fit into the concept of frustrated behavior.

(2) In a recent article (1984) on "civic inclusion," I made the point that the apparently nonrational, self-defeating behavior of lower-class pupils in American and British schools comes from an authority culture that is highly adaptive to the defining characteristic of poverty: high scarcity. The argument needed to make that point is rather complex. Suffice to say here that apathy toward formally offered opportunities (just "getting through" the day, the term, etc.), submissiveness to authoritarian domination, the testing of teachers for what Herbert Foster (1974) has called their "physicality" (including their willingness

to use violence), as well as fitting well into the concept of frustrated behavior, seemed sensible in the milieus from which the pupils came and to which they were headed. In fact, they seemed close to deducible from the objective, exigent conditions, if only we proceed from the postulate that people adapt to situations and manage to think ourselves into the pupils' environments.

Take "physicality." In a setting of pervasive physical insecurity (for instance, on the mean streets, and in the schools themselves) physicality promises at least a possibility of safety. Just as the capacity for fighting was a basis of acceptable domination during the age of early feudalism, so it legitimates teachers to fearful pupils and makes education possible. But, Foster tells us, only a small percentage of "gentle" middle-class teachers ever understand that. Thus they themselves change their good intentions to what is, for them, better adapted (but educationally useless) behavior.

FRUSTRATION-INSTIGATED BEHAVIOR AS ADAPTIVE BEHAVIOR

Maier was criticized by other psychologists for not showing the nature of the link between the experience of frustration and frustrated behavior as a theoretically distinctive response to it (Yates, 1962:30ff.). This seems to me justified. The difficulty arises, in my view, from a point made earlier: Maier's view that frustrated behavior is maladaptive. I would argue that when the most fundamental functional imperatives of existence in societies are considered, frustration-instigated behavior seems just the opposite.

Certain compelling functional imperatives do govern our lives, at a deep level; that is why the imperative to adapt to situations exists in the first place. These fundamental imperatives do not include engaging in and winning competitions that involve "rational choice," like economic or political "market" competitions. Such competitions may be exciting and winning them no doubt *is* pleasant. But the competitions are better regarded as luxuries one can afford only when the elementary imperatives of life have been satisfied and life situations thus provide substantial "degrees of freedom." Up to that point, "struggle" occurs, but that is something different.

What are the elementary imperatives for adaptation? The most fundamental, no doubt, is that emphasized by Hobbes: *survival*. The imperative to survive should not be understood only as sheer physical survival. Often, in social situations, survival refers to somehow "getting through" ordeals, without injurious stress—like getting to the end of an onerous and monotonous workday. For instance, in the case of the lower-class pupils discussed in my 1984 article, surviving often simply meant getting through boring days devoted to trivial, apparently pointless tasks; and it meant getting through school as such without painful exertions, in order to start working life—"real" life. Peter Woods (1979), in a study of a British secondary modern school, found that the behavior of teachers frequently also amounted, at bottom, to what he calls "survival-strategies"—surviving tension and threats created by pupils. And none of the behavior—neither the teachers' nor the pupils'—was discernibly "goal-oriented," if that means aiming at instruction and educational achievement.

A second imperative of existence surely is *low entropy*: a predictable life, not a life seemingly governed by random or arbitrary forces. (Even rats seem to need that.) That low entropy is a fundamental need for people comes out particularly well in R. W. Southern's discussion of the medieval "idea of freedom," in *The Making of the Middle Ages* (1959:107–110). For the medieval mind, Southern states, to be free meant neither the absence of constraints ("freedom from") nor opportunities and resources to realize goals ("freedom to"). It meant not being subject to arbitrary will. In other words, before the condition of being free could be equated with choosing and with realizing chosen goals, freedom was equated simply with predictable existence. And this should not surprise. Without predictability, choosing means to act anomically. Anomie as an intolerable, often life-destroying, burden on individuals has been discussed in studies as diverse as Durkheim's *Suicide* (1952) and DeGrazia's (1948) *Political Community*. It is worst when it is not a special individual but a general social state. Stephen Coleman's excellent (and much neglected) *Measurement and Analysis of Political Systems* demonstrated, with great precision, that much political behavior which we view differently is best regarded as entropy-reducing behavior, including voting and making revolutions.

A third imperative is the reduction of the *precariousness* of life. By this I mean not knowing, with reasonable probability, what one's condition in life will be in any future, near or far—especially, of course, near. "Unpredictability" and "precariousness" are not the same. The first refers to interactions, particularly interactions with authorities and powers. By precariousness I mean *material* uncertainty. The possibility of sudden unemployment, with little or no alternative support, is an obvious example of high precariousness. A more destructive source of it (because it affects all, like a natural disaster) is high inflation. As we know from concrete cases like Israel, people adapt behavior even to egregious inflation—they *must* do so—but the condition defines the adaptation. One such adaptation to precariousness we know from history: the acceptance of authoritative control. Rogowski (1974) has constructed an admirable rational choice theory of legitimacy, in which he makes good use of contract theories. We would do well to look at actual charters and "constitutions" that granted powers "contractually" to great princes. The reasons for the grants (in the West, at any rate) generally were to assure "the security of persons" and to guarantee "the reliability of the currency" (which goes beyond survival, to precariousness even with survival).

What is the link to frustrated behavior? Consider once more the Appalachians. It should be evident that the Appalachian mountaineers are oriented toward all of these imperatives: survival (even if at an abject level), entropy reduction (even if through apparently irrational fixations or regressive beliefs and practices), and reduction of precariousness (even if by chronic dependency, and fleeing from opportunity because of minor mishaps).

CONCLUSION

Frustrated behavior—behavior without goals—is widespread because it has very deep roots in the basic, inescapable imperatives of human existence. Unless we take this fact into account, we will continue procrustean, and certainly not parsimonious, stretching of cost-benefit conceptions to account for phenomena to which they are irrelevant. On the practical side, we will also continue attempts to meliorate conditions that undoubtedly call for improvement, but we will do it in all the wrong ways, doing harm or nothing while trying to do good.

Psychologists like Maier invariably theorized for the sake of therapy. They often failed because *they* were fixated, as it were, on inadequate theoretical perspectives. This charge, I hold, also applies to rational choice theories of politics—for all their ingenuity and elegance. Their key failure comes from the assumption, with which Downs begins, as axiomatic truth: that action always is directed "toward the attainment of conscious goals."

It is not.

REFERENCES

Allport, G. W.; Bruner, J. S.; and Jandorf, E. M. (1941). "Personality Under Social Catastrophe." *Character and Personality*, 4:1–22.

Ball, R. A. (1968). "A Poverty Case: The Analgesic Subculture of the Southern Appalachians. *American Sociological Review*, 33:885–895.

Baruch, D. W. (1940). "Therapeutic Procedures as Part of the Educational Process." *Journal of Consultative Psychology*, 4:165–172.

Caudill, H. M. (1962). *Night Comes to the Cumberlands*. Boston: Little, Brown.

Coleman, S. (1975). *Measurement and Analysis of Political Systems*. New York: Wiley.

DeGrazia, S. (1948). *The Political Community: A Study of Anomie*. Chicago: University of Chicago Press.

Dollard, J., et al. (1939). *Frustration and Aggression*. New Haven: Yale University Press.

Downs, A. (1957). *An Economic Theory of Democracy*. New York: Harper & Row.

Durkheim, E. (1952). *Suicide: A Study in Sociology*. London: Routledge and Kegan Paul.

Eckstein, H. (1984). "Civic Inclusion and Its Discontents." *Daedalus*, *113*:107–146.

Eisenberg, P., and Lazarsfeld, P. F. (1938). "The Psychological Effects of Unemployment." *Psychological Bulletin*, 35:358–390.

Foster, H. L. (1974). *Ribbin', Jivin', and Playing the Dozens*. Cambridge, MA: Ballinger.

Frazier, E. F. (1966). *The Negro Family in the United States* (rev. and abridged ed.). Chicago: University of Chicago Press. (Original work published 1939)

Gaventa, J. (1980). *Power and Powerlessness: Quiescence and Rebellion in an Appalachian Valley*. Urbana: University of Illinois Press.

Laver, M. (1981). *The Politics of Private Desires*. Middlesex: Penguin.

Lewis, O. (1951). *Life in a Mexican Village*. Urbana: University of Illinois Press.

————. (1959). *Five Families: Mexican Case Studies in the Culture of Poverty*. New York: Basic Books.

————. (1966). *La Vida*. New York: Random House.

Maier, N. (1961). *Frustration: The Study of Behavior Without a Goal*. Ann Arbor: University of Michigan Press. (1st ed., 1949)

Matza, D. (1966). "The Disreputable Poor." In N. J. Smelser and S. H. Lipset (Eds.), *Social Structure and Mobility in Economic Development*. Chicago: Aldine.

Merton, R. K. (1949). *Social Theory and Social Structure*. Glencoe, IL: Free Press.

Moynihan, D. P., and Glazer, N. (1966). *Beyond the Melting Pot*. Cambridge, MA: MIT Press and Harvard University Press.

Riker, W. H. (1962). *The Theory of Political Coalitions*. New Haven: Yale University Press.

Rodman, H. (1971). *Lower-Class Families: The Culture of Poverty in Negro Trinidad*. London: Oxford University Press.

Rogowski, R. (1974). *Rational Legitimacy*. Princeton: Princeton University Press.

Schumpeter, J. A. (1943). *Capitalism, Socialism and Democracy*. London: Allen and Unwin.

Simon, H. A. (1976). *Administrative Behavior*. New York: Free Press. (Original work published 1947)

————. (1955). "A Behavioral Model of Rational Choice." *Quarterly Journal of Economics*, 69:99–118.

————. (1982). *Models of Bounded Rationality*. Two volumes. Cambridge, MA: MIT Press.

————. (1983). *Reason in Human Affairs*. Stanford: Stanford University Press.

————. (1985). "Human Nature in Politics: The Dialogue of Psychology with Political Science." *American Political Science Review*, 79:293–304.

Southern, R. W. (1959). *The Making of the Middle Ages*. New Haven: Yale University Press.

Thomas, W. I. (1951). *Social Behavior and Personality*. New York: Social Science Research Council.

Toynbee, A. (1946). *A Study of History*. New York: Oxford University Press.

Valentine, C. A. (1968). *Culture and Poverty*. Chicago: University of Chicago Press.

Wallas, Graham. (1921). *Human Nature in Politics*. New York: Crofts. (Original work published 1908)

Watson, G. (1934). "A Comparison of the Effects of Lax Versus Strict Home Training." *Journal of Social Psychology*, 5:102–105.

Weller, J. E. (1965). *Yesterday's People: Life in Contemporary Appalachia*. Lexington: University of Kentucky Press.

Woods, P. (1979). *The Divided School*. London: Routledge and Kegan Paul.

Yates, A. J. 1962. *Frustration and Conflict*. New York: Wiley.

Chapter

4

Human Agency and Rational Action[1]

David Johnston

The idea of a human agent as rational actor is basic to the economic approach to politics. An individual conceives a desire or goal, chooses an action by comparing this goal with the available alternatives, and acts upon his or her choice. From this basic understanding, the conventional idea of human agency is constructed around two claims:

1. The human being is a causal agent, as opposed to a mere object of causation. In other words, the individual makes *choices* and acts upon them, thereby initiating certain chains of events while allowing others to remain unrealized.
2. The individual's choices are made with certain ends or goals in mind rather than being capricious or random. Choices are *rational* when they can reasonably be expected to advance the agent's ends; an agent is rational when his or her set of ends forms an internally consistent whole.

The conventional idea of human agency and action is a staple of modern social thought and an essential element in the rationalist or, more broadly, intentionalist approach to social inquiry. This approach has been adopted widely in many fields of social science both for explanatory and for normative purposes. The idea has roots in the writings of diverse modern philosophers, including John Locke and Immanuel Kant. It is no great exaggeration to say that this idea expresses a modern alternative to the Aristotelian definition of man as a *zoon politikon* by nature. Where Aristotle argued that human beings are intended for life in a *polis* and are capable of achieving fulfillment only in such a context, many modern thinkers assume that humans are rational, purposive creatures by nature, beings who reach their potential only insofar as they make and act upon choices in accordance with coherent plans.[2]

In many instances, however, actions appear not to conform to the pattern assumed by the rationalist approach to social inquiry. There are two basic problems. First, many actions appear not to result from choices at all, or at least not to result from choices to take those specific actions. Second, where actions appear most clearly to result from choices, the circumstances of choice seem difficult to assimilate to the conventional idea. Often there are unreconciled inconsistencies among the individual's ends. Where such inconsistencies exist, it is difficult to interpret the process of choice along the lines laid down by the conventional idea.

In this essay I propose two informal alternatives to the conventional idea of human agency. The purpose of these alternatives is to represent actions that cannot be described by the conventional idea without straining credibility. My first alternative is built upon the notion of a performance. The key thought is that many actions belong to highly programmed sequences. The actions within such sequences are triggered by the "program" that governs the sequence rather than by a discrete decision or choice. These actions are integral to the sequence's performance. I shall argue that many actions are better accounted for by reference to the notion of a skilled performance than by the concept of choice assumed by the rationalist approach to explanation.

The second alternative is constructed around the concept of deliberation. This alternative is designed to help make sense of actions that occur when the agent's ends are not clearly specified or when he or she possesses conflicting goals. I shall suggest that we can explain these actions more adequately by attempting to understand the processes of deliberative choice than by treating actors as if each possessed a utility function capable of generating a complete and consistent ordering among all alternatives with which he or she might be faced.[3]

My main aim in sketching these two alternatives is to help describe the limitations of the economic approach to the explanation of political behavior. Within specific domains the economic approach can be of considerable heuristic value. In recent years, however, that approach has frequently been applied to problems of social explanation it is ill-suited to address. The notions of performance and deliberation are designed to help reestablish this approach within appropriate bounds.

An additional purpose of these sketches is to call attention to the normative limitations of the conventional idea of human agency. That idea articulates aspirations toward efficacy and purposiveness that have been influential in our culture for the past three centuries or more. These aspirations should be tempered with a grasp of the alternative understandings of human excellence suggested by the notions of performance and deliberation.

I

The first premise of the rational actor approach to social explanation is that human actions result from choices.[4] In many cases, however, the assumption that choices determine actions is highly questionable. Consider my morning drive to the station to catch a train into New York City. From one standpoint this 15–minute episode is a single "action." From another, however, it is a highly complex sequence of actions, many of which require considerable skill. I must get into the car, start it, back out of my driveway, and negotiate a path through a series of stop signs, lights, and traffic until I am able to find my way into a vacant space in the garage adjacent to the station. The number of actions required for the completion of the task is very large. How can these actions best be explained?

The rationalist approach suggests that actions are best explained as if they were the consequences of choices made by an agent in an attempt to advance the agent's ends. When I notice that I am approaching another automobile at excessive speed, I choose to apply my foot to the brake pedal in order to avoid suffering or inflicting personal injury or damage to property. Similarly, I choose to turn the steering wheel from left to right because I wish to execute a right turn. Although advocates of the rationalist approach generally recognize that individuals do not usually consciously choose to take actions of the kinds described, they do maintain that episodes of this kind are best understood as if individuals did make these choices.

One well-known difficulty with any such analysis is that most of the decisions I must make in order to complete the sequence of actions that brings me to the station occur without my consideration of any alternative. Ordinarily the concept of choice is applied to situations in which two or more alternative actions are contemplated. In the case of most of the actions that constitute the sequence under discussion, however, this condition is absent. Often I am not even conscious of the fact that I am performing the actions themselves, let alone of the possibility that I might do otherwise. Yet awareness of and at least some degree of deliberation about alternative possibilities is implied by the concept of choice.

This objection suggests that it might be useful to distinguish various types of decisions. When an actor is aware of and deliberates about alternative possibilities, we can say that he or she *chooses* an action. When these conditions are not met—as they often are not in the case of actions within a sequence like the one described above—we can say that the actor *selects* an action.[5] The concept of selection implies that an alternative decision would be objectively possible, but it does not imply that the decision maker has considered or is even aware of any alternative. It would be within my power to decide *not* to apply my foot to the brake pedal when I notice that I am approaching another automobile at excessive speed. Ordinarily, however, I do not give this possibility a single thought.

Building upon this distinction, we can construct a conception to account for some sequences of actions to which the conditions of choice implied by the rationalist approach seem not to apply. The central idea of this conception is that of a skilled performance, which can be defined by reference to two key features. First, a performance consists of a *programmatic sequence* of actions.[6] The actions which constitute it must be executed in a well-defined order. Variations in this order may be possible, but only within a range permitted by the program. The program defines criteria that the agent applies more or less automatically to select actions within the sequence. In effect, each action is "triggered" by an antecedent event and in turn triggers a subsequent action in a chain that continues until the sequence is completed. Second, the execution of a performance is supported by a considerable amount of *tacit knowledge*.[7] A performer is likely to be unaware of many of the details of his or her performance while it is going on, and would probably be incapable of articulating many of these details at any time. The performer "knows" what to do but would be able to explain only a small portion of this knowledge.

The notion of a performance provides us with an alternative to the explanation suggested by the rationalist approach for the actions that comprise my morning drive to the train station. When I notice that I am approaching another automobile at excessive speed, I react to my perception almost automatically by applying the brakes. No conscious calculation is involved. When I approach a routine right turn, I turn the steering wheel without thinking. Most of the actions required to execute the drive successfully are performed without consideration of an alternative. They are relatively automatic responses triggered by previous actions and by routine situations that arise within a sequence. With a few exceptions, the actions that constitute the sequence are selected, not chosen.

Of course, some of the actions required for successful execution of my drive are *not* automatic. Machlup, whose celebrated analogy between the theory of the maximizing firm and the "theory of overtaking" provoked me to adopt the example of driving in this paper, suggests the following analysis of the decision procedure involved in one action of this kind:

> What sort of considerations are behind the routine decision of the driver of an automobile to overtake a truck proceeding ahead of him at a slower speed? What factors influence his decision? Assume that he is faced with the alternative of either slowing down and

staying behind the truck or of passing it before a car which is approaching from the opposite direction will have reached the spot. As an experienced driver he somehow takes into account (a) the speed at which the truck is going, (b) the remaining distance between himself and the truck, (c) the speed at which he is proceeding, (d) the possible acceleration of his speed, (e) the distance between him and the car approaching from the opposite direction, (f) the speed at which that car is approaching, and probably also the condition of the road (concrete or dirt, wet or dry, straight or winding, level or uphill), the degree of visibility (light or dark, clear or foggy), and the condition of the tires and brakes of his car, and —let us hope—his own condition (fresh or tired, sober or alcoholized) permitting him to judge the enumerated factors (Machlup, 1946:534–535).

Although Machlup acknowledges that the driver envisaged in this scenario will reach his decision without consciously calculating all the enumerated factors, his point is that an explanation of the driver's action must proceed as if such a calculation had taken place. The rational actor model is the applicable explanatory tool regardless of the actor's subjective state of mind.

Despite the complexity of analysis suggested by Machlup's example, one of the most noteworthy things about the approach to explanation he advocates is the amount of relevant information he ignores. While the analogy is intended to focus attention upon the wealth of information to which the decision maker must attend at the moment of decision, it makes no mention of the sequence of events that gave rise to the need for a decision. Even if we were to accept the conclusion that the rational actor model is the appropriate tool for analyzing the driver's *decision*, any explanation of his *action* (overtaking or not overtaking) would have to take cognizance of the sequence of actions that brought the driver to a position behind the truck in the first place. His decision and subsequent action are "set up" by a series of events, most of which can best be accounted for by the notion of a performance, not by the rational actor approach.

Moreover, the agent is rendered capable of making a decision only by the fact that there are so many actions he or she routinely takes without the need for decision or awareness. The importance of this feature of many actions is emphasized by Polanyi:

I shall take as my clue for this investigation the well-known fact *that the aim of a skillful performance is achieved by the observance of a set of rules which are not known as such to the person following them.* For example, the decisive factor by which the swimmer keeps himself afloat is the manner by which he regulates his respiration; he keeps his bouyancy at an increased level by refraining from emptying his lungs when breathing out and by inflating them more than usual when breathing in; yet this is not generally known to swimmers (Polanyi, 1962:49).

Awareness of most of the actions comprising a performance is not only unnecessary for a successful execution; it is often undesirable or even incompatible with a successful performance. A swimmer who attempts to attend simultaneously to all the various subskills required for swimming would probably fail, and would certainly be diverted from the main task—the integration of these subskills into an overall performance. The driver in Machlup's example can decide whether or not to overtake the truck only because he does not have to decide or even think about most of his other, more routine actions.

The importance of this tacit dimension to action is most evident when a skill is being learned. A novice driver or swimmer is typically aware of many more details of the performance than is an experienced practitioner of either of these skills. As the actions involved in the performance as a whole become routinized, the agent's awareness of these actions diminishes, and the quality of the performance improves. The agent who has achieved a certain degree of proficiency can begin to make choices like the decision described by Machlup about whether or not to overtake. The driver is enabled to make this decision by the fact that most of the actions are so thoroughly routinized that they need involve no conscious decision making at all. Decisions generally take place against the background of a performance, the bulk of which is constituted by actions about which no decision is necessary.

In many cases, then, it seems more plausible to account for actions by reference to the conception of a performance than by evoking the idea of rational choice. Actions that are highly routinized or programmed are not chosen except insofar as the sequence to which they belong is chosen. My actions in applying the brakes or turning the steering wheel generally are selected, not chosen. They are entailed by my decision to initiate a larger sequence of actions—namely, my drive to the station.

Moreover, even the initiation of an entire sequence of actions is sometimes better explained as the outcome of a programmed selection procedure than as the consequence of a deliberate choice. My performance of the drive is merely one component of a larger performance that brings me from my home to my office in the morning. The decision to undertake the drive is a programmed element within that larger performance. Like the other components of that larger performance, I usually undertake it without thinking, and certainly without making a conscious choice.

The key thought here is that *sequences of actions can be imbedded within larger sequences*. The decision to initiate a sequence can accordingly be programmed in the same way as are the actions within that sequence.

We might call my drive to the station a *first-order* performance. Its components include a large number of actions that are so highly routinized that I perform them without awareness that I am doing so. A *second-order* performance, then, is a sequence of actions that includes first-order performances among its components. In the example developed above, the morning routine that brings me from my home to my office is a performance of the second order. The program by which that routine is defined includes my (programmed) decision to initiate my morning drive as well as the decisions responsible for initiating the other sequences of action I undertake. Second-order performances can of course be imbedded within higher-order sequences. To extend the example one step further, the second-order performance I have called my morning routine is imbedded within a third-order performance I shall call my workday routine.

The notion of a performance could thus be extended indefinitely. For the purpose of explaining actions, of course, this conception is likely to be of greatest use if its complexity is kept within reasonable limits. My point in calling attention to its potential for extension is to suggest that the concept of performance can help make sense even of relatively extended action sequences. It is not always necessary, and sometimes is not plausible, to explain even the initiation of these sequences—let alone their execution—by reference to the idea of choice.

The claim that actions can sometimes best be explained by reference to the conception of a skilled performance extends a criticism of the rational actor approach to social explanation associated with the concept of bounded rationality. According to Simon's classic papers on this concept, the rationality of actions is generally bounded in part because considerable economies can be achieved by organizing actions into routinized procedures (Simon, 1955). While there is a close link between this aspect of Simon's argument and the conception of a skilled performance for which I have argued here, Simon appears to share the rational actor theorists' assumption that the *basic* category for explaining human action is an individual choice. This reading of Simon's intent is implied, at least, by the argument of a recent paper:

> My main conclusion is that the key premises in any theory that purports to explain the real phenomena of politics are the empirical assumptions about goals and, even more important, about the ways in which people characterize the choice situations that face them (1985:301).

Although Simon is surely right to emphasize the way in which people characterize their choices, the concept of choice may not be as important to the explanation of at least some actions as Simon suggests in this paper. The conception of a skilled performance is designed to account for actions that are better explained as outcomes of programmed decision making than as consequences of a choice of any kind. My argument is that the concept of a performance possesses greater verisimilitude and greater explanatory potential than the intentionalist approach for the purpose of explaining actions of a relatively routinized nature. The concept of a performance imposes far less distortion upon such actions than does the rational actor approach to human action.[8]

II

In many instances, of course, human beings do make choices. However, many situations of choice are difficult to analyze by the means placed at our disposal by the rational actor approach to explanation. The central problem is that choices often are made when the choosing agent's ends are unclear or when conflicts among these ends remain unresolved. Choices made under these circumstances do not seem to be reconcilable with the rational actor approach to the explanation of social actions, which proceeds for the most part on the assumption that individual agents can fruitfully (even if fictionally) be regarded as the possessors of complete and internally consistent sets of ends.

Consider the following example. A young professional woman, having recently given birth to her first child, must decide whether to return to full-time work. Her employer has granted her only the six weeks of maternity leave required by law in the state where she lives and has told her that she must return at the end of that period on a full-time basis or not at all. She is in the early stages of her career in a field with limited opportunities, so a decision not to return to work could place her career in jeopardy. Eventually she decides to resign so that she will be able to devote at least the next year or two to raising her child. Yet her feelings about the decision are highly equivocal. She is torn between the two alternatives because of her awareness that either choice will commit her to sacrificing something she values very highly, and she finds it exceedingly difficult to commit herself to any course of action that would entail such a major sacrifice. Moreover, her equivocal feelings persist even after that commitment has been made. She runs through the decision in her mind many times. A year later she still experiences sentiments of regret for the sacrifice she was unable to avoid.

How can we best account for this woman's experience? The rational actor approach suggests that the woman's decision must be the result of a comparison between her goals or values and the alternatives available to her (the feasible set). Ideally she would prefer both to pursue her career and to spend considerable time with her child. Since no available alternative will permit her to pursue both goals at once, she must clarify and carefully assign relative weights to each of her relevant values in order to make her decision. However, her efforts to clarify her own values are only partly successful. Although those efforts enable her to formulate a value structure with sufficient internal consistency to generate a decision, her prior equivocation and subsequent misgivings indicate that that consistency is fleeting, and that she is unable to achieve a stable reconciliation between the two pulls upon her sentiments. Her equivocal feelings about her own decision indicate that her ends are less internally coherent—and thus less rational—than they might be.

This interpretation of the woman's experience is constructed entirely within the framework defined by the rational actor approach to explanation. Yet what reason do we have for believing that this analysis is accurate? In particular, why should we assume that the young woman ever achieves an internally consistent structure of values, even at the moment of her decision? In light of the deep equivocation with which she viewed her decision in advance and continues to view it in retrospect, it seems doubtful that this assumption is correct.

Imagine by way of an alternative to the rational actor approach that the woman in the example possesses two independent value structures rather than one. These two value structures belong to two distinct personae who happen to be joined within a single biological individual. Each structure is internally consistent, at least with respect to the decision in question here, but the two structures are mutually contradictory: one would have her return to her job without a trace of hesitation, while the other indicates adamantly that her only course is to resign. These two personae are at odds with one another throughout her decision process, including its aftermath.[9]

How does this woman resolve her difficulty? Clearly she cannot do so simply by clarifying and ranking her values. The process of value clarification simply throws into sharp relief the deep and apparently irreconcilable conflict between her two personae. Given the inadequacy of this clarification strategy, the woman has three remaining alternatives:

1. She may attempt to modify either or both of her two personae in order to achieve a reconciliation between their initially contradictory value structures; or
2. She may transform herself radically by discarding one or the other of the two personae; or

3. She may initiate a bargaining process between her two personae in the hope that they will be able to reach some kind of compromise or modus vivendi without erasing the contradiction between them.

Suppose now that each of this woman's two personae is attached to a social role. We might say that she is both a "mother" and a "professional." Her role as a mother defines one of her personae, with its own reasonably well-ordered and stable value structure, while her role as a professional defines another. In neither case is the definition of her role of her own making. Mother and professional are social categories. The woman cannot redefine these categories without enlisting the cooperation of others, nor can she reject the values associated with them without seriously impairing her ability to perform well within these roles. Although each category permits a range of permissible value structures, in both cases the range is constrained.

Under these circumstances, the first of the three alternatives listed above may be closed off. While some degree of modification may be possible, the range of permissible modification is constrained by social norms attached to the two roles this woman has assumed. In this case let us assume that the range is not sufficiently broad to permit a reconciliation. There are practical obstacles that prevent this woman from pursuing both her goals at once *and* normative obstacles that block her attempts to reconcile her two personae with each other.

Only two possibilities remain. The woman may discard one of her two personae, thereby altering her identity substantially. Alternatively, she may retain both personae, despite the recognized conflict between them, and initiate a bargaining process in the hope of achieving a modus vivendi solution.

The latter of these two possibilities describes the alternative pursued by the woman in the example above. The woman is unwilling to discard either of the two personae that define her identity. Her response to her difficult decision suggests instead that a bargaining relationship has been struck up between them. The circumstances are such that on the major issue—whether or not to return to work—it is possible for only one of her two personae to achieve its goals. In this case, the mother has come away with the major prize. It may be, however, that the professional was able to wring concessions from her adversary in the bargain, perhaps including a promise to reciprocate by allowing the woman to return to the job market at an earlier date than the mother would like. In any case, the woman's continuing equivocation and unreconciled regrets testify to the continuing claims of both parties to the bargain. I suggest that this bargaining scenario captures many elements of the process of deliberation about ends to which the rational actor rendition of human action is oblivious. The need to make a genuine choice is created by an inconsistency within the agent's structure of ends and not merely by a need to choose means appropriate to predetermined ends. It may be that in principle such inconsistencies can always be resolved. A virtue of representing deliberative choice in the way I have suggested, however, is that the scenario indicates that such evaluative resolutions may be purchased (at least on some occasions) only at a high price. Given the practical and normative constraints within which the woman must work, she must either sacrifice an important element of her identity or live with ambivalence and second thoughts. Under these difficult circumstances, her adoption of the latter course seems reasonable.

The difference between the rational actor approach and the conception of deliberation developed here is especially clear from the contrasting ways in which these two alternative accounts portray this woman's ambivalence. The framework of analysis defined by the rational actor approach suggests that ambivalence stems from lack of clarity. Once she has succeeded in clarifying her values, her ambivalence should be dispelled, and the woman need have no further misgivings about the choice she has made. The fact that she continues to have equivocal feelings about the decision just shows that her efforts to achieve self-clarification have failed. Viewed from within the framework defined by the concept of deliberative choice, however, the woman's ambivalence is a sign of her clear recognition of the objective conflict between the two personae, or roles, she has assumed. She experiences equivocal feelings because she has achieved self-clarification, not because she has failed to do so. The concept of deliberative choice portrays the woman's ambivalence as the consequence of her clear grasp of her objective situation in the world rather than as a sign of her imperfect rationality.

The concept of deliberation can be used to make sense of a considerable variety of cases that are likely to be distorted or misunderstood by theorists who are wedded closely to the rational actor approach to human action. The notions of bargaining among multiple personae and of identity redefinition it invokes are potentially applicable to many situations in which an agent's ends are unclear or internally inconsistent. The concept of deliberation seems to be an especially useful tool for explaining the process of choice in cases of conflicting commitments or loyalties like those which beset individuals who play multiple roles. Whether one's concern is with a woman attempting to adjudicate between the roles of mother and professional, a public official trying to reconcile the roles of professional administrator and democratic citizen in the face of information about bureaucratic corruption or ineptitude,[10] or the ruler of a Greek *polis* forced to choose between loyalty to his city and love for his daughter,[11] conflicts between roles and the values they impose upon individuals have been a recurrent feature of human life throughout the history of civilization. It is a feature the rational actor approach neglects.

III

The most widely recognized advantage the rational actor approach possesses over rival approaches to social explanation is the great elegance and simplicity of theoretical formulation it allows. Building upon a few simple assumptions, rational actor theorists have shown that it is possible to generate sophisticated models with very interesting implications for our understanding of human action. This advantage was a major factor in the extension of the economic approach into the domain of political explanation initiated by Downs (1957). In addition to this advantage, the rational actor approach appeals to certain widely shared normative inclinations. It represents human beings as causally efficacious and purposive creatures. The rationalist approach thus expresses in formal terms aspirations that have had a powerful influence in shaping Western civilization during the past several centuries. Although some practitioners of the economic approach to politics may be unaware of these normative implications of the rationalist approach to social inquiry, they are almost certainly an important source of its appeal to theoreticians throughout the social sciences. I shall discuss each of these factors behind the current popularity of the economic approach to politics in turn.

Elegance and simplicity—"parsimony," in the jargon of the discipline—are widely regarded as theoretical virtues.[12] Advocates of the economic approach to politics have often cited these virtues as a major factor in favor of their preferred method of political analysis. But the rational actor approach to social explanation does not deliver these virtues in as great a measure as many of its practitioners contend. As Simon (1985) has persuasively argued, the key explanatory feature of any rational choice model that purports to explain real political events is the set of empirical assumptions made by the theory about the goals people pursue and about the ways in which people characterize their own choices. A key assumption in Downs's original work on voting, for example, was that citizens cast their votes "as part of a selection process, not as an expression of preference" (Downs, 1957:48). If this assumption were false, then many of Downs's theoretical propositions would be invalid. Yet it is reasonable to believe that in many situations the assumptions *is* false, and that many citizens cast votes for reasons other than those postulated by the theory. In any case, the only plausible way to determine why people cast their votes as they do is to investigate these reasons through complex empirical research. Theoretical postulation alone is not an effective means of explaining real political events.

I believe we should extend Simon's argument by observing that the explanation of political events is heavily dependent upon empirical research into the routines people learn to perform as well as the goals they choose to pursue. A great deal of human conduct is selected through processes of programmed decision making rather than chosen in the classical sense. The programs or sequences that regulate such conduct are learned; the ability to carry out these sequences is an acquired skill. The only way to construct a plausible explanation of such conduct is to discover the culture-specific practices that govern it. A model built upon the assumption that human conduct can be understood as efficient goal-oriented behavior simply cannot explain many of the actions in which ordinary human beings routinely engage.[13]

Even when human conduct is better understood as a consequence of choice than as an outcome of programmed decision making, the character of people's choices often is not what the rational actor approach would lead one to expect. The making of choices is in part an identity-defining act through which the agent specifies his or her ends as a result of deliberation rather than an exclusively instrumental act in which means are chosen to advance predetermined goals. The expressive voting Downs excluded from his model of democratic electoral behavior is a case in point. It is reasonable to believe that voters sometimes go to the polls primarily in order to register who they are rather than because they believe their votes will affect the outcome of an election. A vote may be a way of establishing one's political identity with others, or perhaps only of affirming it to oneself. In any case, the definition of an agent's ends is a continuous and frequently an inconclusive process. It often does not result in a set of ends or utility function with sufficient internal consistency to justify use of the rational actor approach without the adoption of substantial auxiliary assumptions, as the empirical literature on this topic attests.[14]

I do not mean to suggest that the rationalist approach to human action is devoid of explanatory value. On the contrary, this approach has been put to work fruitfully as an aid to analysis both in works of great theoretical abstraction (e.g., Axelrod, 1984) and in highly specific studies of institutional behavior (e.g., Mayhew, 1974).[15] But the usefulness of these studies is partly a function of their authors' appreciation of the limitations of the economic approach to the analysis of political behavior. A great deal of human conduct occurs under circumstances that are insufficiently similar to those postulated by the rational actor approach for that method to be of great use for the purpose of explanation. The highly touted virtues of elegance and simplicity are very attractive in the abstract. They are less so when their application to real world explanation is achieved at the price of implausibility.

Apart from its alleged explanatory virtues, the rational actor approach is attractive to some writers because it captures and expresses in formal language certain aspirations and desires. The assumption that human beings make choices that determine the course of subsequent events appeals to a desire to see ourselves as efficacious creatures that seems to prevail widely throughout our culture.[16] The assumption that our choices are rationally directed toward coherent ends reinforces a self-image constructed around the notion that humans are purposive beings that appears to have been a dominant theme in Western thinking at least since the Reformation. The rational actor approach often conveys a normative message even when its principal intended purpose is explanatory.[17]

I suggest that the idea of a human agent as rational actor is as flawed normatively as it is imperfect for the purpose of explanation. To be sure, purposiveness and efficacy are admirable attributes in human beings. We have only to consider their opposites, aimlessness and inefficacy, to see why they are considered desirable. But in many areas of life we are neither as purposive nor as efficacious as we sometimes imagine. Moreover, there are reasons to believe that we would not be better off if we were able to make and implement choices more freely and efficaciously than we already do. From a normative as well as an explanatory perspective, the rational actor approach should be supplemented by drawing on the notions of skilled performance and deliberative choice so that its message may be assessed in relation to the alternative understandings of human excellence supported by these theoretical constructs.

The human attribute most prominently featured in the notion of a performance is the capacity for skilled behavior. Almost all human actions of any consequence are performable only because the agent involved has acquired the appropriate skills. Automobile drivers and swimmers, musical performers and athletes all must learn skills at some level of proficiency in order to carry out their activities. For our purposes one of the most noteworthy features of any performance is that the agent's skill at performing is in part a function of his or her ability to forego the making of choices and even to a large degree to suppress awareness of what he or she is doing. Skilled performances are the products of practice, routine, and sometimes monotonous repetition. Imitation is a vital means of acquiring many skills. Within limits there is an inverse relationship between the making of choices and the perfection of skills.

The conventional idea of a human agent as rational actor tends to diminish our understanding and appreciation of the kinds of human excellence that can be achieved through skilled performance. The normative inclinations built into this conventional idea were captured in classic fashion over a century ago by the philosopher John Stuart Mill:

> He who lets the world, or his own portion of it, choose his plan of life for him, has no need of any other faculty than the ape-like one of imitation. He who chooses his plan for himself, employs all his faculties (Mill, 1859/1975:56).

In order to become a skilled performer, however, one *must* allow "the world" a preponderant voice in the choosing of that portion of one's life required for the perfection of the relevant skill. This kind of excellence can be acquired only through mastery of established social practices. This observation is as true of innovative excellence and invention as it is of more strictly imitative performances. Meaningful innovation in all fields builds incrementally upon existing forms.

By contrast with the notion of performance, the concept of deliberation focuses precisely upon that capacity to define one's own ends Mill celebrates as the essential attribute of a distinctively human way of life. Historically this capacity began to achieve prominence in conjunction with a substantial increase in social mobility in Europe after the Reformation.[18] When individuals are involved in multiple roles, and especially when they begin to move with some frequency among roles, conflicts between the diverse evaluative schemes associated with these different roles are likely to occur within persons. The capacity for self-definition celebrated by some modern thinkers and recognized by many others became a possibility—and for many persons a necessity—with the emergence of modern societies organized more around relationships of contract and consent than around ascriptive roles and traditional ties.

The conventional idea of human agency can accommodate the notion that persons define their own ends without difficulty. From a conventional perspective, however, any scheme of ends that falls short of perfect internal consistency demonstrates a failure of rationality. The notion of deliberative choice sketched above casts the everyday phenomenon of evaluative inconsistency in a different light. At the very least it calls attention to the fact that the resolution of internal conflict is not always a cost-free process. In defining their ends or goals, people define their identities. Any event that provokes a person to reexamine one of his or her central ends places that person's identity in question. Despite the conventional equation of rationality with internal consistency, there are some circumstances in which a refusal to resolve internal inconsistencies may be the most reasonable course of action available to the person involved.[19]

The concepts of skilled performance and deliberative choice help formalize and make sense of human experiences and conduct that the conventional idea of a human agent as rational actor neglects. They add complexity and depth to the austere picture around which the economic approach to politics has been constructed during the past several decades. But they do so in ways that are necessary if the idea of a human agent is to have sufficient verisimilitude to perform the explanatory and normative functions for which it is intended. The conventional idea of a human agent elevates certain attributes of human social existence that have been celebrated by philosophers at least from Locke onward from the status of the historically contingent to that of the eternally true. The emendations to that idea made possible by the notions of performance and deliberation can help return the idea of the human being as rational actor to a more modest and more appropriate place.

NOTES

1. I wish to thank Jules Coleman, Charles E. Lindblom, Richard Nelson, and Rogers Smith for reading a draft of this paper and providing me with many useful suggestions for revision. I would also like to acknowledge the American Council of Learned Societies, the Columbia University Council for Research in the Social Sciences, and the National Endowment for the Humanities for financial support that enabled me to compose the paper.
2. For an influential formulation of this view, see Rawls (1980:528–530 and passim). For a brilliant exposition of the contrasting view of human agency articulated in classical Chinese and neo-Confucian thought, see Bloom (1985).
3. Strictly speaking, the rationalist approach does not require that actors be treated as the possessors of utility functions with these characteristics, as Jon Elster has insisted in a long series of studies of rationality and irrationality (see, e.g., Elster 1983, 1984). A great deal of work in modern decision theory is designed to address situations in which these characteristics are absent or are incompletely realized. For an important example, see Levi (1986), and for a valuable review of recent work in this field as a whole, see Abelson and Levi (1985). Nevertheless, the notion that an agent is rational only to the extent to which his or her scheme of ends is complete and consistent remains a crucial point of reference for advocates of the rationalist approach.
4. "An action is the outcome of a choice within constraints" (Elster, 1983:vii). Although Elster is a revisionist of the rational choice approach to social inquiry, this premise, which underlies his work throughout, is purely orthodox.
5. In drawing this distinction, I follow Nelson and Winter (1982:94). My discussion in this section is heavily indebted to this work, especially Chapter 4.
6. My notion of a programmatic sequence, which I have adapted from Nelson and Winter (1982:74–76), seems similar to the concept of a

"learned strategy" developed by Monroe, in the introduction to this volume.

7. For a highly influential formulation of this concept, see Polanyi (1962).

8. For a related discussion of Simon's approach (focusing on the assumption that behavior is necessarily goal-oriented), see Eckstein's essay in this volume.

9. The general idea of treating an agent as the possessor of multiple evaluative schemes is familiar, though underdeveloped. For one well-known formulation (focusing upon the disparity between long-term and short-term evaluations), see Schelling (1978); and for more recent (and slightly more developed) treatments, see Ainslie (1986) and Steedman and Krause (1986).

10. For discussion, see Hirschman (1970).

11. I have in mind here the discussion of Aeschylus's *Agamemnon* in Nussbaum (1986:32–41).

12. As Bernard Williams (1981) has pointed out, however, the ideal of parsimony contains a powerful slant in favor of modern and (loosely) Kantian approaches to normative theory.

13. For a similar claim about a class of actions that cannot be explained by reference to the idea of efficient goal-oriented behavior, see Eckstein's chapter in this volume.

14. This observation is true even in some highly simplified decision situations. For an illuminating discussion, see Tversky and Kahneman (1981).

15. Mayhew's application of the economic approach is highly informal.

16. This desire is one of the subjects of attribution theory in social psychology. For a concise discussion (with references to the major works in the literature), see Rosenberg (1979:70–73).

17. Notice, for example, that Elster consistently describes anything other than perfect coordination and integration within a person's structure of ends as a form of failure (e.g., 1986:3) and treats "regret and incontinence" as "liabilities" from which persons suffer due to "lack of integration" (1986:14) rather than as reasonable responses to excessive restrictions of the feasible set of alternatives.

18. Michel de Montaigne, writing in the late sixteenth century, may have been the first European thinker to argue that the human self defines itself. For this interpretation of Montaigne, see Larmore (1988).

19. For an argument that arrives at similarly skeptical conclusions about the conventional account of human agency and about the importance of formal consistency in particular (though from an angle different from that presented in this essay), see Rorty (1986).

REFERENCES

Abelson, R. P., and Levi, A. (1985). "Decision Making and Decision Theory." In G. Lindzey and E. Aronson (Eds.), *Handbook of Social Psychology* (3rd ed.) (Vol. I). New York: Random House.

Ainslie, G. (1986). "Conflict Among Interests in a Multiple Self as a Determinant of Value." In Elster (1986:133–175).

Axelrod, R. (1984). *The Evolution of Cooperation*. New York: Basic Books.

Bloom, I. (1985). "On the Matter of the Mind: The Metaphysical Basis of the Expanded Self." In D. J. Munro (Ed.), *Individualism and Holism: Studies in Confucian and Taoist Values*. Ann Arbor: University of Michigan, Center for Chinese Studies, pp. 293–330.

Downs, A. (1957). *An Economic Theory of Democracy*. New York: Harper & Row.

Elster, J. (1983). *Sour Grapes: Studies in the Subversion of Rationality*. Cambridge: Cambridge University Press.

———. (1984). *Ulysses and the Sirens* (Rev. Ed.). Cambridge: Cambridge University Press.

———. (Ed.). (1986). *The Multiple Self*. Cambridge: Cambridge University Press.

Hirschman, A. O. (1970). *Exit, Voice and Loyalty*. Cambridge, MA: Harvard University Press.

Larmore, C. (1988). *Scepticism and the Self in Montaigne*. Unpublished manuscript.

Levi, I. (1986). *Hard Choices*. Cambridge: Cambridge University Press.

Machlup, F. (1946). "Marginal Analysis and Empirical Research." *American Economic Review*, 36:519–554.

Mayhew, D. R. (1974). *Congress: The Electoral Connection*. New Haven: Yale University Press.

Mill, J. S. (1975). *On Liberty*. New York: Norton. (Original work published 1859.)

Nelson, R. R., and Winter, S. G. (1982). *An Evolutionary Theory of Economic Change*. Cambridge, MA: Harvard University Press.

Nussbaum, M. C. (1986). *The Fragility of Goodness: Luck and Ethics in Greek Tragedy and Philosophy*. Cambridge: Cambridge University Press.

Polanyi, M. (1962). *Personal Knowledge: Towards a Post-Critical Philosophy*. New York: Harper Torchbooks.

Rawls, J. (1980). "Kantian Constructivism in Moral Theory." *Journal of Philosophy*, 77:515–572.

Rorty, A. O. (1986). "Self-Deception, *Akrasia* and Irrationality." In Elster (1986:115–131).

Rosenberg, M. (1979). *Conceiving the Self*. New York: Basic Books.

Schelling, T. C. (1978). "Egonomics, or the Art of Self-Management." *American Economic Review: Papers and Proceedings*, 68:290–294.

Simon, H. A. (1955). "A Behavioral Model of Rational Choice." *Quarterly Journal of Economics*, 69:99–118.

_____ . (1985). "Human Nature in Politics: The Dialogue of Psychology with Political Science." *American Political Science Review*, 79:293–304.

Steedman, I., and Krause, U. (1986). "Goethe's *Faust*, Arrow's Possibility Theorem and the Individual Decision-Taker." In Elster (1986:197–231).

Tversky, A., and Kahneman, D. (1981). "The Framing of Decisions and the Psychology of Choice." *Science*, 211:453–458.

Williams, B. A. O. (1981). "Persons, Character and Morality." In *Moral Luck*. Cambridge: Cambridge University Press.

Chapter
5

Rational Choice as a Reconstructive Theory

James D. Johnson

INTRODUCTION

Partisans of rational choice theory and of interpretive theory often view their work as mutually and fundamentally incompatible.[1] In this paper I will present theoretical reasons for believing that such views are mistaken. I will proceed from the view that rational choice and interpretation are broadly complementary (Moon, 1975) and indicate more precisely the relation that holds between them.

To do so, I make general claims about the nature of rational choice theory. In order to lend credence to these general claims, however, I focus on the spatial theory of electoral competition, a narrower, highly technical, though central, topic in the rational choice research tradition.[2] Even more specifically I concentrate on game-theoretical representations of spatial theory.[3] General arguments about the nature of a research tradition simply are not compelling unless tied to close analysis of actual practice. I have tried to keep this in mind throughout this chapter. I nonetheless intend my arguments to hold for the rational choice research tradition more generally.

The substance of this essay consists of four sections. In Section 1 I scrutinize and criticize the standard objections to rational choice theory raised by interpretive theorists. I then suggest an alternative, more compelling line of criticism. Both rational choice theorists and their interpretive critics subscribe to the orthodox view of rational choice as a "positive" science. In Section 1 I challenge this consensus as an initial warrant for the more constructive arguments in later sections.

In Section 2 I pursue a nonpositivist rendering of rational choice theory. I argue that, when properly disentangled from his broader theoretical project, Jurgen Habermas's concept of reconstructive social theory can ground such a rendering. The main thrust of my argument is that interpretation and rational choice occupy different but integral positions within a reconstructive enterprise.

In Section 3 I identify the constraints that interpretation imposes upon reconstructive social theory. I try to dispel general qualms about proceeding from the "thick description" of interpretive inquiry to the sort of formal analysis characteristic of rational choice theory. In Section 4 I demonstrate the reconstructive character of rational choice theory in greater detail. Specifically, I explore three common reconstructive techniques employed by rational choice theorists in constructing their models. I conclude by indicating the limits that reconstructive considerations impose upon the scope of rational choice models.

1. RATIONAL CHOICE THEORY AND ITS INTERPRETIVE CRITICS

In this section I begin by assessing the objections that interpretive theorists raise against rational choice analysis. Interpretive theory is exemplified in the writings of Clifford Geertz (1973) and Charles Taylor (1985). It accords overriding importance to "the concrete varieties of cultural meaning in their particularity and complex texture." It consequently focuses inquiry on "the web of language, symbol and institutions" that are the tangible vehicles of cultural significance (Rabinow and Sullivan, 1988:5–6). Interpretive theorists self-consciously reject the positivist theorist's ambition to explain and predict. They instead aspire to describe and explicate the distinctive cultural forms that frame social and political action.

Interpretive theorists criticize rational choice theory for taking the preferences of social and political actors as given. They view this as a theoretically illegitimate attempt to circumvent culturally defined "desirability characterizations." (Taylor, 1985:119) I find this objection, at least in the form in which interpretive theorists typically cast it, to be wanting. But I also argue that rational choice theory does not conform to the central criterion of "positive theory" as typically explicated by its practitioners. I do not intend the arguments of this section as decisive.[4] I view them as an initial warrant for challenging the predominant positivist view of rational choice theory. But I anticipate that this initial warrant will be reinforced by my arguments in subsequent sections.

Interpretive theorists typically hold rational choice models in particularly low esteem. Taylor (1985:103), for example, declares that rational choice models of politics "always end up either laughable, or begging the major questions, or both." Unfortunately, such criticism fails to engage rational choice theorists in a compelling manner.

In the first place, interpretive theorists rarely demonstrate close familiarity with economic or rational choice models (Riker, 1977:16f.; Hands, 1987). As a result, they themselves often end up appearing laughable.[5] Secondly, even partisans of interpretive theory who do examine rational choice models more closely tend in various ways to adopt the standard economist's assumption of "given" preferences (and subsequent neglect of preference formation) as the platform from which to press their point. The problem with this line of attack is that it largely is an external critique.[6] Rational choice theorists readily admit that the assumption of exogenously determined preferences is a lacuna in their technical edifice. But they also deflect scrutiny of such problematic premises by insisting that predictive performance is the fundamental criterion for judging their work.[7] Regardless of whether this defense is justifiable, rational choice theorists tend not to seriously entertain objections to the assumptions upon which they construct their models. So it is perhaps best at least to begin by inquiring whether they adequately adhere to their own criterion of evaluation. I will suggest that they encounter both practical and theoretical problems in trying to do so.

Riker responded to interpretive critics by defending a positivist rendering of social science. He offered micro-economic and rational choice theory as prime examples of positive social science. A central feature in his portrait of positive social science is that it generates predictions that can be subjected to empirical testing, "to repeated efforts at falsification" (1977:15). Economists, however, rarely conform to Riker's methodological strictures.[8] And the general record of rational choice theorists also is lacking on that score.[9] More particularly, even sympathetic observers concede that empirical testing of spatial models has lagged considerably behind their technical sophistication (Poole and Rosenthal, 1984:282; Ordeshook, 1976:298).[10]

I make no claim to assess exhaustively the empirical performance of rational choice electoral models. Nonetheless, the general record offers little solace to those who define rational choice as a positive science. Barry, for example, concludes his discussion of Downs's early statement of the spatial theory of elections as follows:

> [I]t is surprisingly difficult to test . . . Downs's theory. . . . [T]here is more work to be done in establishing precisely what are the conclusions to be drawn from his premises, showing where additional, different or more precise premises are needed to get results, and so on (1978:183).

Yet several years later, after many of the theoretical refinements that Barry recommended (e.g., multidimensional electoral spaces, probabilistic voting, alternative candidate motivations, etc.) had begun to be more systematically incorporated into spatial models, their predictive capacities remained in doubt.[11] The price of greater theoretical sophistication was "considerable confusion about exactly what, if anything, spatial models predict" (Page, 1978:18).

In fact, one empirical prediction is central to spatial electoral models. This is the famous median voter theorem introduced by Downs.[12] Spatial models take "the relationship between preferences and distance" to be fundamentally important in explaining electoral competition. They assume that voter preferences are distributed along one or more dimensions in an electoral space, with each voter having a most preferred position on each dimension. A "candidate is preferred to another by some voter if and only if the candidate's position in the issue space is closer to that voter's ideal point" (Enelow and Hinich, 1984:15, 80). Given these assumptions, the median voter theorem can be roughly stated as follows. In a two-party, majority rule election on a single dimension (with certain assumptions concerning the distribution of voter preferences), both candidates will converge on the ideal point of the median voter. Although Downs formulated this hypothesis for a one-dimensional electoral space, it subsequently was generalized to the multidimensional context (Enelow and Hinich, 1984:24–30; Ordeshook, 1986:165–175).

Empirical studies of the median voter prediction produce results that are at best mixed.[13] The standard procedure for testing this hypothesis is to reconstruct the predictive space for particular elections from survey data. On this basis it is possible to identify the location of candidates relative to the distribution of voter preferences. This has most frequently been done for recent U.S. presidential elections. On this basis Rabinowitz (1978:809–810) concludes that, contrary to what spatial models would predict, candidates in the 1968 and 1972 presidential elections were located at the periphery of the electorate's preference distribution. His conclusion on this point is corroborated by subsequent studies (Poole and Rosenthal, 1984:288).

If such empirical studies confound the median voter prediction, others purport to sustain it. Enelow and Hinich (1984:222) reach a conclusion, opposite to that just sketched, for the 1976 and 1980 elections. But the force of their conclusion is diminished considerably by conceptual difficulties.[14] Enelow and Hinich (1984:221) introduce "nonspatial candidate characteristics" as an additive factor into the utility functions of voters in their spatial model. And they *assume* for methodological purposes that the survey data used to reconstruct the predictive maps of voters in their empirical study also incorporate this factor (1984:80–81, 170–171).

Enelow and Hinich reconstruct the predictive map for the 1976 and 1980 elections as a two-dimensional (social and economic) issue space. But candidate locations in that space are a function not simply of their perceived policy or ideological distance from voters. Candidate locations also reflect what Enelow and Hinich refer to as "the subjectively perceived positions of candidates on the nonpolicy issues of the campaign" among the electorate.[15] They acknowledge that these "nonspatial" considerations temper the positions assigned to various candidates in the predictive space (1984:95, 221). Yet in generating empirical results consistent with the median voter hypothesis, Enelow and Hinich breach the most fundamental assumptions of the spatial framework.[16] They may, in fact, be providing an accurate account of electoral dynamics in American presidential races, but their work does not empirically vindicate the median voter theorem.

The median voter theorem thus illuminates the practical difficulties that rational choice theories encounter in trying to conform to Riker's methodological strictures. But as I mentioned earlier, there also are theoretical problems with defending positive political theory along falsificationist lines.

Rational choice theory is animated by a presumption of rationality (Elster, 1979:116–117).[17] Such a presumption serves as a regulative idea; it does not imply that actors are uniformly or consistently rational. It merely distributes the burden of proof by recognizing that in order to attribute irrationality to social actors, we must presume a background of otherwise rational thought and action. A presumption of rationality is a principle of charity.[18] It mandates that when confronted with seemingly irrational action, the social theorist investigate the broader patterns of action, explore the social or political contexts, within which the perplexing action might be interpreted as rational.

Here I want to trace the implications of this presumption as it interacts with other components of the rational choice research program. Specifically, I want to discuss its relation to the falsificationist criterion of theory evaluation endorsed by those who view rational choice as a positive theory. This clearly is an inquiry into the assumptions of rational choice models. Not all rational choice theorists resist inquiry into basic assumptions (Fiorina, 1975; Page, 1977; Barry, 1982). Two points nonetheless are in order. First, it is not necessary to evaluate rational choice along falsificationist lines (Moon, 1975; Ball, 1976). This is, however, the standard of evaluation typically endorsed by advocates of positive political theory (Riker, 1977:15; Kramer, 1986:12, 15). Second, I am not objecting to the presumption of rationality that animates rational choice theory. And because their own work is constructed upon just such a presumption (e.g., Habermas, 1984:131–134), interpretive theorists cannot afford to object to it either. What follows is a matter of theoretical coherence, not of "realism."

When rational choice theorists claim empirical performance generally and falsification particularly as the basic criterion for assessing their work, they frequently invoke the authority of Karl Popper. Specifically, they refer to Popper's work on the philosophy of natural science (e.g., Riker, 1977:15). They often overlook what Popper (1976, 1985) actually has written on the philosophy of *social* science. This is a critical oversight. According to Popper, much, if not all, of social science incorporates a rationality principle which conforms largely to the presumption of rationality sketched above and which is inconsistent with a falsificationist rendering of social theory.[19]

Popper, like advocates of positive political theory, takes economic theory as the paradigmatic social science. He claims that:

> the theoretical social sciences operate almost always by the method of constructing *typical* situations or conditions—that is, by the method of constructing models. . . . [W]e . . . construct our models by means of *situational analysis*. . . . [O]nly in this way can we explain and understand what happens in society—social events (1985:357–358).

Although Popper insists that there is a "close similarity" between natural and social science explanations (1985:358), situational analysis is on his view the "only" method for generating social explanations. And because the "theoretical reconstructions" (Popper, 1976:103) generated by situational analysis operate upon a presumption of rationality, they are unavailable to the natural sciences.[20]

Situational analysis is animated by the "rationality principle," understood as "the assumption that the various persons or agents involved act adequately or appropriately; that is to say, in accordance with the situation" (Popper, 1985:359). But while Popper repeatedly refers to this as the "animating law" of situational analysis, it is clear that he does not understand it in the same sense as the laws which animate the deductive-nomological explanation championed by positive political theorists. In the first place, Popper does not present the rationality principle as *a priori* true. Yet he also concedes that as a general empirical proposition, it is "clearly false." The rationality principle is both falsifiable and false (Popper, 1985:360–362). The social scientist has a *methodological* commitment to the rationality principle. In situations where an actor proceeds in an apparently irrational manner, social scientists do not jettison the rationality principle. Rather, they respecify the context of interaction in an effort to make sense of the action.[21]

This "method of interpretation" (Popper, 1985:363) is hardly bound to inspire the enthusiasm of positive political theorists committed to constructing deductive-nomological explanations on the received natural science model.[22] They might well object that it does not adequately capture their enterprise.

This objection can be defused by recalling the median voter theorem. Riker offers this as an example of one part of the political world that has "been scientifically explained with empirical laws imbedded in axiom systems" on analogy with natural science explanations.[23] Specifically, he depicts the median voter theorem as driven by "an empirical law-theorem which states that, in a two-candidate context, *a voter* supports *the candidate* who is ideologically closest to himself" (Riker, 1977:22, 23; stress added).

This appears to be precisely the sort of empirical generalization characteristic of a scientific law. But note the ellipsis. The median voter theorem and the broader research program within which it is embedded precisely presume *rational* voters and *rational* candidates. The remainder of the median voter theorem as commonly stated sketches the context, the situation, within which these rational agents interact.[24]

A presumption of rationality animates all of the "scientific laws" of positive political theory, and the methodological commitment to it means that these laws are not candidates for falsification.[25] So while the structure of positive political theory "adds up to the form, at least, of science" (Riker, 1977:27), this appearance is deceptive. It remains to be seen what might actually be going on.

In this section I have claimed that interpretive critics of rational choice generally are unpersuasive. I also have argued that the positivist rejoinder to those critics is inadequate. Even if we accept predictive performance as the primary criterion of theory assessment, rational choice theorists have been lax in attempting to falsify their models. Moreover, especially in the case of spatial electoral theory, the existing record of empirical research on central issues is unimpressive. Beyond these practical difficulties I have presented theoretical reasons for doubting that rational choice can be defended as a positive science.

My purpose has been to suggest that neither the blanket repudiation of rational choice by interpretive theorists nor the uncritical celebration of rational choice as a positive science by many of its advocates is persuasive. As I stated at the outset, I do not intend these arguments as decisive. They do, however, provide initial warrant for an alternative rendering of rational choice theory. I turn to that task in the next section.

2. RECONSTRUCTIVE SOCIAL THEORY

Rational choice theory is grounded in the analytical distinction between parametric and strategic rationality (Elster, 1979:18–19, 117–118). Strategic actors recognize their environment as consisting, in part, of other intentional actors. Parametric actors view their environment as a constant, viewing themselves as engaged in a game with nature.

Jurgen Habermas has elaborated a more complex typology of action. He categorically distinguishes between strategic and communicative action and sets both of these forms of social interaction apart from instrumental (parametric) intervention in the nonsocial world.[26] Strategic action, according to Habermas, is oriented toward individual success—effectiveness in influencing the action of others. Communicative action is oriented toward establishing a context of mutual understanding which enables participants to pursue their individual plans (Habermas, 1984:85f, 285f). Habermas expends considerable energy elaborating a reconstructive account of communicative action. By contrast, he almost entirely neglects strategic action.

My purpose here explicitly is not to explicate Habermas's ambitious theoretical project. In this section I will explore his views on reconstructive theory.[27] By disentangling the idea of reconstructive science from Habermas's broader theoretical undertaking and applying it to the rational choice research tradition, it is possible to lend some independent warrant to his insights regarding the nature of social science. But this is a byproduct of my main task—demonstrating how the conception of a reconstructive theory can sustain an alternative, nonpositivist rendering of the status of rational choice models.

Habermas differentiates "two levels of explication of meaning." The first corresponds to the "thick description" of interpretive theory. He labels it "the understanding of content" and claims that it is "directed . . . to the semantic content of the symbolic formation." The second level, "reconstructive understanding," involves "formal analysis" of the "general cognitive, linguistic or *interactive* competence" of social actors (1979:11–15; stress added). On this view interpretation and formal analysis are simply different dimensions of the same process of inquiry. Here I will suggest in a broad and preliminary way that rational choice generally, and game theory specifically, are modes of reconstructive understanding. More precisely, game theory amounts to the reconstructive understanding of strategic interaction.[28] In Section 4 I will explore several specific techniques employed by game theorists in moving from the understanding of content to reconstructive understanding.

Habermas discusses reconstructive theory largely in the context of his analysis of communicative action. He claims that the reconstructive theorist:

> directs himself to the generative structures of the expressions themselves. . . . He . . . turns away from the surface structure of the symbolic formation. . . . He attempts instead to peer through the surface, as it were, and into the symbolic formation to discover the rules according to which the latter was produced. . . . (1979:12).

As exemplars of this approach, Habermas points to several rather suspect theories of moral and psychological development.[29] Consequently, his views on reconstructive theory largely have been neglected by critics intent on questioning the substance of his theory of communicative action.[30]

Although he concentrates on his theory of communicative action, Habermas (1984:85–88, 285f.) acknowledges both the necessity of incorporating strategic considerations into any adequate social theory and the insights that game theory provides in understanding strategic action. And while he does not explicitly indicate what a reconstructive theory of strategic action might entail, such a theory certainly is sanctioned by the scope that he accords to reconstructive analyses.[31] Several of the characteristics that Habermas attributes to reconstructive understanding are germane to game-theoretical models of strategic interaction.

First, Habermas claims that reconstructive understanding involves formal analysis of generative structures of social interaction. This is precisely the task of game-theoretical models. They show in abstract form how particular social or political outcomes are produced by the interdependent actions of strategic agents.[32]

Second, reconstructive theories aim at "giving accounts of the pretheoretic knowledge and intuitive command" of social actors (Habermas, 1983:260). As noted earlier, rational choice theory is animated by a presumption of rationality. Insofar as this presumption itself presumes a generalized capacity for strategic action (Elster, 1979:15–16, 87), formal rational choice models reconstruct the performance of "strategically competent" actors.[33]

Third, reconstructive theory is empirically grounded:

> . . . [R]econstructive sciences . . . try to make explicit, from the perspective of those participating in discourses and interactions, and by means of analyzing successful or distorted utterances, the pretheoretical grasp of rules on the part of competently speaking, acting and knowing subjects (Habermas, 1987:297–298).

Reconstructive understanding thus presupposes the understanding of content provided by interpretive theory. But it also proceeds beyond such interpretation to analyze "successful or distorted" interactions.

This critical function frequently is acknowledged by advocates of interpretation. Thus Taylor (1985:94–95) claims that the task of social theory is not restricted to explicating the self-understandings constitutive of social practices and institutions but also involves criticizing or challenging those self-understandings. This often involves revealing a causal context within which interaction occurs but which is not recognized by the participants.

The promise of social and political theory is to reduce "to a minimum the sources of opacity in our collective life" (Moon, 1982:177). What interpretive theorists typically refuse to countenance is the possibility that rational choice theory might play such a critical role. But this is precisely what, beginning from a "thin" conception of individual and collective rationality (Elster, 1983:1–15, 26–33), rational choice theory does. As a reconstructive theory, rational choice offers a basis for analyzing the causal context (strategic interdependencies) that holds among rational actors and the various dilemmas, paradoxes, and so on to which it can give rise.[34]

Fourth, reconstructive theories are not simply logical exercises. They not only presuppose detailed empirical understanding, but in turn can be employed as components in empirical studies.[35] Even though they commonly are highly abstract and frequently are counterintuitive, reconstructive theories can potentially be corroborated in an indirect fashion (Habermas, 1983:261).

Finally, unlike positive political theories which aspire to the natural science ideal of prediction and control,[36] reconstructive theory aims more modestly at refining our understanding of social interaction. Game theory specifically and rational choice more broadly can be viewed in precisely this manner. This, in fact, was the position of some early advocates of game theory who viewed it less as a "manipulative technique" aimed at "the enhancement of environmental control" than as "a source of . . . insights into the nature of conflict based on the interplay of decisions" (Rapoport, 1966:203).[37] As a product of reconstructive understanding, the insight afforded by game theoretical analyses potentially is a resource of practical reason.

3. INTERPRETIVE THEORY: THE "UNDERSTANDING OF CONTENT"

Habermas explicitly recognizes that reconstructive understanding proceeds from "the perspective of those participating in discourses and interactions," a perspective that is the product of interpretive understanding of content. Consequently, he expends considerable energy dissecting the various forms of interpretive inquiry (Habermas, 1983; 1984:102–141).

Interpretive theorists tend to be skeptical of the theoretical aspirations embodied in a reconstructive project of the sort that I have sketched. In this section I briefly will explore the place of interpretation within a broader reconstructive undertaking. Since, by design, interpretive theorists eschew explicit methodological precepts, I will not attempt to reconstruct their program in detail. Similarly, I will not attempt to remedy the several misconceptions that rational choice theorists hold regarding interpretation.[38] Rather, I will begin from the views of interpretive theorists themselves and attempt to dispel one source of potential resistance to incorporating their work within a more encompassing theoretical framework.

To start, it is crucial to recognize that the "thick description" produced by interpretive social theorists is itself reconstructive. "In finished anthropological writings . . . what we call data are really our own constructions of other people's constructions of what they and their compatriots are up to" (Geertz, 1973:9). Where rational choice theory reconstructs strategic interaction, interpretive theory reconstructs the symbolic resources that actors use to navigate the social world.

But interpretive theorists might well object that these two sorts of reconstruction are fundamentally at odds. These theorists might complain that, unlike game-theoretical reconstructions of strategic interaction, the interpretive reconstruction of symbolic formations is disciplined by the meanings with which social actors in concrete situations endow actions and events. From this they might infer that by abstracting from concrete detail, formal models eliminate critical features of the situation and thus do irremediable damage to the prospects for adequate understanding.

Something like this complaint seems to motivate the criticism repeatedly voiced by interpretive theorists that rational choice theory is unable to account for preference formation. Thus Taylor (1985:119–123) rejects social theories that seek to "finesse understanding" by circumventing the culturally defined "desirability characterizations" of concrete social actors.[39]

If it were cogent, this line of criticism would raise acute difficulties for the prospects of reconstructive understanding. It certainly would challenge the practice of imputing preference rankings to the strategic actors who inhabit game-theoretical models. Ultimately, however, the position just sketched is not cogent. For interpretive theorists themselves typically reject the notion that their inquiries must proceed in the language of the agents whom they study:

[I]nterpretive social science requires that we master the agent's self-description in order to identify our *explananda*; but it by no means requires that we couch our *explanantia* in the same language. On the contrary it generally demands that we go beyond it (Taylor, 1985:118).

Interpretive theory indicates where inquiry must be grounded, but it does not mandate where it might culminate.[40] More specifically, the "desirability characterizations" of a given population surely restrict where any attempt to reconstruct typical preference orderings must begin.[41] But they need not limit the language in which those orderings might be cast for theoretical purposes (Moon, 1982:167).

Minimally, then, interpretive considerations allow for the shift to reconstructive understanding. But the case can be put more strongly. For in many instances an adequate account of social interaction requires more than interpretation. To take a clear case, if the task of social and political theory is to analyze distorted as well as successful practices and interactions, then it cannot be limited to explicating the self-understandings of participants in those practices. The source of distortion is typically opaque, frequently residing in a causal context that, while framing the actions of social actors, is unrecognized by them. And a proper grasp of such a causal context requires reconstructive understanding generated by formal analysis of the problematic interaction.

In this section I have argued that the claims of interpretive theory do not represent a cogent objection, at the level of general principle, to the quest for reconstructive understanding. In the next section I will explore how and to what degree of success game theorists seek to accommodate interpretive considerations as a practical matter.

4.   RATIONAL CHOICE THEORY: THE "RECONSTRUCTIVE UNDERSTANDING" OF STRATEGIC INTERACTION

The presumption of rationality that animates game theoretical models highlights their reconstructive character. Game theory "does not assume rational behavior; rather it attempts to determine what 'rational' can mean when an individual is confronted with the problem of optimal behavior in games and equivalent situations" (Morgenstern, 1968:62). In order "to determine what 'rational' can mean" in particular situations, game theorists must be sensitive to how they circumscribe the decision context within which actors choose. Their results typically depend directly on the way they *reconstruct* the context of choice.[42]

In this section I will argue that the "mathematical frontier" of rational choice models is set by the ability of theorists to either accommodate or bracket interpretive considerations. I will explore three specific reconstructive techniques that they use for this purpose. The techniques I will discuss are used in making the transition, in Habermas's terms, from "the understanding of content" to "reconstructive understanding."[43] They are employed by rational choice theorists as a means of specifying the decision context in which formal analyses of strategic interaction are set. Before discussing the reconstructive techniques deployed by game theorists, however, I will try to convey exactly how sparse their models actually are and to indicate a theoretical problem that such abstraction raises.

Game theorists model the strategic interdependencies inherent in social and political interaction. In doing so they largely ignore the "incidental details" of those interactions (Schelling, 1960:67, 106). Consequently, and in stark contrast to the accounts typically produced by interpretive inquiry, game theorists proceed from a radically "thin" description of political reality.

The sparse character of game-theoretical representations is readily apparent in spatial electoral models. Shepsle (1986:137–139) identifies four features of what he refers to by turns as the "classic" or the "standard" spatial model of elections.[44] First, the agents populating this model are *anonymous*; they are indistinguishable other than by their preference orderings.[45] Second, the alternatives these anonymous agents confront are *neutral*. Or, more precisely, since the alternatives that agents confront in electoral models are embodied in candidates, those candidates are anonymous. Voters have preferences only over the substantive positions, not the characteristics of various candidates.[46] Third, the agents in these models respond to choice situations in a *uniform* manner; they reveal their preferences over alternatives sincerely. Finally, the agents in spatial electoral models are presumed to be *isolated* from adjoining realms of interaction. In particular, their preferences are presumed to be exogenously generated.

In their paradigmatic form, then, game-theoretical electoral models are inhabited by anonymous, isolated voters who respond uniformly to neutral alternatives (anonymous candidates). Such austere models produce theoretical benefits in the form of heightened insight into the strategic dimensions of political interaction. But they also generate theoretical difficulties that become apparent when we contrast them with the products of interpretive inquiry.

The details from which game-theoretical models abstract are precisely what the interpretive theorist seeks to capture in a thick description of culture. Culture, for present purposes, consists of shared meanings and the symbols and cultural performances in which they are embodied (Geertz, 1973). Such cultural particularities serve to direct the attention of actors in differential ways (Kertzer, 1988; Johnson, 1988).

By abstracting from the incidental details of social and political interaction, game theory potentially falls prey to a common criticism of maximizing models of rational choice. Such models, it is claimed, while adept at incorporating information costs, cannot adequately account for the ways actors differentially focus attention on various strategies, outcomes, and so on.[47]

In constructing their models, game theorists deploy at least three reconstructive techniques in the effort to bracket the issue of attention and the cultural issues that it embodies. The first is the completeness condition on preference rankings. The second is the condition of single-peakedness imposed on preferences. The third is embodied in the conditions of interchangeability and equivalence imposed on the notion of equilibrium. These conditions partially insulate rational choice models from the criticism just mentioned.[48]

An individual has a *complete* (or, as some call it, a connected) preference ordering if, between any two alternatives Q and J, that individual either prefers Q to J, prefers J to Q, or is indifferent between the two.[49] It is plausible to consider this condition "not as a restriction on preferences, but as a guide to modeling" (Ordeshook, 1986:13). More specifically, because completeness insures that "any two alternatives are comparable" (Arrow, 1963:13), it can be used to determine whether the context of choice is adequately characterized. The persistence of literally incommensurable alternatives indicates that the decision context remains improperly specified. In such instances it is presumed that the problem lies not with the completeness condition but with the way in which the choice situation has been circumscribed (Ordeshook, 1986:13).

By imposing the completeness condition on the preferences of relevant agents, game theorists seek to purge incommensurable alternatives from the decision context, thereby partially excluding indeterminacy from their models and reducing the need to have recourse to incidental details in explaining choice. In short, completeness precludes instances of an actor "not knowing, or not even having considered, how an outcome would compare with others." It provides "a common coinage which overcomes the threat of incommensurability" (Hollis, 1987:19, 66). The completeness condition operates to mitigate the issue of how actors focus attention on alternatives by insuring that all alternatives are equally available for consideration.

Yet even if actors have complete preference orderings, further sources of indeterminacy remain. One such source is the problem of indifference. Electoral models typically incorporate indifference as a possible reason for abstention. In that sense indifference arises when the costs associated with voting itself outweigh the expected utility of voting for any available candidate (Enelow and Hinich, 1984:90). But game-theoretical models must also account for a more standard form of indifference. It occurs in situations where, though someone has reasons for selecting either of two alternatives, that individual "has no reason to *prefer* one alternative to the other" (Morgenbesser and Ullmann-Margalit, 1977:768).[50] Here the two alternatives differ along several relevant dimensions in ways that render them equally attractive.[51] The individual consequently has countervailing reasons for selecting either alternative. So, unable to "choose" one alternative over another, the individual must simply "pick" (Morgenbesser and Ullmann-Margalit, 1977).

Game-theoretical electoral models exclude indifference of this latter sort by assuming that preference orderings are *single-peaked*. What are single-peaked preferences?[52] On a vertical axis, represent an individual's ordinal ranking over a set of alternatives arrayed along a horizontal axis. If, as the preference curve moves away from the origin, it rises continuously, falls continuously, or rises to a unique point or plateau and then continuously falls, the preferences are single-peaked (Riker, 1980:12). This condition implicitly homogenizes the range of individual orderings acceptable for aggregation. It imposes consensus by insuring that relevant actors "judge the alternatives consistently with respect to one issue, namely that measured by the dimension on the horizontal axis" (Riker, 1980:12; Mueller, 1979:41, 195). In electoral models this homogeneity is reflected in the common—typically, left/right—dimension(s) that voters are assumed to employ when evaluating alternatives (Downs, 1957:115; Enelow and Hinich, 1984:38, 40, 54).

At the aggregate level single-peaked preferences preclude intransitive social orderings such as cyclical majorities (Riker, 1980:11–12; Austen-Smith, 1983:440). But single-peakedness is a condition on individual orderings. It establishes a common evaluative dimension for *all* actors by establishing that dimension as basic for *each* actor (Enelow and Hinich, 1984:70). Single-peakedness thus reduces the incidence of indifference of the sort intrinsic to "picking" situations by imposing a common dimension for judging alternatives. It relieves game theorists of the need to rely upon cultural particularities in explaining how individuals in picking situations "focus . . . *attention* on some one of the available alternatives" (Morgenbesser and Ullmann-Margalit, 1977:774; emphasis in the original).[53]

The final reconstructive technique that I will discuss involves the conditions of *equivalence* and *interchangeability* commonly imposed on equilibria.[54] Equilibrium concepts are crucial to conceptions of rational choice as a positive theory because they provide the basis for determinant outcomes (Riker, 1980; Ordeshook, 1986:118–119, 98). And equivalence and interchangeability provide bite to the most fundamental equilibrium concepts of game theory (Ordeshook, 1986:146–149).

These conditions address the problem of how an actor will choose when, as "is frequently the case . . . a game will admit a multiplicity of equilibria, *all competing for attention*" (Binmore and Dasgupta, 1986:16; emphasis added). Equivalence simply insures that players are indifferent as to which equilibrium obtains, so long as one of them does. And interchangeability insures that no coordination, implicit or explicit, is required for players to converge on one among the available equilibria (Ordeshook, 1986:148).

In this section I have detailed three reconstructive techniques used by game theorists seeking to purge their models of incidental details. The difficulty for advocates of rational choice is that the techniques discussed here are not sufficient to insulate formal models from the incidental details of strategic interaction. For example, although the most cogent case for assuming complete preferences is convenience in model building, this condition also raises unwanted theoretical questions of endogenous preference change (Elster, 1983:8).[55] Likewise, difficulties arise with single-peakedness as the number of contested dimensions proliferates. With multiple predictive dimensions, cyclical social orderings can result even if voter preferences are single-peaked over each dimension (Davis, et al., 1970:428). And equivalence and interchangeability frequently do not hold in n-person or non-zero sum settings (Ordeshook, 1986:196, 204).[56]

CONCLUSION

Conceiving of rational choice as a reconstructive social theory highlights the restricted scope of highly formalized models of strategic interaction. Formal analysis presupposes some technique for making the transition from the interpretive understanding of content to reconstructive understanding. Indeed, the limits of their reconstructive techniques have induced mathematically oriented game theorists either to restrict their attention to tractable models that generate a unique equilibrium (e.g., Ordeshook, 1986:205, 241) or to turn their attention more systematically toward the study of the "incidental details" of strategic interaction (Riker, 1983, 1984, 1986; Shepsle, 1986).[57] This chastened view again recommends a return to the modest view of game theory endorsed by some of its early advocates.[58] It encourages both interpretive and rational choice theorists to recognize the limits of their respective work and to consider potential links to other modes of inquiry with a greater sense of equanimity.[59]

NOTES

A grant from the Charlotte Newcombe Foundation supported my work on this paper. Jon Elster, David Greenstone, Russell Hardin, Jack Knight, and Kim Stanton provided helpful comments on an earlier version of this paper.

1. See, for example, Riker (1977) and Taylor (1985) respectively. Rather than attempting to define these two approaches, I refer readers to recent anthologies containing representative selections of each. On rational choice, see Barry and Hardin (1982) and Elster (1986b). On interpretive theory, see Gibbons (1987) and Rabinow and Sullivan (1988).

2. The literature on this subject is immense. Downs (1957) is commonly credited with initiating it. For an early statement of theoretical advances, see Davis et al. (1970). I rely upon several very helpful overviews of the literature for more recent developments (Ordeshook, 1976, 1986; Page, 1977; Mueller, 1979; Austen-Smith, 1983; Enelow and Hinich, 1984).

3. Ordeshook (1986:xii–xiii) suggests that game theory is the "integrating force" in rational choice analysis of politics. Although others might contest whether rational choice is quite so homogeneous an undertaking (Hardin, 1987), game theory is surely central to recent developments of the spatial electoral theory. This is because "any theory of electoral competition founded on the spatial framework . . . can be properly formulated as a non-cooperative game in normal form" (Austen-Smith, 1983:445).

4. I am not arguing against the *a priori* possibility of naturalistic social science. Such arguments are unlikely to persuade. (Bernstein, 1978)

5. For instance, Taylor (1985:104) presents the systems theory elaborated by David Easton as an example of an economic analysis of politics. This deficiency recently has been rectified somewhat. See Dyke (1983), McPherson (1983), and Hadari (1987).

6. It is not necessarily an external critique. Dunleavy and Ward (1981) cogently explore the implications for rational choice electoral models of assuming preferences to be exogenously determined. But they do not advocate an interpretive remedy.

7. See, for example, Downs (1957:21) and Enelow and Hinich (1984:2).

8. "Modern economists frequently preach falsificationism . . . but they rarely practice it" (Blaug, 1980:128, 259). And "most economists admit that economic theory fails miserably when judged by . . . falsificationist standards" (Hands, 1985:83).

9. Kramer claims that though rational choice theory initially was driven by empirical concerns, this is no longer the case. He concludes that "formal theory has to some degree evolved away from these empirical roots, and at present much of the sophisticated and rigorous theoretical research has had little interaction with the great body of empirical work on politics. . . . [T]he fact remains that much of formal theory, whether for good reasons or bad, is simply not very rich in testable empirical content at present" (1986:16–17). Compare Elster (1982: 477) and McLean (1986:377, 393).

10. Thus, Austen-Smith (1983), while explicitly reviewing the positive, explanatory aspects of spatial modeling and concluding that it represents a "compelling paradigm," devotes no attention to empirical performance. At an abstract theoretical level, the rarity of equilibria in voting models has raised questions about their general predictive capacities. See the various "disequilibrium" results discussed in Ordeshook and Shepsle, (1982, Chs. 1–5). The contributors to this volume differ in how they assess the scientific prospects of rational choice electoral models in light of their predictive shortcomings, but they largely concede that such shortcomings exist.

11. Many of these theoretical developments had already begun to be made by the time Barry wrote. See, for example, Davis et al. (1970).

12. Riker (1977:23) presents this prediction (albeit with some equivocation) as among three promising results of positive political theory. And Page notes that, at a minimum, some suitably relaxed version of the median voter theorem is "critical to the economic theory of democracy" (1978:20).

13. Mueller (1979:111) rightly cautions that the various assumptions and compromises made in testing spatial models means that empirical results ought to be approached circumspectly. I will make no effort to assess the measurement techniques employed by the studies cited here. Page, who is sensitive to these methodological difficulties, nonetheless draws a rather stark conclusion. "Predictions about parties' and candidates' stands are intended to be a chief payoff of election theories. . . . Where evidence exists, it tends to weigh against many if not all of the leading theories of elections" (1977:658).

14. Fiorina offers the following suggestion: "Do not skip over the technical portion of the model and go directly to the conclusions. Rather, examine carefully the definitions and assumptions of the model. The model's conclusions are implicit in the definitions and assumptions" (1975:154). Enelow and Hinich underscore why his advice is sound.

15. "Nonpolicy issues are relatively fixed characteristics of the candidate that are generally beyond his control, at least for the duration of the campaign. Age, religion, party, and gender are obvious examples of nonpolicy issues. But so are issues such as war, prosperity, prestige abroad, and other conditions that are "givens" of the campaign" (Enelow and Hinich, 1984:37, 174).

16. This is *not* a complaint about measurement technique or other narrowly methodological issues. It is a prior conceptual objection of a sort to which, because of their deductive structure, rational choice theories are especially susceptible. For example, Downs (1957:268–270) attempted to resolve the paradox of voting by claiming that a rational, self-interested individual would willingly incur short-term costs in order to contribute to a long-term social good. This is clearly inconsistent with the basic assumptions of his economic theory of politics (Barry, 1978:20). Similarly, introducing "nonspatial" considerations at a crucial juncture into electoral models assumed to be fundamentally animated by the spatial relation between voter preference and the ideological or policy positions of candidates is conceptually inconsistent.

17. Lukes (1982), Follesdal (1982), and Hardin (1987) discuss various philosophical issues that this presumption involves.

18. There are clearly limits to charity. Some action is irrational. But this should be a conclusion of inquiry, not its point of departure.

19. My views on Popper are very much indebted to the interpretation offered by Hands (1985). Also see Farr (1985).

20. On this point see Elster (1979:1–35). This of course raises difficulties for Popper's (1957:130f.) earlier position on the methodological unity of natural and social science. On this, see Hands (1985).

21. In circumstances where actors proceed in an apparently irrational manner, "it is good policy, a good methodological device, to refrain from blaming the rationality principle for the breakdown of our theory: we learn more if we blame the situational model. . . . In order to understand their (inadequate) actions, we have therefore to reconstruct a wider view of the situation than their own. This must be done in such a way that we can see how and why the situation as they saw it . . . led them to act as they did. . . ." (Popper, 1985:362–363).

22. Rational choice theory does not require this commitment. Davidson (1980) provides solid philosophical arguments for believing that explanations in terms of reasons need not rely upon general laws. Elster (1986a) interprets rational choice explanation along these lines.

23. Riker offers the law of demand in micro-economics as the prototypical social scientific law. This claim is less straightforward than

Riker allows (Blaug, 1980:160–164). And even he concedes that "the closest political scientists have to something similar is the median voter theorem which, however, *lacks an underlying empirical regularity* like the law of demand" (Riker, 1988:255; stress added).

24. Rational choice theorists extend this presumption of rationality to political actors generally and retain it on methodological grounds. Thus "the assumption of rationality serves just about the same function in social science that the principle of mechanism once served in physical science" (Riker, 1977:32). And as Enelow and Hinich (1984:2–3) note, the "model of man" as rational and self-interested that informs spatial theory more specifically is not open to falsification.

25. Again, "the rationality principle . . . does not play the part of an empirical explanatory theory, of a testable hypothesis" (Popper, 1967:360).

26. At least in part, Habermas's theoretical project is driven by what he views as the inadequacies of existing theories of rational action. Although I will not argue this claim here, Habermas does not successfully sustain his categorical distinction between types of action. See Johnson (Forthcoming).

27. Habermas does not systematically present his views on reconstructive theory. In what follows I attempt to articulate his position in a concise fashion. For a brief sketch of Habermas's larger theoretical project, see Johnson (1987).

28. In essence I am arguing that game theory is a form of interpretive inquiry. This position is unorthodox but not unprecedented. Although he does not develop the claim, Follesdal suggests—from a confirmed "empiricist" position, no less—that "game theory is one of the important tools of hermeneutics. Many cases of group behavior that initially may seem puzzling and irrational . . . get simple rational explanations in terms of game theory, and we thereby come to *understand* them" (1979:335).

29. Critics tend to argue that the examples of reconstructive theory that Habermas offers (e.g., Piaget on cognitive development, Kohlberg on moral development) do not have the universal status he claims for communicative rationality. For persuasive arguments on this score from a critic sympathetic to Habermas, see McCarthy (1982).

30. Only one study treats reconstructive theory in any detail. And Alford (1985) is "primarily concerned with the epistemic status" that Habermas claims for reconstructive theory. Alford concludes that reconstruction is differentiated less by any special epistemic status than by the "rational processes" that it takes as its subject

matter (1985:331, 332). This conclusion is compatible with my own skepticism regarding Habermas's broader theoretical project.

31. A reconstructive theory gives "accounts of the pretheoretic knowledge and intuitive command, let us say, of the rule systems by means of which competent subjects generate and evaluate valid expressions and performance." Among the valid performances that Habermas explicitly mentions are "effective instrumental actions" (1983:260). Because Habermas views both instrumental and strategic action as oriented toward success, the structure of his own theory compels him to allow for a reconstructive theory of strategic interaction.

32. Thus "generative models" such as game theory "are not designed to be homologous with observed social regularities; instead they are designed so that they, by specified operations, can *generate* such regularities or forms" (Barth, 1981:9, 32).

33. I am not interested here in the categorical foundations that Habermas seeks to provide for his theory of communicative action. Very roughly, he elaborates a view of "communicative competence" whose central feature is the capacity of social actors to recognize and fulfill the validity claims inherent in speech acts (Habermas, 1979:26–29; 1984:14). By comparison, a "strategically competent" actor might be understood as one capable of recognizing others as equally rational, purposive agents and of accommodating their anticipated plans and actions into his or her own strategies.

34. Strategic interdependencies actually are what von Wright (1971:85) calls "quasi-causal" in the sense that they figure in explanations which connect actions and outcomes in ways that do not invoke nomic conditions (Moon, 1982:162–163). Like Davidson's claims about explanation by reasons, this casts doubt on the prospects of generating the sort of deductive nomological accounts to which positive political theorists aspire.

35. On this view reconstructive theories such as game theory are useful "mainly in illuminating the nature of social interaction and in creating more discriminating categories of sociological analysis" (Elster, 1982:477).

36. This aspiration to "predict and manipulate" is endorsed explicitly by Riker and Ordeshook (1973:5–6). It is implicit in the language of "rational decision engineering" and the "engineering of choice" used by March (1986:143). Few, if any, practical steps have been taken toward fulfilling this aspiration (McLean, 1988).

37. "The ability to *predict* what will go on in the future is often used as a criterion by which to judge inductive theories. In contrast to this, . . . rational choice theories . . . attempt to provide us with ideas

about what *would go on in certain circumstances . . .* to expand our understanding of the possibilities, rather than to explain events" (Laver, 1981:11).

38. If interpretive theorists frequently advance laughable indictments of rational choice theory, "positive" theorists often reciprocate in kind. In part such misconceptions are sustained by the reluctance of interpretive theorists to advance explicit methodological arguments. But misconceptions persist even on issues that are fairly straightforward. For example, Riker burlesques interpretation as "an ungeneralized kind of sympathetic appreciation of particular motives in particular events" (1977:22, 28). This characterization might approximate a crudely Weberian or phenomenological preoccupation with the "subjective meaning" of action. But interpretive theorists consistently reject this view of their work as requiring "empathetic" identification with the subject of inquiry. For a representative sampling, see Winch (1958:119); von Wright (1971:30–31); Geertz (1973); McCarthy (1973); Habermas (1984:109); Taylor (1985).

39. Insofar as it is aimed at rational choice theory, the larger argument of which this criticism is a part is misguided. Taylor insists that an adequate social theory must be interpretively grounded, that it must treat social actors as "*agents*—i.e. beings who act, have purposes, desires" and so on (1985:117, 123). This claim is unobjectionable. But he then indiscriminately lumps "holistic functionalism, . . . individual utility-maximization, or whatever" among the approaches which fail to adequately accommodate agency. Once again, failure to attend to details makes interpretive critics appear laughable. Rational choice can be differentiated from functionalism on precisely the criterion that Taylor insists is crucial to adequate social theory (Elster, 1979).

40. Similarly, Geertz portrays ethnographic interpretation as "microscopic." But he also insists that the locale within which anthropologists study is not ultimately constraining. "The locus of study is not the object of study. Anthropologists don't study villages (tribes, towns, neighborhoods . . .); they study *in* villages. . . . [W]here an interpretation comes from does not determine where it can be impelled to go" (Geertz, 1973:22–23).

41. Sen (1982:71–72, 89) suggests that rational choice theorists ought not to restrict themselves to behavioral evidence of actor's preferences. In so doing he implicitly acknowledges the role of interpretive inquiry. For reservations on this point, however, see Ordeshook (1986:14–15).

42. "In game theory an equilibrium is a prediction, *for a prespecified circumstance*, about the choices of people and the corresponding

outcomes. The prediction generally takes the form 'if the institutional context of choice is ..., and if people's preferences are ..., then the only choices and outcomes that can endure are ... '" (Ordeshook, 1986:xiii).

43. Although I concentrate on the specific techniques used by game theorists in making this transition, it is an important problem for any sort of reconstructive understanding. Habermas (1984:335–337) recognizes it as critical to the formal analysis of speech acts that grounds his theory of communicative action.

44. As the title to his paper suggests, Shepsle is himself engaged in the task of reintroducing "incidental detail" into spatial voting models. Two aspects of his project are noteworthy. First, it explicitly is limited to voting within legislative institutions. And second, the progress of his research program has been "piecemeal" due largely to the constraints imposed by institutional detail (1986:149).

45. This assumption of anonymity is not peculiar to voting models. To take an example from another area of rational choice theory, after making several simplifying assumptions regarding, for instance, the nature of agents and the role of time in bargaining models, Raiffa explains: "The two agents come together to bargain. The setting, the language, the costumes are all irrelevancies for us" (1982:44).

46. Enelow and Hinich (1984:38–39), for example, insist that in constructing spatial models, it is not the particular "political labels" attached to candidates that are important but whether these can be arrayed along one or more evaluative dimensions. While this might be plausible when constructing ideological or policy dimensions, it is difficult to see how such basically idiosyncratic "nonspatial candidate characteristics" as age, race, religion, or gender can be incorporated into the model without stretching the neutrality assumption beyond recognition.

47. "There is ... a fundamental difference between a situation in which a decision maker is uncertain about the state of X and a situation in which the decision maker has not given any thought to whether X matters or not, between a situation in which a prethought event judged of low probability occurs and a situation in which something occurs that has never been thought about, between judging an action unlikely to succeed and never thinking about an action. The latter situations in each pair are not adequately modeled in terms of low probabilities. Rather, they are not in the decision maker's considerations at all. To treat them calls for a theory of attention, not a theory that assumes that everything always is attended to but that some things are given little weight (for objective reasons)" (Nelson and Winter, 1982:67). Also see Simon, (1986:31). This criticism

typically is leveled by theorists of "bounded rationality," not by interpretive theorists. The latter nonetheless provide the resources for a cogent reply.

48. Indeterminacy plagues game-theoretical reconstructions of strategic interaction in two fundamental ways. First, no optimal strategy may exist. Second, no unique optimal strategy may exist (Elster, 1986a:65f.; Ordeshook, 1986:119). The completeness condition is aimed at the problem of existence; single-peakedness and the equilibrium conditions address that of uniqueness.

49. Spatial electoral models from Downs (1957:6) through Enelow and Hinich (1984:65) assume complete preference rankings.

50. This standard sort of indifference draws force from the need to choose one among the proffered options, whereas indifference in spatial models amounts to refusing to choose among the available alternatives. Abstention becomes a third alternative.

51. "Indifference can arise because two options have the same features, like two identical cans of soup, or because they differ in several ways that exactly offset each other in the evaluation of the agent" (Elster, 1986b:17).

52. They are a crucial assumption in spatial models. Downs's median voter result requires single-peakedness (Riker, 1980:12; Austen-Smith, 1983:450). Austen-Smith's review of subsequent developments shows that many of them do so as well. Several alternatives to single-peakedness have been proposed, but these are dismissed as either unwieldy (Ordeshook, 1986:164) or substantively suspect (Niemi, 1983:263).

53. Single-peakedness "seldom appears to be satisfied in the real world" (Riker, 1980:12). Less restrictive conditions such as "semi" or "partial" single-peakedness are most compelling precisely where the range of alternatives open to actors is institutionally or culturally constrained (Niemi, 1983:263–264) or where some political actor can successfully depict the political world as organized along a particular salient dimension (Feld and Grofman, 1986:76). In short, these less restrictive conditions precisely presume some mechanism for directing the attention of voters to particular criteria of evaluation.

54. My attention was drawn to this particular reconstructive technique by Schelling (1960:291–292), who makes similar observations regarding the solution concept expounded by Luce and Raiffa (1957:107f.).

55. See also Page (1977:644–645). Because completeness demands that actors express a preference, or failing that, at least indifference, over all possible options, preferences could change over time as a function of greater experience, increased information, or the availa-

bility of new options. Interpretive critics could sharpen their complaints about rational choice theorists' laxity regarding the issue of preference formation by exploiting this wedge.

56. Echoing a point made by Schelling (1960), Ordeshook explains that in the latter case, "solving such games in the sense of arriving at definite choice predictions may require an appeal to considerations that lie outside of the game's representation" (1986:204).

57. Schelling proved quite prescient on this point. "Preoccupied with the solution to the zero-sum game, game theory has not done justice to some typical game situations or game models and to the 'moves' that are peculiar to non-zero sum games of strategy" (1960:199). Thus game theorists remain preoccupied with modeling elections as zero-sum interactions even while admitting that this represents only "a useful approximation" (Ordeshook, 1986:145). And others have only recently begun systematic study of the incidental details of strategic interaction.

58. "The great philosophical value of game theory is in its power to reveal its own incompleteness. Game-theoretical analysis, if pursued to its completion, perforce leads us to consider other than strategic modes of thought" (Rapoport, 1966:214).

59. I already have cited various instances of intemperance from Taylor as a representative interpretive theorist. A similar intemperance informs statements such as those by Ordeshook (1986:ix), who divides social theory into rational choice theorists attempting "to satisfy a rigid definition of theory" and unspecified others committed only to "some ambiguous criteria of good journalism and insightful comment."

REFERENCES

Alford, C. F. (1985). "Is Jurgen Habermas's Reconstructive Science Really Science?" *Theory and Society,* 14:321–340.

Arrow, K. (1963). *Social Choice and Individual Values* (2nd ed.). New Haven: Yale University Press.

Austen-Smith, D. (1983). "The Spatial Theory of Electoral Competition: Instability, Institutions and Information." *Environment and Planning C: Government and Planning,* 1:439–459.

Ball, T. (1976). "From Paradigms to Research Programs." *American Journal of Political Science,* 20:151–171.

Barry, B. (1978). *Sociologists, Economists, and Democracy.* (2nd ed.). Chicago: University of Chicago Press.

———. (1982). "Methodology Versus Ideology." In E. Ostrom (Ed.), *Strategies of Political Inquiry*. Beverly Hills: Sage.

Barry, B., and Hardin, R. (Eds.) (1982). *Rational Man and Irrational Society.* Beverly Hills: Sage.

Barth, F. (1981). *Process and Form in Social Life*. London: Routledge Kegan Paul.

Bernstein, R. (1978). *The Restructuring of Social and Political Theory*. Philadelphia: University of Pennsylvania Press.

Binmore, K., and Dasgupta, P. (1986). "Game Theory: An Introduction." In K. Binmore and P. Dasgupta (Eds.), *Economic Organizations as Games*. New York: Basil Blackwell.

Blaug, M. (1980). *The Methodology of Economics*. Cambridge: Cambridge University Press.

Davidson, D. (1980). *Essays on Actions and Events*. Oxford: Oxford University Press.

Davis, O., Hinich, M., and Ordeshook, P. (1970). "An Expository Development of a Mathematical Model of the Electoral Process." *American Political Science Review*, 64:426–448.

Downs, A. (1957). *An Economic Theory of Democracy*. New York: Harper & Row.

Dunleavy, P., and Ward, H. (1981). "Exogenous Voter Preferences and Parties with State Power: Some Internal Problems of Economic Theories of Party Competition." *British Journal of Political Science*, *11*:351–380.

Dyke, C. (1983). "The Question of Interpretation in Economics." *Ratio*, 25:15–29.

Elster, J. (1979). *Ulysses and the Sirens*. Cambridge: Cambridge University Press.

———. (1982). "Marxism, Functionalism and Game Theory." *Theory and Society*, *11*:453–482.

———. (1983). *Sour Grapes: Studies in the Subversion of Rationality*. Cambridge: Cambridge University Press.

———. (1986a). "The Scope and Nature of Rational Choice Explanation." In B. McLoughlin and E. LePore (Eds.), *Actions and Event*. New York: Blackwell.

———. (Ed.) (1986b). *Rational Choice*. New York: New York University Press.

Enelow, J., and Hinich, M. (1984). *The Spatial Theory of Voting*. Cambridge: Cambridge University Press.

Farr, J. (1985). "Situational Analysis: Explanation in Political Science." *Journal of Politics*, 47:1085–1107.

Feld, S., and Grofman, B. (1986). "Partial Single-Peakedness: An Extension and Clarification." *Public Choice*, 51:71–80.

Fiorina, M. (1975). "Formal Models in Political Science." *American Journal of Political Science*, 19:133–159.

Follesdal, D. (1979). "Hermeneutics and the Hypothetical Deductive Method." *Dialectica*, 33:320–336.

———. (1982). "The Status of Rationality Assumptions in Interpretation and the Explanation of Action." *Dialectica*, 36:300–316.

Geertz, C. (1973). *The Interpretation of Cultures*. New York: Basic Books.

Gibbons, M., (Ed.). (1987). *Interpreting Politics*. New York: New York University Press.

Habermas, J. (1979). *Communication and the Evolution of Society*. Boston: Beacon Press.

———. (1983). "Interpretive Social Science vs. Hermeneuticism." In N. Haan et al. (Eds.) *Social Science as Moral Inquiry*. New York: Columbia University Press.

———. (1984). *The Theory of Communicative Action* (Vol. 1). Boston: Beacon Press.

———. (1987). *The Philosophical Discourse of Modernity*. Cambridge, MA: MIT Press.

Hadari, S. (1987). "What Are Preference Explanations? The Interpretive Core of Economic Modeling." *Social Science Quarterly*, 68:340–366.

Hands, D. W. (1985). "Karl Popper and Economic Methodology." *Economics and Philosophy*, 1:83–99.

———. (1987). "Review of Charles Taylor's Philosophical Papers." *Economics and Philosophy*, 3:172–175.

Hardin, R. (1987). "Rational Choice Theories." In T. Ball (Ed.), *Idioms of Inquiry*. Albany, NY: S.U.N.Y. Press.

Hollis, M. (1987). *The Cunning of Reason*. Cambridge: Cambridge University Press.

Johnson, J. (1987). "Habermas: The Politics of Theory." *Socialist Review*, 95:133–141.

———. (1988). "Symbolic Action and the Limits to Strategic Rationality." *Political Power and Social Theory*, 7:211–248.

_____ . (Forthcoming). "Habermas on Strategic and Communicative Action." *Political Theory*.

Kertzer, D. (1988). *Ritual, Politics and Power*. New Haven: Yale University Press.

Kramer, G. (1986). "Political Science as Science." In H. Weisberg (Ed.), *Political Science: The Science of Politics*. New York: Agathon Press.

Laver, M. (1981). *The Politics of Private Desires*. New York: Penguin.

Luce, R. D., and Raiffa, H. (1957). *Games and Decisions*. New York: John Wiley and Sons.

Lukes, S. (1982). "Relativism in its Place." In M. Hollis and S. Lukes (Eds.), *Rationality and Relativism*. Cambridge, MA: MIT Press.

March, J. (1986). "Bounded Rationality, Ambiguity and the Engineering of Choice." In Elster (1986b).

McCarthy, T. (1973). "On Misunderstanding Understanding." *Theory and Decision*, 3:351–370.

_____ . (1982). "Rationality and Relativism: Habermas' Overcoming of Hermeneutics." In D. Held and J. Thompson (Eds.), *Habermas: Critical Debates*. Cambridge, MA: MIT Press.

McLean, I. (1988). "Ships that Pass in the Night: Electoral Reform and Social Choice Theory." *Political Quarterly*, 59:63–71.

_____ . (1986). "Review Article: Some Recent Work in Public Choice." *British Journal of Political Science*, 16:377–394.

McPherson, M. (1983). "Want Formation, Morality and Some Interpretive Aspects of Economic Inquiry." In N. Haan et al. (Eds.), *Social Science as Moral Inquiry*. New York: Columbia University Press.

Moon, J. D. (1975). "The Logic of Political Inquiry." In F. Greenstein (Ed.), *The Handbook of Political Science*. Reading, MA: Addison-Wesley.

_____ . (1982). "Interpretation, Theory and Human Emancipation." In E. Ostrom (Ed.), *Strategies of Political Inquiry*. Beverly Hills: Sage.

Morgenbesser, S., and Ullmann-Margalit, E. (1977). "Picking and Choosing." *Social Research*, 44:757–785.

Morgenstern, O. (1968). "Game Theory: Theoretical Aspects." *International Encyclopedia of the Social Sciences* (Vol. 6). New York: Macmillan.

Mueller, D. (1979). *Public Choice*. Cambridge: Cambridge University Press.

Myerson, R. (1986). "An Introduction to Game Theory." In S. Reiter (Ed.), *Studies in Mathematical Economics*. Washington, DC: Mathematical Association of America.

Niemi, R. (1983). "Why So Much Stability?: Another Opinion." *Public Choice, 41*:261–270.

Ordeshook, P. (1976). "The Spatial Theory of Elections: A Review and Critique." In I. Budge et al. (Eds.), *Party Identification and Beyond*. New York: John Wiley and Sons.

———. (1986). *Game Theory and Political Theory*. Cambridge: Cambridge University Press.

Ordeshook, P., and Shepsle, K. (Eds.) (1982). *Political Equilibrium*. Boston: Kluwer-Nijhoff.

Page, B. (1977). "Elections and Social Choice: The State of the Evidence." *American Journal of Political Science, 21*:639–668.

———. (1978). *Choices and Echoes in Presidential Elections*. Chicago: University of Chicago Press.

Poole, K., and Rosenthal H. (1984). "U.S. Presidential Elections 1968–1980: A Spatial Analysis." *American Journal of Political Science, 28*:282–312.

Popper, K. (1957). *The Poverty of Historicism*. New York: Harper & Row.

———. (1976). "The Logic of the Social Sciences." In T. Adorno et al. (Eds.), *The Positivist Dispute in German Sociology*. New York: Harper & Row.

———. (1985). "The Rationality Principle." In D. Miller (Ed.), *Popper Selections*. Princeton: Princeton University Press.

Rabinow, P., and Sullivan, W. (Eds.). (1988). *Interpretive Social Science: A Second Look*. Berkeley: University of California Press.

Rabinowitz, G. (1978). "On the Nature of Political Issues: Insights from Spatial Analysis." *American Journal of Political Science, 22*:793–817.

Raiffa, H. (1982). *The Art and Science of Negotiation*. Cambridge, MA: Harvard University Press.

Rapoport, A. (1966). *Two-Person Game Theory*. Ann Arbor: University of Michigan Press.

Riker, W. (1977). "The Future of a Science of Politics." *American Behavioral Scientist, 21*:11–38.

———. (1982). "Implications from the Disequilibrium of Majority Rule for the Study of Institutions." In Ordeshook and Shepsle (1982).

_____. (1983). "Political Theory and the Art of Heresthetics." In A. Finifter (Ed.), *Political Science: The State of the Discipline*. Washington, DC: American Political Science Association.

_____. (1984). "The Heresthetics of Constitution-Making." *American Political Science Review*, 78:1–16.

_____. (1986). *The Art of Political Manipulation*. New Haven: Yale University Press.

_____. (1988). "The Place of Political Science in Public Choice." *Public Choice*, 57:247–257.

Riker, W., and Ordeshook, P. (1973). *Introduction to Positive Political Theory*. Englewood Cliffs, NJ: Prentice-Hall.

Schelling, T. (1960). *The Strategy of Conflict*. Cambridge, MA: Harvard University Press.

Sen, A. (1982). *Choice, Welfare and Measurement*. Cambridge, MA: MIT Press.

Shepsle, K. (1986). "The Positive Theory of Legislative Institutions: An Enrichment of Social Choice and Spatial Models." *Public Choice*, 50:135–178.

Simon, H. (1986). "Rationality in Psychology and Economics." In R. Hogarth and M. Reder (Eds.), *Rational Choice*. Chicago: University of Chicago Press.

Taylor, C. (1985). *Philosophy and the Human Sciences*. Cambridge: Cambridge University Press.

von Wright, G. (1971). *Explanation and Understanding*. Ithaca, NY: Cornell University Press.

Winch, P. (1958). *The Idea of a Social Science*. London: Routledge Kegan Paul.

Chapter

6

Social Values and Democracy

Anthony Downs

Social values perform important functions in all human societies. They are especially crucial to democracies. Why? Because "government by the people" depends upon widespread acceptance and practice of certain values among the citizenry itself. This essay explores the fundamental nature of social values, why they are important to democracy, some basic realities that underlie the social values vital to democracy, and the specific nature of those values.[1]

WHAT ARE SOCIAL VALUES?

Every society has rules of behavior concerning how people should regard and treat each other in day-to-day living. It also has dominant ways of perceiving key realities important to social life—for example, whether most truth is best learned through acceptance of authority or through open discourse among freely speaking citizens. These rules and perceptions together form the social values of the society.

Social values occur in three basic forms. Some are *internalized fundamental ethical and perceptual beliefs* held by most citizens. Others are *externalized laws and regulations* officially adopted by the government. Still others are *informal customs* not officially adopted as laws. Not all subgroups in the society hold exactly the same social values. But every society has at least some set of such values that are supposed to be common to all its citizens.

Social values are culturally determined, not hereditary.[2] Therefore, every generation of children must be taught these values anew. Teaching citizens, especially the young, to know and accept key social values is a vital function in every society, essential to its order and stability. Yet social circumstances change constantly, and these changes put pressure on systems of social values to change too. The results can be unpredictable shifts in social values over time, plus intergenerational strains caused by such alterations in values.

An example is the current change in values concerning sexuality and the roles of women in society. These shifts result in part from greater availability and use of contraceptives, longer average life spans, higher costs of rearing children and lower economic benefits to each family from doing so, extension of voting franchises to women, more widespread formal education of women, and rising concern about environmental quality as related to population growth. These dynamic factors have affected both the way people perceive reality and their beliefs about how they should behave toward each other.

WHY ANALYZING SOCIAL VALUES IS IMPORTANT[3]

Most non-Marxist economists regard the "preferences" or "tastes" of individuals—including social values as defined above—as a *given* element in the social environment. This perspective applies to individuals considered in their roles as consumers, producers, or citizens. According to this view, economics and economists—and perhaps social scientists generally—have no business analyzing, dealing with, or making prescriptions concerning social values.

This "agnostic" view has been encouraged by (1) the highly subjective nature of ethical and other social values, (2) major controversies among many groups concerning which social values are appropriate, (3) the difficulty of determining empirically the exact nature of social values and of measuring their nature, their extent, or their effects, and (4) strong pressures within the social sciences to emphasize "value-free" analytic methods similar to those used in the natural sciences.

As a result, most economists have focused their analysis entirely upon how the behavior of persons with *given* preferences and tastes (including social values) is, or could be, influenced by institutional arrangements, prices, and other incentives confronting them. This approach assumes some type of incentive scheme can be designed to induce any desired behavior in persons with almost any given values. Therefore, analyzing values is unnecessary to achieving desired social outcomes.

This is an important approach, and has yielded many valuable insights and policy guidelines. In fact, whole theories of political behavior have been built upon this rather narrowly focused "economic" approach. They include my own earlier *Economic Theory of Democracy*.[4]

In contrast to economics, traditional political theory from Aristotle through the mid-twentieth century assumed that one of the central goals of politics was to improve the character of each society's citizens. Having better characters would improve their chances of living "the good life."[5] This traditional approach focused a great deal of attention on which social values were most likely to produce the best society if widely held by the citizenry.

Academic political analysts changed their main focus from ethical and value issues to positivistic empiricism after World War II. Emphasis within the study of politics shifted from studying "what ought to be" to studying "what actually is," "how does it really work?" and "what problems does it generate?" As a result, there was a widespread neglect of ethical issues, including how social values affect the characters of citizens, and which such values create the most desirable social conditions.

In reality, the social values classified by economists as "given" preferences or tastes are extremely important variables in every society. Their nature, and changes in them, greatly affect economic and political behavior and institutions. Many recent pressing domestic and international problems seem insoluble through any rearrangement of incentives. Remedying those problems appears to require changing people's characters and behavior patterns by altering their personal and social values. For example, educational studies show conclusively that children from families in which parents place a high value upon doing well in school do much better than those from families without that value. Also, recent initially-poor immigrant ethnic groups, such as the South Vietnamese, whose values include strong family loyalty and a powerful work ethic, have achieved remarkably swift economic gains. Their economic progress has been far greater than that of other American ethnic groups, such as those inner-city black households in which children are reared by single female parents and ethical pressures among young men both to work and to care for their own children are weak.[6]

In these and other cases, the welfare of both society and many individuals concerned would be greatly improved if they could be induced to behave in accordance with different personal and social values from the ones they now exhibit. Similar emphasis upon the importance of individual character has emerged as crucial concerning policies to combat crime, delinquency, and drug and alcohol abuse.

Therefore, no study of democracy and how it works can be either accurate or comprehensive unless it analyzes the role of social values. In fact, I believe an absolutely crucial ingredient in successful democracies consists in the values in the hearts and minds of the citizenry that support democratic institutions and behavior patterns. Without the prior existence of such values, most democracies would never have been established in the first place.[7] And no democracy can successfully maintain itself over time *as a democracy* unless its citizens' political beliefs and behavior become dominated by social values that support democracy.

KEY REALITIES UNDERLYING DEMOCRATIC SOCIAL VALUES

Using "Realistic" Assumptions

In thinking about social values, it is important to avoid assuming certain conditions exist that are impossible or extremely unlikely in reality, if assuming them makes a significant difference to the conclusions arrived at. For example, much of economic theory assumes that consumers, firms, and other actors have "perfect information" about everything except the future. It is sometimes useful to make that assumption at an intermediate stage of theorizing about the real world. Doing so enables the theorist to estimate what would happen if that unrealistic assumption were true, before subsequently estimating what would happen if it is not. But if there is a big difference between these estimates, then it is illegitimate to base social policies upon the clearly unrealistic assumption.[8]

For this reason, my analysis of social values rejects the use of many purely hypothetical historical or abstract concepts. These include the "utopian societies" of Plato and Thomas More, the "social contract" theories of John Locke, Jean-Jacques Rousseau, and Thomas Hobbes, and the "mental experiments" of John Rawls and Robert Nozick. Instead, I believe any social values capable of being widely accepted by modern citizens must be directly grounded on certain realities they perceive as affecting their own daily lives, both individually and in society.[9]

The Structure of Axioms About Reality

Several such realities are crucial to the social values developed in this essay. They are presented here as eight axioms. These axioms contain both *descriptive* and *normative*, or *moral*, elements concerning how the world really works. I consider them axioms because I do not attempt to prove them, even though I believe they are true. Nor do I consider them to be "self-evident" as defined by formal logic. Rather, these axioms are statements about reality that most people in a democracy must accept as true if democracy is to function effectively. Moreover, I believe most people in modern democracies do indeed believe these axioms are true.

Each axiom has definite moral or normative implications for theorizing about social values. Its validity limits the range of such theories consistent with the reality it describes. Some of these implications will be presented along with the axiom itself. They will be used later in discussions of the specific social values underlying democracy.

My choosing the eight axioms set forth below is admittedly arbitrary. Other analysts might have used a different number, or defined them in some other way. However, I believe these eight form a sufficient foundation for my subsequent analysis of the social values necessary to democracy.

AXIOMS ABOUT THE NATURE OF TWO FUNDAMENTAL SOCIAL ENTITIES

Axiom 1 concerns the reality of individual autonomy. It states that *individual persons are the only true centers of human self-consciousness, and they also have at least some freedom of choice among possible actions open to them*. This axiom implies that individuals are and should be the fundamental units of any social theories and social values. Hence it is quite consistent with the views of John Locke and many subsequent theorists supporting "liberal democracy." However, if it is taken as the *only* key axiom underlying social values, it leads to an atomistic approach of "pure individualism" like that of Thomas Hobbes, Robert Nozick, or James Buchanan and Gordon Tullock.[10] In spite of the popularity of that approach among Americans, I believe it provides an inadequate ethical foundation for successful democracy, for reasons discussed below.[11]

Axiom 2 concerns the reality of social solidarity. It states that *certain societies—from the family through the neighborhood up to whole nations—are also real forces affecting the creation, nature, and behavior of every individual. In fact, no individual person can become human except in a society*. All human beings are created and nurtured within one and usually more societies; none are "pure individuals." No child can become a genuine human being without being strongly molded by social forces, especially the love, views, and actions of the other persons who rear him or her. Therefore, prevailing social perceptions of reality, customs, and values shape the fundamental consciousness of every individual, as well as his or her subsequent behavior.

People have lived in societies throughout human history for several good reasons. Societies permit a specialized division of labor, which immensely increases human productivity. They also improve each person's ability to defend himself or herself from "outside" threats of all types, from natural disasters to military invasions. Moreover, they stimulate human creativity by exposing each individual to a variety of influences and ideas, and by increasing the genetic diversity of the species.

This axiom implies that social values must support the solidarity, maintenance, and appropriate operation of certain key societies, including families. True, no societies have a biological existence or consciousness wholly separate from those of the individual members that comprise them. But many societies exert forces separate from or additional to those of their individual members upon those members and other people. Examples are strong families, religious organizations, nation states, armed forces, large business corporations, and labor unions.

Therefore, societies are not merely aggregates of atomistic individuals with no separate impacts or reality, as many modern political theorists, like Buchanan and Nozick, claim.[12] But neither are societies so dominant that individual choices are entirely subordinate to collective forces such as social class, as most Marxists contend. Both individuals and societies are real elements of life that any set of social values must recognize and relate to each other.

AXIOMS ABOUT THE BEHAVIOR OF PERSONS AND SOCIETIES

Axiom 3 concerns the rationality of average citizens. It states that *normal adult citizens can both recognize and pursue their own interests and the interests of society as a whole with reasonable accuracy and effectiveness, if they have access to sufficient, reliable, and relevant information*. This axiom admittedly contains many ambiguous terms, both descriptive and normative. They include "normal," "the interests of society," "reasonable accuracy," "effectiveness," and "sufficient, reliable, and relevant information." Volumes have been written about what each of these terms might mean. Another ambiguity is what citizens will do when their own interests conflict with what they believe are their society's interests.

It is not possible to resolve these ambiguities here. However, this axiom does not imply that normal citizens are *completely* reasonable, nor that their conclusions about what is in their own interests or the interests of society are *totally* accurate and effective. Rather, it implies that citizens in a democracy accept a basic "common sense" interpretation of the terms in this axiom.

That in turn implies that average adult citizens are rational enough to justify society's entrusting major governmental decisions to them. That is done through the various forms of citizen participation built into democracy. Hence this axiom is a fundamental basis for the "government by the people," or—more accurately—the "government with the consent of the governed"—that constitutes democracy.

This does not mean that the policy choices of average citizens are *optimal*, either for themselves or for society—that is, they do not necessarily *maximize* the welfare of either. Rather, it implies that such policy choices are *satisfactory*, on the average—especially in comparison with choices made through alternative forms of governance.[13]

Many people reject this axiom. They are unimpressed—or even depressed—by the rational capabilities of average citizens, whether acting individually or collectively. They cite numerous instances in which choices made by a majority of citizens in a democracy have proven wrong, ineffective, or downright stupid. So they argue either that most people are not sufficiently rational to make such choices, or that most people will always choose their own interests over society's interest when conflicts between those interests arise.

This argument implies that some other governance arrangement would produce superior results. Hence such critics usually contend it is better to entrust key government decisions—including selection of the government elite—to a small group of especially well-qualified citizens than to the citizenry as a whole. So they reject democracy in favor of some other form of government that puts full government powers in the hands of some special elite or "vanguard"—as in Communist systems. But the wisdom of such nondemocratic solutions is challenged by the next axiom.

Axiom 4 concerns the universality of selfishness. It states that *individuals in all societies tend—when they can—to give higher priority to serving their own interests, and the interests of those dearest to them, than the interests of others not so linked to themselves—even at the cost of sacrificing or exploiting others to benefit themselves*. This axiom is based upon the dualistic theory of human nature found in Judeo-Christian thinking. That theory postulates that all human beings have both ethically positive and ethically negative behavioral potentials. Positively, they can make the socially beneficent rational choices described in Axiom 3. Negatively, people also have a tendency to exploit others for their own benefit. Axiom 4 thus declares that the citizen rationality postulated by Axiom 3 has certain limits.

Axiom 4 has many crucial implications for democratic social values and social policies. The most important is that the power and authority of any one citizen or group of citizens should be limited, because those with great power are likely to use it to exploit others unjustly. That in turn leads to many conclusions about the way governmental and other social powers should be embodied in specific institutions, laws, and social values.

Axiom 5 concerns group identification and loyalty. It states that *in most societies, individuals draw part of their personal identities from membership in relatively cohesive subgroups within the society. Examples are ethnic groups, tribes, and religions.* Even the most mature and sophisticated individuals have usually come out of backgrounds involving specific social subgroups. Therefore, they have absorbed and benefited from many particular cultural values and practices unique to the groups from which they sprang. That form of group identification is desirable both for individuals and for society as a whole, which is enriched by the resulting cultural diversity. Examples of such groups in the United States are Jews, Puerto Ricans, Italians, Baptist fundamentalists, American Indians, Poles, blacks, Catholics, and Swedes.

However, this axiom also implies that the more intensively people identify with specific subgroups, the less likely they are to conceive of all persons within their society as fundamentally equal. But any subgroup identification involving belief in the basic superiority of some types of people over others is harmful to democracy. Such identification occurs when people judge the importance or value of others more from specific subgroup membership than from individual ideas, behavior, or other personal traits. This type of judgment violates the principle of human equality fundamental to democracy. For example, many whites in South Africa believe that all blacks should have fewer political rights and privileges than whites, regardless of the individual characteristics of either whites or blacks. Therefore, intensive subgroup identification can create strong social cleavages within a society that undermine the possibility of effective democracy there. Examples are the contemporary situations in Northern Ireland and Lebanon.

Thus this axiom implies that democracy will work best in societies that do not contain broad, deep, and multidimensional cleavages among major subgroups. When no deep cleavages exist, there is widespread confidence that each group in society does not have to exercise power itself to protect its interests from being grievously damaged by some other group elected to office.

AXIOMS ABOUT CONDITIONS INFLUENCING PERSONAL INTERACTIONS WITHIN SOCIETIES

Axiom 6 concerns inequalities and diversity among persons. It states that *concerning almost all empirically observable dimensions, human persons exhibit a diversity of traits involving substantial inequalities. Moreover, elimination of such inequalities by attaining complete identity among persons is not possible concerning at least those traits that inhere to each person's basic nature.* Inequalities concerning almost all observable dimensions have been the general lot of humanity throughout recorded history. This is true both among societies, and among individuals within each society. Such inequalities arise because of (1) hereditary dissimilarities in traits and abilities, (2) learned differences in abilities and views resulting from upbringing in different families, (3) the tendency for many persons to derive much of their personal identity and many cultural views from different subgroups in society, (4) the division of labor into specialized roles that generate diverse viewpoints and perspectives based upon different knowledge and training, (5) differential levels of effort and skill exhibited by different persons in obtaining valued resources, (6) the fact that governing elites and other powerful groups in each society have disproportionate influence upon social values and disproportionate access to valued resources, and (7) sheer chance.

Some of the traits regarding which people are unequal involve integral elements of their characters or personalities. Examples are intelligence, sense of humor, linguistic capabilities, physical strength, endurance, energy levels, and musical ability. It is not possible to create absolute equality—that is, identity—among different persons concerning such traits without fully controlling both their heredity and the family and subgroup environments in which they are reared. No society has ever been able to exert such control. Nor would it be desirable to do so, because diversity concerning such traits contributes greatly to the richness of social life. Moreover, even if exerting such control were scientifically possible, the loss of individual freedom required would vastly outweigh any resulting benefits.

Thus an implication of this axiom is that achieving complete equality among persons concerning all their traits is neither a feasible nor a desirable social objective. However, it would certainly be possible to attain more equality among persons than now exists concerning certain traits not inherent in their personalities or character. Examples often cited in discussions of social policy include income, wealth, political power, and access to health care and other social services.

Axiom 7 concerns the costliness of information. It states that *information necessary for making effective political and other decisions is scarce and costly in terms of money, time, and effort. Therefore, all political decisions are made in an environment of incomplete data and partial ignorance*. This axiom may seem an obvious characteristic of reality generally, but it is worth emphasizing because it so profoundly affects all social, economic, and political activity.

In a purely theoretical world, every democratic citizen would become well informed about every important issue before voting in any election. In addition, every government official and every candidate running for office would be fully informed about the views of all citizens on every issue. Moreover, citizens, officials, and candidates would all have total information about how alternative policies concerning each issue would actually work, if they were adopted.

But reality is vastly different from this picture, because acquiring accurate information is both difficult and costly. The most important cost is the time any person must spend procuring and studying data in order to become well informed about any complex issue. The amount of information available on each major issue facing a nation's government is enormous. It often exceeds what any one person could absorb even if he or she spent 24 hours a day studying it. Today even trained experts cannot keep up with all the relevant information in their own specialties. Yet the average voter is supposed to pass judgment on proposed policies concerning dozens of extremely complicated issues, ranging from combating new diseases to dealing with military conflict in Central America.

The idea that average citizens can become really well informed about most of the issues facing government is therefore false. So is the belief that government officials have clear ideas about the likely results of the many policy alternatives facing them. This axiom implies that both citizens and government officials must make most key political decisions in an environment containing immense amounts of ignorance and uncertainty that cannot be overcome.

Axiom 8 concerns the inherent interdependencies of social life. It states that *normal life in all societies involves myriad direct interactions among persons that generate complex, overlapping, and immeasurable externalities.* "Externalities" are direct relationships that cause the actions of some people to affect the welfare of others without flowing through markets—therefore, without receiving the voluntary consent of the affected persons. For example, acid rain generated by smoke from Midwest industries reduces the quality of lake environments in the Northeast and Canada. Similarly, noise and air pollution from expressways diminish the quality of life for persons living in nearby neighborhoods. Those adversely affected cannot protect themselves by refusing to enter such relationships, because the direct causative actions of others occur whether they consent or not. This differentiates "externalities" from transactions that take place in markets, in which each party can end any impacts upon itself by refusing to participate. In urbanized societies, because people live so close together and interact so frequently, both beneficial and harmful externalities abound and affect myriad aspects of daily life.

A major implication of this axiom is that no society can govern all its interpersonal relationships through purely voluntary contractual relationships. Too many inescapable direct interactions among persons have effects that are neither totally controllable, voluntarily accepted, nor accurately measurable. Such relationships cannot be governed by formalized contractual relationships. Theories that presume such governance—like that embodied in Nozick's "minimal state"—are to that extent invalid.[14]

Most societies implicitly assume that a rough balance exists for all citizens between the direct benefits they receive from all such unmeasured externalities taken together, and the direct costs imposed upon them by all such externalities taken together. When specific externalities clearly impose much heavier costs than benefits on particular citizens, those citizens should be compensated, preferably by the beneficiaries of the relationships concerned.

OTHER PHILOSOPHIC ASPECTS OF DEMOCRACY'S SOCIAL VALUES

Four other factors have had major effects upon the way the social values of democracy are generated in this analysis. First, a certain amount of logical and actual tension always exists among the realities described above. The spontaneous behavior of individuals, and their tendency to give priority to their own interests, inevitably conflict with the rules set forth to govern every society. They also conflict with society's need to compromise among the interests of its different members in order to make their joint life reasonably harmonious and effective.

Intense loyalties of individuals to specific subgroups within a society also generate conflicts with both individual autonomy and the general rules governing social behavior. In addition, nearly all societies contain one or more hierarchical orderings of status, power, and wealth among their members. That creates tension between those at the top of each hierarchy and those below them. As a result, the social values in democracies—like those in all other societies—contain what seem to be conflicting, inconsistent, or even contradictory elements.

Second, to be widely acceptable in a specific society, the social values underlying its system of government must be consistent with the philosophic views of reality dominant among its members. This is the case even if that philosophic view is not "objectively true"—that is, it does not correspond to empirically or otherwise demonstrable reality. For example, in John Locke's time, the vast majority of the English citizenry believed that God had created the world and "governed" it through a system of "natural laws"—including moral principles—structured into the nature of reality. Hence Locke's system of social values linked two of the realities described above—atomistic individuals and society as a whole—within an overarching context of "natural law" originated by God, who had created both individuals and societies for His own purposes.

But in the late twentieth century, belief in such a built-in system of "natural laws" rooted in divine creation is far from universal among citizens of most democracies. It is particularly lacking among modern politicians and intellectuals, including political scientists, political theorists, and other social scientists. Hence generating social values for democracy by linking individuals and societies through some system of divinely created "natural law" would not ground those values in a perspective widely acceptable to citizens of modern democracies.[15] For that reason, I have not followed such an approach. Rather, I have tried to build the democratic social values in this article upon a philosophic perspective that accepts two key constituent elements of reality. One is individual consciousness, along the lines established by Descartes and Hume. The other consists of certain specific societies, as discussed above.

A third basic aspect is that the social values prevalent in any culture evolve over time, partly in response to their own inherent inner dynamism. That dynamism springs from the fact that at least some social values always embody ideals, and human ideals are never fully achieved in practice. Hence there is always an inner tension, between a culture's aspirations and its current practices, that tends to evoke changes in those practices over time. As a result, the social values supporting democracy generate ongoing changes in social conditions that in turn cause a further evolution of those values over time.

A fourth key philosophical aspect is that, in judging the desirability of living under democracy, those evaluating its overall merits and faults should always compare them with the overall merits and faults of actually available alternative systems, not purely theoretically "ideal" ones. Democracies—especially modern capitalistic ones—have many serious faults. Their drawbacks have evoked legions of critics rightly calling for something better. However, it is well to keep in mind the famous remark of Winston Churchill about democracy:

> No one pretends that democracy is perfect or all-wise. Indeed, it has been said that democracy is the worst form of Government except all those other forms that have been tried from time to time.[16]

It is all too easy to propose some alternative form of government that does not contain some particular flaw perceived in democracy without realistically recognizing the other flaws that that form will contain— especially if it has never been tried in reality. Yet countless critics of democracy fail to describe how the alternative systems they advocate can successfully resolve the very problems and dilemmas they so vehemently attack in democracy. Or they ignore other, worse faults likely to occur in the alternatives they advocate.

SPECIFIC SOCIAL VALUES FAVORABLE TO DEMOCRACY

All societies differentiate between fundamental social values and less basic ones. In fact, the social values most relevant to government in any society can be arranged conceptually into a *value hierarchy* shaped roughly like a pyramid. A small number of fundamental values form the peak of the hierarchy. These fundamental values are *ethical axioms* that need not be proven by reference to other values. They represent the core of what most people in that society believe in their hearts is the truth about how human beings should behave toward each other. Most other social values in the hierarchy are *ethical corollaries* that can be derived from these fundamental values.

True, no one can describe the social values in a particular society's value hierarchy in a wholly unequivocal way. Any such description is bound to be somewhat arbitrary, and therefore subject to dispute. However, a broad consensus among the society's citizens is possible concerning at least some of their most fundamental social values. I will set forth what I believe is a version of democracy's hierarchy of social values that would be accepted by most citizens of most modern democracies—and, particularly, of the United States. These are presented below, beginning with the social values at the top of the value hierarchy described above.

The Ultimate Social Values Supporting Democracy

Almost all observers of democracy would agree that the following social value is at the very peak of the democratic hierarchy of social values:

- *The sanctity of the individual person.* The individual person is the most valuable and precious entity in the visible world.[17] Every person is therefore a repository of ultimate value not to be violated by anyone else.

Unless the vast majority of citizens in a society strongly believe in this value, democracy will not work well—if at all—in that society.

Accepting this value *alone* as fundamental to a democratic (or any other) society is equivalent to placing oneself in the "state of nature" visualized by John Locke and Thomas Hobbes. That state consists of myriad individuals—or perhaps small families—each asserting his or her own intrinsic value, without having established any ethical basis for relating to each other. Yet personal interactions among individuals are the essence of all societies. In my opinion, thus conceptualizing the fundamental values underlying a society in a way that assigns inferior status to the *interactive* aspects of human behavior is both unrealistic and incomplete.

Moreover, it is not clear that anyone can derive, with irrefutable logic, an ethical basis for a democratic society solely from the axiom of the sanctity of individuals. The difficulty of doing so can be inferred from the experience of Locke and Hobbes. Both started from an assumed state of nothing but isolated individuals, but they reached exactly opposite conclusions about the appropriate type of government. Locke favored a limited monarch responsible to the people, whereas Hobbes favored an absolute monarch answerable to no one else. Similarly, John Rawls's attempt to move from something like this one value to an ethical basis for democracy involves very complicated and abstract assumptions that do not seem very realistic to me and to many others.[18]

Therefore, it is necessary to postulate a second, equally fundamental social value at the peak of democracy's value hierarchy—an axiom concerning interactive relationships among persons. The purpose of this value is to establish an ethical basis for such relationships. One simple-sounding version could be a principle found in most religions, in one form or another. The Judeo-Christian version is the "Golden Rule": "Do unto others as you would have them do unto you."[19] Although this version has the virtues of simplicity, aesthetic charm, and familiarity, I propose a more general and therefore more abstract version, as follows:

- *The duty of mutual cooperation with others.* Every person should (1) cooperate with other members of societies in which that person is a member, and from which he or she gains, in actions aimed at their mutual benefit; (2) assist others in need insofar as he or she can without diminishing his or her own welfare below some reasonable minimum; and (3) uphold the system of behavioral rules necessary for harmonious social life in those societies to which he or she belongs.

As stated above, each person's duty of mutual cooperation applies mainly to interactions with other people who meet two conditions. First, those people are also members of societies to which the person involved belongs. Second, that person derives net benefits from membership in those societies. The second condition establishes a moral responsibility for the person involved to contribute to the welfare of such societies, since he or she is gaining from their operations. This moral obligation holds even if the person's membership does not result from voluntary choice. For example, people do not normally become members of particular families through their own choices; they are born into those families. Yet everyone has a moral duty to support and interact with other family members to their mutual benefit. Similarly, most people do not become citizens of a specific nation-state by choice; they are born into it.[20] Yet, insofar as its operations provide them with net benefits compared to the alternatives, they have a moral obligation to contribute to its welfare. However, the duty of assisting other persons in need is not confined to other members of societies to which the person concerned belongs; it extends to all other human beings to at least some degree.

These two ultimate social values are often stated in completely different ways. For example, the Judeo-Christian moral axiom "Love your neighbor as yourself" expresses both the sanctity of the individual person (as "self" and as "neighbor") and the obligation to assist others. From another perspective, the sanctity of the individual person establishes the basis for each individual's *rights*, whereas the obligation to assist and cooperate with others establishes the basis for each individual's *duties and responsibilities*.

Both these ultimate values—like most profoundly important ideas—can be extremely ambiguous in practice. What should be done when Smith's exercise of her rights conflicts with Krumkowski's exercise of his? Similarly, to what extent should any person sacrifice his or her own welfare to assist others? Answering these questions is not primarily a matter of philosophical clarity. Rather, it involves highly personal *prudential choices* that must be made each day by every citizen about what kind of life he or she wants to live.

Why Achieving These Two Ultimate Values Requires Democracy

The two ultimate social values described above can only be fully achieved in a society that has adopted a democratic form of government. Why? Because these two axiomatic values directly imply the validity of all three key principles of democracy, and any society built upon those principles is necessarily a democracy. Those three key principles—which constitute the essence of democracy—are described more fully below.[21]

The axiom of the sanctity of the individual gives rise to the principles of individual liberty and equality. Individual liberty is derived from the inviolability of the individual person. That inviolability implies that each person has certain inalienable rights to live, think, speak, and act freely. Such freedom is necessary for the individual to attain his or her full potential as a human being. Equality is necessary because every person is an ultimate repository of value; hence all persons are equal in some ultimate but abstract and immeasurable sense.

The axiom of the necessity of mutual cooperation with other persons in society, combined with that of the sanctity of the individual, provides a foundation for the principles of citizen participation and equality. Citizen participation is necessary because only cooperative action among many individuals can create and operate a social order that enables people to help each other and to respect the sanctity of the individual. The fundamentally equal value of all persons is implied by each person's obligation to assist persons other than himself or herself.

Moreover, citizen participation in a democracy includes citizen selection of the government elite through periodic, genuinely competitive elections. If this crucial ingredient of democracy is not present in a society, its government elite is almost certain not to uphold the sanctity of individual rights for all citizens, or to treat all citizens equally before the law. Instead, the government elite will provide its own members, and those few other persons who greatly influence whether it remains in office, with treatment superior to that accorded most other citizens. The inferior treatment accorded to others normally includes frequent violations of the sanctity of their individual rights.

Thus all three key principles of democracy both (1) can be derived directly from democracy's two fundamental social values and (2) are necessary to put those two values into practice. This means those two value axioms are fully achievable only in democratic societies.

Second-Level Social Values in a Democracy

It follows from the above analysis that the second level in the overall hierarchy of democracy's social values consists of the three key principles of democracy. These can be briefly stated here as follows:

- *Individual liberty*. Every person has the right to act freely on his or her own behalf. Therefore, every person has certain individual political and social rights that cannot be legitimately taken away from him or her without reasonable cause, even by the state or by society acting as a whole to serve mutual interests.
- *Basic equality*. Every person is fundamentally equal to every other in some abstract sense that transcends empirical observations, even though all are not equal in specific observable traits. Such equality is usually expressed through the ideal of equal treatment of all persons before society's laws.
- *Citizen participation in government*. Government should occur with the consent of the governed, as expressed in periodic elec-

tions to choose the government elite. Citizens should participate in governing themselves in other ways, too, such as holding office, seeking to influence legislative decisions, working in political campaigns. Only through effective citizen participation can the rights of individuals be maintained in the long run.

Lower-Level Social Values in a Democracy

Lower in the hierarchy are several values still essential to the successful operation of democracy but logically derivable from the values on the two higher levels. These lower-level values could conceivably be arranged on several descending levels instead of just one, but I have put them all on one for simplicity. They include the following:

- *Self-reliance*. Each person should basically assume responsibility for his or her own welfare, perhaps aided by other family members. This value is implied by each individual's being accorded the freedom to act by the principle of individual liberty. Presumably, such action is for his or her own benefit. Self-reliance certainly does not preclude cooperating with others at any time, or even receiving unreciprocated aid from them in times of difficulties. But it also expresses the truth that in democracy, since "the people" govern themselves, they are responsible for their own welfare.
- *Limitation of anyone's ability to exercise power over others*. Because human beings tend to exploit others for their own benefit, no one person, organization, or other locus of power should be entrusted with immense authority or power over others that is not somehow limited or checked.
- *Supremacy of the law over individual persons*. No persons—including those in the governing elite—are above the law; all persons should be treated as fundamentally equal by the laws. Everyone is subject to the rules and policies arrived at through legitimate democratic processes that do not violate the basic rights of individuals.
- *Primacy of individuals over groups*. As the "ultimate repositories of value," individuals and families are the most important units in society. Hence they are more important than governments, any political party, or any subgroups within society.
- *Tolerance of differing values and views*. Each person should exhibit a considerable tolerance for views and beliefs different from his or her own. Such tolerance not only should be behavioral but also should express an inner attitude of acceptance concerning the diversity and plurality in society.

- *Willingness to compromise*. Most policies can be fruitfully based upon compromises among groups with differing views, rather than rigid imposition of one group's view upon society.
- *Positive nature of economic competition and limited social conflict*. Economic competition (within legal limits) is generally beneficial to society as a whole because it motivates those engaging in it to perform better than they otherwise would. Conversely, economic monopoly is generally harmful to society as a whole because it permits those engaging in it to exploit others to at least some extent. Also, a certain amount of conflict in society is a necessary—and worthwhile—price to pay for allowing freedom, diversity, competition, and genuinely contested elections.
- *Pursuit of truth through open competition among ideas*. The truth about most subjects is most likely to be discovered in the long run through unrestricted competition among ideas and information concerning that subject, rather than by the pronouncements of any supposed authorities concerning it. Therefore, everyone should be free to express whatever ideas he or she wishes, regardless of the views held by supposed authorities.
- *Desirability of providing social aid to the distressed*. Society should collectively assist those who are in great need through circumstances that are no fault of their own. However, the exact nature and degree of assistance that ought to be provided is often quite controversial.
- *Belief in the effectiveness of democracy*. Democratic decision making and governing processes are effective in governing both society as a whole and most smaller-scale components within society.

Undoubtedly, other ways of defining and arranging the key social values and beliefs underlying democracy could be devised. Other analysts might choose slightly different expressions of the same basic ideas, include some further ideas or omit some included above, or arrange them differently. Nevertheless, I believe the analysis above conveys the value ingredients essential to democracy in a reasonably clear and comprehensive way.

WHY THESE PARTICULAR SOCIAL VALUES ARE CRUCIAL TO DEMOCRACY

Many different social values now exist in various societies throughout the world, or might conceivably exist, that are not included in the set described above. Why do I believe these particular values are crucial to democracy?

The two values set forth above as democracy's ultimate social values are assumed to be true, even though they are not self-evident. If you believe in them, and also subscribe to the eight axioms presented earlier, you will be best off living in a democracy; if you do not, you will not support democracy. The remaining values stated above have been chosen because they either (1) are logically derivable from the two ultimate fundamental values or (2) encourage achievement of the three basic principles of democracy, which are themselves derivable from its two ultimate values.

For example, consider tolerance of differing values and views, and willingness to compromise. If all people are basically equal in value, and each has a right to individual liberties, then each person must tolerate the exercise of that right by others. Therefore, no one can insist upon imposing his or her will upon others, regardless of their views or rights; so a spirit of compromise is essential.

These values in turn imply that the truth can best be found in a free competition of ideas, rather than through dictation by authority figures. Similarly, to implement individual liberty and equality, a democratic society needs to take a positive view of a certain amount of social conflict, including economic competition, as basically healthy, rather than likely to create disruptive disorder.

Self-reliance is related to both individual liberties and citizen participation in government. The purpose of individual liberties is to permit people to act on their own behalf. But that in turn requires their willingness to take the initiative in doing so. Also, citizen participation in government will not be effective unless people are willing to step forward and contribute their own efforts to it.

Seemingly opposite to self-reliance is the desirability of providing aid to the distressed. This value stems from the axiom of equality. If everyone has a certain fundamental value as a human being, he or she should be assisted by others in times of distress.

SOCIAL VALUES AND FACTUAL PERCEPTIONS UNFAVORABLE TO DEMOCRACY

Many societies are based upon social values or beliefs about actual conditions unfavorable to democracy, either as a system of government or as a type of society. For example, in Communist societies, the individual is subordinate to the state and the party, rather than superior to them. And in societies governed by religious leaders of a single faith, as in Iran, skepticism concerning authority may be replaced by devout acceptance of authority.

Values and beliefs unfavorable to democracy are essentially the opposites of those stated above as favorable to democracy; hence they are not named explicitly here. Persons who hold some of these antidemocratic values and beliefs do not necessarily hold all of them simultaneously. But the more dominant such views are in a society, the less likely democracy is to work effectively there.

THE INADEQUACY OF SELF-INTEREST AS THE SOLE MORAL FOUNDATION FOR DEMOCRACY

Many people today believe democracy can work well even if individuals exhibit no social values other than self-interest—as long as political institutions are designed to check those interests. As George Will has said:

> What once was considered a defect—self interestedness—became the base on which an edifice of rights was founded. Modern politics . . . has transformed a fact (man's appetitive nature) into a moral principle: Man should be allowed, even encouraged, to do what he most desires to do (consistent, of course, with other people doing likewise).[22]

The adverse impacts of such unrestrained desire would presumably be offset by appropriate institutional structures. As de Tocqueville observed about Americans over 100 years ago:

> Americans . . . are fond of explaining almost all the actions of their lives by the principle of self-interest rightly understood; they show with complacency how an enlightened regard for themselves constantly prompts them to assist one another and inclines them willingly to sacrifice a portion of their time and property to the welfare of the state.[23]

Not all political historians agree that the Founding Fathers largely ignored the necessity of nurturing social values other than self-interest.[24] However, the idea that individuals ought to openly express their self-interest, rather than suppress it through moral self-control, has become quite prominent in recent American and other social thought. As James Q. Wilson said:

> Modernity . . . involves, at least in elite opinion, replacing the ethic of self-control with that of self-expression.[25]

This emphasis upon self-expression rather than self-restraint also lies at the heart of the therapeutic-managerial view of the self some observers believe has become quite widespread recently:

> The therapeutic attitude . . . begins with the self rather than with a set of external obligations. The individual must find and assert his or her true self because this self is the only source of genuine relationships to other people. External obligations, whether they come from religion, parents, or social conventions, can only interfere with the capacity for love and relatedness.[26]

In fact, this highly subjective view of reality permeates much of modern culture. For example, Daniel Bell contends that modern art differs from traditional art in at least two key ways. One is a changing of the basic concept of space in art:

> In the new conceptions of space, there is an inherent eclipse of distance. Not only is physical distance compressed . . . but the very techniques of the new arts, principally cinema and modern painting, act to eclipse the psychic and aesthetic distance between the viewer and the visual experience. . . . The emphasis in cubism on simultaneity and in abstract expressionism on impact are efforts to intensify the immediacy of the emotion, to *pull the spectator into the action rather than allow him to contemplate the experience.*[27]

Equally important in modern art is a turning away from viewing reality as an objective fact outside the viewer—and so common to all persons—to a subjective view internal to each viewer—therefore potentially different for each.:

> [A] classical principle . . . of most Western art and literature was the idea of *mimesis*, or the interpretation of reality through imitation. Art was a mirror of nature, a representation of life. Knowledge was a reflection of what was "out there," known through a . . . copy of what was seen, as perceived through the senses. Judgment was essentially a contemplation, a beholding of reality, and its *mimesis* was a reflection of its worth.[28]

This objective view of reality is rejected in most modern art:

> Modernism is the disruption of *mimesis*. It denies the primacy of an outside reality, as given. . . . There is an emphasis on the self as the touchstone of understanding and on the activity of the knower rather than the character of the object as the source of knowledge. . . . Activity—making and doing—becomes the source of knowledge. . . . Instead of contemplation, we find substituted *sensation, simultaneity, immediacy,* and *impact.*[29]

Thus a central theme of modern Western culture is the moral obligation of the individual to *express his or her self as subjectively perceived*, whatever the self's nature or contents. That differs radically from the traditional Western cultural emphasis upon *modifying the nature of the self* to be more in accordance with external standards derived from studying both objective reality and society's past experiences. These two views have profoundly different implications for how democratic political systems ought to be structured and operated.

If the primary moral obligation of every individual is self-expression, then the only check upon conflict in society is to arrange external institutions and incentives so that each person's pursuit of unadulterated self-interest is "automatically" balanced against similar pursuits by all other persons. But this means little or no attention is devoted to teaching each person to check his or her passions and desires through self-restraint, self-denial, and moderation in life. These classical virtues are ignored.

But two centuries of experience with American and other democracies strongly imply that this approach often fails. Many social conditions arise under which purely externalized restraints upon individual self-interest cannot achieve adequate social peace and harmony. These conditions are particularly probable in a modern capitalistic society that deliberately inflames people's acquisitive desires to promote economic prosperity. As George Will remarked:

> Many Founders thought that commerce—the submersion of passion and interest in pursuit of private gain—was more reliable than public virtue as a basis of political stability. But . . . democracy subverts itself if it subverts the habits of self-restraint, self-denial, and public spiritedness. That danger defines the drama of democracy in a commercial nation, a nation devoted to inflaming and satisfying appetites.[30]

Belief in the "right" of individuals to indulge in unlimited self-gratification under the guise of "self-fulfillment" or "self-development" embodies an erroneous view of human freedom:

> Freedom is not only the absence of external restraints. It also is the absence of irresistible internal compulsions, unmanageable passions, and uncensorable appetites. From the need to resist, manage, and censure the passions there flows the need to do so in the interest of some ends rather than others. Hence freedom requires reflective choice about the ends of life.[31]

Thus self-interest cannot be the sole moral value in the long-run political life of an effective democracy. There must also be a core of shared *positive moral values* about how people *ought to behave* in social, political, and economic life for the benefit of others and of society as a whole, as well as for their own benefit. Without such values, the unchecked pursuit of self-interest would eventually overcome the values of tolerance, willingness to compromise, and respect for the rights of others that are essential to democracy. That is why the democratic value hierarchy described above has *two* values at its peak—one concerning the sanctity of individuals, and a second concerning each individual's duty to cooperate with others.

Moreover, development of the necessary core of positive and society-regarding moral values within the population cannot simply be left to the unguided operation of self-interest in every group. Rather, the leaders of society must take some specific initiatives to be sure that young people are inculcated with these shared values, even though this is hard to do in a pluralistic society. Failure to discharge this responsibility adequately can have serious adverse consequences for the entire society, as current experience in the United States so clearly demonstrates. However, analyzing the ways in which democracy's social values should be inculcated in its citizenry is beyond the scope of this essay.

CONCLUSION

A vital element in every effective democracy consists of the social values shared by most of its citizens, and built into both their institutions and their everyday behavior patterns. In the past, common belief in these values was grounded on widely shared religious views. Particularly central was the belief that God created the world and built into it certain "natural laws" governing desirable human behavior. But this belief has been greatly eroded in most contemporary democracies by many secularizing forces associated with industrialization and economic modernization. These same forces have caused many social scientists—especially economists—to shy away from analyzing the nature of social values and their functions in economic and political life.

However, several major contemporary social problems in democracies cannot be remedied without changes in the social values of key actors generating those problems. In addition, the central institutions that constitute democracy probably cannot be sustained for long without both reinforcing its key social values in the minds and hearts of existing citizens, and inculcating those values in the minds and hearts of future citizens as they grow up. Two initial steps are essential to achieving these goals. One is to identify the specific social values most important to democracy. The second is to provide some rational arguments supporting those values that are likely to be philosophically acceptable to most modern citizens. This essay has sought to carry out those two steps in a manner consistent with the secular views of most citizens in modern democracies.

NOTES

1. This article is an abbreviated version of two chapters in a book on social values and democracy. The views expressed herein are solely those of the author, and not necessarily those of the Brookings Institution, its trustees, or any of its other staff members.
2. Sociobiologist Edward Wilson contends that thousands of years of human evolution have resulted in definite genetic predispositions toward specific social and individual behavior patterns. Hence the

range of social values consistent with these genetic predispositions is much narrower than the overall range of theoretically possible social values. An example is the tendency of people to divide the world into two groups: those within their own society, to whom they owe considerate treatment, and "outsiders," who can be treated as less than human in many respects. Even so, the "genetically permissible" range of values is so large that culture remains the main determinant of the specific social values that actually exist around the world. See Edward O. Wilson, *On Human Nature* (New York: Bantam New Age Books, 1978).

3. Many of the ideas in this discussion have been taken from James Q. Wilson, "The Rediscovery of Character," *Public Interest* 81 (Fall 1985), pp. 3–16.

4. *An Economic Theory of Democracy* (New York: Harper & Row, 1957).

5. Aristotle, "Nichomachean Ethics," ed. Richard McKeon trans. W. D. Ross, in *Introduction to Aristotle*, Book I, (New York: Random House Modern Library, 1947), pp. 308–331. Specific quotations concerning the goal of political science are as follows:

> What is it that . . . political science aims at and what is the highest of all good achievable by action? Both the general run of men and people of superior refinement say that it is happiness, and identify living well and doing well with being happy. . . . Human good turns out to be activity of the soul in accordance with virtue. . . . We stated the end of political science to be the best end, and political science spends most of its pains on making the citizens to be of a certain character; viz. good and capable of noble acts. . . . Moral virtue comes about as a result of habit . . . none of the moral virtues arises in us by nature . . . the virtues we get by first exercising them . . . we learn by doing them. . . . It makes no small difference, then, whether we form habits of one kind or another from our very youth; it makes a very great difference, or rather *all* the difference.

6. A striking analysis of the values of young black men in such areas is presented in Elijah Anderson, "Sex Codes and Family Life Among Inner-City Youth," in *The Ghetto Underclass: Social Science Perspectives*, ed. W. J. Wilson, *Annals of the American Academy of Political and Social Science* 501 (January 1989).

7. Exceptions are democracies imposed upon previously dictatorial societies by military conquerors (as in Japan in 1945) or democracies formed suddenly out of former colonies (as in many African states from 1950 through 1970).

8. This view that the assumptions underlying theories should be *relatively* realistic differs from the well-known view of Milton Friedman that theories should be judged solely by the accuracy of their

predictions. Friedman correctly points out that no assumptions underlying any theory can be *perfectly* realistic. Why? Because some degree of abstraction is an inherent part of drawing general conclusions from particular cases in this infinitely complex world. Therefore, he argues that assumptions can be as divorced from apparent reality as the theorist desires, as long as the predictions or other implications of the theory are borne out in practice.

However, Friedman's view assumes that the theory's predictions or other implications can be reliably tested empirically. This is not always true. It is particularly unlikely to apply to theories about social values, which involve ethical conclusions rather than factual ones. Moreover, a theory has other purposes besides prediction, such as imparting accurate knowledge about how the world actually works.

9. In the cases of Hobbes and Locke, postulating a "state of nature" in which individuals existed without a prior social order uniting them did have some correspondence to their direct historical experience. Their society had just emerged from a prolonged civil war in which something akin to such a "state of nature" actually existed at times. Moreover, Locke pointed out that the "state of nature" closely corresponded to historic realities in America, since many individuals there lived apart from each other in a wilderness. But even in both these historical cases, social influences had critical impacts upon all individuals to a much greater extent than recognized by the atomistic individualism found in their "states of nature." In the more modern cases of Rawls and Nozick, using purely abstract "mental experiments" as though they were important constituents of historical reality seems to have no similar justification.

10. Hobbes, *Leviathan* (New York: Collier Macmillan, 1977); Nozick, *Anarchy, State, and Utopia* (New York: Basic Books, 1974); Buchanan and Tullock, *Calculus of Consent* (Ann Arbor: University of Michigan Press, 1962).

11. An analysis of the role of Lockean individualism in American political thought is found in Louis Hartz, *The Liberal Tradition in America* (New York: Harcourt Brace Jovanovich, 1955).

12. For example, Nozick states that "there is no *social entity* with a good that undergoes some sacrifice for its own good. There are only individual people, different individual people, with their own individual lives. Using one of these people for the benefit of others, uses him and benefits the others. Nothing more." (*Anarchy, State, and Utopia*, pp. 32–33.)

13. This distinction corresponds to the distinction in formal decision-making theory between *maximizers* and *satisficers*, as developed by James March.

14. See *Anarchy, State, and Utopia*, Chap. 4.
15. It should be clear that this modern view and John Locke's view cannot both be true; at least one of them is "objectively false." Yet I believe useful theories about democratic social values can be constructed on the basis of both these views. Certainly John Locke's view was extremely useful to the political theorists of his day and of many later days. I hope the view set forth here will be useful to political theorists and just plain citizens of modern democracies throughout the world.
16. House of Commons, November 11, 1947. Quoted in *The Oxford Dictionary of Quotations*, 3rd ed., 1980, p. 150, quotation 19.
17. This definition limits the supremacy of human beings to the *visible* world because religious persons regard some *invisible* divinity as superior in value to human beings. I have tried to use a definition that would neither contradict nor affirm that religious view, while getting across the idea of the supremacy of value of human beings *within this world.*
18. See Rawls, *A Theory of Justice* (Cambridge, MA: Harvard University Press, Belknap Press, 1971); Robert Paul Wolff, *Understanding Rawls* (Princeton: Princeton University Press, 1977); Nozick, *Anarchy, State, and Utopia.*
19. In the New Testament, this "Golden Rule" is stated in Matt. 7:12. In the Old Testament, a negatively stated version is found in Tob. 4:16.
20. In theory, they could move elsewhere; hence their remaining within the nation-state where they were born constitutes a type of voluntary choice of being citizens there. However, this conclusion does not apply to citizens of nations that prohibit their members from leaving, as have many Communist countries.
21. This essay does not contain a full explanation of why the three key principles of democracy constitute the essence of that form of government. That explanation is included in earlier chapters of the book from which this essay is drawn, but it is too lengthy to be included here. Unfortunately, the analysis in this chapter suffers from some logical incompleteness because of this unavoidable omission—a fact for which I apologize.
22. *Statecraft as Soulcraft* (New York: Simon and Schuster, 1983), p. 43.
23. *Democracy in America*, Vol. II (New York: Knopf, 1972), p. 122.
24. For example, Michael Novak disputes this view. See *Character and Crime* (Notre Dame, IN: Brownson Institute, 1986), pp. 51–53
25. "The Rediscovery of Character," pp. 3–16, reprinted in Novak, p. 30.

26. Robert N. Bellah, Richard Madsden, William M. Sullivan, Ann Swidler, and Steven M. Tipton, *Habits of the Heart* (New York: Harper & Row, 1986), p. 98.
27. *The Cultural Contradictions of Capitalism* (New York: Basic Books, 1978), p. 106. Emphasis added to the original.
28. Bell, p. 110.
29. Bell, pp. 110–111.
30. Will, p. 66.
31. Will, p. 66

REFERENCES

Anderson, E. (1989). "Sex Codes and Family Life Among Inner-City Youth." In W. J. Wilson, (Ed.) *The Ghetto Underclass: Social Science Perspectives, Annals of the American Academy of Political and Social Science*, 501.

Bellah, R. N., Madsen, R., et al. (1986). *Habits of the Heart*. New York: Harper & Row, p. 98.

Bell, D. (1978). *The Cultural Contradictions of Capitalism*. New York: Basic Books, pp. 106, 110, 111.

Buchanan, J. M., and Tullock, G. (1962). *Calculus of Consent*. Ann Arbor: University of Michigan Press.

Downs, A. (1957). *An Economic Theory of Democracy*. New York: Harper & Row.

Hartz, L. (1955). *The Liberal Tradition in America*. New York: Harcourt Brace Jovanovich.

Hobbes, T. (1977). *Leviathan*. New York: Collier Macmillan.

Novak, M. (1986). *Character and Crime*. Notre Dame, IN: Brownson Institute, pp. 51–53.

Nozick, R. (1974). *Anarchy, State and Utopia*. New York: Basic Books, pp. 32–33.

Rawls, J. (1971). *A Theory of Justice*. Cambridge, MA: Harvard University Press, Belknap Press.

Ross, W. D. (1947). "Nichomachean Ethics." In R. McKeon (Ed.), *Introduction to Aristotle*, Book I. New York: Random House, pp. 308–331.

de Tocqueville, A. (1972). *Democracy in America*, Vol. II. New York: Alfred A. Knopf, p. 122.

Will, G. F. (1983). *Statecraft as Soulcraft*. New York: Simon and Schuster, pp. 43, 66.

Wilson, E. O. (1978). *On Human Nature*. New York: Bantam New Age Books.

Wilson, J. Q. (1985). "The Rediscovery of Character." *Public Interest*, *81*:3–16.

Wolff, R. P. (1977). *Understanding Rawls*. Princeton: Princeton University Press.

Chapter
7

The Rational Actor Approach to Politics: Science, Self-Interest, and Normative Democratic Theory

Mark P. Petracca

The rational choice approach to politics assumes that individual behavior is motivated by self-interest, utility maximization, or, more simply put, goal fulfillment.[1] As "positive theory," rational choice is sternly but sympathetically criticized in this volume and elsewhere for its failure to construct a model of political behavior which accounts for the complexities of human nature and various aspects of organized politics. These worthy criticisms suggest that, in its current configuration, the rational choice approach cannot accurately describe, explain, or predict a great deal of what is most interesting about political life.[2] As a consequence, critics urge various additions to and alterations in the rational choice model to better accommodate political reality. Since many critics share the commitment of rational choice theorists to the scientific study of politics, they advocate modifying and supplementing the rational actor model of political behavior rather than questioning the value of this approach for political explanation and its consequences for democratic political life.

This essay breaks with this line of criticism. Rather than embrace the rational actor model because of its claimed scientific status, I examine the consequences of this approach for normative democratic theory. Specifically, I argue that the value-ladened assumption of the self-interested, maximizing individual is incompatible with the transformation of the individual and the regime which constitutes the sine qua non of many important classical and contemporary normative theories of democracy. As a vehicle to this assessment, I revisit the claim that rational choice is value-free scientific inquiry, evaluate the assumptions upon which the model is constructed, and identify the dangers to democratic politics posed by the economic model of humankind.[3]

THE CLAIMS OF RATIONAL CHOICE

In just three decades, rational choice theory has emerged as one of the most active, influential, and ambitious subfields in the discipline of political science. Rational choice theory is variously praised for its contribution to political theory, wide applicability, explanatory power, influence on public policy, and promising future.[4] Beyond its wide applicability and considerable explanatory power, some theorists also believe that rational choice has directly influenced the course of American public policy.[5]

The impact of rational choice's contributions for future political analysis is calculated by Abrams who concludes that "the material presented here represents the beginning of a theoretical development which will emerge as the preeminent approach to political analysis in the next several decades" (1980:1).[6] For many, then, rational choice may constitute the beginning of political theory.

While it is tempting to speculate about the validity of these claims, that is not the primary task before us. It is, however, germane to ask why rational choice theory has become so popular and influential in the discipline of political science. A look at the rationalization of rational choice offers a preliminary answer to that query and at the same time begins to reveal some of the important consequences of this approach for normative democratic theory.

THE RATIONALIZATION OF RATIONAL CHOICE

The growth of rational choice theory in the discipline of political science is attributable to its close association with the scientific method and its political compatibility with the assumptions of modern liberalism. Students of politics have long searched for and debated the merits of a scientific approach to political inquiry.[7] From the formal founding of the discipline at the turn of the century to the present, many political analysts have aspired to develop a "science of politics."[8] For many scholars a generation or so ago, the commitment to scientific knowledge took the form of behavioral research in politics (see Easton, 1967:133). In the following decade and a half, rational choice has emerged as the new champion of scientific inquiry. Gabriel Almond suggests that with its commitment to formal theory and "formidable array of scientific methodologies—deductive, statistical and experimental"—"it is not surprising that the rational choice and public choice literature flowered . . . and became the cutting edge of 'scientific' political science" (1988:832, 1990b:120–121).[9] Thus rational choice has an innate intellectual appeal to many members of the discipline because of its association with science. Indeed, "rationalist theories are functionallly rational for offering political science a column, figuratively, in the Temple of Science, safe alongside the columns of other disciplines that dwell in American universities" (Ricci, 1984:247).

The pretension of rational choice theory as science serves professional as well as symbolic functions. The professional survival and prominence of the political science discipline is dependent on its ability to identify a body of important knowledge that only its specialized experts can reveal.[10] If almost anyone is capable of important insight and the revelation of vital political knowledge, then the discipline of political science becomes unessential. To put this more forcefully, if the insights of political scientists are no better (or worse) than those of average citizens, then there is no need for a specialized discipline. In sharp contrast to the classical political rationalism of Strauss (1989) or the "tacit knowledge" and wisdom of Wolin (1969), which broaden rather than narrow the appropriate source of political knowledge, rational choice theory justifies the existence of the political science discipline by its claim to specialized, scientific knowledge. Only those with the requisite expertise are capable of the discovery and analysis of political knowledge so essential to modern society. The specialized and scientific qualities of rational choice theory help to justify the unique contribution made by political science to the art of democratic governance and in doing so justify the very existence of the discipline.

Beyond professional benefit, rational choice theory provides a symbolic comfort to many who desire the discipline to be relevant and responsive to the problems confronting the modern world.[11] As a discourse which pervades our daily lives and most of social science practice, rationality is invested with the dual capacities of purpose and control. The discourse of rationality helps confirm our interpretations of the world and opens up the possibility of addressing the problems inherent in that world in a purposeful and systematic fashion. This view has great appeal.[12] In its implicit promise for a better world, the discourse of rationality comforts us in the world we currently inhabit.

Rational choice is also an attractive approach to poltical inquiry because its assumptions are compatible with the essential political requirements and ingredients of modern liberalism. Like the market system they emulate, economic models of political behavior produce a determinate system out of a multitude of conflicting individual wills.

This leads to a stable equilibrium which, in turn, yields the maximum utility for the whole membership of the system. This view helps to explain one of the central problems in American versions of liberal democracy: How do governments "reconcile or balance or hold in adjustment a multitude of diverse and conflicting individual interests" in order to create an equilibrium known as the public interest? As a response to this problem, it is little wonder that "the equilibrium-market model has been irresistible" (Macpherson, 1973:186–187).[13]

These theories reduce the burdens of citizenship and policy aspirations in a modern democracy by maintaining that only certain mechanisms of social choice are feasible. For example, in a defense of "liberalism" over "populism, " Riker opts for a system in which "the function of voting is to control officials, and no more."[14] For Riker, "Liberal democracy is simply the veto by which it is sometimes possible to restrain official tyranny . . . a veto at the margins" (1982:9, 245).[15] In Riker's view of democracy, citizenship and political participation play a role only at the margins in a system dominated by competitive elites.[16] "Such theories," notes Ricci, "serve the larger requirements of liberalism when they avoid suggesting that America needs more preaching of absolute standards, or a rational citizenry more numerous than the number of informed voters who presently inhabit the country" (1984:247). The theoretical and substantive impoverishment of democratic life is one of the most severe consequences of rational choice, a consequence I consider in greater detail below.

Thus the ascendancy of rational choice theory can be understood in terms of its intellectual, professional, symbolic, and political appeal and advantages.

RATIONAL CHOICE THEORY: IS IT SCIENCE?

As indicated above, the banner of science is essential to the vitality, respectability, and growing influence of rational choice theory. For many political scientists, rational choice theory represents a promised land for the scientific study of politics.[17] However, much of the discipline's faith in rational choice theory as a science is misplaced once we consider one of the most important characteristics of social scientific inquiry—that is, the distinction between facts and values.

The cardinal characteristic which defines modern social science for many of its advocates is the distinction between facts and values. What is the essence of this distinction? Consistent with the sine qua non of scientific inquiry, modern social science claims

> to be a science of empirical reality. It does so by contending that only *empirical* evidence is able to confirm or disconfirm social

scientific theories. . . . [It insists] that there is a clear distinction between empirically testable propositions and those which are not, and that social scientific theory consists only of the former. In practice, this distinction is usually expressed as a distinction between empirically testable propositions and propositions which express value judgments (Bergner, 1981:3–4).

Since the founding of the discipline, the distinction between facts and values has been a dominant feature of political science. Some political scientists have explicitly attempted "value-free" research, while others have advocated the importance of such a distinction.[18] The general or dominant view was that political science "studies what is, not what should be" (Catlin, 1927'1964:325). Indeed, Somit and Tanenhaus identified the fact-value distinction as one of their eight "key behavioralist articles of faith" (1967:178). For most political scientists only "empirical (based on observation of the world) and analytic (based on logical derivations from premises)" approaches to political inquiry "qualify as knowledge" (Isaak, 1981:12).[19] Normative propositions are simply value judgments which do not qualify as knowledge. As a result, normative theories of political life are banished to the realm of political philosophy.

Despite the dominance of the fact-value distinction in contemporary political science, it is not without its friendly critics and harsh protagonists. In a forceful criticism of the illusory distinction between facts and values, Strauss argues that modern political science declares

that no value judgments, including those supporting liberal democracy, are rational. . . . The very complex pros and cons regarding liberal democracy have thus become entirely obliterated by the poorest formalism. The crisis of liberal democracy has become concealed by a ritual which calls itself methodology or logic (1962:327).[20]

For Strauss the distinction between facts and values not only is misleading, but also threatens our ability to cope with the crisis of liberal democracy. Bellah and his colleagues offer a similar warning:

Social science as public philosophy cannot be "value free." It accepts the canons of critical, disciplined research, but it does not imagine that such research exists in a moral vacuum. To attempt to study the possibilities and limitations of society with utter neutrality, as though it existed on another planet, is to push the ethos of narrowly professional social science to the breaking point. The analysts are part of the whole they are analyzing. In framing their problems and interpreting their results, they draw on their own experience and their membership in a community of research that is in turn located within specific traditions and institutions. . . . *We cannot deny the moral relationship between ourselves and those we*

are studying without being untrue to both (1985:302–303);
(emphasis added).

Social science cannot adequately respond to the important societal challenges before us if we continue to deny the essential connectedness of
facts and values.

How does rational choice respond to this criticism? On the whole,
rational choice theorists rarely discuss the value neutrality of their enterprise. However, a few important works do make explicit reference to
the "positive theory" of rational choice or the economic approach to politics. Positive theory is presumed to be value-free. Downs says that his
economic model is distinguished from most other economic models of
government on the grounds that his is positive, while the others are normative (1957:20). Riker says that the "main hope for a genuine science
of politics lies in the discovery and use of an adequate model of political
behavior" (1962:8). According to Riker, the use of models aids the cause
of scientific investigation because they carefully exclude normative
features from the axioms or render them conscious, thereby making it
possible to exclude (or control) normative elements from the deduced
generalizations. Buchanan reminds us that "the analysis of public choice
is positive rather than normative. It does not advance propositions that
politicians, bureaucrats, or voters 'should' or 'should not' adopt"
(1984a:442). Finally, Mueller distinguishes between "the positive
theory of public choice, based upon economic man assumptions" and
"normative theories of public choice" (1979:173). By conceding the
existence of normative theories of public choice, much like Downs's
reference to normative economic theories, Mueller intends to persuade
the reader that "positive theories" of public choice are not contaminated
by value judgments. Mueller concludes with a helpful hint for normative theory:

> The challenge normative theory faces is to develop theorems about
> the expression and realization of values, based on generally
> accepted postulates, in the same way positive theory has developed
> explanatory and predictive theorems from the postulates of rational
> egoistic behavior (1979:173).

In other words, normative theories of public choice should be
encouraged to treat values as positive theories treat egoistic behavior—
as assumptions from which particular conclusions are deduced. But, this
recommendation is responsive neither to the harsh criticisms of Strauss
or Bellah nor to the friendly criticisms of rational choice theory by
Almond, Downs, or Eckstein contained in this volume.

Nor are these claims sufficient to persuade perceptive critics (or
even supportive innovators) that rational choice theory contains no
value assumptions or important normative implications. Barry argues
that both "the economic and sociological approaches to politics still trail

shreds of ideology" (1978:173). Barry uses Downs's work as a primary example. For Downs, democracy is a rational end of political activity because it enables individuals to rationally pursue (and often achieve) their self-interest. This perspective not only presumptively values the pursuit of self-interest (even though it is posited as an inherent part of human nature), but more important, it positively evaluates the mechanistic capacity of a democratic regime to respond to the driving force of human nature. This is a normative statement.

However, the value judgments made by rational choice theories are not limited to a preference for a particular set of institutional mechanisms. Judgments also extend to the realm of political principles. The widespread endorsement of the Pareto principle by most rational choice theorists is but one example.[21] "A state of society is Pareto-optimal," as Barry and Hardin explain, "if there is no state of society that is superior to it, that is, no state of society that in moving to it, nobody would be made worse off and at least one person would be made better off" (1982:141). The usual view is that Paretianism is a "weak" value judgment. However, Paretianism also maintains that individual utilities are not comparable. Thus, as Peter Self, points out, "it follows that only the affected individual can accurately judge how far his welfare is reduced by some policy measure. . . . Logically it would rule out any public policy change if anyone objects. Its assumption of the 'non-comparability of utilities', if taken literally, virtually excludes any policy making at all, since someone is likely to claim that his 'welfare loss' is enormous or even infinite . . ."(1985:175–176).[22] Rather than a "weak" value judgment, the Pareto principle represents a rather strong conservative position when it comes to potential public policy making.

The inherently normative quality of rational choice is less of a problem for sophisticated innovators in the field. Elster argues that rational choice explanations require the construction of a normative theory of rational choice:

> The theory of rational choice is, before it is anything else, a normative theory. It tells us what we ought to do in order to achieve our aims as well as possible. It does not tell us what our aims ought to be. . . . In order to know what to do, we first have to know what to believe with respect to the relevant factual matters. Hence the theory of rational choice must be supplemented by a theory of rational belief. Again, this is a normative theory before it is anything else. While the rationality of an action is ensured by its standing in the right kind of relation to the goals and beliefs of the agent, the rationality of beliefs depends on their having the right kind of relation to the evidence available to him (1986:1–2).

If Elster is right, then the very logic of rational choice requires that it be based upon a normative theory of behavior and belief. Arrow concedes the same point: "These conditions are, of course, value judgments and could be called into question; together they express the doctrines of citizens' sovereignty and rationality in a very general form, with the citizens being allowed to have a wide range of values" (1963:30–31). While the inherent value judgments of rational choice may be consonant with the ingredients of modern liberalism, they are no less evaluative or normative, and therefore represent a significant challenge to the status of rational choice theory in the "Temple of Science."

MORE THAN JUST ASSUMPTIONS

A great deal has already been said in this volume[23] and elsewhere[24] about the characteristics of rational choice as political theory. Rational choice theory emerges from classical microeconomics. It is formal, axiomatic, and deductive. As a method of political analysis, then, rational choice operates within the boundaries of two well-known assumptions. The first is methodological individualism and the second is the concept of rationality itself.

Methodological individualism insists that everything about society and social action can be reduced to statements about component individuals.[25] As a result, the way to study politics is to analyze the political behavior of individuals. Most rational choice theorists are fairly unapologetic for the pivotal role that individuals play in their deductive reasoning, frequently to the exclusion of other important variables.[26] Early rational choice innovators (e.g., Buchanan and Tullock, 1962:1), as well as subsequent applicators (e.g., Ordeshook 1986:1), explicitly identify their work in terms of methodological individualism. However, for most practitioners of the rational choice approach, this assumption is so deeply embedded in what they are doing that it need not be explicitly identified or discussed in their analyses.

The problem with methodological individualism is twofold. It encourages a political science which empirically views individual actions as unconditioned by social structures and other supra-individual entities.[27] By focusing on the individual as the appropriate unit for social analysis, methodological individualism nurtures the normative belief that politics should attend and respond to the needs, wants, and preferences of individuals. This stands in sharp contrast to the Platonic view that political life is about the pursuit of wisdom, knowledge, virtue, justice, and the other qualities intrinsic to the "good society."[28]

The assumption of rationality is essentially an assumption about human nature. As a deductive theory the analyst is able to predict that certain actions and consequences will result from basic assumptions about the motivational force of human nature. In the theory of rational choice, there is some variability over the precise qualities of human nature. Definitions range from the somewhat crude and unbridled pursuit of material self-interest to utility maximization to purposive behavior. Beginning with Hume, the following examples illustrate the central tendencies of the various assumptions concerning human nature:[29]

David Hume: Political writers have established it as a maxim, that, in contriving any system of government and fixing the several checks and balances of the constitution, every man ought to be supposed a knave, and to have no other end, in all his actions, than private interest. By this interest we must govern him, and by means of it, make him, notwithstanding his insatiable avarice and ambition, cooperate to public good.[30]

Adam Smith: But man has almost constant occasion for the help of his brethren, and it is in vain for him to expect it from their benevolence only. He will be more likely to prevail if he can interest their self-love in his favour, and show them that it is for their own advantage to do for him what he requires of them. . . . It is not from the benevolence of the butcher, the brewer, or the baker, that we can expect our dinner, but from their regard to their own interest (Smith, 1775/1976:18).

Anthony Downs: We assume that every individual, though rational, is also selfish. . . . Throughout our model, we assume that every agent acts in accordance with this view of human nature. Thus, whenever we speak of rational behavior, we always mean rational behavior directed primarily towards selfish ends. . . . From the self-interest axiom springs our view of what motivates the political actions of party members. We assume that they act solely in order to attain the income, prestige, and power which comes from being in office (1957:27–28).

James M. Buchanan and Gordon Tullock: The basis for the theory of collective choice . . . assumes that the individual, as he participates in collective decisions, is guided by the desire to maximize his own utility and that different individuals have different utility functions. . . . We propose to analyze the results of various choice-making rules on the basis of this behavioral assumption, and we do so independently of the moral censure that might or might not be placed on such individual self-seeking action (1962:25, 30).

William H. Riker: Politically, rational man is the man who would rather win than lose, regardless of the particular stakes (1962:22).

Kenneth Arrow: The condition of rationality [is identified] with maximization of some sort (1963:3).

Mancur Olson: Indeed, unless the number of individuals in a group is quite small, or unless there is coercion or some other special device to make individuals act in their common interest, *rational self-interested individuals will not act to achieve their common or group interests* (1965:2; emphasis in original).

William H. Riker and Peter C. Ordeshook: [A]ctors in society seek to attain their purposes. Persistence in this search, or "goal-directed behavior" to use the current jargon, is the substance of rationality (1973:10).

James Buchanan: [P]ublic choice models . . . embody the presumption that persons seek to maximize their own utilities, and that their own narrowly defined economic well-being is an important component of these utilities (1984b:13).[31]

The phrases "private interest," "self-interest," "utility maximizing," "selfish ends," "maximization," "goal-directed," "purposive behavior," and "egoistic" characterize the economic approach to rationality. What does this tell us about human nature? First, the picture of human nature that emerges from these examples is one of egoistic individuals seeking to maximize their own good or well-being. In the main, proponents of rational choice theory "assume that it is egoistically, individualistically irrational not to maximize one's satisfactions and seek one's own greatest good" (Slote, 1989:7).

However, the implication of the "maximizing individual" is far more pervasive. Many of the influential nonmaximizing conceptions of human nature, such as those proposed by Amartya Sen (1979) and Charles Fried (1970), are likewise trapped in the logic of individual optimization. Despite recent protestations to the contrary, contemporary rational choice theory is no less wedded to the assumption of self-interest than was Adam Smith. While contemporary theorists have lessened the severity of what counts as self-interest (occasionally calling it "purposive" or "goal-directed" behavior), self-interest continues to be the assumption which informs and drives many of the actual rational choice models.

As an empirical question, how accurate are the assumptions of self-interest and utility maximization? Even some proponents concede its limitations. Clearly, humans are social beings, with "choices . . . not rigidly bound to his own preferences only" (Sen, 1977:66).[32] Rational choice's "reductionist individualism," which can easily make sense of all the exchange or market modes of social coordination, cannot accommodate "the permeable, three-dimensional self of the real world—the self which has been fashioned by constant interaction with other selves, in a structure of common traditions, interlocking histories and shared meanings" (Marquand, 1988:266).

Some eminent rational choice theorists have recognized this (e.g., Simon, 1985:303; March and Olsen, 1984:738, 744; Downs, 1988). But far too many are seriously less circumspect (e.g., Brams, 1985:2; Laver, 1981:1–2). The most extreme argument in support of the self-interest or maximization assumption is advanced by Buchanan, who alleges that the burden of proof in this entire matter rests with those who question the validity or usefulness of *homo economicus* as an assumption of rational choice theory (1984b:13–14). Following Buchanan's argument, rational choice theorists are under no obligation to *prove* that their assumption about individual self-interest is accurate. To the contrary, that obligation rests with its critics and those who advocate a different view of human nature.[33]

These assumptions about human nature are of enormous consequence. Assumptions about human nature shape research strategies, which in turn effect political cognition as well as political possibilities and actual behavior. A research strategy determines not only what we see but how we see it, as well as what remains hidden from view.[34] Many things may be obscured by the assumption of self-interest, not just omitted but actually concealed from the analysis.[35] The choice of any model is never benign, never neutral, despite frequent claims to the contrary; instead a model influences the collection and presentation of data and the inferences and conclusions that are drawn for public policy. "Each conceptual framework consists of a cluster of assumptions and categories that influence what the analyst finds puzzling, how he formulates his question, where he looks for evidence, and what he produces as an answer" (Allison, 1971:245).[36] The assumptions of a model matter not only to research but "for the proper design of political institutions" (Simon, 1985:303). For example, the Founders of the American republic were cognizant of the relationship between assumptions about human nature and the design of political institutions.[37] We may pay a high price as a society for the formulation of public policy based on an overly restricted and narrowly constructed model of human nature.[38] Public policy fashioned on the assumption of self-interested behavior may beget precisely such behavior when implemented. For this reason, if no other, the self-interest and maximization assumption of rational choice seems ill suited to the task of political explanation as a prelude to political action.

RATIONAL CHOICE AND DEMOCRATIC GOVERNANCE

One further question of importance remains. What effect will the particular concept of human nature embedded in the theory of rational choice have on the prospects for democratic governance? Belief in the individualist, egoistic, self-regarding consumer "results in a deeply incoherent account of democratic citizenship" (Ball, 1988:142) and produces a political system which shows "a constant bias against (a) action as against inaction, and (b) public interests as against private and sectional interests" (Barry, 1965:280). It is to the consideration of these two important problems for normative democratic theory—the transformation of the individual and of the regime—that we now turn.

Citizenship

A polity constituted by self-interested individuals is incompatible, even antithetical, to the promise of democratic citizenship. The qualities of the individual and the vision of political life supported by rational choice theory present severe limits on the transformation of the self-regarding individual into a citizen. This transformation is one of the essential defining characteristics of many classical and contemporary normative theories of democracy. Citizenship is more than a status; it is also a characteristic of how the individual views the world.

Aristotle's *Politica* is a defense of values which make citizenship central to the good and rational life of humankind. This conception of citizenship came to be embodied in the classical republican tradition. The goal of equality among citizens is achieved when there is reciprocity of ruling and being ruled by in turn and where reason rather than hierarchical status is the governing principle.[39] Citizenship in the *polis* was neither an amalgam nor merely an aggregation of individuals. Instead, the *polis* was an association of households rather than individuals, with membership the key precondition of citizenship. Thus civic life was predicated on the individual's membership in a private association. In this conception of citizenship, the individual does not come to public affairs alone, with only his or her own wants, needs, desires, and preferences. Rather, the individual comes to public life as *part of* a social entity.

The values of the Greek civic ethic are a challenge to modern views of rationality grounded on the view of humans as self-centered, egoistic, infinite consumers. Such individuals were not worthy of admiration and certainly were not individuals capable of democratic governance.

Aristotle's view of citizenship reappears throughout the Enlightenment. Rousseau thought that freedom and effective political life were both dependent upon the creation of citizens.[40] A citizen's attachment to the body politic is not through limited interests but rather, constitutes his or her very identity. Civic attachment and identity, which is far more than self-interest, is the key to classical republican government. Indeed, the central core of classical republicanism, which significantly influenced the founding of the American republic, depends upon human political beings and the opportunities for them to actively take part in government.[41] Thomas Paine was not alone in arguing that a republic can flourish only when most citizens are sufficiently virtuous and public-spirited to sacrifice their own interests for the good of the community.[42] Individuals are naturally sociable, bound together by mutual interest and reciprocal dependence. "Common interest regulates their concerns and forms their laws; and the laws which common usage ordains, have a greater influence than the laws of government" (Paine, in Philp, 1989:69). These are the qualities of citizenship necessary for the progress of civilization. The public good cannot be based on the motive of interest; higher motives are essential for the development and creation of a new republic.

Tocqueville found the heart of American democracy in active civic association. He observed that through active involvement in common concerns, the citizen could overcome the sense of relative isolation and powerlessness resulting from the insecurity of life in a society undergoing the pangs of commercialization. Civic associations were the functional equivalent of the classical polity, in which the social differentiation of individuals could be overcome by an investment in public life. Tocqueville feared that with growing social differentiation, individuals would lose their sense of involvement and worth as well as their identity as citizens. If democracy was to flourish, it would require a complex balance between the organizations of the state, the private citizen, and the associations that mediate between citizen and state. The crucial part of this balance was the civic association, which would transform the self-interest of the individual into the common good by making the individual an active, politically aware subject rather than a passive object of state control. Like Rousseau, Tocqueville believed in the educative benefits of a participatory democracy and embraced the traditional civic-republican notion that human dignity requires the freedom that flourishes only in the context of an active civic community.[43]

John Stuart Mill also strongly believed that active citizenship is an essential condition for effective democratic government. Mill defended representative government on the ground that it enables the citizen to develop an active self-helping character through the educative function of participation. "The maximum of the invigorating effect of freedom upon the character is only obtained when the person is or can look forward to becoming a fully privileged citizen" (Mill, 1861/1962:71). Part of the government's responsibility is to train individuals for full involvement in public life and to provide as many venues for their participation as is possible. For Mill, there is a dual educative function to participation: it makes individuals more capable of protecting their own interests and it enhances moral development. It is through the moral instruction afforded from participation that the individual is transformed into a citizen.

Modern rational choice theory owes its intellectual heritage to Smith and to a lesser extent Hume, but most certainly to the generations of utilitarians, such as Jeremy Bentham and James Mill, who were subsequently criticized by John Stuart Mill. The elder Mill and Bentham defended liberal government on the ground that it was efficient. In contrast, John Stuart Mill defended it because freedom of thought and investigation, freedom of discussion, and the freedom of self-controlled moral judgment and action were good in their own right. For Mill, citizens are neither simply voters nor consumers. Contrary to the economic theory of democracy, citizenship is not equivalent to consumership.[44] The efficient maximization of individual happiness—the essential characteristic of early utilitarianism—means little without the benefits to civilization that are brought about by the active participation of morally empowered citizens.

Since the 1950s democratic theory in American has been dominated by a rejection of classical democratic theories on the grounds that they "were normative and value-laden and replaced by a revisionism which aspired to develop scientific and empirical political theory, firmly grounded in the facts of political life" (Pateman, 1970:3). Under the influence of Schumpeter's writings, a revision of democratic theory took place which viewed competitive elections as the main defining characteristic of modern democracy. With their assumption of humans as economic beings and their minimal expectations for political participation, rational choice theories are completely consistent with revisionist theories of democracy.

After a long period of dormancy, in which revisionist theories were subject to sporadic but forceful criticism, a new stream of creative thinking about democracy has emerged to reinvigorate the democratic imagination (see Keane, 1988).[45] While no single vision of democracy has yet to emerge from this new wave,[46] most of these theorists have a renewed commitment to the virtues of political participation and the necessity of citizenship, even as their theories attempt to respond to the conditions endemic to a postindustrial society. These theorists bring to the study of democratic theory a new passion and vision for citizen engagement even as our expectations for such activity continue to plummet. In contrast, revisionist theories struggled to minimize the activities and responsibilities of citizens in order to reconcile normative theory with empirical political reality. Revisionists not only abandoned a commitment to classical ideas of democratic life but also surrendered to the impoverishment of contemporary political life.

These new perspectives on democracy celebrate and require the development of citizenship as a prerequisite to effective democratic governance and self-rule. Robert Bellah and colleagues advise that the "transformation of the state...should focus on bringing a sense of citizenship into the operation of government itself" (1985:211). The communitarianism advocated by Marquand (1988) is best facilitated by a form of "yeoman democracy" which follows the advice of John Stuart Mill and lets citizens learn these values by "doing" politics. The new vision of democracy requires heightened citizen activity through which individuals develop an appreciation for the public good which transcends their individual interests (Green, 1985:269–271). Even Robert

Dahl, a former revisionist, sees new hope and importance for the development of active and informed citizens through the elimination of fundamental economic inequalities (1985) and the widespread utilization of telecommunications technology (1989:338–339).[47]

The new theorists of democratic engagement see the economic theory of democracy as one of their primary targets for criticism. The work of Benjamin Barber (1985, 1988) is probably the most ambitious attempt thus far to defend participatory democracy against its many modern detractors and to set forth a reform agenda to achieve it. The "democracy" that Barber envisions is not the constitutional liberalism of Riker, the minimal participatory practices of Schumpeter, or the political marketplace of Buchanan. Rather, it is a democracy in which "the citizen is an adept participant in the polity, schooled in the arts of social interaction and marked by the capacity to distinguish the requirements of 'we' styles of thinking from those of 'me' styles of thinking" (1988:218–211). What stands directly in the way of this possibility is the liberal individualism of contemporary political theory and practice, so well exemplified and staunchly defended by rational choice theory.[48] The assumptions of rational choice theory which create a framework for research, influence cognition, and inform political practice make it difficult to develop a citizenry which thinks as a "we" when its entire project of social scientific inquiry has a first-person singular understanding of society and politics.

Indeed, one of the threads which link many of the new theories of democratic engagement is the view that economic models of human beings make the development of citizens and democracy extremely problematic and unlikely. While these new theories may not share a common political agenda, they share this common critique. Our inability to make a commitment to anything beyond self-interest weakens commitments to family and community and leads to the self-absorption that is sometimes called narcissism.[49] This is a fate which we seem destined to follow as the theories of self-interested human beings beget both cognition and practice. It is precisely this sense of interconnectedness which is necessary for effective participatory democracy and which is entirely absent from rational choice theory. The transformation of self-regarding individuals into public-spirited citizens is simply not present in the theories of rational choice.[50]

The growth of economic ways of thinking and speaking is a political danger of the greatest significance. In this sense, unrevised, rational choice theory is inimical to the good society. "The world of preference summation . . . excludes things like good will, education to civic virtue, trust, responsible leadership, community and value consensus" (Bluhm, 1987:289). The result is an intellectual cynicism and sterility which makes a mockery of the democratic promise and moral philosophy.[51]

The Public Good

What about the myth of value neutrality and the capacity of the political regime for transformation? It is primarily the assumption of self-interest which drives the engine of rational choice research.[52] The very logic of the self-interested, utility-maximizing, egoistic individual creates a moral presumption in defense of how economic and political goods are distributed in the status quo. [53] What individuals possess by way of economic and political goods or resources is what they should possess. In turn, this justifies the incentive and political force to preserve the status quo.

"A conservative position about collective action starts from the assumed interest of the individual over protecting his existing assets and freedom of action" (Self, 1985:70). This human tendency is then invoked as the much revered "Pareto principle," a principle which makes the redistribution of economic goods as well as significant political change nearly impossible, given the non-comparability of individual utilities. There are few redistributive policies that can be justified as Pareto-efficient. As a result, the very set of assumptions which drive the theory of rational choice creates a strong moral justification and political force for the current distribution of economic and political goods and resources. This often leads some rational choice theorists to a myopic defense of property rights. Buchanan, for example, gives the "status quo a privileged status, since he maintains that nobody can rightfully be deprived (even by legislation) of what he now has" (Barry, 1989:174). Hence, not only can rational choice be easily used to defend the economic and political status quo, but the very assumptions it makes about human nature compel it to do so.

Without a theory of how political preferences are formed[54] and with a conception of the public good that justifies what the system produces rather than what it might or should produce, rational choice theory logically preserves and conserves a liberal, self-interested, individualistic status quo in which regime stability is valued over political change and an emergent public good. Coupled with its narrow and self-regarding empirical conception of human nature, rational choice theory can be used to justify a government system fraught with political apathy and acquiescence and great inequalities in the distribution of economic goods, political power, and privilege.

Rational choice preserves the status quo because it can offer no sense of a good or desirable society beyond procedural principles for articulating and aggregating individual preferences.[55] Riker's critique of populism leads to the conclusion that "no such thing as the 'public interest' exists" (1982:137). For Buchanan, the common good is a product of the clash of self-interested individuals in the political marketplace.[56] Thus, thanks to the hidden hand of the political marketplace, public policy as it is can be labeled the public interest as it ought to be.[57] By either denying that the public interest exists at all or by contending that what the political system produces is the public interest, rational choice theorists have a strong tendency to preserve existent institutional arrangements for America's version of constitutional democracy and the distributional consequences of those arrangements. This should also easily put to rest the disingenuous idea that rational choice theories are value-neutral.

Thus there are three reasons for the conclusion that rational choice theory is driven to preserve and conserve the present political system along with its many distributional implications. By assuming that human nature is motivated by a quest for the maximization of self-interest, rational choice theories must necessarily credit and respect political outcomes in which individuals act to protect their interests—to preserve an advantage or to ameliorate a disadvantage. Absent a theory of preference formation, this behavior becomes an acceptable norm, perhaps to be channeled, but always to be facilitated. Likewise, the rational choice conception of the common good does little more than justify the outcomes of the current political system on the grounds that this system is preferred to alternative systems.[58]

CONCLUSION

The growing importance of rational choice theory has naturally led me to consider the reasons for its rising influence and whether or not those reasons are valid. I have argued that rational choice theory, as an aspirant to the scientific method, remains embedded in the struggle to separate facts from values, a struggle that may ultimately be impossible if human behavior can simply not be translated into the systematic laws of scientific discourse.[59] I have also considered the consequences of assuming that individuals are self-interested, maximizing, egoistic beings. In particular, I have argued that such assumptions may not only serve to misdirect important research strategies but may also beget a cognition of human nature and a political practice which is incompatible with the transformation of self-regarding individuals into democratic citizens. It serves to preserve and conserve a status quo characterized by great inequalities in political opportunities and economic well-being.

Even if the assumptions of rational choice theory were true and mankind was accurately defined by self-interest and maximizing behavior, we must ask whether this is a permanent state and whether political science should be employed to justify it. As advocates of a nor-

mative theory of political behavior, unwittingly or not, rational choice
theorists limit themselves by ignoring the extent to which the polity
shapes human nature and human potential. As a vision of political life,
rational choice theories help to beget a political reality that is neither
salutary nor authentically democratic.

NOTES

1. For the purposes of this paper, rational choice includes and refers to
   those approaches to the study of political life influenced by the
   economic model of human action captured under the various head-
   ings of public choice, social choice, and collective choice.
2. This volume is a veritable smorgasbord of important omissions committed by prevailing rational choice research. The following list is
   by no means all-inclusive: frustration-instigated behavior (Eckstein), time (Eckstein), culture (Eckstein and Almond), emotional
   bases of behavior (Whitehead), cognitive psychology (Rosenberg),
   social values (Downs), alternative conceptualizations of self-interest
   (Scalia), and moral reasoning and other-regarding behavior (Monroe et al.). This list could be easily expanded by considering the
   rigorous attacks on rational choice theory presented by Ball (1988),
   Bluhm (1987), Hindess (1988), MacIntyre (1988), Mcpherson (1973,
   1977), Plamenatz (1973), Ricci (1984), Self (1985), Simon (1985),
   and Slote (1989).
3. The strident tone of this essay is a personal reaction to the unrelent-
   ing ascendancy of rational choice theory in the social sciences and is
   an attempt to provide a strongly worded counterpoint to the many
   friendly criticisms contained in this volume. I make no apology for
   this tone, even though I recognize that it may offend some readers,
   both critics and sympathizers alike. However, I believe it is necessary as an antidote to the inflated claims of many rational choice
   theorists and to their condescending attitude towards alternative
   methods of political inquiry.
4. Peter C. Ordeshook claims that the well-known books by Downs
   (1957), Black (1958), Riker (1962), and Buchanan and Tullock
   (1962) constitute nothing less than "the beginning of modern political theory" (1986:ix). Economist Gary Becker claims that the
   economic approach "is applicable to *all human behaviour*, be it
   behaviour involving money prices or imputed shadow prices,
   repeated or infrequent decisions, large or minor decisions, emotional or mechanical ends, rich or poor persons, men or women,
   adults or children, brilliant or stupid persons, businessmen or politicians, teachers or students" (1976:8). Richard A. Posner, Becker's

former colleague at the University of Chicago and currently a circuit judge on the U.S. Court of Appeals, extends the application of rational choice theory not only to the development of the law but to the determination and rendering of justice. Posner argues that the widely accepted assumption that "people are rational maximizers of their satisfactions" means "it is no longer absurd to suggest that justice, privacy, primitive law, and the constitutional regulation of racial discrimination might be illuminated by the economic approach" (1983:1, 3). In the preface to *The Rise and Decline of Nations*, Mancur Olson provides another set of strong claims for the broad applicability and explanatory power of the economic approach. We can "extend economic theory in a way that not only explains the 'stagflation' and declining growth rates [of recent years] . . . but also provides a partial explanation of a variety of problems usually reserved for other fields—the 'ungovernability' of some modern societies, the British class structure and the Indian class system, the exceptionally unequal distribution of power and income in many developing countries, and even the rise of Western Europe from relative backwardness in the early Middle Ages to dominance of the whole world by the late nineteenth century" (1982:ix).

5. Nobel Laureate James M. Buchanan concludes that the "rapidly accumulating developments in the theory of public choice . . . have all been influential in modifying the way that modern man views government and political process." "This shift in attitudes toward bureaucracies, politicians, and government," alleges Buchanan, has precipitated "various proposals in the United States, at all levels of government, designed to limit the expansion of governmental power" (1984b:20–21). For elaborations on the conservative policy recommendations of the so-called Virginia School of public choice, see Buchanan, 1984a, 1984b; Buchanan and Tullock, 1962; Buchanan and Wagner, 1977.

6. Not everyone shares Abrams's vision of the future. According to William C. Mitchell, the discipline of political science is not conducive to the postulates of rational choice theory. Mitchell observes that "the basic economic postulate of methodological individualism and its corollaries of self-interest and rationality have never had widespread appeal among political scientists" (1988:115).

7. This is a search which begins with Aristotle and variously continues in the writings of Machiavelli, Hobbes, Locke, Madison, Mill, Burgess, Wilson, Seeley, Merriam, Catlin, Easton, and many others. A reference to even a representative sample of the political writings concerned with a "science of politics" would be cumbersome indeed. The interested reader should consult the following to begin

further consideration of this topic: Easton, 1953; Somit and Tanenhaus, 1967; Collini, Winch, and Burrow, 1983; Ricci, 1984; and Almond, 1988.

8. For a provocative examination of this quest, see Seidelman (1985).

9. Almond's respectful, sympathetic, and largely complimentary remarks about rational choice theory contained in the present volume must be juxtaposed with his far more critical assessment made in 1977 (reprinted as 1990a). Almond's (1990a:49) assessment of the "postulated regularities" of political behavior advanced by Riker and Ordeshook is worth citing at length: "Like the regularities of interest to Riker and Ordeshook, these 'presuppositions' are postulated (specified) *a priori*. They replace the contingent aspects of empirical choice and action with causal and lawlike assumptions. Thus choices are reduced to an algorithm specifying a necessary outcome from a necessary utility calculation. The net result of this substantive reduction is a definition of choice that denies the existence of choice! Certainly this conclusion would appear strange if we were not familiar with the current priority of method over substance in political science." What Almond misses here and in his contribution to this volume is the possibility that the particular assumptions of the "reduction" have very important substantive consequences for the possibilities of democratic governance.

10. See Ricci (1984:246–247).

11. One classic call for a relevant political science is Easton (1969).

12. See Edelman (1988:3–4).

13. A similar explanation is offered by Ricci: "Rational models of man serve liberalism by obviating the need for gaining agreement to principles of collective decisions even as they speak of social choice, by saying that people may be left free to make up their own minds as to whatever course they might wish public policy to take. The liberal tradition says very little about wise and proper directions for public policy ... What liberalism offers, instead, is a vague but comfortable notion that reason will prevail, that people will be rational enough to decide what their community needs and reasonable enough to work together so as to fulfill those needs" (1984:247).

14. For a comparison of the different schools of public choice, see Mitchell (1988).

15. For a lively and forceful attack on Riker's brand of rational choice and resulting liberal democracy, see William T. Bluhm (1987). Also consider Weale (1982).

16. It is more than a coincidence that rational choice theorists frequently adopt the limiting and narrow view of democracy advocated by the revisionist theories of democracy. See Pateman (1970) and Petracca (1986).

17. We do not have time to fully consider whether or not a science of politics is even possible or, for that matter, desirable. However, since the view that a science of politics is both possible and desirable is largely assumed by the vast proportion of the discipline and especially by those adhering to the rational choice approach, a few critical words are in order. It may well be the case that the most important and intrinsically interesting aspects of politics can be neither studied scientifically nor reduced to law-like formulations. In contrast to those who "believe that the fortuitous, the surprising, the unpredicted, arise in politics only because our knowledge of political motions is less adequate than our knowledge of planetary motions," A. C. MacIntyre reminds us that "in political life *fortuna*, the bitch goddess of unpredictability, has never been dethroned." We are advised by MacIntyre: "To any stock of maxims derived from empirically founded generalisations the student of politics must always add one more: 'And do not be surprised if in the event things turn out otherwise'" (1973:228). This view is shared by democratic theorist John Hallowell: "Because man is able to choose between alternative ways of acting and to deliberate upon that choice the behavior of human beings is never as predictable as the behavior of atoms" (1954:104). If political science is to be a "science" at all, it must be a practical one, more like engineering than physics. The problems presented by human beings for scientific study is one we share with all the social sciences. Claude Levi-Strauss expressed it well: "What we as social scientists are trying to do is only to offer better explanations—which cannot be said to be true or false—than those accepted before" (1979:16). Beyond the limitations on a science of politics, there may be a great danger in turning politics into a science because of the potentially disastrous consequences it could have on the future treatment and transformation of human nature. If we guess wrong about human nature, then the political solutions advocated as a result could be completely useless at best and harmful in the worst case.

18. For appropriate examples, see Lowell (1889:8); Catlin (1927/1964:325; 1962); Merriam (1925/1970).

19. Additional examples are probably not needed to evidence the point that the fact-value distinction is an essential part of how the social sciences define themselves. However, the curious reader may also wish to consult Brecht (1959); Van Dyke (1960); Riker, (1962); Pool (1967); Kruskal (1982); or Ricci (1984) for further illustrations.

20. Also see Strauss (1952) and the indictment of empirical theory by Eric Voegelin (1952).

21. For discussions of Pareto optimality, see Riker and Ordeshook (1973:92); Downs (1957:170–198); Mueller (1979:185–206); Fishburn (1973:83–84); Ordeshook (1986:61–77); Brams (1985:156–

157); Rikers (1982:201–202) as well as the extensive discussion in Barry and Hardin (1982:139–142).

22. See Self (1985:75–78).
23. See Whitehead and Almond within.
24. See Almond (1988); Ball (1988); Hindess (1988); MacIntyre (1988); Plamenatz (1973); and Self (1985).
25. According to Karl R. Popper, "the task of social theory is to construct and to analyze our sociological models carefully in descriptive or nominalist terms, that is to say, in terms of individuals, of their attitudes, expectations, relations, etc.—a postulate which may be called 'methodological individualism'" (1957:136). Popper is probably the best single source on this approach to social theory. However, like so many great innovators, Popper is much less certain of the virtues of deductive reasoning than contemporary theorists, who appear unfamiliar with the subtle nature of Popper's analysis.
26. See Hindess (1988:96).
27. See Hindess (1988:36–39).
28. See Bluhm (1987); Strauss (1952, 1973).
29. These examples are presented neither to bludgeon nor persuade the reader. Rather, they are presented to counter the claims by rational choice theorists that the theory has moved away from the economic person model of microeconomics. These citations evidence how pervasive and deeply rooted the self-interest assumption is throughout the realm of rational choice theory.
30. Quoted in Collini, Winch, and Burrow (1983:30).
31. For further examples, see Mitchell (1971:239); Fiorina and Noll (1978:239); Laver (1981:9); Fiorina (1984:84); Mueller (1984:23); Brams (1985:2).
32. For a theoretical perspective, see Barry (1989:285) and for an empirical account, see Marquand (1988:262–265).
33. There are of course many other visions of human nature, some of which will be discussed below. For further discussion, see Bellah et al. (1985); Diamond (1986); Diggins (1986); Duncan (1983); Hallowell (1954); Hofstadter (1986); Jordon (1989); Kelman (1987); Strauss (1952, 1989).
34. On the hidden dimensions of political power, see Petracca (1986:Chs. 2–3).
35. See Simon (1985:303) and Hindess (1988:4).
36. Allison's study of the Cuban missile crisis shows that models not only conceptualize the world in different ways; they conceptualize and represent altogether different worlds or political realities (see Scaff and Ingram, 1987:631). As a result, it is possible that the assumptions embedded in the theory of rational choice also shape political cognition and political behavior.

37. See Diamond (1986); Diggins (1986); Hofstadter (1986); and articles in Grofman and Wittman (1989).

38. The assumption of self-interest contained in the theories of rational choice begets self-interested political behavior. The social, political, and psychological phenomena explicated by Lasch (1979, 1984) and Sennett (1978) are less surprising and far more comprehensible when we view them as reflective of a social theory that sees human nature in terms of self-regarding, egoistic, maximizing, and optimizing individuals.

39. Ironically, in appropriating the notion of "rational action" to the instrumental advance of self-interest, rational choice theorists have done a disservice to the rationalist tradition. As Peter Self explains, "This tradition stresses the significant role of reason over the harmonization of interests and the responsible exercise of individual freedom. Stripped of these conditions, the individual is a bundle of desires and tastes, not a person capable of meaningful choice" (1985:190).

40. Maurice Keens-Soper explains Rousseau's position on the creation of citizens outlined in *The Social Contract*: "The body politic is thus a man-made association of intense, austere, and indivisible unity. It is created in a momentary act of unequivocal self-transformation upon whose constituency its character and continuation is utterly dependent. *The bonds of union thus created rest in the civic virtue of men become citizens.* In the act of association men negate their 'natural' selves by giving themselves wholly new natures of an artificial and social kind. *A citizen is a fresh kind of man* whose identity depends on the state" (1989:179; emphasis added).

41. For a discussion of the connection between classical republicanism and the American founding, see Anastaplo (1989); Diggins (1986); Epstein (1984); and various essays in Horwitz (1986).

42. See Philp (1989:38).

43. This discussion of Tocqueville relies heavily on Sullivan (1986).

44. See Ball (1988:135).

45. Here I am referring to works by Barber (1985, 1988); Bellah et al. (1985; Bobbio (1987a, 1987b); Dahl (1985); Duncan (1983); Green (1985); Harris (1983); essays by Cochrane, Rowbotham, McLean, and Burnheim in a collection edited by Held and Pollitt (1986); Jordon (1989); Mansbridge (1983); Marquand (1988); Miller (1983); Sullivan (1986); Unger (1983, 1987) as well as the important earlier contributions of Bachrach (1967); Cahn (1961); Macpherson (1973, 1977); M. Margolis (1979); Pateman (1970); and Plamenatz (1973).

46. Indeed, many of these works offer very different analyses and prescriptions for democracy. However, they all seem to share an unapologetic commitment to democratic life and a commitment to

do something about it. While we might refer to this growing body of literature as a theory of democratic engagement, in contrast I would characterize democratic revisionism as a theory of civic abandonment and surrender.

47. Active citizenship is required for a reconstructed public philosophy of civic republicanism (Sullivan, 1986:xii); the enhancement of democratic life (Duncan, 1983:203); an active social democracy (Harris, 1983:233); and "empowered democracy," whereby social life will be reconstructed in the authentic image of liberal politics (Unger, 1983:41).

48. Of course, we can easily imagine how rational choice theorists might respond to Barber's indictment and vision. The enlightened thinking of Steven Brams comes most easily to mind: "In my opinion, it is better to have an understanding of what values are at stake, which rational-choice models can clarify, than to engage in a fruitless debate over the oft-touted virtues of democracy" (1985:205–206). Barber's work of course is far more than a celebration of democracy's virtues; it is a plan for the development of strong democracy informed by a vision of a democratic polity. That is far more than can be said about the writings of most rational choice theorists—including the prolific, but largely sterile, writings of Brams.

49. See Sullivan (1986:222).

50. To the contrary, such a transformation, as Barber points out, "requires an understanding of citizenship more vigorous and mutualistic than the one favored by modern social scientists, which identified citizens as private agents pursuing private interests in a political marketplace" (1988:201).

51. As Cropsey put it, now three decades ago, "[T]he self-regarding man is, as such, the opposite of the citizen" (1977:39).

52. I agree with Slote (1989), Bluhm (1987), Bellah et al. (1985), and others who argue that there is really not much of a moral difference between the assumptions of self-interest, maximization, or optimization, all of which create and encourage individuals who are self-regarding and insensitive to the interconnected nature of social existence.

53. A distribution which, by many accounts, is not very equitable. See Page (1983) and Phillips (1990).

54. Rational choice does not have a theory of preference formation. Instead it accepts people's desires as given. As a result, it can explain neither how individual cognition is transformed nor how political regimes are transformed. See Simon (1985); Hector (1987); Plamenatz (1973:150); Ricci (1984:241).

55. See Self (1985:178) and Ricci (1984:243).

56. "The challenge to us, " says Buchanan "is one of constructing, or reconstructing, a political order that will channel the self-serving behavior of participants towards the common good in a manner that comes as close as possible to that described for us by Adam Smith with respect to the economic order" (1978:17). This notion bears a striking resemblance to Dahl's (1956) discussion of "Madisonian democracy."

57. See Ricci (1984:242). Tullock (1970:32–33) takes a position similar to Buchanan.

58. Since threats do exist to the stability of the American regime—from the populists, according to Riker, and from the Leviathan state, according to Buchanan—rational choice theory has also been invoked to support the political agenda of neoconservatism. While it would be a mistake to identify rational choice analysis with some version of the New Right, there is a strong and disturbing tendency by rational choice theorists to deploy their "scientific" prowess on behalf of the New Right's political agenda. Examples to illustrate this point are uncomfortably abundant. There is Riker's (1980) support of fiscal reform at the constitutional level; Buchanan and Wagner's (1977) attack on deficit spending; Buchanan's (1977) defense of property rights; Olson's (1982) call for open and competitive markets; and the "Virginians'" principled rejection of governmental intervention in matters of regulation and social policy (see Mitchell, 1988:106–110).

59. This is probably as it should be. To view humankind as nothing more than a bundle of wants, desires, and preferences, all of which can be explained and predicted by a set of behavioral laws, is to deny the essence of humanity. This essence is as unpredictable as it may be infinitely perfectable. Because we are thinking, self-reflective beings, the rigid formalisms and narrow motivational assumptions of rational choice theory are ill-suited for the purpose of understanding political life.

REFERENCES

Abrams, R. (1980). *Foundations of Political Analysis: An Introduction to the Theory of Collective Choice.* New York: Columbia University Press.

Allison, G. T. (1971). *Essence of Decision.* Boston: Little, Brown.

Almond, G. A. (1988). "Separate Tables: Schools and Sects in Political Science," *PS: Politics and Political Science,* 21:828–842.

———. (1990a). "Clouds, Clocks, and the Study of Politics." In G. A. Almond (Ed.), *A Discipline Divided*. Beverly Hills: Sage. Pp. 32–65.

———. (1990b). "Rational Choice Theory and the Social Sciences." In G. A. Almond (Ed.), *A Discipline Divided*. Beverly Hills: Sage. Pp. 117–137.

Anastaplo, G. (1989). *The Constitution of 1787*. Baltimore: The Johns Hopkins Press.

Arrow, K. J. (1963). *Social Choice and Individual Values* (2nd ed.). New Haven: Yale University Press.

Bachrach, P. (1967). *The Theory of Democratic Elitism*. Boston: Little, Brown.

Ball, T. (1988). "The Economic Reconstruction of Democratic Discourse." In T. Ball (Ed.), *Transforming Political Discourse*. Oxford: Blackwell. Pp. 122–142.

Barber, B. (1985). *Strong Democracy*. Berkeley: University of California Press.

———. (1988). *The Conquest of Politics*. Princeton: Princeton University Press.

Barry, B. (1965). *Political Argument*. London: Routledge and Kegan Paul.

———. (1978). *Sociologists, Economists, and Democracy*. Chicago: University of Chicago Press.

———. (1989). *Theories of Justice: A Treatise on Social Justice*. Berkeley: University of California Press.

Barry, B., and Hardin, R. (Eds.). (1982). *Rational Man and Irrational Society*. Beverly Hills: Sage.

Becker, G. S. (1976). *The Economic Approach to Human Behavior*. Chicago: University of Chicago Press.

Bellah, R. N.; Madsen, R.; Sullivan, W. M.; Swidler, A.; and Tipton, S. M. (1985). *Habits of the Heart*. New York: Harper & Row.

Bergner, J. T. (1981). *The Origin of Formalism in Social Science*. Chicago: University of Chicago Press.

Black, D. (1958). *The Theory of Committees and Elections*. Cambridge: Cambridge University Press.

Bluhm, W. T. (1987). "Liberalism as the Aggregation of Individual Preferences: Problems of Coherence and Rationality in Social Choice." In K. L. Deutsch and W. Soffer (Eds.), *The Crisis of Liberal Democracy: A Straussian Perspective*. Albany: State University of New York Press. Pp. 269–296.

Bobbio, N. (1987a). *The Future of Democracy*. Minneapolis: University of Minnesota Press.

_____. (1987b). *Which Socialism?* Minneapolis: University of Minnesota Press.

Brams, S. J. (1985). *Rational Politics*. Washington, DC: Congressional Quarterly Press.

Brecht, A. (1959). *Political Theory: The Foundations of Twentieth Century Political Thought*. Princeton: Princeton University Press.

Buchanan, J. M. (1977). *Freedom in Constitutional Contract*. College Station: Texas A & M Press.

_____. (1978). "From Private Preferences to Public Philosophy: The Development of Public Choice." In *The Economics of Politics*. West Sussex: Institute of Economic Affairs. Pp. 1–20.

_____. (1984a). "Constitutional Restrictions on the Power of Government." In J. M. Buchanan and R. D. Tollison (Eds.), *The Theory of Public Choice—II*. Ann Arbor: University of Michigan Press. Pp. 439–452.

_____. (1984b). "Politics Without Romance: A Study of Positive Public Choice Theory and Its Normative Implications." In J. M. Buchanan and R. D. Tollison (Eds.), *The Theory of Public Choice—II*. Ann Arbor: University of Michigan Press. Pp. 11–22.

Buchanan, J. M., and Tullock, G. (1962). *The Calculus of Consent: Logical Foundations of Constitutional Democracy*. Ann Arbor: University of Michigan Press.

Buchanan, J. M., and Wagner, R. E. (1977). *Democracy in Deficit*. New York: Academic Press.

Cahn, E. (1961). *The Predicament of Democratic Man*. New York: Dell.

Catlin, G. E. G. (1962). *Systematic Politics*. Toronto: University of Toronto Press.

_____. (1964). *The Scope and Method of Politics*. Hamden, CT: Archon Books. (Originally published in 1927.)

Collini, S.; Winch, D.; and Burrow, J. (1983). *That Noble Science of Politics*. Cambridge: Cambridge University Press.

Cropsey, J. (1977). "On the Relation of Political Science and Economics." In J. Cropsey (Ed.), *Political Philosophy and the Issues of Politics*. Chicago: University of Chicago Press. Pp. 32–43.

Dahl, R. A. (1956). *A Preface to Democratic Theory*. Chicago: University of Chicago Press.

_____. (1963). *Modern Political Analysis*. Englewood Cliffs, NJ: Prentice-Hall.

_____. (1985). *A Preface to Economic Democracy*. Berkeley: University of California Press.

_____. (1989). *Democracy and Its Critics*. New Haven: Yale University Press.

Diamond, M. (1986). "Ethics and Politics: The American Way." In R. H. Horwitz (Ed.), *The Moral Foundations of the American Republic* (3rd ed.). Charlottesville: University of Virginia Press. Pp. 75–108.

Diggins, J. P. (1986). *The Lost Soul of American Politics*. Chicago: University of Chicago Press.

Downs, A. (1957). *An Economic Theory of Democracy*. New York: Harper & Row.

_____. (1988). *The Evolution of Modern Democracy*. Unpublished manuscript. Brookings Institution, Washington, DC.

Duncan, G. (1983). "Human Nature and Radical Democratic Theory." In G. Duncan (Ed.), *Democratic Theory and Practice*. Cambridge: Cambridge University Press. Pp. 187–203.

Easton, D. (1953). *The Political System*. New York: Alfred A. Knopf.

_____. (1967). *A Framework for Political Analysis*. Englewood Cliffs, NJ: Prentice-Hall.

_____. (1969). "The New Revolution in Political Science." *American Political Science Review*, 63:1051–1061.

Edelman, M. (1988). *Constructing the Political Spectacle*. Chicago: University of Chicago Press.

Elster, J. (1986). "Introduction." In J. Elster (Ed.), *Rational Choice*. New York: New York University Press. Pp. 1–33.

Epstein, D. F. (1984). *The Political Theory of the Federalists*. Chicago: University of Chicago Press.

Fiorina, M. P. (1984). "Formal Models in Political Science." In H. Asher, H. F. Weisberg, J. H. Kessel, and W. P. Shively (Eds.), *Theory-Building and Data Analysis in the Social Sciences*. Knoxville: University of Tennessee Press. Pp. 67–93.

Fiorina, M., and Noll, R. (1978). "Voters, Bureaucrats and Legislators." *Journal of Public Economics*, 9:239–254.

Fishburn, P. C. (1973). *The Theory of Social Choice*. Princeton: Princeton University Press, 1973.

Fried, C. (1970). *An Anatomy of Values*. Cambridge, MA: Harvard University Press.

Germino, D. (1972). *Machiavelli to Marx: Modern Western Political Thought*. Chicago: University of Chicago Press.

Green, P. (1985). *Retrieving Democracy*. Totowa, NJ: Rowman and Allanheld.

Grofman, B., and Wittman, D. E. (Eds.). (1989). *The Federalist Papers and the New Institutionalism*. New York: Agathon.

Hallowell, J. H. (1954). *The Moral Foundation of Democracy*. Chicago: University of Chicago Press.

Hardin, R. (1982). *Collective Action*. Baltimore: Johns Hopkins University Press.

Harris, D. (1983). "Returning the Social to Democracy." In G. Duncan (Ed.), *Democratic Theory and Practice*. Cambridge: Cambridge University Press. Pp. 218–234.

Hector, M. (1987). *Principles of Group Solidarity*. Berkeley: University of California Press.

Held, D. (1987). *Models of Democracy*. Stanford: Stanford University Press.

Held, D., and Pollitt, C. (Eds.). (1986). *New Forms of Democracy*. Beverly Hills: Sage.

Hindess, B. (1988). *Choice, Rationality and Social Choice*. London: Unwin Hyman.

Hofstadter, R. (1986). "The Founding Fathers: An Age of Realism." In R. H. Horwitz (ed.), *The Moral Foundations of the American Republic* (3rd ed.). Charlottesville: University of Virginia Press. Pp. 62–74.

Horwitz, R. H. (Ed.). (1986). *The Moral Foundations of the American Republic* (3rd ed.). Charlottesville: University of Virginia Press.

Isaak, A. C. (1981). *The Scope and Methods of Political Science* (3rd ed.). Homewood, IL: Dorsey.

Jordon, B. (1989). *The Common Good: Citizenship, Morality and Self-Interest*. London: Blackwell.

Keane, J. (1988). *Democracy and Civil Sciety*. London: Verso.

Kelman, S. (1987). *Making Public Policy*. New York: Basic Books.

Keens-Soper, M. (1989). "Jean-Jacques Rousseau: The Social Contract." In M. Forsyth and M. Keens-Soper (Eds.)., *A Guide to Political Classics*. Oxford: Oxford University Press. Pp. 171–202.

Kruskal, W. H. (Ed.). (1982). *The Social Sciences: Their Nature and Uses*. Chicago: University of Chicago Press.

Lasch, C. (1979). *The Culture of Narcissism*. New York: W. W. Norton.

———. (1984). *The Minimal Self*. New York: W. W. Norton.

Laver, M. (1981). *The Politics of Private Desires: The Guide to the Politics of Rational Choice*. Middlesex: Penguin.

Lowell, A. L. (1889). *Essays on Government*. Boston: Houghton Mifflin.

MacIntyre, A. C. (1973). "Is a Science of Comparative Politics Possible?" In P. G. Lewis and D. C. Potter (Eds.), *The Practice of Comparative Politics*. London: Longman. Pp. 219–237.

———. (1988). *Whose Justice? Which Rationality?* South Bend, IN: Notre Dame Press.

McLean, I. (1987) *Public Choice: An Introduction*. Oxford: Blackwell.

Macpherson, C.B. (1973). *Democratic Theory: Essays in Retrieval*. Oxford: Clarendon Press.

———. (1977). *The Life and Times of Liberal Democracy*. Oxford: Oxford University Press.

Mansbridge, J. J. (1983). *Beyond Adversary Democracy*. Chicago: University of Chicago Press.

March, J., and Olsen, J. (1984). "The New Institutionalism: Organizational Factors in Political Life." *American Political Science Review*, 78:734–750.

Margolis, H. (1982). *Selfishness, Altruism and Rationality*. Cambridge: Cambridge University Press.

Margolis, M. (1979). *Viable Democracy*. Middlesex: Penguin.

Marquand, D. (1988). "Preceptoral Politics, Yeoman Democracy and the Enabling State." *Government and Opposition*, 23:261–275.

Merriam, C. E. (1970). *New Aspects of Politics* (3rd ed.). Chicago: University of Chicago Press. (Originally published in 1925.)

Mill, J. S. (1962). *Considerations on Representative Government*. Chicago: Regnery. (Originally published in 1861.)

Miller, D. (1983). "The Competitive Model of Democracy." In G. Duncan (Ed.), *Democratic Theory and Practice*. Cambridge: Cambridge University Press. Pp. 133–155.

Miller, N. (1983). "Pluralism and Social Choice." *American Political Science Review*, 77:734–747.

Mitchell, W. C. (1971). *Public Choice in America*. Chicago: Markham.

_____. (1988). "Virginia, Rochester, and Bloomington: Twenty-Five Years of Public Choice and Political Science." *Public Choice*, 56:101–119.

Mueller, D. C. (1979). *Public Choice*. Cambridge: Cambridge University Press.

_____. (1984). "Public Choice: A Survey." In J. M. Buchanan and R. D. Tollison (Eds.), *The Theory of Public Choice—II*. Ann Arbor: University of Michigan Press. Pp. 23–67.

Olson, M., Jr. (1965). *The Logic of Collective Action*. Cambridge, MA: Harvard University Press.

_____. (1982). *The Rise and Decline of Nations*. New Haven: Yale University Press.

Ordeshook, P. C. (1986). *Game Theory and Political Theory*. Cambridge: Cambridge University Press.

Page, B. I. (1983). *Who Gets What from Government*. Berkeley: University of California Press.

Pateman, C. (1970). *Participation and Democratic Theory*. Cambridge: Cambridge University Press.

Petracca, M. P. (1986). *Agenda-Building and National Policy Formation*. Doctoral dissertation, University of Chicago.

Phillips, K. (1990). *The Politics of Rich and Poor*. New York: Random House.

Philp, M. (1989). *Paine*. Oxford: Oxford University Press.

Plamenatz, J. (1973). *Democracy and Illusion*. London: Longman.

Pool, I. de Sola, (Ed.). (1967). *Contemporary Political Science: Towards Empirical Theory*. New York: McGraw-Hill.

Popper, K. (1957). *The Poverty of Historicism*. New York: Harper & Row.

Posner, R. A. (1977). *Economic Analysis of Law* (2nd ed.). Cambridge, MA: Harvard University Press.

_____. (1983). *The Economics of Justice*. Cambridge, MA: Harvard University Press.

Rawls, J. (1971). *A Theory of Justice*. Cambridge, MA: Harvard University Press, Belknap Press.

Ricci, D. M. (1984). *The Tragedy of Political Science*. New Haven: Yale University Press.

Riker, W. H. (1962). *The Theory of Political Coalitions*. New Haven: Yale University Press.

_____ . (1980). "Constitutional Limitations as Self-Denying Ordinances." In W. S. Moore and R. G. Penner (Eds.), *The Constitution and the Budget, 85–90*. Washington, DC: American Enterprise Institute.

_____ . (1982). *Liberalism Against Populism*. San Francisco: W. H. Freeman.

_____ . (1986). *The Art of Political Manipulation*. New Haven: Yale University Press.

Riker, W. H., and Ordeshook, P. C. (1973). *An Introduction to Positive Political Theory*. Englewood Cliffs, NJ: Prentice-Hall.

Schumpeter, J. A. (1975). *Capitalism, Socialism, and Democracy*. New York: Harper Colophon Books. (Originally published 1942.)

Scaff, L. A. and Ingram, H. (1987). "Politics, Policy, and Public Choice: A Critique and Proposal." *Polity, 19*:613–636.

Seidelman, R. (1985). *Disenchanted Realists*. Albany: State University of New York Press.

Self, P. (1985). *Political Theories of Modern Government*. London: Allen and Unwin.

Sen, A. (1977). "Rational Fools: A Critique of the Behavioral Foundations of Economic Theory." *Philosophy and Public Affairs, 6*:53–89.

_____ . (1979). "Utilitarianism and Welfarism." *Journal of Philosophy, 76*:463–489.

Sennett, R. (1978). *The Fall of Public Man*. New York: Vintage Books.

Simon, H. (1985). "Human Nature in Politics: The Dialogue of Psychology with Political Science." *American Political Science Review, 79*:293–304.

Slote, M. (1989). *Beyond Optimizing*. Cambridge, MA: Harvard University Press.

Smith, A. (1976). *The Wealth of Nations*. Edwin Cannan (Ed.). Chicago: University of Chicago Press. (Originally published in 1775.)

Somit, A., and Tanenhaus, J. (1967). *The Development of Political Science*. Boston: Allyn and Bacon.

Strauss, L. (1952). *The Political Philosophy of Hobbes*. Chicago: University of Chicago Press.

_____ . (1953). *Natural Right and History*. Chicago: University of Chicago Press.

_____ . (1962). "An Epilogue." In H. Storing (Ed.). *Essays on the Scientific Study of Politics*. New York: Holt, Rinehart and Winston.

_____. (1973). *What is Political Philosophy?* Westport, CT: Greenwood.

_____. (1989). *The Rebirth of Classical Political Rationalism.* Selected and introduced by T. L. Pangle. Chicago: University of Chicago Press.

Sullivan, W. M. (1986). *Reconstructing Public Philosophy.* Berkeley: University of California Press.

Tarcov, N., and Pangle, T. (1987). "Epilogue." In L. Strauss and J. Cropsey (Eds.). *History of Political Philosophy.* Chicago: University of Chicago Press. Pp. 907–938.

Tullock, G. (1970). *Private Wants, Public Needs.* New York: Basic Books.

Unger, R. M. (1983). *The Critical Legal Studies Movement.* Cambridge, MA: Harvard University Press.

_____. (1987). *False Necessity.* Cambridge: Cambridge University Press.

Van Dyke, V. (1960). *Political Science: A Philosophical Analysis.* Homewood, IL: Dorsey.

Voegelin, E. (1952). *The New Science of Politics: An Introductory Essay.* Chicago: University of Chicago Press.

Weale, A. (1982). "Social Choice Versus Populism, An Interpretation of Riker's Political Theory." *British Journal of Political Science,* *14*:369–385.

Wolin, S. (1969). "Political Theory as a Vocation." *American Political Science Review,* *63*:1062–1082.

Chapter
8

Self-Interest and Democratic Theory

Laura J. Scalia

Rational choice theorists depict democracy as a process of authoritative interactions linking self-interested leaders to self-interested constituents. In this view, rational citizens demand policies in their particular interests and rational leaders execute these demands in order to ensure reelection. Precisely because everyone acts in his or her own interest, policies reflect the people's articulated concerns. Interest-motivated behavior, considered as the foundation of democratic political society, serves the beneficial function of ensuring an electoral connection.

Such a role for self-interest in democracy stands in stark contrast to early nineteenth-century American political thought, which described such unrestricted self-interest as a detriment to democracy, one which would undermine self-government and individual rights. I will argue here that a consideration of these nineteenth-century arguments exposes a critical problem in rational actor explanations of democratic politics. The rational choice assumption that widespread self-interest is natural carries a value connotation which, although "useful," also contains negative consequences. A government which mirrors private concerns is by definition a government susceptible to factional politics. The nineteenth-century arguments about self-interest and democracy clearly suggest that such factionalism can undermine the legitimacy of democracy. Basically, then, while rational choice theory's positioning of self-interest at the core of democratic behavior may "predict" the electoral connection and may occasionally describe actual politics, it also undermines the legitimacy of democracy.

In the first section below, I describe how rational choice theorists describe democracy since they represent a core group which categorically relies on self-interest as *the* motivation behind political behavior in democracies. I then explain why the nineteenth-century American debate over ratification of state constitutions constitutes an appropriate critical evaluation of rational actor theory. Next, I compare rational choice theory to earlier American perspectives on self-interest in democracy. I close by suggesting why the rational choice assumption of self-interest is undesirable as the *sole* foundation of democratic theory. Essentially, I argue that rule by the self-interested means the majority rules for itself. The majority *may* consider the whole; but, by assumption, such consideration is an unexpected, unnecessary addition, not a core part of democratic theory. Given this, I conclude that rational choice theorists are restricted to a narrow view of what democracy can accomplish *vis-à-vis* the public good. Their chosen assumption, derived from economic theory and not political reality, may explain adversarial politics, but it ignores other critical aspects, such as the unitary, the communitarian, or the dialogue aspect of politics.[1] Certainly, while self-interest may explain an important electoral connection, this explanatory power should not drive analysts into a blind embrace of self-interest as the founding motivation of citizenship in a democracy. As nineteenth-century American political thought suggests, such a basis is antidemocratic.

SELF-INTEREST AND DEMOCRACY: THE RATIONAL CHOICE PARADIGM

Rational choice theorists borrow economic assumptions and offer a straightforward model of democracy. They describe democracy as a procedural government wherein rational, egoistic, utility maximizers interact with each other and establish "democratic" relations of power. At the heart of political rationality is the assumption of self-interest. Self-interest motivates all voters and political candidates, and it explains why political alliances exist between the people and their leaders.[2] Self-interest drives voters to choose candidates closest to their particular preferences and political candidates to act as best they can to please constituents. According to the theory, self-interest connects leaders and voters.

While not all rational choice theorists agree how closely their model of democracy mirrors the policies voters personally prefer, all imply that it is self-interest which drives leaders to pay attention to their constituents in some nontrivial way. One group of rational choice theorists, for which Downs is the archetypical spokesman, argue that leaders' perpetual personal concern for reelection allows voters to have their policy preferences transformed *directly* into policies. Because candidates seek to ensure their narrow private concerns (i.e., election and reelection), they forever remain attentive to constituent policy demands. Otherwise, rational voters would simply choose another, more economically rational candidate who would pay attention to their demands.[3] According to the theory, then, because candidates follow an exceptionally narrow private interest,[4] democratic government stays in touch with its people's demands. While this model retains some proponents, most rational choice theorists have since admitted several reasons why the electoral process cannot produce candidates who choose policies directly mirroring constituent preferences, even if it were in their best interest to do so.[5] Riker, among others, takes this view.[6] He denies that candidates can know voter preferences. And even if they somehow ascertained their constituents' preferences on any given issue, they still would not be able to select the most popularly preferred policy. According to this revised rational choice paradigm, neither the democratic procedure nor any other can transform preferences into policies. Popular elections can only veto past legislative polices, can only bar unwanted incumbents from reelection.[7] Although this weakens the extent of the electoral connection between leaders and their voters originally postulated, this type of critique does not negate the supposed effect of self-interested leadership behavior. Yes, the people make choices among leaders who cannot possibly reflect all their current demands; but because self-interested leaders mainly want their constituents to evaluate them more favorably than opponents, over the course of their term they must try and support some of the people's preferences, even if not a strict majority on each and every issue. Since this revised model still maintains that narrowly self-interested incumbents want reelection, surely it assumes that leaders act with this reelection idea in mind, which thereby means new candidates (and old) must align themselves with policies constituents do not reject totally. On the whole, these revisionists may be correct; voters may be choosing among *persons* and not policy platforms. Nevertheless, their evaluation of any given person will never be wholly divorced from his or her policies. This means that even in the revised rational model, the assumption of self-interested candidate behavior implies that rationally driven democratic governments reflect voter preferences in some nontrivial way, albeit not as direct a reflection as originally postulated.[8]

Rational choice theorists similarly assume that the electoral connection arises because voters act in their own self-interest. Citizens have an interest in choosing candidates who have taken policy positions similar to their own. No rational actor would want to help elect someone with policy goals in opposition to his or her own self-interest. Rational voters reject candidates who ignore their preferences and choose candidates who best reflect their demands. These voters knowingly act to form a government in their interests. In other words, because rational citizens care about whom they elect, only candidates who appeal to their constituents' demands (i.e., only rational candidates) gain and retain office.

As with candidates, self-interest among the electorate ensures that government pays attention to many of the demands its people articulate; it ensures that procedural government resembles a democracy.

Oddly enough, rational choice theorists generally do not discuss the logical consequence of an electoral connection based on self-interest.[9] If voters naturally seek leaders that reflect their *self-centered* demands, what does this say for the type of policies that emerge? In the case of the original rational choice democratic model which Downs describes, leaders blindly follow the requests of their constituents; they ignore the content or consequences of the concerns they follow. Rational leaders unquestioningly submit to the policy advice of their constituents, constituents who, by assumption, act solely in self-interest. In the case of the revised model which Riker describes, the democratic process permits voters, regardless of how personally driven their interests are, to decide who stays in positions of power. Leaders cannot act precisely as voters demand, but they necessarily act so as to convince a majority of self-interested constituents that they deserve reelection. In both cases, the rationality of the vote process maintains power for those leaders who somehow or other appeal to the self-interest of their people. Both models logically imply that leaders follow demands originating solely from self-interested voters. Both see voters not as public-spirited citizens concerned with policy consequences for the whole but as private-minded individuals concerned with the consequences policies have on themselves. Thus, according to the rational choice model, government enacts policies strictly in the self-interest of some subset of the constituents.

Of course, when discussing behavior, rational choice theorists do not assume that people only act upon self-interest, narrowly understood. They do not expect voters to rely solely on their egoistic, particularized concerns in every policy situation. For example, Downs specifically denies that he means selfishness in this narrow sense.[10] Likewise, when Buchanan and Tullock discuss self-interest, they speak of self-interest "broadly conceived."[11] In general, rational choice theory allows for benevolent actions, provided they are pursued for an individual's self-interest.[12] Thus, when rational choice theorists say leaders will follow their self-interested constituents, they do not assume that every resulting policy will reflect narrow concerns. Whenever a majority of voters find it in their enlightened self-interest to demand policies or leaders that reflect the good of the nation, rational government will serve collective goods. At the same time, the theory does not distinguish between this and more narrow-minded actions. Whenever a majority of voters act in purely selfish ways, rational government will serve particularized egoistic concerns. Both types of self-interest motivate citizens in politics and thereby have a legitimate place in the electoral process. Whether political actors behave altruistically or egoistically may affect policy content but not the overall rational choice democratic paradigm.[13] For rational choice theorists, interest drives politics, whether that interest is narrow or other-regarding is beside the point.

I find this moral equation of self and other regarding interests, which rational choice theorists make but do not critically assess, detrimental to democratic theory. Their model assumes that every political citizen acts only for him- or herself. The accidental inclusion of the welfare of others in that interest calculation is largely secondary and in part irrelevant. Citizens consider the welfare of others *only* to the extent that welfare benefits themselves. Although postulated as a simple given, this assumption, upon which their whole theory rests, is faulty in a number of ways. First, as other papers in this volume suggest, people do not always act with precise goal-directed behavior in mind.[14] And to the extent people do pursue goals, they do not always act with self-interest in mind.[15] Second, although self-interest does explain individual motivations in certain circumstances, clearly it does not explain motivation in all circumstances. Political issues concern public goods; but most economic theories break down in the presence of public goods. Thus, one might reasonably expect economic behavior to differ from political behavior.[16] Finally, regardless of claims to the contrary, there is a normative bias reflected in the insistence that self-interest best explains individual behavior. On the whole, rational choice theorists genuinely do believe themselves to be simply explaining real political phenomena. However, an acceptance of self-interest as a norm in politics without a commensurate search to deter its negative force means that rational choice theorists build the negative consequences of self-interest into their system of democracy.[17] By offering a theory that unquestionably accepts self-interest as the basis of democratic politics, rational actor theorists have described a system with no defense against factional, antiliberal, democratic politics.

Let me now discuss early nineteenth-century American perspectives regarding self-interest in democracy, perspectives that seriously considered the potential policy consequences of placing self-interest at the foundation of democratic politics. By using their arguments, I will highlight the problems with any model—descriptive or proscriptive—that assumes self-interested behavior while implicitly or explicitly arguing for democratic government.

EARLY NINETEENTH-CENTURY AMERICAN DEBATES ON DEMOCRACY

In the sections to follow, I compare rational choice theory with early nineteenth-century American democratic arguments on the consequences of maintaining self-interest as the sole foundation of democratic theory. In particular, I examine state constitutional convention debates in Iowa (1844 and 1846), Louisiana (1845), Massachusetts (1820), New York (1821 and 1846), and Virginia (1830 and 1850), regarding democratic reforms such as reducing qualifications for electors and representatives, basing representation solely on population, increasing the number of state officers popularly elected, and eliminating restrictions on reelection of the executive branch.[18] These convention debates constitute a sample of American public opinion of the time, opinion regarding the relationship between democracy and self-interest. Let me begin my consideration of early nineteenth-century America by arguing why these nineteenth-century American ideas offer valuable and serious theoretical discussions of democracy, still relevant today.

I first need to address whether its antidemocratic tendencies render American debate in the early nineteenth century irrelevant and inappropriate for contemporary discussions of rational democratic theory. Some historians and present-day democratic theorists argue that early nineteenth-century American debates on suffrage and popular empowerment are limited as examples of democratic debate for a number of reasons. For one thing, delegates never discussed the possibility of direct popular governing.[19] Furthermore, these Americans excluded certain key groups from the franchise.[20] For example, those against reform wanted to enfranchise and give privilege only to those citizens who owned property. The rest of the people, a priori, did not deserve the same participatory privileges.[21] Those for reform may have increased popular control, but they still excluded all women and most blacks and native Americans from the franchise.[22]

Because nineteenth-century Americans embraced leadership selection as popular rule, that does not mean they accepted mere token activity. In the American tradition, the sovereignty of the people and the need for avenues to exercise that valued popular supremacy were essential characteristics of government.[23] Furthermore, delegates at the nineteenth-century conventions believed that by selecting leaders, the people actually ruled themselves, that those who had governing privilege (e.g., the enfranchised, those able to seek election, etc.) had great and sovereign influence.[24] Unlike some delegates today, delegates back then found leadership selection practicably equivalent in importance to actual decision making. In this sense, nineteenth-century Americans considered themselves debating issues regarding true popular government. In addition, whether a state is democratic does not depend solely on how many citizens it excludes from participatory privilege. One would not call a society that excluded 70 percent of its population undemocratic if the 70 percent excluded were all under the age of 18. Any democracy must exclude some from participating in government; how democratic one describes the franchise depends on which exclusions are deemed justifiable and which are not. However, differentiating between democratic exclusions (e.g., the exclusion of aliens, criminals, the insane, or children) and undemocratic exclusions (e.g., the exclusion of the illiterate) is an extremely difficult task, one most democratic theorists avoid completely. Instead, theorists rely on current popular perception to determine the "legitimate" boundaries of democratic inclusion.[25] Although not all openly embraced it, for early nineteenth-century Americans, adult white male suffrage represented universal suffrage. Many no longer found the exclusion of groups, such as the laboring whites or the non-propertied, universally acceptable or "democratically" justifiable, but the enfranchisement of women, slaves, and native Americans had yet to become a political issue.[26] With this in mind, early nineteenth-century exclusions of women, slaves, and native Americans parallel our contemporary universally acceptable exclusions (e.g., children and the insane); both are "democratic" exclusions in their own time.[27]

Although practically everyone at these conventions valued popular rule, not all of them wanted universal suffrage (i.e., universal adult white male suffrage) or direct popular control in areas outside the legislature. Thus, I do not characterize every delegate as a spokesman for democracy. Throughout this essay, I distinguish between those who favored reform and those who preferred to maintain the status quo or even introduce new popular restrictions, by referring to one as democratic and the other as antidemocratic. Those against reform I call the "antidemocrats" because they wanted to limit popular control.[28] They believed that popular sovereignty and majority rule could be sustained by maintaining power in selected "representative" citizens and by keeping the Senate and judiciary in hands other than the populace. Those for reform I call the "democrats" because they wanted to expand the people's power as much as possible.[29] To them, popular sovereignty meant that almost all men shared equally in government, and shared in electing all government representatives, not just assembly members. They believed that the people were not really sovereign unless everyone participated; otherwise, a part enslaved the rest.[30] Although these so-called democrats did not support lifting all popular restrictions, they *never* justified exclusions and instead presented reasons for extending the privileges of popular government. They fought for a more democratic republic.

In short, early American debates on reform resemble contemporary discussions on democracy. Although the American system being debated was less inclusive and less participatory than many democrats today would like, both sides *believed* that reforms would bring democracy to America. Those against reform saw changes as bringing a "democratic" chaos much like the French had experienced.[31] Those for reform believed that changes would make previous democratic principle into a final reality. For both sides reform meant democracy of one sort or another.

VIRTUE AND THE CONSEQUENCES OF SELF-INTEREST IN POPULAR GOVERNMENT: THE EARLY NINETEENTH-CENTURY PERSPECTIVE

Americans in the early nineteenth century believed that popular government reflected the people's preferences, and that this electoral connection existed by definition of what popular government is and ought to be. In contrast to rational choice theorists today, who describe the link between voters and their officers as the direct (and beneficial) consequence of individual self-interest, Americans then saw this link as the normative foundation and the empirical reality of American popular government.[32] Delegates from each side accepted or rejected democratic reform in part because of their understanding of human nature. Those against reform believed that self-interest drove all human actions and that because of such narrow motivation, popular government could never entail universal suffrage or direct selection of every government officer. Some self-interests would bring harm and therefore had to be silenced.[33] Those arguing for reforms rejected the antidemocrats' depiction of human nature. Self-interest did not guide people's action in the political realm; virtue did.[34] However, they admitted that if self-interest so wholly influenced politics, they too would have to reject democracy. In other words both democrats and antidemocrats described unrestricted self-interest in a way quite different from today's rational choice theorists. Self-interest had little independent contribution to the electoral connection, and, whenever unrelated to the public good, self-interest led to faction and particularized popular rule. Narrow self-interest had no place in democracy. To unquestioningly allow unrestricted self-interest in democracy meant the ruin of free government.

State constitution writers worried about the people's nature because public temperament would determine whether popular sovereignty—a key element of republican government—would undermine private rights and the public good, the other two essential attributes of the ideal republic. They wanted to ensure that these values would not conflict with each other. This state-level task resembled Madison's national task of the prior century. For Madison, good republican government must avoid factions, avoid the chance that citizens might be "united and actuated by some common impulse of passion or of interest adverse to the rights of other citizens, or to the permanent and aggregate interests of the community" (Hamilton, et al, 1982:43). Republican government must "secure the public good and private rights against the danger of . . . faction, and at the same time . . . preserve the spirit and the form of popular government" (ibid:45). The people, in their misguided passion, might request policies that hurt the rights of themselves or others. State delegates had to be certain that the constitutions they approved avoided this flaw. While they valued popular government, they knew it afforded the people the opportunity to put dangerous interests into action. State constitutions had to offer "checks" in order to avoid the destruction these passions and interests could potentially bring. Unlike Madison, who believed that the people could never be wholly trusted to act properly and who therefore advocated external checks (a diverse, extended republic) to make the people's passionate self-concerns harmless, most state-level constitutional delegates believed that the republic had to expect better from its citizens. Since the people governed, the republic could not render them powerless. Government had only to trust them as competent decision makers. From the perspective of so many state representatives, if the people were not of good character, no external checks would stop their misguided self-seeking behavior from destroying the public good and private rights. This was the reality of popular government.

Both democrats and antidemocrats believed that all the governors—the people and their leaders—had to act with the good of the state in mind. Rather than making self-interest the base of politics, rather than seeing political participants as acting solely to maximize their own personal gain, early nineteenth-century Americans saw virtue, specifically concern with the public good, as the foundation of good politics.[35] They believed that concern for one's country, not just for one's personal life, had to direct political governors. This way, policies would never reflect narrow constituent concerns and would never harm the public good or private rights.

For democrats, only a virtuous people guaranteed security for the public good and private rights:

> The only effectual guarantee, against the abuse of power in a republic, is to be found, and to be found only, in the virtue and intelligence of the people. . . . While virtuous and intelligent they will do no act of injustice or rapine (Powell, democrat, Virginia delegate, 1830:107).

Without widespread virtue and intelligence among the people, republican government would fail. "Virtue and intelligence are the true basis on which every republican government must rest. When these are lost, freedom will no longer exist" (Buel, democrat, New York delegate, 1821:239).

> Our Republican Institutions rest for their support upon the virtue and intelligence of the people; and if they should not be sufficient to

ensure a faithful and wise administration of the Government, the best hopes for human liberty and happiness which we have cherished must be disappointed (Baldwin, democrat, Virginia delegate, 1830:102).

In so many of their speeches, democrats made claims of this sort. Based on a population committed to furthering the public good, popular government would flourish. If some portion of the population lacked this virtuous commitment, any popularly governed state would face the dangerous possibility of faction and the destruction of liberty.[36]

According to democrats, no other condition besides widespread virtue better preserved self-government from factious ruin. Democrats specifically disclaimed the potential success of many other so-called checks on the people's governing, especially those checks that antidemocrats proposed. To democrats, a corrupted people would always find a voice in republican government. In a free government no special procedure could dispel the people's influence. For example, suppose the people were truly incapable of selecting certain leaders. To remedy this, antidemocrats suggested these leaders be appointed. But according to democrats, the body which would appoint these leaders was one previously elected by the same supposedly incompetent people, and thus the people's corrupting influence would still be felt. By definition, in a republic, all government bodies somehow rested on the people. Without virtue this reliance would always prove destructive. The good republic required a good people. In other words, the nature of the people mattered. To be successful, popular government needed a virtuous people.

Similarly, antidemocrats agreed that the people's nature mattered to the success of popular government. Antidemocrats repeatedly mentioned that good government must work with, not against, the "feelings, habits and modes of thinking of the people" (Young, antidemocrat, New York delegate, 1821:189). Wise government relied on a virtuous people. Virtue was "essential to the very being of a Republic"; it was "the vital spirit which animates healthful liberty" (Leigh, antidemocrat, Virginia delegate, 1830:398). Like their adversaries, delegates against reform argued that without such virtue, popular government could not survive. "Where there is not private virtue, there cannot be public security and happiness" (Story, antidemocrat, Massachusetts delegate, 1820:288). Without virtue, the people might behave adversely to themselves and the state. With it, they might fight against the evils of passionate, factious unions. "Public virtue [is] an influence, which obviates the possibility of corruption" (Leigh, antidemocrat, Virginia delegate, 1830:398).

[K]nowing that our government rests directly on the popular will, that we may preserve it, we endeavor to give a safe and proper

> direction to that public will. . . . [W]e confidently trust . . .
> that . . . good and virtuous sentiments, . . . [will] secure, as well
> against open violence and overthrow, as against the slow but sure
> undermining of licentiousness (Webster, antidemocrat, Mas-
> sachusetts delegate, 1820:315).

Again, without virtue, no constitutional designer should choose popular
government.

Although antidemocrats found virtue necessary, they willingly
tolerated some corruption among the people. So long as the unvirtuous
did not have direct political power, the republic would not suffer from
factions. So when antidemocrats claimed that a virtuous people ensured
against internal republican destruction, they truly meant that republican survival depended on virtuous governors. A virtuous *electorate* protected the republic from the dangers of factions. In this sense, antidemocrats differed from their adversaries regarding the importance of
virtue in society. Democrats found widespread virtue integral. The corrupting influence of the people (if it existed at all) would always reach
government, even if these people had no direct political power. On the
other hand, antidemocrats believed that checks on the people's power
could counterbalance the otherwise impenetrable force of vice among
the people. By restricting the political privileges of those without virtue,
government could avoid factious policies.

At first glance, this view stands in stark contrast to rational choice
theory today. The overriding assumption of early nineteenth-century
Americans was that the very definition of democracy ("self-
government," in their language) meant that popular input would affect
the nature of government policies. At the basis of this government was
citizen concern with the common good. So long as the people were virtuous, they would not seek policies that undermined the public good or
private rights. Without virtue, the people could be expected to unite
into dangerous factions and destroy free government. Yet in rational
choice theory, the people do not a priori have influence on their leaders,
and citizen concern with the common good has no necessary role in
governing. Relying on virtue is not only unrealistic; it does not "predict"
the electoral connection. Instead, in the rational choice view, democracy relies on self-interested citizens. Self-interest brings about what
they view as the end goal of democracy—popularly responsive government. So although early nineteenth-century Americans found no place
for any behavior not directed at the common good, rational choice
theorists find no unique place for behavior directed at that good and
instead argue in favor of a place for self-directed behavior. In this sense,
the two bases of democracy appear radically different.

While nineteenth-century Americans *seemingly* denied any role for
self-seeking rational behavior in politics, their positions do not preclude

a political role for interest. When using the concept of virtue, Americans meant one of two things: either the more classical notion of disinterested action in the name of the good or the altered notion of self-interested action that de facto coincides with the public good.[37] Only the first of these views leaves no normative or descriptive role for self-interest in good governing. In this first case, virtue implies subordinating one's personal concerns to the general welfare of the state. This understanding assumes that conflicts between one's self-interest and the good of one's country exist but that good citizens forgo personal goals when making decisions affecting the community. A virtuous citizen always places love of community and concern for its well-being *above* individual goals. Virtue represents the overcoming of self-interest. In the latter case, a citizen may act virtuously simply by relying on personal desires. Here, citizens do not make benevolent sacrifices for the good of the state, yet the public good emerges. Often, in this conception, individual self-seeking behavior refers to the quest for material gain; the economic growth thereby resulting contributes to the common good.[38] Whatever constitutes the connection, this understanding of virtue as self-interest leading to the common good allows citizens in the political realm to place their individual priorities first, to place their individual concerns over any abstract state concerns. Here, the community still succeeds precisely as it did in the earlier, more classical understanding of virtue. The good arises *as if* citizens had sacrificed for it and not just followed their personal, passionate inclinations.[39] In this second case, self-interested citizens may indeed be virtuous citizens so long as their personal interests coincide with their duties to the state.

In general, nineteenth-century democrats understood virtue in the earlier, more classical sense. Many of those for reform argued that Americans worked for the good of the state regardless of their personal circumstance. They believed that when asked to make decisions on a public issue, citizens would rely on their attachments to the state, attachments they developed from patriotic love of country. "[I]t is safe to trust . . . patriotism which . . . glowed in the bosom of every American" (Dunn, democrat, Louisiana delegate, 1845:108). Democrats believed that the American people—poor and rich alike—were virtuous. "[T]he poor [man] must, and does take as great an interest in the good of the country, as the rich man" (Wilson, democrat, Virginia delegate, 1830:352). "We are as virtuous, as intelligent, and moral as any people under the sun" (Lucas, democrat, Virginia delegate, 1850:355). "The people of this country, above all others, were intelligent and virtuous" (Radcliff, democrat, New York delegate, 1821:286). In other words, to them virtue was not merely some abstract ideal that would enhance good governing; virtue was the reality that allowed America to institute republican government.

For democrats, the proper impetus for political action, although perhaps not benevolent, perhaps not a painful struggle, certainly remained separate from personal, self-centered concerns. "The love of country . . . does not, as seems to be supposed, grow out of the self-love and self-interest of mature years" (Hoge, democrat, Virginia delegate, 1850:174).

> Some gentlemen allege . . . the words *common interest with* and *attachment to* the community, meant neither less [N]or more than a freeholder. According to what dictionary or mode of interpretation this meaning is made out . . . I have not as yet learned (Campbell, democrat, Virginia delegate, 1820:385).

In arguments by democrats, community attachment brought virtue; attachment did not arise from economic conditions or other selfish motives. Democrats believed that people acted for the state's benefit out of love for the country, not out of love of one's personal success. Often, when confronted with the origin of virtue, they specifically noted: *Virtue was not based on self-interest.*[40]

When democrats spoke of virtue as the basis of successful government operation, they did not mean self-interest in disguise. Virtue was a sentiment, a sentiment that people developed toward their country independent of their personal and economic interests. Of course, democrats did not say it was never in one's personal interest to be virtuous, never in one's interest to love and fight for free government. Rather, they argued that virtue had a separate and distinct identity from interest. One could love one's country and govern on its behalf regardless of one's self-interested intentions. For example, one could respect existing property distributions even though those distributions were not in one's personal interest. Widespread self-interest (if coincidental to virtue) had a neutral effect on government policy. However, because self-interest was different from virtue, if citizens acted only to pursue personal gain, their political actions would eventually undermine democracy or any form of popular rule. Government needed virtue, and because interest could signify a lack of virtue, it was dangerous, and became the basis of factious politics. Basically, then, democrats devised a theory of democracy different from rational choice. They described popular government as founded on the motivation they believed prevalent among Americans; they founded popular government on virtue, a concept separate from and often opposed to interest. This view differs dramatically from a theory of democracy which specifically founds popular government on self-interest.

Having noted the above, I must add that rational choice theorists share much in common with nineteenth-century antidemocrats, who argued that individuals (naturally weak) act only in their own interests, and that all *realistic* governments must take this into account.[41] Antidemocrats did not expect individuals to step beyond their own private interests and work for the good of the state. Instead, they believed that everyone did good only out of self-interest. "[I]f we look . . . into the ordinary affairs of men, we shall find that interest is the great spring of action"; interest even motivated so-called good deeds. Love of wealth made agriculture flourish and built cities. Only fame encouraged the soldier to be brave. Want of distinction drove the poet to write. "[H]onorable and intelligent men, with all their devotion to principle, unconsciously [are] influenced by interest" (Scott, antidemocrat, Virginia delegate, 1830:125). From the perspective of antidemocrats, virtue came from self-interest; no one would place abstract state concerns over their personal preferences. Individuals worked for the good of the state only when it was in their self-interest to do so. "[T]o separate interest from duty, [is] to expose virtue to the strongest temptation." It does not work (Stanard, antidemocrat, Virginia delegate, 1830:295). In short, many of those against reform argued that personal interest motivated all actions, including political actions. Furthermore, to the extent people acted virtuously, they did so for personal reasons.[42]

Despite this belief that actions spring from interests, antidemocrats still believed that to be governed well, the state needed to rely on citizens concerned with the public good. Popular government should not ignore the importance of virtue just because people naturally followed their self-interest. Although men would not "benevolently" work for the common good for its own sake, that did not mean men would not work for the good at all. Just as the rational choice theorists describe self-interest broadly understood, antidemocrats spoke of "directed" self-interest. For these delegates, some individuals had a personal interest in serving state interests, and therefore they would naturally pursue virtuous goals. These men with properly directed self-interests deserved the governing privilege. It was in this way that, while in theory governors were concerned with only themselves, in practice their actions would benefit everyone.[43] By giving the governing privilege *only* to such "directed" individuals, states could secure against factious interests. According to antidemocrats, the good constitution writer constructed government so "as to give all [voters], or at least to a very great majority, an interest in its preservation" (Webster, antidemocrat, Massachusetts delegate, 1820:311). This way, voters, who naturally worked only for their own gratification, would actually work for the good of the state as well. Antidemocrats believed that despite its self-centered citizenry, the republic could maintain its necessary foundation of virtue so long as only those citizens whose personal interests coincided with the public good had political power, so long as states selectively chose who governed.

For antidemocrats, empowering only those whose self-interest had virtuous intentions meant making sure property holders had majority power.[44] The property qualification "afforded a conclusive test of attachment to good order and good government" (Grymes, anti-democrat, Louisiana delegate, 1845:104). For these delegates, the common good consisted of property and its preservation,[45] and clearly only property holders held that interest as their own. The propertyless had an interest in undermining the property of others; therefore, they might demand the equalization of property or the heavy taxation of landlords and, in so doing, undermine the common good. In other words, because citizens naturally followed their own self-interest, the state could not trust certain citizens with majority power. Only property owners could follow their natural inclination to benefit themselves and yet ensure the common good; that is, ensure that private property remained secure in government. Thus American state governments must empower only them. In short, for antidemocrats, government could succeed in spite of the prevalence of self-interested behavior, provided the republic *excluded* some self-interested people—those without property—and entrusted the governing privilege only to those personally sharing the common state concerns.

These antidemocrats share a fundamental premise with today's rational choice theorists: popular government cannot escape the inevitable fact that citizens naturally pursue their own self-interests. Writers from these two seemingly diverse traditions agree that voters naturally consult their personal preferences when making public policy choices and that this natural reality does not destroy the chances of a successful popular government. However, in rational choice theory all self-centered preferences belong in government. In theory the system whole-heartedly gains from self-interested behavior, for self-interest creates the electoral connection. Perhaps in part because proponents of this model define self-interest broadly (i.e., because they assume that some actions intended to benefit one's personal situation will also benefit the state), they seemingly ignore the potential of narrow, factional politics. In contrast to our rational choice contemporaries, antidemocrats did worry about the narrow, harmful policies a self-interested citizenry might elect. They therefore distinguished normatively between the two types of interested behavior. They believed that majority pursuit of purely selfish interests, defined as interests not at all related to any notion of the common good, negatively affected resulting government policies. Left undirected, self-interested majorities might enact policies ignorant of and even harmful to more general concerns. Thus, for popular government to survive, antidemocrats denied political voice to self-interests of the narrow, egocentric kind.[46] To antidemocrats, the reality of self-interest mean that *only* those with certain personal interests (one might say only those with virtuous self-interests) should govern. The good republic excluded certain narrow interests from governing; it had to be less than wholly democratic to survive. So while antidemocrats may have agreed with rational choice thinkers that self-interest is at the foundation of popular government, they would not have agreed that all kinds of self-interested behavior rightfully belonged in politics. Self-interest could be tolerated only when it reflected a certain morality, only when it coincided with the antidemocratic understanding of good citizenship. Ultimately, that meant self-interest could be tolerated only in a less than wholly democratic government.

All this strongly suggests that the early nineteenth-century American concern with the outcomes of popular rule entailed a critical appraisal of an unquestioned approval of self-interest in politics. A government that allowed all citizens to pursue their own interests, without also guaranteeing that the personal preferences of these voters reflected the community interests at large, would suffer internal destruction. On a general level, both democrats and antidemocrats agreed that *undirected* self-interested behavior in politics could result in factions and poor government. A good, stable, popularly governed state depended on a virtuous people. Without virtue, self-government would crumble from within. Unvirtuous governors could be expected to forsake state concerns for their own personal gain. On a specific level, antidemocrats believed that although government relied on virtue, it could not ignore the inevitable fact that people acted in their own self-interest. In their view, to operate successfully, popular government had to rely on those whose interests had virtuous intentions. Since not everyone had such enlightened self-interests, popular government should never reach a "democratic" extreme; it should never grant everyone equal power in the governing process. Instead, it should empower only those with interests identical to the common good. For democrats, who never connected virtue to interest, self-interested action in political affairs remained a force potentially able to undermine popular government. To base popular government on self-interest would be to destroy its desirability, for it would represent the establishment of a government prone to corrupt, factious rule. To democrats, virtue represented the foundation of democracy. To replace virtue with interest would deprive popular government of its strongest foundation, of the force that kept it distinct from tyrannous, factional government. In sum, those both for and against reform believed that undirected self-interest could destroy the desirability of popular government. Purely self-interested citizens could not uphold democratic government in theory or practice.

THE CONSEQUENCES OF PLACING SELF-INTEREST AT THE HEART OF DEMOCRACY

What can be learned from the above consideration of nineteenth-century debates on democracy? Clearly, rational choice theorists place self-interest at the heart of democracy. They value self-interest for its procedural benefits, specifically the electoral connection, and generally ignore its effect on policy content. However, as early nineteenth-century American thought on democracy suggests, government by wholly self-interested actors produces no ideal polity. Because the people determine the content of policies, whether the people follow narrow or enlightened self-interest, self-centered or virtuous intentions will affect the desirability of popular rule. Their arguments remind us that the rational choice theory of democracy, which fails to make such distinctions, ends up depicting a government which by definition breeds faction. Furthermore, because rational choice theorists depict citizen activity aimed to benefit the whole society as the exception rather than the rule, these thinkers ignore ideal democracy.

The nineteenth-century American debates highlight three critical problems in the rational choice conception of democracy. First, theorists who adopt the rational choice model of democracy seem to ignore the potentially ill-fated consequences of self-centered citizens in a democracy. They assume that citizens naturally act in their own self-interest, and that leaders, being popularly guided, represent the personal concerns of their constituents. Although they do not deny that sometimes citizens have a personal interest to serve others, according to their standards, it does not matter whether citizens act solely for themselves or whether citizens act for interests of their community, from which they also benefit. However, in politics, especially democratic politics, the *aim* of self-interest has important consequences. Citizen character affects the content of governmental policy. Self-interested behavior does not *uniquely* encourage the electoral connection, and it may produce factious policies. If narrowly self-interested, the winning coalition will include only its own interests. In this case, those without political power lack an advocate for their concerns. If the narrow interests of some conflict with the interests of others, those without political voice can expect polices which are not just disinterested but also *hostile* to their own interests. In both cases, narrow interests mean that government assuredly protects the majority in power. In the case of conflict, narrowly minded governors actually harm the minority. Although rational choice theorists discuss the possibility of a more broadly interested citizenry, because they accept policies of both broad *and* narrow concerns, their rational democracy is sometimes synonymous with rational majority tyranny and sometimes synonymous with an undesirable account of democracy.

Second, it is not surprising that the rational choice image of democracy is one which fuels present-day arguments to limit democracy. Nineteenth-century debates clearly indicate the historical connection between self-interest and arguments against democracy. Just as nineteenth-century antidemocrats believed widespread self-interest meant the populace could not be trusted to rule, many theorists today fear democracy for precisely the same reason: they fear the hostile policies a self-interested majority may inflict upon the minority.[47] In other words, our contemporary skeptics who argue to impose restrictions on majority power often appropriate the precise vision of democracy that rational choice theorists depict, a world of self-interested citizens; but rather than accept it as the reality of the democratic polity, they use it to undermine the viability of popular rule.[48]

Finally, earlier American arguments suggest that insofar as rational choice theorists base democracy on self-interest they may preclude the growth of democratic theory and practice. Assumptions of a self-interested citizenry often are accompanied by assumptions of zero-sum politics. Such an understanding of politics leads too easily to an emphasis on *restraining* institutions and ignores other more democratic possibilities. Most modern theorists scoff at those who suggest that the people can be trusted to rule themselves without restraint. Yet those Americans who fought for democracy and won reform in the early 1800s did so based on precisely this faith, based on the belief that the people would exercise self-restraint in the political realm and would pursue virtuous intentions with beneficial policy results. This more optimistic understanding of popular behavior was one of the distinguishing features of the democratic argument.[49] Without a faith in popular capabilities, the argument for democracy loses much of its attraction.

I do not wish to imply that democracy will be saved as soon as theorists stop *assuming* narrow self-interest and encourage a model of democracy which portrays its people as virtuous.[50] Rather, I intend to suggest that by assuming self-interest as the foundation of popular government and by not differentiating between, and making judgments upon the types of interests people rely on in politics, rational choice theorists are not "simply" developing a value-free empirical description of democratic politics; instead, they are depicting a system of democracy which is narrow, and sometimes undesirable. Too often, they describe a system not wholly based in fact, one that actually perpetuates democratic skepticism. While special interests sometimes can better the whole,[51] they can likewise harm certain sectors of the population.

Describing a government that assuredly considers the concerns of the winning majority—no matter how narrow those concerns—is describing a government that will often neglect the interests of the minority. This is a negative image of democracy. The rational choice view of democracy is thus both unverified and sometimes negative in its depiction of democratic politics. These limitations should lead one to question the utility of adopting self-interest as the *sole* basis of democracy. There *is* a place for self-interest in democracy. It does describe many political actions. But one must recognize, as did early nineteenth-century Americans, that virtue and good citizenship remain a political possibility, a possibility which enhances the theoretical desirability of democracy. Such optimistic accounts of citizen motivation are necessary if we are ever to enhance democratic practice.

In this paper I have utilized early nineteenth-century American understandings about virtue and self-interest to question the value of relying on a rational theory of democracy. As did our intellectual forefathers, our discussions about democracy ought to center on how *varying* citizen motivations affect the nature of popular government. We ought not blindly accept economic assumptions for modeling democratic political behavior. As self-governors, we ought to (at least some of the time) aspire to a more "stately" model.

NOTES

1. See Mansbridge (1980) for a discussion of interests in adversarial versus unitary politics.
2. "We assume that every individual, though rational, is also selfish. . . . [W]henever we speak of rational behavior, we always mean rational behavior directed primarily toward selfish ends" (Downs, 1957:27). See in general Downs (1957, Chs. 3 and 4). "Self-interest, broadly conceived, is recognized to be a strong motivating force in all human activity; and human action . . . is assumed more naturally to be directed toward the furtherance of individual or private interest" (Buchanan and Tullock, 1962:27). In general, see Buchanan and Tullock (1962:17–23). Riker and Ordeshook (1973) also discuss the importance of the self-interest assumption; see pp. 8–37.
3. The argument goes more or less as follows: The people want candidates that best mirror their particular policy preferences. Candidates, interested only in their own power gratification, have no political agenda and therefore act as the people want them to. To attract votes, candidates choose policy positions that best mirror a majority of their constituent demands. (Or, to be more precise, the

winning strategy for a candidate is to take the majority preferred position for each issue. An alternative winning strategy, available only to a challenger, would be to take the majority position for every issue except one.) After they win the election and become representatives of government, candidates—now leaders—continue without an agenda of their own; they continue supporting the people's preferences, this time in the hope of ensuring reelection. Thus, because of their self-interested desire to be reelected, leaders, once in office, serve the people by choosing those policies which best represent a coalition of the majority's articulated interests.

4. For rational choice theorists, candidates only run for office to obtain office. They do not, for example, run for office in the hopes of putting their ideal political vision into action or of influencing the ideological positions of another, more likely successful candidate. (It has been argued that third parties in America exist precisely as such an ideological influencer. See Rosenstone et al. (1984).

5. According to such critics, there are a number of reasons why candidates cannot mirror constituent policy preferences. First, all schemes for aggregating voter preferences remain subject to cycles (see Arrow, 1963) and most schemes do not even guarantee the selection of the most preferred candidate when he exists (see Brams, 1976). Second, the outcome of any election depends as much on the procedure chosen for aggregating preferences as it does on the content of those preferences (see Brams, 1976). Third, naive inconsistencies exist among voter priorities. Voters may prefer one thing in principle, another in practice. (For an old but not outdated analysis of American public opinion, including its many inconsistencies, see Key, 1961.) Finally, preferences vary in intensity, and such variations affect leadership behavior and accountability.

6. See Riker (1982).

7. In fact, for Riker, voters in a democratic government have only one function—to accept or reject the incumbent. This is similar to Schumpeter's view of democratic government (1942).

8. Riker would not agree with this conclusion. He argues there can be no such electoral connection between leaders and voters. But given the other assumptions of his model, some democratic connection, however imperfect, must exist. If it did not, one could not even talk (as Riker himself does) about the vote act symbolizing leadership choice. For a more detailed critique of Riker's position on this issue, see Cohen (1986).

9. Usually, according to the theory, government has no public functions apart from individual wants. (Either that or during the electoral process an "invisible hand" alters individual preferences so that they serve society's needs.) Of course, not all theorists agree

with this happy appraisal of self-interest in democracy. Some theorists who describe American politics as a network of group interactions, where each group represents a different set of self-interested actors, reject the invisible hand thesis. They claim that the special interest of business controls policy and that group politics ignores the greater public good. For examples of this general critique against pluralist democracy, see Lowi (1967, 1969) or McConnell (1966). At the same time, many other group theorists would agree with rational choice thinkers that government should simply serve (or broker among) competing group interests. See, for examples, Bentley (1908), Dahl's earlier work (e.g., 1958 or 1961), and Truman (1951).

10. See Ch. 3 on the logic of voting. Downs says he wants to allow for altruistic behavior as well as selfishness in the narrow sense. Of note, although he claims voters may act with broader intentions, he does not speak of leaders acting with any other intention except the narrow reelection one.

11. See Buchanan and Tullock quote in note 1 above. Also, Riker (1962) devotes much of his opening chapter to the problems with strictly applying *narrow* economic behavioral assumptions to voter behavior.

12. So, for example, a citizen living in Florida may prefer a candidate committed to halting the damage of acid rain, even though the problem does not directly affect that citizen. He is not a lover of nature, nor a producer of antipollutant devices; he has no self-centered connection to the problem. Still, beautiful forests in the North may be in the self-interest of this voter. He might want to boast to his foreign friends of America's beautiful landscaping, to appease his nagging environmentalist friends, to vacation there someday. Somehow or other, he perceives what seems to be a strictly national, other-regarding issue to be of his own personal concern. Therefore, in supporting the environmental candidate, he acts out of self-interest, a self-interest broadly conceived. Such behavior is wholly consistent with the rational choice model, for the behavior remains essentially self-interested.

13. In fact, the type of self-interest one acts upon may affect their theory, especially the certainty of the electoral connection. For example, narrowly self-interested voters may care more about sports than political policies and therefore ignore elections during baseball season (recall that no presidential debates were scheduled during the 1988 World Series). Or they may pay little attention to leadership activity in general throughout the year's sporting events. In other words, "narrow" selfishness among voters may actually prevent them from making *any* demands on their leaders. At the

same time, anything other than narrow, selfish reelection concerns among leaders may also prevent the electoral connection. Candidates may want to support policy initiatives they believe in the best interests of their country and feel it necessary to wholly ignore their constituents except for an occasional campaign deception tactic in order to ensure outcomes that reflect other nonelectoral interests. (For example, a leader might feel it is in his or her self-interest to pursue policies aimed at halting acid rain despite constituent opposition.) Here, broadening the notion of self-interest beyond the reelection concern to include a genuine interest in policies means that a rational candidate may not ensure the supposed "democratic" connection between leaders and voters.

14. See Monroe's essay in this volume, which looks at World War II rescuers of Jews. For a discussion of the psychology literature on this assumption of goal-directed behavior, see the Eckstein or the Rosenberg essay in this volume.

15. Essays in this volume by Margolis and Monroe directly question the extent to which people follow their self interests in calculating actions.

16. Again, see the Margolis essay in this volume.

17. Petracca's essay in this volume describes this and other normative assumptions in rational choice theory from a theoretical perspective.

18. Reforms from 1800 to 1850 represented a significant movement toward democracy in two key ways. They extended the franchise and increased the people's governing influence so that all states allowed almost all freemen to elect their legislative and executive officers. First, regarding the franchise: Delaware, Georgia, and New Hampshire removed all voter restrictions prior to 1800. Massachusetts, Ohio, and Virginia were the last three to maintain a taxation requirement for suffrage; they abolished the requirement around 1850. After that, all states basically had universal white male suffrage, with some states allowing selected free blacks—usually the propertied—to vote as well. For a history of suffrage reforms, see Williamson (1960). Second, regarding how representatives were elected: by 1800, the people directly elected all legislative officers, but only around half the states allowed executive officers to be elected by the people, either directly or indirectly through an electoral college system. (See Lutz, 1980:88.) By 1850, all states had the executive branch popularly elected—directly or indirectly. At the same time, by 1850 and still today, states infrequently adopted a popularly elected judiciary. While more often than not statesmen believed that an elective judiciary took democracy too far, many flirted with the possibility around the mid-nineteenth century.

19. Many critics of democracy say that whenever the people only select leaders, they "govern" by token activity. Theorists criticize leadership selection as an elite, unnecessarily empirical definition of democracy. They argue that only popular decision making and direct participation characterize democracy. See, for examples, Wolff (1970), Pitkin and Shumer (1982), and Walker (1966). Of course, some theorists (such as Schumpeter, 1942) would characterize leadership selection as democracy. Many (for example, see Sartori's latest work, 1987) defend this definition as the only viable account of modern democracy. For a good and more critical perspective of this controversy between elite and participatory theorists, see Skinner (1973).

20. Many historians and political scientists argue over just how democratic America has been since the signing of its Constitution. Their debate often centers on just how many people could vote at the time. For example, Beard (1913/1986) points to the exclusions of women, slaves, the working class, etc., and argues earlier America was a capitalist decision-making society, not a democracy at all. Others, for example Brown (1955, 1956), argue states were quite democratic even during the colonial period. For a critical evaluation of this debate, see Murrin (1965). Most democratic theorists today define democracy in terms of full citizen inclusion. For examples, see Pennock (1979:7), Dahl (1980:101), Simon (1951:77–79), or Macpherson (1973:Ch. 3). Adherents of this view might well consider nineteenth-century America undemocratic.

21. Important to note here, even given their restrictions, by some estimates around 70 percent of the white male population had enough property to vote. The precise percentage is disputed. For example, the data analysis of Bailyn (1969:87) suggests that, by the time of the constitution, somewhere between 50 and 75 percent of the adult white male population could vote, He finds a more precise figure impossible, given the data. Williamson (1960) offers a similar estimation but also offers a state-by-state analysis which demonstrates that how democratic America was cannot be decided at a national level. So, for example, in 1800, some states such as Pennsylvania allowed as much as 90 percent of the adult white male population to vote in all elections, while other states such as New York allowed only about 33 percent of its adult white male population to vote in senatorial elections. Beard (1913/1986:24) argues that qualifications for the franchise vary so much from region to region that all estimations are hopelessly inaccurate. For example, Bruce (1982) breaks down the voting eligibility by region in Virginia in 1829: 73 percent of the adult white male population could vote in the East, 56 percent in the West, and 51 percent in the Valley.

22. Although state constitutions did not start specifically excluding women until the late eighteenth century, women never voted (with the exception of one particular occasion in New Jersey). Women received the vote by national constitutional amendment in 1920, only after a long struggle. For a history of the women's suffrage movement, see Flexner (1970). In addition, while in the early 1800s many Northern states unquestioningly gave the vote to freed blacks, over the next 50 years these states increased restrictions on their franchise, first by introducing a special property qualification for blacks and then by disenfranchising them completely. All blacks received the vote only after the passage of the Fifteenth Amendment and many were unable to exercise their privilege until the mid-1960s. For a study of Negro suffrage, see Olbrich (1912). For an interesting interpretation of why blacks ultimately received the national right to vote, see Porter (1918).

23. The tradition of exercised popular sovereignty had been established in America long ago. For early Americans, tacit consent did not imply self-government. Revolutionary Americans had already rejected the British concept of virtual representation; to accept it now would be contradictory. Americans may not have been whole-heartedly democratic but they did believe popular government required popular *input* of nontrivial consequence. On the English origins of American theories of popular government, dating back to as early as the sixteenth century, see Pole (1966). On the Whig theory of consent and the use of popular participation to demonstrate consent in eighteenth-century America, see Lutz (1980). On the widespread use of participation during the revolution, see Wood (1969).

24. For examples: "The popular feature is the strongest feature of our constitution" (Read, democrat, Louisiana delegate, 1845:744). "[T]he community is the true source of political power" (Wiley, democrat, Virginia delegate, 1850:15). "Ours is a government of the people; it may properly be called self-government. I wish it may be preserved forever in the hands of the people" (Monroe, anti-democrat, Virginia delegate, 1830:429).

25. The question of inclusion remains one of the most difficult for democratic theorists. For a discussion regarding the complications of democratic inclusion, see Whelan (1983). For an even more complicated understanding of the "boundary" problem, taken from a worldwide perspective, see Beitz (1979:Part 3).

26. Never, not once in any of the debates, did I find mention of the proper status for native Americans. Nor did any delegate seriously suggest women be included in the franchise. Women themselves did not begin their quest for civil and political rights until mid-

nineteenth century. (See Flexner, 1970.) While the issue of free negro suffrage generated some debate in the North, especially in New York, Southerners agreed blacks did not deserve the privilege, and delegates in neither region proposed enfranchising slaves.

27. That in no way suggests I would characterize such exclusions as democratic today.

28. These debaters wanted to maintain property and taxation requirements for voting and running for office. They wanted the number of state officers popularly elected minimized and property holdings weighted into representation so as to give extra political power to large landlords and/or slaveowners. While many of these debaters belonged to the Whig Party (or the earlier Federalist Party), even some party Democrats (and earlier Republicans) opposed reform, particularly in the South, where reforms were tied to regional or class—not partisan—conflicts. (See Green, 1930, or Bruce, 1982.) Since my interests lie in distinguishing among Americans according to their positions on reform, I simply call those delegates fighting against the democratic reforms the "antidemocrats" and ignore their party affiliation.

29. These debaters argued for extending the franchise, reducing the qualifications for elected officers, making representation based on population only, and increasing the number of state officers popularly elected. Often these debaters were members of the Democratic (and earlier Republican) Party, but sometimes Whigs (and earlier Federalists) voted with them for reforms. Here, I use the word "democrats" with a small d to indicate that the name does not necessarily imply party preference but simply support of reforms aimed to make the republic more democratic.

30. Democrats often spoke of the disenfranchised as enslaved. "They [nonvoters] are degraded to the condition of slaves, without the right of exercising an opinion of their own" (Ross, democrat, New York delegate, 1821:246). To deny specific individuals the vote was to "politically enslave a portion of our citizens" (Simmons, democrat, New York delegate, 1846:790).

31. Those against reform often referred to the changes as disastrously democratic. Besides predicting that universal suffrage and the proposed additional avenues of popular control would lead to the chaotic situation in France after the Revolution, they argued that reform would cause the downfall of the American republic, just as democracy had destroyed Greece and Rome.

32. Their divergent understanding as to why leaders follow constituent demands questions the role self-interest plays in the electoral connection. Given the potential problems with the self-interest assumption (see note 13 above), perhaps widespread democratic faith and

practice better explains why leaders follow their constituents. By definition, in a democracy the whole people are sovereign decision makers (even if they only indirectly influence decisions through their choices of leadership). Why not attribute the process, the electoral *power* granted to the populace, as the force behind the electoral connection?

33. Of course, not every delegate against reform spoke about human nature. However, those who did speak on the subject found interests at the base of all behavior, political or otherwise.

34. As in the case of antidemocrats, not every delegate for reform spoke about human nature. However, many spoke of the prevalence of virtue, and the vast majority of these delegates mentioned its connection to patriotism and/or denied its association with personal interest.

35. There is much debate over the extent to which early Americans believed virtue helped secure successful republican operations. For example, Appleby (1982) and Diggins (1986) suggest that the founders and thinkers thereafter saw the people as self-interested and acted on this precise assumption. On the other hand, some, like Pocock (1975) and Banning (1986), suggest that leaders at the time of the Constitution and perhaps thereafter relied partially on virtue to protect the American republic from self destruction. Still others, like Wood (1969), describe some Americans (the Anti-Federalists) as relying on virtue and others (the Federalists) as relying on self-interest. Rather than take sides in this ongoing debate—America as liberal or republican—let me say that my findings suggest that all Americans of the early nineteenth century appreciated virtue. That does not mean the delegates themselves were for or against reform for virtuous reasons. Often reformers, though property owners, believed change would benefit them and their party's power. Their discussions regarding virtue simply suggest that they thought good citizenship ought to involve putting one's country before oneself. Likewise, current lip service to self-interest does not mean that all those who espouse this view of politics act only for themselves (e.g., work only to benefit their careers). Nor does it mean that they believe political actors will never act against their personal interests. These theorists simply argue that good citizenship need not involve any benevolent behavior. For the purposes of this essay, I am not interested in why politicians take the positions they do. Rather, I am concerned with the content of their positions and how their beliefs affect the resulting image of government. The purpose of looking at American thinking during the early nineteenth century is to examine an alternative view of how nature affects government ideal. Given this research concern, I need only analyze what

delegates say they think, how they think character affects government; and, in the debate proceedings I read, delegates say they think virtue is essential to successful popular government. Although they did question what virtue meant, they never questioned good government's dependence on it.

36. By liberty they meant both the free exercise of one's sovereignty as well as the secured enjoyment of private rights. For a more detailed discussion of the varying early nineteenth-century American democratic understandings of liberty, see Scalia (1987).

37. See Lutz (1980:8–10). Diggins (1986:19–21) offers a similar dichotomy.

38. Adam Smith makes this case in his famous work *The Wealth of Nations*. Of note, for Adam Smith self-interest in politics is not guided by the same "Invisible Hand" as it is in economics. Instead, Smith argues interest in government requires more moral restraints. See the Whitehead chapter in this volume.

39. It is a variant of this second vision that drives the rational choice model as well as many other present-day favorable depictions of self interest in democracy.

40. Not all Americans for reform who discussed the importance of virtue in the republic went on to define virtue as something unconnected to interest. However, none made the specific equation. That is to say, democrats rarely ever discussed a political role for self-interests.

41. This understanding of human nature as weak and corruptible and of government as unable to rely on anything resembling a human social nature belongs to a cultural tradition already well established among certain intellectual circles and reinforced by certain religious dogmas of the time. See Bruce (1982).

42. This understanding of virtue parallels the more modern conception of virtue mentioned above. As in the case of democrats, not all anti-democrats detailed what they meant by virtue. However, among those that did, interest played a great role.

43. Of course, voters served everyone's public interests, not their personal interests (a blessing in the eyes of antidemocrats, since they saw many, particularly those they denied the vote, as having misdirected personal concerns, concerns that had no place in good government policy). Of note, this so-called protection for everyone and not just governors or a majority thereof is actually questionable. For example, what happens on governmental decisions that have nothing to do with property and related common state concerns? Also, do the propertyless really benefit from state policies protecting a good they presently do not and might never have?

44. To give property majority power, delegates either excluded nonproperty holders from voting entirely or altered representation so that districts with few inhabitants had as many representatives as, if not more than, those regions heavily populated.

45. Equating property with the general good is usually indirectly asserted, using, for example, the common good in one sentence, then replacing the concept with property a few sentences later. Other times antidemocrats reported property as different from but contributing to the public good. "Property becomes the source of comforts. . . . In this way it conduces to the public good" (Story, antidemocrat, Massachusetts delegate, 1820:285–286). In any case, antidemocrats placed a high value on property and its preservation. "Property is the greatest tie of social life. It was to protect property government was first organized" (Beale, antidemocrat, Virginia delegate, 1850:316). Property "is the greatest object of civil society" (Saltonstall, antidemocrat, Massachusetts delegate, 1820:275). Of note, nineteenth-century Americans often believed economic growth and prosperity relied on the nation's maintaining property as its base. Since economic growth was such an important priority for Americans, the antidemocratic connection between property and the common good should be easily understandable. (On the importance of property and economic growth in nineteenth-century America, see Hurst, 1956.)

46. Antidemocrats denied certain groups political voice in one of two ways. Sometimes they completely silenced certain harmful interests—such as nonproperty holders—by denying them the vote. Other times they kept undesirable interests silent—such as city dwellers and nonslave holders—by keeping them in the minority, by giving extra weight in representation to large landowners, country dwellers, and slave holders.

47. It is interesting to note that arguments for minority rights have often been used by those of privilege to keep certain disadvantaged groups politically silent. This is true of the early nineteenth-century American case (see Scalia, 1989) and in the early nineteenth-century British case (see Shapiro, 1988). For a similar argument about discussion of majority rule and minority rights, see Commager (1943).

48. This represents the general liberal fear of majority tyranny best expressed by Tocqueville over a century ago. Berlin (1969), a present-day liberal theorist, echoes these fears. For a second contemporary perspective, see Ortega y Gasset (1932).

49. One has only to read arguments of participatory theorists today (e.g., Pateman, 1970, or Barber, 1984) to realize these thinkers trust

the people's capabilities. In fact, characteristic of their arguments is the belief that democratic institutions will make people even better and more trustworthy citizens.

50. At the same time, I am not completely hostile to the idea suggested by Leo Strauss in many of his critical writings that characterizing the masses as self-interested might in fact encourage them in that direction and lead them away from public responsibilities. Most likely, expectations affect behavior.

51. For a discussion of the sometimes beneficial role of self-interest in democratic politics, see Mansbridge, 1980 and 1986.

REFERENCES

Appleby, J. (1982). "What's Still American in the Political Philosphy of Thomas Jefferson?" *William and Mary Quarterly*, 39:287–309.

Arrow, K. J. (1963). *Social Choice and Individual Values*. New Haven: Yale University Press, second edition.

Bachrach, P. (1967). *The Theory of Democratic Elitism: A Critique*. Boston: Little, Brown.

Bailyn, B. (1969). *The Origins of American Politics*. New York: Knopf.

Banning, L. (1986). "Jefferson Ideology Revisited: Liberal and Classical Ideas in the New American Republic," *William and Mary Quarterly*, 43:3–19.

Barber, B. (1984). *Strong Democracy: Participatory Politics for a New Age*. Berkeley: University of California Press.

Beard, C. A. (1913). *An Economic Interpretation of the Constitution of the United States*. New York: Free Press, (Revised 1986).

Beitz, C. R. (1979). *Political Theory and International Relations*. Princeton: Princeton University Press.

Berlin, I. (1969). *Four Essays on Liberty*. Oxford: Oxford University Press.

Bentley, A. F. (1908). *The Process of Government*. Evanston: The Principia Press.

Brams, S. J. (1976). *Paradoxes in Politics*. New York: The Free Press.

Brown, R. E. (1955). *Middle-Class Democracy and the Revolution in Massachusetts, 1691–1780*. Ithaca, NY: Cornell University Press.

Brown, R. E. (1956). *Charles Beard and the Constitution: A Critical Analysis of "An Economic Interpretation of the Constitution."* Princeton: Princeton University Press.

Bruce, D. D., Jr. (1982). *The Rhetoric of Conservatism: The Virginia Convention of 1829–30 and the Conservative Tradition in the South*. San Marino, CA: The Huntington Library.

Buchanan, J. M., and Tullock, G. (1962). *The Calculus of Consent: Logical Foundations of Constitutional Democracy*. Ann Arbor: University of Michigan Press.

Calhoun, J. C. (1953). *A Disquisition on Government*. New York: Bobbs-Merrill.

Cohen, J. (1986). "An Epistemic Conception of Democracy," *Ethics*, 97:26–38.

Commager, H. S. (1943). *Majority Rule and Minority Rights*. New York: Oxford University Press.

Dahl, R. A. (1958). "A Critique of the Ruling Elite Model." *American Political Science Review*, 52:462–469.

_____. (1961). *Who Governs? Democracy and Power in an American City*. New Haven: Yale University Press.

_____. (1980). "Procedural Democracy," In J. Fishkin and P. Laslett (Eds.), *Politics, Philosophy and Society*, 5th ser. New Haven: Yale University Press.

Diggins, J. P. (1986). *The Lost Soul of American Politics*. Chicago: Chicago University Press.

Downs, A. (1957). *An Economic Theory of Democracy*. New York: Harper & Row.

Flexner, E. (1970). *Century of Struggle: The Woman's Right Movement in the United States*. Cambridge, MA: Harvard University Press.

Green, F. M. (1930). *Constitutional Development in the South Atlantic States, 1776–1860: A Study in the Evolution of Democracy*. Chapel Hill: University of North Carolina Press.

Hamilton, A., et al. (1982). *The Federalist Papers*. New York: Bantam Books.

Hanson, R. (1985). *The Democratic Imagination in America*. Princeton: Princeton University Press.

Hurst, J. W. (1956). *Law and the Conditions of Freedom in Nineteenth Century United States*. Madison: University of Wisconsin Press.

Iowa State Convention. (1900). *Fragments of the Debates of the Iowa Constitutional Convention of 1844 and 1846*. Compiled and edited by B. F. Shambough. Iowa City: State Historical Society of Iowa.

Key, V. O. (1961). *Public Opinion and American Democracy*. New York: Knopf.

Louisiana State Convention. (1845). *Journal of Debates and Proceedings in the Convention of Delegates.*

Lowi, T. (1967). "The Public Philosophy: Interest Group Liberalism." *American Political Science Review*, 61:5–24.

———. (1969). *The End of Liberalism.* New York: W. W. Norton.

Lutz, D. S. (1980). *Popular Consent and Popular Control.* Baton Rouge: Louisiana State University Press.

Mansbridge, J. J. (1980). *Beyond Adversary Democracy.* New York: Basic Books.

———. (1986). *Why We Lost the ERA.* Chicago: University of Chicago Press.

Massachusetts State Convention (1853). *Journal of Debates and Proceedings in the Convention of Delegates, 1820.* Boston: Daily Advertiser.

McConnell, G. (1966). *Private Power and American Democracy.* New York: Random House/Vintage.

Macpherson, C.B. (1973). *Democratic Theory: Essays in Retrieval.* Oxford: Clarendon Press.

Monroe, K. R. (1991). "Editor's Introduction. The Economic Approach to Politics: What Is It? How Useful Is It in Explaining Political Behavior?" In K. R. Monroe (Ed.) *The Economic Approach to Politics.* New York: HarperCollins.

Monroe, K. R.; Barton, M. C.; and Klingemann, U. (1991). "Altruism and the Theory of Rational Action." In K. R. Monroe (Ed.) *The Economic Approach to Politics.* New York: HarperCollins.

Murrin, J. R. (1965). "The Myths of Colonial Democracy and Royal Decline in Eighteenth-Century America: A Review Essay," *Cithara*, 5:53–69.

New York State Convention. (1821). *Reports of the Proceedings and Debates of the Convention of 1821.* Albany: E. and E. Hosford.

New York State Convention. (1846). *Reports of the Debates and Proceedings in the New York State Convention of 1846.* Albany: Office of the Albany Argus.

Olbrich, E. (1912). *The Development of Sentiment on Negro Suffrage to 1860.* Madison: University of Wisconsin Press.

Ortega y Gasset, J. (1932). *The Revolt of the Masses.* New York: Norton.

Pateman, C. (1970). *Participation and Democratic Theory.* Cambridge: Cambridge University Press.

Pennock, R. (1979). *Democratic Political Theory*. Princeton: Princeton University Press.

Petracca, M. P. (1991). "The Rational Actor Approach to Politics: Science, Self-Interest, and Normative Democratic Theory." In K. R. Monroe (Ed.) *The Economic Approach to Politics*. New York: HarperCollins.

Pitkin, H. F. (1969). *Representation*. New York: Atherton.

Pitkin, H. F. and Shumer, S. M. (1982). "On Participation." *Democracy*, 7:43–54.

Pocock, J. A. G. (1975). *The Machiavellian Moment*. Princeton: Princeton University Press.

Pole, J. R. (1966). *Political Representation in England and the Origins of the American Republic*. London:Macmillan.

Porter, K. H. (1918). *A History of Suffrage in the United States*. Chicago: University of Chicago Press.

Rawls, J. (1971). *A Theory of Justice*. Cambridge, MA: Harvard University Press.

Redman, E. (1973). *The Dance of Legislation*. New York: Simon and Schuster.

Riker, W. H. (1962). *The Theory of Political Coalitions*. New Haven: Yale University Press.

———. (1982). *Liberalism Against Populism*. San Francisco: Freeman.

Riker, W. H., and Ordeshook, P. C. (1968). "A Theory of the Calculus of Voting." *American Political Science Review*, 62:25–42.

———. (1973). *An Introduction to Positive Political Theory*. Englewood Cliffs, NJ: Prentice-Hall.

Rosenstone, S.; Behr, R.; and Lazarus, E. (1984). *Third Party Politics in America*. New Haven: Yale University Press.

Sartori, G. (1987). *The Theory of Democracy Revisited* (Parts 1 and 2). Chatham, NJ: Chatham House.

Scalia, L. J. (1987, September 3–6). "American Ideas on the Extension of Suffrage: Implications for Liberal Justifications of Democracy." Paper presented at the annual meeting of the American Political Science Association, Chicago, IL.

———. (1989, August 31-September 3). "Democracy: An Inevitable Invasion of Rights?" Paper presented at the annual meeting of the American Political Science Association, Atlanta, GA.

Schumpeter, J. A. (1942). *Capitalism, Socialism and Democracy*. New York: Harper & Row.

Shapiro, I. (1989). "Three Fallacies Concerning Majorities, Minorities and Democratic Politics." In J. Chapman and A. Wertheimer (Eds.), *Majorities and Minorities: Political and Philosophical Perspectives. Nomos* 32. New York: New York University Press.

Simon, Y. R. (1951). *Philosophy of Democratic Government.* Chicago: University of Chicago Press.

Skinner, Q. (1973). "The Empirical Theorists of Democracy and Their Critics: A Plague on Both Their Houses." *Political Theory, 1*:287–305.

Spitz, E. (1984). *Majority Rule.* Chatham, NJ: Chatham House.

Truman, D. B. (1951). *The Governmental Process.* New York: Knopf.

Virginia State Convention. (1830). *Proceedings and Debates of the Virginia State Convention of 1829–1830.* Richmond: Samuel Shepard.

Virginia State Convention. (1850–1851). *Proceedings and Debates of the Virginia State Convention of 1850–1851.*

Walker, J. L. (1966). "A Critique of the Elitist Theory of Democracy." *American Political Science Review*, 60:285–295.

Whelan, F. G. (1983). "Prologue: Democratic Theory and the Boundry Problem." In J. R. Pennock and J. W. Chapman (Eds.), *Liberal Democracy. Nomos* 25. New York: New York University Press, pp. 13–47.

Whitehead, J. (1991). "Reason and Regulation in Economic Theory." In K. R. Monroe (Ed.), *The Economic Approach to Politics.* New York: HarperCollins.

Williamson, C. (1960). *American Suffrage: From Property to Democracy, 1760–1860.* Princeton: Princeton University Press.

Wilson, J. Q. (1973). *Political Organizations.* New York: Basic Books.

Wolff, R. P. (1970). *In Defense of Anarchism.* New York: Harper & Row.

Wood, G. S. (1969). *The Creation of the American Republic, 1776–1787.* New York: Norton.

Chapter
9

Rational Actor Theory, Social Norms, and Policy Implementation: Applications to Administrative Processes and Bureaucratic Culture

Roger G. Noll and Barry R. Weingast

At the core of most criticism of the rational actor model as a positive theory of human behavior lies the argument that rational actor theory (RAT) is ahistorical and based on methodological individualism.[1] The principal alternative, the communitarian approach, argues that behavior is driven primarily by commonly shared values and conventions which are internal to a society and which have value and meaning primarily, if not solely, within the social context in which behavior takes place. A second critique, while accepting the approach of methodological individualism, argues that rational actor models ignore all motives other than narrow self-interest. These two criticisms are linked in that social norms provide examples of shared communitarian values that conflict with self-interest.[2]

The objective of this paper is to illustrate that rational choice political economy is not necessarily restricted to behavior motivated solely by self-interest, and that social norms can be incorporated into the theory. Specifically, we use a rational choice analysis of administrative procedures and bureaucratic cultures in the implementation of policies to illustrate two points. First, norms as sources of individual preferences pose no serious analytical problem for rational actor theory, which requires only that individuals rationally pursue goals that are consistent and stable. We demonstrate this point by exploring the implications of semi-interdependent preferences as the basis for rational actor theory. Second, to the extent that a person's normative values play an important role in choices of actions, a rational actor can rely on—and make use of—this phenomenon in selecting another rational actor to whom will be delegated decisional authority. The core idea that we seek to elaborate is that political actors, in designing the administrative procedures of an agency and in selecting the problems which an agency's employees will be called upon to solve, create the set of normative values that the agency will seek to serve. In particular, these values will reflect the policy purposes of the coalition that gave rise to a policy at the time of its creation. Moreover, the character of these norms—that is, the extent to which they reflect the narrow self-interest of the winning political officials and their constituents or arise from a broader set of social norms—will depend on the political circumstances giving rise to the policy. Finally, we argue that if our argument is correct, bureaucratic autonomy or discretion is a form of false consciousness. The bureaucratic culture of an agency, having been constructed by rational political actors because of the predictable policies that will flow from it, creates the illusion of autonomy because, if the construction of the agency is sufficiently precise, its constructors need not monitor its performance to assure its compliance with their political objectives.

INTERDEPENDENT RATIONAL ACTOR THEORY

The rationality postulate of our argument is as follows. Regarding actions, we assume that individuals evaluate alternatives according to the extent to which actions are expected to achieve their personal goals. Regarding personal goals, we assume that individuals have interdependent preferences in the following two senses.

First, individuals evaluate actions only in part on the basis of self-interest. They also are other-directed in that they care about the effect of actions on other specific individuals, and to some extent are willing to sacrifice their own well-being in order to benefit others. The extent to which one person cares about another can depend on the latter person's identity, so that, for example, a person may ascribe greater importance to the welfare of his or her own children than to others. Or, in the extreme, a person may be a complete altruist, disregarding personal well-being for the benefit of others.

Second, individual preferences are assumed to be based in part on general perceptions of the characteristics of social justice. Thus we assume that individuals have preferences and take actions based upon such considerations as equity in income distribution, protection of individual rights, or preservation of the natural environment beyond the instrumental effect these social norms might have on the welfare of any specific person.

In the political sphere, we assume that political participation is viewed instrumentally as a means for advancing individual preferences as defined above. For voters, this means supporting candidates for office on the basis of the extent to which the preferences of a candidate are congruent with those of a supporter. Elected officials may be viewed as simply acting on their own preferences, with electoral competition causing some conformance to constituency preferences. Another view, which we believe is more realistic, is that political leaders are selected in part on the basis of their adherence to the representation norm of democracy. That is, they may value office in its own right or as a means to advance their own vision of a just society, but they do so with conscious deference to constituency preferences, either because they believe in representation as a value in its own right or because they view adequate representation as a necessary activity for survival in office long enough to achieve their own purposes.

If candidates are selected on the basis of the policy preferences of constituents, the nature and scope of government depends on the form of the preferences of the electorate. As we have defined them, interdependent preferences can take an infinite variety of forms because we have not specified the relative weights which people assign to their own welfare, to the welfare of other specific individuals, and to social norms. Consequently, as the foundation for a theory of individual behavior, interdependent preferences present a serious danger of tautology. Virtually all behavior can be viewed as consistent with some preference function. And if preferences are simply inferred in ever more elaborate ways from observed behavior, much as Ptolemaic astronomers managed to expand their theory in ever more complex ways to account for new data about the motions of heavenly bodies after the invention of the telescope, the resulting theory will be tautological.

We escape tautology in two ways. First, we consider preferences that represent either specific communitarian values or normative theories from moral philosophy and ethics. Thus we examine the implications of a positive, individualistic theory of behavior in which a rational actor pursues values specified in social norms or individualistic normative theory. Our purpose is to examine the predictions of a theory in which individuals behave as if they were rationally attempting to implement a particular set of social norms or normative values. Second, to the extent that revealed preference arguments are deployed, the purpose is to use revelations in one sphere of behavior to develop predictions in another sphere. We adopt the view that rational actor theory should seek consistency and universality. Consistency refers to the presumption that preferences are stable over time. A person's choices among actions are permitted to evolve only through mechanisms which are part of rational actor theory. For example, the preferences of imperfectly informed actors can change to reflect new information, but these changes must adhere to general principles of rational learning, such as, for example, Bayesian decision theory. Universality means that the same basic theory of individual decisions applies to a wide variety of decisional problems. Here we do not need to invoke a strong form of universalism, such as the presumption that market and political behaviors stem from identical motivations. Instead, we require only that all political behavior be derived from the same theoretical construct. This amounts to using the methods of microeconomic theory, but not necessarily the same assumptions about motives.

To elaborate an infinite variety of admissible interdependent preferences would require an essay of infinite length, so we will provide only a few illustrative examples which help to shed light on our analysis of bureaucratic culture. All examples, however, presume that preferences are, indeed, *semi*-interdependent—that is, that a person's own well-being is accorded at least as much weight as the well-being of another person, and that neither self-interest maximization nor complete altruism accurately describe most behavior.

The first example is the positive theory of a Rawlsian rational actor. Elizabeth Bailey and Robert Willig have formalized Rawls's difference principle in the context of benefit-cost analysis as applied to telephone regulation.[3] Their purpose is to define the circumstances in which a change in policy would be adopted by a decision maker who steadfastly adheres to Rawls's theory of justice. Suppose that individuals are indexed from the poorest ($i = 0$) to the wealthiest ($i = N$) in a society with $N + 1$ members. Let A_i be the net benefits accruing to person i under an existing policy, and B_i be the net benefits accruing from a proposed change. Welfare economics that incorporates the Rawls rule then requires that the following conditions hold true if the policy is to be changed. First, B_0 must exceed A_0 (to make the poorest better off). Second, $B_0 + B_1$ must exceed $A_0 + A_1$ (to assure that the second poorest person is not made so poor as to exceed the poverty of the worst-off person in the initial state). Likewise, for any person $i = k$, the sum of net benefits for everyone from $i = 0$ to $i = k$ must also be greater under B than under A to assure that person k does not sink below the ex ante state of person $i = 0$. Finally, the same condition for $i = N$ requires that net benefits be positive for all citizens taken together, which is the normative criterion of welfare economics.

The Rawlsian semi-interdependent preference structure is most easily represented as follows. Assuming $i = r$ is the Rawlsian, this person can be modeled as maximizing ($B_r - A_r$) within the set of policies satisfying the Rawls criteria as stated above. This amounts to a theory of politics in which there is unanimity that the welfare of the least well-off person should be maximized and that only policies producing aggregate net benefits should be considered. But within this area of agreement, politics will exhibit conventional jockeying for position (based on pursuit of self-interest) for relative rankings above the least well-off.

Alternatively, the semi-interdependent Rawlsian could be imagined to assign relative weights to personal gains ($B_r - A_r$) and the Rawls criteria, implicitly regarding one unit of improvement in the well-being of the worst-off as being worth no more than w_r units of personal sacrifice in net benefits. Thus policy C may be preferred to policy A if A_0 falls short of C_0 by 1 unit but C_r exceeds A_r by more than w_r units. This version of the Rawls rule is quite similar to the notion of "low-cost objectivity" propounded by Harsanyi.[4] Harsanyi proposes a theory of political participation in which citizens select among candidates and/or policies on the basis of social norms and/or normative principles of social welfare as long as they perceive themselves to have sufficiently low personal stakes in the outcome; however, once personal stakes exceed this threshold, political participation becomes motivated by self-interest.

A second example builds from the observation that certain disciplinary specialties socialize their members to adhere to certain social norms or ways of evaluating social states.[5] For example, one theory of the operation of hospitals is derived from a characterization of the norms implanted in physicians by medical education.[6] Likewise, some theories of the behavior of regulatory agencies attribute their procedural complexity to "lawyer dominance"—the behavior of an agency reflects the procedural values drummed into lawyers by legal education.[7]

A useful illustration is derived from the claim that economists tend to be obsessed with economic efficiency. Such an obsession, if accurate, amounts to a normative theory that society ought to be organized in a way that maximizes aggregate wealth. Achieving maximal wealth may require government intervention: pure public goods are a form of wealth, so that taxation and public enterprise are likely to be a necessity, and market imperfections (monopoly, externalities) generate less wealth for their beneficiaries (monopolists, polluters) than they cost their victims. But this caricature of an economist would advocate government intervention only because it increased aggregate wealth, regardless of its distributional consequences or its effects on noneconomic values. Slavery, for example, would be advocated if it increased the aggregate wealth of slaves and owners—a position, as far as we know, which no modern economist has ever actually advanced.

The goal of national wealth maximization is a form of interdependent preference because it explicitly ignores the welfare of the person who holds that peculiar normative view. The semi-interdependent version of unconstrained pursuit of efficiency simply places at least as much weight on one's own wealth as on the wealth of everyone else. To parallel the discussion of the partial Rawlsian, the person who is only partially committed to aggregate wealth maximization (person $i = e$) would be willing to sacrifice no more than w_e in personal wealth to achieve one dollar more in aggregate wealth (and hence $1 + w_e$ in the wealth of others). Our caricature economists, then, will favor breaking up their own monopoly or limiting their own pollution only as long as the benefits to others are sufficiently large to offset their own loss of wealth plus some additional threshold amount. One could easily develop more caricatures of other professionals; energy technologists who steadfastly pursue maximization of the ratio of gross national product to energy consumption, ecologists who seek to minimize change in the genetic inventory of life on earth, geneticists who seek to maximize that inventory by biochemical intervention, neorealists who seek to maximize the political power of the nation in which they reside. Of course, the purpose is not to draw cartoons but to examine the predictions of a theory in which public policy is driven by such preferences, ameliorated only by the parallel pursuit of self-interest by the person holding such views.

The point of an exercise to develop versions of RAT that conform to a variety of different normative values is to employ the power of the method in seeking predictions about behavior and its policy consequences. Regardless of motives, RAT—as a generic use of constrained maximization—will produce certain types of useful insights.

One important deduction from rational actor models is the generalized Slutsky equation, which, in economics, separates the demand for a commodity into a relative price (or substitution) effect and an income (or opportunities) effect. In semi-interdependent preference theory, the Slutsky equation has several useful interpretations. Applied to the trade-off between self-interest and the particular form of other-directedness embodied in the preferences, the key predictions are (1) if for some reason any given degree of altruism requires a greater personal sacrifice, behavior will be more self-interested, and (2) if for some reason a person is afforded greater opportunities (e.g., greater wealth, holding constant whatever gave rise to that person's preferences), greater altruism will be forthcoming (e.g., larger donations to charity). Applied to different norms that might be embodied in the same person's preferences, the Slutsky equation predicts that people will allocate their other-directed effort in activities that produce the greatest benefits to the other people whom they care about at the least personal sacrifice.

A second, less obvious use of RAT applies to learning and intertemporal behavior. RAT provides a theory about how people make inferences and how they take future eventualities into account when taking present actions. In the public sphere, actions do more than generate direct consequences in terms of the delivery of benefits today and tomorrow. They also affect the likelihood of alternative policy actions in the future by altering the relative costs of these alternatives and the set of opportunities available to actors (i.e., they affect prices and income in the Slutsky equation of tomorrow's political actors). The perfect altruist, if rational, responds to incentives in that altruistic benefits will be maximized if other-directed behavior is channeled in directions where opportunities are greater and the costs of effective action are lower. Hence, if today's actions affect tomorrow's opportunities, today's decision maker can affect the actions of tomorrow's altruist.

The salient feature of RAT is that every action is associated with a cost and a benefit, and together these effects produce an incentive. But the concept of incentive is not limited to self-interested costs and benefits, nor to benefits and costs measured in economic terms. The rational altruist seeks to obtain the greatest altruistic gain for the resources available, and so responds to incentives having to do with the relative difficulty of the various forms that altruism can take. Institutions—political as well as economic—affect the opportunities that are available and the relative costs of each. Institutions, in turn, are human constructs. Today's rational altruists, then, will construct institutions on the basis of the relative costs that these institutions will impose on future altruistic actions, seeking to advantage the particular form of other-directedness that is embodied in their preferences.

The semi-interdependent rational actor theory of politics incorporates three distinctly different forms of political contest. Because it embodies self-interest, it includes the narrower struggle among interest groups or other types of egoistic actors. It also incorporates the conflict between self-interest and other-directedness by explicitly incorporating this conflict within the preferences of political actors. Finally, it permits modeling the conflicts among alternative normative values and, especially, how institutions as social constructions allocate effective power among these normative values.

BUREAUCRATIC DELEGATION IN REPRESENTATIVE DEMOCRACY

Our illustrative application of semi-interdependent RAT begins with a series of observations about the procedures used by bureaucracies to make decisions affecting the welfare of citizens. Our discussion focuses on processes in the United States; in the conclusion we speculate on applications elsewhere. One important observation about bureaucracy is that, in the vast majority of cases, day-to-day decisions of bureaucrats are not monitored closely by elected officials, or even by high-level administrative officials who are appointed by elected politicians. For the most part, decisions about contract awards, eligibility for programs, or regulatory rules as they apply to a particular company, industry, or locality are made by professional civil servants. Only occasionally does a matter rise to the attention of the government officials who are presumed to hold the greatest power. Nonetheless, elected political leaders ought to care deeply about bureaucratic decisions. If elected officials actually want policy to serve their own political values, their success will depend on the actions, and hence the values, of bureaucrats who implement the policy. In addition, in order to continue to pursue their own political values, elected officials must gain ratification from their constituents when seeking reelection. And, in a democratic system, their standing with the electorate, and hence their likelihood of survival, depend on the way in which bureaucratic decisions are made. Specifically, if a political leader's constituency does not share the values served by at least some programs, the political leader is likely to face electoral disapproval.

Some conclude from the apparent independent action of the bureaucracy that, indeed, unelected officials actually run the government with little or no effective political control. This interpretation leaves unanswered a massive puzzle: Why would elected political officials permit such a state of affairs? Why would they not intervene to protect their values and interests, and reserve more decision making to themselves or, at least, to people whom they could control? And if political leaders are ineffective and powerless relative to the bureaucracy, why are they so successful in retaining office? And why in any event do constituency-oriented characteristics of programs, such as distributive politics and geographic balance, nonetheless seem to be manifest in many programs implemented by bureaucrats?

Scholars in administrative law provide some answers to these questions. In the United States, a reasonably lengthy and complicated body of law has developed which imposes procedural requirements on bureaucrats who are responsible for implementing policies. Although these procedures differ substantially among programmatic areas and are far too rich for easy characterization, the key features are as follows. First, decisions must be within the scope of the legislative mandate in the statute establishing the program. (In many cases, this is a minor constraint, for statutes are often broad and vague.) Second, decisions must satisfy some standard of rationalizability: the decision must be plausibly based on logic and evidence, and defensible as such. The precise standard varies considerably across programs, as well as the assignment of the burden of proof (e.g., is it on those who would change policy, or those who would defend the status quo?). Third, some degree of openness is usually required. Affected parties are normally given procedural due process—they can plead their case directly to the decision maker—and in almost all circumstances the information upon which the decision is based must be made public if anyone asks for it. Fourth, the question of whether the agency did adhere to its formal procedures is subject to judicial review. That is, a citizen dissatisfied with the result can appeal the decision to the courts, which will examine the agency's compliance with these requirements.

For the most part, scholars of administrative law do not view the development and enforcement of decisional procedures as essentially a political matter. Instead, they attribute most of the development of procedural requirements to the U.S. Constitution and the courts, rather than to Congress and the president. Moreover, they see these requirements as being derived primarily from principles of moral and political philosophy. Essentially, administrative procedures are seen as means for protecting individual rights against arbitrary exercise of the coercive power of government and for carrying forward the pluralist vision of representative democracy.[8] Thus administrative law is regarded as embodying social norms about the relationship between the citizen and the state in a democracy.

The final observation about bureaucracies is that they seem to have operational styles or "cultures," as emphasized particularly in the writings of organizational sociologists and social psychologists. For example, the Social Security Administration (SSA), state employment service agencies, and county welfare agencies all do essentially the same kind of business. They ascertain who is eligible for various forms of public assistance, determine the amount they are entitled to receive, and arrange for payments. (SSA deals with retirement and disability payments, state employment agencies pass out unemployment insurance, and county welfare agencies provide welfare to the poor.) Yet the operating styles of the agencies differ substantially. The retirement program within Social Security is generally administered with the utmost care and respect for the clients; by contrast, the SSA disability insurance program is often confrontational. Candidates for unemployment are typically treated in a rather casual, diffident style; welfare candidates are treated in a rather authoritarian, almost parental manner.[9]

To the extent that an explanation is offered for the differences in the style of administration of similar programs, it usually rests on a combination of the skills and training of the personnel who administer the programs and the likelihood that they must deal with cheaters—that is, people who make false claims for eligibility. Again, the notion that administrative norms for treating clients are rooted in politics is usually not pursued.

The rational actor theory of politics provides insight into the source of differences in the style of administration, which can be illustrated by further analysis of income maintenance programs. The differences in the implementation of income maintenance programs have two connections to a rational choice theory of policy implementation. One is concerned with preferences, and the other with institutional design.

The first connection relates to the preferences of elected officials and their constituents that would be consistent with these differences. Suppose that the generosity and client respect embodied in these programs can be ordered from retirement assistance (the greatest) through unemployment and disability insurance programs (intermediate) to welfare (the least). Assuming a perfectly responsive representative democracy unaffected by differences in wealth and mobilization, purely self-interested preferences would be broadly consistent with these results if the numbers of beneficiaries were also ordered in this way. Taking account of unequal political power, one might expect the ordering to reflect numbers weighted by wealth and participation. Because the two Social Security programs, in a probabilistic sense, provide expected benefits to almost everyone, their constituencies should be the largest and of greatest wealth. Again in a probabilistic sense, a smaller but still large fraction of citizens, including some in the middle but none at the top of the income distribution, enjoy positive expected benefits from unemployment insurance. Finally, welfare has the narrowest constituency. Probabilistically, it has the smallest fraction of the population having positive expected benefits, and the beneficiaries would tend to be those with low wealth and low political organization. Thus the self-interest axiom goes a long way to explain the ordering. But self-interest is not fully satisfying. It surely does not explain why welfare exists *at all*. Moreover, for most citizens private disability insurance is freely available and avoids the substantial internal subsidization from upper- and middle- to lower-income workers that characterizes the federal program. Likewise, the redistribution toward lower-income workers within both retirement and unemployment insurance is not obviously derivable from the self-interest axiom.[10] Thus for either voters or elected officials (or both), the preference structure that appears most consistent with the administration of these programs is semi-interdependent. Specifically, preferences appear to give more weight to lower-income citizens than is consistent with the self-interest axiom, and to apply a social norm which makes distinctions among the causes of low income according to the likelihood that the poor bear some responsibility for their fate.

Given these preferences, the characterization of the administration of these programs is further connected to rational choice by the implication that elected officials can create bureaucratic behavior (norms and conventions) that implements these preferences. Imagine that elected officials desire to create a bureaucratic culture which implements their preferences (whether their own or those of constituents). Presumably they could implement the program themselves, selecting from among themselves the leadership of the bureau. But with numerous programs and scarce politicians, this is not feasible for all programs even if the Constitution allowed it. Even in parliamentary systems which are not so constrained, only one or two elected officials occupy positions in each of a small number of very large ministries, thereby limiting their detailed control of programs.

An alternative to direct political control, which is perhaps less efficient in faithfully reflecting the officials' preferences but which conserves the valuable time of political officials, is to try to organize an imperfect bureaucracy. By selecting its process, the information available to it, and the nature of the people who populate it, elected officials can create norms which predispose their bureaucratic agents to implement the preferences of these officials. Indeed, our inferences about societal preferences regarding income distribution have validity only if political officials can so design an implementing agency. The alternative explanations, of course, are that humans are alike in their preferences, or that bureaucrats inherently tend to overlook their self-interest or the idiosyncratic aspects of their preferences and seek instead to implement the preferences of the political coalition that gave rise to a policy, just as worker bees always seek to serve the interests of the hive and its queen. But if a program is enacted amid controversy by a narrow plurality, these explanations lack plausibility. Our task, then, is to explore how bureaucratic culture is created. Of course, as we have explicated the income maintenance story, our explanation has the distinct ring of post hoc, ergo propter hoc. Henceforth, we will present our theory of administrative process in the proper deductive framework.

In essence, our argument is the following: the principles of administrative law and the organizational culture of an implementing agency are significantly influenced by political actors. That is, the relationship between procedures and culture, on the one hand, and programmatic outcome, on the other, is important, predictable, and, indeed, understood by political actors when they design government agencies. Administrative procedures and organizational structure create a set of decisional norms for an agency, and the norms they induce are predictable and hence controllable. Likewise, the details of eligibility requirements determine the extent to which cheating is likely to be the problem, and the kind of training required of a bureaucrat is governed by the type of screening and client relationship that is created by legislation. Hence bureaucratic cultures are in part created statutorily, and this source of bureaucratic behavior, while seen as norms and conventions within the agency, is in fact an intentional, rationally chosen instrument of public policy.

To say that these variables are influenced by conventional political actions, such as writing statutes, does not answer the question of how they control outcomes. The second part of the argument is that these actions create a relationship between agencies and citizens that recreates the political environment—the relative strengths of parties, values, and interests affected by a program—in the decisional environment of the agency. Thus agency norms serve to enfranchise certain groups (e.g., the retired before Social Security) and disenfranchise others (e.g., healthy males before unemployment and welfare agencies), and the manner in which they do so reflects the balance of political forces that the policy is intended to serve. Thus, agency norms *mirror* the political coalition supporting the program by *stacking the deck* in favor of values pursued by the constituencies who form the support coalition of the program. Agency discretion, then, is a delusion; it reflects the *autopilot* aspect of agency design, which causes agency decisions to respond favorably to shifts in the values and goals of the groups enfranchised before it.

The key idea is the following: the norms and conventions of bureaucratic behavior are linked to the purposeful intent of political leaders. Such an autopilot agency requires no time-consuming and costly monitoring; it is led, more or less on its own by following its norms and conventions, to do what political actors would do if they retained decisional authority. Thus agency norms are an equilibrium in a political struggle, reflecting the policy preferences of the victorious coalition. The absence of monitoring creates within the agency an illusion of discretion, which is itself part of the social construction. Hence the internal perception of autonomous other-directedness within an agency is false consciousness.

PROCEDURES AND NORMS AS SOLUTIONS TO THE COMPLIANCE PROBLEM

To develop the logic underpinning these claims, we begin by defining the problem from the standpoint of elected officials. Consider a new program that elected officials have decided to delegate to a bureaucracy for implementation. Once the agency is given sufficient authority to pursue the goals intended by elected officials, how is it prevented from altering the intentions of political leaders by implementing another policy altogether? We call this the *compliance problem*.[11]

The most obvious answer to this question is that if bureaucrats deviated from the intentions of elected officials, the latter could pass corrective legislation that puts the agency back on track. This answer turns out to be problematic. The reason is that legislation is usually the result of a compromise among elected officials who have different values and goals, different views about the desirability of the status quo, and different support constituencies. As a result, a deviation by the bureaucracy will benefit at least one of the officials who was part of the enacting coalition. This person is likely to reject corrective legislation, so that the deviation has the effect of breaking apart the support coalition that gave rise to the program.[12] Indeed, the members of the coalition may well have failed to agree on the original compromise had they known in advance that the *ex post* deviation would occur—or even had they known it might occur.

To illustrate this point, consider the case of U.S. environmental legislation at any time from 1970 to 1990, through which Congress and the president attempt to design a policy. The main issue of contention is that a majority in Congress prefers giving greater weight to environmentalists' values than to the interests of polluting industries in comparison with the inclinations of the president. These differences typically result in a compromise between the two positions. If the bureaucracy, when asked to implement this compromise, deviates from it by placing greater weight on environmentalists' goals, the congressional majority will prefer the deviation to corrective legislation that forces the bureaucracy back toward the compromise. Similarly, if the bureaucracy deviates toward the interests of polluters, the president will veto corrective legislation. Corrective legislation, therefore, is not an effective device for policing bureaucrats in environmental policy agencies.

The preceding analysis implies that the problem of bureaucratic compliance will loom large in the calculus of elected officials at the time that they create a program. By anticipating the potential for deviations that are difficult to correct after the fact, politicians can develop strategies for attempting to prevent bureaucratic deviations. We argue that procedures play this role and that they do so in three ways.[13] First, some general procedures, applying to all agencies, are designed in part to increase the visibility of possible deviations before they occur and to make them more costly. These general procedures also can implement the general democratic ideals emphasized by scholars of administrative law. Second, new legislation typically imposes specific procedural constraints which stack the deck in favor of certain constituencies (or strike a balance among them) and thereby increase the difficulty of deviating from the compromise intended in the original legislation. Third, by selecting the staff of an agency, the power relations within it, and its informational requirements for decisions, political actors create its bureaucratic culture, which embodies the type of semi-interdependent preferences that the enacting coalition seeks to advantage.

DECK-STACKING IN SPECIFIC POLICY CONTEXTS

In order to achieve their or their constituents' policy preferences, elected officials can be expected to attempt to tailor each statute to reflect the mix of values and constituencies comprising the winning coalition. Procedural and organizational language in statutes, therefore, ought to reflect differences in their political environment (constituency characteristics, underlying political values at stake, and the nature of the problem to be addressed).

In practice, the legislative emphasis on structure and process rather than substance often causes legislation to run on for hundreds of pages. Our hypothesis is that these differences stack the deck in predictable directions. The cases that follow illustrate the use of procedures both for inducing bureaucratic compliance and for creating the norms and culture of an agency. They also reveal the range of procedural options available to politicians.

(1) *Enfranchising new interests*. The rise of environmentalism in the late 1960s led to a series of challenges to existing policy across a range of agencies. Examples are the U.S. Army Corps of Engineers (responsible for flood control and maintenance of waterways and harbors) and the Atomic Energy Commission (or AEC, responsible for promotion and regulation of nuclear power until 1975). In each case the values of the coalition giving rise to the original policy did not include the concerns raised by environmentalists. Hence, when the environmental movement began to attack these programs in agency decision processes, its success was initially quite limited. But political actors, either sharing or responding to these newly emerging values, intervened procedurally by passing the National Environmental Protection Act of 1969 (NEPA). NEPA required all agencies to file environmental impact statements (EIS) concerning proposed actions and projects, thereby forcing agencies to assess the environmental costs of their activity, but not forcing any particular policy response to these assessments. The principal effect of the EIS requirement was to give environmental actors an avenue of participation in agency decisions using terms of reference most amenable to the values of environmentalists. Moreover, their participation could begin much earlier in the process than had previously been possible. Finally, the EIS requirements increased the ability of environmental groups to press suits against agencies in the courts should

the EIS be incomplete or the reasons for ignoring it poorly explicated or nonrationalizable.

The passage of NEPA effectively mirrored the new political environment in agency proceedings, and had substantial effects on policy. The regulation of nuclear power provides an illustration. As originally conceived, the AEC was designed to promote the peaceful uses of nuclear energy. The commission played a role in all aspects of this endeavor, including basic research, the development of prototypes, commercial demonstration, and the regulation of safety. The original culture reflected the values of scientists and engineers who were advocates of nuclear technology, and stressed cooperation between industry and government. Environmentalists threatened this culture, for they held values which were antithetical to the continued use of nuclear power.

The initial reaction by the AEC to intervention by environmentalists was to exclude them. Though the courts made absolute exclusion difficult, the commission was able to minimize the influence of environmentalists. This outcome was consistent with the coalitional agreement giving rise to the AEC.

NEPA altered this outcome by enfranchising the environmentalists before the AEC. This opened both rulemaking and licensing procedures to them, and imposed significant delays in licensing decisions concerning each new power plant. Even though initially the agency rejected all objections by environmentalists, the new procedures and environmentalists' participation concerning EIS added more than a year to the consideration of construction permits at the AEC.[14] This substantially raised the relative costs of nuclear power.

NEPA also transformed the culture of nuclear power regulation, changing it from partnership to confrontation, and from a process dominated by technologists to one empowering lawyers and decision analysts. Greater confrontation and substantive complexity added more delays and the rationalizability requirement led the agency to impose additional safety standards (and, hence, costs). By the mid-1970s, it became unprofitable to build new nuclear power plants in the United States.

(2) *Burden of proof.* One way in which procedures stack the deck is by determining who bears the burden of proof. Consider the Airline Deregulation Act of 1978, which transformed U.S. air transportation policy. Prior to this act, the Civil Aeronautics Board (CAB) required that air carriers proposing price changes show that their proposed prices were neither too high nor too low, but that they were "just, reasonable, and nondiscriminatory." In practice, this meant that if one air carrier filed for a lower rate or a new route, its competitors merely had to petition the CAB, arguing that the proposed change was discriminatory

(i.e., that it discriminated against them). The board would then post-pone the change, pending a hearing in which the burden of proof fell on the applying carrier. The latter had to show that it would not harm other carriers (which was impossible, since a price decrease or a new competitor would surely hurt them). This system benefited established air carriers by strongly inhibiting price competition and new entry. The culture that ensued was one of coziness with the industry. New competitors were kept out and the key dimension of competition among existing competitors—price—was strongly curtailed.

The Airline Deregulation Act dismantled the previous regulatory protection against competition by enacting a provision that reversed the burden of proof from the applying air carrier to those seeking to deny the applicant. By requiring the CAB to authorize a change unless it was inconsistent "with public convenience and necessity," this provision became the basis for initiating substantially greater competition in the industry. The legislation also transformed the culture of the CAB. No longer the guardian protector of existing carriers and their routes, the board now fostered a dynamic, competitive environment.[15]

(3) *Autopilot.* A good example of autopilot is provided by the regulation of cable television by the Federal Communications Commission (FCC). The culture that developed around the regulation of television broadcasting during the early post–World War II era was to insulate broadcasters from competition so as to promote greater "public service" broadcasting addressed to local community needs in a station's area. The local orientation of the public service norm, combined with limited channel allocations, led to an industry in which most communities were served by only a few stations. These stations were highly profitable, providing the opportunity for the FCC to try to impose some unprofitable service requirements.

In the 1960s, cable TV began to pose a major threat to this system because cable imported stations from distant markets to compete with local stations. The FCC reacted by asserting jurisdiction over cable, arguing successfully in the courts that though cable did not use the airwaves, it could alter the effects of regulation of the latter. The commission used its power to freeze the development of cable in the 100 largest markets. But this action was politically unstable, for the support coalition for broadcast policy included the independent stations (e.g., WTBS) which benefited from having their signals imported, and program suppliers, who viewed themselves as benefiting from policies which reduced the market power of networks.

Over the next few years, a political compromise was arranged by Congress and the White House and implemented by the FCC, though without the need for new legislation. Essentially, political actors over-saw a negotiation among the affected parties. The result was a complex set of new regulations and restrictions, which limited, but did not prevent, signal importation and pay-TV on cable. The rules slowed cable development by at least a decade, largely to the benefit of existing television stations, but they did not prevent it.[16]

Eventually, the steady growth of cable along with a dramatic fall in the costs of distributing signals (via satellites) allowed the cable industry to attract significant numbers of customers and, thereby, to become a substantial political player. The FCC reacted to the evolving mix of interests in its environment by reopening the question of cable regulation, eventually increasing the freedom of cable providers.

Cable regulation illustrates the autopilot aspect of administrative procedures—that is, the ability of an existing regulatory regime to adjust to changing circumstance in a manner desired by politicians, yet without the need for new legislation. First, the FCC allowed broadcasters a route to challenge the development of a a new, competing technology before it became a serious threat. Second, the process of investigating the issue provided elected officials with the means for forging a political compromise without recourse to legislative intervention, and the agency implemented the compromise. Third, as cable interests became a potent political force, the FCC institutionalized its representation. By creating a separate bureau for dealing with cable, the FCC removed cable issues from the Broadcast Bureau, which was dominated by broadcast interests. The new Cable Bureau then led the movement to overturn the previous policies and restrictions, in the beginning by granting literally thousands of case-by-case exceptions to the restrictive rules. Again, legislation was not needed. The initial freeze on cable, combined with the institutionalization of its influence, allowed slow growth, leading to the slow transformation of the bureaucratic culture from one dominated by broadcasters to one reflecting a more pluralistic set of interests. Along the way, the cultural norm of "local public service" was replaced by the "marketplace of ideas" as the touchstone of broadcasting policy at the FCC. Eventually, when the deed was accomplished the Cable Bureau was disbanded, and oversight of cable issues returned to the Broadcast Bureau.

CONCLUSION

The arguments presented here illustrate the value of rational choice political theory in providing an answer to an important puzzle—why public organizations and their administrative procedures are constructed with such care and complexity. If policies are inherently conflictual, they necessarily will produce winners and losers. An agreement to change policy is usually an agreement to favor some values over others.

When a new program is designed, part of the challenge for the members of the victorious coalition is to use structure and process to cause the decisions of the agency to be more responsive to the values that the policy is intended to serve and to maintain the political compromises negotiated at the time of enactment. Whether these values are purely self-interested or largely other-regarding is irrelevant to the applicability of the analytic method. Indeed, although bureaucratic culture may take the form of an internal social norm that is other-directed from the perspective of the bureaucrat, the apparent interdependent preferences of the bureaucratic actor may be the product of purely self-interested behavior by the political actors who designed the agency.

The discussion of the three cases illustrates two effects regarding bureaucratic culture. First, the dominant culture that emerges in an administrative regime depends on the nature of the political compromise engineered by politicians. Though these cultures are typically seen as norms and conventions within an agency, in fact they reflect policy decisions by elected officials. In the case of cable TV, the normative values governing broadcast policy changed to reflect a political agreement regarding the balancing of competing interests. This agreement was embodied in agency policy without requiring legislation. Second, a stable culture can be dramatically transformed via new legislation in which procedures, not policy statements, are the instruments of transformation. Enfranchising environmentalists before the AEC challenged the dominant culture of a technocratic partnership between industry and government in the promotion of nuclear power. Reversing the burden of proof in airline regulation transformed an industry from cartel to competition, at least for awhile.

The above discussion focuses on the American context, one notably distinct in Western democracies. Nevertheless, we believe that our basic approach of applying interdependent rational actor theory to understand policy implementation holds in other representative systems. In most parliamentary systems, delegation to the bureaucracy is associated with greater independent authority by bureaucrats. A different version of the compliance problem occurs in parliamentary systems. In Britain, for example, corrective legislation under the government that created a program is less of a problem because of greater party discipline and the dominance of a single branch of government, the House of Commons. Likewise, the need for corrections is reduced by the direct control that the ruling party has over the ministries.

Compliance problems occur in parliamentary systems because a government knows it will not remain in power forever, or at least as long as it would like its programs to endure. The practice of according greater decisional authority to career civil servants who are carefully chosen by the government initiating a program offers a possible solution to this problem. Under such a regime, a new government will not be able quickly and easily to dismantle the whole range of policies of its predecessors. The government which creates a new program, we predict, will use agency design and culture as means for dampening policy changes after the government loses power.

In parliamentary systems, legislation is a less reliable means for establishing procedures, for legislative change in parliamentary systems is relatively easy to undertake. A more reliable approach is to predetermine the norms and conventions of an agency by the appropriate choice of career bureaucrats in positions of authority. Thus decisional authority, as well as the information available in the agency (both necessary components for controlling policy outcomes), rests in nonpolitical officials with predictable values. For a new government to change these outcomes requires considerable time and effort. This reduces the likelihood that a new government will attempt the change, or be successful if it tries to do so. We offer the conjecture that in governmental systems in which legislative change is easy, officials will place greater reliance on creating policy inertia through granting seemingly greater discretionary authority to bureaucrats, and then carefully selecting bureaucrats whose normative values and educational backgrounds best comport with the policy intentions of the government that created the program.

Finally, our analysis provides an illustration of what we believe to be the most important power of rational actor theory. The logic of our argument requires only that political actors pursue goals and have reasonable foresight about the consequences of their actions and the way in which institutional arrangements shape decisions. Self-interest plays no necessary role; social norms and other-directed values were given active force not only in shaping individual preferences but also in adding predictability to the policy outcomes arising from delegation to a bureaucracy. To the extent that people's values and decisional proclivities differ and can be anticipated, bureaucratic cultures can be orchestrated by administrative design. Our evidence suggests that elected political officials know this and use this knowledge as rational actor theory predicts.

NOTES

1. The authors gratefully acknowledge the research support provided by the National Science Foundation, the Smith-Richardson Foundation, and the Hoover Institution, and the patience and insight provided by Kristen Monroe. The authors are, of course, solely responsible for the contents of this paper.

2. A third set of criticisms accepts methodological individualism and egoistic motives but rejects rationality, especially for circumstances

in which individuals are imperfectly informed and/or face probabilistic cause-effect relations. We do not deal with this approach in this essay; however, for a discussion of the relationships between rational actor theory and this approach as applied to the politics of regulation, see Roger G. Noll and James E. Krier, "Some Implications of Cognitive Psychology for Risk Regulation," *Journal of Legal Studies* 18 (1990), pp. 747–779.

3. Robert D. Willig and Elizabeth E. Bailey, "Income Distribution Concerns in Regulatory Policymaking," in Gary Fromm, *Studies in Public Regulation*, Cambridge: MIT Press, 1981.

4. John C. Harsanyi, "Rational Choice Models of Political Behavior vs. Functionalist and Conformist Theories," *World Politics* 21 (1969), pp. 513–538.

5. Peter M. Blau and W. Richard Scott, *Formal Organizations*, San Francisco: Chandler, 1962.

6. Charles Perrow, "Goals and Power Structures: A Historical Case Study," in Eliot Friedson, *The Hospital in Modern Society*, New York: Free Press, 1963.

7. Roger G. Noll, "Government Regulatory Behavior: A Multidisciplinary Survey and Synthesis," in Noll, *Regulatory Policy and the Social Sciences*, Berkeley: University of California Press, 1985.

8. See Richard Stewart, "The Reformation of American Administrative Law," *Harvard Law Review* 88 (1975) pp. 1669–1813, and Cass Sunstein, "Factions, Self-Interest and the APA," *Virginia Law Review* 72 (1986):271–96.

9. For discussions of the implementation of these programs, see Jerry Mashaw, *Bureaucratic Justice: Managing Social Security Disability Claims*, New Haven: Yale University Press, 1983, and the references therein.

10. In related work, Gerald H. Kramer and James M. Snyder derive a theory of the tax burden from the self-interest axiom, which predicts proportional taxes for the bottom half of the income distribution and progressive taxes for the top half. Income distribution programs, or perhaps taxes net of income distribution, plausibly should have the same incidence, but clearly they do not. See Snyder and Kramer, "Fairness, Self-Interest, and the Politics of the Progressive Income Tax," *Journal of Public Economics* 36, (1988), pp. 197–230.

11. For details about the nature of the compliance problem in governmental policy, see Mathew McCubbins, Roger G. Noll, and Barry R. Weingast, "Administrative Procedures as Instruments of Political Control," *Journal of Law, Economics and Organization*, (1987), pp. 243–277.

12. For a detailed exposition of this point, see Mathew McCubbins, Roger G. Noll, and Barry Weingast, "Structure and Process, Politics and Policy: Administrative Arrangements and the Political Control of Agencies," *Virginia Law Review* (1989), pp. 431–482.

13. A fourth (and obvious) mechanism is that politicians can specify policy objectives by writing detailed legislation, so that deviations can readily be policed in the courts. But this is problematic on two grounds. First, as in environmental legislation, efficient policy implementation may require using arcane and changeable technical knowledge, which cannot be anticipated in statutes. Second, it requires that courts not impose their own values in reviewing agency decisions.

14. Linda R. Cohen, "Innovation and Atomic Energy: Nuclear Power Regulation, 1966–Present," *Law and Contemporary Problems* 43 (1980), pp. 67–97.

15. Michael E. Levine, "Revisionism Revisited? Airline Deregulation and the Public Interest," *Law and Contemporary Problems* 44, (1981), pp. 179–195. In subsequent years, this was partially undone by still another procedural maneuver. Congress, in abolishing the CAB, transferred authority for scrutinizing airline mergers to the Department of Transportation, which quickly embarked on a program of allowing the industry to merge to monopoly or tight oligopoly in much of the nation. Normally, mergers are policed by the Federal Trade Commission or the Department of Justice. In this case, the DOJ opposed nearly all of the mergers; therefore, it is quite likely that had airline mergers been placed within the procompetitive culture of DOJ, rather than the proindustry culture of DOT, the airline industry would not have become as concentrated.

16. For more details on the development of the 1972 "cable accords," see Roger G. Noll, Merton J. Peck, and John J. McGowan, *Economic Aspects of Television Regulation*, Washington, DC: Brookings Institution, 1973.

REFERENCES

Blau, P. M., and Scott, W. R. (1962). *Formal Organizations*. San Francisco: Chandler.

Cohen, L. R. (1980). "Innovation and Atomic Energy: Nuclear Power Regulation, 1966–Present." *Law and Contemporary Problems*, 43:67–97.

Harsanyi, J. C. (1969). "Rational Choice Models of Political Behavior vs. Functionalist and Conformist Theories." *World Politics,* *21*:513–538.

Levine, M. E. (1981). "Revisionism Revisited? Airline Deregulation and the Public Interest." *Law and Contemporary Problems,* *44*(1):179–195.

Mashaw, J. (1983). *Bureaucratic Justice: Managing Social Security Disability Claims.* New Haven: Yale University Press.

McCubbins, M.; Noll, R. G., and Weingast, B. (1987). "Administrative Procedures as Instruments of Political Control." *Journal of Law, Economics and Organization,* 3(2):243–277.

——— (1989). "Structure and Process, Politics and Policy: Administrative Arrangements and the Political Control of Agencies." *Virginia Law Review,* 75(2):431–482.

Noll, R. G. (1985). "Government Regulatory Behavior: A Multidisciplinary Survey and Synthesis." In R. G. Noll (ed.), *Regulatory Policy and the Social Sciences.* Berkeley: University of California Press.

Noll, R. G., and Krier, J. E. (1990). "Some Implications of Cognitive Psychology for Risk Regulation." *Journal of Legal Studies,* 18.

Noll, R. G., Peck, M. J., and McGowan, J. J. (1973). *Economic Aspects of Television Regulation.* Washington, DC: Brookings Institution.

Perrow, C. (1963). "Goals and Power Structures: A Historical Case Study." In E. Friedson (ed.), *The Hospital in Modern Society.* New York: Free Press.

Snyder, J. M. and Kramer, G. H. (1988). "Fairness, Self-Interest, and the Politics of the Progressive Income Tax." *Journal of Public Economics,* 36(2):197–230.

Stewart, R. (1975). "The Reformation of American Administrative Law." *Harvard Law Review,* 88.

Sunstein, C. (1986). "Factions, Self-Interest and the APA." *Virginia Law Review,* 72.

Willig, R. D., and Bailey, E. E. (1981). "Income Distribution Concerns in Regulatory Policymaking." In Gary Fromm (ed.), *Studies in Public Regulation.* Cambridge, MA: MIT Press.

Chapter
10

Rational Choice: Theory and Institutions

Robert Grafstein

Institutions! Individuals! said Cranly,
you're a foolish bloody young man.

James Joyce,
A Portrait of the Artist as a Young Man

Cranly is not alone in disdaining analyses of individual-institution relations. For a time, rational choice theory prided itself on being as ainstitutional as possible. Fortunately, the last 10 years have seen the tide turn. In the name of the new institutionalism, it is now widely appreciated that institutions help explain how the same set of preferences produces different outcomes when aggregated in different social settings. Furthermore, increasing numbers of rational choice theorists realize that much of the stability one finds in social life would be inexplicable in the absence of institutional constraints on choice. Yet ironically, rational choice theory's conception of institutions, rooted in game theory, falters at the very task for which it was designed—namely, to explain the stable interdependence of rational actors in social situations.

This is not to denigrate game theory. Given the far-ranging genius of its founder, this theory may have been one small step for John von Neumann but it was one giant step for the rational choice approach. Rather than conceiving the agent as optimizing over alternative states of nature, von Neumann and Morgenstern (1953) saw that a rational actor would also take into account the existence of other rational decision makers. Social interdependence was finally recognized in a formal way.

The contrast implicitly drawn between rational action in natural and social settings, however, has not been an unalloyed benefit for the rational choice approach. One result has been a weakened appreciation of the extent to which an institution, like nature itself, constrains human behavior. This may seem an odd claim to make in light of the growing influence of the new institutionalism. But on the standard rational choice account, we will see, institutional analysis so-called serves more to summarize or describe behavioral regularities than to explain them in terms of institutions. In what follows, I will (1) demonstrate how the standard game-theoretical characterization of political institutions is inadequate and (2) in light of that discussion, suggest a replacement derived from evidential decision theory's version of rationality (see Jeffrey 1983). This replacement is better able to recognize the distinct impact of institutional circumstances on the ostensibly independent deliberations of rational decision makers.

THE STATE OF NATURE

A natural, and naturalistic, way to explore the role of institutions is to ask what problems they would solve for a collection of individuals who, lacking them, exist in a state of nature. It is routine to model this state of affairs as a Prisoners' Dilemma, which I present here in its normalized two-person form:

	B_1	B_2
A_1	y, y	0, 1
A_2	1, 0	x, x

where the utilities for agents A and B, who face alternatives (A_1, A_2) and (B_1, B_2) respectively, are structured so that $0 < x < y < 1$. According to the standard analysis, the payoff for each of the rational agents is the suboptimal x, since each reasons that A_2 (resp. B_2) is preferable to A_1 (resp. B_1) regardless of the other player's behavior. This, in turn, opens the door for the introduction of institutions as a means to achieve the superior result, y, for both.

Before we move to institutional solutions, however, it will be helpful to examine the agents' reasoning a little more carefully. If both players are rational, and this is common knowledge, why would players expect to find themselves in the asymmetrical positions (A_1, B_2) or

(A_2, B_1)? By the symmetry of their situations, some argue, what is rationally prescribed for the one is rationally prescribed for the other. This suggests their real choices are between (A_1, B_1) and (A_2, B_2). If so, the argument concludes, both would expect to come to the same conclusion that the former is better than the latter (Rapoport, 1966:141–142).

Or suppose neither agent can be sure the other agent is identically rational (Hardin, 1982:151–152). Still, each player might believe that the decisions of the two players are highly correlated. This does not guarantee that the expected utility of A_1 (resp. B_1) will be greater than the alternative (Jeffrey, 1981:485). Yet under some circumstances, one might claim, the reasoning leading to suboptimal results is inappropriate.

Those who see the need for institutional resolutions of the Prisoners' Dilemma have not been particularly impressed with this line of argument. The interplayer correlations, however high, should be disregarded on the standard view, since neither player's choice has any power to affect the choice of the other, who in fact may have already acted. Thus in selecting A_2, player A is not biasing the game toward (A_2, B_2) over (A_1, B_1) so much as biasing it toward (A_2, B_2) over (A_1, B_2). In fact, on the standard view A_2 remains preferable even when the interplayer correlation is perfect. For in the game under consideration, even a perfect correlation cannot nullify the objective causal independence of the two players' physical actions (Harper, 1985:221–223).

This interpretation of game theory goes back to von Neumann and Morgenstern (1953:41–43), who regard the fundamental rules of the game as a "physical background" against which unique or multiple solutions to the game emerge from the rational calculations of the players.[1] As we now see, this implicit contrast between player choices and physical givens resurfaces in the Prisoners' Dilemma as the idea that rational players can and do bracket out interplayer correlations when making their decisions. Since these correlations are social, not physical facts such as those dictated by the rules of the game, they need not be incorporated in the players' decisions about the best way to behave given their physical circumstances.[2]

The players, on the other hand, must confront their disappointing physical circumstances. One way, of course, is for the players to optimize within the constraints of those circumstances, though the result, x for each, is socially suboptimal. Another way, associated with social contract theory, is to assume that players can alter the Prisoners' Dilemma game itself. The trick is for them either to agree to a set of binding rules (a constitution) leading to better outcomes, or to recognize a third party who will directly enforce the superior outcome (A_1, B_1). By changing the structure of payoffs, agents embed them in a wider game in which the original Prisoners' Dilemma is but one (default) outcome. The players, therefore, are no longer confined to that Prisoners' Dilemma (Buchanan, 1975).

Stated crudely, institutions emerge because rational agents prefer institutional order to the anarchy of the state of nature. And clearly this preference for institutional order over anarchy is merely an induced preference reflecting each agent's underlying interest in the outcomes that are more likely to occur within institutions. Institutions are simply instruments for achieving these results.

The catch is to explain how these instruments bind the people who employ them. The social contract approach faces serious problems on this score (Grafstein, 1988). First, it is difficult for residents of the state of nature to secure an agreement to transcend the Prisoners' Dilemma, particularly for a more realistically sized society than the one just considered. This problem is substantial, notwithstanding the possibility of selective incentives offered by organizations and the efforts of political entrepreneurs (Hardin, 1982; Coleman, 1988:266–276).

Second, the contract establishing an institution requires players to have ex ante preferences for alternative rules, systems of authority, or constitutions. The crucial institutions do not evolve as solutions to Prisoners' Dilemma games but are supposed to emerge full-blown from the heads of the participants.[3] Nominally prepolitical actors are thus required to have quite an elaborate political psychology, even granting the "as if" sense of rational choice (Plott, 1972).

Third, institutions created in this way are extremely vulnerable to the kind of rational considerations that first spawned them. Those who support the agreement ex ante often have good reasons to dodge or renegotiate the agreement ex post. On the other side of the equation, those who ostensibly enforce the agreement face considerable incentives to violate or exploit it. The difficulties principals have controlling their agents (Pratt and Zeckhauser, 1985) can be exacerbated when the constitutional system itself is the subject of the contract. Institutional machinery, once established, also represents a significant lure to subjects seeking rents available to rulers and their partners (Coleman, 1988:266–276; Brennan and Buchanan, 1985; Vanberg and Buchanan, 1989:54–56).

This last collection of problems is an outgrowth of the first two. On the social contract view, the Prisoners' Dilemma is avoided by embedding it in a larger game sustained by players who can survey the enlarged set of possibilities. But this capacity to assess the state of nature and find it wanting in light of better alternatives is of a piece with the capacity to scrutinize and transcend the resulting institutional arrangements (Buchanan, 1975). The power to leave the wilderness is also the power to return. When institutions are understood in the manner of social contract theory, in short, they exist on the sufferance of the participants. So long as institutions are continuing objects of choice, the choosers, in the end, will not be the objects of institutions.[4] This, in effect, is the message of the third set of problems just outlined.

MODERN STATE OF NATURE THEORY

There is no gainsaying the empirical or theoretical legitimacy of social contract theory's claim that constitutions and the like do not always evolve but can be—indeed have been—intentionally created (Witt, 1989). Nor has social contract theory exhausted all the potential ways of resolving many of the difficulties raised above. What is important for present purposes, however, is the very conception of institutions undergirding the theory's insight into the creation of institutions. Social contract theory thinks institutional participants remain, analytically speaking, in a state of nature, since even existing institutional arrangements are always compared with other possibilities. There are always alternative institutions in consideration and the bottom line, reverting to ordered anarchy, is a live option.

Institutions understood this way are not just empirically precarious in ways further theoretical analysis may allow us to discount. Their precariousness is built into the very structure of the theory, making their utility and influence somewhat baffling. Though by no means illusory on the social contract view, institutionalized patterns of behavior lack any independent binding power. Like the interplayer correlations discussed earlier, they represent social facts that are not among the unalterable givens built into the game (in this case, the expanded game encompassing the Prisoners' Dilemma). They are the objects of a continuing choice whether to maintain or recall them.

Social contract theory's judgment that the agents who create institutions and the agents who dissolve them are essentially operating within the same analytical framework thus magnifies the empirical problem of accounting for institutional stability. By way of solution, Shepsle (1989:137–138, 144; 1986) suggests that a fundamental temporal asymmetry—institutions are first created and only then have their effects—serves to weaken the impact of this analytical homogeneity.

Once created, institutions become the background against which the decision to dissolve them must be calculated. And just as the framework of the Prisoners' Dilemma encourages the formation of institutions, so does the institutional framework discourage its own dissolution. Atomized social contract theory, in contrast, is seriously handicapped by its insistence that outcomes in institutional settings are purely "preference-driven" (Shepsle, 1989:136). Once institutions are chosen, their structures induce behavioral equilibria that would not otherwise exist.

As a solution to the problem faced by social contract theory, the upshot of Shepsle's insight is said to be this: "Like relationships, institutions may be thought of as part of what embeds people in social situations. They are the social glue missing from the behavioralist's more atomistic account" (1989:134). I think Shepsle is right about the significance of institutions. Yet on those very grounds, I doubt whether his account of institutions is complete.

Since Shepsle accepts social contract theory's explanation of institutions, his analysis of institutional effects must hinge on features of institutional life that are consistent with social contract theory's creation scenario. With this in mind, he appeals to transaction costs and risk aversion as frictions hampering deviance from institutional order. Existing institutions represent a familiar and settled pattern of behavior, whereas deviations involving more than one player will typically exact substantial transaction costs. The familiar is also expected. The much greater uncertainty attached to deviation will induce risk-averse players into continued conformity. In sum, deviation from the institutional regime is fraught with relatively high uncertainty and low expected utility. What the institutionalization of behavior means, in contrast, is that agents are better able to anticipate the behavior of others.

Yet this way of embedding people in social situations is not qualitatively different from the atomized theory's. The original social contract analysis recognized that since each agent's results depend on the choices of others, all must reason strategically in light of everyone's preferences and alternatives. Supplementing this game-theoretical insight, Shepsle insists that these agents are also entitled to factor in their uncertainties about the likelihood of alternative outcomes and the costs of obtaining them. To put it directly, on this interpretation individuals face a game whose payoffs reflect their fully calculated opportunity costs. This seems less a radical departure from atomized contract theory than an intelligent modification. If the original theory is preference-driven, Shepsle's is preference-and-belief-driven. What structures as such induce or do remains unclear.

The new institutionalism, in sum, continues to assume that the facts of social life, even the facts of institutional order and structure, are objects and products of individual choice in a way that the rules of the underlying game are not and cannot be if the notion of a game-theoretical framework for choice is to make sense. Accordingly, it inherits social contract theory's original problem: How can institutional structures induce anything when they themselves are still subject to the instrumental calculations of those ostensibly influenced by them?

[S]ince institutions and rules are the products of human choice, we should assume that like other choices, they are designed to attain some preferred set of outcomes. And, when such outcomes cannot be attained under them and when some set of persons possesses the appropriate means, those institutions will either be modified or bypassed (McKelvey and Ordeshook, 1984:201).

The conventional view of institutions is conventionalist to its core.

Before exploring how this excessive conventionalism might be extruded from the theory of institutions, I want to consider one version of the new institutionalism that more pointedly distinguishes itself from the social contract approach. Schotter (1981), among others, avoids appealing to a synoptic act contractually establishing a polity. He proposes instead an "organic" theory in which institutions are conceived as the unintended products of an evolutionary process.

The initial state of nature, according to Schotter, is best modeled as a Prisoners' Dilemma supergame, an infinite sequence of ordinary (i.e., static) Prisoners' Dilemma games. Cognizant of this sequence, agents do not confront supergames one iteration at a time. They adopt policies about how they should choose contingent on the previous choices of the other participants. As a result, Schotter demonstrates, tacit behavioral norms can develop that perform the crucial function of institutions in social contract theory: at the limit they lead rational players to produce the superior outcome (A_1, B_1), believing with near certainty that unilateral deviation from it will be disadvantageous. Though a set of rules which participants confront, institutions are also *solutions* to supergame problems rooted in the state of nature (Schotter, 1981:155).

In effect, this simulation of social-contract institutions achieves for its players the kind of social embeddedness Shepsle associates with institutions, yet apparently without the implausible psychological machinery of social contract theory. As a result, institutions are not *created* in the sense envisioned by contract theory. The more accurate reading, however, is that while Schotter's scheme does not require the full machinery *initially*, the relevant psychological paraphernalia of the social contract is in place by the time the evolutionary process reaches equilibrium (Grafstein, 1988). At equilibrium, specifically, players are required to have accurate expectations about everyone's behavior, which Schotter expressly equates with knowledge by all of the institutional norms (read: the rules or regularities of behavior). They must also know that all others conform to the norms, that everyone knows that they all know, and conform to, the institutional norms, and so on.[5] Ultimately, then, the full psychological machinery must be in place in order for institutions, as Schotter defines them, to exist. Institutions continue to be products of those who calculate within them. Social contract theory delayed, it turns out, is not social contract theory denied.

INSTITUTIONS RECONSIDERED

Let me summarize the conclusions so far. If the new institutionalism is correct, institutions have consequences that atomized rational choice theory fails to capture. Because methodological individualism is hard to give up, many theorists, as we have seen, find that the best way to accommodate this effect is to pack all the institutional details, the regularities of behavior variously called norms or rules, into the heads of the participants. Acting on this knowledge, participants continually reinvent the institution—that is, reproduce the behavioral patterns associated with it. The institution as such does nothing.

The attraction of defining institutions in terms of rules of this sort is that rules can be ambiguously understood either as abstract entities— universals—capable of being apprehended by one or more people, or as the internalized counterpart of those entities. Asked, then, to explain what institutions are, one can talk about public rules to which people conform; asked to explain why the rules are effective, one can talk about their psychological efficacy, normative or prudential. The efficacy of institutions can still be explained in individualistic, psychological terms.

The costs are threefold. One, the underlying conceptualization trades on ambiguity. Two, the psychology imputed to rational agents becomes less plausible. Three, the notion of active, institutional constraints on behavior must be sacrificed. And all this is by definitional or conceptual requirement; it is not the result of empirical findings. Institutions, in any case, are reduced to institutionalized patterns of behavior. In fact, they essentially become the products of self-fulfilling hypotheses: they serve as information confirming the expectations of the participants, who are really responsible for these patterns of behavior *qua* patterns. On this reading, institutions are no more active, let us say, than a dead deer that confirms to the hunter that he or she can stop shooting.[6]

The first cost is philosophical, so less obviously pressing. The second cost is significant, yet is one that rational choice theorists have consistently been willing to bear. The third cost is perceived as a conceptual nicety, if it is perceived as a cost at all. I am suggesting that the three are linked in ways that make the psychologizing of institutions a serious threat to the coherence of the standard approach, which recognizes institutional constraints only by dissolving them. In the end, these constraints are seen as collectively self-willed.

The awkwardness of this solution becomes particularly apparent in those theories with the strongest rationality assumptions and, therefore, those most comfortable with the internalization of institutions. An advocate of those strong assumptions, Lucas chides opponents of internalization by noting that "conventions and institutions do not simply come out of the blue, arbitrarily imposing themselves on individual agents" (1981:4). Rational participants, efficiently processing all available information, can detect any institutionalized patterns of behavior they witness and, accordingly, can choose whether to maintain them.

This conclusion, however, does not directly follow from strong rational choice assumptions. While institutions do not come out of the blue, they do not necessarily come out of agents' heads. For agents, like any social scientists, cannot be sure they are using correctly specified models. Given limited information, agents can find it difficult to decide which institutional model really obtains. If so, even fully rational agents need not converge to a common institutional interpretation. They can infer different models or arrive at different estimates of its parameters (Frydman and Phelps, 1983).

The possibility that the inferences of rational agents will not converge raises two related issues bearing on the problem of institutions in rational choice theory. One, whether rational agents converge to a so-called rational expectations equilibrium may rest, in part, on their ability to discover the true model. To say this much, we must already distinguish the social structure in which people operate from the structures even fully rational agents may perceive.[7]

To see how far this distinction can lead, consider that even if agents do converge to the same model, they may not converge to what otherwise would be considered the true model. In an economy, for example, the resulting equilibria can be influenced by stochastic variables extrinsic to the fundamental forces understood to drive that economy (Cass and Shell, 1983). These oddities have been labeled "sunspot equilibria" to allude to the random and ostensibly irrelevant events on which they can depend.

Two, the derivation of sunspot equilibria, like the debate over rational expectations generally, centers understandably enough on the proper incorporation and modeling of expectations. It may be, for example, that a necessary condition for the existence of an equilibrium, sunspot or not, is the initial or eventual homogeneity of perceived and actual participant beliefs (Phelps, 1983; Frydman, 1982). In light of this, Frydman and Phelps suggest that "institutions and social norms external to markets may play important roles" (1983:11) in providing the homogeneity successful rational expectations models require. Or in the somewhat more dramatic formulation of a noted economist:

> Expectations of natural events cause no problem. But expectations of a higher order—expectations of others' expectations—force economics away from this traditional safe haven. Where such expectations are important to an area of study, we shall find ourselves—God forbid!—in the same barrel with sociology and political science (Cagan, 1983:45).

Rational expectations equilibria, then, seem to demand homogenous beliefs. Homogeneous beliefs, in turn, seem to demand social norms or institutions.

In the work of Shepsle and Schotter, the institutionalization of behavior is tantamount to the homogenization of beliefs concerning the norms or rules of behavior. Yet homogeneity, it turns out, is not inevitable even when agents form expectations rationally. Rational expectations are no substitute for institutional analysis.[8]

And a fortiori, the traditional rational choice approaches of Buchanan, Shepsle, and Schotter are no substitute for institutional analysis. They too try to tame institutions by boosting the assumed cognitive capacities of participants, who must internalize the institution's rules. Accordingly, these approaches do not, in the end, recognize the extent to which participants may have unintended, partial, or incompletely understood behavioral relations with institutions. As a result, institutions are not the glue joining agents so much as handcuffs to which all parties have keys.

"The whole of Roman law may not have sprung fully formed from any one person's forehead, but its bits and pieces, much like the bits and pieces of a European cathedral built over many centuries, were surely the result of human agency" (Shepsle, 1989:145). Why not go further? Even the institutional pieces people create may not be intended as such, and, accordingly, the aggregate institution may never be intended or even encompassed as a single entity in their calculations.

To go further, we must appreciate that an institution, unlike a convention, should not be defined as an intended object of agent decision making. It should be understood as an arrangement of expectations and behavioral dispositions such that agents, rationally using their information, are led to reproduce the arrangement in question.[9] Understood this way, institutions typically relieve individuals of the full obligations of supervision and forecasting.[10] The choice, then, between institutions that arbitrarily impose themselves on individual agents and institutions that agents knowingly impose on themselves is too stark.

To make myself clear, I do not propose we *define* institutions as unintended or incompletely understood. This is an empirical issue. My point is just the opposite: for extraneous and unconvincing reasons, rational choice theory has forced itself to define institutions in a way that seriously limits these empirical possibilities a priori.

One impediment to recognizing this, I suspect, has been that the institution-as-creation theme seems inescapable. If institutions are not creations, they must be granted a distinct ontological status and this, many theorists feel, is no solution at all. True, the basic rules of a game—the structure of physical possibilities—already enjoy an independent status. But since they are constituted by the facts and laws of nature, their independence is unproblematic (unless you are a philosopher of science). To count institutions as distinct entities, on the other hand, seems a throwback to some atavistic form of holism.

For the record, I think it is possible to define institutions as distinct entities having empirically contingent relations with their participants. The solution, I have argued (Grafstein, 1988), is to interpret them as physical aggregates of their membership, limited to the times these members happen to be doing whatever is institutionally relevant. On this interpretation, the institution is not necessarily the object participants conceive it to be, but it is not supernatural either, its existence being no more or less problematic than that of the participants themselves.[11]

EXPECTATIONS AND INSTITUTIONS

> If the leaders of a country's economic policy are determined to embark on a program of disinflation, then they ought ... to devise a way to convey the idea that expectation of disinflation should be presumed, that it should be taken to be a fact.... In any case, there seems to be a need for a symbol, a catalyst, that will precipitate the expectation on the part of all persons that a certain desired expectation has become general, shared (Phelps, 1983:40).

The homogeneity of beliefs does not fall out of rational expectations assumptions about markets.

Much as the new institutionalism has learned to substitute supergame equilibria for the Leviathans of social contract theory, the alternative conception of institutions presented at the end of the preceding section would substitute institutions for the signals from authorities Phelps invokes to homogenize beliefs. Specifically, occupying an institutional role can itself be a signal about expectations.

Participants typically enter an institution not knowing all the details of its structure, its history, or the preferences and beliefs of every other agent. They are, in short, playing a game of incomplete information. Yet they may know they have distinct roles to play—say as voters—leading to outcomes that depend not just on any one of them but on the actions of those who also occupy roles within the institution.

What makes the institutionalization of expectations a fact for participants, I suggest, is their sense, by virtue of their occupying an institutional role, that their behavior is a good index of the behavior of other participants. These beliefs need not be based on a knowledge of everyone's biographies or sociodemographic data. To the extent institutionalization matters, their beliefs reflect a contextual fact about those in institutional roles, determined by a myriad of forces of concern only to social scientists and busybodies. The behavioral result is what counts: each sees his or her actions as linked, as a matter of institutionalized fact, with the actions of others.

Agents in roles discern, in particular, an unavoidable stochastic interdependence between their behavior and that of others within the institution (unavoidable, of course, does not mean inexplicable). If this relation were merely a matter of social convention, they could mentally step outside their roles in order to decide whether it was best to act with or against the statistical relation. But this is an institution. Their very ruminations contrasting inside and outside, indeed the contrast between inside and outside itself, are institutionally defined. The statistical relations will shadow them, appearing each time they calculate the expected utility of possible actions.

There is a decision theory capable of attending to these institutional interdependencies. According to Jeffrey (1983), rational agents choose the action yielding the highest expected utility conditional on that action. The conditional expected utility of an act might reflect, in particular, the act's stochastic dependence with the acts of others insofar as the likelihood of alternative outcomes partly depends on those other acts. If, then, one sees the conformity of others to institutional regularities of behavior as stochastically dependent on one's own decision to conform, the rational incentive to deviate, free-ride, or otherwise take advantage of the existence of the institution is reduced. In a stable institutional setting, the principle of maximizing conditional expected utility can make conformity to socially optimal behavior much more inviting, from a self-interest standpoint, than it might otherwise seem.

In place of the standard characterization of what otherwise would be a Prisoners' Dilemma, one now finds that the probability of identical behavior on the part of institutional participants is high and the probability of different behavior is correspondingly low.[12] The new renormalized expected utilities might in fact become:

	B_1	B_2
A_1	1, 1	0, x
A_2	x, 0	y, y

where $0 < x < y < 1$. What I have done, in other words, is to combine the utility and probability matrices to produce the expected utility for each outcome.[13] When the joint probability for (A_1, B_1) is high enough, its expected utility exceeds that of (A_2, B_2), which in turn exceeds the off-diagonal utilities whose initially high values are subject to heavy discounting. Under these circumstances, conformity to institutional regularities can be rational for agents maximizing conditional expected utility.

Earlier, this strategy for reinterpreting the Prisoners' Dilemma was shunted aside in the face of apparently strong objections. It is time to reconsider them. The principal complaint is that the probabilities built into conditional expected utilities are fooling the agents who rely on them. Since agents do not have the power to affect the behavior of others, stochastic dependencies are no guide to the specific consequences of particular actions. Probabilities notwithstanding, truly rational actors will choose the "hard-headed" acts A_2 and B_2 and hope for the best.

If one takes the original Prisoners' Dilemma to be the normal-form game agents are confronting, then it is true that allowing players to defer to stochastic dependencies makes a hash of ordinary game-theoretical reasoning. The calculation of mixed-strategy Nash equilibria, as one example, assumes that an agent's strategies can vary independently of the hypothetical mixed strategies imputed to the other agents (Harper, 1985:221–223). This independence is even assumed in Aumann's (1987) analysis of correlated equilibria, which otherwise allow players to take advantage of any possible stochastic dependencies of their strategies.

But it is wrong to assume additionally that agents maximizing conditional expected utility within institutions still implicitly act within the original Prisoners' Dilemma. It takes a careful assessment of the agents' situation to determine what game they are in fact playing. If, for example, there is no exit option, the Prisoners' Dilemma fully describes their circumstances and, *pace* social contract theory, they are required to play within it. In other game-like situations, however, the institutional dependencies I have in mind may be as unavoidable as the constraints modeled by the Prisoners' Dilemma. If so, they become built-in features of the game.

Following an idea of Harsanyi (1967–1968), we can think of each player A in this revised game as facing a player B, drawn from a pool of alternates. Some percentage of these alternates are exact clones of A, who, as far as A can tell, will decide to do B_k whenever A chooses A_k ($k = 1, 2$); and some percentage of these alternates will do B_j ($j \neq k$) whenever A chooses A_k. A can anticipate whether the possible players B have clonelike or anticlonelike attributes only up to a probability distribution.[14]

This stochastic element is thus built into the structure of the game independently of the agent's willingness to recognize it. Stochastic dependence, therefore, should be distinguished from the agent's voluntary adoption of mixed strategies. Mixed strategies, on the other hand, do raise an interesting problem for the conceptualization of stochastic dependence. Agents adopt a mixed strategy by using a randomizing device to select the pure (i.e., nonstochastic) strategies they will play. In such a case, would a rational actor take seriously any remaining dependence between the chosen strategy and the strategies of others? Is not the very purpose of mixing to prevent the exploitation of such relationships?

If a player is unable, or unwilling, to be committed irrevocably to the outcome of a random process for choosing strategies, then the statistical dependencies for pure strategy choices regain their importance. If, on the other hand, full commitment to a mixed strategy is possible, then "such a commitment should itself be considered an action" (Aumann, 1987:11). As Owen puts it, the random choice of a pure strategy is irrational; what can be rational is the choice of a randomization scheme (1982:13). If so, the decision to use the specific mixed strategy under the circumstances prompting this choice can itself be subject to unavoidable stochastic dependencies.[15]

In general, then, if there is institutionalized interdependence, statistical relations among the acts of distinct agents are unavoidable and can be properly factored in when the agent determines what is rational. On pain of embracing purely ad hoc resolutions of this issue, those who would object to this approach, we have seen, must be prepared to discount such dependencies even when they are perfect —that is, even when both A and B are certain the outcome (A_j, B_k) $(j \neq k)$ will not occur. On this dissenting view, in fact, A's knowing for certain that B's actions perfectly depend on A's makes it all the more worthwhile for A to choose A_2 when otherwise inclined to choose A_1.

Such is the radical freedom from social connections the dissent—the standard view—presupposes. Even knowing for certain there will be a particular outcome is not supposed to limit A's freedom to choose another, since the dissenting view is prepared to distinguish strictly between (1) A's choices and their consequences, which are subject to A's free intervention, and (2) everything else in the world which might be fixed and determined. The dissent's insistence on concerning itself with A's causal influence may seem hard-headed, but the metaphysics lurking in the background is quite delicate.[16]

CONCLUDING REMARKS

The standard view of rational choice has the weight of history on its side: the history of game theory as standardly interpreted, the legacy of that interpretation reflected in social contract theory, and, finally, the continued role of state of nature theory in the new institutionalism. If, however, we are ready to surrender the sharp distinction between forces of nature, on the one side, and the forces or facts of society, on the other, we may find ourselves with a more coherent conception of rational choice and institutions, not to mention one more likely to fit the behavior observed in real social settings and experimental simulations of Prisoners' Dilemmas.

Institutions presumably differ from social structures because they entail a greater degree of awareness or recognition on the part of members. They differ from conventions to the extent that they exist independently of the will of participants. A conception of institutions anchored in evidential decision theory is designed to reconcile these ostensibly opposing considerations. In contrast to the standard alternative, agents using evidential theory can comprehend the institutional facts their behavior helps collectively to reproduce without deluding themselves into thinking that mere comprehension necessarily makes these facts any less potent or any more subject to their personal whims. Institutional embeddedness matters because individuals, acting on this comprehension, must still act within the institutional constraints they now understand in the guise of conditional expectations.

On this interpretation, existing institutions are not at the mercy of time-travelers whose baseline for judgment is an ancient state of nature. The baseline for judgments made from within institutions is nothing other than the institutional status quo. This means that institutions are the framework in which agents make decisions concerning the inventory of possible acts, alternative collective arrangements, and the opportunities for leaving or reforming the social order. Though these institutions may not be there at the end of the day's calculations, they are unavoidably there at the beginning.

NOTES

1. For a more recent example, Harsanyi and Selten note that games of incomplete information arise because, inter alia, "players may have limited information about . . . the *physical consequences* to be produced by alternative strategy combinations" (1988:10).

2. As we will see later, Harsanyi (1967–1968) introduces an intermediate case in which an agent playing a game of incomplete information calculates the likely behavior of others based on his or her beliefs about shared attributes. But this agent can exploit these statistical relations by acting independently of them.

3. Shepsle (1989:138–143) notes that ex ante deliberations about the creation of an institution are subject to great uncertainty, and hardly any resulting institution can be expected to be truly "renegotiation-proof." This only extends the range of demands on social contractors who must anticipate that the original setup may encompass a procedure for institutional change (e.g., amendments) that makes the process of renegotiation part of the institution (p. 143).

4. I have argued elsewhere (Grafstein, 1990) against this postulated asymmetry between institutional order, which in analytical terms is precarious, and the ordered anarchy of the state of nature, which serves as the ultimate default option for all rational actors. Recently, Schmidt-Trenz (1989) has shown in detail how calculations leading to state-of-nature equilibria are affected by institutional possibilities, just as equilibrium institutions are affected by the possibility of anarchy.

5. Schotter's analysis, like many others, is inspired in this respect by Lewis (1969).

6. Along the same lines, Taylor (1989:135–138) complains that the standard rational choice definition of norms conflates them with whatever is normal practice (perhaps assisted by sanctions). Taylor's substitute notion is that norms involve normative beliefs. This substitute at least captures the idea that (institutional) norms do not merely describe actual behavior but have some distinct binding power.

7. See Aumann (1987:8–9) for an interesting discussion of this issue; cf. the response by Pettit and Sugden (1989:178).

8. This conclusion, of course, cannot pretend to offer a final judgment on rational expectations. It does show the sort of considerations that must at least be entertained by those attempting to reach such a verdict. What matters is the implicit acknowledgement that institutions can have a distinct impact on an agent who fully exploits information when trying to understand them.

9. The contrasting tendency to see institutions as solutions to game-theoretical problems, rather than the structures within which these problems are solved, can be traced back to the fundamental conventionalism I have been arguing against (see Grafstein, 1983).

10. See Gehlen (1964) for the unburdening role of institutions, though on his view they mitigate the individual's reliance on instincts.

11. Following Davis and North (1970), Bromley (1989:22–33) notes the possible confusion between institutions as rules and institutions as the organizations defined by those rules. Like most in the rational choice tradition, he opts for the former, giving insufficient consideration, I believe, to the problems with this approach. "Thus, it is not 'the rule', as such, that can explain behavioral regularities, but the social facts or constraints that induce individuals to act in accordance to the rule" (Vanberg, 1986:78).

12. Note that the dependence at stake reflects conditional probabilities, not mere coincidence. The dependence signifies not merely the fact that $\text{prob}[\,(A_1 \,\&\, B_1) \textit{ or } (A_2 \,\&\, B_2)\,]$ is high; rather, $\text{prob}(B_1|A_1)$ and $p(B_2|A_2)$ are both high. The former fact does not imply the latter.

13. For details, see Jeffrey (1983), who supports the standard recommendation and, therefore, does not endorse the application of evidential decision theory in this particular form to the Prisoners' Dilemma. For reasoning in the opposite direction, see, for example, Price (1986) and Seidenfeld (1985).

14. Harsanyi assumes that agents playing games of incomplete information will incorporate these statistical relations among player attributes into their calculations of expected utility (1967–1968:322–329). In a sense, I have suggested that we should extend these calculations to cover behavioral dispositions as attributes. In a full rational expectations model, of course, these probability distributions would be inferred from information given to players within the model.

15. This can be viewed as expanding on an observation by Shubik: "Sometimes one can step outside the usual conceptual framework of game theory and regard the probabilities [of mixed-strategy equilibria] as subconscious behavioral parameters rather than conscious choices" (1982:250).

16. The dissenters' reasoning faces the complications attending any seriously worked out causal analysis of decision making, which evidential decision theory is designed to avoid (see Eells, 1985, versus Levi, 1985). By the same token, there are some situations in which, on any view, A and B would be fools to let stochastic dependencies inspire their choices. They should go to a doctor when they are sick, for instance, even though there is a correlation between going to the doctor and being terminally ill. Fortunately, the foolish and wise uses of stochastic dependence can be distinguished within evidential decision theory (Price, 1986).

REFERENCES

Aumann, R. J. (1987). "Correlated Equilibria as an Expression of Bayesian Rationality." *Econometrica*, 55:1–18.

Brennan, G., and Buchanan, J. M. (1985). *The Reason of Rules: Constitutional Political Economy*. Cambridge: Cambridge University Press.

Bromley, D. W. (1989). *Economic Interests and Institutions*. New York: Blackwell.

Buchanan, J. M. (1975). *The Limits of Liberty*. Chicago: University of Chicago Press.

Cagan, P. (1983). "Comment." In Frydman and Phelps (1983), pp. 41–45.

Cass, D., and Shell, K. (1983). "Do Sunspots Matter?" *Journal of Political Economy*, 91:193–227.

Coleman, J. L. (1988). *Markets, Morals and the Law*. Cambridge: Cambridge University Press.

Davis, L. E., and North, D. C. (1970). "Institutional Change and American Economic Growth: A First Step Toward a Theory of Institutional Innovation." *Journal of Economic History*, 30:131–149.

Eells, E. (1985). "Levi's 'The Wrong Box'." *Journal of Philosophy*, 82:91–104.

Frydman, R. (1982). "Towards an Understanding of Market Processes: Individual Expectations, Learning and Convergence to Rational Expectations Equilibrium." *American Economic Review*, 72:652–668.

Frydman, R., and Phelps, E. S. (Eds.). (1983). *Individual Forecasting and Aggregate Outcomes*. Cambridge: Cambridge University Press.

Gehlen, A. (1964). *Urmensch und Spätkultur*. Frankfurt am Main: Athenäum.

Grafstein, R. (1983). "The Social Scientific Interpretation of Game Theory." *Erkenntnis*, 20:27–47.

———. (1988). "The Problem of Institutional Constraint." *Journal of Politics*, 50:577–599.

———. (1990). "Missing the Archimedean Point: Liberalism's Institutional Presuppositions." *American Political Science Review*, 84:177–193.

Hardin, R. (1982). *Collective Action*. Baltimore: Johns Hopkins University Press.

Harper, W. (1985). "Ratifiability and Causal Decision Theory: Comments on Eells and Seidenfeld." *PSA 1984*, 2:213–228.

Harsanyi, J. C. (1967–1968). "Games with Incomplete Information Played by 'Bayesian' Players, I–III." *Management Science*, *14*:159–182, 320–334, 486–502.

Harsanyi, J. C., and Selten, R. (1988). *A General Theory of Equilibrium Selection in Games*. Cambridge, MA: MIT Press.

Jeffrey, R. (1981). "The Logic of Decision Defended." *Synthese*, 48:473–492.

———. (1983). *The Logic of Decision*. Chicago: University of Chicago Press.

Levi, I. (1985). "Epicycles." *Journal of Philosophy*, 82:104–106.

Lewis, D. K. (1969). *Convention: A Philosophical Study*. Cambridge, MA: Harvard University Press.

Lucas, R. E., Jr. (1981). *Studies in Business-Cycle Theory.*. Cambridge, MA: MIT Press.

McKelvey, R. D., and Ordeshook, P. C. (1984). "An Experimental Study of the Effects of Procedural Rules on Committee Behavior." *Journal of Politics*, 46:182–205.

Owen, G. (1982). *Game Theory*. Orlando, FL: Academic Press.

Pettit, P., and Sugden, R. (1989). "The Backward Induction Paradox." *Journal of Philosophy*, 86:169–182.

Phelps, E. S. (1983). "The Trouble with 'Rational Expectations' and the Problem of Inflation Stabilization." In Frydman and Phelps (1983), pp. 31–41.

Plott, C. R. (1972). "Individual Choice of Political-Economic Process." In R. G. Niemi and H. F. Weisberg (Eds.). *Probability Models of Collective Decision Making*. Columbus, OH: Merrill.

Pratt, J. W., and Zeckhauser, R. J. (Eds.). (1985). *Principals and Agents: The Structure of Business*. Cambridge, MA: Harvard Business School Press.

Price, H. (1986). "Against Causal Decision Theory." *Synthese*, 67:195–212.

Rapoport, A. (1966). *Two-Person Game Theory*. Ann Arbor: University of Michigan Press.

Schmidt-Trenz, H.-J. (1989). "The State of Nature in the Shadow of Contract Formation: Adding a Missing Link to J. M. Buchanan's Social Contract Theory." *Public Choice*, 62:237–251.

Schotter, A. (1981). *The Economic Theory of Social Institutions*. Cambridge: Cambridge University Press.

Seidenfeld, T. (1985). "Comments on Causal Decision Theory." *PSA 1984*, 2:201–212.

Shepsle, K. A. (1986). "Institutional Equilibrium and Equilibrium Institutions." In H. Weisberg (Ed.), *Political Science: The Science of Politics*. New York: Agathon.

———. (1989). "Studying Institutions: Some Lessons from the Rational Choice Approach." *Journal of Theoretical Politics*, 1:131–147.

Shubik, M. (1982). *Game Theory and the Social Sciences*. Cambridge, MA: MIT Press.

Taylor, M. (1989). "Structure, Culture and Action in the Explanation of Social Change." *Politics & Society*, 17:115–162.

Vanberg, V. (1986). "Spontaneous Market Order and Social Rules." *Economics and Philosophy*, 2:75–100.

Vanberg, V., and Buchanan, J. M. (1989). "Interests and Theories in Constitutional Choice." *Journal of Theoretical Politics*, 1:49–62.

von Neumann, J., and Morgenstern, O. (1953). *Theory of Games and Economic Behavior*. New York: Wiley.

Witt, U. (1989). "The Evolution of Economic Institutions as a Propagation Device." *Public Choice*, 62:155–172.

Rationality and Interpretation: Parliamentary Elections in Early Stuart England

John Ferejohn

INTRODUCTION

It is sometimes thought that rational choice and interpretive explanations of social phenomena are intrinsically opposed to each other in the sense that if one is successful in accounting for something, the other must be either wrong or superfluous. In this essay I try to show why this view is not only incorrect but is also profoundly unproductive in helping us to a richer understanding of social life.

I shall argue that rational accounts and interpretive accounts are or can be complementary in an important sense. Both interpretive and rational explanations are inherently incomplete as accounts of action. At best either type of explanation can eliminate certain patterns of action as inconsistent, but they cannot fully account for social action. Fortunately, the incompleteness of each kind of explanation can be (partly) overcome by appeal to the other.

To demonstrate this claim, I examine the institutions and practices of parliamentary selection as they operated in early seventeenth-century England. There are two broad historical accounts of these practices and institutions: Whig and revisionist. Whig history sees parliamentary elections of that period as similar to elections anywhere, anytime: elections are simply contests for votes among politicians ambitious to obtain office and implement their policies. In order to win office, competing politicians devise programs, aimed at attracting support, develop organizations to mobilize this support, and attempt to manipulate the franchise to their advantage. Seventeenth-century practices and institutions were, to be sure, imperfect versions of more modern ones. Electoral institutions were young then and easily subverted or deflected in practice. Thus they were more tarnished by corruption, ineptness, and casualness; but once account is taken of these superficial imperfections, the logic of electoral competition was pretty much the same then as now.

The revisionist account of this period rejects this view as anachronistic and constructs in its place a self-consciously "interior" (or cultural) interpretation of the perceptions, identities, and meanings of the seventeenth-century English in order to understand the practices by which members of Parliament were chosen. For the revisionists, these practices were not aimed at winning or holding office or implementing rival policies but were aimed, instead, at recognizing and reinforcing local social solidarity by suppressing competition in an ordered hierarchical society. Thus seventeenth-century electoral practices are really best seen as vestiges of a recent medieval past and not as harbingers of an era of democratic Enlightenment.

These two accounts, the one anachronistic, the other antiquarian, are sometimes thought to stand as irreconcilable alternatives in the historiography of the period. I shall show that each approach contains both rational and interpretive aspects and that each is necessary for an understanding of the practices of the period, and specifically for a richer understanding of how these practices changed in the course of the "long century."

RATIONAL AND CULTURAL EXPLANATION

If, as I claim, rational and interpretive accounts are complementary, why is it that practitioners of each see them in conflict? Part of the reason lies in their differing conceptions of the feasible aims of social science. Generally speaking, rational choice theorists aim at developing theories that can explain and predict observed patterns of behavior and practice. They are committed to a particular kind of philosophy of science, one which attempts to produce lawlike claims about measurable phenomena and in which one theory is judged better than another only if it provides a coherent account of a wider range of observed data.

Interpretivists, [1] on the other hand, reject the possibility of prediction in this sense.[2] For them the proper aim of social science is to interpret practices, behaviors, and institutions by reconstructing the meanings that infect them, by understanding how the agents constitute themselves, their values, and their preferences, in relation to their actions. Charles Taylor, one of the most articulate defenders of this approach and one who is at pains to emphasize the differences between culturalist-interpretivist and positivistic approaches (with which he would place rational choice theory), argues that social sciences cannot hope to predict behavior. At best, social science is an ex post enterprise in which we can hope only to come to some understanding of events and practices after the fact.[3]

Nevertheless, there are criteria for judging among cultural accounts. For example, one account of an event, practice, or institution—one construction of meanings and understandings—is better than another if it can explain (in the sense of making more comprehensible) more aspects of the event, practice, or institution than another.[4] Thus, at minimum, interpretivists seem committed to a coherence test, but, insofar as the demand of comprehensibility is fleshed out, they might endorse a larger set of comparative criteria for judging theories.

Leaving aside issues of measurement, there is nothing in this comparative principle that should seem inhospitable to the rational choice theorist. Rational choice theory is, in this sense, an interpretive theory that constructs explanations by "reconstructing" patterns of meanings and understandings (preferences and beliefs) in such a way that agents' actions can be seen as maximal, given their beliefs. In this sense the logic of rational choice and the logic of interpretivist or culturalist approaches are similar: start with observed data (behavior including documents and letters, practices, institutions) and reconstruct actors and their inner attributes (meanings, beliefs, values) in such a way that the data are as fully explained or accounted for as possible. As Jon Elster argues, both are forms of intentional explanation and are at least formally similar in that respect.[5] Moreover, cultural or interpretive accounts, if they are to ring true to us, must have some aspect of rationality embedded in them. To understand someone's actions implies at minimum that if we had their goals, beliefs, and opportunities, their actions would be plausible choices for us.[6]

The main differences between the approaches seems to lie elsewhere. At the most abstract level, rational choice theorists are committed to a principle of universality: (all) agents act always to maximize their well-being as they understand it, based on their beliefs, preferences, and strategic opportunities. This commitment to a universal description of agents is what permits rational choice theorists to believe in the possibility of prediction as well as ex post explanation. Culturalists argue either that this commitment is so weak as to be without meaning, or that it is merely an article of faith and that there is no a priori reason to believe that the similarity of human agents is particularly extensive.[7] Humans are simply too reflexive, too self-conscious, and too malleable for such universalistic claims to have much truth or power. Instead, interpretivists proceed by taking the data of a given situation, event, or practice and reconstruct meanings and understandings specific to agents in those circumstances. This "thick" description of an event or "text" and its meanings to participants is supposed to stand as an explanation of the event or practice.

At a more concrete level, it is necessary to distinguish among various types of accounts offered by rational choice theorists. In what I call a "thin-rational" account, the theorist assumes only that agents are (instrumentally) rational, that they efficiently employ the means available to pursue their ends. In a "thick-rational" account, the analyst posits not only rationality but some additional description of agent preferences and beliefs. Thick-rational choice theorists generally assume that agents in a wide variety of situations value the same sorts of things: for example, wealth, income, power, or the perquisites of office. A substantial part of the power of a rational choice approach comes from (thickly) specifying the "objective function" of the agents in a way that is separable from the context of decision.

For example, neoclassical consumer theory is essentially a thin-rational account, since it is based only on the assumption that individuals act as though they are maximizing something, although that thing is specified formally only under the name of "utility." The other component of neoclassical economics, the theory of the firm, is based on the thick-rational assumption that firms act as profit maximizers.[8]

While culturalists criticize thin-rational accounts on the grounds that they seem empty, their criticism of thick-rational accounts is that they are anachronistic (when applied to distant times) or ethnocentric (when applied to distant places or peoples). Thick-rational accounts, even where they might seem plausible, are flawed because they contain no theory determining the selection of agent identities, values, beliefs, and strategic opportunities. Without such a theory, there is no (nonethnocentric) reason to make the types of universal assumptions found in thick-rational accounts: that economic actors are wealth maximizers, that politicians are eager to pursue office, and so forth. These things may all be true of the world we live in, but, without further justification, there is no warrant for exporting such assumptions across expanses of time and space.[9]

TWO KINDS OF INCOMPLETENESS

Interpretivists are characteristically suspicious of general claims about human nature, preferring to see individuals as plastic and malleable and as possessed of a wide range of capacities. Thus they often limit attention to the self-interpretations of the agents and ignore other information about human agents that may be available to the analyst. But by restricting the range of observations to a specific time and place and by resisting the urge to attribute universal attributes to actors, they inevitably expand the range of defensible alternative theories or understandings of a given situation. While the domain of observations that can be employed to discriminate among theories is fixed and finite, the set of theories that can be "fit" to these observations is infinite.

This inability to eliminate alternative accounts is the price of the interpretivist's "open-mindedness." Interpretivists sometimes deal with this indeterminacy by trying to explain social action in terms of intersubjective meanings embedded in institutions and practices.[10] Intersubjective or cultural meanings limit the beliefs, self-interpretations, and values available to individuals so that many logically conceivable patterns of practice and behavior may be eliminated. Of course, such accounts leave open two questions: first, how does the analyst arrive at, or "infer," an interpretation or cultural description (the hermeneutical circle)? Second, how fully can such a description delimit agent characteristics and choices?

None of this is to say that culturalists never propose specific interpretations. Often they do. However, the jump to a specific account is not dictated by their method at all but is driven instead by some intuition external to it. Taylor asks how we can convince another person of the correctness of our interpretation of a text. He says that we must

> try to show him how it makes sense of the original nonsense or partial sense. But for him to follow us he must read the original language as we do.... If he does not, what can we do? The answer, it would seem, can only be more of the same.... Success here requires that he follow us in these other readings, and so on, it would seem, potentially forever. We cannot escape an ultimate appeal to a common understanding of the expressions."(1985:17)

Taylor seems to suggest that if different analysts consider the same event, and they come to different coherent interpretations, there would be no criterion within the approach to decide between them. Taylor calls this appeal to the intuition of the interpreter the "hermeneutical circle"; I call it incompleteness.[11]

If interpretive methods are weak in failing to discriminate sharply among alternative explanations, rational choice theories share a similar indeterminacy, though for different reasons. A rational choice account of an interaction—a rational reconstruction—aims to explain a social action by reconstructing the agents' beliefs, values, and strategic opportunities (everything there is that is relevant to choice) and showing that the outcome corresponds to equilibrium behavior in this situation or game. An account of an interaction is completely successful if the outcome can be shown to be the unique equilibrium in the resulting game.

Recent work in game theory, however, has shown that in a very wide class of situations of strategic interaction—indeed, in virtually any game that takes place over time or in which there is a nontrivial informational structure—almost any outcome can occur in some game-theoretical equilibrium. This indeterminacy, often called the "folk theorem" by game theorists, suggests that unless we substantially enrich the concept of rationality itself, or supplement it with extra assumptions about human nature, rationality by itself cannot fully account for the selection of one outcome rather than another. In this sense, the naive hope of complete rational reconstruction—the reductionist project—cannot work. At best, rational reconstruction may be necessary for an explanation of social action; it cannot be sufficient.

It is useful to give an example of the reach of the folk theorem to show how it applies to an apparently familiar and misunderstood problem: the infinitely repeated Prisoners' Dilemma game. In the one-shot or stage game, there is a unique equilibrium in which neither player cooperates. As is well known, under pretty general conditions, in repeated play there is another equilibrium in which both players cooperate each time. People sometimes conclude from this observation that repeated play leads to cooperation and that the cooperative outcome is a prediction of the repeated-play Prisoners' Dilemma. The folk theorem, however, says that in fact there are a lot of other (indeed, infinitely many) equilibrium outcomes sustainable in this game: specifically, any outcome in which both players receive more than they would in the noncooperative outcome. For instance (assuming that the values attached to outcomes satisfy a certain condition), the players could take turns cooperating and defecting.[12] There is nothing internal to game theory or rational choice theory that allows the analyst to "predict" the play of one such equilibrium rather than another, so that the prediction of cooperation in this setting does not follow from principles of rationality but from some other (nonrational) assumption about how the game will be played.

To obtain a unique prediction, we need to appeal to an auxiliary principle that would allow the agents to coordinate their behavior on a specific equilibrium. In the Prisoners' Dilemma, for example, the game is usually presented in a symmetric form in which the analyst's eye is drawn to the symmetric equilibrium in which both players cooperate. Obviously, this symmetry is artificial in the sense that it has nothing intrinsically to do with the characteristic feature of Prisoners' Dilemmas—that equilibrium play is not efficient—and would not be expected to occur naturally in many situations.

While there is little agreement among game theorists as to what kinds of auxiliary assumptions are most plausible for selecting among equilibria, many theorists, beginning with Thomas Schelling,[13] have appealed to intersubjective or cultural understandings which permit the actors to focus on one equilibrium among many. In effect, in order to carry out a complete game-theoretical analysis of a game with multiple equilibria, one must assume that somehow it is common knowledge among the agents exactly which equilibrium is being played.[14] Nothing internal to the theory of games, or in the nature of rationality, will accomplish this.

While each approach is plagued by characteristic indeterminacy, these indeterminacies can be partially alleviated by appeal to the other approach. The culturalist can narrow the range of plausible interpretations of an event or practice by appealing to (universal or at least broadly shared) principles of consistent purposive action implied by the possibility of intersubjective comprehensibility. The rational choice theorist may be able to select among equilibria by appealing to culturally shared understandings and meanings necessary to select among strategic equilibria.[15]

The source of this theoretical complementarity is found not in sheer coincidence but in the nature of the relationship between the sphere of action or choice and the sphere of meanings or understandings.[16] In social action, human agents make strategic or allocative choices while simultaneously enacting (ontologically) prior understandings about the nature of the strategic situation in which they find themselves, the characteristics or identities of the players (including themselves), and the common understandings or expectations as to how the game will be played. Thus, when it comes to explaining action, rational accounts, no less than interpretive ones, must appeal to principles external to the individual agents. That appeal may be to historical practice or to cultural expectations, but in any case it remains ad hoc and external to the theory.

Thus neither rational nor interpretive accounts can wholly succeed in explaining social events and practices. Because human practices and institutions are located on the boundary between the sphere of action— where they are constrained by the logic of rational choice and calculation—and the sphere of meanings—which is constrained by subtler ideational logics—they cannot be completely understood without taking both spheres into account. In the end, while neither rational nor interpretive approaches can offer sufficient accounts of social institutions and practices, each can claim to offer necessary components of an adequate explanation.

Obviously, this account of the differences and similarities between rational and cultural accounts is stylized and overemphasizes their differences. For that reason, it is useful to see how these approaches might work together in a practical case. The example is drawn from the literature on electoral institutions and practices in early seventeenth-century England, a period in which institutions associated with elections were varied and unsystematized, in which the franchise was ambiguous and unclear, and in which the practices associated with nominations and voting were diverse.

The central controversies in the historiographical literature on this period turn on the question of whether we should look at the elections of this period as forerunners or precursors of present elections (in which candidates compete for office by bidding for votes with policies and ideologies, the franchise is well defined, and the practices of voting are legally codified and enforced) or whether, instead, we should recognize from the outset that these practices really had little to do with what we think of as electoral politics, but were aimed at reinforcing local hierarchical social structures.

As I construe it, this debate is really between nascent thick-rational choice theorists—Whig historians[17]—and culturalist (interpretive) revisionists. I shall claim that both of their accounts are intrinsically incomplete in the sense outlined above and that each would be improved by recognizing a contribution from the other perspective.[18] In the next section I shall set out what I understand to be an agreed upon description of electoral practices in the period and then briefly summarize the interpretations of the Whigs and the revisionists, with which I shall be concerned.

ELECTIONS IN EARLY STUART ENGLAND

In early seventeenth-century England, elections to the House of Commons were rarely contested: in the first two elections of the century, less than 20 of the more than 400 seats were fought.[19] In most constituencies, there were the same number of aspirants for seats as there were seats available. Typically, these aspirants possessed certain social characteristics. In the larger and more prestigious county seats, they were typically high gentry, ranking just below the peerage. In the boroughs and towns, they were often magistrates, candidates nominated by patrons, or neighboring gentry. In all cases, they were men of social distinction. Moreover, they were not anonymously drawn from the upper class; virtually everyone who stood for election (correctly) expected to win the seat based on the specific social characteristics of his family and his place within it.

Parliamentary seats in the counties were largely kept in families, while in the boroughs they often adhered to the family of a patron or to a local office such as that of recorder or high steward. In virtually every constituency, expectations as to who had the right to be "selected" for

Commons were settled and consensual and for that reason contests seldom arose.

Where a contest threatened, somehow one or more of the candidates would somehow be induced to withdraw, presumably to prevent the contest from occurring. A number of institutional devices existed which helped organize this phenomenon. The least visible but most widespread was of course the shared understandings and expectations of the aspirants themselves. Men did not stand for seats that someone else "deserved." But where these understandings were unclear or contested, local officials intervened and employed rotation, lot, and other forms of negotiation as ways of rationing access to office. Only where aspirants could not agree on such a method was there resort to contest, or, to use a more evocative phrase, "trial by election."

Historians hold divergent views of elections in the early seventeenth century. From the Whig perspective—stripped of its apologetic and celebratory aspects—elections then, as now, were contests for valuable political office among ambitious power and wealth seekers. For Whig historians, there was much at stake in elections even in the early part of the century. Those who attained office were able to influence the course of the king's (expensive) foreign policy through the revived use of impeachment and withholding of subsidies, persecute (or prevent the persecution of) Catholics, affect royal grants of monopoly and patent, obtain patronage from the Court or from high-ranking peers, or manipulate tax assessments for their own benefit or that of their neighbors. If the level of competition was low, Whiggish historians tried to explain it by appeal to the manipulation of elections or of Parliament, or by alleging the coercion of the electorate by the Court, powerful families, or oligarchies.

For Whig historians, the Stuart years were marked by a growing opposition between the Court and the Parliament, particularly the House of Commons. The Parliaments of those years, it is claimed, faced with impecunious and ambitious monarchs who required more and more money to carry out foreign adventures or to indulge in extravagant vices, bargained for increased control of their own membership and agenda. The pulling and hauling of this bargaining, the struggles over the right to lay taxes and to influence courts of law, the extent of the royal prerogative in foreign policy, are what characterize the politics of the early Stuart years.

Whig accounts emphasize the growing importance of the electorate as an increasingly legitimate arbiter of disputes over office, the growth in the franchise in both counties and boroughs, and the increase in the frequency of contests over the early part of the century.[20] They emphasize, too, the seizure by the House of Commons of the right to settle election disputes. As J. H. Plumb says, "the Commons took upon themselves the more fundamental questions of parliamentary franchises, the revival of representation in boroughs where it had lapsed, and even the question of new enfranchisement, matters hitherto falling within the prerogatives of the Crown"(1969:95).

Whigs showed that the electorate underwent steady and dramatic expansion, partly as the result of the effects of inflation on the ancient 40-shilling freehold requirement, and partly as the result of parliamentary actions aimed directly at widening the borough franchise.[21] This larger electorate was much less controllable by patrons or courtiers and was therefore more often appealed to in disputes about office. Wallace Notestein(1924), focusing on internal parliamentary developments, emphasizes the creation of new institutions in the House of Commons, particularly the Committee of the Whole,[22] as a barrier to Court influence. He argues that the Committee of the Whole was a device that permitted Parliament to appoint its own presiding officer, to make its own rules of debate, and more efficiently to conduct its business.[23] And, as Parliament gained increasing control over legislation and over the conduct of its own affairs, as it gained increasing control over election disputes, as, in brief, it became a regular and somewhat independent part of government, the value of office increased and the level of competition increased as well. Thus, for the Whigs, we may see in this period the emergence of modern parliamentary forms, of the electorate as an institution, of contests, and of insulation of Parliament from the executive.

For the Whigs, to the extent that elections in this period fail to resemble their modern successors, the reasons are to be found either in an extensive social and political consensus, the tiny size and relative homogeneity of the electorate, or in the imperfect institutions and practices of the time.[24] These institutions and practices still permitted coercion, manipulation, and confusion, and, as these institutional defects were remedied,[25] elections (and other institutions) came to resemble modern ones more closely.

REVISIONIST INTERPRETATION

Revisionists argue that the Whig view of seventeenth-century parliamentary electoral practices fails for several reasons. Fundamentally, it is claimed, the Whig account employs a misleading and extraneous teleology[26] and imposes on past institutions and practices false and foreign readings. Whig teleology led historians to explain the absence of competition, the infrequency of genuine contests, and the invisibility of elections themselves, by appealing to underlying or latent forces: Court influence through patronage, electoral corruption, and the like. The revisionists claim that direct evidence of these phenomena are either weak or lacking. Revisionists argue that citizens were neither manipulated nor coerced into electing their betters to parliamentary seats. Patronage practices, for example, are not evidence of the capture of unwilling boroughs by powerful aristocrats. Rather, boroughs sought patrons for the services they could provide and generally entered voluntarily into the protection of influential courtiers. As to electoral corruption, revisionists generally see the alleged occurrences as instances in which socially legitimate actors undertook to forestall divisive electoral contests.

Revisionists emphasize that Parliament was still, at this period, only an occasional assembly in which seats were not considered especially valuable; that sometimes seats would go unfilled because of the absence of nominations. Indeed, the surviving correspondence among potential candidates and patrons suggests that candidates felt more a sense of obligation to serve than an ambition to do so.

For revisionists, the cause of electoral quiescence is found instead in the (real or ideal) fundamental unity of society and in the consensual recognition of the merit of certain people and families. Revisionists deny that much was at stake in the making of policy by Parliament; indeed, they see Parliament as an episodic social event more than as an institution: "Parliaments, if they are to be seen in perspective, should not be seen as the makers of the major historical events of the 1620s, but as *ad hoc* gatherings of men reacting to events taking place elsewhere"(Russell, 1979:1). The members were not struggling to make their mark on policy; that right they freely accorded to the king. Instead they met to give substance to the king's requests and to make the voice of the "country" heard.

In any case, if policy is conceded to the king, there was little left in Westminster to fight over; electoral politics was all about local social recognition rather than control over legislation. The lack of electoral competition was the result primarily of the broad agreement over who deserved office, to the underlying appeal of the ideal of unity, and not to manipulation, coercion, or any such thing.

Revisionists also deny that there was much opposition between the Court and the Parliament, emphasizing instead the willingness of Parliament men to play their accustomed supporting role for the king's policies. They do not see any real growth in partisanship or ideology until well into the 1640s, and interpret Whiggish accounts of partisanship as placing an ex post interpretation on what was really a succession of isolated disputes, traceable more to strong personalities or to simple misunderstandings or miscalculations than to any coherent sense of party.

Mark A. Kishlansky(1986) argues that we should not try to understand this period through contemporary eyes at all; such an attempt would mislead us into thinking that elections of this period were sufficiently like present-day elections that they should be understood as mere precursors, or pale reflections, of our contemporary versions. Instead, we should interpret the past in terms of contemporaneous meanings. We should recognize that there was nothing predetermined about the way modern elections are conducted, that the past might have led to many different histories. We should reconstruct the meanings that contemporaries brought to the choice of members of the Commons. We should strip away the interpretative baggage of nearly four centuries and try to see how the process looked and felt to those who might have been candidates or constituents then. We should be careful not to assume just because the same or similar words are used to describe a phenomenon, that contemporaries understood those words as we do.

Thus the practices of that period should not be seen as imperfect or unperfected versions of modern practices. In the case of voting, for example, most parliamentary selections in the early Stuart period were settled by what was called "giving voices" or the "shout." People assembled at an announced location and shouted, sometimes for hours, the name of their preferred candidates, after which a magistrate would declare a winner or winners. This practice looks similar to the voice vote of modern Parliaments, but Kishlansky cautions us that "giving voices meant giving assent, agreeing to something rather than choosing it. Actually giving voices meant appearing at the place of election to shout or say aye to the proposal of the nominee's name. The shout was a ritual of affirmation and celebration. As a process, it was both anonymous and unanimous. It was the very opposite of voting"(1986:10–11). Obviously, much rests on the observation that there were very few contests. What, after all, could all these people have been doing except celebrating, out there in a field shouting at the top of their lungs, drinking ale and wine supplied by the nominees, when there was no contest, no alternative candidates, no choice?

And what were they celebrating? The answer to this question provides a key to Kishlansky's interpretation of the selection of members for the Commons. English society of that period was marked by hierarchy and associated notions of honor, deference, and merit. Access to Parliament and other office was held as a matter of right by those deserving of social distinction. This was clearest in the case of the House of Lords but was almost as true in the case of Commons. Selection to the House of Commons was, according to Kishlansky, a public recognition of social merit, not the outcome of a contest among ambitious aspirants to public office. "In the counties the keynotes of parliamentary selection were honor and deference. Men were chosen members of Parliament or given the right to nominate on the basis of criteria largely social in nature"(Kishlansky, 1986:14). He goes on: "[I]n the early modern world there was no separation between the social and the political. Authority was integrated. Personal attributes, prestige, standing, godliness—were all implicit in officeholding"(1986:15–16).

Elections, Kishlansky says, had little to do with what policy was made, and ideology played no role in selection because the men who were sent to Parliament were not sent there in order to do anything specific. They were sent because of who they were, not because of what they or their supporters wanted to accomplish. "There is almost no evidence upon which to base the assumption that there was a connection between the selection of members to Parliament and the activities of members of Parliament." Thus electoral contests were not struggles over alternative policies but were instead "bitter personal or local feuds that rent the social fabric of the community." Contests were marked by social dislocation, riots, ambushes, lawsuits, and "were a catastrophe for the community and were seen as such"(1986:16,17,18).

Contests were dangerous because they "could become a vehicle for widening local and familial feuds and an open challenge to the magistracy"(1986:71). When candidates undertook to bid for votes, to "labour for voices," they risked not only humiliating rejection but also the social peace.

> [A]n electoral contest would divide county society into warring groups; such a duel could only leave disfiguring scars. To cast down this gauntlet was to place high value on family honor, for the innocent would be victimized with the guilty. . . . An electoral contest might become an occasion for sedition and treason".(Kishlansky, 1986:95–96.)

Kishlansky sees the rare occurrence of a poll—a recording of each eligible individual's vote—which is indisputable evidence of a contest, as a violation of deeply held social norms. "By counting each man as one, the meanest freeholder equal to the worthiest gentleman, the community violated every other social norm by which it operated." The progression from the voice to the "view" (in which partisans gathered in separate groups to be viewed) to the poll or vote was degenerative: the voice or shout was a celebration, rather than a method of determining majorities; the view was "equally useless as a means of fixing size, though it was exceedingly helpful if those taking it wanted to know which candidate had the support of county leaders." "A poll was good for one thing only . . . it was a somber affair. It was a solution akin to Solomon's judgement—equitable but not efficacious." In his discussion of a case in which a sheriff went to great lengths to resolve a contest, Kishlansky noted that, "as always, the sheriff was exceedingly reluctant to hold a poll."(Kishlansky, 1986:61,62,71.)

Thus, on Kishlansky's theory, the celebration marked the unity of a social order that was reflected once again in the uncontested selection of candidates in the constituency. While the candidates supplied the wine and the food and the people freely supplied their voices, it was not an exchange and certainly not a competition. The "conventions of the selection process were not shadows behind which lurked ambition and the hunger for power."(1986:23.) Indeed, service in Parliament was neither widely nor deeply desired.[27] The commitment of resources by the candidates normally had nothing to do with persuading citizens to vote one way or another. Instead, an election was a festive affirmation of unified social and political order in which honor and merit were recognized in voluntary deference, and in which those of high social standing—the candidates and their families—simply did their part by providing food and drink.

What is important here is to see that the uncontested selection was the normal case not only in the sense that this was what ordinarily occurred, but also in the sense that it was the normatively desired, healthy, peaceful method by which communities recognized rather than chose their representatives. Contests were breakdowns, symptoms of failure, of uncontrolled tensions and hostilities.

For Kishlansky, parliamentary selection in the early part of the seventeenth century contrasts strikingly with the more modern practices of election after the Restoration. Under the later Stuarts, contests were frequent and were routinely expected, campaign expenditures escalated dramatically,[28] the franchise was steadily widened and clarified,[29] the rules of election were codified, and ideology became more central to the choice of members. Elections became more what we would think of as choices of representatives. Older social meanings began to decay and even seemed archaic.

According to Kishlansky, the cause of this shift was the shattering of English social unity during the Civil War. Localities no longer possessed a consensual unified hierarchy of desert and merit, but were sharply divided along religious and ideological lines. Old institutional forms and practices could no longer contain social conflict and disagreement, and so these institutions and practices began to atrophy. Formal political institutions and practices—elections, Parliament, administration, legal systems—began to separate from and become more autonomous of a deeply divided social world, because the older hierarchy-based mechanisms would no longer serve.

In the end, the empirical-basis revisionist response to the Whigs rests importantly on the observation that there is simply too little contestation for office for the Whig account to be sustained. While it is true that the number of contested seats increased sixfold, from 15 in 1604 to 91 in the Long Parliament,[30] even this number represents much less than a quarter of the available places. If office was valuable, office seekers ambitious, and electorates relatively large and hard to control, why were there still so few electoral contests?[31] Why, instead, did so many parliamentary seats remain uncontested in the same families that had held them under Elizabeth? The revisionists undercut the Whig attempt to invoke corruption, coercion, and patronage by interpreting these as accepted and legitimate social practices which, while possibly limiting contestation, actually point to the necessity for another interpretation of electoral practices altogether.

A RATIONAL CHOICE ACCOUNT: WHIGGERY REVIVED

To the modern cephologist, an era without competition for seats is not incomprehensible. A good deal of empirical and theoretical effort has gone into trying to understand the relatively low level of competition for congressional seats in the last 30 years, and it has become clear that even where national office is valuable, the franchise is relatively broad and clearly defined, and politicians ambitiously seek election—in other words, even where standard Whiggish assumptions hold—the level of observed competition need not be very high.

While this is not the place to develop a fully specified model of elections, it is useful to give a very simple model that illustrates the main lines of a revised Whig account. I shall assume only that a parliamentary office has some value to whoever holds it and construct a game-theoretical model in which electoral contests are rare. Specifically, I shall argue that we can understand electoral phenomena in this period as the realization of an implicit form of collusion in which potential aspirants for office implicitly agree not to contest seats.

Suppose, for the purposes of argument, that there is a constituency with one seat and two potential candidates and that (for both candidates) the costs of running a campaign is c and the benefits of office, b, where $b/2 < c$. Furthermore, assume that election is symmetric in the sense that if two candidates enter the race, each has the same expectation of winning. Then, if only one candidate enters the race, his or her expectation is $b - c > 0$, while if both enter, each expects $b/2 - c < 0$. In a noncooperative analysis of this game, in which the players make their choices independently, there are two pure strategy equilibria: each with exactly one candidate entering, and one mixed-strategy equilibrium in which each candidate enters with probability $2(1-c/b)$. Thus, in this model, even though office is valuable and politicians are ambitious, competition for office will not necessarily occur.

In the mixed-strategy equilibrium, competition may occur, but if c is relatively large (compared to b), the probability of a contest would be very low. Moreover, the presence of a mixed-strategy equilibrium in which there is competition is the result of the assumption that strategies are announced simultaneously, surely an artificial feature of the example. If announcements are sequential, this equilibrium disappears and all that remains are pure strategy equilibria. In fact, if the candidates have full information about the strategic structure of the game, it is difficult to construct situations in which competition can be observed in equilibrium.

While this example leaves out nearly everything that an actual rational choice account would wish to include (variable campaign costs, private information as to the value of office to each of the candidates, consideration of timing, and the like), it is rich enough to illustrate the indeterminacy of the rational choice explanation. There is nothing internal to the account that explains why one equilibrium rather than another is observed. When, as always, there are more candidates and more strategic opportunities, this indeterminacy becomes even more substantial.

Now suppose, to change the example slightly, that $b/2 - c > 0$. In a (noncooperative) Nash equilibrium, both candidates will surely enter and competition will be observed. Of course, if the situation of the candidates is not symmetric, so that one candidate is much more likely to win than the other, then only the advantaged candidate may enter. Thus we see that (at least in a thick-rational account of this type) competition will occur in some circumstances and not in others. In fact, by comparing this case with the previous one, we might conclude that if the value of political office increases or if the costs of running decreases, the amount of competition will increase.

However, the structure of the model suggests another possibility. In any equilibrium in which there is competition, campaign expenditures are simply thrown away by the candidates. If the two candidates could somehow "agree" (whether explicitly or tacitly) not to compete with each other and, instead, to rotate in office so that only one would enter at each election, it is easy to see (as long as elections are sufficiently frequent) that both would be better off than in any of the noncooperative equilibria described above.

Thus if there is a way for the candidates to arrange to "collude," or to come to an enforceable agreement as to who shall stand and who shall stand down, each can avoid costly campaigning. If methods permitting such collusion are available, the model suggests that they will be used in order to realize gains from exchange. Indeed, it seems that agreements would be resorted to more frequently when the value of office is relatively high and the candidates symmetrically situated, since otherwise the candidates might easily come to their own implicit understandings as to who will enter and under which circumstances.

The claim that early seventeenth-century elections can be understood as collusive outcomes raises two issues: How are collusive arrangements agreed to? How are they enforced? Put another way, we might ask about which conditions are most propitious for the formation and enforcement of such collusive arrangements. In our discussion of the revisionists, we have already seen evidence of enforcement mechanisms. Kishlansky and others document the fear of social disorder that is expected to attend electoral contests, and the possibility—indeed the likelihood—of prolonged feud among powerful families, leading to fighting and deaths following the violation of electoral understandings. The chain of dismal consequences that might be expected to follow the failure to carry out such an understanding is documented as well in John Neale's(1949:122–131) account of a contest in Rutland.

While enforcement mechanisms would seem to be abundantly available in a closed hierarchical society, it is less obvious how they would work in practice. The possibility of enforcing collusion depends on the availability of beliefs, practices, and institutions permitting the enforcement of understandings when they threaten to break down.[32] Kishlansky demonstrates that both formal institutions and informal normative structures geared to enforcing collusive arrangements of the sort suggested here existed during this period. He gives a number of examples from both counties and boroughs of local officials arranging collusive outcomes when a contest threatened. "No parliamentary selection that threatened to degenerate into a contest was without plans for settling the issue peaceably. . . . [A]ttempts at composing potential contests were made initially by an appeal to the community's leadership. . . . [I]f noblemen or magistrates could not successfully intervene to compose potential conflicts, then responsibility fell to the returning officer in the boroughs and to the sheriff in the counties."(1986:55–57.)

Even if enforcement mechanisms are available, it is less obvious just how contestants might be expected to come to an understanding as to who shall stand for the seat in the first place. After all, there is a pervasive distributional issue of who shall share the gains from office, one in which there is a genuine possibility of conflict. Here again, shared expectations associated with a hierarchical society would seem to play the key role. Kishlansky argues that, early in the century, each locality had its own consensually recognized social hierarchy and that only families near the top of that hierarchy were thought to have a legitimate expectation of a seat in the House of Commons. Neale too illustrates the fact that very few families were thought to have a historic claim on a seat and, even within families with legitimate claims, the (socially valued or disvalued) attributes of the individual aspirants imposed further restrictions on potential candidates. Thus I argue that the interior understandings of early Stuart England had the effect of allowing costly contests to be avoided.

While the game-theoretical model is an alternative interpretation of the practices and institutions associated with early Stuart elections, it can also be employed to suggest hypotheses as to the conditions under which we might expect contests to arise. For example, the ease with which collusive outcomes can be "agreed upon" depends on the restriction of the set of potential candidates to a small number. If there are a great number of candidates who may (legitimately) declare their intent to stand for office, and thereby demand some sort of satisfaction in exchange for "standing down," it may be impossible to prevent contests from occurring. Any collusive arrangement would be subject to entry by another candidate demanding satisfaction.

This raises questions as to how the field of candidates is restricted: Is the distribution of wealth so skewed that only a few could afford to run? Or is there some sort of (cultural) expectational phenomenon that restricts the number of "legitimate" aspirants to a small set of families? How does this set of expectations relate to the religious divisions of the period? If parliamentary office became more valuable during the century, or if consensual beliefs and expectations as to existence and legitimacy of local hierarchy declines, we would expect that more candidates would wish to stand in every sort of seat and this would make collusion more difficult to arrange and enforce. If the costs of defeat became more onerous, and here the evidence is more ambiguous, the incentives to collude would increase and the level of competition should fall.[33]

To take another example, insofar as rotation or lot—both of which depend on repeated elections rather than wealth transfers as the method of inducing potential challengers to withdraw—are the main "coins" of exchange in preventing contests, collusive outcomes would be more likely when elections are frequent than when they are not. Thus, after Charles refused to call Parliaments for the 11 years after 1629, it is not surprising that the number of contests doubled.

Perhaps, too, different types of constituencies arrived at different sorts of equilibria. It may be the case that the value of office varied according to the type of constituency or that entry barriers—whether rooted in an intersubjectively agreed upon claim to the seat or in the distribution of wealth, in the size or diversity of the constituency, or in some other factors—were stronger in some places than others.

So far I have assumed that the agents face no informational problems in executing collusive arrangements; if information as to the costs and benefits of all courses of action is commonly known to all agents, none would have any reason to depart from the agreement. But if information as to the benefits and costs of actions is privately held by individuals, someone may rationally defect from the arrangement. Such failures to keep to accepted arrangements can arise as a part of equilibrium play in a game of incomplete information. These occasional departures from expected behavior would then be punished by other agents. The punishments, if they are costly to carry out, would have to be severe enough to deter too frequent violations.

Thus Kishlansky's description of the disruptive social consequences of a contest can be given a game-theoretical interpretation. A collusive outcome is based on an (implicit) promise or contract among potential candidates. Some candidates are supposed to stand aside in the expectation of future rewards. Thus the low levels of competition could be evidence not of the relative unattractiveness of office (as Kishlansky argues) but of successfully executed collusion instead.

Indeed, on the rational account, the occurrence of a contest is evidence that someone has broken a promise. Thus it is not surprising (even to moderns) that the matter is understood or interpreted by participants as a question of honor or integrity. It is a question of honor. An important social norm has been violated; someone has been, or appears to have been, dishonest and so others are right to cast doubt upon his word or his character. In the rational account, this is exactly the interpretation that agents should give to the outbreak of a contest. Moreover, these natural feelings of outrage provide support for the retaliatory actions that must be undertaken to deter future occurrences of this sort. The point is that the rational account provides an "interior" description of the significance and meanings of events, and this account is consistent with the documentary evidence found in Kishlansky's book.

DISCUSSION

At one level, the revisionist account can be seen simply as a thick-rational choice explanation. The revisionist takes hierarchical values as given and unproblematic for most people in the early part of the century and interprets their actions as optimal, given these values. If contests are considered disastrous not merely to the candidates but to the whole of local society, then perhaps it is not too surprising that great collective efforts would be spent in avoiding and suppressing them. But that seems to be only a small part of the real value of the revisionist story.

The more important contribution of revisionism is in its narrative aspect: the reconstruction of a worldview in which not only are hierarchy, order, and solidarity valuable, but a world lacking them is inconceivably chaotic and disorienting. The interpretive reconstruction of this world requires the incorporation of religious or sacred values at the center of ordinary life; it requires that we see the local stakes of political disruption as vastly more significant to most people than distant and abstract goings-on in London or Europe. And, most important for our purposes here, it helps us to see how natural and how "unchosen" local society and social expectations were or appeared to be to people of that time.

Neo-Whig theory is aimed at explaining exactly the same facts described by the revisionists. It is aimed at showing that nothing in the revisionist interpretation excludes the possibility that elections in the early seventeenth century were fundamentally similar to those today. This does not imply that a Whiggish account is either better or more plausible: it is a different reconstruction of institutions, practices, meanings, and even of self-understandings—a forward-looking rather than backward-looking one—from the one that Kishlansky proposes.

The rationally reconstructed Whig account is, however, incomplete in certain important ways. Centrally, it lacks any way of selecting which of the many possible equilibria will be played. Indeed, it contains no internal reason to believe that collusive equilibria could be reached or sustained. It does not say who will stand and who will not; it makes no unique prediction as to the level of competition: it is as consistent with high levels of competition as with lower ones.

The weakness of Whig accounts is exactly what is endemic in any rational choice or reconstructive explanation. Such accounts cannot, even in principle, explain why one set of intersubjective or cultural understandings prevailed at a given time rather than some other, or why, among all of the possible equilibria, the specific collusive equilibrium I have identified ex post is the one that occurred rather than some other. Such accounts cannot say, for example, why the rivalry in Sommersetshire was between the Phelips and the Pouletts or why that in Rutland involved the Noels and the Harringtons, and not other families. They cannot explain why these families claimed seats, why others generally deferred to their claims, or why, when contests occurred, they took the form they did. They cannot explain why there were contests in these places and times and not in others. There are many different equilibrium outcomes, each of which seem plausible, ex ante, and which cannot be reduced on purely game-theoretical grounds. Like Taylor's hermeneutics or like Kishlansky's historical description, the game-theoretical analysis is stronger as an ex post account than as prediction.

It is here that an interpretivist approach offers a valuable and unique contribution. There is something in the meanings shared by members of that time and place, in their identities and self-understandings that make some equilibrium outcomes not just plausible but more natural, and even more inevitable than others. Interpretivists are right to suggest the self-understandings of members of a hierarchical and unified society as the likely source of this selection. But if appeals to tradition and to the internal norms of an ordered society are essential components of explanation, they do not exclude that part of explanation that results from principles of rationality, thin or thick. However they construct their worlds, agents' actions must make sense to themselves as in some way not merely appropriate but as representing the best actions they could choose.[34]

But this is only part of what the interpretivist has to offer. The fact that cultural or intersubjective understandings may select among equilibria might be called an exterior or formal relationship between theories of interpretation and choice. Intersubjective understandings happen to play the part of the auxiliary hypothesis, or "focal point," permitting agents to coordinate their strategic behavior in complex social interactions. There is as well the possibility of interior or substantive connections between the two approaches: What is the structure of the set of ideas and interpretations that can be held by actors? Do these intersubjective understandings obey an autonomous dynamic, or is their evolution affected by how they affect the choice of actions? Reciprocally, does the choice of an action in one circumstance somehow limit ensuing cultural or intersubjective understandings?

I think that the debate between neo-Whigs and revisionists helps us to explore some of these interior issues. The revisionist description suggests a view in which intersubjective understandings are given or evolve relatively autonomously and in which the relationship between culture and action is unidirectional. Culturally constituted agents interpret their situations and actions in terms of an autonomously generated and sustained systems of values, beliefs, and understandings. The neo-Whig account envisions more of a symbiotic relationship between interpretation and action. Actor preferences, beliefs, and identities may be given (by biological, social, or cultural processes or by the structure of the strategic setting), but the structure of cultural understandings that permit social coordination—the identification and value of hierarchy and one's place in it—may also be partially determined by the nature of the coordination problem itself.

It seems as wrong to overemphasize the differences among cultures and historical milieus as to overemphasize their similarities. There is much in the revisionist or interpretivist account of seventeenth-century elections that cannot be explained by traditional Whig theory, but we do not need to see the early seventeenth century as a separate world existing on the other side of a fundamental and radical divide in English history in order to comprehend its electoral practices. We do not need to deny that office was valuable, that Parliament was becoming an important source of policy and saw itself so, or that motivations of politicians then were similar to those of today. These claims may all be true or false, of course; the revisionist interpretation remains plausible. But it is not inevitable, and more important, it is not inconsistent with a deeper reconstruction of Whig theory.

NOTES

1. In this essay I will identify the culturalist position with interpretivist or hermeneutical ones. In fact, there are a wide range of alternative positions which can be distinguished. For present purposes the critical feature of these approaches is in what I will call the ethnographic starting point: the proper place to begin social analysis is with the meanings embedded in the social practices in question. These intersubjective meanings, or cultural elements, form the basis for the identification of actors and their choices. The main differences among different schools seems to be in how deeply (beyond the meanings shared consciously by the actors) the interpretation can or must go. That question is unimportant for this essay and is, therefore, left in this note.

2. To take just one prominent example, MacIntyre rejects the widely accepted Hempelian covering law version of social science on the grounds that social phenomena are inherently unpredictable. See Chapter 8 of Alasdair MacIntyre (1981).

3. The "most fundamental reason for the impossibility of hard prediction is that man is a self-defining animal" (Charles Taylor, 1985:55).

4. Taylor says that "a successful interpretation is one which makes clear the meaning originally present in a confused, fragmentary, cloudy form" (1985:17). He goes on to say that the test of the correctness or adequacy of an interpretation is that it "makes sense of the original text: what is strange, mystifying, puzzling, contradictory, is no longer so, is accounted for" (1985:17). I read this statement to imply the criterion for ranking interpretive theories given in the text.

5. Elster, 1983.

6. I believe that a somewhat stronger claim than this can be defended—namely, that an adequate interpretation of behavior must satisfy the requirement that actors are behaving as though they are trying to maximize something. If this is not true of an interpretation, it must be the case that the explanation can account for the choice of some action from a set of alternative actions, $\{a_1, a_2, \ldots a_k\}$ such that the actor prefers a_i to a_{i+1} for all i and a_k to a_1. In my view such an account does not permit us to understand the agent's actual choices by appeal to his or her values or beliefs. For if

the agent made any choice from this set of actions, there would have been some other action that was preferable but which, for some reason, wasn't chosen. The explanation must rest on what that reason is and not on the agent's preferences among the actions.

7. Clifford Geertz rejects the search for universals among anthropologists on the grounds that such "universals" will necessarily be so empty as to tell us little about actual humans in any society. He asks: "What, after all, does it avail us to say . . . that 'morality is a universal, and so is enjoyment of beauty, and some standard for truth,' if we are forced . . . to add that 'the many forms these concepts take are but products of the particular historical experience of the societies that manifest them' ? " Geertz, 1973:41.

8. Theorists regard thin-rational accounts, when available, as more fundamental than thick-rational ones. Thus theoretical developments in the theory of the firm have been aimed at constructing a thin justification of the profit-maximizing assumption. This has proceeded on two levels: externalist theories of "natural selection" and internalist theories of agency relationships in the organization of economic enterprises.

9. Ironically, once these claims are stripped of their pejorative tone, rational choice theorists generally accept them in the sense that they regard thick assumptions as in need of justification. While some theorists move immediately to Friedman's pragmatic justification that if a theory "works," there is no need to question its assumptions, most others recognize that assumptions are predictions of a theory too and try to justify thick-rational assumptions either as approximations or as "placeholders" for some deeper (i.e., thinner) theory that will appear later on. See Almond (this volume) for an alternative view of thin and thick rational choice explanations.

10. Some interpretivists stop short of attributing unambiguous causal force to cultural meanings: Geertz writes that the central problem of his approach is "to conceptualize the dialectic between the crystallization of such directive 'patterns of meaning' and the concrete course of social life" (1973:250).

11. This stance seems to leave interpretivists with little more than a coherence test in comparing different explanations. Indeed, Geertz acknowledges that there are "serious problems of verification . . . of how you can tell a better account from a worse one. . . . The force of our interpretations cannot rest, as they are now so often made to do, on the tightness with which they hold together. . . . Nothing has done more, I think, to discredit cultural analysis than the construction of impeccable descriptions of formal order in whose actual existence nobody can quite believe" (Geertz, 1973:16,18).

12. Technically, in a repeated Prisoners' Dilemma game, any outcome which guarantees the players more than they would receive in the "defect-defect" equilibrium can be supported in an equilibrium.

13. Schellins, 1960.

14. By "common knowledge" I mean the following: X is common knowledge among a set of agents if each knows X; each one knows that each knows X; each knows that each knows that each knows X; and so on, "all the way down."

15. Admittedly, this use of culture within rational choice explanation is functionalist: culture performs the function of selecting among alternative equilibria. Obviously, the account is incomplete as it stands and requires a deeper investigation of "selection" principles among cultural elements or meanings, something I am unable to do in the present essay. The question is this: is it the case that cultural elements that permit coordination in (game-theoretical) social interaction are "selected over" or survive longer than those that do not?

16. I do not mean to imply by this terminology that I regard these domains as in any sense autonomous. Indeed, the larger point of this essay is precisely that the two spheres are interconnected in ways that have to be better understood if we are to understand either of them. See James Johnson, 1988, 1990.

17. Derek Hirst puts the Whig perspective thus: "The corollary of the assertion that the electoral system . . . was forming in this period is that these were its early days. A normal accompaniment of the initial stages of any development is a measure of uncertainty and confusion. . . . But, for our purposes, the important point about elections is that they should be contested" (1975:12).

18. While I focus on divergent explanations of seventeenth-century electoral practices, the reader should be aware that this debate recurs in other periods. For a revisionist account of Victorian elections, for example, see Vincent, 1966.

19. Historians of the period disagree as to what constitutes evidence of a contest but, as far as I can tell, most would probably agree that the number of contests was not far from this estimate. This number of contests represents a modest increase from the estimated number in the Elizabethan period. The number of contests began to increase more rapidly in the 1620s and 1640s.

20. Hirst, 1975.

21. Revisionists argue that these attempts must be seen as piecemeal accommodations and not as part of a coherent program aimed at franchise expansion.

22. "By the twenties nearly all important questions are referred to this Committee" (Notestein, 1924:37).

23. "Whether or not there was any connexion between the development of this new procedure and the close relations between the King and Speaker, it is certain that the Commons found it a convenience of the Committee plan that the Speaker could no longer regulate debates. The Committee of the Whole House usually chose men who were not Privy Councillors as chairmen" (1924:37).

24. "Political consensus and the more or less effective workings of the patronage system averted both elections and the open agitation of issues" Hirst, 1975:1.

25. Plumb and others describe electoral manipulation by sheriffs, biased polling practices, and other procedures conducive to manipulated elections.

26. Even modern Whigs exhibit this tendency. Hirst betrays a tendency to look toward the future when he argues that "a reluctance to come to terms with integral parts of the electoral process was visible in this period. Contests were uncommon, unpopular, and not fully accepted for what they were. Even the straightforwardly numerical proposition of a majority was not wholly clear of doubt" (1975:16). Or, again: "[P]eople were only beginning to feel their way towards an appreciation of the existence of elections and an electorate" (p. 21).

27. "[S]essions were of uncertain duration; and the preparations and pains of travel could be repaid by sudden dissolution as in 1584 or 1614" (Kishlansky, 1986:24).

28. "Costs increased ten- or twenty-fold, with no logical limit based on competition or constituency. Rising costs were simply the result of the presence of free-spending competitors trying to feed an insatiable electorate" (Kishlansky, 1986:20).

29. "Once majorities were the requirement for selection then the question of who held rights of participation became paramount" (Kishlansky, 1986:20).

30. These numbers are computed from a table in Hirst, (1975:216–222).

31. Kishlansky writes that "in itself, an increase or decrease in the number of contested elections provides little guidance to the social and political changes of the early seventeenth century. Those who count contests inhabit the same sort of dream world as those who counted manors" (1986:76).

32. The connection of collusive opportunities with institutions is not necessary from a game-theoretical view, though it seems natural enough in the present case. In repeated play situations, "collusive"

outcomes can be sustained through "tacit" coordination, which entail the threat of punishment for deviation from collusive behavior. Indeed, it is not clear, in repeated play settings, just what observational difference there is between what we ordinarily think of as an institution and tacit collusive equilibria.

33. Kishlansky reports two offsetting tendencies over the course of the century. On the one hand, the actual amounts spent on campaigning increased because of the increased frequency of contests. On the other, the humiliation of suffering an electoral rejection diminished as the contests came to seem more "normal."

34. In this we must take account of informational limitations and inter-subjective understandings of the strategic structure of interaction.

REFERENCES

Elster, J. (1983). *Explaining Technical Change*. Cambridge: Cambridge University Press.

Geertz, C. (1973). *The Interpretation of Cultures*. New York: Basic Books.

Hadari, S. (1989). *Theory in Practice: Tocqueville's New Science of Politics*. Stanford: Stanford University Press.

Hirst, D. (1975). *The Representative of the People?* Cambridge: Cambridge University Press.

Johnson, J. (1990). "Rational Choice and Culture: Skeptical Remarks on 'The Renaissance of Political Culture.'" Northwestern University working paper.

————. (1988). "Symbolic Action and the Limits to Strategic Rationality." *Political Power and Social Theory*, 7:211–248.

Kishlansky, M. A. (1986). *Parliamentary Selection: Social and Political Choice in Early Modern England*. Cambridge: Cambridge University Press.

MacIntyre, A. (1981). *After Virtue*. Notre Dame: University of Notre Dame Press.

Neale, J. (1949). *The Elizabethan House of Commons*. Harmondsworth: Penguin.

Notestein, W. (1924). *The Winning of the Initiative by the House of Commons*. London: Oxford University Press.

Plumb, J. H. (1969). "The Growth of the Electorate in England from 1600 to 1715." *Past and Present*, vol. 42.

Russell, C. (1979). *Parliaments and English Parliaments 1621–1629*. Oxford: Oxford University Press.

Schelling, T. (1960). *Strategy of Conflict*. Cambridge, MA: Harvard University Press.

Taylor, C. (1985). "Interpretation and the Sciences of Man." *Philosophy and the Human Sciences, Philosophical Papers 2*, Cambridge: Cambridge University Press.

Vincent, J. (1966). *The Formation of the British Liberal Party*. New York: Scribner.

Chapter

12

The Relational Boundaries of Rationality

Michel Crozier

Neither the theories of the market nor the neoinstitutional theories can provide a satisfactory answer to the problems of the opposition between individual choices and collective outcomes, or even between short-term and long-term self-interested behavior. For such an answer, we must turn to a discussion of the relational boundaries of individual choices. Doing so can help us understand how aggregation of choices really takes place and can, furthermore, help us integrate in a more rational way the indispensable moral and cultural dimensions of individual choice.

The model of the hidden hand is quite rightly viewed as a positive discovery which still stands as the founding paradigm of modern economics. But it should also be viewed as it appeared to eighteenth-century thinkers, as a countermodel to the then still dominant paradigm of the sovereign and the state as embodiment of the general interest. The originators of economics intended that barriers to trade, monopolistic practices, and doctrines of the state were to be exposed as built on a false model of rationality. Because of such a perspective, classical economists were led to believe that the model of the market was in the nature of things and that there were no intellectual alternatives.

The victory of a Marxist revolution in Russia and its attempt to create an economy, indeed, an entire society, on an alternative (even an opposite) paradigm challenged this basic creed once again. The broad appeal of Marxism and its international influence made it necessary to admit that an alternative model was at least theoretically possible. The recent resounding failure of the Socialist economies in Eastern Europe now appears to have ended the fundamentalist debate concerning whether a priori schemes of resource allocation could meet the challenge of modern complexity. We appear to have been led once again to the conclusion that the market is the only efficient economic model. It is precisely the resolution of this one question concerning the economic model that makes it more imperative to reexamine the founding paradigm of rational action. The problems now do not concern the fight against traditional conservative hierarchies or against the Socialist totalitarian state as a bogeyman but rather the relationships between individual choices and collective outcomes in a context of accelerating complexity and change.

In retrospect, the 1960s debate concerning incrementalism and the science of muddling through may be considered a first attempt at reappraising the foundations of classical political economic liberalism in view of the results of concrete practical policies. This attempt dealt very well with the fallacy of an a priori general interest, but it neglected entirely to inquire about the different structures of the various markets, how these structures were (and still are) built consciously and unconsciously, and what the possible role of collective institutions may be in shaping them and in the indirect shaping of the results they will produce. The present-day debate revolves much more around the fundamentals.

GAME THEORY'S DILEMMA

One such fundamental can be illustrated by the dilemma of game theory. I do not believe that analysts have sufficiently explored the conditions of a "good" solution to the prisoner's dilemma. If the prisoners pursue their own individual self-interest "rationally," they will end up with the worst possible outcome for both of them. But they also can trust each other enough to accept the risk of retreating from their own immediate interest in favor of a common solution that will benefit each of them. The key variable in that case is trust. If there is no possibility of communication, trust does not make any sense rationally. Reduced to the logic of individual rationality within an open market, the operators cannot work together unless there is a possibility for them to bargain. And there cannot be bargaining without the building of a system of communication, which is a relational construct.

How can we analyze trust in that case? It is neither as an internalization of the collective good nor as a moral imperative. It is a relational construct. I trust John because over time I built a relationship that is strong enough for each of us to know the other will live up to his word. Such knowledge and belief may be developed through very different experiences, from the sheer terror of certain religious or moral training to the more commonly employed trial and error process that occurs in a rewarding environment. What is decisive is the result, which can be considered as a self-fulfilling prophecy.

It will be argued, of course, that this example is not relevant because communications and information are always possible at a cost; and if cost is taken into account, then we return to the concepts of classical rationality. I would maintain, on the contrary, that there is a part of this dilemma present in most transactions, because the most useful or vital information is not available and/or because in the final analysis it can be considered a more "parsimonious" behavior to trust one's partners than to check in a precise way all possible information.

Trust, moreover, cannot be understood only from the perspective of a dual relationship. It takes place within groups and among all sorts of organizational configurations. If we consider these configurations as games, they are not two-person zero-sum games but rather multiperson non-zero-sum games. Within such games, participants not only are led to trust each other through socialization, but they also recognize the collective results of such patterns of trust and they realize that they will be punished if they are not trustworthy. This does not mean that they will not cheat. Experience shows that some of them cheat often, and many cheat sporadically. But cheating does not occur enough to change the basic pattern and the outcome. Furthermore, good behavior is also rewarded and may provide clear advantages, such as positions of honor or even of material gratification, which are built into the social fabric.

Let us now question the epistemological status of a proposition that says that (1) only trust makes it possible to move from one zero-sum game to a non-zero-sum game that is, from the maximization of individual self-interest to a game designed to bring a more positive collective outcome; and (2) trust is a relational construct that cannot be explained in terms of simple economic rationality.

The traditional view of rationality has not rejected this sociological dimension as a background to rational markets.[1] But it has tended to minimize it and to relegate it to the domain of historical genesis. Economists might eventually accept the idea that there are limits (indeed, changing limits) of rationality, but they have had difficulty conceptualizing the extent to which this sociological dimension is critical in understanding the transformation, the development, and the renewal of the present-day functioning of sophisticated markets.

The economists' position may have been intellectually useful when the first order of business was to maintain and extend the principles of rationality from constant attack. But its value diminishes in the new environment of a much more complex service society, in which new markets or new games develop continually. New, more intense interdependencies and networking systems and the development of parasitism as a way to use and misuse some market positions oblige one to deal with the issue of rules from a sociological angle. A network of subcontractors built on an immediate short-term cost-benefit rule appears to be much less efficient than a system built on longer-term relations of trust which permit cooperation. Conversely, when the financial game explodes and the financial markets change nature, one is led to rediscover the basic limits that had previously prevented change; the "club" was capable of maintaining a regular kind of game which, within certain limits, was compatible with a slow evolution, not because of the legal constraints but because it was working on an extremely strong relational construct of trust.

RELATIONAL CONSTRUCTS AND SIMON'S LIMITED RATIONALITY

I have argued that analyzing the relational aspects of the structures and workings of markets makes it possible to understand their parochial aspects. Behind the general framework of market rationality, we find specific rationalities associated with the relational constructs that maintain them. To make sense of our world using the concept of rationality, we need a more encompassing theory of rational choice that could take into account its relational aspect. We can begin to construct such a relational theory of rational choice if we accept the limited rationality paradigm of Herbert Simon in an extended way. The key element to discuss from this perspective is the criteria of satisfaction used by human beings in choosing a satisfactory solution, without attempting the vain pursuit of the optimum. If we were able to calculate the optimum, we would escape the boundaries that prevent the application of pure rationality. Simon demonstrated that we cannot attain an optimum, not because of the heavy search costs but rather because, for cognitive reasons, the human mind works only sequentially and cannot work under the assumptions of optimization. James March subsequently suggested that the satisficing model is more functional anyway because it is compatible with an experimental learning paradigm which reflects the lifelong learning process we all undergo.[2]

But how do human beings develop criteria of rationality? I believe we can conceptualize such criteria as direct and indirect relational constructs. Criteria of satisfaction must be learned by individuals within the boundaries of their immediate human environment. Socialization shapes more than values and personalities; it also entails inculcating capacities of reasoning and methods of logic. Moreover, people do not reach the adult world of rational calculus with the tools already perfected to make rational choices. They will continue to learn much more through further socialization. They will change and may even undo certain patterns of childhood socialization, particularly insofar as their later experiences teach them that the childhood patterns are inappropriate.

Let us summarize. People do not maximize their interests in the abstract. They choose the first satisficing solution they find acceptable under the specific criteria they have developed. These criteria are personal; but since they have been developed through socialization, they are therefore culture-bound. We learn these cultural criteria through what is accepted within our own society, within our subculture, and within our smaller immediate environment. Acceptable norms of accountability (e.g., the returns on investment which dominate business life) are cultural constraints. It is rational to operate in this manner because others operate that way. We may innovate in adopting new, more significant criteria. We may cheat. We may try to outperform our competitors by playing a nonrational game. But this can all be understood only with reference to these cultural criteria.

But this is not enough to take us to the root of the problem. Let us consider the individuals who make choices as players within a game. They will more specifically choose the first acceptable solution that makes it possible for them to win or to maintain themselves in the relational game they are playing with their peers, their partners, and their subordinates or superiors. Their criteria of satisfaction will therefore be strongly influenced by the nature of the game in which they operate. Most players will choose the move that permits them to win in the game or to stay in it even if it is not quite rational from the point of view of the collective outcome of the players. In practice, players will search for the solution that meets their minimum criteria of satisfaction from the point of view of global rationality, while at the same time meeting the minimum criteria of satisfaction from the perspective of their own place in the game. Their rational behavior is game-bound as well as culture-bound. To improve the rationality of choices within an organization, it is more important to improve the functioning of the games that limit the rationality of the operators than to impose more strict rules.

Does this formulation make a difference? Does it matter so much if we put these considerations at the heart of the reasoning, instead of taking them into account only as exceptions to the principle, exceptions that are not meaningful enough to warrant a restructuring of the whole approach? Let me address these questions by reference to a specific market case examined from this perspective: the artichoke market in Brittany. This particular market was to be radically transformed within a very short time from a disorganized feudal market to a modern, efficient one. Because this case was so unusual in its clarity, it allows us to look, as if through a magnifying glass, at forces that operate more opaquely in many other cases.

Artichokes are a perishable good that cannot easily be stocked. Another problem is that the market is periodically disturbed by overproduction. The market had been dominated up to the 1960s by the middlemen, who controlled the big retail market in Paris. Producers felt very strongly about what they called their exploitation by these middlemen, who could wait long enough to force the price down as soon as there was a significant increase in production. Producers deplored what they called false bargaining because they were at the mercy of the middlemen. They united around very crude slogans to take charge of the wholesale job. Their social movement (or demonstration) was successful politically but could not yield any economic results. The producers were forced to recognize that middlemen were indispensable. Once the producers recognized that they could not organize direct sales to retailers, they then turned to building a new and more open market where middlemen would play their role but within the confines of an open market. Disastrous downturns in terms of overproduction would then be eliminated, as would individual cheating on both sides. The specific mechanism that they chose (called the "Dutch auction") worked very well. Ten years later, when we analyzed its functioning, it was considered a great success by all the concerned participants, middlemen included.

When we analyzed the genesis and the functioning of the Brittany artichoke markets in the light of our proposed paradigm stressing the relational construct, two kinds of key problems required attention. Both can have a direct impact on public policies:

1. *Markets are delicate relational constructs.* Historically, the acceptance of this impressively rational structure was not easy. It did not win acceptance on its rational merit alone but also because of social and relational reasons. It was a difficult, even an improbable, relational construct. Once the concept was borrowed (and reformulated) from operating experiences in the Netherlands, it appeared both simple and yet almost impossible to introduce. Resistance was strong, not only from the middlemen but also from many producers. Vested interests were at stake, of course; but the difficulty was enhanced because it entailed moving from one type of game to a very different one, and in moving all at once and with no one trying to escape.

The solution was a political one. The movement of young farmers produced two strong leaders who were extremely active during the transition period. They used their charisma to organize the majority of the producers to support this new rational scheme and to force the minority to go along. They then attacked the middlemen by taking the risk of refusing to sell to those who did not accept the rules they had declared. As in any kind of strike, a strong moral, if not physical, coercion was present. This could work because of the keen knowledge of the social milieu shown by the leaders, as well as from the fact that they could rely on the members of close-knit, small rural communities to maintain relations of trust and solidarity during a risky operation. The success of the group gave immediate results to each of the participants and thus helped maintain the system in operation. A board was elected to supervise the management of the market and to ensure that the rules were respected. Its transparence for the middlemen as well as for the producers made it possible to maintain trust. Because rewards were apparent and cheaters were fined, it had become rational for each participant to play the game and obey its rules on both sides.

French state agricultural authorities were very much impressed by the success of the artichoke growers. They decided to introduce the same Dutch auction patterns to manage a number of key perishable goods markets. But there was no social movement in existence in these arenas, nor was there any other way to develop trust. Although the government technocrats were convinced that a rational model could win acceptance solely on the merit of its rationality, they were wrong. The rational reorganization did not work. The technocrats had to abandon their attempts very quickly. Our analysis of several of these counterexamples where attempts to replicate the artichoke market failed, even though they were just as rational in their market arrangements, should be convincing evidence for those skeptics who minimize the importance of the social context of such rational arrangements.

2. *The imperfectibilities of a market may be rational solutions to relational problems.* When we analyzed the present functioning of the artichoke market, it became clear that it was not as perfect as the theory supposed. Separate arrangements were not entirely absent between the middlemen and the individual producers. These developed around problems of delay, regularity, and the quality of production. They were known and tolerated by the board, whose members, as a matter of informal policy, wanted to maintain legitimacy through social trust and thus had to strike a difficult balance between recognizing special interests and preventing the latter from being a threat to the equilibrium. They even used these arrangements to explore new ways to regulate the market. In order to maintain trust, one has to accept stretching the meaning of the rules. Paradoxically, it was found empirically that being completely rational was not the most rational course in view of the relational constraints. The best way to maintain the social trust that makes it possible to maintain the rule of the market was to tolerate some breaches of these very rules.

A THEORY OF POLITICAL RATIONALITY

For the last 20 or 30 years, several attempts have been made to apply the rational model of economics to other fields, especially to political behavior. I will not deny the suggestive insights that were derived from these attempts to borrow from economics. What I do question, however, is the possibility of building a general theory of political rationality. It seems to me that the successive disappointments documented elsewhere in this volume were to be expected. The relational theory of rationality gives us some interesting clues regarding these difficulties.

Politics cannot be considered principally as a zero-sum game or even as a non-zero-sum game of transferring money or goods. It does not deal directly enough with allocating resources. The more basic role of politics concerns the regulation of the games that make it possible for human beings to cooperate fruitfully in a complex and active society.

Markets (and even games) are not natural givens. Specific rationalities are associated with relational constructs. It follows that the influence one can exert on relational constructs may be a determining factor. Politics does not create relational constructs. Whenever it tries, it fails. But politics can—and most modern citizens think it should—regulate relational constructs. Furthermore, human beings are not completely irresponsible regarding what they are offered by society. They have the possibility of choosing between the games that are offered to them. These offers are increasingly numerous and complex. Their individual choices may put a lot of pressure on them, especially with bureaucratized organizations that may be forced to restructure because of rapid attrition. But markets also disappear if the relational constructs on which they rely disappear. Examples are numerous in everyday economic life. One very simple example is the individual French bakery shops. To be efficient and profitable economically, these shops require a great amount of trust between the two persons who occupy complementary roles: the blue-collar baker and his white-collar wife.[3] If French working couples cannot practice that game successfully anymore, the bakery business declines, even though it seems a good business rationally; industrial bakeries will take over. Conversely, people can also help demolish old games and build new ones, such as was demonstrated in our example of the artichoke growers in Brittany.

As societies and economies become more complex and change more rapidly, a great deal of human activity at the top level has to do with changing the rules of old markets, with creating new ones, and with intervening to arrange and regulate and develop new "metamarkets" to take care of conflicts and change. (The same process occurs at many operational levels, not just at the top.) The role of politics is more and more associated with these activities. If we put it in a larger perspective which encompasses the political aspect of management, this has always also been the major function of private management.

There is a rationality in politics, but it cannot be conceptualized by the workings of a determined political market. Politics does not deal with aggregating direct, quantifiable interests, whether individuals or groups. It does not allocate goods, the value of which can be understood clearly and immediately. Of course it serves human interests, but it does so only indirectly. And people cannot accurately predict how they will themselves benefit from the restructuring of an institutional market. Nor can they predict the consequences of a decay in an institutional market.

Even in cases (such as welfare) in which we see direct money transfers from the haves to the have-nots, a more thoughtful analysis helps us to discover that the more basic impact has always been to change (sometimes radically) the markets themselves (in this example, the medical and social services). The political marketplace cannot be understood, therefore, by employing the logic of either the perfect economic market or the conventional imperfect market. The political marketplace should be considered as a metamarket, or perhaps as an articulate conglomerate of metamarkets which deals not with the allocation of resources but rather with the regulation and management of complex systems of markets and quasi-markets.

RELATIONAL CONSTRUCTS THAT SHAPE POLITICAL RATIONALITY: IDENTITY

Relational constructs that help shape our rationality have another basic dimension: trust is built over time. Once it is built into a market, it looks God-given. But it is not. We are reminded that it is human-made wherever it disintegrates or when markets have to be built up from scratch, as is currently happening in East European Socialist societies. From an individual point of view, time makes it possible to anticipate and to learn. It helps in the balancing of short-term with long-term interests. Learning through a relational construct to extend our time horizon will change our choices and even our logic.

I cannot deal here with the collective aspects of the time element in the development of a relational construct. But I would like to say a few words on the individual learning processes because they lie at the root of our concepts of rationality.

If one agrees that the processes through which we learn about rationality are contextual and specifically relational, one is led to believe that they are associated with the building of our identity. Therefore, our choices to commit ourselves to a specific game and to play in it according to a specific rationality will be connected with our identity.

Our methods of playing may even be considered a part of our identity. They are rational from a broader, individual point of view. If I have built an identity as a trustworthy person, I will trust a partner.[4] I will refrain from cheating my partner not because I want to escape punishment or for some religious or ideological reasons, but rather because trust is part of my identity as a reliable person. If an opportunity arises when my self-interest is clearly contrary to that reliable behavior, I could lie to others and even to myself. But this has a cost, especially because identity requires consistency. From a rational self-interested point of view, it will be more rewarding to sacrifice immediate self-interest in order to maintain one's identity. Here, of course, values interfere. But values, we must recognize, are part of identity. They help shape our personality. We may get many rewards from the assertion of our commitment to our identity, since we will be proud of it in a relational context.

Solitary commitments and sacrifices to causes that do not bring relational rewards are very unusual. But they do exist. They may be understood as a means of innovation. In that case, one will be appealing to relational construct as well as to values.

The emphasis on one's own identity entails liabilities. It prevents us from being abstractly rational and from seizing many opportunities. But identity is a basic asset for a personality. It is associated with critical psychological feelings, even physical feelings as well. Maintaining a posture corresponding to our identity may lead to self-sacrifice, such as it does for the captain who perishes with the sinking ship, or for a decent nonpolitical person who takes tremendous risks in hiding Jews chased by the Nazis during World War II.[5] This can be considered irrational. But such individuals often view their deeds as rational choices *in view of* the identity they have built. They were giving an example. They were trying to maintain values that gave a meaning to their lives. They were helping to build better human games, and they had a chance of success.

NOTES

1. The chapter by Whitehead in this volume addresses this issue more fully.
2. "For a Technology of Foolishness," in *Organizations for the Future*, ed. H. Leavitt et al. (New York: Praeger, 1974).
3. This can be seen in the classic French film "*La femme du boulanger.*"
4. See Graham Greene, *The Heart of the Matter*, for a novelist's characterization of this phenomenon.

5. This question is also discussed in this volume in the chapter by Monroe, Barton, and Klingemann.

REFERENCES

Greene, G. (1978). *The Heart of the Matter*. New York: Penguin.

March, J. (1974). "For a Technology of Foolishness." In H. Leavitt et al. (Eds.) *Organizations for the Future*. New York: Praeger.

Chapter
13

Altruism and the Theory of Rational Action: An Analysis of Rescuers of Jews in Nazi Europe

Kristen R. Monroe, Michael C. Barton, and Ute Klingemann

I never made a moral decision to rescue Jews. I just got mad. I felt I had to do it. I came across many things that demanded my compassion.—Otto, German rescuer of Jews in Nazi Europe.

It's pretty near impossible not to help—Margot, German-Dutch rescuer

What can an empirical analysis of altruism suggest about the theory of rational action? Is human behavior as related to conscious calculations of individual self-interest as proponents of the theory have implied? We focus on these questions via in-depth interviews with 13 individuals whom most of us would consider unusual exemplars of ethical behavior: rescuers of Jews in Nazi-occupied Europe. These individuals form the altruists in our sample. Their interviews are contrasted with interviews from a baseline sample, consisting of entrepreneurs (who exemplify archetypical rational actors) and ordinary Europeans who lived in Nazi-occupied Europe but who did not participate in rescuing Jews.[1] A detailed narrative and survey analysis of these interviews is then utilized to evaluate specific explanations of altruism advanced by rational actor theorists.

Rational actor explanations of altruism traditionally stress a cost-benefit calculus, psychic gratification, expectations of reward, the availability of resources, clusters of altruists, and theories of goods altruism, participation altruism, or reciprocal altruism. Our analysis suggests that none of these explanations adequately accounts for rescue behavior. On the basis of this, we conclude that there are definite limitations to any theory which makes self-interest the norm of human behavior, which locates the mechanism behind behavior so exclusively in decisions rooted in conscious choice, and which is predicated on the primacy of the individual as the basic actor in society.

In the first part of this essay we describe our theoretical orientation, methodology, and sample. We next utilize rescue behavior to assess the particular explanations of altruism which have been developed based on rational actor theory. Finally, we offer an alternative explanation of rescue activity, stressing identity and self-recognizing choice. In our conclusion, we particularize the implications of our examination for the theory of rational action.

THEORETICAL FRAMEWORK, METHODOLOGY, AND SAMPLE

We focused on the cognitive frameworks of rescuers. We defined cognitive frameworks broadly, to include that particular part of an individual's beliefs about how the world works that is used to organize and make sense of reality. (See Axelrod, 1973, or Monroe, 1991, for details). Within this general framework, we wanted to determine whether an individual's perception of himself or herself in relation to others influences behavior. Our conceptual framework thus emphasizes an individual's self-perception and identity formation. (See Crozier's chapter in this volume.)

Let us summarize our research methodology, which is described elsewhere in greater detail (Monroe, 1991). We began with an unstructured discussion of the respondent's life, stressing his or her self-perception and worldview, particularly as these relate to behavior toward others. This unstructured part of the interview was inspired by traditional ethnographic work in anthropology (Goffman, 1959), by the self-revelation technique of psychotherapy (Kohut, 1985), by Turner's (1987) work on self-categorization, and by the cognitive framing work pioneered by Bruner (1988). This information was elicited in response to the question: "Tell me something about yourself and, in particular, how you came to save someone from the Nazis." Our goal here was to determine how the concept of self determines behavior. We hoped that this part of the interview, in which the subject was given a limited time period (one to two hours) to relate critical facts, would reveal the subject's inner sense of self. Our hypothesis was that one's sense of self determines how one perceives the world and one's place in it. This perceptual location of self in relation to others then constitutes a cognitive framework which acts to delineate and define the boundaries of possible behavior, particularly in regard to other people. The concept of framing seemed especially relevant for work on rationality, since experimental work on rationality and cognition stresses the need to understand the actor's views of the world (cf. Simon, 1984; Kahneman, Tversky, and Slovic, 1982).

The second part of the interview consisted of open-ended questions asked from a 14-page questionnaire administered over several sessions, ranging from two to eight hours. This survey was a comprehensive, systematic posing of questions designed to determine the subject's cognitive framework and to test specific findings on altruism asserted by scholars from Hume (1939) to Trivers (1971). Questions clustered into 10 specific categories: (1) family background, (2) political views, (3) group ties, (4) situational factors, (5) views on human nature, (6) duty, (7) view of self, (8) expectations, (9) costs, and (10) empathy. We hoped this would enable us to query all subjects on central issues and to test prior work through specific hypotheses, especially those topics not raised in the initial part of the interview. Our intention in both parts of the interview was to elicit critical information from the respondent in his or her own words, as a conversation or narrative. Traditional content analysis or coding of responses was not performed at this stage.[2]

Rescuers' names came from Yad Vashem, an Israeli agency established to honor Holocaust victims and their rescuers. All the rescuers were thus gentiles who were identified and certified (either by Yad Vashem or by the West Berlin Senate) as rescuers of strangers who were Jewish victims of Nazi aggression. Four rescuers living in Berlin were interviewed in German. The rest now reside in the United States; their interviews were conducted in English.

Rational actors were represented by entrepreneurs, matched as closely as possible to rescuers by age, gender, religion, and socioeconomic characteristics. (See Schumpeter, 1958, for the classic discussion of entrepreneurs as the quintessential rational actors.) For the most part, entrepreneurs were identified by personal connections. The mutual friend was asked to describe the research project briefly and ask if the entrepreneur would be willing to be interviewed. If the response was yes, we telephoned to describe the project and ask if we could send a copy of the questionnaire for the subject to see exactly what questions would be posed. During a follow-up phone call (usually two weeks later), individuals who agreed to be interviewed were reminded that we would be asking personal questions concerning early childhood experiences, ties to family, money, and philanthropic activities. "Would this make you uncomfortable?" The answer was always no, except for one entrepreneur who preferred not to discuss his income and who was therefore not interviewed. Rescuers were contacted initially by letter; the follow-up procedure was the same as described above for the entrepreneurs.[3]

We also interviewed a sample of five ordinary Europeans who had lived in Nazi-occupied Europe but who had not rescued Jews.[4] We tried to suspend judgment of these people, treating them as baseline data rather than as bystanders. But we did ask them extensive questions about the war and their actions toward the Jews.

Interviews with all our respondents were taped with audio equipment. Once the interview was transcribed, it was sent to the respondent for approval. Any material the respondent felt was too private—or simply wanted deleted for any reason—was excised from the transcript.[5] All interviews were conducted between March 1988 and January 1990, either by telephone or in person.[6] Our shortest interview lasted 2 hours. Our longest interview ran close to 20 hours. A narrative analysis of the edited transcriptions (ranging from 10 to 150 pages) then formed the foundation for the analysis. Each transcribed interview was analyzed independently by three to six analysts, who later met and discussed their classifications of the transcript. In particular, the analysts were asked to identify sections of the interview which revealed information on specific hypotheses found in the literature. (For example, did the subject come from a tight-knit community? Did he or she believe that people had a duty to help others?)

Since our interest here is in altruism, our emphasis is on extensive analysis of the interviews with the 13 rescuers; these are contrasted with findings from interviews from 6 entrepreneurs and 5 Germans who did not rescue Jews.[7] Rescuers include the following: Bert (a Dutch upholsterer), Bethe (a Berlin Quaker), Leonie (a 17-year-old Dutch girl who later became a psychotherapist), Irene (a Polish nursing student impressed into slave labor), Ursula (an upper-class Berlin woman with a famous family background), Maruska (a Silesian countess and social rebel who became a veterinarian traveling with a circus), Margot (a wealthy German who lost her citizenship because she refused to support Hitler), Tony (a young Dutch cavalry officer), Wilhelmina (a Berlin orthopedist who owned two drugstores), Alida (a Dutch housewife with eight children), Otto (a German-Czech engineer), Peter (an army officer and minor official in the Slovakian puppet government), and Knud (a Danish printer serving in the wartime police force).[8] Analysis of the interviews from our baseline sample is utilized primarily for contrast and background.[9]

TESTING RATIONAL ACTOR EXPLANATIONS OF ALTRUISM

Rational actor theory has been widely utilized to explain collective action and altruism.[10] The theory itself has been heralded as a useful "comprehensive" theory "applicable to all human behavior," from suicide to marriage and discrimination (Becker, 1976:8).[11] Our in-depth interviews with these 13 rescuers, however, suggest certain limitations to this perspective.[12] To test the rational actor explanations of altruism more fully, let us examine each of the rational actor explanations by considering more detailed evidence from the rescuers. When appropriate, we will contrast this evidence with the findings from our baseline data sources. Our goal here is not to explain altruism itself; rather, we examine the theory of rational action by determining the theory's ability to explain significant political behavior that deviates from the norm of self-interest.[13]

Cost-Benefit Calculus

Let us begin by considering the traditional idea that behavior results from a cost-benefit calculus. Were the rescuers aware of the costs or at least the risks and the potential costs involved in helping Jews? Yes.

Interviewer Have you always been conscious of the possible risks and consequences of your actions?

Maruska Of course. It would have been a bit naive not to know the consequences all this implied (p. 8).

Bethe We knew the risk was there. We knew what could happen. If they had caught us, we would have been taken away. The children would have been taken away. We absolutely knew this. But when they're standing at the door and their life is threatened, what should you do in this situation? You could never do that [turn them away] (p. 26).

Interviewer So you were quite aware of the big risk you took?

Wilhelmina Yes, yes. Of course (p. 3).

Were these costs relevant to their actions? No. All the rescuers knew the danger and the risks to their own and their families' safety. But they disregarded their own safety as a "cost." This is well demonstrated by one example. Irene was a Polish woman in slave labor, working as a housekeeper for a German Major when she hid 12 Jews in the Major's villa. The morning of the day Irene was caught hiding Jews, she had been forced to witness a public execution of a Polish family (including their young children) who had hidden Jews. Despite this stark and immediate reminder of the fate of rescuers, however, when *she* was discovered, her only request was that the German Major turn her in and let the Jews go free:

Irene One day in September, the end of September, I was in town. Suddenly, out of nowhere the Gestapo was pushing everyone from the streets to the marketplace. And they forced us to witness a Polish couple with two little children and a Jewish couple with a child being hung in the middle of the marketplace. And they forced us to watch to see what happens when someone befriended a Jew.

I closed my eyes. I could not watch. But you can hear the breathing, the cries of the children. And I was like a zombie, numb. There were signs on every street corner saying, "This town is Jew-free, and whoever will help escaped Jew descendants is dead." So I knew what could happen. But that doesn't matter—I mean, they were human beings. I knew I didn't have to help; I took the responsibility. . . . But I was shaken that day, seeing those children hung. Coming to the villa I opened the door. I closed the door. I even locked it but I pulled the key out. Usually I pulled the key and put it in the inside lock and turned it in the lock, so when the Major would come in he could not walk in; he would have to ring the bell. But that day I was so shaken up that I took the key and walked straight into the kitchen. I put the things down. I came back with something, put it on the sink, and I was looking white like the snow. I was trembling. Four of the [Jewish] girls came out, as they usually did when I was alone in the kitchen. The door was locked and we had a warning system. They knew I was not normal and they asked me what happened. I said, "I'm catching cold." I could not tell them what I witnessed because it would put a guilt in them; I could not do it. And I was standing with the door open and the Major walked in on us.

Interviewer And he saw you?

Irene He saw me and he saw the four girls. He was just standing. His eyes was unbelieving. His skin was shaking. He looked like he'd seen a ghost, and without saying one word he turned around and went to his library. Well, I had to go and face him. There was no other way. He knew [some of] them from the laundry room. When I went in he began to scream and yell at me, "How did you dare to do so? Behind my back! I trusted you. I give you home, I give you protection. Why?"

Well, by that time I was crying. And I said, "They are my friends. Nobody has a right to kill. I didn't have a home to take them to. . . . Please forgive me." I kneeled down. I was kissing his hand. I was holding to his knees. I was praying and pleading. I said, "It's my fault. Let them go. I take the punishment." I did see something in his eyes, you know. Just a moment of hope. But he said, "I have to go now. When I come back we will talk" (pp. 24–25).

The Major did relent and agreed to keep Irene's secret on condition that she be his mistress.

We found that the potential costs—the danger, the risks to their safety, the tension, the inconvenience—were viewed strategically; they affected how a rescuer might proceed with the rescue activity, but they did not affect whether or not the rescuer would try to save someone. Tony best articulates this idea, as he explains that he was painfully aware of the costs of his actions but that he viewed such costs as tactical considerations, irrelevant to the basic rescue action itself:

Interviewer Let me ask you a little bit about the costs of your actions. Were you conscious of the potential costs for you and for your family?

Tony Yes. As I said, those are decisions everybody makes every single day of their lives. Anytime you drive to downtown Los Angeles, you totally accept random challenges. You don't give it a second thought. Sometimes you think about it a little bit.

Interviewer But what you did was a little more dangerous than going to downtown Los Angeles.

Tony Yes. It is more dangerous. But actually you don't realize how dangerous driving is. Look at the statistics of the people that get killed each year. There are more people killed each year driving than were killed in the whole of the Vietnam war. So it's funny how the mind adjusts.

Interviewer You didn't think about the risks?

Tony We were cautious. It's just like you are in driving. You say, "I'm taking a risk driving there. It's dangerous driving at rush hour. Maybe I won't take the freeway." You take certain precautions.

Interviewer The idea that you could be losing your life for this, it never really affected you?

Tony Oh, it sunk in at times. But it's just like flying. I'm going to fly [next week]. I know we've just had three major air crashes and I really don't like flying. But what am I going to do about it? Not go on the trip?

Interviewer So does a calculus of the risks have any relevance to your decision to undertake the action?

Tony Not too terribly much . . .

Interviewer Let me be sure I understand you. Is what I'm hearing you say is that there is a conscious calculus that goes on, but that it's a strategic kind? But that this calculus does not really have any impact on the decision to help other people, to rescue people. Is that what you are saying?

Tony Yes, it is (pp. 88–92).

Benefits, Expectation of Reward

If they ignored costs, what about benefits? None of our rescuers acted in expectation of reward. Indeed, this is a necessary qualifying factor for being honored by Yad Vashem. None of our rescuers helped Jews in return for money, jewelry, or other goods. Only rarely did the rescuers accept money for food or other expenses from their Jewish guests, even when the guests offered it or when it was badly needed. In fact, many rescuers (e.g., Margot's father and Otto) spent much of their own money in obtaining false papers, bribing officials, and transporting Jews out of Nazi-occupied Europe. Beyond this, even after the war, when rescuers often became eligible for compensation by the reinstated governments, most refused to take any money:

Bert ... The Underground had plenty money and they promised to pay back everything that was lost.... I paid one time on five tons of potatoes... that I picked up and I never got that money back, but I didn't care (p. 86A).

Interviewer You've mentioned before that the two girls had money. Did they ever offer you any?

Bethe No, they never offered us any, but on the other hand, we never asked for any. What we could offer them for food was so little that it would not have been right to ask. But even if we'd had more, I wouldn't have accepted (p. 33).

Several rescuers told us that Nazi sympathizers often helped Jews late in the war as insurance against a Nazi defeat. They felt only scorn for these people, although they were glad that these selfish actions did at least result in more people being saved. And they all uniformly expressed contempt for the many people who exploited the plight of the Jews for their own material gain. "It stinks a little bit," Bert said (p. 117A).

Beyond material benefits, the honors or thanks the rescuers received were not sought, and were as often as not a source of embarrassment as one of pride:

Interviewer Now many people would say that what you did was an extraordinarily good deed and that you should be rewarded.

Margot That's what they say now. The hell with it. I don't want any reward (p. 68).

Maruska refused her medal from Yad Vashem because she saw her actions in saving Jews as a blow against prejudice and she felt the Israeli actions in Sidon constituted persecution of the Arabs (p. 6). Alida did not know she had even been identified as a rescuer until she spoke with us. And Leonie refused the Yad Vashem award, saying she had not really done enough to deserve it.

Was the praise of others a factor in their decision to save Jews? No. Many central European rescuers suffered harsh social ostracism for their acts, even after the war (Oliner and Oliner, 1988). None of our rescuers experienced this, but several mentioned the subtle ridicule of rescuers after the war (e.g., Tony, Bert). Wilhelmina commented that no one in her immediate social milieu admired her for her efforts in saving Jews (p. 6). And Bert told us that no one after the war commented on his actions at all. Most striking of all, all of the rescuers said they never expected praise for their actions:

Interviewer Was the opinion of others important to you? Of people on whose judgment you set great store?

Wilhelmina . . . but nobody knew about that (p. 10). . . . Later I became an "Unbesungener Held" [unsung hero] and I thought then, "Great, now you've got this record of honour." I always took much pride in that. But I never made use of it that I had this or so. Never. I was only proud inside, just for me (p. 7).

For all of the rescuers, then, the honors they later received—usually more than 30 years after the rescue—were peripheral. For most of the rescuers, the honors were nice and something which gave them pleasure. But for none of them was the honor ever central. For the rescuers, the act was the end. Saving someone's life was reward enough. Irene articulated this succinctly:

I did not realize then because I didn't do it for money or glory or anything. But the older I get, the more I feel I am very rich. . . . I would not change anything. It's a wonderful feeling to know that today that many people are alive and some of them married and have their children, and that their children will have children because I did have the courage and . . . the strength . . . (p. 42).

Participation Altruism

If rescue activity was not undertaken for material gain or honors—what rational actor theorists would call "goods" altruism—what about "participation" altruism, a concept referring to people who help others in order to feel good about themselves (Becker, 1976)? Were rescue activities pursued because they made rescuers feel better about themselves? *Did* it affect the way they felt about themselves? We found no evidence of this first phenomenon and very little of the second. Bethe and Margot articulate the attitude expressed by our rescuers on this point:

Interviewer How did your rescue activities make you feel about your-
self? (Margot shook her head.) It didn't affect you?
Margot Nothing special, no.
Interviewer Was it important to you that you were the one who saved
the people?
Margot No. They just had to be saved (p. 55).

We also asked explicitly whether the rescuers could distinguish between
a concern that the Jews were saved or that they be the ones to save
them. No one mentioned the latter:

Interviewer Was it of importance to you that the two young girls and
the mother with her son were being helped, or was it important to
you that it was you who did it?
Bethe That they were being helped. It was not important that we did
it. But because they came to us and had nobody else, we helped them
(p. 29).

In contrast, we should note that this was not the case for the
rational actors in our baseline sample. The entrepreneurs all said that
giving to and helping others made them feel good about themselves.
They mentioned the value of being part of a social network; some gave
in order to incur benefits for their businesses or families. Perhaps
because of this, they tended to give more readily to people they knew
directly, to local causes rather than to people far away. (One
entrepreneur even structured his contributions as loans, not uncondi-
tional gifts.) None of this appeared to be true for the rescuers.

Psychic Goods: A "Taste" for Altruism

The argument that altruism is a "psychic good" is closely related to the
concept of participation altruism and is an often cited explanation of
altruism. Do altruists simply have a taste for helping others, a taste
which produces an unusual utility function? We found this explanation
both the most powerful and the most frustratingly tautological. It is
extremely difficult to operationalize in a way that allows one to set a test
by which it can be reliably accepted or rejected. Beyond the psychic
pleasure in feeling good about oneself (already discussed above), what
can we examine to determine whether altruists simply have a "taste" for
altruism? We might ask whether rescuers performed other altruistic acts
to determine whether they demonstrated altruistic behavior frequently
enough to reveal an underlying preference for altruism. We might look
at the need to atone for past wrongs. Or we could try to measure their
pleasure (or utility) in feeling they were living up to the expectations of
a critical role model or to abstract ethical standards by saving Jews.

We tried to test these vague ideas. We asked our rescuers whether they felt their actions would (or were intended to) atone for past wrongs. We found no one at all in our sample who said they acted to alleviate past guilt. Nor did we find any pattern in adherence to particular ethical or religious standards. Rescuers came from all religions; they also were found among agnostics and atheists. For the most part, rescuers had been given high ethical standards by a critical role model. But this was not true for all rescuers. (Wilhelmina, for example, said she'd had no role model as a child.) And the role models mentioned specifically varied greatly. Furthermore, we found that all our rational actor respondents *also* had role models. As best we could ascertain, the moral messages transmitted by role models appeared to be virtually the same for both rescuers and for rational actors: honesty, fairness, justice, equality, respect for other people. We found no significant differences in the messages received by our altruists and by those in our baseline sample.[14]

In general, we also found that those in our baseline samples would rank just as high as our selfless individuals on conventional measures of morality. We also noted that during the war our rescuers deviated wildly from the standards they claimed to have been given by their role models. "Always tell the truth, that's my motto!" Peter told us. "But, Peter," we protested, "you just told us you lied like crazy during the war." Peter laughed. "Oh, well, that was different" (Peter, Tape 2). Since some earlier works on altruism (Rushton and Wiener, 1975; Rushton, 1980; Bandura, 1971; Eisenberg, 1987) which found social learning and role models to be critical predictors of altruism failed to control adequately for baseline data, this point must be reiterated. Our findings suggest that the entrepreneur, the rich person who gives no significant amount of money, the Germans who did not rescue Jews—all these individuals seem to evidence equally high ethical standards on conventional measures of morality (Kohlberg, 1976; Maslow, 1962). They have analogous experiences with critical role models. We conclude, therefore, that pursuing the ingrained values of a role model or the desire to please a role model cannot be judged a critical determinant of altruism. At best, it is a necessary but not a sufficient condition. This finding also suggests that altruism may differ in critical ways from other forms of ethical development, a finding we address later.

The idea of an underlying taste or preference for altruistic behavior is even harder to test. We do find surprisingly consistent behavior among our rescuers. Altruistic behavior seems evidenced at an early age and appears constant throughout life. Most of the rescuers said they were unchanged by their rescue activities:

I've always been a person who liked to give, and I've kept that 'til today (p. 9). . . . All the money I've had I gave . . . to these social places. . . . I send a lot of money [to good causes] (pp. 6–7).

This consistent pattern of concern for others is demonstrated by other rescuers as well. Most of the rescuers we interviewed lived very modestly, several almost in poverty. Yet despite limited financial means, most continue to give a surprising amount of their small incomes to charities. Bert has raised several children in informal adoptive arrangements, with no monetary compensation. Both he and Tony have saved people from drowning. (Tony lives near the Pacific Ocean and has saved 18 people.) Bethe cared for her baby brother after her mother died, demonstrating a surprising sensitivity and concern for someone so young and in mourning herself. During the war, Margot, Otto, Tony, and Ursula hid political prisoners as well as Jews. And both Irene and Maruska specifically identified their actions in saving Jews as part of a lifetime struggle against persecution:

Maruska I belong to a class of people who have been vigilant from youth on (pp. 4–5). . . . When somebody by nature has a relatively strong personality, then he also should use it to defend and to protect people who don't have this [kind of personality] (p. 6).

Interviewer Your help for persecuted Jews . . .

Maruska I'd like to generalize this. I helped persecuted people. Whether they were Jews, politically persecuted people or otherwise persecuted, was not important to me at all. I'd like to emphasize this. Here in Berlin-Kreuzberg [a working-class section of Berlin, populated by foreign workers] I live in a corner which is explosive, too. When policemen act evilly during their operations, which happens quite often, I'm always ready to go down on the street and to defend the people. I've always been doing this (pp. 6–7).

Interviewer So you are still on the side of the persecuted?

Maruska Yes, of course. You cannot just look at all this and do nothing. During my whole life, I've always been intervening in things I found unjust. As a child, I already acted like this (p. 11).

This suggests that rescue actions were part of a consistent pattern of helping others. Whether the mere consistency of altruistic behavior is enough to confirm the psychic goods argument seems doubtful to us, but our doubt may reflect our belief that the idea of psychic goods is so all-encompassing that it can mean anything and thus cannot be tested reliably.

Clusters of Altruists

Do clusters of similarly motivated actors encourage altruism? We found no evidence of this, with group support being only a secondary factor for our rescuers. Those rescuers (Margot, Otto, and Tony) who were active in organized political resistance movements undertook their political action simultaneously with or after initiating rescue actions. Rescuing Jews was not seen as another form of political resistance to the Nazi regime. Nor did anyone undertake rescue activities in order to obtain ties in a group or to experience social prestige or group fellowship, as is often cited as a motivation for cooperation and altruism (Trivers, 1971; Axelrod, 1984). In part, this is because danger necessitated ad hoc arrangements. Rescue networks "came up by themselves. As the need arose, people ended up getting involved" (Tony, p. 87). Rescue networks did not serve as clubs which one wished to join.[15]

What about the more subtle cluster concept often utilized to explain cooperation? This idea suggests that cooperators could find resources around them to support their cooperation; therefore, a tendency toward altruism (or cooperation) would be reinforced by contact with other altruists. Assessing the evidence on this aspect of the clustering effect is complex, both because the danger of rescue action necessitated secrecy and because any ongoing rescue action often required some tacit support or assistance from others, either by giving food, misfiling papers, or simply looking the other way (cf. Ursula, p. 14; Irene, p. 41).[16] On the whole, the evidence here is negative. Bethe said she knew that other Quakers probably also hid Jews but she never discussed it with any of them since it was too dangerous (p. 33). Bert mentioned farmers who gave him food, or who sold it to him very cheaply; he assumed they suspected he had Jews to feed and no food rations. But he—and all other rescuers—stressed that rescue activity was never discussed with others unless it was absolutely necessary, simply because of the danger involved in such activities:

> I knew of 10 or 12 families that . . . have Jews. I knew of one case that went wrong. . . . People knew of them [these families] because of their extraordinary needs [for food]. There was always a set of people who know not to ask [questions]. . . . I always go alone when [what I do would] have endangered . . . all the people in the house [the hidden Jews and my own family]. When they put those irons on you, you never know how far they can go to make you become a betrayer or something (Bert, Tape 4).

No rescuer we spoke with was recruited into rescue activities, although both Margot and Otto were recruited for their political activities.[17] Married or engaged rescuers (cf. Bert, Otto, Wilhelmina, Alida) often worked with their spouses, but this was not always the case. Maruska and Margot kept their actions hidden from everyone, including their fiancés.[18] Several rescuers had to go against critical loved ones in order to rescue Jews. Leonie, for example, was 17 years old and staying with her older sister in Rotterdam when the Allies liberated her home in southern Holland. Yet she took in two Jewish girls over the strenuous objections of this sister, on whom Leonie was totally dependent at that time. Alida's father chastised her for endangering her own children for strangers.

If clusters of altruists did not provide the appeal of empathy or duty sufficient to encourage altruism, what about sanctions? Were people who refused to help Jews threatened by rescuers? Did this phenomenon encourage rescue activity? Not at all. In fact, any sanctions served to treat rescuers more as defectors from the regime, with severe punishments instituted for those who saved Jews. At this more general level, we found no evidence that clusters of rescuers could defend themselves against defectors (presumably these might be represented by the Quislings in occupied countries) by cooperating with one another and doing better as a group than the defectors. The biographical and historical evidence of this period suggests exactly the contrary; at least until the very last days of the war, the rescuers were mercilessly turned in by the Quislings, who were rewarded by the Nazi regime.

In most of their actions, then, rescuers operated on their own, without encouragement from others and without formal group support. Rescuers were not recruited into tight groups, as were some resistance workers. Nor did the loose support networks which did exist provide the kind of tight group membership for which people would risk their lives. Finally, because of the danger and the extremity of the methods of torture, most rescuers isolated themselves from loved ones who might otherwise have encouraged them in their activities.

Resource Hypothesis

Is altruism a luxury, to be indulged in only after more basic, self-interested needs are satisfied? Do people strike some balance between what they are willing to do for others and what they have already done for themselves? Does having more encourage one to give more? These are variations on the rational actor explanation that views altruism as a resource. We found that this explanation held true for typical rational actors, who were more likely to take care of the needs of their own families before they considered giving to strangers. The nonrescuers we interviewed also often said they had nothing to give to Jews, since their own families were so destitute. Rational actors appear to make some conscious calculation about what they could afford to give and what they needed or wanted to keep or pass on to heirs. Entrepreneurs who gave money did say that it was easier to give once one had cared for one's needs and had extra resources (Monroe, 1991). None of this was the case for our rescuers, however, to whom actual resources seemed secondary details.

The general context of war meant that everyone experienced at least some shortages and physical hardship. Particularly during the Hunger Winter of 1944, food was scarce all over Europe and the limitations on ration coupons meant that rescue activities drained away the already scarce resources designated for food and fuel. Beyond this shared wartime limitation on resources, however, there was great variation in the resources individual rescuers brought to their situation. Wilhelmina and Ursula were reasonably comfortable economically. Margot and Otto were wealthy but lost most of their wealth because of their activities. In contrast, Alida had eight children who often went hungry to feed their Jewish guest, and Bethe was quite poor, living with her husband and three small children in one room so their Jewish guests could have the other room (Bethe, p. 24). The most extreme conditions were experienced by Tony and Knud (condemned to death and living underground), by Irene (living the precarious existence of a slave laborer), and by Otto (arrested and in various concentration camps). The critical point is that rescuers did not attend first to their own needs and then to the needs of others, as traditional theories of needs hierarchy suggest (Maslow, 1962). Indeed, rescuers made no distinction between their own needs and those of their Jewish guests. "Every other person is basically you," Tony told us (p. 1). "Gradually, by opening your eyes, you see that . . . everyone is you. . . . It's the mirror, again. . . . That's the kind of attitude you have for most of these rescues" (p. 81).

Beyond food and financial resources, none of these rescuers had tremendous resources in other significant areas. Irene was a young Polish girl, barely 20, cut off from her family by the war. She had been raped, beaten, and left for dead in the snow by Russian solders. She eventually ended up in a German slave labor camp, living in one room in back of the kitchen in a diner where German soldiers were fed. Yet she managed to hide 12 Jews in a German Major's villa, and she smuggled German food to other Jews hidden in the nearby forest. Leonie was only 17 and staying with her sister in Rotterdam, cut off from her home in Southern Holland, which had been liberated by the Allies. Despite her sister's objections, she hid 2 Jewish girls for three days in her sister's house.[19] Knud and Tony spent the war in hiding, sleeping wherever they could. At great risk to his own safety, Otto worked out deals with particular guards so he could continue his rescue activities even after he was sent to concentration camps. Margot was stripped of her German citizenship because of her refusal to support Hitler. She spent the war in Holland as a divorcée with two young children in the precarious position of a suspect and stateless person. She was quite active in rescue activity even though she was arrested six times and lost contact (temporarily) with her children as a result of this. Both she and Wilhelmina had fiancés who were killed because of the women's rescue activities.[20]

This did not alter their behavior. In sum, then, all of the rescuers acted even though they lacked what the traditional hierarchies of needs suggest are the apparent imperatives necessary for performance of selfless action: food, fuel, safety, emotional support from families or friends, love.

Assessing Rational Actor Explanations of Altruism

At this point, let us summarize what our interviews with rescuers of Jews suggest about rational actor explanations of altruism. In support of the rational actor approach, we find a consistent pattern of altruism. Altruism is demonstrated early in life for our rescuers and it remains a consistent part of their behavior. Beyond this, however, we find only the most spurious evidence of rescuers behaving altruistically because of their role models. Most of our rescuers had role models, but so did the rational actors we interviewed. As best as we can ascertain, the ethical messages transmitted to the two samples—"do good, work hard, be fair"—are identical. This suggests that role models per se are not critical determinants of altruism.

In contrast, we found much evidence weighing against the kinds of explanations of altruism developed using rational actor theory. We find no evidence of a need to atone for past wrongs, no evidence of either goods or participation altruism, no clusters of altruists, no expectation of reward, and no cost-benefit calculus. Given all this, we conclude that rational actor theory is of little or no use in explaining rescue activity.

IDENTITY, COGNITIVE FRAMEWORKS, AND RESCUE BEHAVIOR

Since traditional rational actor explanations of altruism do not explain rescue behavior, what does? For an answer, we turned to social cognition, which suggests that different perceptions of human nature, perhaps stemming from different perceptions of self in relation to others, would affect one's altruistic behavior. Did we find critical differences here? If so, what does this in turn reveal about the theory of rational action?

We noted clear differences in cognitive outlook, although not the ones we had expected from the literature or from our hypotheses.[21] Initially, we had expected to find differences in worldview between altruists and traditional rational actors, with altruists demonstrating a more communitarian *Gemeinschaft* and economic man a *Gesellschaft* view of the world as one in which individual ties come through conscious volitional associations (Tönnies, 1957). We found only limited evidence of this.

Shifts in cognitive outlooks were too subtle to be bifurcated. In a broader study of altruism, we did find shifts occurring, with philanthropists falling somewhere between the entrepreneurs and the rescuers (Monroe, 1991). But the critical dimension was not a view of human nature, as we had expected. All of the individuals discussed in this essay (rescuers, nonrescuers, and entrepreneurs alike) felt that human nature was mixed, sometimes good, sometimes bad. Most rescuers felt self-interest was to be expected in human behavior (cf. Maruska, p. 10, and Wilhelmina, p. 5).

While we did find that other-directed behavior was associated with close group ties for traditional rational actors, membership in a particular group did not explain rescue activity. To our surprise, our findings did not support traditional wisdom dating from Hume; group ties and identification do *not* seem to be critical predictors of altruism. At least in our small sample, rescuers were just as likely to be loners as they were to belong to tight-knit groups. Bert, Alida, and Irene, for example, came from very tight-knit communities; in contrast, Margot and Maruska were raised as international cosmopolitans, and Tony characterized himself as one caught between the national, religious, linguistic, and cultural differences of his Dutch father and his Belgian-French mother.

What about relations with Jews or toward Germany? Was there a consistent pattern for rescuers in this area? Some rescuers had known Jews well before the war (Otto, Tony, Margot, Bethe, and Wilhelmina). Others had grown up with anti-Semitic parents (Maruska's mother) or had never experienced much contact with Jews (Bert, Alida). Prior attitudes toward Germany, while varied, could not be characterized as anti-German. This was particularly interesting, since non-German rescuers might quite reasonably be expected during a war to voice anti-German attitudes or patriotic feelings of national identity. Yet surprisingly, no one characterized their rescue actions as patriotic, political, or anti-German. In fact, despite the horrors of the war, *none* of our non-German rescuers made anti-German statements. (Bert said he had felt sorry for the Germans after the Versailles Treaty.) Only Margot (born a German) made any critical comments about German character. Furthermore, we noted earlier that none of the rescuers said they began or took part in rescue activities *because* they were members of any particular group, be it religious, political, or social. In contrast, group ties were significant for rational actors. The individuals in our baseline sample said they were likely to give money mainly to familiar people or to local groups, to people and causes with which they had some empathetic tie or identification.[22]

Identity as One with All Humankind, Not Traditional Empathy

We explored the idea of empathy, a phenomenon noted by analysts as early as Hume (1939) and Adam Smith in *The Theory of Moral Sentiments* (1953). We defined "empathy" as the act of putting oneself in another's place and behaving ethically toward another because "that could be me." We found subtle but important distinctions to be made between empathy in this traditional sense and what we would characterize as an identity perception as part of a common humanity. The rescuers were remarkably unaffected by the kind of phenomenon which Rawls (1971) describes in his veil of ignorance metaphor. They were not rescuers because they knew they could be in a similarly needy position. To expand upon Rawls's metaphor, their fellow feeling was more the kind that would prompt them to specify ethical institutions even if they knew in advance that *they* would be the philosopher king in any political or social system. In this, rescuers seem to approach the concept of "fellow feeling" described by Smith in *The Theory of Moral Sentiments*.[23] This fellow feeling appears to us to be much broader than the particular group ties which drive traditional concepts of empathy. Traditional usage of empathy suggests viewing both oneself and the person being aided as having something specific in common—for example, "I helped them because they were also Polish, female, mothers," and so on, as opposed to the idea that "I would help any human being." The subtle distinction here can best be documented by an extensive excerpt from our interview with Irene, an excerpt which begins by sounding as if the bond were this traditional empathy but which reveals something subtly different as Irene explains her actions more fully:

Irene Well, we did have in common that we were all separated. I was not with my parents. In a way, I was persecuted too. I was not free.

Interviewer You identified with them?

Irene Yes.

Interviewer Was there a kind of bond or empathy that you had?

Irene Yes. We created a bond between us because they told me their story. Then I knew some of them, like Franka. I knew her parents. Remember I went to the ghetto to get her one time when her parents were taken. There was a bond between us.

Interviewer I know this is a difficult question to answer, but if you try to compare what it was that caused you to rescue people, what was more important? You said there was a bond, a kind of feeling there of empathy, identifying with them, because you were all separated from your family.

Irene Yes, because we were all persecuted.

Interviewer Now you've also said that you felt that you were a part of a common humanity.

Irene It did not matter to me that they were Jewish. Because I was not raised with anti-Semitism. If they would be another nationality, it would mean to me the same thing. They were persecuted.

Interviewer But suppose you had not been persecuted. Suppose you had been treated just fine by the Germans. Would you still have saved them?

Irene Yes, I would. Just because I am not persecuted, I can still see that they [the Germans] are persecuting people; they are hurting them. The Germans have no right to do this.... And they are hurting the people.

Interviewer So would you say your actions were motivated less by identifying with them [the Jews] and more from a feeling that we're all human beings?

Irene Yes. That has to be done. Nobody can do this. We have all the same rights (pp. 44–46).

Margot also articulated this more succinctly:

Interviewer Was empathy a part of it at all?
Margot Meaning what?
Interviewer A feeling that this could be me?
Margot No, I never even thought of it (p. 67).

This perception of self as part of a common humanity—as opposed to more specific personalistic ties to family, local interests, or even country—most aptly captures the systematic and consistent differences in cognitive view between traditional rational actors and rescuers:

Tony ...[W]e all are like cells of a community that is very important; not America, I mean the human race... (p. 1).

Interviewer In terms of your basic identity, is it more Polish or more someone who protects persecuted people? You talked [earlier] about being a member of a family of man.

Irene Yes, That's what it is. This was more because I thought that we all belong to one human family.

Interviewer So that's a more basic identity for you, even than being Polish?

Irene Yes. That's true (pp. 39–40).

Our rescuers are what can best be characterized as John Donne's people.[24] They need not send to know for whom the bell tolls. They know. And this perception of themselves as one with all humankind is such an intrinsic part of their cognitive orientation, of the way they define themselves, that they need not stop to make a conscious decision when someone knocks at the door asking for help. We heard phrases such as the following from all our rescuers. "You help whoever you can when you are asked" (Margot, p. 39). "You help people because you are human and you see that there is a need. . . . There are things in this life you have to do and you do it" (Bert, p. 12).

Bethe . . . one day our oldest—he was about eight—said to me: "Tell me, Mom, we haven't enough for ourselves to eat, but we have always guests. They eat here and live here, and we haven't enough for ourselves."

Interviewer And what did you answer?

Bethe I knew at this moment that I must now answer so that he would understand that it was necessary. So I told him: "Listen, these are people like you and me. The possibility to live in an apartment has been taken away from them. They will be sent to the concentration camp." (I explained what a concentration camp is.) "And they don't get coupons [food ration coupons] anymore and they don't know how to live. They would have to die or go to the concentration camp, and there they'll also die if we don't help them." Then he said: "This is quite different." And from then on he shared every apple, everything he received as a present (pp. 24–25).

Identity as Limiting Perceived Choice Options

Because the rescuers' identities were so strong, there was no conscious choice for them to make in the traditional sense of assessing options and choosing the best one. Instead, their perception of themselves in relation to others limited the options available *to them*. Certainly, they knew most people did not risk their lives to save Jews and so they knew that theoretically this choice was available. But they did not believe this choice was an option for them.

We asked rescuers how they began their activities, how they made their decision to risk their lives for strangers. Margot best summarizes the extent to which a rescuer's identity delineated the available options so effectively that it essentially precluded making a decision:

Interviewer You started out, really before we even started the interview, talking about making conscious choices. And you said you didn't think you operate that way. Was there really a conscious choice that you made?

Margot I don't make a choice. It comes, and it's there.

Interviewer It just comes. Where does it come from?

Margot I don't know. I don't think so much because I don't have that much to think with. . . .

Interviewer It was just totally nonconscious?

Margot Yes. You don't think about these things. You can't think about these things. It happened so quickly.

Interviewer But it isn't really totally quickly, is it? There's a tremendous amount of strategic planning that has to be done [to do what you did].

Margot Well, I was young. I could do it. Today I don't know. I'd have to try it. But I was 32 years old. That was pretty young.

Interviewer You didn't sit down and weigh the alternatives?

Margot God, no. There was not time for these things. It's impossible.

Interviewer So it's totally spontaneous? It comes from your emotions?

Margot Yes. It's pretty near impossible not to help. You couldn't do that. You wouldn't understand what it means. Suppose somebody falls in the water, as I said before. You want to think, "Should I help or should I not?" The guy would drown! You know, that's no way.

Interviewer How about the repercussions of your actions? Did you think about what might happen because you were doing this?

Margot You don't think about it. No way.

Interviewer You didn't worry about possible consequences for you? For your family?

Margot No. No way (p. 54).

Interviewer How did all this start, I mean that besides the Blochs, you took other Jews into your house?

Ursula This happened bit by bit. Two sisters, musicians, came one day to our house. . . . We went upstairs, and then they asked, "Couldn't we stay here?" Only then did I notice what was going on. At first, I had understood nothing at all. So they were standing in our house, and we knew that if we kicked them out, they'd go into the Wannsee [drown themselves in Lake Wann]. So I told them, "You better stay here." And they stayed in our house for months.

Interviewer Did you carefully consider your decision to take the two into your house and were you aware of all the consequences?

Ursula But there wasn't any time for that (p. 15).

Interviewer But why, why did you do that at all?

Ursula . . . [I]t happened quite by itself, this situation. There were these two girls standing there. . . . You were simply confronted with this situation (p. 17).

Bert also tells of coming home to find Henny (the first Jew they saved) at his house. "Suddenly, I know why she comes. 'She stays,' I say" (Land-Weber, p. 3 of chapter on Bert).

Furthermore, even after they had been forced to evaluate the costs, there still was no conscious choice for rescuers to make; rather, it was a recognition that they were a certain kind of person and that this meant they *had* to behave in a certain way. This does not mean they were not conscious of a choice being made. It meant that they knew that the choice had already been made for them by who they were.

Interviewer Let me ask you what really is the hardest question for me to understand. What do you think it was that made you able or willing to risk your life, when so many other people did not?

Margot Well, I think it's just me (p. 56).

Interviewer Did the idea ever come to mind to not act as you did?

Bethe No, I don't think so. . . . [I]t was difficult sometimes. But we would never have turned anybody out. We would never have considered it. . . . [W]e knew that we would expose them to death (p. 33).

Interviewer Did you have the feeling that it was your obligation to help your Jewish friends? Even if you risked your own life with this?

Wilhelmina But we had to do that; they needed us. First of all we had a very precious group of people and I simply considered it a matter of course (p. 7).

"One cannot really act otherwise." "There was no decision to make. I didn't really think about it. What else could I do?" We heard these words paraphrased over and over, from all our rescuers. It is interesting that several of the Germans in our baseline sample echoed a similar idea of no choice available to them; but nonrescuers also added an expression of poignant isolation, viewing themselves as individuals who were alone and helpless: "But what could I do to help, I, just one person alone against the Nazis?" (Freida, Tape 1).

This almost instinctive response seemed more credible for the heroes we interviewed in our broader survey, people who were presented with an immediate life or death situation which is soon resolved when one jumps in the lake or walks away. But the rescuers had ample time to rethink the costs of their actions. They were forced to develop elaborate strategic arrangements to obtain food when they had no ration coupons, to dispose of refuse for additional people, to deal with illnesses and births and the myriad other parts of life in close quarters. The ongoing nature of their activities makes the evidence here all the more striking. Surely, during the long nights spent by Otto in the concentration camps or by Irene in the Major's bed, one would become conscious of what one had done. Yet all of our rescuers insisted, over and over again, that there was no choice to make.

In part, then, it is the very ongoing nature of rescue activity which leads us to emphasize rescuers' identity construct in our explanation of altruism. Rescuers felt that "all human beings belong to one . . . family" (Irene, p. 40; Tony, p. 1). Their perception of themselves as part of a common humanity formed such a central core of their identity that it left them no choice in their behavior toward others. Even though, in most cases, their awareness of this identity was not conscious and the behavior was spontaneous, it was, in our view, the critical factor in their actions. Bethe succinctly captured both this sense of oneness with humankind and the nonconscious aspect of rescuers' activities. "When one knows that one is bound into a bigger entity, then one cannot really act otherwise. But this enlightenment really comes only with old age" (p. 28).

This shared perception of themselves as part of a common humanity thus seems to be what distinguishes rescuers from other individuals. It is what guides their actions in saving others. It is what limits their perceived choice options and makes their actions emanate from non-conscious sources. We should note that it provides a striking contrast to the self-image of nonrescuers. What emerged for nonrescuers was a picture of people who saw themselves as helpless, isolated individuals, rather than as members of a common humanity. From this group, we often heard: "But what could I do... one individual, alone against the Nazis?" (Freida, Tape 1). From the rescuers we heard: "But what else could I do? It's pretty near impossible not to help" (Margot, p. 1).

IMPLICATIONS OF FINDINGS

We have presented excerpts from interviews with 13 rescuers of Jews in Nazi-occupied Europe. What does this evidence suggest about the theory of rational action? In *The Economic Approach to Human Behavior*, Becker presents a strong argument that the "comprehensive" nature of rational actor theory makes it "applicable to all human behavior" (1976:8):

> The heart of my argument is that human behavior is not compart-mentalized, sometimes based on maximizing, sometimes not, some-times motivated by stable preferences, sometimes by volatile ones, sometimes resulting in an optimal accumulation of information, sometimes not. Rather, all human behavior can be viewed as involving participants who maximize their utility from a stable set of preferences and accumulate an optimal amount of information and other inputs in a variety of markets.
>
> If this argument is correct, the economic approach provides a unified framework for understanding behavior that has long been sought by and eluded Bentham, Comte, Marx, and others (Becker, 1976:14).

Our analysis of the rescuers documented here is in sharp contrast to Becker's claims. We would not assert that rational actor theory is totally wrong; but we do argue that rescue activity clearly demonstrates that at least *some* human behavior cannot be explained by this economic approach. Even if we are extremely cautious in interpreting the implications of our findings, three points seem clear.

1. *The empirical existence of altruism sets limits to a theory based on self-interest.* Rescuer activity constitutes a significant theoretical challenge to the fundamental assumption of self-interest which lies at the heart of the theory of rational action (Meyers, 1983; Mansbridge, 1990). The rescuers demonstrate that self-interest is not always the dominant force motivating human behavior. Over and over, even when we pressed them during the interviews, the rescuers uniformly insisted that while they knew the costs of their actions, they disregarded these costs (including the possible loss of life) as relevant determinants of behavior.[25] They neither expected nor considered possible rewards for their acts. They did not think in terms of a cost-benefit calculus. No matter how rare an empirical phenomenon, rescue activity thus constitutes an important theoretical challenge to any theory (be it neoclassical economics, Darwinian biology, or Freudian psychology) which makes self-interest its cornerstone.

Economists did not, of course, originally develop the theory of rational action to explain altruism. Yet increasingly, social scientists have seen this theory offered as a comprehensive construct useful in explaining human behavior in social areas far beyond the market situations from which it first emerged. Analysts have applied this theory to everything from political phenomena such as democracy and discrimination to the most personal social acts such as marriage and suicide. Because of this somewhat indiscriminate application of rational actor theory, an empirical analysis which demonstrates that there are clear limits to the theory must take on a significance of some theoretical importance. In particular, it suggests we should stop straining to fit all behavior into this theoretical framework. We also must stop grafting on artificial factors to make the theory conform to reality. Instead, we should move to identify more precisely those situations in which the theory *does* explain reality and to specify those situations in which it does *not* have high predictive or explanatory value.

We suspect that political behavior is a complex area in which the theory's usefulness varies greatly, depending on the particular political action. Rational actor theory may work well in explaining conscious political actions which are clearly based on perceived self-interest, such as coalition formation. It may be less satisfactory in explaining political phenomena (such as voting) in which much of the decision to act (vote), and even the particulars of the action (vote choice) themselves, may be prompted by less conscious concerns. Obviously, these matters need to be explored more fully. What is abundantly clear to us, however, is that insofar as rescue activity constitutes an important form of political behavior, any theories of rational action which are applied to political behavior must be modified in a fundamental way to allow for individuals' concerns for others, even when this concern entails sacrifice of one's own welfare.

2. *Behavior is more than the product of conscious choice*. Rescuers made no conscious decision when they rescued Jews. Any conscious decision making entered only at a strategic level, focusing on how best to go about effecting the rescue, rather than on whether or not to attempt the rescue itself. The conscious element of rescue behavior thus appears to be limited to arranging the specific daily logistics of rescue activity. The initial actions in sheltering Jews were usually described as spontaneous. All our rescuers insisted that they simply saw no other option available to them. Their awareness of life around them made it abundantly clear that there *was* the option of turning away Jews or of simply doing nothing. They knew that most people did exactly that. But they also knew that they could not accept such an option for themselves. The rescuers thus suggest that certain behaviors arise spontaneously, resulting from deep-seated dispositions which form one's central identity. These behaviors are not the product of conscious choice. This conclusion, if accurate, may or may not constitute a critical challenge to rational *actor* theory, which requires only that actors behave *as if* a rational decision-making calculus has been formed. But it does suggest that we need drastic modifications in rational *choice* theory, in which the decision-making process is assumed to follow a conscious and consistent goal-directed maximization (Riker, 1962). In particular, it suggests that certain behaviors—and these may well entail the most significant personal and political choices we make—are not the result of conscious choice at all.

3. *Our identity constructs limit our perceived options*. Instead of conscious choice, rescue activity appears to reflect an unconscious recognition (a) that the rescuer was a certain kind of person and (b) that this basic identity construct necessarily entailed and precluded certain kinds of behavior. For rescuers, the concept of a cost-benefit calculus became meaningless, since to indulge in proscribed behavior would necessitate a fundamental shift in the actor's basic identity construction.[26] This particular perception of self in relation to others was the common—and therefore, we believe, the critical—cognitive factor in rescue activities.[27]

The importance of identity suggests to us that cognitive frameworks, especially the view of self in relation to others, are critical in understanding political behavior, behavior which by its very nature involves others. We believe that this cognitive framework may be the link between the theory of rational action and cultural theory and should be a major area of focus for scholars interested in constructing future positive political theory.

At this point, we still find it difficult to disentangle the complex relationship between identity (which delineates choices nonconsciously) and simple conscious and perhaps volitional adherence to particular moral values. We are aware that rational choice theorists could simply argue that altruists' values differ from those of other actors. We believe that this intellectual sleight of hand skirts the issue. (Certainly it conflicts with our above-described evidence on the pattern of moral values transmitted to our respondents and with the findings presented in the Oliner and Oliner, 1988, study of rescuers.) Our impression of rescuers is that they do not consider the individual the basic actor in society. All of our interviews point to the idea that rescuers view themselves as part of a shared humanity rather than as individual beings, separate and distinct from others. In part, we conclude this on the basis of the rescuers' repeated assertions that they did what anyone else would have done, that their extraordinary actions were nothing unusual, nothing special, when clearly this was not the case:

Interviewer What did you receive these decorations [from Yad Vashem and the Decoration of Merit from the Federal Republic of Germany] for?

Bethe We got them for things that go without saying. If things had been right, all people would have acted this way (p. 23).

Interviewer Could you try to explain why you, precisely, together with your mother, took upon yourselves these enormous risks to help persecuted people? Many, many people did nothing. . . .

Ursula On the contrary, I always had the feeling that we, too, still did not enough. . . . I always think we had done far too little; my mother and me. We did far too little, we should have done much more. When I hear from others what they have done . . .! (p. 17).

Interviewer Let's talk again about your rescue actions. How did all this begin?

Maruska How did all this begin? . . . I hid and protected Jews. I gave them a chance to find shelter in my house. This was quite normal, nothing extraordinary (p. 12).

We also base our conclusion, however, on more explicit statements of a common humanity. While we did hear echoes of empathy and duty from our rescuers, these seemed a minor part of their actions; a common bond among humankind seemed a much more important and more frequently voiced factor for rescuers:

Interviewer The things you have done, did you do them more out of a sense of duty or rather was it pity? If you think once again of these two musicians . . .?

Ursula I cannot really explain that. At that time one did that spontaneously. Of course there was pity and it was a sense of duty. But basically, it was quite normal that you had to do that (pp. 17–18).

Interviewer Do you consider it to be your duty to help someone in difficulties, even if that exposes you or people who are close to you to danger?

Ursula This is a strange question. It's difficult to answer this question after 40 or 50 years. At that time, one had quite another attitude than at the present prosperous time. We were simply much more welded together, we and our Jewish friends. We knew they needed us (p. 20).

Perhaps Tony captured most succinctly what we have so clumsily tried to analyze:

Tony I was to learn to understand that you're part of a whole and that just like cells in your own body altogether makes your body, that in our society and in our community that we all are like cells of a community that is very important; not America, I mean the human race, and that you should always be aware that every other person is basically you. You should always treat people as though it is you, and that goes for evil Nazis as well as for Jewish friends who are in trouble. . . . [Y]ou should always have a very open mind in dealing with other people and always see yourself in those people, for good or for evil both (p. 1).

"Part of a whole . . . every other person is basically you." "One cannot really act otherwise." "You help people because you are human." Statements like these were the clues which helped us distinguish between actions motivated by a conscious adherence to a system of moral values and acts motivated by a sense of personal identity in which choices serve more as self-affirmations and less as options. We believe the fact that none of our rescuers mentioned a specific moral, political, or philosophical credo suggests that identity is primary. Certainly, it seems logical that identity, which is formed so early in life, becomes central. But we recognize that this is not the same thing as definitively disentangling the relationship between personal identity and adherence to moral values in any scientific manner. Nonetheless, we would argue that if one conceives of oneself as a certain kind of individual, then decisions become less choices between alternatives and more a recognition, perhaps an inner realization, which reflects a statement of who one is at the most fundamental level of self-awareness. This self-recognition involves an acceptance that only certain options are available to one because of this perception of self. How one's basic identity develops, the importance of culture and socialization in this process, and whether the cognitive view of self can provide the link between rational actor theory and cultural theory—all these questions remain beyond the scope of this essay.[28]

NOTES

Acknowledgments. Many people provided generous assistance in this project. First and foremost are the kind people who endured long interviews which invoked deeply personal memories, often of difficult times. To protect their privacy, we may not thank them publicly, but our thanks are deeply felt. Eva Fogelman assisted in identifying Americans honored by Yad Vashem. Ellen Land-Weber allowed us to quote from her book manuscript, as did Dr. Philip Alexander from his unpublished tapes with Bert. Generous research funds were provided by the University of California at Irvine Academic Senate Committee on Faculty Research, by the Earhart Foundation, and by Juergen Falter. Special thanks go to David Easton, Joseph Cropsey, Howard Margolis, Harry Eckstein, Wil Lampros, Hans-Dieter Klingemann, and the anonymous referees, all of whom provided valuable suggestions or comments on our work at various stages. Wilma Laws, Cheryl Larsson, and Ziggy Bates typed the manuscript. Susan Lee transcribed the English interview. The German interviews were translated and transcribed by A. Dallendörfer, Michelle Mueller, and Ute Klingemann. An abbreviated version of this paper appears in the October 1990 issue of *ETHICS*.

1. Because of space constraints, the interviews with members of the baseline sample are discussed only as contrasting corroboration that the rescuers do differ from typical rational actors. See Monroe (1991) for fuller details of our broader survey on altruism, which also included interviews with philanthropists and heroes (honored by the Carnegie Hero Commission for risking their lives to save strangers from natural disasters, accidents, or human violence).

2. Edited transcripts of the interviews will be published so that scholars utilizing diverse methodologies, from interpretive analysis to content analysis and Q-sorts, may reanalyze our date. (See Monroe, 1991, for samples of questions.) The interviews with Bert, Alida, and Peter were only partially transcribed because of the bilingual aspect of their interviews. Some quotations are from notes taken during the interview or from the taped interviews. For Bert, we also quoted from the transcript of Philip Alexander's interview, in which case an "A" follows the page number. Quotations from all other interviews are identified by the rescuer's name or pseudonym, tape number, or page on their transcript.

3. Eventually, we found that the rescuers preferred not to see the questionnaire in advance, appearing somewhat overwhelmed by the formality of a long questionnaire.

4. Additional background knowledge of nonrescuers came from Ute Klingemann's interviewing of bystanders as part of the Altruistic Personality Survey described in Oliner and Oliner (1988).

5. We were surprised how rarely anyone asked to delete material from the interview. Rescuers occasionally asked to delete the names of well-known people who were still living and who might be injured by public knowledge of their wartime activities. (For example, we were told that the father of a well-known American businessman made his money as a bunker builder for the Germans.) No one ever asked to delete any information because it reflected badly on himself or herself.

6. We experimented with telephone interviews to determine whether the potential increase in anonymity and the decrease in visual cues justified the loss in personal contact. As far as we could ascertain, the benefits attached to a telephone interview seemed greater than its costs.

7. Further interviews with nonrescuers have been conducted but have not yet been fully analyzed. Preliminary analysis of these interviews corresponds with the general findings presented here.

8. Eight of the 13 rescuers are women. This slight oversampling of women resulted from two factors: (1) gender differences in life expectancy and (2) our desire to interview as many German rescuers as possible. Because most German men were in the military service, they were therefore effectively removed from the pool of potential rescuers. (Peter is an exception here.) However, Alida's husband (now dead of natural causes), Margot's father, and Wilhelmina's fiancé (presumed to be killed by the Nazis because of his rescue activities) shared in their rescue efforts.

9. Although in-depth narrative interviews of matched samples have a long and respectable tradition in social science, those readers used to large sample studies may desire reassurance on the small size and the extent to which we may have cued or led the subject. We were sensitive to both these factors. The full transcripts reveal the extent to which we bent over backward not to lead the subject. The excerpt from Tony (quoted below) contains his first words in our first telephone interview. They are striking because they capture the essence of our conclusions on altruism, but even more so because they could not possibly have been cued in any way, since the only information Tony had from us was a written note that we were interviewing rescuers. We reprint this transcript in full to demonstrate the extent to which Tony's answer was not cued in any way:

Interviewer Hello, Tony. This is Kristi Monroe. Thank you for agreeing to speak with me. Is it all right if I record our conversation?

Tony Yes, of course.

Interviewer Good. I'm pushing the record button now. Would you like me to tell you a little bit about what I'm doing?

Tony Yes, I'd love that.

Interviewer Okay. I've been interested in altruism partly because it's an interesting phenomenon in and of itself, but also because it deviates from the way that social theory usually argues that people behave. I've been looking at certain kinds of rescue behavior and certainly, to me, rescue behavior falls into that category. I've been interviewing rescuers and asking people to tell me their story—to let me get to know them—their family background, things like that—and then tell me what happened during the war because that's always interesting.

Tony Sure.

Interviewer And then I have some questions which I've been asking people and which look at the social science predictors of altruism. Originally I was just interested in it [this interview] from that point of view. And I will be doing a book on that [on altruism]. But what I've found out in doing the interviews is that some of the stories people are telling me in and of themselves are so interesting that I probably will be doing another book, just on some of the stories and analyzing them a little bit. So what I will do is send you the transcript [and] let you look it over. There will be lots of mistakes in terms of spelling, names, of course, things like that, that I won't catch, and the typist won't catch.

Tony Of course.

Interviewer I want you to have a chance to look at it because a lot of times I know people will say things that maybe they didn't want to have made public in any way. And then if you say it's okay [I'll analyze the interview].

Tony Yes.

Interviewer And I want you to have an opportunity to think about it. Primarily, I've never done interviews with people before and I want to be very sensitive to not invade anyone's privacy. That's my main concern. What I'd like to do is talk [with you for] about 30–45 minutes each phone call. But you stop me when you get tired. And then later [when we finish talking on the phone] I can send you the transcribed material and we can get together, 'cause I'd like to meet you.

Tony Fine.

Interviewer Why don't you tell me a little bit about yourself.

Tony Well, you were talking about altruism. I have very strong thoughts about altruism. I'm not talking about the suicidal type of thing. That's totally different. Risking your life, that's not a form of altruism. Personally, I'm not particularly Christian, insofar as men believing in the Resurrection of the Lord and stuff like that. But I do believe that one of the most important teachings in Christianity is to learn to love your neighbor as yourself. And I was to learn to understand that you're part of a whole; that just like cells in your own body altogether make your body, that in our society and in our community, that we all are like cells of a community that is very important. Not America. I mean the human race. And that you should always be aware that every other person is basically you. You should always treat people as though it is you. And that goes for evil Nazis as well as for Jewish friends who are in trouble or anything like that. You should always have a very open mind in dealing with other people and always see yourself in those people, for good or for evil both (Tony, verbatim quote from Tape 1).

10. See Arrow, 1975; Wintrobe, 1981; Valavanis, 1958; Margolis, 1982; Frohlich, 1974, 1975; Hirschleifer, 1977, 1981; Fitzgerald, 1975; Landes, 1978; Landes and Posner, 1978; Becker, 1976; Kolm 1983.

11. Although Becker's work may constitute the most extreme statement of the universal egoism assumption, many works document the extent to which the assumption of individual self-interest constitutes the heart of rational actor theory (see Frank, 1988; Mansbridge, 1990; Myers, 1983; Hirschman, 1977, inter alia).

12. In a broader examination of the rational actor analyses of altruism, we found that these explanations did have some predictive power in accounting for the limited volunteer and charitable activities undertaken occasionally by entrepreneurs and a limited usefulness in explaining giving by philanthropists. (See Monroe, 1991.)

13. Rational actor explanations of altruism are subtle and interwoven. For clarity of presentation, we have tried to discuss and offer evidence on the theory's different aspects, recognizing that doing so creates some artificial separateness and that an explanation stressing a cost-benefit calculus may relate closely to one stressing psychic gratification, and so on.

14. It was interesting that our rescuers voiced the same phrases as our baseline respondents—for instance, "always tell the truth," "never lie." And yet we'd remind rescuers that they had told many lies during the war. "You should have heard what [lies] I told them [the Germans]! I didn't believe it myself" (Margot, p. 54). Rescuers saw nothing incongruous about this. These rescuers were not and did not claim to be saints.

15. *Interviewer* When people talk about philanthropy, one of the explanations that is often given is that people feel they're part of a network. Because other people they know are giving money, they feel they want to give, too. Or they feel they *should* give money. In other words, partly they give money because they want to feel part of the crowd. Was this factor relevant in any of your rescue activities?
    Tony No.

16. Maruska eventually became engaged to one of the Jewish men she was hiding, but the encouragement she received from him was obviously not the cause of her rescue activity since she met him only *after* he was hidden in her home. Also, he was a victim, not another rescuer.

17. Margot was recruited for resistance work after she had already begun her rescue activities.

18. Such secrecy was prudent, although it occasionally went tragically awry. Margot's fiancé naively went to the Gestapo to find out why

Margot had been arrested. The Gestapo questioned Alfred about Margot's activities and beat him to death because he could tell them nothing.

19. Because her sister was very frightened by this, Leonie contacted the Dutch Underground about moving the girls elsewhere. Leonie eventually engaged in more extensive rescue activity, including taking 100 sick, starving children on a surreptitious barge journey to Friesland, assisted only by her sister and one other woman.

20. Wilhelmina's fiancé simply disappeared. Since both he and Wilhelmina had been active in rescue work, Wilhelmina presumed the Gestapo killed him. Margot's fiancé was killed because of his association with her, even though he was not involved in her activities.

21. In our interviews, we used cognitive frameworks interchangeably with worldview in order to make it clear to our respondents what we were asking.

22. *Interviewer* Do you feel that you are trying in some sense to repay people who helped you when you had a [disabled] child in this situation? Or is it more that you can just empathize [with people with disabled children]?
    Philanthropist I can just empathize. I think it's more that. It's an empathy for anyone that has a problem. I do empathize with.... I know it's harder [having a disabled child], and I know that they have a lot of hurt inside, and that it takes a lot more to do what we just normally take for granted, so therefore I really appreciate that effort that they made (Mary, a philanthropist, p. 50).

23. While Smith referred to the concept as both "fellow feeling" and "sympathy," the concept seems closer to contemporary common language usage of the term "empathy."

24. "No man is an island, Intire of itself; every man is a peece of the Continent, A part of the Maine; If a clod bee washed away by the Sea, Europe is the lesse, as well as if a promonterie were, As well as if a Mannor of thy friends or of thy owne were; Any man's death diminishes me, Because I am involved in Mankinde; and therefore never send to know for whom the bell tolls; it tolls for thee" Donne, Devotions XVII.

25. We have tried through extensive quotations to capture both how hard we pushed rescuers on this point and their exasperation as a result of our persistence.

26. Whether such a shift occurred in nonrescuers is, of course, a possibility. We are exploring this question in future work.

27. See Crozier, in this volume, on the importance of identity for rationality.

28. Two additional questions, also too broad to be discussed adequately here, are nonetheless of direct concern for scholars interested in ethical behavior and therefore should be mentioned briefly. (1) What is

the relation of altruism to ethical behavior? (2) What is the driving force behind altruism?

We noted that the rescuers did not "fit" into any of the traditional developmental frameworks designed to explain and predict ethical behavior (cf. Maslow, 1962; Kohlberg, 1976; or Adorno et al., 1950). This surprised us and suggests the need to distinguish more carefully between altruism and traditional forms of ethical behavior in future discussions. In particular, we should design research to discover the extent to which altruism and ethical behavior are the same. The two may overlap. But altruism may differ significantly at critical points from other forms of ethical behavior. This may suggest why altruism is best explained through an identity construct and through one's self-perception in relation to others and why the developmental hierarchies or traditional socioeconomic predictors (such as religion) fail to successfully predict altruism. All of this suggests the need for further work.

Second, although the present discussion has focused on the cognitive explanation of altruism, we have also noted that rescuers always discussed their acts as emanating from the passions, not the intellect. This is at odds with a major Western tradition in discussions of ethical behavior since Plato and Kant. This tradition locates the origins of ethical behavior as emanating in reason's control of the passions. (See Frank, 1988; Hirschman, 1977.) In sharp contrast to this accepted wisdom, all of our rescuers appeared to be driven by their emotions to save others, with all of them clearly stressing the nonconscious and nonconsequentialist aspect of their behavior. None of our rescuers explained his or her behavior by reference to any well-developed system of ethical action which reason discovered for them. We asked Margot: "Do you have any particular ethical credo that has guided your life? Any system of ethical beliefs?" "No," she replied (p. 54). We never heard: "It would have been 'un-Christian' or 'wrong' to turn away Jews." Instead, our questions met with a look of surprise, followed by a return query: "But how could you do anything else?" These explanations—often uttered with some exasperation as we pressed the rescuers on this point—always focused on the nonreasoning part of one's character, emanating from the emotions rather than from the intellect or from the triumph of reason over passion. This sounds closer to the kind of moral sense theory which was so critical in Adam Smith's first book and which appeared later in Darwin's discussion of morality and evolution (Darwin, 1936; Schwartz, 1986). It seems particularly ironic, then, that while Smith's use of "fellow feeling" credited humankind with an instinctual response toward others which is caring and ethical, Smith's followers have largely overlooked this aspect of Smith and have instead emphasized self-interest as a scientifically established fact of life around which political and social institutions *must* be constructed if they wish to be successful. We hope that a closer analysis of altruism will encourage the rereading of Smith necessary to reinterpret economic theory in the broader and more humane context in which Smith originally crafted it.

REFERENCES

Adorno, T., et al. (1950). *The Authoritarian Personality*. New York: Norton.

Arrow, K. (1975). "Gifts and Exchanges." In E. Phelps (Ed.), *Altruism, Morality, and Economic Theory*. New York: Sage.

Axelrod, R. (1984). *The Evolution of Cooperation*. New York: Basic Books.

_____. (1973). "Schema Theory: An Information Processing Model of Perception and Cognition." *American Political Science Review*, 67:1248–1266.

Bandura, A. (1971). *Social Learning Theory*. Englewood Cliffs, NJ: Prentice-Hall.

Becker, G. (1976). *The Economic Approach to Human Behavior*. Chicago: University of Chicago Press.

Bruner, J. (1988). *Actual Minds, Possible Worlds*. Cambridge, MA: Harvard University Press.

Darwin, C. (1936). *The Origin of Species and the Descent of Man*. New York: Modern Library.

Eisenberg, N. (1987). "The Development of Prosocial Values." In N. Eisenberg, J. Reykouski, and E. Staub (Eds.), *Social and Moral Values: Individual and Societal Perspectives*. Hillsdale, NJ: Erlbaum.

Fitzgerald, B. (1975). "Self-Interest or Altruism: Corrections and Extensions." *Journal of Conflict Resolution, 19*(3):462–478.

Frank, R. H. (1988). *Passions Within Reason*. New York: Norton.

Frohlich, N. (1974). "Self-Interest or Altruism: What Difference?" *Journal of Conflict Resolution, 18*:55–73.

_____. (1975). "Comments in Reply." *Journal of Conflict Resolution, 19*:480–483.

Goffman, I. (1959). *The Presentation of Self in Everyday Life*. Garden City, NY: Doubleday-Anchor.

Greenstein, F. I., and Tarrow, S. (1970). *Political Orientations of Children: The Use of a Semi-Projective Technique in Three Nations*. Beverly Hills, CA: Sage.

Hirschleifer, J. (1977). "Shakespeare vs. Becker on Altruism: The Importance of Having the Last Word." *Journal of Economic Literature*, 15(2):500–502.

————. (1981). "Comment on 'It Pays to Do Good. . . .'" *Journal of Economic Behavior and Organization*, 2:387.

Hirschman, A. O. (1977). *The Passions and the Interests*. Princeton: Princeton University Press.

Hume, D. (1939). *A Treatise of Human Nature*. London: Oxford University Press.

Kahneman, D., Tersky, A., and Slovic, P. (1982). *Judgment Under Uncertainty: Heuristics and Biases*. Cambridge: Cambridge University Press.

Klingemann, U. (1985, June 18–21). "The Study of Rescuers of Jews in Berlin." Paper presented at the annual meeting of the International Society of Political Psychology, Washington, DC.

Kohlberg, L. (1976). "Moral Stages and Moralization: The Cognitive-Developmental Approach." In T. Lickona (Ed.), *Moral Development and Behavior*. New York: Holt, Rinehart and Winston.

Kohut, H. (1985). *Self-Psychology and the Humanities*. New York: Norton.

Kolm, S. C. (1983). "Altruism and Efficiency." *Ethics*, 94(1):189–265.

Land-Weber, E. *Rescuers*. Unpublished manuscript.

Landes, W. (1978). "Salvors, Finders, Good Samaritans, and Other Rescuers: An Economic Study of Law and Altruism." *Journal of Legal Studies*, 7:83–97.

Landes, W., and Posner, R. A. (1978). "Altruism in Law and Economics." *American Economic Review*, 68(2):417–421.

Mansbridge, J. (Ed.) (1990). *Beyond Self-Interest*. Chicago: University of Chicago Press.

Margolis, H. (1982). *Selfishness, Altruism and Rationality*. Cambridge: Cambridge University Press.

Maslow, A. H. (1962). *Toward a Psychology of Being*. Princeton: van Nostrand.

Monroe, K. (In press 1991). "John Donne's People: Explaining Altruism Through Cognitive Frameworks." *Journal of Politics*, 53(2):(May 1991).

Myers, M. (1983). *The Soul of Modern Economic Man*. Chicago: University of Chicago Press.

Oliner, S., and Oliner, P. (1988). *The Altruistic Personality*. New York: Free Press.

Rawls, J. (1971). *A Theory of Justice*. Cambridge, MA: Harvard University Press.

Riker, W. H. (1962). *The Theory of Political Coalitions*. New Haven: Yale University Press.

Rushton, J. P. (1980). *Altruism, Socialization and Society*. Englewood Cliffs, NJ: Prentice-Hall.

Rushton, J. P., and Wiener, J. (1975). "Altruism and Cognitive Development in Children." *British Journal of Social and Clinical Psychology*, 14(1):341–349.

Schumpeter, J. (1958). *Capitalism, Socialism and Democracy*. New York: Harper & Row.

Schwartz, B. (1986). *The Battle for Human Nature: Science, Morality and Modern Life*. New York: Norton.

Simon, H. (1984). "Human Nature and the Study of Politics." *American Political Science Review*, 79(2):293–304.

Smith, A. (1953). *The Theory of Moral Sentiments*. London: Bohn.

Tönnies, F. (1957). *Community and Association (Gemeinschaft und Gesellschaft)* (C. P. Loomis, Trans.). East Lansing: Michigan State University Press.

Trivers, R. (1971). "The Evolution of Reciprocal Altruism." *Quarterly Review of Biology*, 46:35–57.

Turner, J. (1987). *Rediscovering the Social Group: A Self-Categorization Theory*. New York: Blackwell.

Valavanis, S. (1958). "The Resolution of Conflict When Utilities Interact." *Journal of Conflict Resolution*, 2:156–169.

Wintrobe, R. (1981). "It Pays to Do Good. But Not More Good Than It Pays." *Journal of Economic Behavior and Organization*, 2(3):201–213.

Chapter

14

Incomplete Coercion: How Social Preferences Mix with Private Preferences

Howard Margolis

Rational choice models traditionally assume actors pursue individual self-interest and nothing else. In recent years, though, it has become increasingly common to see variants of the traditional model amended to allow for motivation beyond material self-interest. But even these broader models easily lead to paradoxes in various perfectly ordinary situations, such as those involved in choosing whether, and how, to vote. The dual-utilities model proposed in *Selfishness, Altruism and Rationality* (Margolis, 1982) was devised in response to such paradoxes, and the present essay considers some implications of that model for the very important contexts in which social behavior is neither purely voluntary nor fully coerced. The quickest summary of the basic model is provided by the slogan "Neither Selfish Nor Exploited": "NSNX," with NS pronounced to rhyme with "Ms." and NX pronounced just as it is spelled: so, "Niz-Nex."[1]

After reviewing the basic model, I describe a special, but socially pervasive and crucial, set of contexts in which it may be more than usually clear that NSNX yields implications qualitatively different from any plausible variant of the standard model, even allowing for one or another of the usual hedges, such as psychic income, consumption value of doing good, and so on. I label the context "incomplete coercion," referring to situations in which there is a coercive threat, but in which successful social action is possible only if compliance far exceeds what can be accounted for by rational deterrence. The principal technical content consists in showing how NSNX yields an unexpected consequence in the context of incomplete coercion. I conclude by sketching some ideas about how the rival inferences from NSNX versus the standard economic model might be tested.

SKETCH OF THE NSNX MODEL

Nobody is puzzled when a colleague says of a piece of legislation: "I would be personally better off without it, but in terms of the public interest, I hope it passes." It would be hard to make sense of such remarks, which all of us have heard and most of us have made, unless people have a sense of social preferences which is distinct from their sense of private preferences. No one has been able to make much sense of such commonplace acts (contributing to a charity or to public television, helping a stranger, or bothering to vote), other than in terms of social motivation or something functionally equivalent to that.

Readers who follow the rational choice literature will be aware of various formulations which work no better than, but at least as well as, directly postulating social preferences in accounting for phenomena such as voting. We often say we vote because we like to vote, feel good about voting, want to look like a good citizen, or perhaps feel a duty to be a good citizen. Most often, all these are just ways of saying that we are behaving (on this occasion) *as if* we are moved by social rather than narrowly self-interested preferences. So if we don't vote, the standard model explains that choice as a natural response to the microscopic significance of one vote; and if we do vote, then any of the possibilities mentioned above seem to serve about equally well to patch things up.

We might have a theory with more analytical bite, however, if we could specify something about *when* a person acts as if moved by social preferences, and *how* such motivation might interact with private preferences.

What we want is a rule, or set of rules, that will determine when a marginal bit of resources will be allocated to satisfy social, rather than private, preferences. The choice could concern time, or material resources, or the favor of other actors, but for simplicity I will just speak of the "marginal dollar." We want some procedure which will govern the *balance*, or *equilibrium*, between spending on social as against private preferences. Translated into a person's subjective sense of things, what we want is a specification that could capture our sense of doing our *fair share*, so that we feel *neither selfish nor exploited* in the way spending is allocated between private and social interests. This is the NSNX model.

It turns out that a simple pair of rules seems to provide all we need (Margolis 1982:39). Rule 1 concerns what I will call the *value ratio*: meaning the ratio between the value of spending a marginal dollar on its best social use, as against the best private use. For this notion to be well defined, private and social values must be on a common scale, and the common scale that is relevant here is the individual's own sense of social values.[2] From the social perspective (even though it is the individual's own social perspective, not something external to the individual), the social value that could come from spending the dollar will almost always be greater than the private value. So by itself Rule 1 would almost always favor allocating the dollar socially. But Rule 2 concerns the special *weight* given to (or the multiplier favoring) the individual's private spending. That weight is almost always greater than (and never less than) 1, so that Rule 2 by itself almost always favors private spending. Equilibrium occurs when the two rules are just in balance, in the way I will now describe.

Here are the two rules.[3]

Rule 1. Other things equal, the more social utility I can get with a marginal dollar relative to the private utility I can get, the *more* likely I will be to allocate the dollar to my social preferences.

Rule 2. Other things equal (in particular, even if the marginal value ratio of Rule 1 is unchanged), the larger my social spending relative to my private spending, the *less* likely I am to allocate yet another dollar to social spending.[4]

So as already suggested, we have a pair of rules, of which the first can be seen as favoring social spending, and the second restraining it.

Let G' be the value of a marginal dollar if spent on social (group-interested) preferences. Let S' be the corresponding value if the dollar is spent on private (self-interested) preferences. G'/S' is then the value ratio needed for Rule 1. It is the ratio between the value of group-interested, social use of the dollar as against self-interested, private use of the dollar. The bigger that ratio (other things equal) the more likely it is that the dollar will be spent on group-interest. The smaller the value ratio, the more likely it is that the dollar will be spent on self-interest.

Let W be the weight needed to handle Rule 2. Specifically, W must govern how far the person favors self-interest over group-interest. To be consistent with Rule 2, W must always be at least 1, and always increase when a dollar is allocated socially and decrease when a dollar is allocated privately. So the effect of W, aside from the exceptional context in which $W = 1$, is always to provide a multiplier to the private value.[5]

The resulting equilibrium process can be envisioned in terms of a seesaw, with W on one side balancing against G'/S' on the other.[6] Spending a dollar in a particular way can affect G'/S' by changing numerator or denominator or (when there is a significant interaction effect) perhaps both. For self-interested spending, we ordinarily expect (but the model does not require) diminishing marginal utility. But for group-interested spending, essentially constant marginal social value is common (though again, not required by the model.) If we consider the effect of an ordinary citizen's contribution to some public good—say a voluntary donation to the Red Cross, or the non-voluntary payment of an assessment—then to a very good approximation, G' will be constant across the range affected by a single chooser. But cases also arise where marginal utility is clearly decreasing or even increasing for social use of resources, the latter producing (among other things) the "I am spending more time on this than I intended" syndrome.

Now in addition to possible effects on the marginal values (G' and S'), spending a dollar *must* also affect W, since if the dollar is spent privately it will decrease W, and if spent socially it will increase W. If a person is out of equilibrium with $WS' > G'$, resources will be shifted toward private spending, decreasing W and ordinarily increasing G'/S', hence moving the individual toward a balance with $W = G'/S'$; and the converse will hold when the person is out of equilibrium favoring social spending.

Summing up: From Rules 1 and 2, a person will allocate a marginal dollar to group-interested G-spending if $WS' < G'$, allocate it to self-interested S-spending if $WS' > G'$, and will be in equilibrium, and so not moved to shift the balance of spending one way or the other, when $WS' = G'$. Or we can write the same equilibrium condition as $W = G'/S'$, which has the virtue of emphasizing the balancing of the conflicting pressures from the value ratio in Rule 1 versus the weight favoring self-interest in Rule 2: in terms of the NSNX intuition, balancing the sense a person has of not wanting to be selfish against the sense that a person also has of not wanting to be exploited.

Figure 1 shows the equilibrium process. Along the vertical axis we have scales for both the weight (W) and the value ratio (G'/S'), as on the analogous diagram for market equilibrium we would have both supply and demand measured on the vertical axis. But here the values are those of some particular individual (call her Smith). On the horizontal axis, we have the fraction of Smith's resources that have been allocated to group-interested spending (G-spending). At the origin Smith is spending 100 percent of her resources on self-interest, and nothing at all socially. On the right of the figure, she is spending 100 percent of her resources socially, with nothing left for her private interest.

Consider the particularly salient case in which in fact diminishing marginal utility holds. For that common case, G'/S' must decline as we move to the right in the diagram. For Smith is spending less on herself, so S' (marginal utility of private spending) would be increasing. G' correspondingly will be decreasing or perceptibly constant (since if Smith is one person in a large society, G' would not ordinarily be noticeably affected by the spending of any single person.) Whether the decline in G' is perceptible or not, the value ratio (G'/S') must be getting

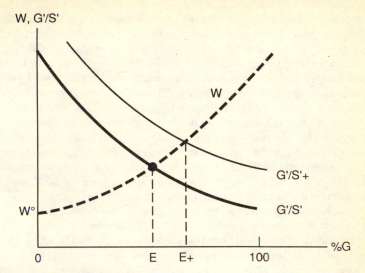

Figure 1. NSNX equibilrium

smaller. Hence the curve for G'/S' must slope downward from left to right, as shown.

The rising curve measures W. We can set $W = 1$ when the share of Smith's resources allocated to G-spending is zero (so in this extreme condition, no special weight is given to Smith's private interest.) But from Rule 2, W must slope upward, as shown, as the fraction of G-spending increases. Equilibrium occurs at the point labeled E, where $W = G'/S'$.

Suppose Smith found herself at some point to the right of E, where $W > G'/S'$. Then by shifting resources to favor her private interests, she could restore herself to equilibrium. For that would move her left in the figure, decreasing W and increasing G'/S'.

Or suppose Smith's wealth increases. Then for any fraction of wealth allocated to G-spending, the amount left for S-spending will be larger, hence S' smaller. For Smith as one citizen in a large society, G' would ordinarily be sensibly constant. So the increase in Smith's wealth implies an increase in G'/S' at each possible allocation, which would shift the G'/S' curve upward (to $G'/S'+$, in Figure 1). Her equilibrium allocation would therefore shift to the right, to $E+$. So an almost immediate implication of NSNX is that, other things equal, as wealth increases, the share of resources spent on what an individual takes to be social spending would tend to increase. In the language of economics, social spending turns out to be a superior good, though in another sense Smith is also becoming more selfish: W is increasing. All this is spelled out in more detail, with concrete illustrations, in Margolis 1982.

Although I cannot here provide the detailed articulation of the model, one point that is especially important is that for actual spending (in contrast to the abstract group-interested G-spending and self-interested S-spending considered so far) there will rarely be pure G- or S-spending. Almost any way that Smith might use a dollar would yield some S-utility and also some G-utility. Of course, in many contexts one or the other is insignificant. But for a large class of cases both elements are essential. If you contribute to public television, you are doing what you presumably think is something socially useful; but the organization may also send you some private gift, such as a coffee mug, or a T-shirt. A man may volunteer time and money to what he takes to be a good social or political cause; but doing so might also be good for business, or get him invited to a party he'd enjoy attending.

The NSNX logic emphasizes the essentially mixed character of the motivation that governs most real choices (Margolis 1982:25, 51–55; 77–81). Social motivation is not treated as an escape hatch, to be used when the usual self-interest assumptions get into trouble; not does allowing for social motivation involve shifting moral gears or any more schizophrenic mental feats. Smith is not strictly selfish most of the time, then abruptly a social paragon on certain other occasions. She is moved all the time by social as well as private motivation, and her spending is allocated in a way that (following the logic of the rationality assumptions that underlie the model) seeks to exploit complementarities in her spending opportunities, to reach the most favorable return to social interests consistent with a given loss to self-interest. Of the set of such allocations, she will choose that which puts her at (or as close as feasible to) NSNX equilibrium.

In sum, then, the model deals with the establishment of an equilibrium between social and self-interested spending by an individual, as well as with choices within each category. And while a dollar of Smith's spending could be almost pure S-spending (self-interested, private) or almost pure G-spending (group-interested, social), very often the dollar is some nontrivial mixture in between.

INCOMPLETE COERCION

The issue of incomplete coercion arises whenever social behavior is pushed along by coercion (or coercive threats) but only incompletely so. This, in fact, is the usual situation.

No society could function if its citizens obeyed its laws and social norms only to the extent that coercion in some form enforced compliance. In particular, the point continues to hold even if we understand "coercion" broadly, so that it includes social pressure as well as police power. Putting the point in a more dramatic way, no society could function well if its citizens would routinely cheat whenever no one is looking. And similarly, at the other extreme, there is no large society in which social motivation is so powerful and uniform that the society could rely entirely on voluntary compliance, or do without coercion. To understand actual societies, we need to understand behavior that falls between these two polar cases of pure coercion (in which social behavior is forthcoming just to the extent that a sufficient deterrent threat is present) and pure voluntary contribution (in which free-riding is a freely available option, but individuals choose to contribute their full share anyway.)[7]

Now for many contexts it is not easy to show how the NSNX model yields testable inferences which diverge from *any* plausible variant of the standard rational choice model. For in one way or another (such as the ways mentioned early in this chapter), it is usually possible to fix up the standard model to allow for social motivation, or something functionally equivalent. A little inventiveness will usually suffice to specify a variant of the standard model which behaves tolerably in the context at issue. The weakness of the standard model shows up when additional inferences are teased out of the variant model (beyond the particular context it was designed to fit), or when variants of the model are compared across contexts. Then it can be seen how coherence has been blurred by slipping from one version of rational choice to another as contexts shift. An approach which needs to be so flexible in shifting ground ex post might be at least embarrassed.

However, in the context of incomplete coercion, a situation can be identified where the standard and NSNX models lead to results so directly in conflict that perhaps a particularly striking confrontation might be arranged. The NSNX inference we are going to reach is likely to strike a reader as counterintuitive or even obviously wrong. So if the reasoning I will go through is correct, and the effect then turns up, that is the most satisfying sort of theoretical result: a surprising prediction which turns out to be valid. If it doesn't show up, that would be an embarrassment for supporters of NSNX, but (so far as I can detect) not much of an addition to the world's misery, since their number is certainly not large and may not be plural.

BACKGROUND OF THE FORMAL ARGUMENT

Compliance with law and social norms does not take the form of a neat dichotomy between compliance and noncompliance. Instead, we have a spectrum that runs from strict compliance with the spirit as well as the letter of the law through compliance lightened by legal but perhaps unfair avoidance (loopholes) and aggressive but not unambiguously illicit evasions to unambiguous evasions, but on a scale short of what would plausibly be punished by criminal penalties and then outright and substantial criminal behavior. Along this sequence there are no clear lines between the categories. This spectrum of compliance also would not exactly coincide with the sociological notion of distance from prevailing norms. Some things which are clearly illegal are acceptable in terms of perceived norms (failing to report your poker winnings on your tax return) and vice versa (neglecting to leave a restaurant tip).[8]

On the NSNX argument, how individuals choose with respect to this continuum will be influenced by how they stand with respect to NSNX equilibrium. The line of analysis to follow considers how that equilibrium (defined above) would change with changes in the enforcement environment. The next few paragraphs introduce the analytical setup.

For the argument at hand, it is convenient to rewrite the equilibrium condition in the form $G'/W = S'$. Hence in each of Figures 2–6, NSNX equilibrium occurs at the intersection of the S' and G'/W curves (instead of at the intersection of W and G'/S' curves, as in Figure 1).[9] I focus the discussion on a concrete context (compliance with tax laws), though as already stressed, the social importance of incomplete coercion is far broader, and in fact pervasive.

Now the more our sample chooser (Smith) evades, the higher the risk of getting caught, and the more significant the penalties will be if she is caught. Put another way, we expect the marginal risk of evasion to increase as evasion increases. Consequently, what Smith would give up to avoid that marginal risk also will be increasing. And since the value of a marginal dollar evaded is not $1, but only $1 *minus* the utility loss incurred by the risk from evading that dollar, the *net* marginal value of an evaded dollar (that is, after discounting for the marginal risk of evasion) must decrease as evasion increases.

In Figures 2–6, the horizontal axis shows the amount Smith evades. Moving from left to right, we go from 0 evasion at the origin, to 100% evasion at T, where the amount Smith evades is equal to the total tax she owed.

The vertical axis measures both S' (marginal private value of a dollar to Smith) and also G'/W (marginal social value of a dollar to Smith deflated to allow for the special weight given to self-interest.) The value to Smith of a dollar of tax evaded *before* deflating for the risk of evasion is just $1 across the entire range of possibilities. The upper horizontal line, intersecting the vertical axis at value = $1, shows that constant marginal value to Smith.[10] The curve labeled S' in Figures 2–6 then shows the net value to self-interest of evaded dollars.

At the origin, where Smith has not yet evaded at all, there is no risk: the evaded dollar is worth a full dollar. But risk grows as evasion grows, so that the net value must always decline as we move right in the figure (i.e., as evasion increases). Eventually this net value becomes negative. The risk of further evasion (which exposes not only that marginal dollar of evasion to penalty but also increases the risk that other evasions will be exposed and punished) eventually becomes larger than the dollar gained by evasion. Then the deterrent threat is sufficiently potent to make the expected gain of further evasion negative. This occurs at C in the figures, where coercion is at last completely effective.

A strictly self-interested chooser would evade so long as S′ > 0, paying a tax of T − C, but evading up to C.

But suppose that Smith is not strictly self-interested: in particular, suppose that even aside from the risk of evasion, an evaded dollar is not worth as much to Smith as an honest dollar. Empirically, we know that something like this is common. The tax system depends heavily (but far from exclusively) on what the Internal Revenue Service calls "voluntary compliance" (Roth et al., 1988).

Within the standard model Smith's attitude might be rationalized in various ways parallel to those illustrated earlier for rationalizing taking the trouble to vote, so that although we are now allowing for social motivation, it is still within the orthodox framework. For this orthodox social motivation, the marginal value curve would lie below the curve reflecting only Smith's self-interest. Either of the dashed curves labeled S′* and S′** in Figure 2 illustrates that possibility.

Since either of the dashed curves intersects the horizontal axis at C*, whichever held, social Smith pays more taxes (T − C*) and evades less (C*) than strictly self-interested Smith. But in terms of the standard model, we can reinterpret the situation as a peculiar sort of complete

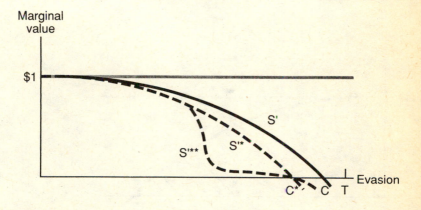

Figure 2. Compliance for self-interested and for (orthodox) social motivation

coercion by redefining coercion to consist of two elements: an external element (threat of punishment) plus an internal element (conscience, or whatever). Smith evades up to the point at which this total coercion eliminates any incentive to further evasion. Strict self-interest is the case in which internal coercion is zero.

Figure 3 next shows the analogous situation for NSNX. If taxpaying were completely voluntary (if there were no coercion at all) then every dollar paid would be a voluntary contribution, and by Rule 2 would increase W. But since there is completely effective coercion beyond C, Smith on net is sacrificing self-interest only on taxes paid to the left of C. The extent of that sacrifice is not the whole sum evaded, but measures only as much as the shaded area under the S′ curve to the left of C. That area shows the net private cost of compliance.

So if we imagine Smith as she contemplates her taxes, the net value of every dollar she chooses to pay to the left of C is a form of socially motivated spending, increasing the shaded area, hence increasing W, hence (since G′ will be effectively constant in this context) decreasing the value of G′/W at each point relative to what it would have been if she had evaded that dollar. Consequently a curve measuring G′/W must slope down from right to left (that is, it slopes down as Smith evades less), as shown in Figure 3. NSNX equilibrium occurs at E, where G′/W = S′. So Smith pays not only the T − C tax which is consistent with strict self-interest, but also C − E where coercion is incomplete.

Figure 4 shows incomplete coercion for both the NSNX equilibrium and for orthodox social motivation overlaid on the same diagram. The solid S′ curve again shows the strictly self-interested incentives. For NSNX we would also have the G′/W curve, yielding an equilibrium at E, as just described in connection with Figure 3. For an orthodox model

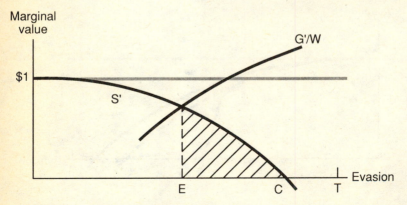

Figure 3. Compliance for NSNX motivation

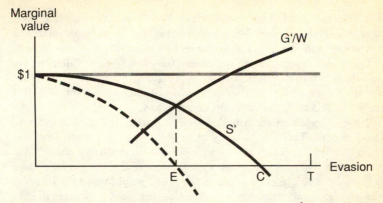

Figure 4. Overlay of compliance for orthodox versus NSNX motivation

(some version of the "internal + external coercion" discussed in connection with Figure 2), the same outcome could be shown by using the dashed curve lying below the S' curve in Figure 4. The S' curve shows the effect only of external coercion (physically effective surveillance and enforcement, perhaps bolstered by social pressure). The dashed curve shows that effect, plus internal constraints (conscience, or whatever). Thus, we have arranged things so that both orthodox social Smith and NSNX Smith exhibit the same choice. For both, self-interest alone would lead to evasion out to C where coercion is complete, but social motivation accounts for a degree of (externally) incompletely coerced compliance, down to E.

COMPARATIVE STATICS FOR NSNX VERSUS THE STANDARD MODEL

But these models yield conflicting implications for a shift in deterrence, which can be seen most clearly by considering the special case where the change in deterrence happens to increase only the risk of evading taxes Smith is paying already.

For the standard model, the situation is simple.

Suppose, for example, that a change in withholding regulations makes it harder to evade taxes on some type of income, but that Smith in fact is already reporting that income anyway. Using Figure 2 again, let the S'* curve show the total (social plus self-interested) incentive to Smith prior to an increase in risk of evasion, and S'** the more severe risk after the increase. So the S'* curve lies below the S' curve because it allows for social motivation as well as external coercion to influence

Smith's choice. The S'^{**} curve lies below the S'^* curve because it allows, further, for the increase in deterrence imposed by the stronger reporting requirement. But this latter shift comes in the special way mentioned, such that we are looking at an increase in the effectiveness of deterrence, which shifts Smith's marginal value curve from S'^* down to S'^{**}, but leaves the intersection with the horizontal axis unchanged: for S'^{**}, just as for S'^* in Figure 2, the intersection comes at C^*.

What is the effect on orthodox Smith? Nothing. She still evades to C^* and pays the balance. In terms of strict self-interest, with either the S'^* or S'^{**} curve, coercion is no longer complete. Smith is paying $C-C^*$ taxes that she would evade if strictly self-interested. Changed incentives that shifted the risk of evasion across the board would move the location of the equilibrium in the obvious direction (increasing evasion if risks decrease, and the converse). But the particular change in incentive shown in Figure 2 has no effect on Smith's choice.

But for NSNX a contrary conclusion holds.

To see this, first consider the shifted S' curve shown as the dashed curve sloping down from left to right in Figure 5. Compared to the situation of Figure 4, the risks of evasion have declined; perhaps, for example, because the personnel available for auditing taxes has been cut. Since the risk of evasion *decreases*, the net value of each dollar evaded *increases*, and the (shifted) S' curve now crosses the horizontal axis at C^* in Figure 5.

For the strict self-interest case, Smith would increase evasion to C^*. An analogous result would hold for the orthodox version of social motivation.

For the NSNX case, the situation is more complicated. When the costs of evasion become less, the G'/W curve will also be shifted. An evaded dollar that was worth a dime to S-Smith is now worth (say) 25 cents. The G-cost of compliance with respect to that dollar is correspondingly larger; and the same holds for each other dollar for which the private net value (if evaded) is positive. So W increases, hence G'/W decreases at each such point. So a shift upward of the S' curve (less coercion) produces an accompanying shift downward of the G'/W curve. The shading in Figure 5 shows the G-cost of complying to the original equilibrium level (E), and the white space between the S' curve and the dashed shifted S' curve above the shading represents an additional G-cost when evasion becomes less risky. The resulting shift downwards in the G'/W curve is shown by the dashed curve marked G'/S'^*.

Hence, NSNX implies two effects of a decline in the cost of evasion. Even if the G'/W curve were unaffected, the equilibrium level of compliance would fall (the equilibrium level of evasion would shift to the right), where the original G'/W intersects the dashed (shifted) S' curve.

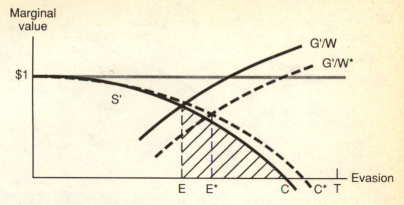

Figure 5. Shift in NSNX compliance when risk of evasion falls

As drawn, this shift would be slight, and it is not specifically marked on the figure. But as would be expected, a relaxation of the risks of evasion leads (as in the standard model) to an increase in evasion. However, for NSNX, the shift up of the S′ curve itself produces a shift down in the G′/W curve, shifting the level of evasion further, to E*. And a converse argument must hold for a case where risks are increased for units before C, directly shifting the S′ curve down, hence indirectly shifting the G′/W curve up.

With that in hand, we can now see how a situation could be defined which yields a particularly sharp test of the NSNX model. For as we have already noticed in the discussion of Figure 2, on the standard model (even when allowing for social motivation) increasing the cost of evasion only for taxes that are already being paid could never increase compliance. But for NSNX that would not be so. W at any point to the left of C is contingent on the area under the S′ curve between C and that point. Hence if the risk of evasion for inframarginal units is more severe (which means that the area under the revised S′ curve will become smaller), then even if the intercept of S′ (C in the figures) is unchanged, at each point W will become smaller (just the converse of the reasoning to explain an increase of W in connection with Figure 5). Hence the G′/W curve will now lie above the original curve. Hence the equilibrium level of evasion will shift to the left (i.e., increasing compliance).

Figure 6 illustrates this special case where increased deterrence happens to be effective just in the range from E to C; that is, it is effective with respect to just those dollars of compliance that Smith pays even though in strict self-interest she would do better to evade. The dashed line shows the altered S′ curve over that range. Evasion is riskier, hence

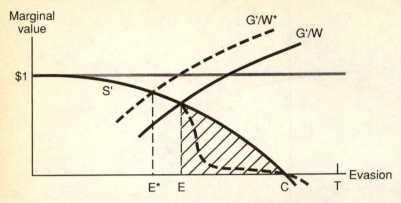

Figure 6. Shift in NSNX compliance under the "Giffen" condition

the dashed curve falls below the original S′ curve, but only for dollars that Smith has been socially motivated to pay already. On the standard model, even a standard model fixed up to allow for a measure of social motivation (say in the way sketched a few paragraphs back), this would have no effect on Smith's behavior. But if NSNX is correct we should get a shift (from E to E*) favoring compliance, since there is an indirect effect from the resulting shift in W, hence in the G′/W curve. And this occurs even though, as can be seen in the figure, we have arranged things such that the direct incentive to comply is not changed at all (the portion of the S′ curve between E* and E is exactly what it was originally).

ANALOGUE OF A GIFFEN GOOD

Conceptually, indeed, there must be cases in which a shift in the deterrence regime that would tempt a self-interested actor to *increase* evasion would lead actual taxpayers (if the NSNX model is correct) to respond in the opposite way. This would occur in the odd case in which a change in the enforcement regime were such as to increase risks of evasion in the interval from a bit to the right of E to C, but decrease the risk in the immediate vicinity of E. The curve would be that of Figure 6 but with a segment lying just above the original S′ curve, instead of just below it, in the immediate vicinity of E.

For orthodox social motivation this should yield an increase in evasion: orthodox Smith is just indifferent between evading and complying at E, so any decrease in risk at that point would tip her to a bit of further evasion. But for NSNX Smith, the indirect effect (from the

overall decrease in the area under the S' curve from E to C) would dominate the direct effect from a slight decrease in risk very near E.

Empirically, this odd possibility may be no more important than
the case of a Giffen good in a standard analysis, to which it is weakly
analogous.[11] But as with the Giffen good, going through the argument
carefully enough to satisfy yourself that this odd circumstance is at least
conceptually possible is a good way to sharpen your sense of how the
analysis works.

LOOKING FOR AN EMPIRICAL TEST

My general point is that if NSNX holds, we must expect significant
interactions between coerced and socially-motivated compliance. This
has consequences which are very broad.[12] The possibility of a change in
deterrence of the special sort illustrated by Figure 6 does not of itself
have any deep social significance. But such situations should occasionally be available for analysis, providing a particularly sharp test of the
NSNX model. We can expect to occasionally encounter actual situations
which happen to approximate these conditions, providing a natural
experiment, if we are alert to the possibility. We can also expect that
opportunities for explicit experiments would also occasionally arise in
the course of the recently expanding work on social choice simulations.

Although I have stressed that the general argument is not at all limited to the particular case of tax evasion, that does provide one promising area for sharp testing. For in the transition to the major revisions of
the Internal Revenue Service code in recent years, we can expect that
classes of taxpayers probably in fact exist which meet the criteria for the
test. For example, where a strengthening of reporting requirements for
a particular sort of income would have an effect (for that subset of taxpayers who were already complying) that reasonably approximates that
shown in Figure 6; that is, such that the shift in deterrence affects neither taxable dollars beyond C, nor interior to E, so that the only effect is
(equivalent to) the special effect on the S' curve shown in the figure.

On the other hand, even though appropriate classes of taxpayers
could be identified in principal, there are strong confidentiality safe-
guards with respect to tax returns, and in general there would be problems in convincingly maintaining *ceteris paribus* conditions. Nevertheless a useful empirical test might be available here, especially since questions of tax compliance have been the focus of much research in recent
years.[13]

The second salient possibility is provided by the lively research
activity on "social dilemmas" (for example, Dawes, van de Kragt, and
Orbell, 1990). Here there may be ongoing work in which some feasible

variant of the usual protocols (one which would be irrelevant in terms of the standard model) would meet the conditions specified for the NSNX effect worked out here.

Overall, considering the pervasiveness of incomplete coercion as a characteristic feature of all functioning societies, there should be many situations that yield natural experiments approximating the special context I have been describing. Since the analysis suggests that in general we ought to expect important interactions between coercion and voluntary compliance, other opportunities should exist for sharp testing of NSNX inferences. But close empirical familiarity, not a general theoretical argument such as presented here, is needed to recognize good candidates for testing these ideas.

On the other hand, empirical familiarity absent the sort of theoretical argument sketched here is also unlikely to recognize the opportunity. For as has often been noted, it can be hard to see even what is plainly in sight unless you are prepared to see it.

NOTES

1. In earlier work I have referred to the model as a "fair share" or as a "dual-utilities" model. But the "NSNX" designation seems to succeed better in conveying the essential character of the argument.
2. Although the scale is common, the two sources of utility nevertheless remain distinct: there is no overall maximand. The model involves irreducibly *dual* utilities. The point, which is counterintuitive but essential to a clear understanding of how the model works, is spelled out in detail in Margolis 1990a.
3. In Margolis 1982 (Chapter 3), I sketch a Darwinian derivation of the rules.
4. Economists, especially, are tempted to read Rule 2 as merely an addendum to Rule 1 that postulates diminishing marginal utility for socially motivated spending. But as stressed in Margolis 1982 and elaborated in Margolis 1990a, that is a mistaken reading. The parenthetical clause is intended to preempt that misreading.
5. The special case where $W = 1$ occurs only when no resources at all have been used socially. For the balance of the argument I will suppose $W > 1$, which in fact would almost always hold empirically.
6. I use seesaw diagrams to illustrate the equilibrium process in more detail in Margolis 1990a.
7. The theme of incomplete coercion is developed further in two recent articles (Margolis 1990b, 1991).
8. Considering the nature of such a spectrum is the principal theme of Margolis 1990b.

9. So the setup here differs from that of Figure 1 only in the entirely trivial respect that it is convenient to arrange the diagrams to yield an equilibrium where $S' = G'/W$, rather than where $W = G'/S'$.

10. Besides taking the marginal utility of a dollar as constant, I will use several other simplifying assumptions harmless for the context at hand. In particular, completely coerced taxes are charged entirely to S-spending; and the net private value of any taxes paid beyond that are charged entirely to G-spending. In fact, this is generally a good approximation (under the theory) of typical real contexts. But important exceptions arise. See Margolis 1982:51–55 and 160–64 for discussion of these notions.

11. So-named after the economist who first noticed the possibility. A Giffen good is a staple (not luxury) good defined by the peculiar property that as the price increases over some range, demand also increases (instead of falling). As here, the effect depends on an odd set of circumstances, but one that should occur occasionally in natural settings, and which can be obtained by manipulation in experimental settings.

12. Levi (1988) develops this theme.

13. For a review of the issues and survey of the literature, see Roth et al. (1988). The argument of the present paper was first sketched out as a paper commissioned for this NSF study.

REFERENCES

Carroll, J. (1986). "A Cognitive-Process Analysis of Taxpayer Compliance." Sloan Working Paper. Cambridge, MA: Massachusetts Institute of Technology.

Dawes, R., van de Kragt, A. J., and Orbell, J. (1990). "Cooperation for the Benefit of Us—Not Me, or My Conscience." In Mansbridge, J., ed., *Beyond Self-Interest*, (Chicago: University of Chicago Press), 97–110.

Graetz, M., et al. (1986). "The Tax-Compliance Game." *Journal of Law, Economics, and Organization*.

Levi, M. (1988). *Of Rule and Revenue*. Berkeley: University of California Press.

Margolis, H. (1982). *Selfishness, Altruism and Rationality*. Cambridge: Cambridge University Press; paper reprint (1984), Chicago: University of Chicago Press.

———. (1987). *Patterns, Thinking and Cognition*. Chicago: University of Chicago Press.

———. (1990a). "Dual-utilities and Rational Choice." In Mansbridge, J., ed., *Beyond Self-Interest*. Chicago: University of Chicago Press, 239–253.

———. (1990b). "Equilibrium Norms." In Hardin, R., ed., *Symposium on Norms in Moral and Social Theory* (special issue of *Ethics*, July 1990, 821–837).

———. (1991), "Social Equilibrium." In Zeckhauser, R., *The Strategy of Choice* (Schelling festschrift), forthcoming 1991.

Posner, R. (1985). "An Economic Theory of the Criminal Law." Working paper. Chicago: University of Chicago Law School, Program in Law & Economics.

Roth, J. A., Scholz, J. T., and Witte, A. D. (eds.) (1988). *Taxpayer Compliance*. Washington: National Academy of Sciences.

Chapter
15

Rational Maximizing in Economic Theories of Politics

Gregory S. Kavka

Please sir, I want some more.—Charles Dickens, Oliver Twist

In recent decades, the discipline of economics has become imperialistic, expanding its methodological tentacles into such "noneconomic" areas of human endeavor as law, international relations, and family life. Nowhere has this invasion been more extensive, or successful, than in the field of politics. While I believe that the economic approach to politics is illuminating and has produced many useful insights, I fear that there is some misunderstanding about *how* the application of economic methodology produces these insights. In particular, I believe that it is important to clarify the precise role, in economic theories of politics, of the central economic idea that individual agents should be viewed as rational utility maximizers.

POLITICAL AGENTS AS UTILITY MAXIMIZERS

Modern economic theory postulates that individual agents are rational choosers, in the sense that their choices among outcomes reflect a complete transitive ordering of these outcomes and that their choices among probabilistic combinations of outcomes are consistent with the standard probability calculus. Indeed, twentieth-century theorists have demonstrated that if an individual's choices satisfy certain plausible axioms embodying these two ideas, then that individual's preferences may be represented by a utility scale that is unique up to a linear transformation.[1] In other words, if one acts rationally (in the sense defined by the axioms), a utility scale can be constructed such that one always acts as though one were maximizing one's expected utility (or degree of overall preference satisfaction) as represented by that scale. Economic theories of politics attempt to use the idea that individuals are rational utility maximizers, in this sense, to understand the behavior of voters, office seekers, elected officials, and bureaucrats. They aim thereby to describe, explain, and—ultimately—predict the behavior of political actors in an accurate, systematic, and coherent way.

Obviously, no proponent of this ambitious project expects it to be perfectly successful. The complexities of human social behavior are probably too great ever to be represented with full accuracy by such abstract models. Furthermore, both common sense and recent empirical observations by cognitive psychologists indicate that people often act irrationally, in the sense of violating the axioms of the theory of utility maximization.[2] Nonetheless, we might realistically hope that enough people act rationally enough of the time in their political behavior for economic theories of politics to yield descriptions, explanations, and predictions which are frequently useful approximations to the truth. This may especially be so when, as is often the case in politics, we are dealing with the aggregate results of the behavior of large numbers of people (e.g., in elections). For in such circumstances, unless there is a greater tendency toward irrationality among those of particular political persuasions, we could expect the effects of irrationality to, on average, cancel each other out, so that there is little net effect on the ultimate outcome. And we may, therefore, without much distortion, treat that outcome as the result of purely rational behavior on the part of the political participants (e.g., voters).

It should be also be noted that, *sometimes*, the idea that political actors are rational maximizers of their own utilities is right on the mark. My favorite illustration of this concerns a visit some years ago by my wife to her parents, who were retired and living in an apartment not far from the ocean. On this visit, my wife noticed some literature that her father had been passing out for a candidate in a local election. The literature noted that the candidate had been endorsed by the farm workers' union, favored curbs on real estate development, and took other liberal stands on political issues. My wife, aware that her father was (to say the least) considerably to the right of her on the American political scale, said: "Dad, I know why I would support this candidate, but why in the world do *you* support her?" His brief reply, sure to gladden the heart of any economic theorist of politics, was: "Rent control. It's the only issue."[3] (This true story, like the one to follow below,[4] has a happy ending: the candidate won, rent controls were imposed, and my in-laws are still living in their pleasantly located apartment.)

THE ROLE OF AUXILIARY ASSUMPTIONS

The question I wish to raise and explore concerns *how* the idea of political actors as rational utility maximizers functions in economic theories of politics. The first suggestion that comes to mind is that, as in familiar theories of consumer behavior, postulating utility-maximizing agents provides an axiomatic foundation from which useful conclusions may be directly deduced. If one actually looks at how economic theories of politics proceed, however, one finds that matters are somewhat more complicated. The economic notion of utility maximization is purely formal and, by itself, guarantees only certain formal properties of individuals' choice behavior—for instance, transitivity of choices, and representability of preferences by indifference curves. Hence much of the actual work in economic theories of politics is done by what I call "auxiliary assumptions,"[5] substantive assumptions about the specific motivations, preferences, and aims of agents in various political contexts. Some examples of such assumptions are listed by Peter Ordeshook:

> [E]lection candidates prefer winning to losing, . . . bureaucrats prefer increased budgets for their bureaus to smaller ones, . . . firms prefer higher to lower profits, and . . . the desire for reelection provides legislators with their principal motivation.[6]

Now there are two key points to notice here. Utility-maximizing assumptions are often superseded early in economic models of politics by auxiliary assumptions of this kind, which are assumed to serve as appropriate proxies for utility maximization itself. But economic theorists of politics sometimes overlook the fact that their auxiliary assumptions are not strictly implied by utility maximization, and they even go so far as to treat mutually inconsistent auxiliary assumptions as equivalent to utility maximization (and to each other).

Consider, for example, Anthony Downs in his pathbreaking *Economic Theory of Democracy*. At the end of Chapter 2, he slides—without comment—from the position that office seekers are utility maximizers in the sense of seeking personal rewards of income, prestige, and power, to the further claims that their main goal is winning elections, and that their actions are "all aimed at maximizing votes."[7] And it is the latter vote-maximizing postulate that Downs goes on to use in constructing his account of democratic elections. However, even if we allow that rational candidates seek solely to maximize personal rewards by being elected to public office, it does *not* follow that they will seek to maximize *votes*. For elections have extreme threshold effects in terms of producing personal utility for candidates, with winning office being much more important than margin of victory. This point was well made by John F. Kennedy during the 1960 presidential campaign when he was questioned for the umpteenth time by reporters about whether his wealthy father, Joseph P. Kennedy, was buying the election for him. In reply, the candidate joked that he had just received a message from the elder Kennedy saying, "Don't spend a dollar more than necessary. I'll be damned if I'm going to pay for a landslide." (This story's happy ending: lore has it that the Democrats bought or stole just enough votes in Texas and Illinois to keep Richard Nixon out of the White House for eight more years.)

Kennedy's point has serious implications as regards Downs's position. Personal utility-maximizing office seekers will aim more at maximizing the probability of winning elections (and the accompanying perquisites of office) than at maximizing their vote totals or pluralities. Given uncertainty, of course, these two maximizing aims will often produce the same electoral strategies.[8] But not always. Candidates trailing badly in the polls, for example, may improve their chances of winning an election by adopting highly risky strategies that reduce the expected percentage (or number) of votes they will win. They accept the likelihood of a worse shellacking at the polls in order to give themselves a better chance of pulling an upset. Walter Mondale's selection of Geraldine Ferraro as his vice-presidential running mate in 1984 might well have been an instance of this phenomenon.[9]

Of course, writers since Downs have explicitly recognized the difference between vote (or plurality) maximizing and personal utility maximizing, in the sense of seeking the greatest social and material rewards available through elective office. But even when recognized, the difference is often ignored or set aside, as when William A. Niskanen writes that "the choice between these two types of models may be deferred."[10] And, indeed, it is more fruitful to plow ahead, constructing models of political phenomena based on specific substantive auxiliary assumptions, than to worry too much about whether such assumptions are always compatible with one another, or with empirical data about frequent inconsistencies in individuals' actual choice behavior. If, however, our aim is to understand the role of utility maximizing in such economic theories of politics, we must pay attention to these differences. For they suggest that utility maximization has some other function in addition to its role as an axiom that enables us to construct models of consistent behavior by political actors.

UTILITY MAXIMIZING AS AN IDEA GENERATOR

If the notion of political agents as rational utility maximizers does not serve solely as an axiomatic ground of deductive inferences in economic theories of politics, what additional role does it play? My claim is that it also functions as an *idea generator*—something which stimulates by analogy, similarity, or association, useful hypotheses or assumptions in the minds of theorists. To explain the concept of an idea generator, I will digress a bit into a subject about which (unlike politics and economics) I know something: the philosophy of Thomas Hobbes.

Hobbes, as is well known, was a mechanist who believed that the world consists solely of matter in motion, and that, in particular, thoughts, desires, people, and social institutions are nothing but complex configurations of matter in motion. Various commentators have even argued that Hobbes's moral and political conclusions follow directly from his mechanistic conception of people and the world.[11] But this, I believe, is a mistake. As pointed out in the opening chapter of my *Hobbesian Moral and Political Theory*, Hobbes rests very few of his moral and political doctrines on mechanistic premises, and where he does do so, other, more compelling defenses of these doctrines are available to him.[12]

This is not to say, however, that Hobbes's mechanism had no influence on his moral and political philosophy. The influence was simply not in the form of deduction (or even induction) from mechanistic assumptions. Instead, thinking of people, and social institutions, on the model of complex machines, generated in Hobbes's fertile philosophical mind certain useful insights into moral and political phenomena. Viewing humans as systems of matter in motion leads naturally to two key ideas: their likelihood of impinging upon one another, and their constant need for resources to fuel their ongoing motions. These ideas, in turn, suggest two main motives that lead to Hobbes's famous war of all against all: the need for present and future resources, and the desire for security against others' potential aggressions. Similarly, viewing the state or commonwealth as a machine suggests two other ideas of which Hobbes made good use. The state is an artificial entity designed to serve the purposes of its creators rather than purposes of its own. And those purposes are best discerned by (hypothetically) dissolving that state into its constituent parts and imagining how and why the state might be created out of those parts.[13]

The main suggestion I wish to make in this essay is that, in addition to serving as a postulate of formally consistent behavior, utility maximization functions in economic theories of politics much as mechanism functions in Hobbes's moral and political philosophy: that is, as an idea generator. More specifically, the general idea of political agents as rational utility maximizers generates at least three sorts of auxiliary assumptions, from which hypotheses about political behavior in various contexts are deduced or inferred.

First, the idea of utility or personal preference satisfaction suggests (though it does not strictly imply) that the motives of political actors are more often personal than public, moral, or ideological—that is, that citizens tend to vote their pocketbooks rather than their civics books. This is an important substantive idea which distinguishes economic theories of political behavior both from moralistic theories which suppose that political actors primarily seek to promote public welfare, and from sociological theories which posit individual agents following group norms or promoting class interests.

Second, the notion that people are rational maximizers leads naturally to the supposition that, in various political contexts, they seek to maximize some quantifiable good—for instance, a candidate's plurality or probability of being elected. As we have seen, such suppositions are not deductive consequences of utility maximization, and different ones may, in some contexts, conflict with one another. Nonetheless, the idea of such maximization may still prove fruitful in understanding political phenomena. Indeed, given our practical inability to measure peoples' utility scales, assuming maximization of some other measureable variable (such as votes) in specific contexts often provides the only way of generating testable hypotheses in economic theories of politics. And even when the formal theory of utility maximization fails (because people's choices are not fully rational and consistent), auxiliary maximization assumptions may provide useful explanations of their behavior. For example, one might be able to explain the frequent physically self-sacrificing behavior of many athletes by supposing that they aim to maximize team victories, or the probability of their team winning a championship, even if their preferences among athletic and nonathletic outcomes do not form a coherent overall ordering.[14] Further, individuals may deliberately aim to maximize some readily measureable quantity, such as wealth, because this makes the process of monitoring progress and adjusting behavior for success easier.

Third, the utility-maximization idea is also useful in suggesting that political actors have various motives which they may have to trade off against one another, and that different agents may assign different priorities to different motives. Thus, for example, recent works have considered some of the implications of elected representatives' having to allocate their time between leisure and public duties, or between constituent service aimed at reelection security and legislative activity aimed at achieving peer approval.[15]

On the issue of priorities, the idea of utility maximization has the virtue of being broad enough to encompass all kinds of motives—including moral and public-spirited ones—and therefore is consistent with economic models of politics that allow different political actors to act differently. For instance, such models need not imply that candidates in two-party presidential elections will converge in their issue positions to capture the median voter. Some candidates may rather be right than president. In each election there is likely to be some significant issue on which most voters reject the analytically right position (for example, that, given realistic estimates of economic growth, spending cannot be maintained and deficits reduced without tax increases) in favor of some alterative (such as voodoo economics). The candidate who prefers to be right will adopt the minority position here. But the candidate who prefers election should then be able to win by disagreeing on this matter, while adopting an identical position to that of the opponent on other issues. In this way, the simple idea of different goal priorities among candidates, which is generated by (but not logically entailed by) the notion of agents as utility maximizers, helps us understand why those candidates who prefer to be right are more often right, while those who prefer to be president more frequently occupy the White House.

It may be observed, at this point, that there is some tension between this idea of motivational diversity and the first two types of ideas generated by utility maximization—dominance of personal motives and maximization of specific quantitative variables. For diversity allows for the potential importance of altruistic, moral, and ideological motives, and suggests tradeoffs among different motivations rather than maximization of a single motive. However, given that none of the specific auxiliary assumptions in question is logically entailed by the idea of rational utility maximization, this tension is no sign of inconsistency or incoherence. Utility maximization generates a variety of assumptions or hypotheses about motivations which can be modeled or tested in specific political contexts. In some contexts, certain of these will be most productive, while, in others, rather different assumptions may be more appropriate. For example, in understanding congressional campaign strategies, we may do best by assuming that candidates seek to maximize a single variable (for instance, probability of election). But in understanding time allocation among activities of congressional incumbents, we may achieve better explanations by positing tradeoffs between reelection security (achieved by constituent service) and approval by congressional peers (achieved by legislative diligence).[16]

It would be nice if at this point I could give a useful account of *how* general notions like mechanism or utility maximization generate useful middle-level theoretical hypotheses or auxiliary assumptions in political theory. But this task is beyond me, and, in any case, would take us far afield into difficult issues in the philosophy of science concerning the so-called "logic of discovery."[17] Much fearing to tread there, I will limit myself to two brief observations. First, in this essay's title, I refer to economic theories (in the plural) of politics because different (and sometimes incompatible) theories may derive from different auxiliary assumptions generated by the common notion of rational utility maximization. I do not want to assert that there is a single economic theory of politics unified by the idea of rational maximization. The relation of idea generation, which holds between that notion and specific auxiliary hypotheses, is probably too weak to ground such a grand unification. Second, discussions of scientific discovery often focus on the question of how data lead to general theories or hypotheses explaining them, while my notion of idea generation concerns abstract general principles leading to more concrete and testable middle-level hypotheses and assumptions. Idea generation, in my sense, concerns the logic of discovery looking downward rather than upward.

Setting these murky matters aside, suppose that utility maximization does serve, in the various ways listed above, as an idea generator for substantive auxiliary hypotheses that do much of the actual work in economic theories of politics. What does this imply about the status of such theories? I believe that it strengthens, rather than weakens, them, as potential descriptive-explanatory theories of political behavior. My observations appear to weaken economic theories of politics only if one adopts an overidealized view of theories as being like systems of geometry, with a few basic general assumptions logically implying a whole structure of interesting consequences. By emphasizing the important role of substantive auxiliary hypotheses in economic theories of politics, I am suggesting that supporters of such theories hold in check any ambitions they may have for achieving geometry-like unity and simplicity.

The reason this would be a wise course is twofold: rational utility maximization is neither an accurate descriptive theory of human behavior[18] nor a sufficient axiomatic ground of the main insights already achieved in economic theories of politics. Viewed, however, partly as an idea generator, utility maximization has proved to be quite useful in producing auxiliary assumptions that help us understand and explain various political phenomena. Nor, in this role, is it necessary for success that the rational utility-maximizing account of human behavior be true, or even approximately true. So long as it generates auxiliary assumptions that are themselves close enough to being true to yield useful predictions, hypotheses, and explanations, the utility-maximizing idea has a positive part to play in advancing our understanding of politics.

ECONOMIC THEORY AND POLITICAL THEORY

My argument that utility maximizing functions partly as an idea generator in economic theories of politics is based on the use, in such theories, of substantive auxiliary assumptions about the motivations of agents. But are not similar auxiliary assumptions employed in straight economic theories—for instance, the theories of consumption, production, and markets? Indeed, they are, as illustrated in Ordeshook's above-quoted list of auxiliary assumptions, which includes the assumption that firms prefer higher profits to lower ones. Further, as is well known, there is a potential tension between this assumption and the general economic idea of agents as personal utility maximizers. If managers who make business decisions aim to maximize their own incomes, prestige, and job security, they may not act to maximize profits for the firm.

These observations raise an interesting question about economic theory itself, and the role in it of the idea of utility maximization. Do auxiliary assumptions play an indispensable role here too, and does the idea of utility maximizing therefore have an idea-generating function as well as a formal axiomatic one? A positive answer to this crucial question is implied by looking at the theory of consumer behavior in markets, the area of economics in which we might most be inclined to say that the main results are direct deductions from the formal theory of utility maximization.

If we look at representative expositions of this theory, we find that even here certain auxiliary assumptions—such as infinite divisibility of goods and convexity of utility functions—are generally used to supplement the formal notion of utility maximization. One such assumption, "that more is better,"[19] may be called the Oliver Twist assumption, in honor of the Dickens character who made the famous statement quoted in this essay's epigraph. D. H. Winch, in proving the Pareto-optimality of the equilibrium state in a perfectly competitive market, explicitly relies on this version of that assumption:

> [A]n individual's utility depends entirely on the volumes of commodities he consumes and factor services he provides. He will always be assumed to choose to consume more, or at least not less, of a commodity and to provide less, or at least not more, of a factor service.[20]

Similarly, Daniel M. Hausman, in his list of the fundamental assumptions of equilibrium theory, includes:

> If option x is acquiring commodity bundle x' and option y is acquiring commodity bundle y' and y' contains at least as much of each commodity as x' and more of at least one commodity, then all agents prefer y to x.[21]

The claim embodied in the Oliver Twist assumption—that in market transactions, people prefer to get more and give less—is minimal and plausible. But even it is substantive; at least as long as "commodities" is used in its usual sense to refer to material goods, and labor is regarded as a paradigm factor service.[22] For there is no inconsistency with the formal axioms of utility maximization if one prefers 100 widgets to 1,000, or working 60 hours a week for one's salary to working 40 hours for equal remuneration. Indeed, in special situations, this minimalist auxiliary assumption may even be inaccurate. A workaholic may genuinely prefer to do more work for the same pay, and some professional athletes may be telling the truth when they say they love their work so much that they would play for free if they had to (that is, they would prefer working without pay to not working without pay).

In the full development of consumer theory, and in other areas of economic theory, the needed auxiliary assumptions are much stronger and more controversial than the claim that people prefer to consume more and surrender less. Consider again the central assumption of the theory of firms—that they act to maximize profits. Nonowning managers make many business decisions, and individual managers may be presumed to aim rationally at fulfilling their own personal goals. Therefore, treating firms as profit maximizers requires the additional assumption that managers can best fulfill their personal goals by maximizing firm profits, rather than firm size, their own visibility within the business community, or their own reputation among their peers and subordinates. Various procedural devices can be used to close the potential gap between firm profits and individual incentives—profit-sharing plans for managers, close supervision of managers by stockholders, and the threat of hostile takeovers of firms that are not maximally efficient. But the need for such devices is itself evidence that the key motivation assumption of the theory of firms is neither empty, trivial, nor fully accurate.

If it is true that both a standard economic theory and economic theories of politics rely on substantive auxiliary assumptions generated by (but not deduced from) the idea of utility maximization, can we generalize about which sort of theory employs stronger or more controversial auxiliary assumptions? It would be wrong, I think, to suppose that economics proper always uses weaker (hence less risky) assumptions about motivations than are used in economic theories of politics. For example, it seems a more accurate approximation that candidates aim to maximize their chances of being elected than that firms aim to maximize their profits. On the other hand, it is politics and not economics that encompasses the phenomenon most intractable to analysis in terms of rational utility maximization. This is the well-known tendency of many individuals (including the present writer) to take the time and trouble to vote in national elections in which their chance of affecting the outcome is, for all practical purposes, equal to zero. Here it seems that rationalist explanations in terms of the intrinsic pleasures of voting (or wildly inflated beliefs in the efficacy of one's vote) are less promising than nonrationalist explanations in terms of social norms, ideological commitment, and symbolic expression. I know of no problem in economics proper (though there may be some) that is so recalcitrant to analysis in terms of rational utility maximization.

Setting this particular problem about voting aside, I am inclined to draw the same conclusion about the role of utility maximization in economic theory as stated earlier about political theory. Utility maximization functions not only as a formal axiom but also as an idea generator that suggests to economic theorists certain substantive auxiliary assumptions about the motivations of economic actors (for example, that firms seek to maximize profits, that workers seek to maximize income and minimize labor expended, and that consumers prefer to pay less and get more). These auxiliary assumptions, in turn, are essential to the derivations of the substantive conclusions and predictions of economic theory (for instance, that in perfectly competitive markets, equilibria will be optima).

These observations are of some significance for the following reason. As noted earlier, cognitive psychologists have observed that people very frequently do not obey the formal axioms of utility maximization. To the extent that we believe that successful theories should rest on approximately accurate assumptions, this would make us worry about the status of economic theory. If, however, approximately accurate auxiliary assumptions often stand proxy for the frequently violated axioms of utility maximization, we may feel somewhat more sanguine about the prospects of economic theory. And we may better appreciate the importance of the theory of utility maximization, which not only provides the axiomatic grounding for formal economic models but also generates many of the substantive auxiliary assumptions needed to derive interesting conclusions from those models.

Not everyone would agree that the success of a theory depends on the accuracy of its assumptions. Most notably, Milton Friedman has argued that theoretical assumptions are fully justified if the resulting theory yields adequate predictions, regardless of the accuracy (or inaccuracy) of the assumptions themselves.[23] This seems to me an overly instrumentalist conception of theoretical adequacy. We want our theories to help us *understand* the world as well as help us cope with it. Even a perfect predictor whose workings we do not follow would not help us understand the phenomenon it predicts.[24] Nor would understanding emerge from a theory that turns inaccurate assumptions into accurate predictions, unless accompanied by a metatheory that explains how error gets transformed into truth within the theory. On the other hand, a theory that deduces approximate truths from approximately accurate assumptions does provide a measure of real understanding. For it enables us to see why and how the theory yields adequate predictions. Thus, recognizing that the notion of utility maximization serves to generate fairly accurate substantive assumptions about human motivations in economic theories of politics and economics should encourage us to hope that such theories will continue to provide us with useful insights about these domains of human endeavor.[25]

NOTES

1. Some classic sources are Frank P. Ramsey, "Truth and Probability," in *The Foundations of Mathematics and Other Essays*, ed. R. B. Braithwaite (London: Routledge, 1931); John von Neumann and Oskar Morgenstern, *Theory of Games and Economic Behavior* (Princeton: Princeton University Press, 1944); and Leonard J. Savage, *The Foundations of Statistics* (New York: Wiley, 1954). The Ramsey-Savage approach allows subjective probabilities, as well as utilities, to be derived from the agent's choice dispositions.

2. See, for example, Daniel Kahneman and Amos Tversky, "Prospect Theory: An Analysis of Decision Under Risk," *Econometrica* 47 (1979), pp. 263–291; and Ward Edwards, "The Theory of Decision Making," in *Decision Making*, ed. Edwards and Amos Tversky (Harmondsworth: Penguin, 1967).

3. Theorists worried about the irrationality of voting in elections whose outcomes we are highly unlikely to affect might not regard my father-in-law's acts as fitting their conception of rationality. However, this was a municipal election in a small city, and my father-in-law passing out literature door to door could have had a nonnegligible chance of influencing the election outcome.

4. Only a modicum of academic decorum restrained me from subtitling this essay "Two Anecdotes in Search of a Connecting Idea."

5. These assumptions are auxiliary to the formal theory of rational choice (or revealed preference). But some of them may function as axioms in certain specific formulations of economic and political theories, and then be contrasted with further "auxiliary assumptions." See, for example, the essays by Edward J. Green and by Daniel M. Hausman in *Philosophy in Economics*, ed. Joseph O. Pitt (Dordrecht: Reidel, 1981), in which the term "auxiliary" seems to be used in this way. The former use of "auxiliary" (that is, auxiliary to the formal theory of rational choice or utility maximization) will be employed throughout this essay.

6. *Game Theory and Political Theory* (Cambridge: Cambridge University Press, 1986), p. 15.

7. *An Economic Theory of Democracy* (New York: Harper & Row, 1957), pp. 34–35. Downs is talking about the aims of *parties* conceived as teams of office seekers. But he explicitly disavows that parties aim at vote maximizing as a means to promote their long-term

interests as ongoing entities (p. 174). Hence the specific points made in the text about individual office seekers apply equally to Downs's parties.

8. Indeed, Ordeshook points out (pp. 161–162) that if an election is perfectly symmetric, with symmetric uncertainties, the same outcomes result (that is, are equilibria) whether candidates aim at maximizing pluralities or probabilities of election.

9. We might call this a Hobbesian strategy, in view of Hobbes's remark that "there is no . . . such hope to mend an ill game, as by causing a new shuffle." (*Leviathan*, ed. C. B. MacPherson [Harmondsworth: Penguin, 1968], Ch. 11, p. 162).

10. "Economic and Fiscal Effects on the Popular Vote for President," in *Public Policy and Public Choice*, ed. Douglas W. Rae and Theodore J. Eismer (Beverly Hills: Sage, 1979), p. 97.

11. See, for example, M. M. Goldsmith, *Hobbes's Science of Politics* (New York: Columbia University Press, 1966); and J. W. N. Watkins, *Hobbes's System of Ideas*, 2nd ed. (London: Hutchinson, 1973).

12. Gregory S. Kavka, *Hobbesian Moral and Political Theory* (Princeton: Princeton University Press, 1986), pp. 10–18.

13. Hobbes also makes use of the idea of the state as an organism. See *Leviathan*, Ch. 29.

14. Of course, such behavior could be explained by other hypotheses— for instance, that athletes tend to be risk seekers or heavy time discounters.

15. See Tyler Cowen, Amihai Glazer, and Henry McMillan, "Rent-Seeking Promotes the Provision of Public Goods," typescript, University of California, Irvine, 1988; and Thomas E. Cavanagh, "Rational Allocation of Congressional Resources: Member Time and Staff Use in the House," in *Public Policy and Public Choice*, ed. Rae and Eismer.

16. Cavanagh, "Rational Allocation of Congressional Resources."

17. See Norwood Russell Hanson, *Patterns of Discovery* (Cambridge: Cambridge University Press, 1965).

18. See references in note 2.

19. Hal Varian, *Microeconomic Analysis* (New York: Norton, 1978), p. 81. Varian says that the formal version of this assumption is usually "much stronger than we need." However, the supposedly weaker assumption he offers in its place, on p. 82, seems to presuppose that more is better.

20. *Analytical Welfare Economics* (Harmondsworth: Penguin, 1971), p. 33.

21. "Are General Equilibrium Theories Explanatory?" in *Philosophy in Economics*, ed. Pitt, p. 18.

22. The terms "commodity" and "factor services" could be used purely formally to refer to whatever the agent wants more of, and wants to provide less of, respectively. However, as soon as this theory is applied to provide predictions or explanations involving commodities like pork bellies and factor services like labor, the purely formal interpretations of these terms will no longer suffice.
23. *Essays in Positive Economics* (Chicago: University of Chicago Press, 1953), Part I.
24. It might help indirectly. For example, if the predictions enable me to get rich playing the state lottery, I can hire the best thinkers and teachers to help me understand the world.
25. I am grateful to the American Council of Learned Societies and the Ford Foundation for fellowship support, and to Tyler Cowen, David Estlund, Alan Nelson, and Brian Skyrms for comments on an earlier draft of this essay.

REFERENCES

Cavanagh, T. E. (1979). "Rational Allocation of Congressional Resources: Member Time and Staff Use in the House." In D. W. Rae and T. J. Eismer (Eds.), *Public Policy and Public Choice*. Beverly Hills: Sage.

Cowen, T., Glazer, A., and McMillan, H. (1988). "Rent-Seeking Promotes the Provision of Public Goods." Typescript. Irvine, CA: University of California Press.

Downs, A. (1957). *An Economic Theory of Democracy*. New York: Harper & Row.

Edwards, W. (1967). "The Theory of Decision Making." In W. Edwards and A. Tversky (Eds.), *Decision Making*. Harmondsworth: Penguin.

Friedman, M. (1953). *Essays in Positive Economics*. Chicago: University of Chicago Press.

Goldsmith, M. M. (1966). *Hobbes's Science of Politics*. New York: Columbia University Press.

Green, E. J., and Hausman, D. M. (1981). In J. C. Pitt (Ed.), *Philosophy in Economics*, Dordrecht: Reidel.

Hanson, N. R. (1965). *Patterns of Discovery*. Cambridge: Cambridge University Press.

Hausman, D. M. (1981). "Are General Equilibrium Theories Explanantory?" In J. C. Pitt (Ed.), *Philosophy in Economics*. Dordrecht: Reidel.

Hobbes, T. (1968). *Leviathan*, C. B. MacPherson (Ed.). Harmondsworth: Penguin.

Kahneman, D., and Tversky, A. (1979). "Prospect Theory: An Analysis of Decision Under Risk." *Econometria*, 47:263–291.

Kavka, G. S. (1986). *Hobbesian Moral and Political Theory*. Princeton: Princeton University Press.

Niskanen, W. A. (1979). "Economic and Fiscal Effects on the Popular Vote for President." In D. W. Rae and T. J. Eismer (Eds.), *Public Policy and Public Choice*. Beverly Hills: Sage.

Ordeshook, P. C. (1986). *Game Theory and Political Theory*. Cambridge: Cambridge University Press.

Ramsey, F. P. (1931). "Truth and Probability." In R. B. Braithwaite (Ed.), *The Foundations of Mathematics and Other Essays*. London: Routledge.

Savage, L. J. (1954). *The Foundations of Statistics*. New York: John Wiley.

Varian, H. (1978). *Microeconomic Analysis*. New York: W. W. Norton.

von Neumann, J., and Morgenstern, O. (1944). *Theory of Games and Economic Behavior*. Princeton: Princeton University Press.

Watkins, J. W. N. (1973). *Hobbes's System of Ideas*, (2nd ed.). London: Hutchinson.

Winch, D. H. (1971). *Analytical Welfare Economics*. Harmondsworth: Penguin.

Rationality, Markets, and Political Analysis: A Social Psychological Critique of Neoclassical Political Economy

Shawn Rosenberg

Following the seminal work of Anthony Downs (1957), neoclassical economics has been applied to the study of politics with increasing frequency and influence. In this tradition, the political arena is regarded as a competitive marketplace. Voters are assumed to be self-interested consumers. Their political participation is then regarded as an attempt to "buy" preferred government action by supporting the candidate who espouses policies closest to their preferences. Candidates are assumed to act like profit-maximizing producers. Their political decision-making is thus viewed as an effort to make marginal changes in their product— that is, the policies they advocate—in order to increase their share of the popular vote.

These simple assumptions of maximizing consumer-voters and producer-candidates set the stage for the formal modeling of the classic liberal vision of government as the executor of popular demand. Economic theory is then invoked to elaborate and explore variations of the basic model in order to discover the effects of various mechanisms of preference aggregation and negotiation on collective or public choices. Analysis extends to evaluation when these collective choices are judged in terms of their efficiency. The standard here is the maximization of the utility of each of the individual citizens. The result is an approach with considerable theoretical power, one which has yielded interesting insight into such diverse phenomena as political campaign strategy, coalition formation, voting behavior, and the provision of collective goods. (For classic examples, see Downs, 1957; Buchanan and Tullock, 1962; Riker, 1962; Olson, 1965).

My aim in this essay is to offer a careful assessment of this approach from my perspective as a political psychologist. In so doing, I follow a long tradition in cognitive and social psychology which has challenged the view that individuals are rational. From early work such as that of Bartlett (1932) to more contemporary efforts such as that of Tversky and Kahneman (1974) and Kahneman, Slovic and Tversky (1982), psychologists have offered an abundance of argument and evidence regarding the flawed or bounded capacity of individuals to perceive, interpret, remember, calculate, and decide. Most economists, however, do not regard this research to be particularly relevant to their inquiry. (This view is articulated in the Wittman chapter in this volume.) Following this lead, political economists (I use the term narrowly here to refer to those who adopt a neoclassical view) have also ignored the psychological studies of cognition. Direct exhortations regarding the limited value of the economists' assumption of substantive rationality and the need to examine political cognition empirically (e.g., Abelson, 1975; Simon, 1985) have had little impact.

With this in mind, I begin my argument by examining the theoretical basis for the economists' decision not to consider seriously the limitations inherent in how people think. Discussion here focuses on the allied concepts of narrow rationality and market discipline. I then continue by suggesting that although most economic inquiry may be justified in ignoring the empirical research on cognition and rationality, political economic inquiry is not. Having thus presented the theoretical rationale for a consideration of the nature of people's cognitive processes, I then briefly review the relevant psychological research and discuss its implications for political analysis. Finally, I consider the expressly political ramifications of the conclusions drawn. The question of a possible ideological bias inherent in the economic approach is raised here.

ECONOMIC AND POLITICAL MARKETS

It is a matter of some confusion that economists use the term "rational" to describe their *Homo economicus*. In both common and philosophical parlance, the term evokes the notion of an active human being who makes choices by (1) searching for relevant information, (2) integrating this information in an appropriate manner, (3) drawing on logic and experience to assess the consequences of the various alternatives, and (4) adopting the course best suited to his or her needs. Yet it is apparent that in most cases economists demand little of this of their rational actor. Rather, they posit a decision maker who is only "narrowly" rational and claim that this restricted view of an individual's capacity provides a sufficient foundation for their analyses. The nature of this concept of narrow rationality and the justification for analysis based upon it are central to economic inquiry and deserve closer consideration.

Many economists preface their work by clearly stating that their conception of rationality is a narrow one. As apparent from its use, this narrow rationality is best considered not as a noun but as an adjective. It is invoked to describe action which is oriented by specific goals. The conceptual focus thus quickly shifts away from reasoning to preferences. To meet the criteria of narrow rationality, it is stipulated that these preferences must be coherent and ordered transitively (if a is preferred to b and b is preferred to c, then a is preferred to c). Defined in this way, this concept of rationality appears to eliminate the need for a consideration of the way in which individuals collect, interpret, and use information when making choices. Clearly these concerns are not addressed directly. Nonetheless, closer examination suggests that they remain central. If we "unpack" what it means to act in a goal-oriented way, it is apparent that the pursuit of one's goals requires an initial determination of the options available and their consequences. For preferences to guide action effectively, individuals must choose on the basis of a full consideration of the alternatives, this involving several steps beginning with the search for all relevant information and carrying through to the calculation of expected utilities. Despite this fact, economists pay little attention to the theoretical niceties of specifying the nature of this consideration of alternatives, nor, as mentioned earlier, do they consider the relevant evidence of the nonrational or irrational processing of information to be particularly significant.

To understand this apparently cavalier attitude, it is necessary to consider the economist's definition of the arena in which the rational actor participates. The arena here is the marketplace. As conceived by the economist, it is a demanding and unforgiving forum for action. The failure to act rationally is subject to immediate retaliation. When one actor fails to respond to the market situation in a way which maximizes his or her utility, other actors immediately capitalize on this failure and exploit it to their own advantage. In the process, the gains of the first actor are diminished. Thus, in the ongoing exchange of the market, a clear and immediate price is paid for the failure to act rationally—that is, in a manner consistent with one's preferences. In economic terms, the market disciplines those who participate in it.

Such a venue requires little of the players in order for them to behave rationally. Although any single decision considered in isolation may require prodigious judgment, the discipline of the marketplace provides an excellent regimen for training. The back and forth of ongoing exchange provides a clearly defined reward structure to guide behavior and ample opportunity to learn. Generally speaking, choices are made among well-specified goods, they lead to consequences with clear costs and benefits, and decisions are made frequently. Simple learning from experience is therefore facilitated. Consequently, over time and across actors, action will tend to become rational even if the individuals involved do not possess the full competence required to produce such action on their own. Thus the economic model may require rational action, but the rationality of action does not depend on the full rationality of individuals (as sophisticated processors of information). Instead, it depends only on their simple capacity to learn from rather clearly structured experience. In this sense, rationality is a product not of individuals but of the context of their interaction. Adopting this view, economics defines its subject matter such that the concerns of epistemology and cognitive psychology are largely irrelevant.

In this light, it is clear that the economic analysis of political life carries with it either the controversial claim of broad rationality or, more frequently, the more palatable assumption of narrow rationality. In the latter case, the approach depends less on assertions regarding the abilities of individuals and more on claims regarding the qualities of the marketplace in which those individuals interact. To assess the appropriateness of this approach to the study of politics, two questions must be addressed: (1) To what extent is the political marketplace similar to or different from the economic marketplace? (2) If there are differences, what is their significance?

In response to the first question, an examination of the arena of political exchange suggests that it is quite different from the marketplace postulated by the economist. This is true in several respects. Each one suggests a weakness in the feedback loop which links the conditions and consequences of action to the choices an individual makes. Together they suggest that unlike the economic marketplace, the political arena does not provide an effective training ground for decision making. To begin with, the consequences of political choice tend to be quite remote from the individual actor, both in time and space. When you buy a pair of shoes, you quickly discover through wearing and later window shopping whether your decision was an optimal one. The feedback is direct and immediate. In political life, when you support a policy and vote for a candidate, the consequences are generally quite removed from the choice made. For example, you may vote for a presidential candidate in the hope of improving your personal economic circumstances, but an improvement in the national economy may take many months or years, and its consequences for one's own pocketbook are generally quite indirect.

Apart from its remoteness, the learning environment of political decision making tends to be ambiguously defined. In the case of purchasing shoes, the specification of the product is clear: the shoes are made of leather, vinyl, or cloth; they are for casual or dress wear; they are double- or single-stitched; they are offered at a particular price, and so on. One has good information on what one is buying. In addition, one has personal experience of the consequences of one's consumer choice. You observe directly how comfortable the shoes are, how often you wear them, and how long they last. The rewards associated with the purchase are clear. Characteristically, political decisions involve alternatives which are more complex and ambiguous, and the outcomes are more difficult to discern. For example, in matters of national security or social welfare, it is difficult (1) to determine the real nature of the goods involved, (2) to calculate the expected utility of complex alternatives, and (3) to discern later what the real outcomes were which followed from a choice made.

Finally, the political marketplace does not afford the number of learning experiences provided in the ideal economic marketplace. In the case of household items like soap or canned tuna, one has frequent opportunity to choose among alternatives and experience the consequences of the choices made. In the case of politics, however, this frequency of choice is not available to candidates or voters. Most people participate in elections only every four or perhaps every two years. Consequently, they have comparatively little opportunity to act and thus to learn from their mistakes. (Of course, this particular problem exists to a lesser extent for political leaders and legislators, who generally have the opportunity to make decisions more often. Nonetheless, the preceding two problems remain.)

In sum, politics confronts the individual actor with choices in which the alternatives are often ambiguously defined and complex, the consequences of choice are remote and difficult to identify, and the opportunity for decision making is relatively rare. Arguably the existence of any one of these features, and certainly the combination of them, disrupts the feedback loop necessary for learning. As a result, the political marketplace differs importantly from the marketplace defined in economic theory in that it lacks the requisite structure to enforce market discipline.

THE ROLE OF PSYCHOLOGY IN THE STUDY OF AN UNDISCIPLINED POLITY

The argument has been made that the political marketplace lacks the feedback structure and consequently the discipline of the marketplace of economic theory. Let us now consider the implications of this argument. Most important, it suggests that the quality of individuals' actions is no longer ensured by the strictures imposed by the interactional setting in which the individuals are engaged. Instead, how they act will reflect more their own intrinsic capacities to gather, interpret, and integrate information relevant to the decisions they make. Given this greater dependence of action on cognitive capacity, the exchange between people and thus the character of the political marketplace itself will necessarily be a function of the qualities of the individuals involved. (Of course, the concern here is not with personal preferences and collective values—at least initially—but rather with the quality of individuals' reasoning and the structural parameters of exchange.) In this sense, the economic study of politics is, by virtue of its subject matter, more dependent on a broader conception of rationality than that normally employed in economic theory. The simple capacity to learn is not enough. As a result, the descriptive account of how individuals cognize the world and how they make choices becomes pertinent.

At issue here is whether the individual has the requisite cognitive capacity to overcome the obstacles of ambiguity, indirectness, remoteness, and infrequency which disrupt the flow of feedback following political action and is therefore able to sustain the normal functioning of market discipline in the political arena. The answer to this question clearly depends on the evidence provided by the descriptive research in cognitive and social psychology. A brief review, one that is more illustrative than comprehensive, is offered here.

The fully rational processing of information required by judgment under conditions of political action involves several steps, from the initial identification of alternatives, to the search for and attention to the information available, through the interpretation and integration of that information for the purpose of making a decision. As we shall see, the research suggests that people's information processing at each step tends to be significantly suboptimal. It is important to remember that any single decision depends on all the steps; thus the effects of the errors at each step are compounded in the final result.

Let us begin with the ways in which individuals initially search for relevant information when confronted with a problem or choice. One interesting line of research suggests that this search tends to be biased by the individual's preconceptions. People tend to look for information which confirms their initial assumption regarding the problem at hand.

They are less likely to search for evidence which informs by disconfirming. For example, given an initial belief (even a very weak one) that John is extroverted, one will respond to a request to discover what John is like by searching for evidence which is likely to confirm extroversion and by neglecting to make inquiries which might reveal evidence of introversion (e.g., Snyder and Swann, 1978). This bias in information processing suggests that prejudices are maintained not only by discounting the evidence available to us but also by the kind of information we initially collect for subsequent processing. The political implications are clear. Transposed to the domain of electoral politics, for example, this suggests that people's search for information regarding the various candidates will be biased by their initial impressions of them. All other things being equal, these voters will therefore begin their deliberations with a distorted view of the choices available to them.

Problems are also evident at the next step of information processing, those of attending to the information at hand. The research suggests that there are various forms of distorting biases operating here. For example, several studies have demonstrated that a person's view of a social event is directed by the relative salience of the various elements in the information field. A person attends more to that which is somehow different, more vivid, or more personally significant. This feature is then overemphasized, and insufficient account is taken of other factors. Significantly, this bias in attention influences people's analysis and explanation of events (e.g., Taylor and Fiskey, 1975, 1978; McArthur, 1981). Moving to the political domain, this suggests that individuals would be more likely to attend to actors or events which were somehow salient (e.g., the unusual case of a black politician in a normally white field of candidates, or the vivid case of terrorist acts in the midst of more abstract social or economic forces) and therefore would ascribe too much influence to them. This would in turn bias their understanding of the political situations and choices they face.

The research on individuals' perception of the information to which they do attend also indicates problems of another kind. A key factor here is the bias in perception and memory created by the impact of preexisting frames of reference or schemas. In a classic study, Bruner demonstrated how prior assumptions of the relative criminality of blacks and whites led Harvard undergraduates to misperceive a robbery such that they incorrectly remembered that it was a black rather than a white who had brandished a weapon (Bruner, 1958). Other research ranging from recent work on eyewitness testimony to personality assessment provides further evidence of these schema-related biases in perception and memory (e.g., Bartlett, 1932; Higgins, Rholes, and Jones, 1977; Cantor and Mischel, 1977; Loftus, 1979; Taylor and Crocker,

1981). Work of this kind helps illuminate such political phenomena as the lingering impact of traumatic political events, like Munich or Vietnam, on the later judgments of foreign policy decision makers. It also contributes to an understanding of how partisans can maintain their image of both their own and opposing parties.

After gathering and interpreting information, the next step in rationally judging a situation requires recognizing correlational relationships across time and space in order to make causal attributions and categorical placements. Again we find evidence of inadequate information processing. This has been attributed to a number of sources. One is the failure to incorporate certain kinds of relevant data when integrating the information available. For example, the research on causal attribution suggests that in the attempt to determine why an individual responded as he or she did to a particular situation, people have trouble incorporating abstract or statistical information on how most people tend to respond in that circumstance (e.g., Nisbett and Borgida, 1975). In an interesting and politically relevant study reported by Nisbett and Ross (1980), viewers were presented with a video news clip on welfare abuse by mothers which included both a filmed interview with a welfare mother and statistical information on the degree of abuse. The two kinds of information were at odds with each other: one kind suggesting welfare abuse was flagrant and the other suggesting it was quite moderate. Consistent with other research on causal attribution, the study found that the interview influenced viewers more than the statistical information.

Other research has suggested that people's attempts to integrate information are plagued by a tendency to perceive relationships in a way consistent with schematic preconceptions or evaluative biases. This research indicates that people do not consider evidence of correlation directly, but rather rely on their preconceptions and "discover" relationships which are consistent with them. A good example is provided in a study conducted by Chapman and Chapman (1969). They presented clinical psychologists with a set of drawings by psychiatric patients. Each drawing was identified only by a label indicating the nature of the psychological disorder of the patient. Unbeknownst to the clinicians, the disorder labels were randomly assigned to the drawings, ensuring that there was no significant correlation between the labels and any characteristics of the drawings. The clinicians were asked to evaluate the diagnostic power of the drawings. In the present terminology, they were asked to assess the level of correlation between qualities of the drawings and the type of disorder of the patient. In response, the clinicians claimed to discover relationships between the patients' disorders and the characteristics of their drawings—relationships reflecting their preconceptions (e.g., faces drawn by paranoids were darker and more angular)—where in fact no real relationships existed. Turning to politics, with all its attendant ambiguities, we would expect these failings and biases in categorization and causal attribution to play an important role. My own research on the images of political candidates shows clear evidence of people's tendency to make schema-driven character judgments on the basis of the most minimal information—for example, a single photograph (Rosenberg and McCafferty, 1987). Other work has indicated how party and ideological schemas affect candidate evaluation (e.g., Lau, 1986; Lodge and Hamil, 1986).

In addition to this specifically cognitive psychological research, other work has demonstrated how the desire to retain consistent evaluations of persons or events can also lead to distorted judgments of causality (e.g., Heider, 1958; Abelson et al., 1968). A politically relevant example is provided by a study of the attribution of causality for various events or circumstances in the Middle East (e.g., Israeli military superiority, Arab support in the United Nations, etc.). Examining the causal attributions made by Arab and Israeli graduate students, clear evidence was found that members of both groups tended to explain events so as to bolster both their positive image of their own group and their negative image of the enemy (Rosenberg and Wolfsfeld, 1977).

Finally, there is the issue of the individual's ability to engage in the requisite computations to make appropriate decisions in situations involving uncertainty and probability. In a series of influential studies conducted in the 1970s, Tversky and Kahneman (1974) have documented that individuals do not engage in the full computation necessary. Instead, they rely on various shortcuts or heuristics. In studies of decision making under risk, other types of biases have been discovered. For example, it appears that individuals are risk aversive when dealing with probable gains, but risk seeking when confronted with probable losses. This research also shows how sensitive individuals' preferences are to substantively meaningless changes in how alternatives are framed (e.g., Quattrone and Tversky, 1988).

To summarize, the research in cognitive and social psychology suggests that people do not have the information-gathering, interpretive, or computational skills required to properly recognize, remember, comprehend, and evaluate the circumstances and consequences of choices made under conditions typical of political life. Returning to our consideration of economic rationality, it is apparent that citizens lack the requisite cognitive ability to overcome the obstacles to the flow of feedback in the political marketplace. We may therefore expect that the polity will lack the discipline typical of the marketplace defined by the economic theorist. Consequently, we cannot assume that the rationality of individuals' actions will be ensured by the structure of the interactional setting. Instead, we must recognize that how people act will importantly be affected by their own limited capacities to process information.

The foregoing review of the psychological literature suggests that individuals will not behave "as if" they were rational—that is, in a way which maximizes their utility—under conditions which disrupt feedback. Under such conditions, we would therefore expect the attendant market inefficiencies and irregularities. Such inefficiencies are certainly characteristic of politics. But we need go no further than empirical research in economics itself to find support for our expectations. For example, the evidence suggests that in the case of markets for goods which require complex computation to evaluate alternatives (e.g., the market for insurance policies with varying provisions), consumers appear to make irrational choices with resulting market inefficiencies. Consumers also have difficulty making rational choices in the case of goods (e.g., whiskey, perfume, or cosmetics) where the benefits are hard to assess. In such cases, the market is flooded by the manipulative efforts of advertisers to define those benefits for the consumer (Comaner and Wilson, 1979; Gelatin and Leiter, 1981; Greer, 1984; Telser, 1964).

OPENING PANDORA'S BOX: NONRATIONALITY, LACK OF DISCIPLINE, AND THE INFUSION OF MEANING

What is the implication of the foregoing conclusion that the *Homo politicus* is a nonrational or subrational actor participating in an arena of exchange in which he or she is not effectively disciplined? To begin with, it suggests that the choices people make and the strategies they pursue will not be a direct function of the objective conditions of their action. This follows directly from the recognition that those conditions are so ill-defined, complex, and remote that individuals are unable to properly judge alternatives and recognize their consequences. This is not to say that their action will be random and that political inquiry is reduced to raw description. Rather, it is to suggest that the conditions to which they are responding are not simply objectively determined, but are in an important sense subjectively constructed. People's choices and actions are structured, but in a way which reflects how they perceive and understand the world. Political theory and explanation must therefore focus on the quality of their reasoning.

It should also be apparent that the argument here is not simply psychological or individualist in nature. It also has consequences for how we conceive the domain of interpersonal exchange. Remember that the individual is now assumed to direct his or her action in light of subjectively constructed understandings rather than in terms of some straightforward recognition of objective conditions. Placing individuals in relation to one another, we have a situation in which people are interacting with one another through the medium of their subjective constructions. Each individual is responding to others or a situation according to his or her subjective definition of the circumstances. In return, other individuals respond to the first's subjectively determined actions in terms of their own reconstructions of it. In this manner, the participants' subjective understandings not only mediate their interaction; they actually constitute the conditions of that interaction. Consequently, the domain of politics must be viewed as having not only an objective reality but an intersubjectively structured one as well. Thus political realities must be discursively interpreted as well as referentially identified and explained.

Our analysis forces us to leave behind the solid comfort of the objectivism and empiricism of the theoretical economist for the more elusive ground of subjectivity, with the attendant vagaries of more unfamiliar epistemologies. It is clear that effective political inquiry will require both a theory which elucidates the nature of the subjective qualities of action and a method appropriate to the subject matter. The psychological research discused earlier, despite its pretensions, fails us here. What it offers is more revealing description than theoretical insight. Currently popular "theories" such as schema theory, heuristics, or prospect theory consist of little more than a few key concepts which are defined more with respect to specific examples or particular experiments than in terms of their place in some broader theory of mind. Nonetheless, the research does illuminate some of the basic contours of subjectivity and thus suggests the direction in which more theoretical efforts must go.

Almost from its inception, the research on cognition has been dominated by two quite distinct views of perception and understanding. Each defines cognition as a quality of mind. However, one does so in a way which excludes considerations of culture and society, and the other does so in a way which makes these considerations quite central. The first focuses on the definitional and computational qualities of mind. It is exemplified in a variety of work, from that on perceptual gestalts (e.g., Koffka, 1935) and cognitive consistency (e.g., Heider, 1958; Festinger, 1957) to the more recent work on heuristics (e.g., Kahneman, Slovic, and Tversky, 1982). The emphasis here is on how the workings of the mind reflect its own internal logic quite apart from any influence of social environments. If external considerations are introduced, they are biologically rather than sociologically oriented. The second view focuses on how the mind's organization of incoming data reflects the imprint of culture. It is exemplified in the research on schemas and scripts (for a good review, see Fiske and Taylor, 1984). A key claim here is that while schemas structure perception, inference, and memory, they are determined by culturally available knowledges and regularities of social experience. Although they diverge significantly, both views of cognition have generated vast bodies of research which largely validate the orientations adopted. For present purposes, we need only draw on this result and recognize the need to differentiate our concept of subjectivity so as to acknowledge its two distinct dimensions, one personal and the other cultural.

In the light of this discussion of the cognitive psychological research and the earlier analysis of the political marketplace, it is possible to discern the outlines of the kind of theory needed to guide political inquiry. First, such a theory must specify the nature of both subjective and intersubjective or cultural constructions of politics. To this end, it must build on the work already done by psychologists adopting one or the other of the orientations mentioned above. Second, it must clarify the nature of the relationship between these two levels of construction—that is, it must indicate how construction at each level shapes and is shaped by construction at the other. Here, there is a need to go beyond the division of labor which currently structures cognitive psychological research and separates that work from sociology. Third, such a theory must indicate how these subjective constructions are related to the objective conditions of political exchange. Again the analysis must recognize the complex and recursive nature of the causal connections. Subjective constructions emerge in response to and are constrained by objective conditions, and at the same time they contribute to the constitution of those conditions.

Arguably, the attempt to provide such an elaboration once again occupies the center stage of theoretical inquiry (e.g., Giddens, 1984; Habermas, 1984/1987). For present purposes, however, a consideration of the issues regarding the particular theory to be adopted may be deferred to another time. The critical point to be made here is that political inquiry cannot rely on the concept of rationality, either broad or narrow, nor can it be premised on the simple objectivism of neoclassical economic theory.

NEOCLASSICAL ECONOMICS AS AN IDEOLOGICAL ENTERPRISE

Thus far, my critique of neoclassical political economy has focused on issues directly relevant to the study of political behavior. Evidence and argument regarding the nature of political exchange and political cognition were invoked to assess the appropriateness of certain key assumptions underlying the economist's approach. This led to the conclusion that this approach was ill-suited to the study of political behavior.

While the foregoing argument stands on its own, the analysis of rationality and political exchange has broader implications. On the one hand, it extends to epistemological concerns regarding the nature of the relationship between analysis and ideology. On the other, it pertains to basic theoretical questions regarding how the domain of politics should be defined. Both these concerns are briefly brought to light in this final section through a consideration of the inherently ideological quality of neoclassical economics. Put in less inflammatory terms, my critique leads to a consideration of neoclassical economics as a political theory.

For the most part, questions of ideology and political theory are denied or ignored by both economists and those political scientists who apply their approach to politics. With regard to matters of ideology, the economist draws a clear distinction between theory and analysis, on the one hand, and values and ideology, on the other. The former is the route to an unfettered, universal truth; the latter to distortion and relativity. The economist solves the problem of ideology by purging inquiry of any particular value orientation. To achieve ideological neutrality, all that is required is an analysis which avoids, at least at the outset, the advocacy of a value position. A good example of this reasoning is provided in Mancur Olson's discussion of the relationship between economics and the other social sciences. With regard to the ideological bias of economics, he writes:

> The great economists of the late eighteenth and nineteenth centuries, like many major theorists, were often inspired to intellectual innovation by immediate practical problems. They were for the most part caught up in the political controversies of their time and were sometimes passionate ideologues. Most of them, at least in Great Britain, were advocates for the rising middle class and the mercantile and industrial interests (1969:140).

Referring to the present, he later adds:

> Indeed, economic theory has escaped the original ideological limitations on its generality to such an extent that I have read some interesting work by people who, as I later learned, were avowed Communists (1969:142).

In drawing such a clear distinction between analysis and value, economists are guided by the largely unreconstructed epistemology of the nineteenth-century liberalism out of which modern economics emerged. In this view, analysis or reason is conceived as a process of definition and understanding. All individuals (including theorists) are assumed to be rational and thus able to reason in fundamentally the same way. In this sense, the process of reasoning has a universal quality. In contrast, ideology is defined as a product. It is a matter of values and preferences which result from the varying circumstances of individual and collective experience. Ideologies are therefore psychologically and culturally relative phenomena.

Our earlier analysis of cognition and rationality suggests that this distinction between reason and ideology is not a viable one. First, the evidence suggests that reason, like ideology, is not universal. At the level of particular understandings, the research on schematic reasoning suggests that there is considerable variation in the causal relationships individuals will perceive and the categories they will define. At a more general level, the research on adult cognitive development suggests that the structure of reasoning may vary across individuals. Thus variation in the nature of reasoning extends to the formal quality of the associations people forge and the kinds of objects they can think about. In my own research, I have provided evidence of this in respect to people's reasoning about political phenomena (Rosenberg, 1987, 1988a, 1988b). Second, the psychological research also suggests that reason, like ideology, is a cultural and historical product. Again, this is true at two levels. On the one hand, schema theorists argue that the connections people make are a product of schemas available in the general culture (indeed, from this perspective, culture is best thought of as a store of schemas). On the other hand, many cognitive development theorists argue that people's cognitive development depends on the structure of the social environment to which they are exposed (e.g., Vygotsky, 1962; Luria, 1976; Dasen, 1977; Rosenberg, 1988b). Third, the evidence also suggests that ideology, like reason, is a process and that there is an isomorphic relationship between the activity of understanding and that of valuing. Looking at particular connections between events or objects, balance theorists have argued the formal identity of unit relations (based on dispassionate cognition) and sentiment relations (based on evaluatively motivated judgment) (Heider, 1958). Similarly, some cognitive developmentalists have argued a structural correspondence between cognition, on the one hand, and moral judgment and political evaluation, on the other (Piaget, 1965; Kohlberg, 1981/1984; Rosenberg, 1988b).

Together, the foregoing three points suggest that reason and ideology are best understood not in terms of a radical distinction but rather in terms of their interpenetration or commonality. Both terms may be more fruitfully defined with reference to a single concept of ideological reasoning. As a cognitive activity, ideological reasoning yields a definition of the nature of political life (its constituent forces and their dynamics) and a complementary determination of the values which do and should orient political action. The results of a single process, these analytical and evaluative constructions are structurally related. This is the case for both the classical ideologies of the eighteenth and nineteenth centuries and the great religions which preceded them. It also holds for the common (and only apparently incoherent) ideologies constructed by average citizens.

Returning to the economist's view of his or her own political position, we may now more clearly recognize the ground on which that view rests. The claim of ideological neutrality depends on a narrow conception of ideology as evaluation independent of cognition. This in turn depends on an epistemology which does not recognize the cultural or political relativity of reasoning nor the constructive and definitional quality of ideology. Here psychological research has been marshaled to raise questions regarding the appropriateness of this view. It is worth noting that this epistemology has been subject to sweeping and widespread attack in philosophical circles as well. In any case, the economist's implicit epistemology and the particular version of social science which follows from it represent but one of many alternatives, each of which is marked by its own particular political ideological implications.

Like its epistemology, the political ideology of neoclassical economics reflects its roots in the philosophy and politics of classic eighteenth- and nineteenth-century liberalism. So grounded, it adopts an approach to the study of human exchange which focuses on the individual. This individual is a rational, independent being capable of self-reflection, insight, and critique. The polity is an aggregate outcome, the product of individual-level actions and forces. These may be channeled by particular circumstances or institutional regulations, but the latter are readily subject to individuals' comprehension and ultimately to their control. In this context, the individual is defined as the basic unit of analysis and thus becomes the building block for political theory and explanation. Similarly, the individual provides the standard for evaluation. Individuals are the source of value in political life, and all collective outcomes are judged in terms of their individual consequences. Moreover, given the abstract or general terms in which "the individual" is defined, the consequences for different individuals are judged equally. This introduces the extra-individual concern with justice alongside that of the individual considered in isolation.

Critiques, such as the one offered here, which debunk this conception of the individual as either broadly or narrowly rational, necessarily lead to a view of political life which focuses less on individuals. People are assumed to be inadequately equipped to realize or even recognize their best interests. Their action (its logic and value orientation) is understood less in terms of personal volition and more in terms of social structural determination. Thus, in both analysis and evaluation, individuals come to be regarded more as the objects rather than the subjects of political life. The focus shifts to the collectivity considered on its own terms. Politics is no longer considered so much in terms of individuals' preferences and decisions but rather in terms of extra-individual phenomena such as community, culture, class, and social structure. Moreover, whereas the latter are understood to penetrate and shape individuals' conceptions, the nature of these social phenomena are not assumed to be directly accessible to them. Consequently, to understand politics, individuals and theorists must supplement observation with insight, interpretation, or critique. Depending on the direction taken, this focus on collectivities may have various political ideological consequences. For example, it may lead to the epistemological skepticism and accompanying political paternalism of classical conservatism or to the dialectics and attendant critical point of view of developmental sociologies (e.g., the historical materialism of Marx, the evolutionary sociology of Hobhouse, or the communicative rationality of Habermas).

The point here is not so much to suggest that the ideological vision implicit in neoclassical economic theory is incorrect, although the argument clearly leads in that direction. Rather, the aim is to suggest that (1) the economist's approach is such that it obscures its own ideological foundations; (2) the definitions and mode of analysis of neoclassical economic theory are structured by classical liberalism and therefore contemporary applications of that theory necessarily express that particular political point of view; (3) although frequently a matter of confusion for the economist, the theoretical arguments surrounding the application of economics to politics necessarily raise fundamental questions of ideology and value. This may help explain some of the fire and obstinacy, the flag waving and flag burning, surrounding the advocacy and critique of the application of neoclassical economics to the study of politics. It is not simply a matter of what is correct and incorrect, but also a question of what is right and wrong.

REFERENCES

Abelson, R. A. (1975). "Social Psychology's Rational Man." In S. I. Benn and G. W. Mortimore (Eds.), *Rationality and the Social Sciences*. London: Routledge and Kegan Paul.

Abelson, R. P., Aronson, E., McGuire, W. J., Newcomb, T. M., Rosenberg, M. J., and Tannenbaum, P. H. (Eds.). (1968). *Theories of Cognitive Consistency: A Sourcebook*. Chicago: McNally.

Bartlett, F. A. (1932). *Remembering*. Cambridge: Cambridge University Press.

Bruner, J. (1958). "Social Psychology and Perception." In E. Maccoby, T. Newcomb, and E. Hartley (eds.), *Readings in Social Psychology*. New York: Holt.

Buchanan, J. M., and Tullock, G. (1962). *The Calculus of Consent: Logical Foundations of Constitutional Democracy*. Ann Arbor: University of Michigan Press.

Cantor, N., and Mischel, W. (1979). "Prototypes in Personal Perception." In L. Berkowitz (ed.), *Advances in Experimental Social Psychology* (Vol. 12). New York: Academic Press.

Chapman, L. J., and Chapman, J. P. (1969). "Illusory Correlation as an Obstacle to the Use of Valid Psychodiagnostic Signs." *Journal of Abnormal Psychology, 14*:271–280.

Comaner, W., and Wilson, O. (1979). "The Effect of Advertising on Competition: A Survey." *Journal of Economic Literature*, pp. 453–476.

Dasen, P. (1977). *Piagetian Psychology; Cross-Cultural Contributions*. New York: Gardner Press.

Downs, A. (1957). *An Economic Theory of Democracy*. New York: Harper & Row.

Festinger, L. (1957). *A Theory of Cognitive Dissonance*. Stanford: Stanford University Press.

Fiske, S. T., and Taylor, S. E. (1984). *Social Cognition*. Reading, MA: Addison-Wesley.

Gelatin, M., and Leiter, R. (1981). *Economics of Information*. Boston: Martinus Nijhoff.

Giddens, A. (1984). *The Constitution of Society*. Berkeley: University of California Press.

Greer, D. (1984). *Industrial Organization and Public Policy*. New York: Macmillan.

Habermas, J. (1984/1987). *The Theory of Communicative Action* (Vols. 1 and 2). Boston: Beacon.

Heider, F. (1958). *The Psychology of Interpersonal Relations*. New York: Wiley.

Higgins, E. T., Rholes, W. S., and Jones, C. R. (1977). "Category Accessibility and Impression Formation." *Journal of Experimental Social Psychology, 13*:141–154.

Kahneman, D., Slovic, P., and Tversky, D. (Eds.). (1982). *Judgment Under Uncertainty: Heuristics and Biases*. New York: Cambridge University Press.

Koffka, K. (1935). *Principles of Gestalt Psychology*. New York: Harcourt Brace and World.

Kohlberg, L. (1981/1984). *Essays on Moral Development* (Vols. 1 and 2). New York: Harper & Row.

Lau, R. R. (1986). "Political Schemata, Candidate Evaluations, and Voting Behavior." In R. R. Lau and D. O. Sears (Eds.), *Political Cognition*. Hillsdale, NJ: Erlbaum.

Lodge, M., and Hamil, D. (1986). "A Partisan Schema for Political Information Processing." *American Political Science Review*, *80*:505–519.

Loftus, E. F. (1979). *Eyewitness Testimony*. Cambridge, MA: Harvard University Press.

Luria, A. R. (1976). *Cognitive Development: Its Social and Cultural Foundations*. Cambridge, MA: Harvard University Press.

McArthur, L. Z. (1981). "What Grabs You? The Role of Attention in Impression Formation and Causal Attribution." In E. T. Higgins, C. P. Herman, and M. P. Zanna (Eds.), *Social Cognition: The Ontario Symposium*. Hillsdale, NJ: Erlbaum.

Nisbett, R. E., and Borgida, E. (1975). "Attribution and the Psychology of Prediction." *Journal of Personality and Social Psychology*, *32*:932–943.

Nisbett, R. E., and Ross, L. (1980). *Human Inference: Strategies and Shortcomings of Social Judgment*. Englewood Cliffs, NJ: Prentice-Hall.

Olson, M. (1965). *The Logic of Collective Action*. Cambridge, MA: Harvard University Press.

———. (1969). "The Relationship Between Economics and the Other Social Sciences: The Province of a Social Report." In S. M. Lipset (Ed.), *Politics and the Social Sciences*. New York: Oxford University Press.

Piaget, J. (1965). *The Moral Judgment of the Child*. New York: Free Press.

Riker, W. (1962). *The Theory of Political Coalitions*. New Haven: Yale University Press.

Quattrone, G. A., and Tversky, A. (1988). "Contrasting Rational and Psychological Analyses of Political Choice." *American Political Science Review*, 82:719–736.

Rosenberg, S. W. (1987). "Reason and Ideology: Interpreting People's Understanding of American Politics." *Polity*, *20*:114–144.

———. (1988a). "The Structure of Political Thinking." *American Journal of Political Science*, *32*:539–566.

———. (1988b). *Reason, Ideology and Politics*. Princeton: Princeton University Press.

Rosenberg, S. W., and McCafferty, P. (1987). "The Image and the Vote: Manipulating Voters' Preferences." *Public Opinion Quarterly, 51*:31–47.

Rosenberg, S. W., and Wolfsfeld, G. (1977). "International Relations and the Problem of Attribution." *Journal of Conflict Resolution, 21*:75–103.

Simon, H. A. (1985). "Human Nature in Politics: The Dialogue of Psychology with Political Science." *American Political Science Review, 79*:293–304.

Snyder, M., and Swann, W. B. (1978). "Hypothesis Testing Processes in Social Interaction." *Journal of Personality and Social Psychology, 36*:1202–1212.

Taylor, S. E., and Crocker, J. (1981). "Schematic Bases of Social Information Processing." In E. T. Higgins, C. P. Herman, and M. P. Zanna (Eds.), *Social Cognition: The Ontario Symposium*. Hillsdale, NJ: Erlbaum.

Taylor, S. E., and Fiske, S. T. (1975). "Point-of-View and Perceptions of Causality." *Journal of Personality and Social Psychology, 32*:439–445.

———. (1978). "Salience, Attention and Attribution: The Top of the Head Phenomena." In L. Berkowitz (Ed.), *Advances in Experimental Social Psychology* (Vol. 11). New York: Academic Press.

Telser, L. (1964). "Advertising and Competition." *Journal of Political Economy*, pp. 537–562

Tversky, A., and Kahneman, D. (1974). "Judgment Under Uncertainty: Heuristics and Biases." *Science, 185*:1124–1131.

Vygotsky, L. S. (1962). *Thought and Language*. Cambridge: MIT Press.

Contrasting Economic and Psychological Analyses of Political Choice: An Economist's Perspective on Why Cognitive Psychology Does Not Explain Democratic Politics

Donald Wittman

It has been more than 30 years since Anthony Downs (1957) published *An Economic Theory of Democracy*. Since that time the economist's concept of rational action has invaded all aspects of political theory. Researchers with training in other disciplines, such as Coleman (1986) and Hechter (1987) in sociology, and even Marxists, such as Przeworski (1987), have incorporated economic man into their models of political behavior. The greatest challenge to this classic approach to rationality comes from the cognitive psychologists. With their more mathematical training and their experimental methods, they have had the confidence to confront economics in a serious way.

In this chapter, I argue that cognitive psychologists, despite their impressive experimental results, have little to add to our understanding of politics. The psychological work which claims to demonstrate that agents make mistaken and biased judgments, primarily because they choose schemata which are the most available rather than the most fruitful (Kahneman and Tversky, 1984), remains little more than a hodgepodge of contradictory results. Some of the supposed evidence against the economic model of rationality is in fact supportive. Furthermore, any attempt to generalize to the real world from their experimental results is extremely suspect. Their work underemphasizes the importance of competitive markets, incentives, and the law of large numbers. The primary emphasis of this chapter is therefore a counterattack on the relevance of cognitive psychology for political behavior rather than a direct defense of the economic approach itself.

Before proceeding, it is useful to consider the contrasting views of economists and cognitive psychologists. The two major approaches to human decision making are global optimization and bounded rationality.[1] Each of these, in turn, can be conveniently divided into two subheadings. Global optimization is typically associated with neoclassical economics: the individual maximizes his or her utility. When outcomes do not take place with certainty but with probability less than one and greater than zero, then economists have typically assumed that individuals maximize expected utility as defined by von Neumann and Morgenstern (1947) and Savage (1954). A more recent tradition still allows for utility maximization, but under different assumptions from those employed by von Neumann and Morgenstern. Proponents of this newer tradition include Fishburn (1988) and Machina (1989), as well as Tversky and Kahneman (1974).[2] In these maximization models, making the decision is generally treated as costless, although there are models of optimal search when search is costly.

In contrast, the bounded rationality literature emphasizes that information acquiring and processing is costly and that various cognitive shortcuts are used. The typical economic approach to bounded rationality is that individuals chose optimal rules of thumb. For example, traffic signals generally remain green longer for the more heavily traveled street because the total value of time is typically greater for the larger number of people on the heavily traveled street than for the fewer number of people on the cross street, even though this may not always be the case (see Wittmann, 1982). As another example, bounded rationality prevents complete contingent contracts from being written since they would be infinitely long; so liability for breach of contract is substituted.

Cognitive psychologists tend to argue that individuals employ simplifying heuristics without paying attention to their instrumental use; hence, systematic judgmental errors may arise from the viewpoint of goal maximization. For example, a person might only remember the first (or last) evidence he or she hears even though optimality might suggest weighting all evidence equally. As another example, the way an argument is framed may alter a person's choice even though the content of the argument is the same in both cases. With regard to this latter example, some cognitive psychologists have argued that such "framing" effects violate fundamental notions of rationality because the person makes inconsistent decisions.[3] Hence cognitive psychologists emphasize the biases and mistakes in decisions, at times arguing that individuals are irrational, [4] while economists tend to emphasize that the rules chosen for making decisions are optimal given the constraints of bounded rationality.[5]

In this chapter, I argue in favor of the economist's concept of rational decision-making over the cognitive psychologist's notion of rational decision-making when issues of bounded rationality arise. I also argue in favor of the von Neumann–Morgenstern postulates over other global maximization approaches in explaining political behavior. Furthermore, I suggest that the rise of political institutions has greatly mitigated the problems of bounded rationality and that therefore optimization models may be more appropriate than bounded rationality models in explaining democratic politics.

In the first section, I consider framing effects. Numerous cognitive psychology experiments have shown that individual decisions are greatly influenced by the way questions are worded (framed). I argue that the relevance of these experiments for explaining democratic politics is nill. In the real world, numerous institutions arise to counteract such errors. Thus, the experiments themselves are misleading since they do not account for learning, experience, competition, adequate incentives, or institutional response. Section two considers risk-preference. Cognitive psychology experiments have shown that people prefer gambles over an equivalent sure loss (in expected value terms) although they will not undertake fair gambles when the expected gain is positive. However, such behavior is not found in economic and political markets. Furthermore, if individuals had such attitudes toward risk, they would make book against themselves: the person would pay to be in the gamble. But once facing the gamble, the person would pay not to be in the gamble; and so on. This is clearly counterfactual. Section three considers psychology experiments demonstrating biased judgments. I argue to the contrary—that in the context of the experimental setup, individuals are making decisions consistent with good scientific procedure. Section four focuses on the role of anomalies. Although some cognitive psychological models are consistent with anomalous political and economic market behavior, normal market behavior is held anomalous from the viewpoint of these same models. In Section five, I argue that inherent unobservables, such as subjective probabilities, allow the cognitive psychologist too many degrees of freedom to make post hoc explanations. Section six argues against those cognitive psychologists who claim that preferences are volatile and dependent on intersubjectively construed meanings. If one were to seriously believe in this view, then cognitive psychology could not be used to predict democratic behavior since there would be few stable relations between objective measures and voter choices. Finally, in the last section, I argue against the rationale for choosing cognitive shortcuts without considering their instrumental role in achieving goals.

FRAMING AND THE RATIO-DIFFERENCE PRINCIPAL

Prospect theory is a set of propositions regarding human cognition. Major components include the S-shaped value function, framing effects, and biased subjective probabilities (to be discussed below).[6] Kahneman and Tversky (1984) view prospect theory as a descriptive theory of human behavior in contrast to economic theory, which they claim is merely prescriptive. They argue that there are predictable biases in human cognition that make people behave differently (in a systematic fashion) from the way predicted by economic theory. Some of this behavior violates the fundamental tenets of rationality (for example, the framing effects considered below), while other behavior violates economic notions of rationality but, possibly, not other notions of rational behavior. Quattrone and Tversky (1988) have applied prospect theory to politics. They have designed experiments which they believe demonstrate the superiority of prospect theory over economic theory in explaining political behavior. In this and the following sections, I argue to the contrary by showing that economics is much more successful than prospect theory is at describing *actual* political and market behavior.

Quattrone and Tversky present some experimental data demonstrating that voter behavior is irrational.[7] In one of their experiments, their subjects did not find much difference between policies with 92 percent employment and 98 percent employment (the latter being only slightly better), even though they found a great deal of difference between 8 percent unemployment and 2 percent unemployment (the former being 4 times as bad).[8] Of course, 2 percent unemployment is equivalent to 98 percent employment, so objectively the differences are the same.

What implications does this have for the rationality of democratic politics? I would argue none, whatsoever. It is quite easy to make mistakes when the mistakes are unimportant to *all* the participants. This is the case for Quattrone and Tversky's experiment, where no one loses money, or more important, loses his or her job if someone makes a mistake. Indeed, almost all of their experiments are plagued by the problem that errors in judgment are not costly and there is no chance for long-run learning and survival. In fact, these are not experiments as much as surveys of people for their answers to hypothetical situations.

There have been other studies of framing involving monetary incentives, but the incentives for making the correct choice have been very slight. Consider for example, experiments 7 and 8 reported in Tversky and Kahneman (1987). When subjects were given the choice between options A and B, they always chose B. When subjects were given the choice between C and D, they chose C 58 percent of the time, although C is equivalent to option A, and B is equivalent to option D.

Option A: 90% win $0, 6% win $45, 1% win $30, 1% lose $15, 2% lose $15.
Option B: 90% win $0, 6% win $45, 1% win $45, 1% lose $10, 2% lose $15.
Option C: 90% win $0, 6% win $45, 1% win $30, 3% lose $15.
Option D. 90% win $0, 7% win $45, 1% lose $10, 2% lose $15.

Even though this experiment provides monetary rewards for optimal behavior, the economic loss from suboptimal behavior is minor. Harrison (1989) calculated that Kahneman and Tversky's experimental procedure (only 1 in 10 students actually got to play the gamble) meant that a wrong decision cost the student only 2 cents in expected value terms. The failure to create significant economic incentives is quite common in experimental work. To frame the argument from a different prospective: given the insignificant economic incentives for optimal behavior in most experimental settings, one should be surprised when experimental results do confirm economic theory.

In contrast, in the real world, politicians are competing for office. If the incumbent frames the argument in terms of unemployment, the opposition can frame the argument in terms of employment or show that the two methods are equivalent. Since elections are a zero-sum game, it will pay one or the other of the politicians to inform the voters of the mistake. Hence, even if framing can alter voters' perceptions and choices, we will not observe voters fooled by the frame.[9]

Furthermore, people often argue over politics, but the experiment did not allow the students to get together and discuss the issue. Someone might have observed the equivalence and pointed it out to the others. Unlike the experimental design, numerous democratic institutions are designed to elicit more informed choices. Consider the U.S. Congress. There are specialized committees, large professional staffs, and floor debates between those with opposing views.[10]

More important, economic and political institutions may arise so that people implicitly make the right choices. Consider the previous lottery problem, in which individuals mistakenly choose C over D. Since both of these are risky, individuals may prefer some sure thing over the gamble. Knowledgeable financiers (those people who know that D is better than C) will be willing to offer more money (since the net gain is positive) to those individuals who have chosen D. Hence uninformed individuals will choose D over C, not because they realize that it yields a higher expected payoff but because they get a higher price for this lottery. The same type of analysis holds in the political sphere. Knowledgeable politicians can use the political system to ensure voters against risk. The knowledgeable politician may not even tell the voters which policy he or she will be undertaking but may just be able to promise them more by chosing D over C. Alternatively, government policies may promise more to voters who have chosen occupations with D payoffs. Hence, the uninformed voters implicitly make the correct choice even though they would make the incorrect choice in the absence of intervening institutions.[11]

A third problem is that the framing effect is unlikely to be observed in many other experiments (or in real life, for that matter). Consider the following "experiments": (1) High school seniors are broken into two groups. The first group is told that 1 in 5 applicants is accepted to University of California, Berkeley. The second group is told that 4 out of 5 applicants are rejected by Berkeley. The students are queried about their decision whether to apply. (2) Consumers are broken into two groups. The first group is told that a six-pack of Pepsi costs $1.89 and then told that a six-pack of Coca-Cola costs an additional $.11. The second group is first told that a six-pack of Coca-Cola costs $2.00 and then told that a six-pack of Pepsi costs $.11 less. The consumers are queried about which soft drink they intend to buy. (3) Voters and 1988 presidential candidates are broken into two groups. The first group is told that a poll showed that 44 percent of the voters favored Bush and that he was 2 percentage points ahead of Dukakis. The second group is told that a poll showed that 42 percent of the voters favored Dukakis and that he was 2 percentage points behind Bush. The two groups are queried about their decision to vote. Although I have not run these experiments, I doubt that the two groups would behave differently despite the different frames. The reason is that individuals have more experience with these issues and therefore are less likely to be fooled by the frames. To paraphrase Tversky and Kahneman (1987:86), subjects are fooled by frames only when they are naive and the framing is nontransparent. But as people become more knowledgeable (as would be the case in a political campaign), the framing becomes more transparent.[12] Other cognitive tasks generate canonical representations automatically and effortlessly. For example, visual objects do not appear to change in shape, size, or color when we move around them or when illumination varies, and the active and the passive voice are often not distinguished by the listener. The key to the existence of the canonical form is the extent of experience. The experimental tests of framing catch the inexperienced.

THE S-SHAPED UTILITY CURVE AND THE REFERENCE EFFECT

The most analytic part of prospect theory is the S-shaped utility function. In standard economics, utility is a concave function of wealth and invariant to present position (see Figure 1). In prospect theory, the status quo is typically at the origin (see Figure 2).[13] The S-shaped utility function is concave (risk averse) for gains and convex (risk preferring) for losses, and the utility increase from a gain in wealth is always less than the utility decrease from an equivalent loss in wealth (i.e., $U(|x|)-U(0) < U(0)-U(-|x|)$, where 0 is the status quo).

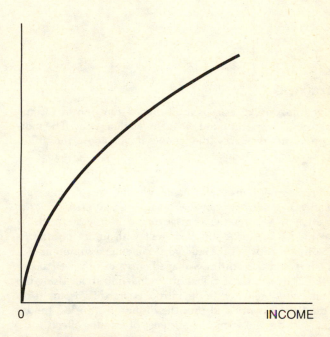

0   INCOME

CONCAVE UTILITY FUNCTION

Figure 1. Utility (vertical axis) is a concave function of income (horizontal axis). The individual is risk averse (the gamble line is below the utility function) and the function is the same regardless of the person's present wealth (0 on the horizontal axis represents 0 income).

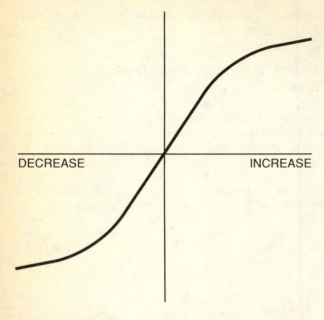

THE S-SHAPED CURVE

Figure 2. Utility (the vertical axis) is an S-shaped function of income (the horizontal axis). The status quo is at the inflection point. The individual is risk preferring for losses (the gamble line is above the utility function) and risk averse for gains.

People can rank order their preferences (although their rankings are situation dependent). Their behavior over compound lotteries (lotteries to play lotteries) now violates the von Neumann–Morgenstern utility postulates, but their behavior is still consistent with utility maximization. Thus the dispute between the standard economic assumption of a fixed concave curve and the shifting S-shaped curve of prospect theory lies wholly within the confines of global utility maximization. Using the two by two framework presented in the introduction, this dispute takes place within the first category and thus the dispute is at a less fundamental level than the dispute about the existence of framing effects.

Quattrone and Tversky present a number of experimental results that contradict the standard economic utility function and support the S-shaped utility function. For example, they report that the majority of experimental subjects prefer a 50/50 chance of losing $200 or losing nothing over a certainty of losing $100.[14] Since a person with an S-shaped utility function prefers a gamble when facing a loss, the experimental results are consistent with prospect theory. In contrast, the

results contradict the standard economic model which predicts a preference for the sure loss since the individual is always risk averse. Both
models predict that people will prefer a sure gain of $100 to an even
chance of a 0 gain and a gain of $200.

The problem here is that we do not observe market behavior
coinciding with this experimental behavior. For example, consider fire
insurance. We do not observe the following policy being written: If
your house burns down, you will be given a lottery. Half the time the
company will reimburse you for the cost of rebuilding your house; half
the time not only will you absorb the cost of rebuilding your home, but
you will also pay the company an amount equivalent to the cost of
rebuilding your house.[15] Since insurance companies deal with the law of
large numbers, they are risk neutral. Since individuals are risk preferring for losses (according to prospect theory), individuals would either
pay right now for this privilege or accept a worse lottery with only a 45
percent chance of being reimbursed.

There may be objections to this example. So let us try another one.
Financial markets have developed all kinds of instruments. Perhaps it is
time for those who believe in the S-shaped curve to develop the following mirror stock. If the price of stock X goes up, the mirror stock price
sells at the same price as stock X. If the price of the stock goes down
(say, by $100), the owner of the mirror stock is given a lottery (50%
chance of losing $200 dollars, 50% chance of losing nothing). Since a
"majority' of people prefer such an option over the sure loss, they will
pay a premium for owning mirror stock. Since the owner of the lottery
faces many gambles, he or she is virtually indifferent and therefore will
be willing to provide such a gamble. But this is not the end of this winning idea. When the stock actually goes down in price, the owner of the
lottery can offer the buyer of the mirror stock an option not to be in the
lottery. Since the stock has now gone down in price, the status quo has
shifted and the lottery represents a gain of 100 or a loss of 100 vis-à-vis
the new status quo. Thus the owner of the stock is now risk averse to
such a gamble and will pay the lottery owner money not to play the lottery![16] The lottery owner is still indifferent, since the outcome of many
gambles is equivalent to the sure thing, and therefore will gladly take
money from the owner of the mirror stock. It is important to realize
that for such a market to exist, we need only a small percentage of people behaving the way Quattrone and Tversky predict. The fact that we
do not observe such markets in the real world suggests that the S-shaped
curve is not descriptive of even a minority of people.

The S-shaped curve is also used to explain multiattribute loss aversion. As already noted, the S-shaped curve is steeper on the bottom,
making losses more acutely felt than gains. Thus if I have 3 pears, I may
not trade them for 4 apples because the utility loss from the 3 pears
outweighs the utility gain of the 4 apples. Furthermore, contrary to

ordinary economic intuition, if I start with 4 apples, it is quite likely that I will not trade them for 3 pears because, once again, the loss is felt more than the gain. Quattrone and Tversky provide experimental evidence (problems 5 and 6) that support their theory. Numerous other studies yield similar results (see Cummings et al., 1986, for a summary of earlier work and Knetsch, 1989, for an example of more recent research in this genre).

Typically, these experiments do not involve real-world characteristics such as experiential feedback, information gathering, or markets. For example, the experimental subject does not choose between items where the price is known. Recent experimental work by economists (Coursey, Hovis, and Schulze, 1987) demonstrates that the differential between loss and gain behavior diminishes significantly (but not completely) when there are market mechanisms.[17] Furthermore, the experiments usually do not involve repetition (for a counterexample, see Kahneman, Knetsch, and Thaler, 1987), and when there is repetition it does not involve alternating experiences (for example, in round one, the person receives 3 pears; round two, 4 apples; round three, 3 pears).

Multiattribute reference point theory has all the problems of the single-dimensional S-shaped curve, plus a few additional ones. Certainly, problems arise when the attributes become more similar. What if three red pears can be traded for four green pears (or four red pears with slightly different shapes)? It is doubtful that they would attain similar results (preference for the status quo). This suggests that one need not make decisions in the way characterized by multiattribute prospect theory.

It is useful to consider the political implications of this theory if it were true. Multiattribute loss aversion, in particular, and the S-shaped curve, in general, imply a great preference for the status quo. Thus they are good at predicting why things remain the same, but not so good at predicting why they change.[18] To illustrate, consider arms control and arms races. Quattrone and Tversky (1988:726) apply the loss aversion theory to explaining arms control. I will quote at length:

> Loss aversion may play an important role in bargaining and negotiation. . . . [E]ach party may view its own concessions as losses that loom larger than the gains achieved by the concession of the adversary (Bazerman, 1983; Tversky and Kahneman, 1987). In negotiating over missiles, for example, each superpower may sense a greater loss in security from the dismantling of its own missiles than it senses in a gain in security from a comparable reduction by the other side.

This is a nice example, and it has a certain air of plausibility about it (perhaps because it suggests why arms control agreements are so difficult to make). Unfortunately the same logic predicts that arms races are unlikely, a situation which appears to be counterfactual. The logic proceeds as follows: Each party knows that if it increases its missiles, the other party will increase its missiles also. Each superpower may sense a smaller gain in security from increasing its missiles than it senses in a loss in security from a comparable increase in missiles from the other side.

Preference for the status quo may have important implications for welfare theory. For example, since losses are felt more acutely than gains, the sum total of human happiness is reduced if a rich person donates money or food to a poor person (unless one assumes that poor people have steeper S-shaped curves).

BIASES FROM PRIORS

Snyder and Swann (1978), among others, have shown that search tends to be biased by the individual's preconceptions. They demonstrated that people search for evidence which is likely to confirm and neglect disconfirming evidence. In their experiment, subjects were more likely to find evidence that X was an extrovert when told beforehand that X was extroverted. Applying these results to politics, Rosenberg, in this volume, argues that voters' perceptions of the various candidates will be biased by their initial impressions and as a result they will tend to have a distorted view of the choice offered.[19]

Generalizing from these experimental results is highly suspect. Priors are less important, the more evidence is accrued. If the subjects had known X for a week, a month, or a year, then the effect of the original statement by the researcher concerning X's extroversion would have been reduced considerably. Also, in politics there are at least two sides trying to argue their case. If the researcher labeled Y an introvert, someone else, possibly Y, might argue that he or she was an extrovert. In this way initial biases might be overcome.[20]

A similar argument can be used against Rosenberg and McCafferty (1987), who demonstrated that a single photograph (flattering or not flattering) could influence the subject's judgment about a "candidate." Of course, in this experiment the photograph was an important piece of information about the pretend candidate (even though Rosenberg and McCafferty view it as being minimal). In the real world, the voter has numerous opportunities to view the characteristics of the real candidate. One picture or even one television interview may not be so influential. But even if photographs do influence, this does not mean that voters use inappropriate or biased heuristics. Would you want to have a president who laughed when the occasion called for being serious?

From another point of view, Snyder and Swann's experimental results not only are consistent with good judgment but also are in accord with sound scientific procedure. It would be foolish to reverse your views if some new evidence slightly supported the contrary view. Furthermore, the subject did not expect to be lied to by the experimenter. Perhaps the subject was too embarrassed to report contrary evidence or possibly the subject just trusted the professional's opinion.[21] In the real world, the voter has better priors about the reliability of people. Perhaps the voter will discount a statement because it comes from a politician and is likely to be self-serving, or perhaps the voter will believe it because it comes from a longtime, trusted friend.

THE ROLE OF ANOMALIES

Both some ecological data and experiments by cognitive psychologists and economists have highlighted anomalous behavior from the viewpoint of economic theory. This is important work, but it should be remembered that these results are anomalies. In this section, I make the following arguments regarding anomalies: (1) the anomalies are the exception rather than the rule; (2) some of these anomalies are predicted by cognitive psychology, but then standard behavior becomes anomalous from the viewpoint of cognitive psychology; (3) some of the economic anomalies are also anomalies for cognitive psychology; (4) the anomalies tend to be second-order effects; and (5) anomalies must remain the unexplained residual until we have a coherent theory to explain a significant portion of the anomalous and nonanomalous behavior.

A number of empirical studies of financial markets have found anomalies from the point of view of economic theory. Indeed, supporters of prospect theory now regularly trot out these studies in their counterattacks on economic theory (see, for example, Frey and Eichenberger, 1989; Kahneman and Tversky, 1987; and Thaler, 1987). However, these anomalies are not supportive of prospect theory either. Consider the oft-mentioned example of the January effect. The historical record shows that purchases made on December 30 of shares in small businesses yield higher than average returns, contrary to economic theory [22] Is this predicted ex ante by prospect theory? If it is, does prospect theory also predict that, consistent with expected utility maximization, there is no February, March, April, etc., effect (or transportation or industrial index effect)?[23] Do we want to throw out economic theory because it does not explain the special case, or do we keep the theory because it explains the typical case?

The cognitive psychologists have developed theories to explain some of the anomalous experimental behavior, but normal behavior then becomes anomalous in their models. Earlier, I argued that individuals with S-shaped utility functions would make book against themselves and that hitherto unknown financial instruments would arise. More important, certain regularities of aggregate market behavior, such as stock prices being martingale-like (today's price is an unbiased predictor of tomorrow's price), would probably not exist if people actually behaved according to the tenets of prospect theory.[24] I use the word "probably" because the implications of prospect theory for market behavior are not well delineated, and, depending on which aspects of the theory are emphasized, one might arrive at contrary conclusions. However, it appears that such concepts as the representative heuristic and framing would lead to predictable patterns (for example, if the price went up today, it will go up again tomorrow), contrary to the general record of stocks.

Observed voting regularities become puzzling if one believes in framing effects and the importance of the status quo or reference point in determining preferences. Consider the observed positive relationship between income and voting for the Republican Party. Prospect theory emphasizes changes in income from the status quo rather than the level of income in explaining behavior. Hence a believer in prospect theory would not, in general, expect to find correlations between income levels and voting behavior; rather, the believer in prospect theory would expect that people whose income was higher than usual would vote Republican.

Despite cognitive psychology's belief in the manipulability of voters, we observe rational voting behavior. Afro-Americans generally voted for the Republican Party after the Civil War. Since the Depression they have voted for the Democratic Party. Do we want to explain this phenomena as maximizing, or as a systematic judgmental error because of framing and other cognitive shortcuts? I prefer to emphasize the optimality rather than the biases in judgment explanation.

It is not surprising that psychological theories do not do very well in explaining aggregate political and economic phenomena, since that is not the arena of comparative advantage for psychologists. But political and economic markets and institutions create incentives, information, and the appropriate division of labor so that welfare is increased over what it would be if individuals acted in isolation. Contrary to the expectations of cognitive psychology, the experimental research on aggregate political behavior and on economic markets strongly supports the expected utility maximizing models.[25] Political experiments have shown that allocations are near the core (Plott, 1979) and that voters can make intelligent judgments from low levels of political information (McKelvey and Ordeshook, 1985). Market experiments show an uncanny ability for market outcomes to aggregate disparate sources of private information (see, for example, Copeland and Friedman, 1987; and Friedman et al., 1984) and to overcome some of the failures of individual decision making in non-market settings (see, for example, Duh and Sunder, 1985; and Plott and Wilde, 1982, who show that the base-rate fallacy and the "representativeness" heuristic no longer hold in experimental market settings).

In earlier sections, I argued that political and economic institutions, either real or incorporated into the design of experiments, will tend to undermine some of the previous experimental results of prospect theory. However, it is quite likely that improved experimentation will still find some effect (albeit diminished) and that some of these anomalies will persist in the real world. However, to the degree that these anomalies exist, they will tend to have second-degree effects. That is, by far the major point predictor will be the expected utility hypothesis; biases from other effects will be small compared to the range of possible biases and smaller than the transaction costs needed to correct the biases.

Consider the "hot hand fallacy." Cognitive psychologists have shown that fans believe that player performance is autocorrelated rather than being based on longer run averages. For example, if a basketball player has the following history: 0 1 0 1 0 1 1 1 0 0 (where 1 stands for making a basket; 0 stands for missing), fans believe that the player is less likely to be successful on the next attempt than if the player had the following history: 0 1 0 0 0 0 1 1 1 1, even though the facts demonstrate that the likelihood of success is the same in each case (see Gilovich et al., 1985).

How far does this effect carry over into the betting market? Point spreads (basketball team A will beat team B by 10 points) are set by bookmakers so that the amount bet on each side is balanced. If there is an efficient betting market so that bets reflect the behavior of knowledgeable statisticians, then teams with win streaks will beat the point spread 50 percent of the time; if the distribution is symmetric, the average differential between the actual point spread and the betting point spread will be zero. On the other hand, if individuals who believe in the hot hand fallacy dominate the betting market, then teams with win streaks will beat the point spread less than 50 percent of the time and the differential between the actual and the betting point spread will be negative (since the hot hand fallacy would lead bettors to overestimate the actual spread).[26] Now the economic rationality hypothesis predicts a point, while the hot hand predicts an interval.[27] If the hot hand fallacy also predicted a point, then we could readily establish a metric. In the absence of one, I will suggest a reasonable lower bound: the hot hand fallacy should lead to bettors' overestimating point spreads by at least 1 point. Camerer (1989) shows that differential between the actual and the betting point spread is only 0.2. Another test, more economic in flavor, is that the extent of the spread should be less than the transaction costs. In this case, the cost of betting (10 percent of the win) is greater than the advantage of betting against the team with the win streak, so there are no positive profits to be made.

Expected utility (or any other) theory does not have as precise predictions for political markets as it does for financial and betting markets. According to Riker, one of the few established theoretical relations is Duverger's law. Duverger's law says that majority rule systems (such as the electoral system that existed in France until recently) will have more political parties than plurality rule systems (such as the electoral system in the United States) because expected utility maximization by the voter means that the voter will not want to waste a vote for a third party under the latter system. What does prospect theory predict? Perhaps nothing, perhaps anything, and quite possibly the following. Strong version: Multiattribute loss aversion predicts one-party rule in all democratic systems because voters value losses from the status quo more than gains. Weak version: Multiattribute loss aversion predicts that there are no radical parties in either system because voters weigh losses more than gains. Then again, Duverger's law might be consistent with prospect theory if multiattribute risk aversion is relatively unimportant in voting. In other words, in the political world, prospect theory, at best, explains only minor deviations from the important observed regularities.

Turning to the fifth point, cognitive psychology is not a unified theory but a set of often inconsistent descriptive hypotheses. The fact that some data are consistent with certain cognitive hypotheses while other data are consistent with other cognitive hypotheses does not imply that there is any consistent subset of cognitive hypotheses that can supplant economics as the primary explainer of political behavior.[28]

POST HOC EXPLANATIONS

Although experiments in cognitive psychology tend to be rigorous, the application of the experimental results to real-world events is quite slippery. In general, cognitive psychologists have too many fudge factors that allow them to explain any *particular* real-world event ex post. These fudge factors arise because, in their theories, objective reality may or may not coincide with subjective beliefs and utility functions are not stable. Since subjective beliefs can only be inferred from behavior, starting with a small set of observed behavioral relations, one can, without too much trouble, infer some subjective beliefs consistent with the objective reality.[29]

Consider Quattrone and Tversky's use of the S-shaped curve (1988). They argue that incumbents profit from good times and that challengers, whose policies are always more of a gamble, profit from bad times. That is, one gambles on losses and takes the sure thing on gains. But one would think that the status quo point represents the existing economic and political conditions under the incumbent (indeed, the authors argue this very same point later in the article). Therefore, no matter how bad objective reality is, the voter does not vote for the riskier opposition candidate if the expected outcome is about the same.[30] Of course, it is not hard to anticipate their counterargument that the status quo might not change quickly and that the voters' frame of reference is based on the historical record. They key point here is that if the researcher has a wide latitude in saying where the choices are on the subject's utility curve (both choices in the upper half, both choices in the lower half, one choice in the lower half and the other choice in the upper half), the researcher can always fit the theory to the facts. Everything is explained ex post, but nothing is predicted ex ante. This is an especially critical problem in utility theory because we do not see the utility function directly; rather, its shape is determined from observation of behavior.

Another source of fudging is subjective probability. Prospect theory allows subjective probabilities to differ from objective probabilities. Prospect theory assumes that individuals underestimate very low objective probabilities (the likelihood is viewed as being zero), overestimate low objective probabilities, and underestimate medium and mildly high objective probabilities. The degree of over- or underestimation is not specified and the terms *very low*, *low*, and so on are vague, allowing the researcher considerable latitude. Consider the following "real-world" lottery: A 10 percent chance of losing $100 and a 90 percent chance of losing nothing versus a sure loss of $10. If people choose the lottery, cognitive psychologists might say that the results are predicted by prospect theory, since the S-shaped curve predicts that people are risk preferring for losses (the issue of subjective probability would probably not arise); if people choose the sure loss of $10, then they might say that the results are consistent with prospect theory because people overestimate low probabilities and therefore become risk averse, their subjective expected loss from the lottery being greater than the loss from the sure thing. Economists have no such latitude; they believe that, on average, a person's subjective probability is an unbiased estimate of the objective probability. Because subjective probabilities and the shape of the utility can only be inferred from behavior (they cannot be measured like blood alcohol content), one needs to be especially cautious so that unseen parameters are not altered to explain the outcome.

THE IMPLICATIONS OF RESEARCH IN COGNITIVE PSYCHOLOGY

"[T]he research in cognitive and social psychology suggests that people do not have the information-gathering, interpretive, or computational skills required to properly recognize, remember, comprehend, and evaluate the circumstances and consequences of choices made under conditions typical of political life" (Rosenberg, this volume p. 394).[31]

Suppose, for the sake of argument, that Rosenberg's characterization is correct for the majority of voters. Does this mean that voters will act contrary to their own interests? I think not. In numerous other areas, individuals do not have the "requisite skills" yet they make the correct decisions. For example, most people do not know the difference between clidinium and cimetidine, but they do not need to; they rely on their doctor and their druggist to give them the correct prescription. And probably a majority of people do not have either the inclination or the cognitive capacity to forecast weather (a highly technical field). But there is no need to; they just have to listen to the weather reports.

In the political sphere, a number of institutions arise which reduce the cognitive load on the average voter. For example, parties and candidates develop reputations so that voters do not have to delve into all the details—voters will not confuse Ted Kennedy with Jack Kemp. Pressure groups may also be a good source of information if your goals coincide with those of the particular pressure group. If you believe that abortion is wrong, you can ask your local pro-life group for information on the candidates. One can also ask trusted and knowledgeable friends for their advice.

Furthermore, democratic politics, because it relies on majority rule, can work very well despite the presence of a large number of poorly informed voters who make distorted (possibly irrational) judgments. And, of course, certain people without adequate cognitive skills (children) are not allowed to vote.

There are numerous articles in cognitive psychology demonstrating the limited cognitive abilities of human beings. For example, people have a hard time remembering a sequence of random digits. But what are the implications of limited memory? Not that humans do not make use of numerical sequences, but that they find substitutes (such as telephone books) for mere memory. If we were to take the results of cognitive psychology experiments at face value, we would claim that an extensive telephone system would be impossible because people do not have the cognitive capability to remember all the necessary numbers. No psychologist would make such claims, but similar generalizations regarding the efficacy of democratic institutions are frequently made from experimental results.

Again for the sake of argument, assume that the cognitive psychologists are correct in characterizing voters as having unstable preferences and being prone to mistaken judgments. If their views are true, the cognitive psychologist will be able to predict laboratory outcomes but not political behavior, because in the real world there are so many influences, incorrect heuristics, approaches to framing the political choices, possible priors, and other ways that actors infuse the world of

politics with their subjectively (and intersubjectively) construed meanings (Rosenberg, this volume), that one would have no hope of determining which is operative. Therefore cognitive psychology would rarely
be useful in predicting any ecological data beyond the arguments that
either things tend to be the same or they are random.[32]

DOES A THEORY OF COGNITIVE FAILURE MAKE SENSE?

Tversky and Kahneman (1974) have argued that people choose schemata which are the most available rather than the most useful. Other
psychologists view people as cognitive misers who minimize information
processing.[33] This is a very strange utility function: the only costs are
decision-making costs. There are no benefits. If this were true, people
could just choose the first possible alternative, or flip a coin, and so on.
Obviously, this is not the answer. Rather, the more appropriate answer
is that people balance off the marginal expected gain from additional
information and cognition with the marginal expected decision-making
cost.[34] If making a mistake involves little cost (e.g., answering a survey
question in a cognitive psychology experiment), then little cognition will
be employed; if making mistakes involves considerable cost (e.g., purchasing equipment for the military), then more detailed schemata and
complicated heuristics will be employed[35] and, more important, more
learning, consulting, and division of intellectual labor into cognitively
manageable tasks will be undertaken. In a nutshell, the more important
the decision, the more likely that the actual decision will approximate
the decision that would occur if all relevant information were available
and correctly processed. Also, as a general rule, one would expect that
the cognitive heuristic chosen to solve a problem would be an unbiased
predictor.[36] Thus, if the loss function were symmetric (an overestimate
is as bad as an underestimate), we would observe both over- and
underestimates and the expected error would be zero. If biases were
predictable, then one could add an additional heuristic to account for
them. For example, a contractor can add up all normal costs and then
add 10 percent for all costs that were not explicitly considered.

Quattrone and Tversky's experiments demonstrating economic irrationality have comparable implications for the experimental work on
optical illusions. Yes, people do make errors in perception (and cognition), often because the rules which usually work misguide in the particular situation (for example, the lines converge; therefore, the object
looks far away, but in fact the object is close). However, no one hauls a
sailboat to a mirage.

CONCLUDING REMARKS

Does the cognitive psychologist's model of man provide an adequate basis for our understanding of democratic politics? No. Cognitive psychology experiments do not account for political institutions, competition, comparative advantage, or significant experience and incentives. Some experimental results ostensibly revealing faulty judgment, in fact, demonstrate optimal decision making within the context of the experiment. Nor does the real world provide much support for the cognitive psychologist's model of man either. While some market anomalies (from the viewpoint of economics) can be explained in a post hoc fashion by some cognitive psychology models, standard political and economic behavior then becomes anomalous from the perspective of cognitive psychology. Finally, cognitive psychology does not encompass a unified body of research but rather a collection of often internally inconsistent hypotheses and results. It is clearly inappropriate to pick and choose where each is successful and then treat the whole corpus of work in cognitive psychology as a single contender with economics for explaining political behavior.

If my arguments are correct, psychologists in the future should emphasize humanity's cognitive successes rather than its mistakes and political scientists should study how political institutions correct for any remaining biases inherent in individual decision making.

NOTES

Acknowledgments. My thanks to Kristen Monroe and Dan Friedman for valuable comments.

1. For a discussion of whether this decision making is conscious or not, see the introductory remarks to this book.
2. Some of these approaches will be presented in greater detail below.
3. One could stretch the concept of rationality so far as to claim that such inconsistent choice was rational if the benefit of making a more correct decision was outweighed by the extra decision-making cost.
4. Cognitive psychologists have had a varied response to the concept of irrationality. Some have argued that human behavior may be irrational either from a goal oriented perspective or from the viewpoint of logical consistency. Others have argued that behavior is always rational although there may be systematic judgmental biases.
5. Of course, not all economists are in the "economist" camp nor are all cognitive psychologists allied with the "cognitive psychology" camp.

6. I will not discuss either the Allais paradox or preference reversal. Both of these experimental results contradict some basic tenets of expected utility maximization. However, the implications of these experimental results for political behavior are more opaque than the experimental results that I consider here.

   The experiments showing preference reversal and the Allais paradox tend to be more immune to some of my criticisms. For example, these experiments often involve monetary incentives (although the amount the subject loses when making a nonoptimal decision is often slight).

7. Those who find the word "irrational" too charged can substitute the phrase "contradicts fundamental notions of economic rationality" for "is irrational."

8. Quattrone and Tversky (1988): problems 9 and 10. See also problems 11 and 12.

9. My arguments against this and other experiments in cognitive psychology should not be taken as arguments against experimental technique but, rather, as an assertion that the wrong experiments have been made. For example, one might have an experiment where two of the subjects run for office and they get paid for winning. The candidates could frame the information in any way and then the other subjects would vote. Of course, even here the stakes are never as high as in the real world, nor is the time for learning as long.

10. For a more extensive discussion of information and democratic institutions see Wittman (1989).

11. A properly designed experiment might allow for such institutions to arise.

12. McNeil et al. (1982) show that specialists are also victims of framing. In their experiment, they asked subjects to decide between two cancer treatments (surgery or radiation). Each treatment had 3 mortality (or in the reverse frame, survival) rates: death during treatment, death after one year, death after five years. However, doctors have more experience with bivariate choices. I would expect to see much smaller effects of framing if the statistic for death (or survival) after one year were eliminated, and virtually no effect of framing if the only difference in the two methods were survival rates after five years.

13. Quattrone and Tversky are more vague. They use the term "neutral reference point." In some of their examples, the status quo is this neutral reference point.

14. Quattrone and Tversky report four experiments (problems 1–4) that have political choice rather than income streams, but they are just variants of the $100 sure thing versus the 0–$200 lottery.

15. In the United States, gambling is illegal in most states, but one might observe arbitrage over different risk portfolios or other behavior by the individual which yields a similar result.

16. "Making book" against oneself is always a possibility when individuals have S-shaped curves. Machina (1989) has argued that making book against oneself need not arise if history is important (that is, the path to the present state is not ignored). In our present example, the fact that the person chose the mirror stock in round one may influence the person not to choose the sure thing over the lottery in round two, when the price of the mirror stock has fallen, even though the person might choose the sure thing in round two if he or she had not purchased the mirror stock in round one. This nonseparability of history (one must even consider outcomes that might have occurred in the past but didn't) creates an enormous cognitive load unknown to expected utility maximization. For a person who is easily fooled by frames and chooses all kinds of cognitive shortcuts, such hypercalculation would appear unlikely. Furthermore, making book against oneself is still possible if the person was not aware of the contingency (in this case, the ability to get out of the lottery if the stock does fall) when the first decision was made. This problem can be circumvented if the person contemplates such a possibility when making the original choice. But again the assumption that people who are so easily fooled by frames make such complicated decisions stretches the limits of internal consistency.

17. See Knetsch and Sinden (1984), who argue against the methodology used in Coursey and Stanley's earlier paper.

18. But this tendency for the status quo is counterbalanced by the variability of framing, which induces changes in behavior even though the objective circumstances do not change.

19. It is interesting to note that Tversky and Kahneman (1974) have contrary experimental results showing that people underweigh their Bayesian priors.

20. An experimental test could be designed to test this proposition.

21. A number of experiments "demonstrating" biased choice (or irrational behavior) by the subject appear to be unbiased (or more rational) once we consider the overall context of the experiment.

22. This anomaly is so well known that financial columns (see, for example, the *Santa Cruz Sentinel*, December 17, 1989) are now advising people to buy stock in small firms in December. Of course, if this advice is heeded, the anomaly will disappear.

23. There are other calendar-based anomalies, but they are not consistent with each other.

24. "Martingale-like" refers to the fact that the general pattern of indi-

vidual stock prices (day to day or hour to hour) is more like a martingale than any pattern in which future price changes are a function of past price changes.

25. Arrow (1982), Russell and Thaler (1985), and Miller (1987) have argued that markets need not correct irrational behavior. However, the examples that Arrow and Miller provided were odd. Arrow assumed that rational investors cared only about the present but that the irrationality involved speculation about the effect of expenditures on research and development in the distant future. However, in the real world, different firms have different expenditure profiles on research and development and different horizons for coming to fruition. The rational investor with a short-term horizon can choose firms where the payoff from R&D will be manifest in the near future. Miller argued that rational investors could not sell short if they felt that stock prices would fall, because of the high transaction costs of selling short over a significant time period. However, there are numerous alternatives to selling short, including organized future markets, forward contracts, and an active option market where speculators may buy a put option. Thaler argued that such mechanisms do not occur in other areas (consumer markets and political markets). However, the market for advice is still available. People pay for lawyers, consumers shop at stores with good customer service, voters discuss the issues, and politicians consult pollsters.

26. The hot hand fallacy may not carry over to team performance. Unfortunately, there is no well defined betting market for individual shooting performance.

27. Cognitive psychology typically gives less precise predictions. It should be remembered that if we hold to a concave utility function and the von Neumann-Morgenstern postulates, then betting is "irrational" when the expected payoff is not positive.

28. Even if we restrict the comparison to experimental studies without market mechanisms, there are numerous "descriptive" hypotheses with strong experimental results contrary to prospect theory (see Camerer, 1989, who shows, among other things, that prospect theory cannot explain the degree to which fanning out varies with payoffs).

29. A large body of real-world facts might pin down the subjective reality of the voter.

Of course, economists have their fudge factors also, but virtually all the fudge factors available to economists are available to those who believe in prospect theory, but the reverse is not the case (utility functions cannot shift and biased mistakes do not last).

30. Note that ordinary economic theory predicts risk aversion and hence preference for the incumbent, other things being more or less equal.

31. With this dismal view of human cognition, one wonders how people could have designed democratic institutions in the first place.

32. Consider first the issue of framing. "Framing is controlled by the manner in which the choice problem is presented as well as by norms, habits and expectancies of the decision-maker" (Tversky and Kahneman, 1987). Since we are unlikely to know what frames the voter has heard or any of the other characteristics, the whole concept is likely to be useless for predicting aggregate voting patterns. Tversky and Kahneman (1974) also consider judgmental heuristics which may lead to biased decision making: judgment by representativeness, judgment by availability, and judgment by adjustment. Each of these depends on the special history of the voter and would in general be impossible to determine outside an experimental setting or large catastrophic events. All of these factors are to be considered in addition to the voter's preferences.

33. Lau (1986) uses the term "cognitive miser."

34. Cognition is not minimized but rationed like other scarce commodities. It is not free, but it is not infinitely costly either. Hence there are tradeoffs between time spent cogitating and time spent at other activities.

35. See Lodge and Hamil (1986) for a survey of results showing that experts use more detailed and sophisticated schemata. Leland (1988) posits that individuals approximate their utility function because inexperience and/or cognitive limitations make the "true" utility function inaccessible. Because of finite resources this approximation is limited to N steps in a step-function estimation, with the optimal approximation defined as that minimizing the expected squared error. His theory is able to explain many of the findings of prospect theory for situations of low information and reduces to ordinary expected utility as experience accumulates. Friedman (1989), in a variant of the Leland model, assumes that utility is weighted by sensitivity (a finite resource). For low levels of information, the value function looks like an S-shaped curve. As experience accumulates, the value function looks more like the standard concave utility function.

36. See Beach and Mitchell (1978), who argue that the appropriate cognitive rule of thumb is chosen for the situation, and Christensen-Szalanski (1980) for some experimental confirmation. Also see the work by Thorngate (1980), who shows that heuristics can often pick the best of several alternatives across a range of alternatives.

REFERENCES

Arrow, K. (1982). "Risk Perception in Psychology and Economics." *Economic Inquiry, 20*:1–9.

Bazerman, M. H. (1983). "Negotiator Judgment." *American Behavioral Scientist, 27*:211–228.

Beach, L. R., and Mitchell, T. R. (1978). "A Contingency Model for the Selection of Decision Strategies." *Academy of Management Review, 3*:439–449.

Brookshire, D. S., and Coursey, D. S. (1987). "Measuring the Value of a Public Good: An Empirical Comparison of Elicitation Procedures." *American Economic Review, 77*:554–566.

Camerer, C. F. (1987). "Do Biases in Probability Judgment Matter in Markets? Experimental Evidence." *American Economic Review, 77*:981–987.

———. (1988). "An Experimental Test of Several Generalized Utility Theories." *Journal of Risk and Uncertainty, 1*:61–104.

———. (1989). "Does the Basketball Market Believe in the 'Hot Hand'?" *American Economic Review, 79*:1257–1261.

Christensen-Szalanski, J. J. J. (1980). "A Further Examination of the Selection of Problem-Solving Strategies: The Effects of Deadlines and Analytic Aptitudes." *Organizational Behavior and Human Performance, 25*:107–122.

Coleman, J. S. (1986). *Individual Interests and Collective Action: Selected Essays.* Cambridge: Cambridge University Press.

Copeland, T., and Friedman, D. (1987). "The Effect of Sequential Information Arrival on Asset Prices." *Journal of Finance, 42*:763.

Coursey, D. L., Hovis, J. L., and Schulze, W. D. (1987). "The Disparity Between Willingness to Accept and Willingness to Pay Measures of Value. *Quarterly Journal of Economics, 100*:679–690.

Cummings, R. G., Brookshire, D. S., David, S. and Schulze, W. D. (1986). *Valuing Environmental Goods: An Assessment of the Contingent Valuation Method.* Totowa, NJ: Rowman and Allanheld.

Downs, A. (1957). *An Economic Theory of Democracy.* New York: Harper & Row.

Duh, R. R., and Sunder, S. (1985). *Incentives, Learning and Processing of Information in a Market Environment: An Examination of the Base Rate Fallacy.* Working paper 1985-5. Minneapolis: University of Minnesota, Department of Accounting.

Einhorn, H. J. (1981). "Behavioral Decision Theory: Processes of Judgment and Choice. "*Annual Review of Psychology, 32*:53–88.

Eisner, R., and Strotz, R. H. (1961). "Flight Insurance and the Theory of Choice." *Journal of Political Economy*, 69:355–368.

Fishburn, P. C. (1988). *Nonlinear Preference and Utility Theory*, Baltimore: Johns Hopkins Press.

Frey, B. S., and Eichenberger, R. (1989). "Should Social Scientists Care About Choice Anomalies?" *Rationality and Society*, 1:101–122.

Friedman, D. (1989). "The S-Shaped Value Function as a Constrained Optimum." *American Economic Review*, 79:1243–1248.

Friedman, D., Harrison, G., and Salmon, J. (1984). "The Informational Efficiency of Experimental Asset Markets." *Journal of Political Economy*, 92:349–408.

Gilovich, T., Vallone, R., and Tversky, A. (1985). "The Hot Hand in Basketball: On the Misperception of Random Sequences." *Cognitive Psychology*, 17:295–314.

Green, J. (1987). "Making Book Against Oneself: The Independence Axiom and Nonlinear Utility." *Quarterly Journal of Economics*, 104:785–796.

Harrison, G. W. (1989, November). *Expected Utility Theory and the Experimentalists*. Working paper. Albuquerque: University of New Mexico, Department of Economics.

Hastie, R. (1985). *Political Cognition*. Hillsdale, NJ: Erlbaum.

Hechter, M. (1987). *Principles of Group Solidarity*. Berkeley: University of California Press.

Kahneman, D., Knetsch, J. L., and Thaler, R. H. (1987). "Fairness and the Assumptions of Economics." In R. M. Hogarth and M. W. Reder (Eds.,), *Rational Choice*. Chicago: University of Chicago Press.

Kahneman, D., Slovic, P., and Tversky, A. (1982). *Judgment Under Uncertainty: Heuristics and Biases*. New York: Cambridge University Press.

Kahneman, D., and Tversky, A. (1984). "Choices, Values, and Frames." *American Psychologist*, 39:341–350.

Kleidon, A. W. (1987). "Anomalies in Financial Economics: Blueprint for Change?" In R. M. Hogarth and M. W. Reder (Eds.), *Rational Choice*. Chicago: University of Chicago Press.

Knetsch, J. L. (1987). "The Persistence of Evaluation Disparities." *Quarterly Journal of Economics*, 102:691–695.

———. (1989). "The Endowment Effect and Evidence of Nonreversible Indifference Curves." *American Economic Review*, 79:1277–1284.

Knetsch, J., and Sinden, J. A. (1984). "Willingness to Pay and Compensation Demanded: Experimental Evidence of an Unexpected

Disparity in Measures of Value." *Quarterly Journal of Economics,* 99:507–521.

Kunreuther, H. R., Ginsberg, R., and Miller, L. (1978). *Disaster Insurance Protection: Public Policy Lessons.* New York: Wiley.

Kunreuther, H., and Slovic, P. (1978, May). "Economic Psychology and Protective Behavior." *American Economic Review. Papers and Proceedings, 68:*64–69.

Lau, R. R. (1986). "Political Schemata, Candidate Evaluations, and Voting Behavior." In D. O. Sears (Ed.), *Political Cognition.* Hillsdale, NJ: Erlbaum. Pp. 95–126.

Leland, J. (1988). *A Theory of "Approximate" Expected Utility Maximization.* Working paper. Pittsburgh: Carnegie Mellon University, Department of Social and Decision Sciences.

LeRoy, S. (1989). "Efficient Capital Markets and Martingales." *Journal of Economic Literature,* 27:1583–1622.

Lodge, M., and Hamil, D. (1986). "A Partisan Schema for Political Information Processing." *American Political Science Review, 80:*505–519.

Machina, M. (1989). "Dynamic Consistency and Non-expected Utility Models of Choice Under Uncertainty." *Journal of Economic Literature,* 27:1622–1688.

McKelvey, R. D., and Ordeshook, P. C. (1985). "Elections with Limited Information: A Fulfilled Expectations Model Using Contemporaneous Poll and Endorsement Data as Information Sources." *Journal of Economic Theory* 3655–85.

McNeil, B. J., Pauker, S. G., Sox, H. C., Jr., and Tversky, A. (1982). "On the Elicitation of Preferences for Alternative Therapies." *New England Journal of Medicine* 306:1259–1262.

Massaro, D., and Friedman, D. (1990). *Models of Integration Given Multiple Sources of Information. Psychological Review* 97:225–252.

Miller, E. (1987). "Bounded Efficient Markets: A New Wrinkle to the EMH." *Journal of Portfolio Management, 13:*4–13.

Olson, M., Jr. (1969). "The Relationship Between Economics and the Other Social Sciences: The Province of a Social Report." In S. M. Lipset (Ed.), *Politics and the Social Sciences.* New York: Oxford University Press.

Plott, C. (1979). "The Application of Laboratory Experimental Methods to Public Choice." In C. Russel (Ed.), *Collective Decision Making: Applications from Public Choice Theory.* Baltimore: Johns Hopkins University Press. Pp. 137–160.

_____ . (1987). "Rational Choice in Experimental Markets." In R. Hogarth and M. W. Reder (Eds.), *Rational Choice*. Chicago: University of Chicago Press. Pp. 117–143.

Plott, C. R., and Wilde, L. L. (1982). "Professional Diagnosis Versus Self-Diagnosis: An Experimental Examination of Some Special Features of Markets with Uncertainty." In V. L. Smith (Ed.), *Research in Experimental Economics* (Vol. 2). Greenwich, CT: JAI.

Pratt, J. U., Wise, D., and Zeckhauser, R. (1979). "Price Differences in Almost Competitive Markets." *Quarterly Journal of Economics*, 93:189–211.

Przeworski, A. (1987). "Marxism and Rational Choice." *Politics and Society*, 16:1389–1409.

Quattrone, G. A., and Tversky, A. (1988). "Contrasting Rational and Psychological Analyses of Political Choice." *American Political Science Review*, 82:719–736.

Riker, W. (1982) "The Two-party System and Duverger's Law: Essay on the History of Political Science." *American Political Science Review*, 76:753–766.

Rosenberg, S. W., and McCafferty, P. (1987). "The Image and the Vote: Manipulating Voters' Preferences." *Public Opinion Quarterly*, 51:31–47.

Russell, T., and Thaler, R. (1985). "The Relevance of Quasi-Rationality in Competitive Markets." *American Economic Review*, 75:1071–1082.

Samuelson, W., and Zeckhauser, R. (1988). "Status Quo Bias in Decision Making." *Journal of Risk and Uncertainty*, 1:7–59.

Savage, L. (1954). *The Foundation of Statistics*. 2d rev. ed. New York: Wiley.

Schoemaker, P. J. (1982). "The Expected Utility Model: Its Variants, Purposes, Evidence and Limitations." *Journal of Economic Literature*, 20:529–563.

Schotter, A. (1981). *The Economic Theory of Social Institutions*. Cambridge: Cambridge University Press.

Shapira, Z. (1986). "The Implications of Behavioral Decision Making Theory to Economics." In H. MacFayden (Ed.), *Economic Psychology: Intersections in Theory and Application*. Amsterdam: Elsevier.

Shiller, R. J. (1987). "Comments on Miller and Kleidon." In R. Hogarth and M. W. Reder (Eds.), *Rational Choice*. Chicago: University of Chicago Press. Pp. 317–321.

Simon, H. (1955). "A Behavioral Model of Rational Choice." *Quarterly Journal of Economics, 69*:99–118.

Slovic, P., Fischhoff, B., and Lichtenstein, S. "Behavior Decision Theory." *Annual Review of Psychology, 28*:1–39.

Snyder, M., and Swann, W. B. (1978). "Hypothesis Testing Processes in Social Interaction." *Journal of Personality and Social Psychology, 36*:1202–1212.

Thaler, R. H. (1987). "The Psychology and Economics Conference Handbook: Comments on Simon, on Einhorn and Hogarth, and on Tversky and Kahneman." In R. M. Hogarth and M. W. Reder (Eds.), *Rational Choice*. Chicago: University of Chicago Press.

Thorngate, W. (1980). "Efficient Decision Heuristics." *Behavioral Science, 25*:219–225.

Tversky, A., and Kahneman, D. (1971). "Belief in the Law of Small Numbers." *Psychological Bulletin, 76*:1105–1110.

_____ . (1974). "Judgment Under Uncertainty: Heuristics and Biases." *Science, 211*:1124–1131.

_____ . (1987). "Rational Choice and the Framing of Decisions." In R. Hogarth and M. W. Reder (Eds.), *Rational Choice*. Chicago: University of Chicago Press. Pp. 67–94.

Tversky, A., and Sattath, S. (1979). Preference Trees. *Psychological Review, 86*:542–573.

Von Neumann, J., and Morgenstern, O. (1947). *Theory of Games and Economic Behavior*. Princeton: Princeton University Press.

Wittman, D. (1982). "Efficient Rules in Highway Safety and Sports Activity." *American Economic Review, 72*:78–90.

_____ . (1989). "Why Democracies Produce Efficient Results." *Journal of Political Economy, 97*:1395–1424.

Index

marginalist model, 53, 54–55, 63–67, 68
future research and, 7–19
human agency and, 94–109
   conventional idea of, 94–95
   deliberation concept and, 95, 101–105, 107, 108
   performance concept and, 95, 96–101, 106, 107–108
interdependent, 238–243
   policy implementation and. *See* Bureaucracy
modification of, 3, 19–22, 171, 340–341
origins of, 1–2
subdisciplines of, 2
topical purview of, 2–3
Rational choice theory. *See also* Economic theory of politics; Rational action theory
appeal of, 172–174
assumptions of, 5–6, 38–41, 49
   about human nature, 178–181
   rationality presumption and, 117–119, 121
   methodological individualism and, 17, 38, 178
claims of, 172
of coalitions, 40, 44–48
   assumptions of, 46–48
   cabinet formation in, 44–46
   games theory and, 76
   historical studies in, 46
   of Riker, 40, 44
complementary to interpretive theory, 279–280, 285–286
in Stuart England electoral study, 286–299
conscious calculus requirement of, 14, 341

democratic model and, 181–187, 204, 205–208, 220–222
   critique of, 181–187
distinction from rational action theory, 2
frustrated behavior and, 75–91
   adaptive, 83, 89–91
   aggressive, 81–82, 85–86
   contexts for, 88–89
   in experimental settings, 79–84
   fixated, 80–81, 85
   regressive, 78–79, 82, 85
   resigned, 82
   in social settings, 84–85
goal-directed behavior and, 8–9, 74, 75–78, 341
indeterminacy of, 283–285
institutions and, 259–273
interpretive critics of, 114–119, 123–124, 282
versus interpretive theory, 280–282
liberalism and, 172, 173–174
neglect of social science literature, 48–49
neoconservatism and, 195
as normative, 18, 176–178
prehistory of, 32–36
as reconstructive, 113–114, 120, 124–128
as science, 36–38, 172–173, 174, 178
theorists of, 38–43
   core, 38–41
   peripheral, 42–43
Rationality
bounded, 5–6, 77, 100–101
and cognition, 391–397, 421–422
citizen, 148–149
narrowed, 388–389

About the Authors

Gabriel A. Almond was educated at the University of Chicago, where he received his PhB and PhD (1932, 1938). He has taught at Brooklyn College, Yale, Princeton, and Stanford universities, among others. His major works include *American People and Foreign Policy* (1950), *The Appeals of Communism* (1954), *The Politics of the Developing Areas* (1960), *The Civic Culture* (1963), *Comparative Politics* (1966, 1978), *Crisis, Choice, and Change* (1973), and *The Civic Culture Revisited* (1980). Among his many professional honors and activities, Almond has served as the chair of the Committee on Comparative Politics, Social Science Research Council (1954–1963), as president of the American Political Science Association (1966), and was the recipient of the James Madison award in 1982. He is a Fellow of the American Academy of Arts and Sciences and a member of the American Philosophical Society and the National Academy of Science.

Michael C. Barton received his graduate degree in politics from The University of California at Irvine.

Michel Crozier is Senior Research Professor at the Centre National de la Recherche Scientifique, the director of the Centre de Sociologie des Organisations, and the director of the Post-Graduate School of Sociology at the Institut d'Etudes Politiques de Paris. He has been a visiting professor at Harvard University and at the University of California at Irvine. A prolific writer on politics and society, Crozier is best known for *The Bureaucratic Phenomenon* (1964), *The World of the Office Worker* (1971), *The Crisis of Democracy* (with Huntington and Kabanuki, 1975), *Actors and Systems*, (1977, 1980) and *Le Mal Americain* (1980).

Anthony Downs received his BA in political theory and international relations from Carleton College, from which he graduated Phi Beta Kappa and summa cum laude in 1952. After receiving his MA and PhD in economics from Stanford University, Downs taught at the University of Chicago in the economics and political science departments from 1959 to 1962. He served as economic consultant at the Rand Corporation from 1963 to 1965 and then worked in the private sector, specializing in real estate and urban economics, until he joined the Brookings Institution in 1977 as a Senior Fellow. While Downs is best known for his two classics, *An Economic Theory of Democracy* (1957) and *Inside Bureaucracy* (1967), he has also published more than 300 articles and has written *Who Are the Urban Poor?* (1968, 1970), *Racism in America* (1970), *Urban Problems and Prospects* (1972, 1976), *Opening Up the Suburbs* (1973), and *Urban Decline and the Future of American Cities* (1985). Downs is currently working on a major study of the evolution of democracy.

Harry H. Eckstein received his BA (1948) from Harvard, where he was elected to Phi Beta Kappa in 1947. He received his PhD from Harvard in 1953 and taught there from 1954 to 1959, when he joined the faculty at Princeton, eventually serving as the IBM Professor in the Department of Politics from 1969 to 1980. He is currently a Distinguished Professor at the University of California at Irvine. Eckstein has been a Guggenheim Fellow (1974–1975), a Fellow of the American Academy of Arts and Science, chair of the Program Committee for the American Political Science Association (1966–1967), APSA vice-president (1981–1982), and the chair in the Department of Politics and Society at UC Irvine. Among his many works are *Division and Cohesion in Democracy* (1966), *Patterns of Authority* (1975), and *Pressure Group Politics* (1960). Eckstein has published widely in professional journals and served as editor of *World Politics* from 1960–1966.

John Ferejohn received his BA from San Fernando Valley State College (1966) and his PhD from Stanford (1972). A past Fellow at the Brookings Institution (1970–1971) and at the Center for Advanced Study in Behavioral Sciences (1981–1982), Ferejohn received a Guggenheim Fellowship in 1981–1982 and was elected to the American Academy of Arts and Sciences in 1985 and the National Academy of Science in 1988. Currently the William Bennett Munro Professor of Political Science at Stanford and Senior Fellow at the Hoover Institution, Ferejohn has also taught at the California Institute of Technology. Widely published in political science, he is best known for *Pork Barrel Politics: Rivers and Harbors Legislation, 1947–68* (1974) and *The Personal Vote: Constituency Service and Electoral Independence* (1987).

Robert Grafstein received his BA with honors at the University of Pennsylvania (1969) and his MA and PhD in political science from the University of Chicago (1974, 1977). Currently associate professor of political science at the University of Georgia, he has published widely in leading journals in political science and philosophy, such as *American Political Science Review*, *Journal of Politics*, *Polity*, and *Philosophical Studies*. Grafstein serves on the editorial board of *Social Science Quarterly*.

James D. Johnson is completing his dissertation, entitled "Symbol and Strategy: On the Cultural Analysis of Politics," at the University of Chicago. He is the author of articles and reviews in *Political Power and Social Theory*, *Political Theory*, and *Ethics*. Johnson is currently assistant professor of political science at Northwestern University.

David Johnston divided his undergraduate studies between Harvard and Swarthmore, and graduated with distinction in political science from Swarthmore (1972). He took an MPhil at Oxford (1975), writing his thesis entitled "The Will in the Philosophy of Hegel." For his PhD from Princeton (1981), he wrote the dissertation "The New Sovereign and the Modern Subject: An Interpretation of Hobbes's Political Theory." Johnston has taught at both Yale and Columbia, where he is currently associate professor in the Department of Political Science. He has written widely on political theory and is best known for *The Rhetoric of Leviathan: Thomas Hobbes and the Politics of Cultural Transformation* (1986).

Gregory S. Kavka received his BA magna cum laude from Princeton (1968) and his PhD in philosophy from the University of Michigan (1973). He taught at UCLA from 1972 to 1979 and is currently professor of philosophy at the University of California, Irvine. The recipient of many honors, Kavka is active professionally, serving on the editorial board of *Ethics*. He is the author of numerous articles on ethics and on social and political philosophy, as well as the author of *Hobbesian Moral and Political Theory* (1986) and *The Moral Paradoxes of Nuclear Deterrence* (1987).

Ute Klingemann, a graduate of Cologne University, is a doctoral candidate in political science at the Free University in Berlin, where she is currently working as a research associate at the Center for Social Research. Her main areas of interest are social psychology and mass communication. Klingemann has been a research affiliate of the Center for Survey Research (ZUMA) at the University of Mannheim, and at the Max Planck Institute for Human Development and Education in Berlin. She has published on the perception of the BILD Zeitung in the West German populace.

Howard Margolis was educated at Harvard (BA, 1953) and MIT (PhD, 1979). He has wide experience in academics and government, serving as assistant to the secretary of defense from 1962 to 1964, as a political writer for both the *Bulletin of Atomic Scientists* and the *Washington Post* (1964–1965), a Research Fellow at the Center for International Studies at MIT, and as visiting Fellow at both the Russell Sage Foundation (1981–1982, 1983–1984) and the Institute for Advanced Study in Princeton (1982–1983). Margolis has taught both politics and economics at the University of California at Irvine and is currently professor in the Graduate School of Public Policy at the University of Chicago, where he also teaches in the college and the Fishbein Center for History of Science and Medicine. Widely published in political science journals, Margolis is best known as the author of *Selfishness, Altruism and Rationality* (1982, 1984) and of *Patterns, Thinking and Cognition* (1988).

Kristen Renwick Monroe was graduated with honors from Smith College (1968) and received her MA and PhD from the University of Chicago (1970, 1974). She was a LaVerne Noyes Fellow at the University of Chicago (1970–1972), a Killam Fellow at the University of British Columbia in political economy and econometrics (1975–1976), and a Fellow at the Center of International Affairs at Princeton (1983–1984). An associate professor in politics and society at the University of California at Irvine, Monroe has also taught at NYU, Princeton, NYU School of Law, and State University of New York at Stony Brook. She was the founder and for 10 years the chair of the International Political Science Association's research group on Political Support and Alienation and is also active in the American Political Science Association. Monroe is the author of *Presidential Popularity and the Economy* (1984) and the editor of *The Political Process and Economic Change* (1983). She is spending the 1990–91 academic year as a Visiting Fellow at the Woodrow Wilson School at Princeton University to complete a book, entitled *John Donne's People*, on altruism and rationality.

Roger G. Noll is Morris Doyle Centennial Professor of Public Policy at Stanford University in the Department of Economics. He has also served as the Institute Professor of Social Science at the California Institute of Technology, as a Senior Fellow at the Brookings Institution, and as senior economist on the president's Council of Economic Advisers. Noll has published 6 books and over 100 articles on such topics as the economics of television, environmental regulation, health care financing, the economics of sports, the politics of regulatory policy, and the positive theory of electoral competition. His most recent book, co-authored with Linda R. Cohen, is *The Technology Pork Barrel* (1990).

Mark P. Petracca received his BA in government from Cornell University (1977) and an MA and PhD in political science from the University of Chicago (1979, 1986), where he was a Hilman Scholar and held both Hawley and Merriam fellowships. Currently assistant professor in politics and society at the University of California at Irvine, Petracca has taught at the University of Chicago, Amherst College, and Beijing University. Co-author of *The American Presidency* (1983), he has also published articles on the administrative state, democratic theory, political consultants, and constitutional reform. Petracca is currently working on a book entitled *Presidential Scorecard* and is editing two books, on interest group politics and American public policy.

Shawn Rosenberg was graduated with honors in political science from Yale (1972), studied as a special student in psychology and social relations at Harvard, received an MLitt from Oxford (1982), and studied as a postdoctoral fellow in political science and social psychology at Harvard (1978–1980). Rosenberg is currently an associate professor of politics and psychology at the University of California, Irvine. His research has focused on social theory, ideology, and political behavior. Widely published in political science and political psychology journals, Rosenberg has published *Reason, Ideology and Politics* (1988) and co-authored *Political Reasoning and Cognition* (1989). He was awarded the Erik Erikson award for early career contribution to political psychology given by the International Society for Political Psychology.

Laura J. Scalia was graduated with honors in mathematics and political science from New York University, where she was elected to Phi Beta Kappa. She received her MA, MPhil, and PhD (1983, 1984, 1991) from Yale University; her dissertation is entitled "Liberalism and Democracy in Nineteenth-Century America: Implications for a Liberal Democratic Theory." She has recently joined the Department of Political Science at the University of Houston as an assistant professor.

Barry R. Weingast, a member of the research staff of the Hoover Institution at Stanford University, previously taught in the School of Business at Washington University in St. Louis. His primary areas of research are the positive theory of political institutions, the politics of regulatory policy, and the role of politics in shaping the development of economic institutions. His most recent publications include articles on the political origins of the savings and loan crisis, the role of government in the creation of capital markets in seventeenth-century England, and the distributional objectives of the first U.S. regulatory agency, the Interstate Commerce Commission, at the time of its enactment.

Jaan W. Whitehead received her BA with honors in economics from Wellesley College (1964) and an MA in economics from the University of Michigan (1966). She worked for a number of years as an economist for private industry and for the Federal Reserve Board, then went on to receive her MA and PhD from the Department of Politics at Princeton University (1988). Her doctoral dissertation is a critical analysis of the origins and theoretical structure of public choice theory. She is now working on a book entitled *Political Philosophy and Public Choice Theory: Economic Myths and Political Reality*. Whitehead is currently a visiting assistant professor at Georgetown University.

Donald Wittman received his BA from the University of Michigan (1964) and his MA and PhD from the University of California at Berkeley (1966, 1970). He has published widely on politics and economics in journals such as *American Political Science Review*, *Journal of Legal Studies*, *Public Choice*, *Journal of Conflict Resolution*, and *Journal of Political Economy*. Wittman taught political science at the University of Chicago from 1974 to 1976 and is currently professor of economics at the University of California at Santa Cruz.